The Norton Book of American Short Stories
edited by Peter Prescott

The Norton Book of Light Verse
edited by Russell Baker

The Norton Book of Modern War
edited by Paul Fussell

The Norton Book of Nature Writing
edited by Robert Finch and John Elder

The Norton Book of the Sea
edited by John O. Coote

The Norton Book of Travel
edited by Paul Fussell

THE NORTON BOOK OF
FRIENDSHIP

THE NORTON BOOK OF FRIENDSHIP

Edited by EUDORA WELTY

 and RONALD A. SHARP

W · W · NORTON & COMPANY · NEW YORK · LONDON

Printed in the United States of America.

Since this page cannot legibly accommodate all the copyright notices,
pages 609–615 constitute an extension of the copyright page.

The text of this book is composed in Avanta (Electra),
with the display set in Bernhard Modern.
Composition and manufacturing by the Haddon Craftsmen, Inc.,
Book design by Antonina Krass.

First Edition.

Library of Congress Cataloging in Publication Data
The Norton book of friendship / edited by Eudora Welty and Ronald A. Sharp.
p.   cm.
Includes index.
1. Friendship—Literary collections.   I. Welty, Eudora, 1909–
II. Sharp, Ronald A.
PN6071.F7N58   1991   91-2879
808.8′0353—dc20

ISBN 0-393-03065-2

W. W. Norton & Company, Inc, 500 Fifth Avenue, New York, N.Y. 10110
W. W. Norton & Company Ltd., 10 Coptic Street, London WC1A 1PU

1 2 3 4 5 6 7 8 9 0

To the memory of
Robert Woodham Daniel
through whose friendship
the editors first became friends

We are a pair of moles burrowing
away in the same direction.

—Ivan Turgenev to Gustave Flaubert,
26 May 1868

CONTENTS

II   CLASSIC ESSAYS · 65

III   LETTERS: GROUP 1 · 99

IV POETRY · 129

V AFFINITIES: GROUP 1 · 207

VI THE BIBLE · 221

VII SHAKESPEARE · 237

VIII LETTERS: GROUP 2 · 257

IX SHORT STORIES · 267

X LETTERS: GROUP 3 · 363

XI   AFFINITIES: GROUP 2 · 391

XII   MEMOIRS AND HISTORIES · 427

XIII   LETTERS: GROUP 4 · 471

XIV   AFFINITIES: GROUP 3 · 483

XV   Further Essays · 511

XVI   Fables, Legends, and Folktales · 529

XVII   AFFINITIES: GROUP 4 · 541

XVIII   LETTERS: GROUP 5 · 555

XIX FAREWELLS · 589

ACKNOWLEDGMENTS

For their kind assistance we wish to thank Jami Peelle, Helen and Elizabeth Forman, Timothy Seldes, Barbara Dupee, Saskia Hamilton, Ed Barber and Robin Mendelson at Norton, the students in Mr. Sharp's seminars on the literature of friendship, and Inese Sharp.

INTRODUCTION BY
RONALD A. SHARP

Most afternoons if you enter the Windsor Room at the Sheraton Hotel in Jackson, Mississippi, you will find neatly arranged rows of chairs, a table and a lectern at the front of the room, a coffee urn and doughnuts tucked in the corner for the moment when the sales seminar or the Rotary Club meeting takes its break. In the spring of 1990, when I asked the hotel manager if Eudora Welty and I could rent this room to work on our book, he was more than a little puzzled: "You want to rent a conference room to write a book?"

"Sort of," I replied. "And we'd like everything moved out of the room and replaced with as many long tables as you can fit."

"Long tables? You want long tables for writing a book?"

"Not exactly for writing. For *arranging.* For *organizing.*"

We had reached that moment in the creation of any anthology when the sheer mass of material was becoming overwhelming. Having spent more than two years finding, reading, and considering literally thousands of stories, poems, essays, folktales, memoirs, letters, and fables about friendship, we had sifted our selections to the hundreds, and while three hundred may be far less than three thousand, keeping three hundred pieces in mind still requires considerable mental housekeeping. We had decided from the outset that, rather than imposing a thematic, chrono-logical, or generic organization at the beginning of our search, we would first gather the works we liked and wanted to include and then deter-mine what shape the material itself demanded. The moment of reckon-ing had arrived, and the question was how to organize this wonderfully diverse material into a coherent anthology.

Who has the fiercer rage for order, the artist or the scholar, is hard to say. But it was Eudora who had the brilliant idea of renting the Windsor Room. When she writes fiction she puts bits and pieces of stories or novels into a file, and when she is ready to start shaping the material, she spreads out the scraps of paper on a bed or a table or the floor, so that she can see it all in one place, and then she actually "pins" together the various pieces into a whole. "Shaping a book is a physical process," she says, and that is precisely what we discovered that afternoon in the Windsor Room.

After spreading out everything from our "yes pile"—the name we had affectionately come to use for the group of works that had survived our necessarily ruthless screening—we spent hours and hours wandering up and down the rows between the tables, juxtaposing a poem and a memoir here, shifting a story there; shamelessly congratulating each other on the brilliance of our selections at one moment, and worrying about an omission at another moment. As we moved among our selections, as we shuffled and rearranged and reordered over a thousand pages of manuscript and fussed over a detail of excerpting here and a matter of balance or chronology there, we found ourselves reading poems and letters and memoirs aloud, declaiming some of them in full histrionics, others with quiet reverence, relishing both the variety and the echoes, and feeling simultaneously the high playfulness of creation and a curiously modest pride—characteristic perhaps of the work of editors as opposed to authors—of the kind that one might imagine grandparents feel, or great-grandparents, spending a few hours with their great-grandchildren, all brought together for the first time in one place.

By the time we left the Windsor Room and headed for a celebratory dinner, the book had literally taken shape beneath our hands. It is a shape that, as a quick glance at the table of contents will indicate, does not define itself along strictly chronological, generic, or thematic lines, but rather incorporates all three of those traditional organizational principles in what we hope is (to borrow a phrase from the poet Robert Herrick) a "sweet disorder." Our intention is to allow the work we have selected to be viewed from a variety of perspectives. Some of it is organized generically (e.g., poems, short stories) and some of it thematically (e.g., Invitations, Farewells), though as "The Walrus and the Carpenter" and Colette's wonderful vignette about her mother's spider friend illustrate, we have tried to avoid thinking of our thematic categories as narrow bins in which to collect and distribute the feed.

The generically defined sections allow some of the material to be considered alongside other works in the same genre, though within those sections we have varied the criteria for ordering: in the poetry section, for example, the arrangement is chronological by date of author's birth, whereas in the memoir section we have attempted instead to place pieces in revealing juxtapositions. Without forcing all of our selections into a chronological sequence, we have provided various opportunities— in the poetry section, for example, and in the clusters of letters that are scattered throughout the book in roughly chronological order—for those who want to consider the subject in an historical context. In a similar manner we have here and there placed a self-contained cluster of pieces, such as the grouping of Coleridge, Lamb, and Dorothy Wordsworth, or of Lowell, Taylor, and Heaney, which we call "Affinities." These clusters contain works that, despite being in a variety of genres and often on a variety of themes, in various ways refer to or illuminate each other or the mutual friendships of their authors. And then there are Shakespeare's works and the Bible, which we have felt it best to let stand alone.

Like our organizational scheme, our working definition of friendship has been, we hope, neither too loose nor too rigid but rather elastic. Though it is not inappropriate to imagine friendship between lovers, or between parents and children, or between husbands and wives, we have by and large emphasized nonsexual relationships of mutual regard and affection between people who are not kin. Though it is misleading and fruitless to draw strict boundaries around categories that, after all, vary greatly from one culture, and one historical era, to another, we have tried to avoid letting the concept of friendship expand endlessly to include any kind of decent behavior, goodwill, or benevolence. But this is a tricky business in a culture like ours, in which there are best-sellers with titles like *How to Be Your Own Best Friend,* or murderers, like the infamous Yorkshire killer, heir to Jack the Ripper, who apparently left a note with one of his victims quoting a popular song: "I want to thank you for being a friend." In this regard Dr. Johnson's quip about poetry has seemed to us the better part of wisdom about friendship as well: "What is poetry?" Boswell asks Johnson in his *Life.* "Why, sir," Johnson replies, "it is much easier to say what it is not. We all *know* what light is; but it is not easy to *tell* what it is."

Dr. Johnson's remark may soothe the anthologists' anxiety that before selecting their material they must have an unimpeachably precise definition of their subject. But while it may be reassuring to realize that we can happily agree on what does *not* relate to our subject, the real problem for us was not finding material but choosing from the enormous abundance of it. As with any anthology, readers will compile their own list of outrageous omissions. My own begins with Plato, Plutarch, Virgil, and the *Gilgamesh,* and comes up through Kant, Tennyson, Pushkin, Sand, Anne Frank, and M.F.K. Fisher, among hundreds of others. Particularly when one begins, as we did, with the assumption that everything is fair game—in any language, any literature, any period, any culture—the sense of omission can be overwhelming. But having agreed to open up the book in this way, we also agreed that, without being inattentive to matters of balance and representation, we would not try to make this into a textbook that adequately and justly represents various literatures, cultures, periods, and interests. We were not intent on establishing a canon but rather on bringing together our favorite writing about friendship.

Nor were we immune to the anthologist's fantasy of reading everything ever written on the subject and representing every conceivable perspective in a book that would be the last word on friendship unto eternity. But particularly with a subject as vast as friendship, one quickly discovers that as soon as one reads and smugly crosses off a dozen works from one's greatest hits list (which runs to the thousands from the outset), one finds another couple dozen the next week. The list may shrink in the course of a week or a month, but over a period of years—such is the perverse logic of anthologizing—it will mushroom. Sooner or later one realizes there is no help for it.

After deciding that we should not include excerpts from novels or plays (with the exception of Shakespeare), we found our task a bit simpler. But could we really compile an anthology of writing about friendship and not include *Don Quixote, Pride and Prejudice, Cranford, Great Expectations, Middlemarch, Huckleberry Finn, Tonio Kröger, Women in Love, Invisible Man, The Golden Notebook,* or *Sula?* The list could go on for pages. It seemed to us, however, that excerpts from nonfictional prose could more readily stand alone than excerpts from novels or plays, and we would, in any case, have a dozen short stories and Shakespeare.

Still, we were left with the question of how to choose from among the thousand or so pieces that we proposed to each other, since we only had room for roughly a fifth of them. Over the course of two years, Eudora and I photocopied possible selections, sent them to each other, then met periodically to decide which ones to include. As a preliminary means of gauging our evaluation of a proposed selection, we improvised our "Four-Star Softshell Crab Rating System," which came to us in the glow of culinary inspiration following our first dinner together.

Eudora and I had met eight years earlier and had exchanged a few letters in the interim, but this was our first extended time together. A few years before that, I had proposed a friendship anthology to a dozen publishers, and their response was unanimous: Friendship? Who's interested in friendship? It was not, they felt, a topic that would engage their readers.

When, in 1986, Norton began the series of anthologies of which ours is a part, I contacted the company to see if it might be interested, and indeed it was. The person who, in all the world, seemed to me the ideal coeditor for such a book was Eudora Welty. Her fiction, I felt, suggested the kind of compassion, vitality, generosity, and comic understanding that also characterize the best friendships; and she herself, from all accounts, had a genius for friendship in her own life. On the wild, one-in-a-million chance that she might actually want to join me in this project, I wrote her a letter and sent it along with the prospectus that I had drawn up for Norton. Not long afterward we were eating softshell crab together at Nick's Restaurant in Jackson, and I began to understand at first hand why she was such a legendary friend.

Whether something important has changed in the decade since those publishers declared friendship a topic unworthy of an anthology, or whether they simply misread the public interest, is not entirely clear. Surely the concerns and writings of both feminists and gays have focused new attention on matters of friendship. Moreover, as a result of the strains and fractures of the family, friendship seems more and more to be functioning, if not as a surrogate family, then at least as an increasingly important source of support and affection. But if friendship has taken on a new prominence and new dimensions, it has done so in a society in which not even intellectuals are familiar with the long tradition of writing about the subject. Ask any English professor for a list of works that deal with love, sex, or marriage, and you will hear a dozen rattled off without a pause. But ask the same question about friendship and, after the first couple items, you are likely to hear a loud silence. The subject of friendship seems to have been relegated to the cultural attic, and in the rare moments when it has been brought downstairs, it appears to have fallen into the hands of pop psychologists and self-help enthusiasts. For thousands of years, friendship was a major philosophical subject, the subject—as Wayne Booth has observed—"of thousands of books and tens of thousands of essays, [but] it has now dwindled to the point that our encyclopedias do not even mention it."

Why, then, have we maintained such stringent economies in both the analysis and the praise of friendship? As many of the selections in this book indicate, the subject has scarcely been ignored in modern literature; but somehow friendship as a serious subject has been buried or obscured in such a way that there is little serious public discussion of it beyond the occasional talk show and the how-to-do-it paperbacks that sometimes turn up on airport bookracks. At best it has seemed that friendship has acquired the allure of an anachronistic virtue, something of the charm of nostalgia.

Yet many people clearly feel, even if they do not acknowledge, that friendship is central to their lives. What is it, then, that accounts for the odd gap between our high regard for friendship and our relative silence about it? Perhaps friendship has slipped into an imaginative realm

around which, for the time being, some inner cultural necessity has
erected barriers against verbal inspection, in order to protect it from a
harsh environment.

By "harsh environment" I mean not only the narcissism, rootlessness,
alienation, and violence that seem to characterize much of our contemporary culture. I also mean that major tendency of twentieth-century
thought to explain all phenomena, including friendship, by tracing their
origins to the genes, the economy, or the unconscious, or to self-interest
or a series of power relations. Pretending to expose "bottom-line" motives beneath lofty feelings, these reductive forms of explanation patron-
ize friendship at best, and discredit it at worst.

The same, unfortunately, is true at the other end of the spectrum. If
friendship has had its problems with cynicism, it has had equal problems
with sentimentality. Much of friendship's currency in our time has been
in the platitudes of warmth and coziness that fill the popular "friendship
lines" of greeting cards; in the saccharine and desperate intimacies and
dependencies of soap-opera friendships; and in the endless commercial
parade of buddies playing racquetball before they reach for their Mi-
chelob or hop into their Toyota.

Friendship has had a hard go of it, for it has been distorted by both
sentimentality and cynicism. The sentimental view is based on the assumption that friendship moves and breathes in a realm of pure ether,
utterly free from the sublunar corruptions of competition, aggression,
and self-interest—to say nothing of politics, economics, and history. The
cynical view operates on the equally erroneous assumption that having
identified the presence of these factors, we have both provided a sufficient explanation of friendship and discredited its pretensions.

Over the course of the last decade when I have been writing about
friendship and working on this anthology, I have been advised time and
again to include a chapter or a section on betrayal, to concentrate on the
way friends manipulate each other, or to include this or that wonderful
illustration of the power games that friends play with each other. When
I mentioned the topic, people often assumed that the focus would be on
the failures of friendship (whereas Eudora and I have been much more
interested in successful friendship: how it works when it does work).
Clearly these reactions reveal something of friendship's particular difficulty in our culture, and one element of that difficulty is the knee-jerk
terror of sentimentality. Perhaps it protects us from commitments that
we are unable to make, but I find this endemic fear of sentimentality at
least as inhospitable to the flourishing of friendship as the actual sentimentality of our commercial icons.

Whatever the cause, our failure to take on the matter of friendship
has impoverished our relationships as deeply as it has our discourse. For

our language of friendship and our conceptions of it affect the way in which we actually experience friendship: our expectations, our hopes, our fears, our satisfactions, and our disappointments. It seems clear that friendship has been relegated to the cultural attic as much out of fear of sentimentality as out of a sense that it can easily be explained away as self-interested. This book takes a humbler stance before the complexities and mysteries of friendship than that of the cynic, and a more tough-minded view than that of the sentimentalist. In so doing it attempts to bring friendship downstairs again: to recover a lost tradition, to make this recently invisible subject visible again, and return it to the center of our lives.

INTRODUCTION BY
EUDORA WELTY

From the beginning of our plans as editors for the *Norton Book of Friendship,* we found ourselves the richer for the differences between us. One is an academic, the other a writer of fiction. One is a man, one a woman. We are of different ages and backgrounds and come from different parts of the country, though we both were graduated from colleges in the Middle West. The scholar-professor was born to be at home with statements on the nature of Friendship and what defined it—or indeed was proof of it; the fiction writer bound to seek among works of the imagination, showing forth Friendship, obliquely and dramatically, through its various aspects. We found our separate approaches congenial and promising. When we set our various choices side by side (each of us chose in either category) we found that rather than denying, or diminishing, each other, they opened ways for each other. Sometimes they suggested an unexpected tie.

In any case, we join in the two best ways for the purpose of editing a reader on Friendship: we both are readers, and we both are friends. Ronald Sharp and I are even friends of the same old friend; some years ago when I was visiting him in Ohio, he introduced us to each other.

That is to say, friendship was blessing our partnership. It *is* a blessing. As is true of all friendships: it might not have happened—and it did.

Not surprisingly, our search for entries took on the character it did because of the essential nature of the subject. "Friendship" is inherently a magnet. As with its own drawing power, it locates and draws to the surface, spreads before our eyes poems, stories, essays, letters, in the widest variety. The qualities of playfulness and frivolity adhere to friendship as rightfully as those of devotion, heroism, sacrifice, of meditation and retrospect. The Irish drinking song "The Rakes of Mallow" has a place here as well as Yeats's poem "The Municipal Gallery Re-visited."

Certainly friendship has proved a magnet to literature, an everlasting magnet. History, poetry, drama, letters have been drawn to the subject of friendship, not simply to celebrate it but to discover, perceive, learn from it the nature of ourselves, of humankind, the relationships we share in our world.

Friendship has inherited its literary treasury; it lies in the language. In the pages ahead are the classic statements; the indispensable questionings and answerings; the reasonings, the definitions. And in that treasury's further stores of pure gold are the works of the imagination, some old as time, some coined only yesterday.

A resident sense of discovery led the editors on; so did memory. (The pleasure of running to find a passage in a beloved book and finding what was supposed to be there *still there!*) Sometimes we could claim equal reward: we had made the identical discovery—at the same time, but while Ron was in Ohio and I was in Mississippi. How reassuringly filled with coincidence is friendship itself!

We counted on our meetings: showing our finds, making proposals for where each should go, offering our trades, then finding room for everything—for the time being. Ron generously undertook all the traveling; the book was made, unmade, and remade in Jackson. And yet, all the way, it seemed that a very solid undertaking was on serene and unendangered course. Its movement was steady, even on balance, I thought. And certainly, the reason for its progressing in safety was, once again, its subject.

Through our method of setting out our combined choices into the single sweeping view on the table or the floor, unexpected affinities offered themselves sometimes before our eyes. That was one way by which our work advanced. In the sheer pleasure of being led on by our own book, we often broke out laughing.

We spotted irresistible pairs of poems, entries whose origins were more likely to have made them incompatible. Seen together, their differences were not as interesting as their kinships. We saw again that friendship acts as a magnet, draws to it something of a circle of its own, poems, stories, or letters. We were looking at a form for putting together our book: the constellation. The one that was apparent from the first is the one that leads off our book: we gave it the name "Invitations."

Should we try to include the novel? Which novel? Any specific question comes down, of course, to the basic question: which would be preferable, too little of Jane Austen, or none at all? If you cut *Emma,* such a wonderful novel of friendship, you would have to curtail Miss Bates, and this would be intolerable all around. We must leave out *Emma.* Miss Bates, who always found it hard not to go on talking about the blessings of friendship ("How shall I ever enumerate the dishes?") will go slighted one more time.

Of course we couldn't have *A Passage to India*, or any partition of *Swann's Way*. But neither could we include "Death in Venice," or *Fallen Idol* by Graham Greene, or *The Turn of the Screw*, where James slowly turns a household friendship for us until it shows a side of spiritual possession. All are novels on the subject of friendship and none will permit us to cut them. Nor the still shorter novel, like *Billy Budd*, which through its very tightness and tautness is the more vulnerable to loss. Just as one word could not be added to this penetrating novel of a friendship, not one word must be allowed subtracted from it.

Excerpting *must* diminish a novel, in respects still other than its length. Its charge of intent, its buildup of moral force, the full chord of its implications of meaning, its full stretch of time and reach of place, its power of drama—of course, most of all, its drama—are affected by meddling with its form. Interfering with its place, its timing, its focus, its symmetry and harmony of structure, would rob it of its identity, something which without any question goes in one piece.

A work of fiction is a world, single and complete and self-contained—altogether unlike life, though *like* life is what it must seem. It exists, as it was made, by one imagination. Any part of it partakes of its whole, and the pleasure of reading the novel comes partly from experiencing the delicate intimacy of its construction.

Lack of space is not the only reason for our omitting novels. The flawless comedies of P. G. Wodehouse, in which friendship takes most often a leading role (the Code of the Woosters calls for deeds of rescue, following which—the way it turns out—the rescuer must in his turn be rescued), will not transplant into the wide, general garden of the Friendship Book. As V. S. Pritchett has pointed out, Wodehouse's gift lay in writing fantasy; he was constructing a sealed-off and perfectly consistent world to itself which, to the very extent of its perfection and consistency and delight, does not exist at all except on its own terms.

The letters the *Book of Friendship* brings together have been written, at some point, from a battlefield in France, from a stretch on the Concord or the Merrimack River, from a deathbed in Rome, from a medieval tower in Ireland, from a cell in Reading Gaol, from a stagecoach bounding over a road in Austria with the youthful Mozart inside it jotting down a note to offer Joseph Haydn the dedication of his Six String Quartets.

All letters, old and new, are the still-existing parts of a life. To read them now is to be present when some discovery of truth—or perhaps untruth, some flash of light—is just occurring. It is clamorous with the moment's happiness or pain. To come upon a personal truth of a human being however little known, and now gone forever, is in some way to admit him to our friendship. What we've been told need not be momentous, but it can be as good as receiving the darting glance from some very bright eye, still mischievous and mischief-making, arriving from fifty or a hundred years ago.

The letters here are many and different, but they make us positive that the story of a life is ever present in each one, running just beneath the skin of its words. To some extent this is true of all letters for the reason that their writers' lives *are* still attached to them. Their lives have been attached to their letters since the day they were written.

Of all our entries, the letters offer the fewest generalizations on the subject of friendship. They lead us into a gallery of portraits. Some, with or without design, are self-portraits.

Edward Lear, who is everywhere known now for his inspired nonsense writings and drawings, in his own time made his living as a painter of landscapes. While living in Hastings, he was a neighbor of Tennyson. They became friends; the two regularly took their walks together, Tennyson reciting to Lear his day's achievement. And how congenial the cadences must have been to the author of "Far and few, far and few/ Are the lands where the Jumblies live./ Their heads are green and their hands are blue,/ And they went to sea in a sieve."

Lear worshiped Tennyson for his love of beauty. Under the inspiration of friendship and admiration, he was struck with the idea of illustrating Tennyson's poems: he wrote to ask Mrs. Tennyson.

It was the poet's "genius for the perception of the beautiful in landscape," he wrote, "which I am possibly more than most in my profession able to illustrate, not—pray understand me—from any other reason than that I possess a very remarkable collection of sketches from nature in such widely separated districts of Europe, not to say Asia and Africa." Tennyson, Emily let him know, did not object.

Edward Lear made his uncertain living by painting landscapes on commission. The hoped-for opportunity would come through various titled friends and acquaintances who had a desire for large paintings of remote sites in the reaches of the Empire or beyond. Lear would spend months in carrying a commission out.

He was a lonely man who loved children. He would go alone, traveling by necessity on foot into Syria, for example, then setting up his easel to make his delicate pencil and watercolor sketches (that are today so highly prized) which were intended to serve him as a notebook of information and color cues. He was unable to resist penciling in the margins nonsense notes to himself, still visible today. On return to his studio back home, he would spend the winter working the sketches up into oil paintings. He would carry them out according to Victorian standards: of giant size, densely and meticulously filled in, suitable for hanging in castle halls.

Lear worked when he could, for thirty-five years, proceeding from paintings to engravings, "vainly seeking," he wrote Mrs. Tennyson, "a method of doing them whereby I can eventually multiply my 200 designs by photograph or autograph or sneezigraph or any other graph." Toward the end of his life, tired and ill and unable to work, he lost heart and admitted that his plan had come to grief. The sheer size of his attempted gift had defeated him.

His genius lay in the effortless and spontaneous creation of nonsense. Any sample of it lives for us now, as fresh as the day it was first set down on some scrap of paper, perhaps to please a child the artist might have noticed running about in a lonely hotel dining room. What Lear would have wished to live forever was the set of illustrations to Tennyson's poems: the two hundred of them completed and dedicated, a monument to his friendship with the Laureate.

We include here some of his letters of progress; he only dared write them to *Mrs.* Tennyson.

Friendship pervades English literature, but not absolutely. It had better not be looked for in Mother Goose. Our nursery rhymes are in every respect callous, impervious to feelings. This callousness may have been deliberately cultivated in the earliest moral tales for children, to make childhood stronger, the better able to bear without tears anything that life ahead had in store.

We take note in this book that friendship sometimes simply does not "take." "I do not love thee, Dr. Fell" is the riddlelike expression of this.

We acknowledge friendship that has gone down to failure in its inception. Francis Parkman's great historical account of early European arrivers in North America tells how the native inhabitants, who watched their sails approach, greeted the strangers as they stepped ashore by offering them gifts and hospitality and shelter; with guidance into the wilderness that lay ahead. Thus began one long career of giant failure in friendship, never to be eradicated.

It will have been noticed that we have not omitted love from the *Book of Friendship*. Friendship and love are not arbitrarily divided here, any more than they are in life. They know each other and avail themselves of each other. The solidest friendship is that of friends who love one another.

Neither have we omitted death. A lasting literature of friendship has risen out of grief. Lines written in mourning fill some necessity for a

completion to the celebration of a friendship: the Chinese poems of
farewell upon a journey; Achilles' storm of pure rage at the messenger's
news of the death of Patroclus in the *Iliad;* Lorca's lament for the death
of a great bullfighter: his compulsive reiteration that it had happened at
five o'clock in the afternoon. There is the unbearable: Keats's message of
the close approach of his own death, written in the last of his letters to
his friend Brown: "I can scarcely bid you good bye even in a letter. I
always made an awkward bow."

And the indomitable: Swift's "Verses on the Death of Dr. Swift," the
poem that erects the poet's own life to memory, the ferocity of a passion
that stands alone, as a giant rock stands, assaulted by the thundering sea
around it.

Lately, in my old age, it has seemed to me, when friends meet to hold
a public service to pay tribute to one of their number who has died, that
without words to that effect ever being said, they are drawing a circle
around that friend. Speaking in turn one after the other, joining themselves together anew, they keep what they know of him intact. As if by
words expressed they might turn friendship into magic, the magic that
now, so clearly, it had been.

Did friendship between human beings come about in the first place
along with—or through—the inspiration of language? It can be safe to
say that when we learned to speak to, and listen to, rather than to strike
or be struck by, our fellow human beings, we found something worth
keeping alive, worth the possessing, for the rest of time. Might it possibly
have been the other way round—that the promptings of friendship
guided us into learning to express ourselves, teaching ourselves, between
us, a language to keep it by? Friendship might have been the first, as well
as the best, teacher of communication. Which came first, friendship or
the spoken word? They could rise from the same prompting: to draw
together, not to pull away, not to threaten any longer.

Friendship lives, as do we ourselves, in an ephemeral world. How
much its life depends on the written word. The English language itself is
friendship's greatest treasure. The title of a dedicatory poem by Ben
Jonson is "To the Memory of My Beloved, the Author, Mr. William
Shakespeare, and What He Hath Left Us." Do we not *owe* friendship,
as we owe Shakespeare, to language?

Ronald Sharp and I thought, on completing our choices for *The Norton Book of Friendship,* that friendship could be said to begin at the
point where it offers itself: with invitation. Now we bring the book to a
close in the same way, with an ancient song called "The Irish Dancer":

> I am of Ireland
> And of the holy land

Of Ireland.
Good sir, pray I thee,
Of sainte charity
Come and dance with me
In Ireland.

PART I

INVITATIONS

An onion with a friend is a roast lamb.

—Egyptian proverb

PO CHÜ-I

Invitation to Hsiao Chü-shih

(Written when Governor of Chung-chou)

Within the Gorges there is no lack of men;
They are people one meets, not people one cares for.
At my front door guests also arrive;
They are people one sits with, not people one knows.
When I look up, there are only clouds and trees;
When I look down—only my wife and child.
I sleep, eat, get up or sit still;
Apart from that, nothing happens at all.
But beyond the city Hsiao the hermit dwells;
And with *him* at least I find myself at ease.
For *he* can drink a full flagon of wine
And is good at reciting long-line poems.
Some afternoon, when the clerks have all gone home,
At a season when the path by the river bank is dry,
I beg you, take up your staff of bamboo-wood
And find your way to the parlour of the Government House.

Translated by Arthur Waley

BEN JONSON

INVITING A FRIEND TO SUPPER

Tonight, grave sir, both my poor house and I
    Do equally desire your company;
Not that we think us worthy such a guest,
    But that your worth will dignify our feast
With those that come; whose grace may make that seem
    Something, which else could hope for no esteem.
It is the fair acceptance, sir, creates
    The entertainment perfect, not the cates.
Yet shall you have, to rectify your palate,
    An olive, capers, or some better salad
Ushering the mutton; with a short-legged hen,
    If we can get her, full of eggs, and then
Lemons, and wine for sauce; to these, a coney
    Is not to be despaired of, for our money;
And though fowl now be scarce, yet there are clerks,
    The sky not falling, think we may have larks.
I'll tell you of more, and lie, so you will come:
    Of partridge, pheasant, woodcock, of which some
May yet be there; and godwit, if we can;
    Knat, rail and ruff, too. Howsoe'er, my man
Shall read a piece of Virgil, Tacitus,
    Livy, or of some better book to us,
Of which we'll speak our minds, amidst our meat;
    And I'll profess no verses to repeat;
To this, if aught appear which I not know of,
    That will the pastry, not my paper, show of.
Digestive cheese and fruit there sure will be;
    But that which most doth take my muse and me
Is a pure cup of rich Canary wine,
    Which is the Mermaid's now, but shall be mine;
Of which had Horace or Anacreon tasted,
    Their lives, as do their lines, till now had lasted.

Tobacco, nectar, or the Thespian spring
   Are all but Luther's beer to this I sing.
Of this we will sup free, but moderately;
   And we will have no Poley or Parrot by;
Nor shall our cups make any guilty men,
   But at our parting we will be as when
We innocently met. No simple word
   That shall be uttered at our mirthful board
Shall make us sad next morning, or affright
   The liberty that we'll enjoy tonight.

HORACE

EPISTLE 1.5

Torquatus, if my tiny couches can hold you, and my herbs
And greens—and not too much of them—can satisfy your stomach,
I'll wait for you, here at home, when the sun goes down.
Our wine will be from marshy Minturné, near Petrinum,
And only as old as Statilius Taurus' second consulate:
If you've anything better, send it—or drink what I give you.
The fire has been bright and hot, for you, and my furniture's clean.
Forget ambition and the making of still more money, forget
Your famous clients: tomorrow is Caesar's birthday,
Everyone's allowed to relax and to sleep. No one will mind
If we stretch a summer's night with pleasant talk.
     What good are Fortune's gifts, unused? Worry
For what your heir will have and you're halfway along
The road to madness. I'll take the first cup, I'll wear
The first flowers: who cares—not me!—how it looks?
Wine was made for miracles, and makes them: it reveals secrets,
Our hearts go leaping high, and higher, cowards run
Into battle, anxiety lifts from our backs, even art opens
Itself. Whose tongue can resist hot wine? Even grinding
Poverty falls away, and a man feels free.

My duty (cheerfully assumed) will be to keep you
From dirty napkins, which wrinkle your nose, to save you
From faded couches, which offend your eyes, to offer you cups
And plates bright as a mirror, to let no one in who would carry out
What good friends say inside: equal with equal,
Equally met.
　　　Butra will come, and Septus,
And Subinus too—if no one offers him better, no woman
Offers herself. Bring anyone you like, I have room
—Though too many sweating guests can turn into fragrant goats.
Write me, tell me how many, then leave law and lawyers—
And escape from that client, waiting to ambush you out in the hall!

Translated by Burton Raffel

JAMES BOSWELL

From THE LIFE OF SAMUEL JOHNSON

Sunday, 16 April 1775

. . . I regretted that I had lost much of my disposition to admire, which
people generally do as they advance in life. JOHNSON. "Sir, as a man
advances in life, he gets what is better than admiration—judgement, to
estimate things at their true value." I still insisted that admiration was
more pleasing than judgement, as love is more pleasing than friendship.
The feeling of friendship is like that of being comfortably filled with
roast beef; love, like being enlivened with champagne. JOHNSON. "No,
Sir; admiration and love are like being intoxicated with champagne;
judgement and friendship like being enlivened. . . ."

COLETTE

From My Mother's House

Have you ever heard tell of Pelisson's spider that so passionately loved music? I for one am ready to believe it and also to add, as my slender contribution to the sum of human knowledge, the story of the spider that my mother kept—as my father expressed it—on her ceiling, in that year that ushered in my sixteenth spring. A handsome garden spider she was, her belly like a clove of garlic emblazoned with an ornate cross. In the daytime she slept, or hunted in the web that she had spun across the bedroom ceiling. But during the night, towards three o'clock in the morning, at the moment when her chronic insomnia caused my mother to relight the lamp and open her bedside book, the great spider would also wake, and after a careful survey would lower herself from the ceiling by a thread, directly above the little oil lamp upon which a bowl of chocolate simmered through the night. Slowly she would descend, swinging limply to and fro like a big bead, and grasping the edge of the cup with all her eight legs, she would bend over head foremost and drink to satiety. Then she would draw herself ceilingwards again, heavy with creamy chocolate, her ascent punctuated by the pauses and meditations imposed by an overloaded stomach, and would resume her post in the centre of her silken rigging.

Translated by Enid McLeod and Una Troubridge

LEWIS CARROLL

The Walrus and the Carpenter

The sun was shining on the sea,
Shining with all his might:

He did his very best to make
   The billows smooth and bright—
And this was odd, because it was
   The middle of the night.

The moon was shining sulkily,
   Because she thought the sun
Had got no business to be there
   After the day was done—
"It's very rude of him," she said,
   "To come and spoil the fun!"

The sea was wet as wet could be,
   The sands were dry as dry.
You could not see a cloud, because
   No cloud was in the sky:
No birds were flying overhead—
   There were no birds to fly.

The Walrus and the Carpenter
   Were walking close at hand;
They wept like anything to see
   Such quantities of sand:
"If this were only cleared away,"
   They said, "it *would* be grand!"

"If seven maids with seven mops
   Swept it for half a year,
Do you suppose," the Walrus said,
   "That they could get it clear?"
"I doubt it," said the Carpenter,
   And shed a bitter tear.

"O Oysters, come and walk with us!"
   The Walrus did beseech.
"A pleasant walk, a pleasant talk,
   Along the briny beach:
We cannot do with more than four,
   To give a hand to each."

The eldest Oyster looked at him,
   But never a word he said:

The eldest Oyster winked his eye,
  And shook his heavy head—
Meaning to say he did not choose
  To leave the oyster-bed.

But four young Oysters hurried up,
  All eager for the treat:
Their coats were brushed, their faces washed,
  Their shoes were clean and neat—
And this was odd, because, you know,
  They hadn't any feet.

Four other Oysters followed them,
  And yet another four;
And thick and fast they came at last,
  And more, and more, and more—
All hopping through the frothy waves,
  And scrambling to the shore.

The Walrus and the Carpenter
  Walked on a mile or so,
And then they rested on a rock
  Conveniently low:
And all the little Oysters stood
  And waited in a row.

"The time has come," the Walrus said,
  "To talk of many things:
Of shoes—and ships—and sealing-wax—
  Of cabbages—and kings—
And why the sea is boiling hot—
  And whether pigs have wings."

"But wait a bit," the Oysters cried,
  "Before we have our chat;
For some of us are out of breath,
  And all of us are fat!"
"No hurry!" said the Carpenter.
  They thanked him much for that.

"A loaf of bread," the Walrus said,
  "Is what we chiefly need:

Pepper and vinegar besides
    Are very good indeed—
Now if you're ready, Oysters dear,
    We can begin to feed."

"But not on us!" the Oysters cried,
    Turning a little blue.
"After such kindness, that would be
    A dismal thing to do!"
"The night is fine," the Walrus said.
    "Do you admire the view?

"It was so kind of you to come!
    And you are very nice!"
The Carpenter said nothing but
    "Cut us another slice:
I wish you were not quite so deaf—
    I've had to ask you twice!"

"It seems a shame," the Walrus said,
    "To play them such a trick,
After we've brought them out so far,
    And made them trot so quick!"
The Carpenter said nothing but
    "The butter's spread too thick!"

"I weep for you," the Walrus said:
    "I deeply sympathize."
With sobs and tears he sorted out
    Those of the largest size,
Holding his pocket-handkerchief
    Before his streaming eyes.

"O Oysters," said the Carpenter,
    "You've had a pleasant run!
Shall we be trotting home again?"
    But answer came there none—
And this was scarcely odd, because
    They'd eaten every one.

CHARLES LAMB

To Thomas Manning

22 September 1800

Dear Manning

You needed not imagine any apology necessary. Your fine hare and fine birds (which just now are dangling by our kitchen blaze) discourse most eloquent music in your justification. You just nick'd my palate. For, with all due decorum & leave may it be spoken, my worship hath taken physic for his body to day, and being low and puling requireth to be pampered. Foh! how beautiful and strong those buttered onions come to my nose. For you must know we extract a divine spirit of Gravy from those materials, which duly compounded with a consistence of bread & cream (y'clept bread sauce) each to each giving double grace, do mutually illustrate and set off (as skilful gold-foils to rare jewels) Your partridge, pheasant, woodcock, snipe, teal, widgeon, and the other lesser daughters of the *Ark* . . . My friendship, struggling with my Carnal & *fleshy* prudence (which suggests that a bird a man is the proper allotment in such cases) yearneth sometimes to have thee here to pick a wing or so. I question if your Norfolk sauces match our London culinarie.

ROBERT BURNS

Here's a bottle and an honest friend

Here's a bottle and an honest friend!
What wad ye wish for mair, man?

Wha kens, before his life may end,
What his share may be of care, man.

Then catch the moments as they fly,
And use them as ye ought, man:—
Believe me, happiness is shy,
And comes not ay when sought, man.

RAYMOND CARVER

My Boat

My boat is being made to order. Right now it's about to leave
the hands of its builders. I've reserved a special place
for it down at the marina. It's going to have plenty of room
on it for all my friends: Richard, Bill, Chuck, Toby, Jim, Hayden,
Gary, George, Harold, Don, Dick, Scott, Geoffrey, Jack,
Paul, Jay, Morris, and Alfredo. All my friends! They know who they
    are.
Tess, of course. I wouldn't go anyplace without her.
And Kristina, Merry, Catherine, Diane, Sally, Annick, Pat, Judith,
    Susie, Lynne, Cindy, Jean, Mona.
Doug and Amy! They're family, but they're also my friends,
and they like a good time. There's room on my boat
for just about everyone. I'm serious about this!
There'll be a place on board for everyone's stories.
My own, but also the ones belonging to my friends.
Short stories, and the ones that go on and on. The true
and the made-up. The ones already finished, and the ones still being
    written.
Poems, too! Lyric poems, and the longer, darker narratives.
For my painter friends, paints and canvases will be on board my boat.
We'll have fried chicken, lunch meats, cheeses, rolls,
French bread. Every good thing that my friends and I like.
And a big basket of fruit, in case anyone wants fruit.
In case anyone wants to say he or she ate an apple,

or some grapes, on my boat. Whatever my friends want,
name it, and it'll be there. Soda pop of all kinds.
Beer and wine, sure. No one will be denied anything, on my boat.
We'll go out into the sunny harbor and have fun, that's the idea.
Just have a good time all around. Not thinking
about this or that or getting ahead or falling behind.
Fishing poles if anyone wants to fish. The fish are out there!
We may even go a little way down the coast, on my boat.
But nothing dangerous, nothing too serious.
The idea is simply to enjoy ourselves and not get scared.
We'll eat and drink and laugh a lot, on my boat.
I've always wanted to take at least one trip like this,
with my friends, on my boat. If we want to
we'll listen to Schumann on the CBC.
But if that doesn't work out, okay,
we'll switch to KRAB, The Who, and the Rolling Stones.
Whatever makes my friends happy! Maybe everyone
will have their own radio, on my boat. In any case,
we're going to have a big time. People are going to have fun,
and do what they want to do, on my boat.

WANG WEI

To the Bachelor of Arts P'ei Ti

Of late during the sacrificial month, the weather has been calm and
clear, and I might easily have crossed the mountain. But I knew that you
were conning the classics and did not dare disturb you. So I roamed
about the mountain-side, rested at the Kan-p'ei Temple, dined with the
mountain priests, and, after dinner, came home again. Going north-
wards, I crossed the Yüan-pa, over whose waters the unclouded moon
shone with dazzling rim. When night was far advanced, I mounted
Hua-tzŭ's Hill and saw the moonlight tossed up and thrown down by the
jostling waves of Wang River. On the wintry mountain distant lights
twinkled and vanished; in some deep lane beyond the forest a dog barked
at the cold, with a cry as fierce as a wolf's. The sound of villagers grinding

their corn at night filled the gaps between the slow chiming of a distant bell.

Now I am sitting alone. I listen, but cannot hear my grooms and servants move or speak. I think much of old days: how hand in hand, composing poems as we went, we walked down twisting paths to the banks of clear streams.

We must wait for Spring to come: till the grasses sprout and the trees bloom. Then wandering together in the spring hills we shall see the trout leap lightly from the stream, the white gulls stretch their wings, the dew fall on the green moss. And in the morning we shall hear the cry of curlews in the barley-fields.

It is not long to wait. Shall you be with me then? Did I not know the natural subtlety of your intelligence, I would not dare address to you so remote an invitation. You will understand that a deep feeling dictates this course.

Written without disrespect by Wang Wei, a dweller in the mountains.

Translated by Arthur Waley

SAPPHO

Horses in Flowers

Come out of Crete
And find me here,
Come to your grove,
Mellow apple trees
And holy altar
Where the sweet smoke
Of libanum is in
Your praise.

Where Leaf melody
In the apples
Is a crystal crash,

And the water is cold.
All roses and shadow,
This place, and sleep
Like dusk sifts down
From trembling leaves.

Here horses stand
In flowers and graze.
The wind is glad
And sweet in its moving.
Here, Kypris [ ]*
Pour nectar in the golden cups
And mix it deftly with
Our dancing and mortal wine.

Translated by Guy Davenport

ROBERT FROST

THE PASTURE

I'm going out to clean the pasture spring;
I'll only stop to rake the leaves away
(And wait to watch the water clear, I may):
I shan't be gone long.—You come too.

I'm going out to fetch the little calf
That's standing by the mother. It's so young
It totters when she licks it with her tongue.
I shan't be gone long.—You come too.

*Illegible words in the manuscript.

V. S. PRITCHETT

THE EVILS OF SPAIN

We took our seats at the table. There were seven of us. It was at one of those taverns in Madrid. The moment we sat down Juliano, the little, hen-headed, red-lipped consumptive who was paying for the dinner and who laughed not with his mouth but by crinkling the skin round his eyes into scores of scratchy lines and showing his bony teeth—Juliano got up and said: "We are all badly placed." Fernando and Felix said: "No, we are not badly placed." And this started another argument shouting between the lot of us. We had been arguing all the way to the restaurant. The proprietor then offered a new table in a different way. Unanimously we said: "No," to settle the row; and when he brought the table and put it into place and laid a red and white check tablecloth on it, we sat down, stretched our legs, and said: "Yes. This table is much better."

Before this we had called for Angel at his hotel. We shook his hand or slapped him on the back or embraced him and two hung on his arm as we walked down the street. "Ah, Angel, the rogue!" we said, giving him a squeeze. Our smooth Mediterranean Angel! "The uncle!" we said. "The old scoundrel." Angel smiled, lowering his black lashes in appreciation. Juliano gave him a prod in the ribs and asked him if he remembered, after all these years, that summer at Biarritz. When we had all been together? The only time we had all been together before? Juliano laughed by making his eyes wicked and expectant, like one Andalusian reminding another of the great joke they had had the day poor So-and-So fell down the stairs and broke his neck.

"The day you were nearly drowned," Juliano said.

Angel's complexion was the colour of white coffee; his hair, crinkled like a black fern, was parted in the middle, he was rich, soft-palmed, and patient. He was the only well-dressed man among us, the suavest shouter. Now he sat next door but one to Juliano. Fernando was between them, Juan next to me, and at the end Felix. They had put Caesar at the head of the table, because he was the oldest and the largest. Indeed, at his age he found his weight tiring to the feet.

Caesar did not speak much. He gave his silent weight to the dinner,
letting his head drop like someone falling asleep, and listening. To the
noise we made, his silence was a balance and he nodded all the time
slowly, making everything true. Sometimes someone told some story
about him and he listened to that, nodding and not disputing it.

But we were talking chiefly of that summer, the one when Angel (the
old uncle!) had nearly been drowned. Then Juan, the stout, swarthy one,
banged the table with his hairy hands and put on his horn-rimmed
glasses. He was the smallest and most vehement of us, the one with the
thickest neck and the deepest voice, his words like barrels rumbling in a
cellar.

"Come on! Come on! Let's make up our minds! What are we going to
eat? Eat! Eat!" he roared.

"Yes," we cried. "Drink! What are we going to drink?"

The proprietor, who was in his shirt-sleeves and braces, said it was for
us to decide. We could have anything we wanted. This started another
argument. He stepped back a pace and put himself in an attitude of
self-defence.

"Soup! Soup? Make up your minds about soup! Who wants soup?"
bawled Juan.

"Red wine," some of us answered. And others: "Not red, white."

"Soup I said," shouted Juan. "Yes," we all shouted. "Soup."

"Ah," said Juan, shaking his head, in his slow miserable disappointed
voice. "Nobody have any soup. I want some soup. Nobody soup," he said
sadly to the proprietor.

Juliano was bouncing in his chair and saying, God, he would never
forget that summer when Angel was nearly drowned! When we had all
been together. But Juan said Felix had not been there and we had to
straighten that matter out.

Juliano said: "They carried him on to the beach, our little Angel on to
the beach. And the beach superintendent came through the crowd and
said: 'What's happening?' 'Nothing,' we said. 'A man knocked out.'
'Knocked out?' said the beach superintendent. 'Nothing,' we said.
'Drowned!' A lot of people left the crowd and ran about over the beach
saying: 'A man has been drowned.' 'Drowned,' said the beach superintendent. Angel was lying in the middle of them all, unconscious, with
water pouring out of his mouth."

"No! No!" shouted Fernando. "No. It wasn't like that."

"How do you mean, it wasn't like that?" cried Juliano. "I was there."
He appealed to us: "I was there."

"Yes, you were there," we said.

"I *was* there. I was there bringing him in. You say it wasn't like that, but it was like that. We were all there." Juliano jumped protesting to his feet, flung back his coat from his defying chest. His waistcoat was very loose over his stomach, draughty.

"What happened was better than that," Fernando said.

"Ah," said Juliano, suddenly sitting down and grinning with his eyes at everyone, very pleased at his show.

"It was better," he said.

"How better?" said Juliano.

Fernando was a man who waited for silence and his hour. Once getting possession of the conversation he never let it go, but held it in the long, soothing ecstasy of a pliable embrace. All day long he lay in bed in his room in Fuencarral with the shutters closed, recovering from the bout of the day before. He was preparing himself to appear in the evening, spruce, grey-haired, and meaty under the deep black crescents of his eyebrows, his cheeks ripening like plums as the evening advanced, his blue eyes, which got bloodshot early, becoming mistier. He was a man who ripened and moistened. He talked his way through dinner into the night, his voice loosening, his eyes misting, his walk becoming slower and stealthier, acting every sentence, as if he were swaying through the exalted phase of inebriation. But it was an inebriation purely verbal; an exaltation of dramatic moments, refinements upon situations; and hour after hour passed until the dawn found him sodden in his own anecdotes, like a fruit in rum.

"What happened was," Fernando said, "that I was in the sea. And after a while I discovered Angel was in the sea. As you know, there is nothing more perilous than the sea, but with Angel in it the peril is tripled; and when I saw him I was preparing to get as far away as possible. But he was making faces in the water and soon he made such a face, so inhuman, so unnatural, I saw he was drowning. This did not surprise me, for Angel is one of those men who, when he is in the sea, he drowns. There is some psychological antipathy. Now, when I see a man drowning my instinct is to get away quickly. A man drowning is not a man. He is a lunatic. But a lunatic like Angel! But unfortunately he got me before I could get away. There he was," Fernando stood up and raised his arm, confronting the proprietor of the restaurant, but staring right through that defensive man, "beating the water, diving, spluttering, choking, spitting, and, seeing he was drowning, for the man *was* drowning, caught hold of me, and we both went under. Angel was like a beast. He clung to me like seaweed. I, seeing this, awarded him a knock-out— zum—but as the tenacity of man increases with unconsciousness, Angel stuck to me like a limpet, and in saving myself there was no escape from saving him."

"That's true," said Angel, admiring his fingernails. And Caesar nodded his head up and down twice, which made it true.

Juan then swung round and called out: "Eat! Food! Let us order. Let us eat. We haven't ordered. We do nothing but talk, not eat. I want to eat."

"Yes, come on," said Felix. "Eat. What's the fish?"

"The fish," said the proprietor, "is bacalao."

"Yes," everyone cried. "Bacalao, a good bacalao, a very good one. No, it must be good. No. I can't eat it unless it's good, very good *and* very good."

"No," we said. "Not fish. We don't want it."

"Seven bacalaos, then?" said the proprietor.

But Fernando was still on his feet.

"And the beach inspector said: 'What's his name and address and has he any identity papers?' 'Man,' I said, 'he's in his bathing dress. Where could he keep his papers?' And Juan said: 'Get a doctor. Don't stand there asking questions. Get a doctor.' "

"That's true," said Juan gloomily. "He wasn't dead."

"Get a doctor, that was it," Angel said.

"And they got a doctor and brought him round and got half the Bay of Biscay out of him, gallons of it. It astonished me that so much water could come out of a man."

"And then in the evening"—Juliano leaped up and clipped the story out of Fernando's mouth. "Angel says to the proprietor of the hotel—"

Juan's head had sunk to his chest. His hands were over his ears.

"Eat," he bawled in a voice of despair so final that we all stopped talking and gazed at him with astonishment for a few moments. Then in sadness he turned to me, appealing. "Can't we eat? I am empty."

". . . said to the proprietor of the hotel," Fernando grabbed the tale back from Juliano, "who was rushing down the corridor with a face like a fish. 'I am the man who was drowned this morning.' And the proprietor who looked at Angel like a prawn, the proprietor said: 'M'sieu, whether you were drowned or not drowned this morning, you are about to be roast. The hotel is on fire.' "

"That's right," we said. "The hotel was on fire."

"I remember," said Felix. "It began in the kitchen."

"How in the kitchen?"

This then became the argument.

"The first time ever I heard it was in the kitchen."

"But no," said Angel, softly rising to claim his life story for himself. Juliano clapped his hands and bounced with joy. "It was not like that."

"But we were all there, Angel," Fernando said; but Angel, who spoke very rapidly, said:

"No and no! And the proof of it is. What was I wearing?" He challenged all of us. We paused.

"Tripe," said Juan to me, hopelessly wagging his head. "You like tripe? They do it well. Here! Phist!" he called the proprietor through the din. "Have you tripe, a good Basque tripe? No? What a pity! Can you get me some? Here! Listen," he shouted to the rest of the table. "Tripe," he shouted, but they were engrossed in Angel.

"Pyjamas," Fernando said. "When you are in bed you wear your pyjamas."

"Exactly, and they were not my pyjamas."

"You say the fire was not in the kitchen," shouted Fernando, "because the pyjamas you were wearing were not yours!" And we shouted back at Angel.

"They belonged to the Italian Ambassador," said Angel, "the one who was with that beautiful Mexican girl."

Then Caesar, who, as I have said, was the oldest of us and sat at the head of the table, Caesar leaned his old big pale face forward and said in a hushed voice, putting out his hands like a blind man remembering:

"My God—but what a very beautiful woman she was," he said. "I remember her. I have never in my life," he said speaking all his words slowly and with grave concern, "seen such a beautiful woman."

Fernando and Angel, who had been standing, sat down. We all looked in awe at the huge, old-shouldered Caesar with his big pale face and the pockets under his little grey eyes, who was speaking of the most beautiful woman he had ever seen.

"She was there all that summer," Caesar said. "She was no longer young." He leaned forward with his hands on the table. "What must she have been when she was young?"

A beach, the green sea dancing down white upon it, that Mexican woman walking over the floor of a restaurant, the warm white houses, the night glossy black like the toe of a patent shoe, her hair black. We tried to think how many years ago this was. Brought by his voice to silence us, she was already fading.

The proprietor took his opportunity in our silence. "The bacalao is done in the Basque fashions with peppers and potatoes. Bring a bacalao," he snapped to a youth in the kitchen.

Suddenly Juan brought his fists on the table, pushed back his chair, and beat his chest with one fist and then the other. He swore in his enormous voice by his private parts.

"It's eleven o'clock. Eat! For God's sake. Fernando stands there talking and talking and no one listens to anybody. It is one of the evils of Spain. Someone stop him. Eat."

We all woke up and glared with the defiance of the bewildered, rejecting everything he said. Then what he said to us penetrated. A wave roared over us and we were with him. We agreed with what he said. We all stood up and, by our private parts, swore that he was right. It was one of the evils of Spain.

The soup arrived. White wine arrived.

"I didn't order soup," some shouted.

"I said 'Red wine,' " others said.

"It is a mistake," the proprietor said. "I'll take it away." An argument started about this.

"No," we said. "Leave it. We want it." And then we said the soup was bad, and the wine was bad and everything he brought was bad, but the proprietor said the soup was good and the wine was good and we said in the end it was good. We told the proprietor the restaurant was good, but he said not very good—indeed, bad. And then we asked Angel to explain about the pyjamas.

PART II

CLASSIC ESSAYS

*Of all the means to insure happiness
throughout the whole of life, by far
the most important is the acquisition
of friends.*

—*Epicurus*

ARISTOTLE

From Nicomachean Ethics

(Aristotle's remarks are essentially a reconstruction of notes from his lectures. Brackets [] indicate additions made by the translator for the sake of clarity.)

Friendship also seems to hold states together, and lawgivers apparently devote more attention to it than to justice. For concord seems to be something similar to friendship, and concord is what they most strive to attain, while they do their best to expel faction, the enemy of concord. When people are friends, they have no need of justice, but when they are just, they need friendship in addition. . . .

. . . There are three kinds of friendship, corresponding in number to the objects worthy of affection. In each of these, the affection can be reciprocated so that the partner is aware of it, and the partners wish for each other's good in terms of the motive on which their affection is based. Now, when the motive of the affection is usefulness, the partners do not feel affection for one another *per se* but in terms of the good accruing to each from the other. The same is also true of those whose friendship is based on pleasure: we love witty people not for what they are, but for the pleasure they give us.

So we see that when the useful is the basis of affection, men love because of the good they get out of it, and when pleasure is the basis, for the pleasure they get out of it. In other words, the friend is loved not because he is a friend, but because he is useful or pleasant. Thus, these two kinds are friendship only incidentally, since the object of affection is not loved for being the kind of person he is, but for providing some good or pleasure. Consequently, such friendships are easily dissolved when the partners do not remain unchanged: the affection ceases as soon as one partner is no longer pleasant or useful to the other. Now, usefulness is not something permanent, but differs at different times. Accordingly, with the disappearance of the motive for being friends, the friendship, too, is dissolved, since the friendship owed its existence to these motives.

Friendships of this kind seem to occur most commonly among old people, because at that age men do not pursue the pleasant but the beneficial. They are also found among young men and those in their prime who are out for their own advantage. Such friends are not at all given to living in each other's company, for sometimes they do not even find each other pleasant. Therefore, they have no further need of this relationship, if they are not mutually beneficial. They find each other pleasant only to the extent that they have hopes of some good coming out of it. The traditional friendship between host and guest is also placed in this group.

Friendship of young people seems to be based on pleasure. For their lives are guided by emotion, and they pursue most intensely what they find pleasant and what the moment brings. As they advance in years, different things come to be pleasant for them. Hence they become friends quickly and just as quickly cease to be friends. For as another thing becomes pleasant, the friendship, too, changes, and the pleasure of a young man changes quickly. Also, young people are prone to fall in love, since the greater part of falling in love is a matter of emotion and based on pleasure. That is why they form a friendship and give it up again so quickly that the change often takes place within the same day. But they do wish to be together all day and to live together, because it is in this way that they get what they want out of their friendship.

The perfect form of friendship is that between good men who are alike in excellence or virtue. For these friends wish alike for one another's good because they are good men, and they are good *per se* [that is, their goodness is something intrinsic, not incidental]. Those who wish for their friends' good for their friends' sake are friends in the truest sense, since their attitude is determined by what their friends are and not by incidental considerations. Hence their friendship lasts as long as they are good, and [that means it will last for a long time, since] goodness or virtue is a thing that lasts. In addition, each partner is both good in the unqualified sense and good for his friend. . . . Moreover, time and familiarity are required. For, as the proverb has it, people cannot know each other until they have eaten the specified [measure of] salt together. . . . The wish to be friends can come about quickly, but friendship cannot. . . .

To be friends with many people, in the sense of perfect friendship, is impossible, just as it is impossible to be in love with many people at the same time. For love is like an extreme, and an extreme tends to be unique. . . .

Good will looks like a friendly relationship, but friendship it is not. For we can have good will toward people we do not know and the fact that we have it may remain unnoticed, but there can be no friendship in such circumstances. That has already been stated. But good will is not even affection: it lacks intensity and desire, the qualities which [always] accompany affection. Further, affection involves familiarity, whereas good will can arise on the spur of the moment, as it does, for example, toward competitors in a contest: a spectator may come to have good will for a competitor and side with him without giving him any active assistance. For, as we said, the good will comes on the spur of the moment and the love is superficial.

So it seems that good will is the beginning of friendship, just as the pleasure we get from seeing a person is the beginning of falling in love. For no one falls in love who has not first derived pleasure from the looks of the beloved. But if someone finds joy in the looks of another, he is not in love with him for all that: [he is in love only] if he longs for the beloved when he is away and craves his presence. Thus, it is likewise impossible to be friends without first feeling good will toward one another, but people who have good will for one another do not therefore feel mutual affection. For they only wish for the good of those toward whom they have good will, without giving them active assistance in attaining the good and without letting themselves be troubled in their behalf. Hence one might call good will "friendship" in an extended sense, but it is inactive friendship. . . .

Is the need of friends greater in good fortune or in bad? Men seek them in both: in bad fortune they need their assistance, and in good fortune they need people with whom to live together and to whom they will be able to do good, since men wish to be beneficent. Accordingly, friends are more indispensable in bad fortune; and that is why the useful kind of friend is needed in such situations. But it is nobler to have friends in good fortune, and for that reason people look for good men [as their friends when they are well off], because it is more desirable to do good to them and to spend one's time with them.

The very presence of friends is pleasant in both good and bad fortune. Pain is alleviated when friends share the sorrow. In this connection, the question might be raised whether friends share a burden, as it were, or whether the truth is rather that the pain is reduced by the pleasantness which their presence brings, and by the thought that they are sharing the sorrow. Let us dismiss the question whether the alleviation is brought about by these or by some other factors. At any rate, it is evident that [friendship] brings about what we have said it does.

It seems that the presence of friends consists in a mixture of several factors. The very sight of friends is pleasant, especially at a time of misfortune, and it provides some relief from pain. For, if a friend is tactful, seeing him and talking to him are a source of comfort, since he knows our character and the things which give us pleasure or pain. But on the other hand, it is painful to see him pained by our misfortunes, for everyone tries to avoid being the cause of a friend's pain. For that reason, manly natures take scrupulous care not to let their friends share their pain, and, unless a man is extremely insensitive to pain, he cannot bear the pain which [sympathy for him] gives his friends. In general, such a person does not let others join in his lamentations, because he himself is not given to lamenting. But womenfolk and womanish men enjoy it when others join their mourning, and they feel affection for them as being their friends and sharers of their sorrow. Still, it is the better type of man whom we must obviously imitate in all matters.

In good fortune, the presence of friends brings with it a pleasant way of passing one's time and the pleasant thought that they are pleased by the good we are enjoying. This is a reason for thinking that we ought to be eager to invite our friends to share our good fortunes, since it is noble to do good, and to be reluctant to ask our friend to share our misfortunes, since one should let others participate as little as possible in what is evil. Hence the saying: "That I'm unfortunate is enough." We should invite our friends to come to our side chiefly when a little trouble on their part will mean a great benefit to us.

Conversely, it is perhaps fitting for a man to go unasked and eagerly to a friend in misfortune: doing good is the mark of a friend, and especially to do good to those in need without being asked, since that is nobler and more pleasant for both partners. It is also fitting to join eagerly in the activities of a friend who is enjoying good fortune, for here, too, friends are needed; but we should take our time in going to enjoy the fruits of their good fortune, for to be eager to receive a benefit is not noble. Still, we should perhaps scrupulously avoid the reputation of being disagreeable in rejecting their kindnesses, for that happens occasionally. So we see that the presence of friends is desirable in all circumstances.

Translated by Martin Ostwald

CICERO

From ON FRIENDSHIP

(The speaker is Laelius, whose friend Scipio Africanus has recently died.)

. . . I am particularly comforted by the fact that I am free of that error which in most men is the usual cause of anguish at the passing of friends. I do not feel that Scipio has suffered any misfortune; I am the one who has suffered misfortune, if any has occurred. But to be crushed by grief at one's own misfortunes is the act not of a man who loves his friend, but of one who loves himself. . . .

. . . Still, the joy that I gain from looking back upon our friendship causes me to conclude that my life has been rich and good, simply because I spent it in Scipio's company. He and I stood side by side in our concern for affairs of state and for personal matters; we shared a citizen's home and a soldier's tent; we shared the one element indispensable to friendship, a complete agreement in aims, ambitions, and attitudes. Therefore I do not take so much delight in that reputation for wisdom which Fannius mentioned a moment ago—and it isn't deserved, anyway—as I do in the hope that for all time to come men will remember my friendship with Scipio. And I cherish this hope the more because in all the course of history men can name scarcely three or four pairs of friends; to this category, I venture to hope, men will assign the friendship of Scipio and Laelius. . . .

. . . And so, if you want a philosophical disquisition on friendship, I suggest that you ask it of those who make a profession of such things. All I can do is to urge you to put friendship ahead of all other human concerns, for there is nothing so suited to man's nature, nothing that can mean so much to him, whether in good times or in bad. . . .

Now friendship is just this and nothing else: complete sympathy in all matters of importance, plus goodwill and affection, and I am inclined to think that with the exception of wisdom, the gods have given nothing finer to men than this. Some people place wealth ahead of it, some good health, some power, some honors, a good many even pleasure. This last, of course, is on the mere animal level; the others are unstable things that one can never be sure of, since they depend not upon our own efforts, but upon fickle Fortune. Those who say that virtue is man's highest good, are of course very inspiring; but it is to this very virtue that friendship owes its beginning and its identity: without virtue friendship cannot exist at all. . . .

Now friendship possesses many splendid advantages, but of course the finest thing of all about it is that it sends a ray of good hope into the future, and keeps our hearts from faltering or falling by the wayside. For the man who keeps his eye on a true friend, keeps it, so to speak, on a model of himself. For this reason, friends are together when they are separated, they are rich when they are poor, strong when they are weak, and—a thing even harder to explain—they live on after they have died, so great is the honor that follows them, so vivid the memory, so poignant the sorrow. That is why friends who have died are accounted happy, and those who survive them are deemed worthy of praise. Why, if the mutual love of friends were to be removed from the world, there is no single house, no single state that would go on existing; even agriculture would cease to be. If this seems a bit difficult to understand, we can readily see how great is the power of friendship and love by observing their opposites, enmity and ill will. For what house is so firmly established, what constitution is so unshakable, that it could not be utterly destroyed by hatred and internal division? From this we may judge how much good there is in friendship. . . .

. . . I have done a lot of thinking about friendship, and over and over again in the course of my reflections it has seemed to me that the most important question arising in connection with it is this: do men desire friendship because of their own feebleness and inadequacy, with the idea that by exchanging mutual services they may be able to give and to receive things that would be beyond their individual and separate powers? Or is this only a *result* of friendship, and there should be some other reason for it, something deeper and finer, and lying closer to man's very nature? For it is love *(amor),* the thing that gives us our word for friendship *(amicitia),* that provides the first impulse toward mutual regard. Advantages, you see, are garnered in many cases even by men who are the objects of simulated friendship, who are esteemed only for the sake of convenience. But in friendship there can be no element of show or pretense; everything in it is honest and spontaneous.

And so I should say that friendship takes its beginning from our very nature rather than from our sense of inadequacy, that it is due to an inclination of the heart together with a feeling of affection rather than to a consideration of the advantages which we might derive from the relation. . . .

. . . It is true, of course, that such a feeling of affection is placed on a firm basis only after they have received kindnesses from these persons, have seen evidence of their interest in them, and have come to be on a footing of intimacy with them; when that first affectionate impulse of the heart has been augmented by these considerations, then there bursts forth a great and wonderful glow of love. If anyone thinks that this is to be attributed to a mere sense of inadequacy—that it exists solely to provide men with assistance in the achieving of their ambitions—he surely leaves friendship with a very humble beginning, with a base and ignoble birth, so to speak. Why! He wants it to be the child of insufficiency and poverty! If this were so, the less confidence a man had in himself, the better suited would he be for friendship—but this is far from the truth.

For the more confidence a man has in himself, the more he finds himself so fortified by virtue and wisdom that he is completely self-sufficient and believes that his destiny is in his own hands, so much the better will he be both at making and at keeping friends. Just think! Did Africanus have some "need" of me? Of course not, nor I of him. Why, no! I cherished him because, in a way, I looked up to his virtue; he, me, because of an opinion not altogether low, perhaps, that he had formed of my character; and our affection for each other grew as we were thrown more and more together. To be sure, many great advantages came to us both from our association, but it was not in expectation of these that we first began to feel drawn toward each other.

For we do not exercise kindness and generosity in order that we may put in a claim for gratitude; we do not make our feelings of affection into a business proposition. No, there is something in our nature that impels us to the open hand and heart. . . .

. . . Well, then, dear friends, you shall hear what Scipio and I between us used to say on those many, many occasions when we were discussing friendship. You know, of course, that he always insisted that there was nothing harder than to maintain a friendship all the way to the last day of life, so often did it happen that interests did not agree, or there was a difference of opinion on political matters; he used to remark, too, that men's characters frequently suffer change, sometimes through ill fortune, sometimes with the increasing burden of years. As proof of these statements he used to take the analogy of boyhood, remarking that the friendships of boys were often laid aside along with the toga of childhood.

In cases where they were continued on into adulthood, he noted that they were still sometimes broken up by rivalry, either for a wife, or for some other advantage which the two could not obtain simultaneously. . . .

He used to say, too, that friendships were violently and in many cases

quite properly broken up when men demanded of their friends something that was morally reprehensible, for example, that they assist in
immorality, or aid in an illegal act. In these instances, men who refused
their help, however honorable such refusal might be, nonetheless could
be charged with violating the laws of friendship by those they refused to
go along with; and these latter, who made bold to demand complete
compliance from their friends, would say that they were showing, by the
very fact of such a demand, that they themselves would do anything
whatever for a friend's sake. This sort of complaint, he said, not only
frequently destroyed friendships of long standing, but even became the
source of enduring enmity. These, he declared, were the deadly perils, so
to speak, that overhung friendship, and they were so numerous that, as
he said it appeared to him, the avoiding of them required not only
wisdom but also sheer good luck. . . .

. . . Wrongdoing, then, is not excused if it is committed for the sake of
a friend; after all, the thing that brings friends together is their conviction of each other's virtue; it is hard to keep up a friendship, if one has
deserted virtue's camp. . . .

Let us, then, lay down this law for friendship: we must not ask wrong-
ful things, nor do them, if we are asked to. . . .

There are certain individuals, you know, who, I hear, are adjudged
wise men in Greece, and who—so it seems to me—have arrived at some
very remarkable conclusions—but there is no question which they cannot solve with those razor-sharp wits of theirs! In part, these thinkers
have concluded that men should shun too intimate friendships, for fear
that one man might find himself in difficulties on behalf of more individuals than just himself; after all, each of us has more than enough
troubles of his own, and, say they, it is not comfortable to be too deeply
involved in the troubles of others. The most expeditious course, they
assert, is to keep the reins of friendship as slack as possible, so that one
may pull up on them or loosen them at will; for the key to the happy life
is freedom from care, and the soul cannot enjoy this if, so to speak, a man
is required to produce it for others besides himself.

Others of these wise men, so they tell us, express an idea that shows
even less regard for human nature. They say . . . that friendship is
desirable for the sake of protection and assistance, not of goodwill and
charity; thus the less any individual has of moral and physical strength,
the more he demands friendship. This, they say, is why mere weak
women are more anxious for the protection afforded by friendship than
are men, poor men more anxious than rich men, and the unfortunate
more than those who would be considered lucky.

What a magnificent philosophy! Why! They take the very sun from
the heavens, I should say, when they take friendship from life, for of all

the gifts the gods have given us, this is our best source of goodness and of happiness. What, after all, is this "freedom from care" that they talk about? In appearance, it is seductive indeed, but in actual fact it is something that in many circumstances deserves only contempt. For it is not in accord with sound principle to refuse to undertake any honorable proposal or course of action, or having once undertaken any such thing, to refuse to go through with it, for fear one may lose one's peace of mind. . . .

And so, if pain does touch the heart of the wise man—and it certainly does, unless we are of the opinion that every vestige of human feeling has been rooted out of him—what earthly reason can be offered for excising friendship, root and branch, from life, for fear that it may become the cause of some slight hardship on our part? For if we remove all feeling from the heart, what difference is there, not, I hasten to say, between a man and an animal, but between a man and a rock or a stump or anything else of the kind? No, we must turn a deaf ear to those who insist that virtue is something hard and steely, so to speak. On the contrary, in many respects, and especially in friendship, it is soft and malleable, so that when our friends are blessed, it expands, and when they suffer misfortune, it contracts. No, indeed! That pain which we frequently must suffer on our friends' behalf is not an adequate reason for banishing friendship from our lives, any more than the cares and troubles which accompany virtue are reason for rejecting it. . . .

. . . For there is nothing more productive of joy than the repayment of kindness, or the sharing of interests and exchange of favors. . . .

And, you know, I surely think that those who form friendships for the sake of advantage destroy the link in friendship that is most productive of affection. It is not so much what we gain from our friend as the very love of the friend itself that gives us joy, and what we get from a friend gives us joy since it comes to us with love. . . .

. . . No, truly: friendship does not follow upon advantage, but advantage upon friendship. . . .

But—for here I go back to Scipio again, who was always talking about friendship—he constantly objected to the fact that in all other matters men were extremely careful; they could tell you how many goats and sheep they had, but not how many friends; in acquiring the former they took great pains, but in choosing friends they were careless, and did not even have signs, so to speak, or marks by which to judge which individuals were likely to make good friends. Obviously it is the reliable, the well-adjusted, and the loyal who should be chosen, but of this kind of people there is a great shortage, and in any case it is hard to pick them out unless one has had experience. But where is the experience to be gained except in friendship itself? Friendship comes before the ability to judge people, and thus precludes the opportunity to gain experience. . . .

. . . Ennius may be right when he says "A friend in need is a friend indeed." Still, the fact remains that the two things which most commonly prove men to be unreliable and weak are these: if, when they are prospering, they drop their friends, or if when their friends are in trouble, they desert them. And so, when anyone in either of these circumstances has shown himself a man of conviction, reliable, and loyal, we are bound to adjudge him one of a very rare species of men—a species virtually divine.

Now the foundation of that steadfastness and loyalty for which we are looking in friendship is trust, for nothing endures that cannot be trusted. The man we choose should be honest too, and unpretentious and congenial—with interests and concerns like our own. All of these qualities are related to trust, for we can have no trust in a devious and deceitful character, and the man whose interests are not like ours and who is not by nature sympathetic to us, cannot be either a trustworthy or reliable friend. We should add as a further point that he should not take delight in bringing charges against us nor believe them when they are brought; these qualities are related to that loyalty which I have already discussed. And so what I said in the beginning is true, that friendship cannot exist except between truly good men. Now it is the plain duty of a good man—and we may well call this "good man" our true philosopher—to keep two principles ever before him in the matter of friendship: first, that there be no element of deception or hypocrisy, for it is more characteristic of a gentleman to hate quite openly than to conceal his true opinion behind a front; second, not only to refuse to listen to accusations made by anybody against his friend, but to be himself above suspecting him—not be always thinking that his friend has done something wrong.

A man ought in addition to have a certain graciousness of speech and manners, for this adds no mean zest to friendship. People speak of rectitude, too, and of an all-pervading seriousness; the latter, to be sure, does impart solidity, but friendship must be more relaxed and less constricting and more pleasurable, and more inclined to affability and congeniality in all aspects.

At this point a question of some difficulty arises: are there any circumstances in which new friends, found worthy of friendship, should be put ahead of old friends, as, for example, we commonly put fresh young horses ahead of old, worn-out ones. No man worthy of the name will feel any hesitation here, for we have no right to get tired of friendships as we do of other things. It is always true that the old and familiar, like wines which can stand aging, is bound to have the best savor, and there is real truth in the familiar saying that people must eat many a peck of salt together if they are to know the full meaning of friendship. . . .

. . . old friendships must always have their proper place reserved for them, for nothing carries the weight of the old and familiar. . . .

Speaking in general terms, we must sit in judgment on our friendships after we have reached physical and intellectual maturity. There may be some individuals who in their earlier years were enthusiastic about hunting or ball-games; we are under no obligation to keep them in a relation of intimacy because we liked them at a time when we shared their enthusiasms. By any such principle as that, we shall be bound to reserve the greatest share of our affection for our nurses and tutors, just for old time's sake. We must not forget them, of course, but our relations with them must be judged by some other standard. Under any other rule, stable and lasting friendships cannot exist. For men's ways of acting and thinking change, and with them their interests, and when interests become different, friends begin to grow away from each other. . . .

. . . It happens many times in life that important considerations compel us to part from our friends. Anyone who tries to keep us from doing what we must and should in such cases, simply because he cannot bear the thought of losing us, is weak and self-indulgent, and for that very reason no true friend. . . .

. . . Sometimes, of course, wrongdoing that is completely intolerable flares up, and in such instances it is neither right nor honorable—in fact it is simply impossible—to refrain from an immediate act of divorce and separation.

Most commonly, however, a gradual change in character or in interests takes place, or people fall into disagreement about politics. . . .

. . . There is a degree of respect which we must pay to a friendship that has been: we must see that the wrong lies always on the side of the one who has done the injury, and not on the side of the one who has suffered it. In general, there is only one way to foresee and guard against all faults and hurts of this kind: we must not be too quick to bestow our affections, and we must not bestow them on men unworthy of them.

Now the men who are worthy of friendship are those who possess within themselves something that causes men to love them. They are a rare species—but of course the really fine is always rare, and there is nothing harder than to find something which in all respects is perfect of its kind. But the vast majority of mankind recognize nothing as good in the human sphere unless it be something profitable. In the matter of friends, as if they were so many domestic animals, they lavish their affections chiefly on those from whom they expect to derive the highest profit.

As a result, they know nothing of friendship in its finest and most natural guise—the friendship that is desirable for its own sake—and they set before themselves no image of the true nature and significance of friendship. For a man loves himself not in order to exact from himself some pay for his affection, but simply because every man is by his very nature dear to himself. Unless this same principle is transferred to friendship, a man will never find a true friend, for the true friend is, so to speak, a second self. . . .

. . . One could make up a long list of things that seem wonderful to some people, but which many, many others deem completely valueless. But all men, to the last man, are in agreement on the subject of friendship. . . .

. . . Yes, friendship is a kaleidoscopic and complicated thing; it affords many possible grounds for suspicion and offense, but a truly wise man always finds it possible to avoid them or smooth them over or put up with them. One thing however must be shunned, and that is hypersensitivity, if we are to preserve the mutual confidence and practical value of friendship. For it often happens that friends must be admonished and even reprimanded, and this we must take in good part when it is offered in a spirit of charity. . . .

. . . In this whole matter, then, we must be reasonable and cautious. We may admonish, but we must not scold; we may reprimand, but we must not humiliate. . . .

It is an essential part of true friendship, then, to offer and to receive admonition; but it must be offered courteously, not peremptorily, and received with forbearance, not with resentment. By the same sign, we must maintain that there is no danger more deadly to friendship than servility, sycophancy, flattery—put as many names as you like upon it, but let it be branded as the vicious practice of disloyal, untruthful men, who measure everything they say by what people want to hear, and never anything by the truth.

Now in all matters, hypocrisy is vicious (for it distorts and destroys our judgment), but it is particularly inimical to friendship, for it makes honesty impossible, and without honesty the word "friendship" has no meaning. For the essence of friendship consists in the fact that many souls, so to speak, become one, and how can that take place if even in the one individual the soul is not single and forever the same, but various, changeable, kaleidoscopic? . . .

. . . For in friendship unless, as we say, you see the naked heart and let your own be seen, there is nothing that you can deem trustworthy or reliable, not even the mere fact of loving and being loved, since you cannot know how genuine the sentiment is. . . .

I tell you, Gaius Fannius, and you, Quintus Mucius: it is virtue, yes virtue, that initiates and preserves friendship. For it is virtue that is the source of the rational, the stable, the consistent element in life. When virtue raises herself up and displays her light, and sees and recognizes the same light in another, she moves toward it and shares reciprocally in that which the other possesses; from this a flame bursts forth, whether of love or of friendship. Both terms after all are derived from the verb "to love" *(amor, amicitia, amare),* and "to love" means nothing but to cherish the person for whom one feels affection, without any special need and without any thought of advantage—although advantage in fact does grow out of friendship, even if one does not seek it. . . .

But since human life is a fragile and unstable thing, we have no choice but to be ever on the search for people whom we may love, and by whom we may be loved in turn, for if charity and goodwill are removed from life, all the joy is gone out of it. As far as I am concerned, although Scipio was taken away from me unexpectedly, he is still living and will live forever, for it was the man's virtue that I loved, and this has not been destroyed; it is still as bright as day to me—and not only to me, who had it always before me: it will shine in all its glory and splendor for generations to come. No man will ever see greater visions or dreams without feeling that he must set Scipio before him as a record to know and a pattern to follow.

For my own part, of all the good things I have had, whether they were special blessings or the normal events of life, I know of nothing that I could compare with the friendship of Scipio.

Translated by Frank O. Copley

MICHEL DE MONTAIGNE

From OF FRIENDSHIP

It* was shown to me long before I had seen him, and gave me my first knowledge of his name, thus starting on its way this friendship which together we fostered, as long as God willed, so entire and so perfect that

* *Voluntary Servitude,* a book written by Etienne de la Boétie, to whom Montaigne refers in this sentence and throughout the essay.

certainly you will hardly read of the like, and among men of today you see no trace of it in practice. So many coincidences are needed to build up such a friendship that it is a lot if fortune can do it once in three centuries.

There is nothing to which nature seems to have inclined us more than to society. And Aristotle says that good legislators have had more care for friendship than for justice. Now the ultimate point in the perfection of society is this. For in general, all associations that are forged and nourished by pleasure or profit, by public or private needs, are the less beautiful and noble, and the less friendships, in so far as they mix into friendship another cause and object and reward than friendship itself. Nor do the four ancient types—natural, social, hospitable, erotic—come up to real friendship, either separately or together.

From children toward fathers, it is rather respect. Friendship feeds on communication, which cannot exist between them because of their too great inequality, and might perhaps interfere with the duties of nature. For neither can all the secret thoughts of fathers be communicated to children, lest this beget an unbecoming intimacy, nor could the admonitions and corrections, which are one of the chief duties of friendship, be administered by children to fathers. . . .

Truly the name of brother is a beautiful name and full of affection, and for that reason he and I made our alliance a brotherhood. But that confusion of ownership, the dividing, and the fact that the richness of one is the poverty of the other, wonderfully softens and loosens the solder of brotherhood. Since brothers have to guide their careers along the same path and at the same rate, it is inevitable that they often jostle and clash with each other. Furthermore, why should the harmony and kinship which begets these true and perfect friendships be found in them? Father and son may be of entirely different dispositions, and brothers also. He is my son, he is my kinsman, but he is an unsociable man, a knave, or a fool. And then, the more they are friendships which law and natural obligation impose on us, the less of our choice and free will there is in them. And our free will has no product more properly its own than affection and friendship. Not that I have not experienced all the friendship that can exist in that situation, having had the best father that ever was, and the most indulgent, even in his extreme old age, and being of a family famous and exemplary, from father to son, in this matter of brotherly concord:

> Known to others
> For fatherly affection toward my brothers.
>
> —Horace

To compare this brotherly affection with affection for women, even though it is the result of our choice—it cannot be done; nor can we put the love of women in the same category. Its ardor, I confess—

> Of us that goddess is not unaware
> Who blends a bitter sweetness with her care
>
> —Catullus

—is more active, more scorching, and more intense. But it is an impetuous and fickle flame, undulating and variable, a fever flame, subject to fits and lulls, that holds us only by one corner. In friendship it is a general and universal warmth, moderate and even, besides, a constant and settled warmth, all gentleness and smoothness, with nothing bitter and stinging about it. What is more, in love there is nothing but a frantic desire for what flees from us:

> Just as a huntsman will pursue a hare
> O'er hill and dale, in weather cold or fair;
> The captured hare is worthless in his sight;
> He only hastens after things in flight.
>
> —Ariosto

As soon as it enters the boundaries of friendship, that is to say harmony of wills, it grows faint and languid. Enjoyment destroys it, as having a fleshly end, subject to satiety. Friendship, on the contrary, is enjoyed according as it is desired; it is bred, nourished, and increased only in enjoyment, since it is spiritual, and the soul grows refined by practice. During the reign of this perfect friendship those fleeting affections once found a place in me, not to speak of my friend, who confesses only too many of them in these verses. Thus these two passions within me came to be known to each other, but to be compared, never; the first keeping its course in proud and lofty flight, and disdainfully watching the other making its way far, far beneath it.

As for marriage, for one thing it is a bargain to which only the entrance is free—its continuance being constrained and forced, depending otherwise than on our will—and a bargain ordinarily made for other ends. For another, there supervene a thousand foreign tangles to unravel, enough to break the thread and trouble the course of a lively affection; whereas in friendship there are no dealings or business except with itself. Besides, to tell the truth, the ordinary capacity of women is inadequate for that communion and fellowship which is the nurse of this sacred bond; nor does their soul seem firm enough to endure the strain of

so tight and durable a knot. And indeed, but for that, if such a relationship, free and voluntary, could be built up, in which not only would the
souls have this complete enjoyment, but the bodies would also share in
the alliance, so that the entire man would be engaged, it is certain that
the resulting friendship would be fuller and more complete. But this sex
in no instance has yet succeeded in attaining it, and by the common
agreement of the ancient schools is excluded from it. . . .

I return to my description of a more equitable and more equable kind
of friendship. *Only those are to be judged friendships in which the characters have been strengthened and matured by age* [Cicero].

For the rest, what we ordinarily call friends and friendships are nothing but acquaintanceships and familiarities formed by some chance or
convenience, by means of which our souls are bound to each other. In
the friendship I speak of, our souls mingle and blend with each other so
completely that they efface the seam that joined them, and cannot find
it again. If you press me to tell why I loved him, I feel that this cannot be
expressed, except by answering: Because it was he, because it was I.

Beyond all my understanding, beyond what I can say about this in
particular, there was I know not what inexplicable and fateful force that
was the mediator of this union. We sought each other before we met
because of the reports we heard of each other, which had more effect on
our affection than such reports would reasonably have; I think it was by
some ordinance from heaven. We embraced each other by our names.
And at our first meeting, which by chance came at a great feast and
gathering in the city, we found ourselves so taken with each other, so
well acquainted, so bound together, that from that time on nothing was
so close to us as each other. He wrote an excellent Latin satire, which is
published, in which he excuses and explains the precipitancy of our
mutual understanding, so promptly grown to its perfection. Having so
little time to last, and having begun so late, for we were both grown men,
and he a few years older than I, it could not lose time and conform to the
pattern of mild and regular friendships, which need so many precautions
in the form of long preliminary association. Our friendship has no other
model than itself, and can be compared only with itself. It is not one
special consideration, nor two, nor three, nor four, nor a thousand: it is I
know not what quintessence of all this mixture, which, having seized my
whole will, led it to plunge and lose itself in his; which, having seized his
whole will, led it to plunge and lose itself in mine, with equal hunger,
equal rivalry. I say lose, in truth, for neither of us reserved anything for
himself, nor was anything either his or mine.

When Laelius, in the presence of the Roman consuls—who, after
condemning Tiberius Gracchus, prosecuted all those who had been in

his confidence—came to ask Caius Blossius, who was Gracchus' best friend, how much he would have been willing to do for him, he answered: "Everything." "What, everything?" pursued Laelius. "And what if he had commanded you to set fire to our temples?" "He would never have commanded me to do that," replied Blossius. "But what if he had?" Laelius insisted. "I would have obeyed," he replied. If he was such a perfect friend to Gracchus as the histories say, he did not need to offend the consuls by this last bold confession, and he should not have abandoned the assurance he had of Gracchus' will. But nevertheless, those who charge that this answer is seditious do not fully understand this mystery, and fail to assume first what is true, that he had Gracchus' will up his sleeve, both by power over him and by knowledge of him. They were friends more than citizens, friends more than friends or enemies of their country or friends of ambition and disturbance. Having committed themselves absolutely to each other, they held absolutely the reins of each other's inclination; and if you assume that this team was guided by the strength and leadership of reason, as indeed it is quite impossible to harness it without that, Blossius' answer is as it should have been. If their actions went astray, they were by my measure neither friends to each other, nor friends to themselves.

For that matter, this answer has no better ring than would mine if someone questioned me in this fashion: "If your will commanded you to kill your daughter, would you kill her?" and I said yes. For that does not bear witness to any consent to do so, because I have no doubt at all about my will, and just as little about that of such a friend. It is not in the power of all the arguments in the world to dislodge me from the certainty I have of the intentions and judgments of my friend. Not one of his actions could be presented to me, whatever appearance it might have, that I could not immediately find the motive for it. Our souls pulled together in such unison, they regarded each other with such ardent affection, and with a like affection revealed themselves to each other to the very depths of our hearts, that not only did I know his soul as well as mine, but I should certainly have trusted myself to him more readily than to myself.

Let not these other, common friendships be placed in this rank. I have as much knowledge of them as another, and of the most perfect of their type, but I advise you not to confuse the rules of the two; you would make a mistake. You must walk in those other friendships bridle in hand, with prudence and precaution; the knot is not so well tied that there is no cause to mistrust it. "Love him," Chilo used to say, "as if you are to hate him some day; hate him as if you are to love him." This precept, which is so abominable in this sovereign and masterful friendship, is healthy in the practice of ordinary and customary friendships, in regard to which we must use the remark that Aristotle often repeated: "O my friends, there is no friend."

In this noble relationship, services and benefits, on which other friendships feed, do not even deserve to be taken into account; the reason for this is the complete fusion of our wills. For just as the friendship I feel for myself receives no increase from the help I give myself in time of need, whatever the Stoics say, and as I feel no gratitude to myself for the service I do myself; so the union of such friends, being truly perfect, makes them lose the sense of such duties, and hate and banish from between them these words of separation and distinction: benefit, obligation, gratitude, request, thanks, and the like. Everything actually being in common between them—wills, thoughts, judgments, goods, wives, children, honor, and life—and their relationship being that of one soul in two bodies, according to Aristotle's very apt definition, they can neither lend nor give anything to each other. That is why the lawmakers, to honor marriage with some imaginary resemblance to this divine union, forbid gifts between husband and wife, wishing thus to imply that everything should belong to each of them and that they have nothing to divide and split up between them.

If, in the friendship I speak of, one could give to the other, it would be the one who received the benefit who would oblige his friend. For, each of them seeking above all things to benefit the other, the one who provides the matter and the occasion is the liberal one, giving his friend the satisfaction of doing for him what he most wants to do. When the philosopher Diogenes was short of money, he used to say that he asked it back of his friends, not that he asked for it. And to show how this works in practice, I will tell you an ancient example that is singular.

Eudamidas of Corinth had two friends, Charixenus, a Sicyonian, and Aretheus, a Corinthian. When he came to die, he being poor and his two friends rich, he made his will thus: "I leave this to Aretheus, to feed my mother and support her in her old age; this to Charixenus, to see my daughter married and give her the biggest dowry he can; and in case one of them should chance to die, I substitute the survivor in his place." Those who first saw this will laughed at it; but his heirs, having been informed of it, accepted it with singular satisfaction. And when one of them, Charixenus, died five days later, and the place of substitute was opened to Aretheus, he supported the mother with great care, and of five talents he had in his estate, he gave two and a half to his only daughter for her marriage, and two and a half for the marriage of the daughter of Eudamidas, holding their weddings on the same day.

This example is quite complete except for one circumstance, which is the plurality of friends. For this perfect friendship I speak of is indivisible: each one gives himself so wholly to his friend that he has nothing left to distribute elsewhere; on the contrary, he is sorry that he is not double, triple, or quadruple, and that he has not several souls and several wills, to confer them all on this one object. Common friendships can be divided up: one may love in one man his beauty, in another his easygoing ways, in another liberality, in one paternal love, in another brotherly love, and so forth; but this friendship that possesses the soul and rules it with absolute sovereignty cannot possibly be double. If two called for help at the same time, which one would you run to? If they demanded conflicting services of you, how would you arrange it? If one confided to your silence a thing that would be useful for the other to know, how would you extricate yourself? A single dominant friendship dissolves all other obligations. The secret I have sworn to reveal to no other man, I can impart without perjury to the one who is not another man: he is myself. It is a great enough miracle to be doubled, and those who talk of tripling themselves do not realize the loftiness of the thing: nothing is extreme that can be matched. And he who supposes that of two men I love one just as much as the other, and that they love each other and me just as much as I love them, multiplies into a fraternity the most singular and unified of all things, of which even a single one is the rarest thing in the world to find.

The rest of this story fits in very well with what I was saying, for Eudamidas bestows upon his friends the kindness and favor of using them for his need. He leaves them heirs to this liberality of his, which consists of putting into their hands a chance to do him good. And without doubt the strength of friendship is shown much more richly in his action than in that of Aretheus.

In short, these are actions inconceivable to anyone who has not tasted friendship, and which make me honor wonderfully the answer of that young soldier to Cyrus, who asked him for how much he would sell a horse with which he had just won the prize in a race, and whether he would exchange him for a kingdom: "No indeed, Sire, but I would most willingly let him go to gain a friend, if I found a man worthy of such an alliance." That was not badly spoken, "if I found one"; for it is easy to find men fit for a superficial acquaintance. But for this kind, in which we act from the very bottom of our hearts, which holds nothing back, truly it is necessary that all the springs of action be perfectly clean and true.

In the relationships which bind us only by one small part, we need look out only for the imperfections that particularly concern that part. The religion of my doctor or my lawyer cannot matter. That consideration has nothing in common with the functions of the friendship they owe me. And in the domestic relationship between me and those who serve me, I have the same attitude. I scarcely inquire of a lackey whether he is chaste; I try to find out whether he is diligent. And I am not as much afraid of a gambling mule driver as of a weak one, or of a profane cook as of an ignorant one. I do not make it my business to tell the world what it should do—enough others do that—but what I do in it.

> That is my practice: do as you see fit.
>
> —Terence

For the familiarity of the table I look for wit, not prudence; for the bed, beauty before goodness; in conversation, competence, even without up-rightness. Likewise in other matters.

Just as the man who was found astride a stick, playing with his children, asked the man who surprised him thus to say nothing about it until he was a father himself, in the belief that the passion which would then be born in his soul would make him an equitable judge of such an act, so I should like to talk to people who have experienced what I tell. But knowing how far from common usage and how rare such a friendship is, I do not expect to find any good judge of it. For the very discourses that antiquity has left us on this subject seem to me weak compared with the feeling I have. And in this particular the facts surpass even the precepts of philosophy:

> Nothing shall I, while sane, compare with a dear friend.
>
> —Horace

The ancient Menander declared that man happy who had been able to meet even the shadow of a friend. He was certainly right to say so, especially if he spoke from experience. For in truth, if I compare all the rest of my life—though by the grace of God I have spent it pleasantly, comfortably, and, except for the loss of such a friend, free from any grievous affliction, and full of tranquillity of mind, having accepted my natural and original advantages without seeking other ones—if I compare it all, I say, with the four years which were granted me to enjoy the sweet company and society of that man, it is nothing but smoke, nothing but dark and dreary night. Since the day I lost him,

> Which I shall ever recall with pain,
> Ever with reverence—thus, Gods, did you ordain—
>
> —Virgil

I only drag on a weary life. And the very pleasures that come my way, instead of consoling me, redouble my grief for his loss. We went halves in everything; it seems to me that I am robbing him of his share,

Nor may I rightly taste of pleasures here alone,
—So I resolved—when he who shared my life is gone.

—Terence

I was already so formed and accustomed to being a second self everywhere that only half of me seems to be alive now.

Since an untimely blow has snatched away
Part of my soul, why then do I delay,
I the remaining part, less dear than he,
And not entire surviving? The same day
Brought ruin equally to him and me.

—Horace

There is no action or thought in which I do not miss him, as indeed he would have missed me. For just as he surpassed me infinitely in every other ability and virtue, so he did in the duty of friendship.

Why should I be ashamed or exercise control
Mourning so dear a soul?

—Horace

Brother, your death has left me sad and lone;
Since you departed all our joys have gone,
Which while you lived your sweet affection fed;
My pleasures all lie shattered, with you dead.
Our soul is buried, mine with yours entwined;
And since then I have banished from my mind
My studies, and my spirit's dearest joys.
Shall I ne'er speak to you, or hear your voice?
Or see your face, more dear than life to me?
At least I'll love you to eternity.

—Catullus

Translated by Donald M. Frame

FRANCIS BACON

From OF FRIENDSHIP

A principal fruit of friendship is the ease and discharge of the fulness and swellings of the heart, which passions of all kinds do cause and induce. We know diseases of stoppings and suffocations are the most dangerous in the body, and it is not much otherwise in the mind; you may take sarza to open the liver, steel to open the spleen, flower of sulphur for the lungs, castoreum for the brain, but no receipt openeth the heart but a true friend, to whom you may impart griefs, joys, fears, hopes, suspicions, counsels, and whatsoever lieth upon the heart to oppress it, in a kind of civil shrift or confession. . . .

. . . The parable of Pythagoras is dark but true: *Cor ne edito; Eat not the heart.* Certainly if a man would give it a hard phrase, those that want friends to open themselves unto are cannibals of their own hearts. But one thing is most admirable (wherewith I will conclude this first fruit of friendship), which is, that this communicating of a man's self to his friend works two contrary effects, for it redoubleth joys, and cutteth griefs in halfs. For there is no man that imparteth his joys to his friend, but he joyeth the more, and no man that imparteth his griefs to his friend, but he grieveth the less. . . .

The second fruit of friendship is healthful and sovereign for the understanding, as the first is for the affections. For friendship maketh indeed a fair day in the affections from storm and tempests, but it maketh daylight in the understanding out of darkness and confusion of thoughts. Neither is this to be understood only of faithful counsel, which a man receiveth from his friend; but before you come to that, certain it is that whosoever hath his mind fraught with many thoughts, his wits and understanding do clarify and break up in the communicating and discoursing with another; he tosseth his thoughts more easily; he marshalleth them more orderly; he seeth how they look when they are turned into words; finally, he waxeth wiser than himself; and that more by an hour's discourse than by a day's meditation. . . .

Add now, to make this second fruit of friendship complete, that other point which lieth more open and falleth within vulgar observation, which is faithful counsel from a friend. Heraclitus saith well in one of his enigmas, *Dry light is ever the best.* And certain it is that the light that a man receiveth by counsel from another is drier and purer than that which cometh from his own understanding and judgement, which is ever infused and drenched in his affections and customs. So as there is as much difference between the counsel that a friend giveth, and that a man giveth himself, as there is between the counsel of a friend and of a flatterer. For there is no such flatterer as is a man's self, and there is no such remedy against flattery of a man's self as the liberty of a friend. . . .

After these two noble fruits of friendship (peace in the affections, and support of the judgement), followeth the last fruit, which is like the pomegranate, full of many kernels; I mean aid and bearing a part in all actions and occasions. Here the best way to represent to life the manifold use of friendship is to cast and see how many things there are which a man cannot do himself, and then it will appear that it was a sparing speech of the ancients, to say *that a friend is another himself,* for that a friend is far more than himself. Men have their time, and die many times in desire of some things which they principally take to heart, the bestowing of a child, the finishing of a work, or the like. If a man have a true friend, he may rest almost secure that the care of those things will continue after him. So that a man hath, as it were, two lives in his desires. A man hath a body, and that body is confined to a place, but where friendship is, all offices of life are as it were granted to him and his deputy. For he may exercise them by his friend. How many things are there which a man cannot, with any face or comeliness, say or do himself? A man can scarce allege his own merits with modesty, much less extol them; a man cannot sometimes brook to supplicate or beg; and a number of the like. But all these things are graceful in a friend's mouth, which are blushing in a man's own. So again, a man's person hath many proper relations which he cannot put off. A man cannot speak to his son but as a father; to his wife but as a husband; to his enemy but upon terms; whereas a friend may speak as the case requires, and not as it sorteth with the person. But to enumerate these things were endless; I have given the rule, where a man cannot fitly play his own part; if he have not a friend, he may quit the stage.

SAMUEL JOHNSON

From THE RAMBLER, No. 64

(Saturday, 27 October 1750)

Idem velle, et idem nolle, ea demum firma amicitia est.
—Sallust, De Coniuratione Catilinae, xx.4

To live in friendship, is to have the same desires and the same
aversions.

When Socrates was building himself a house at Athens, being asked by
one that observed the littleness of the design, why a man so eminent
would not have an abode more suitable to his dignity? he replied, that he
should think himself sufficiently accommodated, if he could see that
narrow habitation filled with real friends. Such was the opinion of this
great master of human life, concerning the infrequency of such an union
of minds as might deserve the name of friendship, that among the multi-
tudes whom vanity or curiosity, civility or veneration, crouded about
him, he did not expect, that very spacious apartments would be necessary to contain all that should regard him with sincere kindness, or
adhere to him with steady fidelity.

So many qualities are indeed requisite to the possibility of friendship,
and so many accidents must concur to its rise and its continuance, that
the greatest part of mankind content themselves without it, and supply
its place as they can, with interest and dependance. . . .

That friendship may be at once fond and lasting, there must not only
be equal virtue on each part, but virtue of the same kind; not only the
same end must be proposed, but the same means must be approved by
both. We are often, by superficial accomplishments and accidental endearments, induced to love those whom we cannot esteem; we are sometimes, by great abilities and incontestable evidences of virtue, compelled
to esteem those whom we cannot love. But friendship, compounded of
esteem and love, derives from one its tenderness, and its permanence
from the other; and therefore requires not only that its candidates should

gain the judgement, but that they should attract the affections; that they should not only be firm in the day of distress, but gay in the hour of jollity; not only useful in exigences, but pleasing in familiar life; their presence should give chearfulness as well as courage, and dispel alike the gloom of fear and of melancholy.

To this mutual complacency is generally requisite an uniformity of opinions, at least of those active and conspicuous principles which discriminate parties in government, and sects in religion, and which every day operate more or less on the common business of life. For though great tenderness has, perhaps, been sometimes known to continue between men eminent in contrary factions; yet such friends are to be shewn rather as prodigies than examples, and it is no more proper to regulate our conduct by such instances, than to leap a precipice, because some have fallen from it and escaped with life.

It cannot but be extremely difficult to preserve private kindness in the midst of publick opposition, in which will necessarily be involved a thousand incidents, extending their influence to conversation and privacy. Men engaged, by moral or religious motives, in contrary parties, will generally look with different eyes upon every man, and decide almost every question upon different principles. When such occasions of dispute happen, to comply is to betray our cause, and to maintain friendship by ceasing to deserve it; to be silent, is to lose the happiness and dignity of independence, to live in perpetual constraint, and to desert, if not to betray: and who shall determine which of two friends shall yield, where neither believes himself mistaken, and both confess the importance of the question? What then remains but contradiction and debate? and from those what can be expected, but acrimony and vehemence, the insolence of triumph, the vexation of defeat, and, in time, a weariness of contest, and an extinction of benevolence? Exchange of endearments and intercourse of civility may continue, indeed, as boughs may for a while be verdant, when the root is wounded; but the poison of discord is infused, and though the countenance may preserve its smile, the heart is hardening and contracting.

That man will not be long agreeable, whom we see only in times of seriousness and severity; and therefore, to maintain the softness and serenity of benevolence, it is necessary that friends partake each others pleasures as well as cares, and be led to the same diversions by similitude of taste. This is, however, not to be considered as equally indispensable with conformity of principles, because any man may honestly, according to the precepts of Horace, resign the gratifications of taste to the humour of another, and friendship may well deserve the sacrifice of pleasure, though not of conscience.

It was once confessed to me, by a painter, that no professor of his art ever loved another. This declaration is so far justified by the knowledge of life, as to damp the hopes of warm and constant friendship, between men whom their studies have made competitors, and whom every favourer and every censurer are hourly inciting against each other. The utmost expectation that experience can warrant, is, that they should forbear open hostilities and secret machinations, and when the whole fraternity is attacked, be able to unite against a common foe. Some however, though few, may perhaps be found, in whom emulation has not been able to overpower generosity, who are distinguished from lower beings by nobler motives than the love of fame, and can preserve the sacred flame of friendship from the gusts of pride, and the rubbish of interest.

Friendship is seldom lasting but between equals, or where the superiority on one side is reduced by some equivalent advantage on the other. Benefits which cannot be repaid, and obligations which cannot be discharged, are not commonly found to increase affection; they excite gratitude indeed, and heighten veneration, but commonly take away that easy freedom, and familiarity of intercourse, without which, though there may be fidelity, and zeal, and admiration, there cannot be friendship. Thus imperfect are all earthly blessings; the great effect of friendship is beneficence, yet by the first act of uncommon kindness it is endangered, like plants that bear their fruit and die. Yet this consideration ought not to restrain bounty, or repress compassion; for duty is to be preferred before convenience, and he that loses part of the pleasures of friendship by his generosity, gains in its place the gratulation of his conscience.

From THE RAMBLER, NO. 40

(Saturday, 4 August 1750)

Felicia and Floretta had been bred up in one house, and shared all the pleasures and endearments of infancy together. They entered upon life at the same time, and continued their confidence and friendship; consulted each other in every change of their dress, and every admission of a new lover; thought every diversion more entertaining whenever it happened that both were present, and when separated justified the conduct, and celebrated the excellencies of one another. Such was their intimacy, and such their fidelity; till a birthnight approached, when Floretta took one morning an opportunity, as they were consulting upon new cloaths, to advise her friend not to dance at the ball, and informed her that her performance the year before had not answered the expectation which her other accomplishments had raised. Felicia commended her sincerity, and thanked her for the caution; but told her that she danced to please herself, and was in very little concern what the men might take the liberty of saying, but that if her appearance gave her dear Floretta any uneasiness she would stay away. Floretta had now nothing left but to make new protestations of sincerity and affection, with which Felicia was so well satisfied, that they parted with more than usual fondness. They still continued to visit, with this only difference, that Felicia was more punctual than before, and often declared how high a value she put upon sincerity, how much she thought that goodness to be esteemed which would venture to admonish a friend of an error, and with what gratitude advice was to be received, even when it might happen to proceed from mistake.

In a few months Felicia, with great seriousness, told Floretta, that though her beauty was such as gave charms to whatever she did, and her qualifications so extensive, that she could not fail of excellence in any attempt, yet she thought herself obliged by the duties of friendship to inform her, that if ever she betrayed want of judgment, it was by too frequent compliance with solicitations to sing, for that her manner was somewhat ungraceful, and her voice had no great compass. It is true, says Floretta, when I sung three nights ago at Lady Sprightly's, I was hoarse with a cold; but I sing for my own satisfaction, and am not in the least pain whether I am liked. However, my dear Felicia's kindness is not the less, and I shall always thinks myself happy in so true a friend.

From this time, they never saw each other without mutual professions of esteem, and declarations of confidence, but went soon after into the country to visit their relations. When they came back, they were prevailed on, by the importunity of new acquaintance, to take lodgings in different parts of the town, and had frequent occasion when they met, to bewail the distance at which they were placed, and the uncertainty which each experienced of finding the other at home.

Thus are the fondest and firmest friendships dissolved, by such openness, and sincerity, as interrupt our enjoyment of our own approbation, or recall us to the remembrance of those failings, which we are more willing to indulge than to correct.

It is by no means necessary to imagine, that he who is offended at advice, was ignorant of the fault, and resents the admonition as a false charge; for perhaps it is most natural to be enraged, when there is the strongest conviction of our own guilt. While we can easily defend our character, we are no more disturbed at an accusation, than we are alarmed by an enemy whom we are sure to conquer; and whose attack, therefore, will bring us honour without danger. But when a man feels the reprehension of a friend seconded by his own heart, he is easily heated into resentment and revenge, either because he hoped that the fault of which he was conscious had escaped the notice of others; or that his friend had looked upon it with tenderness and extenuation, and excused it for the sake of his other virtues; or had considered him as too wise to need advice, or too delicate to be shocked with reproach: or, because we cannot feel without pain those reflections roused, which we have been endeavouring to lay asleep; and when pain has produced anger, who would not willingly believe, that it ought to be discharged on others, rather than on himself?

The resentment produced by sincerity, whatever be its immediate cause, is so certain, and generally so keen, that very few have magnanimity sufficient for the practice of a duty, which, above most others, exposes its votaries to hardships and persecutions; yet friendship without it is of a very little value, since the great use of so close an intimacy is that our virtues may be guarded and encouraged, and our vices repressed in their first appearance by timely detection, and salutary remonstrances.

It is decreed by providence, that nothing truly valuable shall be obtained in our present state, but with difficulty and danger. He that hopes for that advantage which is to be gained from unrestrained communication, must sometimes hazard, by unpleasing truths, that friendship which he aspires to merit. The chief rule to be observed in the exercise of this dangerous office, is to preserve it pure from all mixture of interest or vanity; to forbear admonition or reproof, when our consciences tell us that they are incited not by the hopes of reforming faults, but the desire of shewing our discernment, or gratifying our own pride by the mortification of another. It is not indeed certain that the most refined caution will find a proper time, for bringing a man to the knowledge of his own failings, or the most zealous benevolence reconcile him to that judgment, by which they are detected; but he who endeavours only the happiness of him whom he reproves will always have either the satisfaction of obtaining or deserving kindness; if he succeeds, he benefits his friend, and if he fails, he has at least the consciousness that he suffers for only doing well.

From The Idler, No. 23

(Saturday, 23 September 1758)

Life has no pleasure higher or nobler than that of friendship. It is painful to consider, that this sublime enjoyment may be impaired or destroyed by innumerable causes, and that there is no human possession of which the duration is less certain.

Many have talked, in very exalted language, of the perpetuity of friendship, of invincible constancy, and unalienable kindness; and some examples have been seen of men who have continued faithful to their earliest choice, and whose affection has predominated over changes of fortune, and contrariety of opinion.

But these instances are memorable, because they are rare. The friendship which is to be practised or expected by common mortals, must take its rise from mutual pleasure, and must end when the power ceases of delighting each other.

Many accidents therefore may happen, by which the ardour of kindness will be abated, without criminal baseness or contemptible inconstancy on either part. To give pleasure is not always in our power; and little does he know himself, who believes that he can be always able to receive it.

Those who would gladly pass their days together may be separated by the different course of their affairs; and friendship, like love, is destroyed by long absence, though it may be encreased by short intermissions. . . .

No expectation is more frequently disappointed, than that which naturally arises in the mind, from the prospect of meeting an old friend, after long separation. We expect the attraction to be revived, and the coalition to be renewed; no man considers how much alteration time has made in himself, and very few enquire what effect it has had upon others. The first hour convinces them, that the pleasure, which they have formerly enjoyed, is for ever at an end; different scenes have made different impressions, the opinions of both are changed, and that similitude of manners and sentiment is lost, which confirmed them both in the approbation of themselves.

Friendship is often destroyed by opposition of interest, not only by the ponderous and visible interest, which the desire of wealth and greatness forms and maintains, but by a thousand secret and slight competitions, scarcely known to the mind upon which they operate. There is scarcely any man without some favourite trifle which he values above greater attainments, some desire of petty praise which he cannot patiently suffer to be frustrated. This minute ambition is sometimes crossed before it is known, and sometimes defeated by wanton petulance; but such attacks are seldom made without the loss of friendship; for whoever has once found the vulnerable part will always be feared, and the resentment will burn on in secret of which shame hinders the discovery. . . .

Friendship has other enemies. Suspicion is always hardening the cautious, and disgust repelling the delicate. Very slender differences will sometimes part those whom long reciprocation of civility or beneficence has united. Lonelove and Ranger retired into the country to enjoy the company of each other, and returned in six weeks cold and petulant; Ranger's pleasure was to walk in the fields, and Lonelove's to sit in a bower; each had complied with the other in his turn, and each was angry that compliance had been exacted.

The most fatal disease of friendship is gradual decay, or dislike hourly encreased by causes too slender for complaint, and too numerous for removal. Those who are angry may be reconciled; those who have been injured may receive a recompence; but when the desire of pleasing and willingness to be pleased is silently diminished, the renovation of friendship is hopeless; as, when the vital powers sink into languor, there is no longer any use of the physician.

JAMES BOSWELL

From THE LIFE OF SAMUEL JOHNSON

. . . I have often thought, that as longevity is generally desired, and, I believe, generally expected, it would be wise to be continually adding to the number of our friends, that the loss of some may be supplied by others. Friendship, "the wine of life," should, like a well-stocked cellar, be thus continually renewed; and it is consolatory to think, that although we can seldom add what will equal the generous *first-growths* of our youth, yet friendship becomes insensibly old in much less time than is commonly imagined, and not many years are required to make it very mellow and pleasant. *Warmth* will, no doubt, make a considerable difference. Men of affectionate temper and bright fancy will coalesce a great deal sooner than those who are cold and dull.

The proposition which I have now endeavoured to illustrate was, at a subsequent period of his life, the opinion of Johnson himself. He said to Sir Joshua Reynolds, "If a man does not make new acquaintances as he advances through life, he will soon find himself left alone. A man, Sir, should keep his friendship *in constant repair.*"

Friday, 10 April 1772

A question was started, how far people who disagree in any capital point can live in friendship together. Johnson said they might. Goldsmith said they could not, as they had not the *idem velle atque idem nolle*—the same likings and the same aversions. JOHNSON. "Why, Sir, you must shun the subject as to which you disagree. For instance, I can live very well with Burke: I love his knowledge, his genius, his diffusion, and affluence of conversation; but I would not talk to him of the Rockingham party." GOLDSMITH. "But, Sir, when people live together who have something as to which they disagree, and which they want to shun, they will be in the situation mentioned in the story of Bluebeard: 'You may look into all the chambers but one.' But we should have the greatest inclination to look into that chamber, to talk of that subject." JOHNSON. (with a loud voice.) "Sir, I am not saying that *you* could live in friendship with a man from whom you differ as to some point: I am only saying that *I* could do it. . . ."

Friday, 19 September 1777

. . . We cannot tell the precise moment when friendship is formed. As in filling a vessel drop by drop, there is at last a drop which makes it run over; so in a series of kindnesses there is at last one which makes the heart run over.

PART III

LETTERS: GROUP 1

Your third Chamber of Life shall be a lucky
and a gentle one—stored with the wine of love—and
the Bread of Friendship.

—John Keats

WOLFGANG AMADEUS MOZART

To Joseph Haydn

Vienna, 1 September 1785

To my dear friend Haydn.

A father who had decided to send out his sons into the great world, thought it his duty to entrust them to the protection and guidance of a man who was very celebrated at the time and who, moreover, happened to be his best friend.

In like manner I send my six sons to you, most celebrated and very dear friend. They are, indeed, the fruit of a long and laborious study; but the hope which many friends have given me that this toil will be in some degree rewarded, encourages me and flatters me with the thought that these children may one day prove a source of consolation to me.

During your last stay in this capital you yourself, my very dear friend, expressed to me your approval of these compositions. Your good opinion encourages me to offer them to you and leads me to hope that you will not consider them wholly unworthy of your favour. Please then receive them kindly and be to them a father, guide and friend! From this moment I surrender to you all my rights over them. I entreat you, however, to be indulgent to those faults which may have escaped a father's partial eye, and, in spite of them, to continue your generous friendship towards one who so highly appreciates it. Meanwhile, I remain with all my heart, dearest friend, your most sincere friend

W. A. Mozart

To Baron Gottfried von Jacquin

Prague, 14 January 1787

. . . At six o'clock I drove with Count Canal to the so-called Bretfeld ball, where the cream of the beauties of Prague are wont to gather. Why—

you ought to have been there, my friend! I fancy I see you running, or rather, limping after all those pretty women, married and unmarried! I neither danced nor flirted with any of them, the former, because I was too tired, and the latter owing to my natural bashfulness. I looked on, however, with the greatest pleasure while all these people flew about in sheer delight to the music of my *Figaro,* arranged for quadrilles and waltzes. For here they talk about nothing but *Figaro.* Nothing is played, sung, or whistled but *Figaro.* No opera is drawing like *Figaro.* Nothing, nothing but *Figaro.* Certainly a great honour for me! . . . When I remember that after my return I shall enjoy only for a short while the pleasure of your valued society and shall then have to forgo this happiness for such a long time, perhaps for ever, then indeed I realize the extent of the friendship and regard which I cherish for your whole family. Now farewell, dearest friend, dearest Hinkity Honky! That is your name, as you must know. We all invented names for ourselves on the journey. Here they are. I am Punkititi—My wife is Schabla Pumfa. Hofer is Rozka-Pumpa. Stadler is Nàtschibinitschibi. My servant Joseph is Sàgadaratà. My dog Gaukerl is Schamanuzky—Madame Quallenberg is Runzifunzi—Mlle Crux Ps—— Ramlo is Schurimuri. Freistädtler is Gaulimauli. Be so kind as to tell him his name. Well, adieu. . . .

Translated by Emily Anderson

SAMUEL JOHNSON

To George Strahan

Thursday, 14 July 1763

Dear George

To give pain ought always to be painful, and I am sorry that I have been the occasion of any uneasiness to you, to whom I hope never to [do] any thing but for your benefit or your pleasure. Your uneasiness was without any reason on your part. . . . You are not to imagine that my friendship is light enough to be blown away by the first cross blast, or that my regard or kindness hangs by so slender a hair, as to be broken off by the unfelt weight of a petty offence. I love you, and hope to love you long. You have hitherto done nothing to diminish my goodwill, and though you had done much more than you have supposed imputed to you my goodwill would not have been diminished.

I write thus largely on this suspicion which you have suffered to enter your mind, because in youth we are apt to be too rigorous in our expectations, and to suppose that the duties of life are to be performed with unfailing exactness and regularity, but in our progress through life we are forced to abate much of our demands, and to take friends such as we can find them, not as we would make them.

These concessions every wise man is more ready to make to others as he knows that he shall often want them for himself; and when he remembers how often he fails in the observance or cultivation of his best friends, is willing to suppose that his friends may in their turn neglect him without any intention to offend him.

When therefore it shall happen, as happen it will, that you or I have disappointed the expectation of the other, you are not to suppose that you h[ave lost me] or that I intended to lose you; nothing will [remain but] to repair the fault, and to go on as if it ne[ver had] been committed,

> I am Sir Your affectionate s[ervant]
> Sam: Johnson

To James Boswell

Thursday, 9 September 1779

My Dear Sir

Are you playing the same trick again, and trying who can keep silence longest? Remember that all tricks are either knavish or childish; and that it is as foolish to make experiments upon the constancy of a friend, as upon the chastity of a wife. . . .

To Hester Thrale

Thursday, 13 November 1783

Dear Madam

Since you have written to me with the attention and tenderness of ancient time your letters give me a great part of the pleasure which a life of solitude admits. You will never bestow any share of your good will on one who deserves better. Those that have loved longest, love best. A sudden blaze of kindness, may by a single blast of coldness be extinguished, but that fondness which length of time has connected with many circumstances and occasions, though it may for a while [be] suppressed by disgust or resentment with or without a cause, is hourly revived by accidental recollection. To those that have lived long together every thing heard and every thing seen recals some pleasure communicated, or some benefit confered, some petty quarrel or some slight endearment. Esteem of great powers or amiable qualities newly discovered may embroider a day or a week, but a friendship of twenty years is interwoven with the texture of life. A friend may be often found and lost, but an *old Friend* never can be found, and Nature has provided that he cannot easily be lost. . . .

Write soon again to
Madam Your most humble servant
Sam: Johnson

JONATHAN SWIFT

To the Rev. James Stopford

20 July 1726

. . . I fear I shall have more than ordinary reasons to wish you a near neighbour to me in Ireland; and that your company will be more necessary than ever, when I tell you that I never was in so great a dejection of spirits. For I lately received a letter from Mr. Worrall, that one of the two oldest and dearest friends I have in the world is in so desperate a condition of health, as makes me expect every post to hear of her death. It is the younger of the two, with whom I have lived in the greatest friendship for thirty-three years. I know you will share in my trouble, because there were few persons whom I believe you more esteemed. For my part, as I value life very little, so the poor casual remains of it, after such a loss, would be a burden that I must heartily beg God Almighty to enable me to bear; and I think there is not a greater folly than that of entering into too strict and particular a friendship, with the loss of which a man must be absolutely miserable; but especially at an age when it is too late to engage in a new friendship. Besides, this was a person of my own rearing and instructing, from childhood, who excelled in every good quality that can possibly accomplish a human creature.—They have hitherto writ me deceiving letters, but Mr. Worrall has been so just and prudent as to tell me the truth; which, however racking, is better than to be struck on the sudden.—Dear Jim, pardon me, I know not what I am saying; but believe me that violent friendship is much more lasting, and as much engaging, as violent love. Adieu. . . .

ALEXANDER POPE

To Jonathan Swift

August 1723

I find a rebuke in a late Letter of yours that both stings & pleases me extreamly. Your saying that I ought to have writt a Postscript to my friend Gay's, makes me not content to write less than a whole Letter, & your seeming to receive His kindly gives me hopes you'll look upon this as a sincere effect of friendship. Indeed as I cannot but owne, the laziness with which you tax me, & with which I may equally charge you (for both of Us I beleive have had & one of Us has both had & given a surfeit of writing) so I really thought you would know yourself to be so certainly entitld to my Friendship, that twas a possession, you cou'd not imagine needed any further Deeds or Writings to assure you of it. It is an honest Truth, there's no one living or dead of whom I think oft'ner, or better than yourself. I look upon You to be, (as to me) in a State between both: you have from me all the passions, & good wishes, that can attend the Living; & all that Respect & tender Sense of Loss, that we feel for the Dead. Whatever you seem to think of your withdrawn & separate State, at this distance, & in this absence, Dr Swift lives still in England, in ev'ry place & company where he woud chuse to live; & I find him in all the conversations I keep, & in all the Hearts in which I wou'd have any Share. We have never met these many Years without mention of you. . . .

15 October 1725

. . . I really enter as fully as you can desire, into your Principle, of Love of Individuals: And I think the way to have a Publick Spirit, is first to have a Private one: For who the devil can believe any man can care for a hundred thousand people, who never cared for One? No ill humoured man can ever be a Patriot, any more than a Friend. . . .

22 August 1726

Many a short sigh you cost me the day I left you, and many more you will cost me, till the day you return.* I really walk'd about like a man banish'd, and when I came home, found it no home. 'Tis a sensation like that of a limb lopp'd off, one is trying every minute unawares to use it, and finds it is not. I may say you have used me more cruelly than you have done any other man; you have made it more impossible for me to live at ease without you: Habitude itself would have done that, if I had less friendship in my nature than I have. Besides my natural memory of you, you have made a local one, which presents you to me in every place I frequent: I shall never more think of Lord Cobham's, the woods of Ciceter, or the pleasing prospect of Byberry, but your Idea must be join'd with 'em; nor see one seat in my own garden, or one room in my own house, without a Phantome of you, sitting or walking before me. I travell'd with you to Chester, I felt the extream heat of the weather, the inns, the roads, the confinement and closeness of the uneasy coach, and wish'd a hundred times I had either a Deanery or a horse in my gift. In real truth, I have felt my soul peevish ever since with all about me, from a warm uneasy desire after you. I am gone out of myself to no purpose, and cannot catch you. *Inhiat in pedes* † was not more properly apply'd to a poor dog after a hare, than to me with regard to your departure. I wish I could think no more of it, but lye down and sleep till we meet again, and let that day (how far soever off it be) be the morrow. Since I cannot, may it be my amends that every thing you wish may attend you where you are, and that you may find every friend you have there in the state you wish him or her; so that your visit to us may have no other effect, than the progress of a rich man to a remote estate, which he finds greater than he expected; which knowledge only serves to make him live happier where he is, with no disagreeable prospect if ever he should chuse to remove. May this be your state till it become what I wish. But indeed I cannot express the warmth, with which I wish you all things, and myself you. Indeed you are engraved elsewhere than on the Cups you sent me,

---

*This letter was written after Swift's first visit to Pope at Twickenham.
†"Gapes after the feet."

(with so kind an inscription) and I might throw them into the Thames without injury to the giver. I am not pleas'd with them, but take them very kindly too: And had I suspected any such usage from you, I should have enjoyed your company less than I really did, for at this rate I may say

Nec tecum possum vivere, nec sine te.†

I will bring you over just such another present, when I go to the Deanery of St. Patrick's; which I promise you to do, if ever I am enabled to return your kindness. *Donarem Pateras,* ** &c. Till then I'll drink (or Gay shall drink) daily healths to you, and I'll add to your inscription the old Roman Vow for years to come, VOTIS‡ X. VOTIS XX. My Mother's age gives me authority to hope it for yours. . . .

3 September 1726

. . . And for me, I assure you I love the world so well, and it loves me so well, that I care not in what part of it I pass the rest of my days. I see no sunshine but in the face of a friend. . . .

19 December 1734

. . . I am truly sorry for any complaint you have, and it is in regard to the weakness of your eyes that I write (as well as print) in folio. You'll think (I know you will, for you have all the candor of a good understanding) that the thing which men of our age feel the most, is the friendship of our equals; and that therefore whatever affects those who are stept a few years before us, cannot but sensibly affect us who are to follow. It troubles me to hear you complain of your memory, and if I am in any part of my constitution younger than you, it will be in my remembring every thing that has pleased me in you, longer than perhaps you will. The two summers we past together dwell always on my mind, like a vision which gave me a glympse of a better life and better company, than this world otherwise afforded. I am now an individual, upon whom no other depends; and may go where I will, if the wretched carcase I am annex'd to did not hinder me. . . . I wish to God we could once meet again, before that separation, which yet I would be glad to believe shall re-unite us: But he who made us, not for ours but his purposes, knows whether it be

†"I can live neither with you nor without you."
**A reference to Horace's Ode 4.8, which begins: "I would generously give my friends dishes and welcome bronzes."
‡"Vows."

for the better or the worse, that the affections of this life should, or
should not continue into the other: and doubtless it is as it should be. Yet
I am sure that while I am here, and the thing that I am, I shall be
imperfect without the communication of such friends as you; you are to
me like a limb lost, and buried in another country; tho' we seem quite
divided, every accident makes me feel you were once a part of me. I
always consider you so much as a friend, that I forget you are an author,
perhaps too much, but 'tis as I would desire you would do to me. . . .

25 March 1736

. . . My understanding indeed, such as it is, is extended rather than
diminish'd: I see things more in the whole, more consistent, and more
clearly deduced from, and related to, each other. But what I gain on the
side of philosophy, I lose on the side of poetry: the flowers are gone,
when the fruits begin to ripen, and the fruits perhaps will never ripen
perfectly. The climate (under our Heaven of a Court) is but cold and
uncertain: the winds rise, and the winter comes on. I find myself but
little disposed to build a new house; I have nothing left but to gather up
the reliques of a wreck, and look about me to see what friends I have!
Pray whose esteem or admiration should I desire now to procure by my
writings? whose friendship or conversation to obtain by 'em? I am a man
of desperate fortunes, that is a man whose friends are dead: for I never
aimed at any other fortune than in friends. As soon as I had sent my last
letter, I received a most kind one from you, expressing great pain for my
late illness at Mr. Cheselden's. I conclude you was eased of that friendly
apprehension in a few days after you had dispatch'd yours, for mine must
have reached you then. I wondered a little at your quære, who Cheselden
was? it shews that the truest merit does not travel so far any way as on the
wings of poetry; he is the most noted, and most deserving man, in the
whole profession of Chirurgery; and has sav'd the lives of thousands by
his manner of cutting for the stone.—I am now well, or what I must call
so.

I have lately seen some writings of Lord B's, since he went to France.
Nothing can depress his Genius: Whatever befals him, he will still be
the greatest man in the world, either in his own time, or with posterity.

Every man you know or care for here, enquires of you, and pays you
the only devoir he can, that of drinking your health. Here are a race
sprung up of young Patriots, who would animate you. I wish you had any
motive to see this kingdom. I could keep you, for I am rich, that is, I have
more than I want. I can afford you room for your self and two servants; I
have indeed room enough, nothing but myself at home! the kind and
hearty house-wife is dead! the agreeable and instructive neighbour is

gone! yet my house is inlarg'd, and the gardens extend and flourish, as knowing nothing of the guests they have lost. I have more fruit-trees and kitchen-garden than you have any thought of; nay I have good Melons and Pine-apples of my own growth. I am as much a better Gardiner, as I'm a worse Poet, than when you saw me: But gardening is near a-kin to Philosophy, for Tully says *Agricultura proxima sapientiae.* * For God's sake, why should not you, (that are a step higher than a Philosopher, a Divine, yet have too much grace and wit than to be a Bishop) e'en give all you have to the Poor of Ireland (for whom you have already done every thing else) so quit the place, and live and die with me? And let *Tales Animae Concordes* † be our Motto and our Epitaph.

30 December 1736

Your very kind letter has made me more melancholy, than almost any thing in this world now can do. For I can bear every thing in it, bad as it is, better than the complaints of my friends. Tho' others tell me you are in pretty good health, and in good spirits, I find the contrary when you open your mind to me: And indeed it is but a prudent part, to seem not so concern'd about others, nor so crazy ourselves as we really are: for we shall neither be beloved or esteem'd the more, by our common acquaintance, for any affliction or any infirmity. But to our true friend we may, we must complain, of what ('tis a thousand to one) he complains with us; for if we have known him long, he is old, and if he has known the world long, he is out of humour at it. If you have but as much more health than others at your age, as you have more wit and good temper, you shall not have much of my Pity: But if you ever live to have less, you shall not have less of my Affection. A whole People will rejoyce at every year that shall be added to you, of which you have had a late instance in the publick rejoycings on your birth-day. I can assure you, something better and greater than high birth and quality, must go toward acquiring those demonstrations of publick esteem and love. I have seen a royal birth-day uncelebrated, but by one vile Ode, and one hired bonfire. Whatever years may take away from you, they will not take away the general esteem, for your Sense, Virtue, and Charity.

The most melancholy effect of years is that you mention, the catalogue of those we lov'd and have lost, perpetually increasing. How much that Reflection struck me, you'll see from the Motto I have prefix'd to my Book of Letters, which so much against my inclination has been drawn from me. It is from Catullus,

*"Agriculture is next to wisdom."
†"Such souls in harmony."

Quo desiderio veteres revocamus Amores,
Atque olim amissas flemus Amicitias!*

. . . You ask me if I have got any supply of new Friends to make up for those that are gone? I think that impossible, for not our friends only, but so much of our selves is gone by the mere flux and course of years, that were the same Friends to be restored to us, we could not be restored to our selves, to enjoy them. But as when the continual washing of a river takes away our flowers and plants, it throws weeds and sedges in their room; so the course of time brings us something, as it deprives us of a great deal; and instead of leaving us what we cultivated, and expected to flourish and adorn us, gives us only what is of some little use, by accident. Thus I have acquired, without my seeking, a few chance-acquaintance, of young men, who look rather to the past age than the present, and therefore the future may have some hopes of them. If I love them, it is because they honour some of those whom I, and the world, have lost, or are losing. Two or three of them have distinguish'd themselves in Parliament, and you will own in a very uncommon manner, when I tell you it is by their asserting of Independency, and contempt of Corruption. One or two are link'd to me by their love of the same studies and the same authors: but I will own to you, my moral capacity has got so much the better of my poetical, that I have few acquaintance on the latter score, and none without a casting weight on the former. But I find my heart harden'd and blunt to new impressions, it will scarce receive or retain affections of yesterday; and those friends who have been dead these twenty years, are more present to me now, than these I see daily. You, dear Sir, are one of the former sort to me in all respects, but that we can, yet, correspond together. I don't know whether 'tis not more vexatious, to know we are both in one world, without any further intercourse. Adieu. I can say no more, I feel so much. . . .

23 March 1737

Tho' you were never to write to me, yet what you desired in your last, that I would write often to you, would be a very easy task: For every day I talk with you, and of you, in my heart; and I need only set down what that is thinking of. The nearer I find myself verging to that period of life which is to be labour and sorrow, the more I prop myself upon those few supports that are left me. People in this state are like props indeed, they cannot stand alone, but two or more of them can stand, leaning and

*"With that heartache with which we renew old loves, and weep over friendships long since lost."

bearing upon one another. I wish you and I might pass this part of life together. My only necessary care is at an end. I am now my own master too much; my house is too large; my gardens furnish too much wood and provision for my use. My servants are sensible and tender of me; they have inter-married, and are become rather low friends than servants: and to all those that I see here with pleasure, they take a pleasure in being useful. I conclude this is your case too in your domestic life, and I sometimes think of your old house-keeper as my nurse; tho' I tremble at the sea, which only divides us. As your fears are not so great as mine, and I firmly hope your strength still much greater, is it utterly impossible, it might once more be some pleasure to you to see England? . . .

Would to God you would come over with Lord Orrery, whose care of you in the voyage I could so certainly depend on; and bring with you your old housekeeper and two or three servants. I have room for all, a heart for all, and (think what you will) a fortune for all. We could, were we together, contrive to make our last days easy, and leave some sort of Monument, what Friends two Wits could be in spite of all the fools of the world. Adieu.

JEAN-JACQUES ROUSSEAU

To Madame d'Épinay

17 December 1756

Diderot has written me a third letter, when sending back my papers. Although you informed me in yours that you were sending me the parcel, it reached me later by another route, so that when I received it I had already finished my answer to Diderot. You must be as tired of this long bickering as I am worn out by it.* Therefore, let us say no more about it, I beg you.

But where have you got the idea that I shall complain of you also? If I had anything to complain of, it would be that you show too much con-

*When Rousseau and Denis Diderot quarreled, Madame d'Épinay tried to reconcile them and suggested that perhaps Rousseau would complain about her next.

sideration for me, and treat me too kindly. I frequently need to be scolded more than that. I like a tone of rebuke when I deserve it. I believe that I should be the kind of man to regard it sometimes as a kind of friendly cajolery. But it is possible to quarrel with a friend without treating him with contempt; one can very well call him a beast, but one will never call him a rascal. You will never let me hear you say "that you think you are doing me a favour in thinking well of me." You will never insinuate to me that, "upon looking closely, there would be much esteem to abate." You will not tell me "could there be any further good in saying anything about that?" This would not only be insulting me, but also insulting yourself; for it does not become honourable people to have friends of whom they think ill; if it had happened to me, in regard to this point, to wrongly interpret anything said by you, you would certainly hasten to explain your idea to me, and you would be careful not to keep up the same observations, coldly and harshly, in the wrong sense which I might have attributed to them. What, Madame, do you call that? a form, an exterior?

Since we are discussing this subject, I should like to make a declaration to you as to what I require from friendship, and as to what I desire to exhibit in it in my turn.

Blame freely what you find blamable in my rules, but do not expect to find me easily departing from them; for they are drawn from my disposition, which I cannot alter.

In the first place, I wish my friends to be my friends, and not my masters; to advise me without claiming to control me; to enjoy all kinds of rights over my heart, none over my freedom. I consider those persons very singular who, under the name of friends, always claim to interfere in my affairs without telling me anything about theirs. Let them always speak to me freely and frankly; they can say anything to me; contempt excepted, I allow them everything. The contempt of a person who is indifferent to me is a matter of indifference; but, if I were to endure it from a friend, I should deserve it. If he has the misfortune to despise me, let him avoid telling me, let him leave me; that is what he owes to himself. With that exception, when he remonstrates with me, whatever tone he adopts, he is within his rights; when, after having listened to him, I follow my own inclination, I am within mine; and I greatly dislike anyone to keep eternally chattering to me about what is over and done with.

Their great anxiety to do me a number of services which I do not care about is wearisome to me; it seems to imply a certain air of superiority which is displeasing to me; besides, everyone can do as much. I prefer them to love me and let themselves be loved; that is what friends alone can do. Above all, I am indignant when the first new-comer is able to compensate them for my loss, while I cannot endure anyone's society but theirs in the world. Nothing but their affection can make me endure their kindnesses, but when I once consent to receive them from them, I wish them to consult my taste and not their own; for we think so differently upon so many things, that often what they consider good appears to me bad.

If a quarrel occurs, I should certainly say that he who is in the wrong ought to apologise first; but that means nothing, for everyone always thinks that he is in the right; right or wrong, it is for him who has begun the quarrel to put an end to it. If I take his censure ill, if I am annoyed without reason, if I put myself in a passion at the wrong moment, he ought not to follow my example; if he does, he certainly does not love me. On the contrary, I would have him treat me with affection; do you understand, Madame? In a word, let him begin by soothing me, which will certainly not take long, for there has never been a fire at the bottom of my heart which a tear could not extinguish. Then, when I am softened, calmed, ashamed, and covered with confusion, let him scold me, let him tell me what I have done, and assuredly he will have no reason to complain of me. If it is a question of a trifling detail, which is not worth clearing up, let him drop it; let the aggressor be the first to hold his tongue, and let him not make it a foolish point of honour always to have the advantage. That is how I wish my friend to act towards me, as I am always ready to act towards him in a similar case.

On this point, I could mention to you a little instance of which you have no suspicion, although it concerns you; it has to do with a note which I received from you some time ago, in answer to another with which I saw you were not satisfied, and in which, as it seems to me, you had failed to understand what I meant. I answered properly enough, or at least I thought so; my reply certainly was in the tone of true friendship, but, at the same time, I cannot deny that there was a certain amount of warmth in it, and, reading it again, I was afraid that you would be no better pleased with it than with the first; immediately, I threw my letter in the fire; I cannot tell you how pleased I felt to see my eloquence consumed in the flames; I said nothing more to you about it, and I believe that I gained the honour of being beaten; sometimes it only needs a spark to kindle a conflagration. My dear, kind friend, Pythagoras said that one should never poke the fire with a sword; this maxim seems to me the most important and the most sacred law of friendship.

I require from a friend even a great deal more than all I have just told you; even more than he must require from me, and than I should require from him, if he were in my place, and I were in his.

As a recluse, I am more sensitive than another man; if I am wrong in my behaviour to a friend, he thinks of it for a moment, and then a thousand distractions cause him to forget it for the rest of the day; but nothing distracts my attention from any wrong done by him to me; I cannot sleep; I think of it the whole night long; when walking by myself, I think of it from sunrise to sunset; my heart has not a moment's respite, and the harshness of a friend causes me, in a single day, years of grief. As an invalid, I have a right to the indulgence which humanity owes to the weakness and temper of a sufferer. Who is the friend, who is the honourable man who ought not to be afraid of grieving an unhappy man tormented by a painful and incurable malady? I am poor, and it seems to me that I deserve considerate treatment on this account still more. All these indulgences that I require you have shown to me without my mentioning them, and surely it will never be necessary for me to ask them from a true friend. But, my dear friend, let us speak frankly; do you know any friends that I have? On my honour, it has been my good fortune to learn to do without them. I know many persons who would not be sorry that I should be under obligation to them, and many to whom in fact I am, but hearts fit to respond to mine—ah! it is enough to know one.

Do not therefore be surprised if my hatred for Paris increases; I get nothing from it but annoyance, with the exception of your letters; I shall never be seen there again. If you wish to remonstrate with me upon this point, and even as forcibly as you please, you have the right to do so; your remonstrances will be well received and will be—useless; after that, you will abandon them. Do just as you think fit in the matter of M. d'Holbach's book, except as to taking the edition upon your hands; that is a way of getting a book purchased by force, and of putting one's friends under contribution. I do not like anything of that kind.

I thank you for Anson's Voyages; I will send the book back to you next week.

Excuse the erasures; I am writing to you at my fireside, where we are all assembled. The women-folk are exhausting, in company with the gardener, the history of all those who have been hanged in the country, and to-day's gazette is so full of news, that I do not know what I am saying. Goodbye! my kind friend.

ROBERT BURNS

To Captain Richard Brown

Mauchline 21ˢᵗ May 1789

My dear Friend,

I was just in this country by accident and hearing of your safe arrival, I could not resist the temptation of wishing you joy on your return— wishing you would write me before you sail again—wishing you would always set me down as your bosom-friend—wishing you long life & prosperity & that every good thing may attend you—wishing Mʳˢ Brown and your little ones as few of the evils of this world as is consistent with humanity—wishing you & she were to make two at the ensuing lying-in with which Mʳˢ Burns threatens very soon to favor me—wishing that I had longer time to write you at present—& finally, wishing that if there is to be another state of existence, Mʳˢ Brown, Mʳˢ Burns, our little ones in both families, & you and I in some snug paradisical retreat, may make a jovial Party to all eternity! Amen!!!—

There is a lad, a James Miller, a surgeon from this place that I hear is to sail your Passenger.—He is a good, honest blunt lad, by no means destitute of abilities; and the son of a most respectable man, a particular friend of mine. Should it be in your power to oblidge him in any little civility, it would oblidge me likewise.—Farewell! God bless you! my long-loved, dearest friend!!!—I have time for no more than that I am ever,

Most sincerely yours,
Robert Burns

MARY WOLLSTONECRAFT
SHELLEY

To Jane Williams

Albaro. Jan^ry 12th [1823]

A letter from you, dearest Jane, although a melancholy one, is the source of great delight to me. I live in a state of such complete isolation that the voice of affection comes to me like the sounds of remembered music. I am indeed alone. You, my best girl, have some two or three, I hope many more, who love you; who sympathize in your sorrows & to whom you can speak of them. I have none; and the feeling of alienation which seems to possess the very few human beings I see, causes a kind of humiliating depression that weighs like a fog about me. Yet I ought not to complain. God knows that except yourself & now & then Trelawny I wish to see none but those I do see. And those are three. LB. is all kindness—but there is more of manner than heart, or to speak more truly, I am satisfied with the little he bestows—It is much & it is nothing. It is much in the way of what is called *essential* service, in that way it is *every thing* I can desire—It is nothing for my heart, but then that restless piner seeks nothing from him. Marianne is very good. She does all she can to make me comfortable—but her heart is not an universe—it has received within itself her husband & children, & the gates are closed. Is Hunt then the object of my complaint. This is too bad; but he does not like me—I feel & know this; he has never forgiven my resistance to his intolerable claims at Pisa—He avoids walking with (———), nor does he refrain at times from saying bitter things. I am a coward—I hate contention & I disdain the victory—I wish only to fly—I am enthrawled & feel my chains & bolts.

Yet this after all is nothing. Sometimes he stirs my torpid blood, & when I am very miserable, will cause my tears to flow—Yet now when at night all is quiet and my thoughts resume their usual train—it seems nothing. For in truth I live little in this world—I live on the past & future and the present, day by day, fades like the figures on a lantern. I dare not look on it; I hate every thing about me, all my feelings—the air—the light; I desire death & it comes not; I look on my poor boy, & for worlds I would not die to leave him; every sentiment I have contends one with the other—& I have no refuge. The cup is very deep from which I drink, and all its ingredients are bitter.

So, my own Jane, we two poor creatures compare notes of misery. . . .

You see how selfish I am and that I talk only of myself. Yet I think of you & my heart is with you in your ruined *sanctum.* Your children must employ you somewhat, & I hope you read, for in books we live in a peaceful world; & save that to which the imagination carries us to among the dead, the best the earth affords. If you can get it pray read Sir Philip Sidney's "Arcadia"—It is a beautiful book; its exquisite sentiments and descriptions would have delighted you in happier days, perhaps they will now. It is pleasant to me to think that we both turn our eyes to the same spot for our place of rest. Come to Florence, my dear Jane, & let us see if mutual affection will not stand us in some stead in our calamities— Our fate is one, so ought our interests here to be; we can talk eternally to each other of our lost ones, and surely they would be best pleased to find us together. I will deserve your love—if love can buy its like; and with me—perhaps you may attain the peaceful state you desire—I might ease you of some of your cares—& your affection to me would be a treasure. . . .

—Last night, dear Jane I dreamt of them.* He was looking well & happy & I was transported to see him—I asked Ned if the men in the fishing boat could not have saved them—he replied no—for though they appeared near the high waves rendered it impossible for them to approach—Had you not a dream, where the same answer was given. Would that I could dream of them thus every night & I would sleep for ever

Kiss your Children for me, & teach my little God-daughter that there is one in Italy who loves her.

Your very Affectionate
Mary W. Shelley

---

*Mary's husband Percy Shelley and his friend (and Jane's common-law husband) Edward Williams, who had drowned together six months earlier.

JOHN KEATS

To J. H. Reynolds

[21 September 1817]
Oxford Sunday Morn

My dear Reynolds./

So you are determined to be my mortal foe—draw a Sword at me, and I will forgive—Put a Bullet in my Brain, and I will shake it out as a dewdrop from the Lion's Mane;—put me on a Gridiron, and I will fry with great complancency—but, oh horror! to come upon me in the shape of a Dun! Send me Bills! as I say to my Taylor send me Bills and I'll never employ you more. . . .

For these last five or six days, we have had regularly a Boat on the Isis, and explored all the streams about, which are more in number than your eye lashes. We sometimes skim into a Bed of rushes, and there become naturalized riverfolks,—there is one particularly nice nest which we have christened "Reynolds's Cove"—in which we have read Wordsworth and talked as may be. I think I see you and Hunt meeting in the Pit.— What a very pleasant fellow he is, if he would give up the sovereignty of a Room pro bono—What Evenings we might pass with him, could we have him from M^rs H—Failings I am always rather rejoiced to find in a Man than sorry for; for they bring us to a Level. . . .

Yours faithfully
John Keats

To Benjamin Bailey

Friday Jany 23rd [1818]

My dear Bailey,

Twelve days have pass'd since your last reached me—what has gone through the myriads of human Minds since the 12th we talk of the immense number of Books, the Volumes ranged thousands by thousands—but perhaps more goes through the human intelligence in 12 days than ever was written. How has that unfortunate Family lived through the twelve? One saying of your's I shall never forget—you may not recollect it—it being perhaps said when you were looking on the surface and seeming of Humanity alone, without a thought of the past or the future—or the deeps of good and evil—you were at the moment estranged from speculation and I think you have arguments ready for the Man who would utter it to you—this is a formidable preface for a simple thing—merely you said; *"Why should Woman suffer?"* Aye. Why should she? "By heavens I'd coin my very Soul and drop my Blood for Drachmas."! These things are, and he who feels how incompetent the most skyey Knight errantry its to heal this bruised fairness is like a sensitive leaf on the hot hand of thought. Your tearing, my dear friend, a spiritless and gloomy Letter up to rewrite to me is what I shall never forget—it was to me a real thing. Things have happen'd lately of great Perplexity—You must have heard of them—Reynolds and Haydon retorting and recrimminating—and parting for ever—the same thing has happened between Haydon and Hunt—It is unfortunate—Men should bear with each other—there lives not the Man who may not be cut up, aye hashed to pieces on his weakest side. The best of Men have but a portion of good in them—a kind of spiritual yeast in their frames which creates the ferment of existence—by which a Man is propell'd to act and strive and buffet with Circumstance. The sure way Bailey, is first to know a Man's faults, and then be passive, if after that he insensibly draws you towards him then you have no Power to break the link. Before I felt interested in either Reynolds or Haydon—I was well read in their faults yet knowing them I have been cementing gradually with both—I have an affection for them both for reasons almost opposite—and to both must I of necessity cling—supported always by the hope that when a little time—a few years shall have tried me more fully in their esteem I may be able to bring them together—the time must come because they have both hearts—and they will recollect the best parts of each other when this gust is overblown. . . .

> Your most affectionate friend
> John Keats—

To J. H. Reynolds

Teignmouth May 3ᵈ [1818]

My dear Reynolds.

What I complain of is that I have been in so an uneasy a state of Mind as not to be fit to write to an invalid. I cannot write to any length under a dis-guised feeling. I should have loaded you with an addition of gloom, which I am sure you do not want. I am now thank God in a humour to give you a good groats worth—for Tom, after a Night without a Wink of sleep, and overburdened with fever, has got up after a refreshing day sleep and is better than he has been for a long time; . . . it is impossible to know how far knowledge will console us for the death of a friend and the ill "that flesh is heir to—With respect to the affections and Poetry you must know by a sympathy my thoughts that way; . . . I have often pitied a Tutor who has to hear "Nom: Musa"—so often dinn'd into his ears—I hope you may not have the same pain in this scribbling—I may have read these things before, but I never had even a thus dim perception of them; and moreover I like to say my lesson to one who will endure my tediousness for my own sake—After all there is certainly something real in the World—Moore's present to Hazlitt is real—I like that Moore, and am glad [that] I saw him at the Theatre just before I left Town. Tom has spit a leetle blood this afternoon, and that is rather a damper—but I know—the truth is there is something real in the World Your third Chamber of Life shall be a lucky and a gentle one—stored with the wine of love—and the Bread of Friendship. . . .

Your affectionate friend
John Keats.

To Benjamin Bailey

[21, 25 May 1818]
Hampstead Thursday—

My dear Bailey,

. . . I have this morning such a Lethargy that I cannot write—the reason of my delaying is oftentimes from this feeling—I wait for a proper temper—Now you ask for an immediate answer I do not like to wait even till tomorrow—However I am now so depressed that I have not an Idea to put to paper—my hand feels like lead—and yet it is and unpleasant numbness it does not take away the pain of existence—I don't know what to write—Monday—You see how I have delayed—and even now I have but a confused idea of what I should be about my intellect must be in a degen[er]ating state—it must be for when I should be writing about god knows what I am troubling you with Moods of my own Mind or rather body—for Mind there is none. I am in that temper that if I were under Water I would scarcely kick to come to the top—I know very well 't is all nonsense. In a short time I hope I shall be in a temper to fell sensibly your mention of my Book—in vain have I waited till Monday to have any interest in that or in any thing else. I feel no spur at my Brothers going to America and am almost stony-hearted about his wedding. All this will blow over—all I am sorry for is having to write to you in such a time—but I cannot force my letters in a hot bed—I could not feel comfortable in making sentences for you—I am your debtor—I must ever remain so—nor do I wish to be clear of my rational debt—There is a comfort in throwing oneself on the charity of ones friends—'t is like the albatros sleeping on its wings—I will be to you wine in the cellar and the more modestly or rather indolently I retire into the backward Bin, the more falerne will I be at the drinking. . . .

> Your's affectionately John Keats—

To James Rice

Well Walk—Novr 24—[1818]

My dear Rice,
   Your amende honorable, I must call "un surcroît d'amitié"* for I am not at all sensible of any thing but that you were unfortunately engaged and I was unfortunately in a hurry. I completely understand your feeling in this mistake, and find in it that ballance of comfort which remains after regretting your uneasiness—I have long made up my Mind to take for granted the genuine heartedness of my friends notwithstanding any temporery ambiguousness in their behaviour or their tongues; nothing of which how[ev]er I had the least scent of this morning. I say completely understand; for I am everlastingly getting my mind into such like painful trammels—and am even at this moment suffering under them in the case of a friend of ours. I will tell you—Two most unfortunate and paralel slips—it seems downright preintention. A friend says to me "Keats I shall go and see Severn this Week" "Ah" says I "You want him

---

*"Amende honorable" means "full apology." "Un surcroît d'amitié" means "an excess of friendship."

to take your Portrait" and again "Keats" says a friend "When will you come to town again" "I will" says I "let you have the Mss next week" In both these I appeard to attribute and interested motive to each of my friends' questions—the first made him flush; the second made him look angry—And yet I am innocent—in both cases my Mind leapt over every interval [between] to what I saw was per se a pleasant subject with him—You see I have no allowances to make—you see how far I am from supposing you could show me any neglect. I very much regret the long time I have been obliged to exile from you—for I have had one or two rather pleasant occasions to confer upon with you—What I have heard from George is favorable—I expect soon a Letter from the Settlement itself—

Your sincere friend
John Keats

I cannot give any good news of Tom—

To Benjamin Bailey

14 August 1819

. . . One of my Ambitions is to make as great a revolution in modern dramatic writing as Kean has done in acting—another to upset the drawling of the blue stocking literary world—if in the course of a few years I do these two things I ought to die content—and my friends should drink a dozen of Claret on my Tomb. . . .

Ever your sincere friend
John Keats

To Charles Brown

(Names missing in the manuscript are supplied in brackets by the editors.)

22 September 1819

. . . Now I am going to enter on the subject of self. It is quite time I should set myself doing something, and live no longer upon hopes. I have never yet exerted myself. I am getting into an idle minded, vicious way of life, almost content to live upon others. In no period of my life have I acted with any self will, but in throwing up the apothecary-profession.

That I do not repent of. Look at [J. H. Reynolds]: if he was not in the law he would be acquiring, by his abilities, something towards his support. My occupation is entirely literary; I will do so too. I will write, on the liberal side of the question, for whoever will pay me. I have not known yet what it is to be diligent. I purpose living in town in a cheap lodging, and endeavouring, for a beginning, to get the theatricals of some paper. When I can afford to compose deliberate poems I will. I shall be in expectation of an answer to this. Look on my side of the question. I am convinced I am right. Suppose the Tragedy should succeed,—there will be no harm done. And here I will take an opportunity of making a remark or two on our friendship, and all your good offices to me. I have a natural timidity of mind in these matters, liking better to take the feeling between us for granted, than to speak of it. But, good God! what a short while you have known me! I feel it a sort of duty thus to recapitulate, however unpleasant it may be to you. You have been living for others more than any man I know. This is a vexation to me; because it has been depriving you, in the very prime of your life, of pleasures which it was your duty to procure. As I am speaking in general terms this may appear nonsense; you perhaps will not understand it: but if you can go over, day by day, any month of the last year,—you will know what I mean. On the whole, however, this is a subject that I cannot express myself upon. I speculate upon it frequently; and, believe me, the end of my speculations is always an anxiety for your happiness. This anxiety will not be one of the least incitements to the plan I purpose pursuing. I had got into a habit of mind of looking towards you as a help in all difficulties. This very habit would be the parent of idleness and difficulties. You will see it is a duty I owe myself to break the neck of it. I do nothing for my subsistence—make no exertion. At the end of another year, you shall applaud me,—not for verses, but for conduct. If you live at Hampstead next winter——I like [Fanny Brawne?] and I cannot help it. On that account I had better not live there. While I have some immediate cash, I had better settle myself quietly, and fag on as others do. I shall apply to Hazlitt, who knows the market as well as any one, for something to bring me in a few pounds as soon as possible. I shall not suffer my pride to hinder me. The whisper may go round; I shall not hear it. If I can get an article in the "Edinburg", I will. One must not be delicate. Nor let this disturb you longer than a moment. I look forward, with a good hope, that we shall one day be passing free, untrammelled, unanxious time together. That can never be if I continue a dead lump. . . . I shall be expecting anxiously an answer from you. If it does not arrive in a few days, this will have miscarried, and I shall come straight to [Bedhampton or Chichester?] before I go to town, which you, I am sure, will agree had better be done while I still have some ready cash. By the middle of

October I shall expect you in London. We will then set at the Theatres.
If you have any thing to gainsay, I shall be even as the deaf adder which
stoppeth her ears. . . .

To C. W. Dilke

[22 September 1819]
Winchester Wednesday Eve—

My dear Dilke,
     . . . Talking of Pleasure, this moment I was writing with one hand, and
with the other holding to my Mouth a Nectarine—good god how
fine—It went down soft pulpy, slushy, oozy—all its delicious embon-
point melted down my throat like a large beatified Strawberry. I shall
certainly breed. Now I come to my request. Should you like me for a
neighbour again? Come, plump it out, I wont blush. I should also be in
the neighbourhood of Mrs Wylie, which I should be glad of, though that
of course does not influence me. Therefore will you look about Mar-
sham, or rodney street for a couple of rooms for me. Rooms like the
gallants legs in massingers time "as good as the times allow, Sir." I have
written to day to Reynolds, and to Woodhouse. Do you know him? He
i[s] a Friend of Taylors at whom Brown has taken one of his funny odd
dislikes. I'm sure he's wrong, because Woodhouse likes my Poetry—
conclusive. I ask your opinion and yet I must say to you as to him, Brown
that if you have any thing to say against it I shall be as obstinate & heady
as a Radical. . . .

Ever your sincere friend
John Keats—

To the George Keatses

20, 21, 24 September 1819

     . . . I must tell you a good thing Reynolds *did:* 't was the best thing he
ever *said.* You know at taking leave of a party at a door way, sometimes a
Man dallies and foolishes and gets awkward, and does not know how to
make off to advantage—Good bye—well—good-bye—and yet he does
not—go—good bye and so on—well—good bless you—You know what

I mean. Now Reynolds was in this predicament and got out of it in a very witty way. He was leaving us at Hampstead. He delay'd, and we were joking at him and even said, "be off"—at which he put the tails of his coat between his legs, and sneak'd off as nigh like a spanial as could be. He went with flying colours. . . . From the time you left me, our friends say I have altered completely—am not the same person—perhaps in this letter I am for in a letter one takes up one's existence from the time we last met—I dare say you have altered also—every man does—Our bodies every seven years are completely fresh-materiald—seven years ago it was not this hand that clench'd itself against Hammond—We are like the relict garments of a Saint: the same and not the same: for the careful Monks patch it and patch it: till there's not a thread of the original garment left, and still they show it for St Anthony's shirt. This is the reason why men who had been bosom friends, on being separated for any number of years, afterwards meet coldly, neither of them knowing why—The fact is they are both altered—Men who live together have a silent moulding and influencing power over each other—They interass-imulate. 'T is an uneasy thought that in seven years the same hands cannot greet each other again. All this may be obviated by a willful and dramatic exercise of our Minds towards each other. . . . Now the first political duty a Man ought to have a Mind to is the happiness of his friends. . . .

Your affectionate and anxious Brother
John Keats

To John Taylor

22 September 1820

[The Testament]
In case of my death this scrap of Paper may be serviceable in your possession.

All my estate real and personal consists in the hopes of the sale of books publish'd or unpublish'd. Now I wish *Brown* and you to be the first paid Creditors—the rest is in nubibus*— but in case it should shower pay my Taylor the few pounds I owe him.
My Chest of Books divide among my friends—

*"In the clouds."

To Charles Brown

Saturday Sept 28 *[actually 30 September 1820]*
*Maria Crowther off Yarmouth isle of wight—** *

My dear Brown,
The time has not yet come for a pleasant Letter from me. I have delayed
writing to you from time to time because I felt how impossible it was to
enliven you with one heartening hope of my recovery; this morning in
bed the matter struck me in a different manner; I thought I would write
"while I was in some liking" or I might become too ill to write at all and
then if the desire to have written should become strong it would be a
great affliction to me. I have many more Letters to write and I bless my
stars that I have begun, for time seems to press,—this may be my best
opportunity. We are in a calm and I am easy enough this morning. If my
spirits seem too low you may in some degree impute it to our having
been at sea a fortmight without making any way. I was very disappointed
at not meeting you at bedhampton, and am very provoked at the
thought of you being at Chichester to day. I should have delighted in
setting off for London for the sensation merely—for what should I do
there? I could not leave my lungs or stomach or other worse things
behind me. I wish to write on subjects that will not agitate me much—
there is one I must mention and have done with it. Even if my body
would recover of itself, this would prevent it—The very thing which I
want to live most for will be a great occasion of my death. I cannot help
it. Who can help it? Were I in health it would make me ill, and how can
I bear it in my state? I dare say you will be able to guess on what subject
I am harping—you know what was my greatest pain during the first part
of my illness at your house. I wish for death every day and night to
deliver me from these pains, and then I wish death away, for death
would destroy even those pains which are better than nothing. Land and
Sea, weakness and decline are great seperators, but death is the great
divorcer for ever. When the pang of this thought has passed through my
mind, I may say the bitterness of death is passed. I often wish for you
that you might flatter me with the best. I think without my mentioning
it for my sake you would be a friend to Miss Brawne when I am dead.
You think she has many faults—but, for my sake, think she has not
one——if there is any thing you can do for her by word or deed I know
you will do it. I am in a state at present in which woman merely as
woman can have no more power over me than stocks and stones, and yet

---

*Keats had contracted tuberculosis and, on doctor's orders, had set sail for the milder
climate of Rome, where he died a few months later at the age of twenty-five.

the difference of my sensations with respect to Miss Brawne and my Sister is amazing. The one seems to absorb the other to a degree incredible. I seldom think of my Brother and Sister in america. The thought of leaving Miss Brawne is beyond every thing horrible—the sense of darkness coming over me—I eternally see her figure eternally vanishing. Some of the phrases she was in the habit of using during my last nursing at Wen[t]worth place ring in my ears—Is there another Life? Shall I awake and find all this a dream? There must be we cannot be created for this sort of suffering. The receiving of this letter is to be one of yours—I will say nothing about our friendship or rather yours to me more than that as you deserve to escape you will never be so unhappy as I am. I should think of—you in my last moments. I shall endeavour to write to Miss Brawne if possible to day. A sudden stop to my life in the middle of one of these Letters would be no bad thing for it keeps one in a sort of fever awhile. Though fatigued with a Letter longer than any I have written for a long while it would be better to go on for ever than awake to a sense of contrary winds. We expect to put into Portland roads to night. The Captn the Crew and the Passengers are all illtemper'd and weary. I shall write to dilke. I feel as if I was closing my last letter to you—My dear Brown

Your affectionate friend
John Keats

Rome. 30 November 1820.

My dear Brown,
'Tis the most difficult thing in the world to me to write a letter. My stomach continues so bad, that I feel it worse on opening any book,—yet I am much better than I was in Quarantine. Then I am afraid to encounter the proing and conning of any thing interesting to me in England. I have an habitual feeling of my real life having past, and that I am leading a posthumous existence. God knows how it would have been—but it appears to me—however, I will not speak of that subject. I must have been at Bedhampton nearly at the time you were writing to me from Chichester—how unfortunate—and to pass on the river too! There was my star predominant! I cannot answer any thing in your letter, which followed me from Naples to Rome, because I am afraid to look it over again. I am so weak (in mind) that I cannot bear the sight of any hand writing of a friend I love so much as I do you. Yet I ride the little horse,—and, at my worst, even in Quarantine, summoned up more puns, in a sort of desperation, in one week than in any year of my life. There is one thought enough to kill me—I have been well, healthy, alert &c, walking with her—and now—the knowledge of contrast, feeling for

light and shade, all that information (primitive sense) necessary for a poem are great enemies to the recovery of the stomach. There, you rogue, I put you to the torture,—but you must bring your philosophy to bear—as I do mine, really—or how should I be able to live? Dr Clarke is very attentive to me; he says, there is very little the matter with my lungs, but my stomach, he says, is very bad. I am well disappointed in hearing good news from George,—for it runs in my head we shall all die young. I have not written to [William Haslam?] yet, which he must think very neglectful; being anxious to send him a good account of my health, I have delayed it from week to week. If I recover, I will do all in my power to correct the mistakes made during sickness; and if I should not, all my faults will be forgiven. I shall write to [C. W. Dilke?] to-morrow, or next day. I will write to [Richard Woodhouse?] in the middle of next week. Severn is very well, though he leads so dull a life with me. Remember me to all friends, and tell [J. H. Reynolds?] I should not have left London without taking leave of him, but from being so low in body and mind. Write to George as soon as you receive this, and tell him how I am, as far as you can guess;—and also a note to my sister—who walks about my imagination like a ghost—she is so like Tom. I can scarcely bid you good bye even in a letter. I always made an awkward bow.

God bless you!
John Keats.

PART IV

POETRY

The bird a nest, the spider a web, man friendship.

—William Blake

HOMER

From THE ILIAD

So these fought on in the likeness of blazing fire. Meanwhile,
Antilochos came, a swift-footed messenger, to Achilleus,
and found him sitting in front of the steep-horned ships, thinking
over in his heart of things which had now been accomplished.
Disturbed, Achilleus spoke to the spirit in his own great heart:
"Ah me, how is it that once again the flowing-haired Achaians
are driven out of the plain on their ships in fear and confusion?
May the gods not accomplish vile sorrows upon the heart in me
in the way my mother once made it clear to me, when she told me
how while I yet lived the bravest of all the Myrmidons
must leave the light of the sun beneath the hands of the Trojans.
Surely, then, the strong son of Menoitios has perished.
Unhappy! and yet I told him, once he had beaten the fierce fire
off, to come back to the ships, not fight in strength against Hektor."
     Now as he was pondering this in his heart and his spirit,
meanwhile the son of stately Nestor was drawing near him
and wept warm tears, and gave Achilleus his sorrowful message:
"Ah me, son of valiant Peleus; you must hear from me
the ghastly message of a thing I wish never had happened.
Patroklos has fallen, and now they are fighting over his body
which is naked. Hektor of the shining helm has taken his armour."
     He spoke, and the black cloud of sorrow closed on Achilleus.
In both hands he caught up the grimy dust, and poured it
over his head and face, and fouled his handsome countenance,
and the black ashes were scattered over his immortal tunic.
And he himself, mightily in his might, in the dust lay
at length, and took and tore at his hair with his hands, and defiled it.
And the handmaidens Achilleus and Patroklos had taken
captive, stricken at heart cried out aloud, and came running
out of doors about valiant Achilleus, and all of them

beat their breasts with their hands, and the limbs went slack in each of
them.
On the other side Antilochos mourned with him, letting the tears fall,
and held the hands of Achilleus as he grieved in his proud heart,
fearing Achilleus might cut his throat with the iron. He cried out
terribly, aloud, and the lady his mother heard him
as she sat in the depths of the sea at the side of her aged father,
and she cried shrill in turn, and the goddesses gathered about her,
all who along the depth of the sea were daughters of Nereus.
There as he sighed heavily the lady his mother stood by him
and cried out shrill and aloud, and took her son's head in her arms,
    then
sorrowing for him she spoke to him in winged words: "Why then,
child, do you lament? What sorrow has come to your heart now?
Speak out, do not hide it. These things are brought to accomplishment
through Zeus: in the way that you lifted your hands and prayed for,
that all the sons of the Achaians be pinned on their grounded vessels
by reason of your loss, and suffer things that are shameful."
    Then sighing heavily Achilleus of the swift feet answered her:
"My mother, all these things the Olympian brought to
    accomplishment.
But what pleasure is this to me, since my dear companion has perished,
Patroklos, whom I loved beyond all other companions,
as well as my own life. I have lost him, and Hektor, who killed him,
has stripped away that gigantic armour, a wonder to look on
and splendid, which the gods gave Peleus, a glorious present,
on that day they drove you to the marriage bed of a mortal.
I wish you had gone on living then with the other goddesses
of the sea, and that Peleus had married some mortal woman.
As it is, there must be on your heart a numberless sorrow
for your son's death, since you can never again receive him
won home again to his country; since the spirit within does not drive
    me
to go on living and be among men, except on condition
that Hektor first be beaten down under my spear, lose his life
and pay the price for stripping Patroklos, the son of Menoitios."
    Then in turn Thetis spoke to him, letting the tears fall:
"Then I must lose you soon, my child, by what you are saying,
since it is decreed your death must come soon after Hektor's."
    Then deeply disturbed Achilleus of the swift feet answered her:
"I must die soon, then; since I was not to stand by my companion
when he was killed. And now, far away from the land of his fathers,
he has perished, and lacked my fighting strength to defend him.

Now, since I am not going back to the beloved land of my fathers,
since I was no light of safety to Patroklos, nor to my other
companions, who in their numbers went down before glorious Hektor,
but sit here beside my ships, a useless weight on the good land,
I, who am such as no other of the bronze-armoured Achaians
in battle, though there are others also better in council—
why, I wish that strife would vanish away from among gods and
    mortals,
and gall, which makes a man grow angry for all his great mind,
that gall of anger that swarms like smoke inside of a man's heart
and becomes a thing sweeter to him by far than the dripping of honey.
So it was here that the lord of men Agamemnon angered me.
Still, we will let all this be a thing of the past, and for all our
sorrow beat down by force the anger deeply within us.
Now I shall go, to overtake that killer of a dear life,
Hektor; then I will accept my own death, at whatever
time Zeus wishes to bring it about, and the other immortals. . . ."
                        [Book 18, ll. 1–38, 70–116]

    But the lords of Achaia were gathered about Achilleus
beseeching him to eat, but he with a groan denied them:
"I beg of you, if any dear companion will listen
to me, stop urging me to satisfy the heart in me
with food and drink, since this strong sorrow has come upon me.
I will hold out till the sun goes down and endure, though it be hard."
    So he spoke, and caused the rest of the kings to scatter;
but the two sons of Atreus stayed with him, and brilliant Odysseus,
and Nestor, and Idomeneus, and the aged charioteer, Phoinix,
comforting him close in his sorrow, yet his heart would not
be comforted, till he went into the jaws of the bleeding battle.
Remembering Patroklos he sighed much for him, and spoke aloud:
"There was a time, ill fated, o dearest of all my companions,
when you yourself would set the desirable dinner before me
quickly and expertly, at the time the Achaians were urgent
to carry sorrowful war on the Trojans, breakers of horses.
But now you lie here torn before me, and my heart goes starved
for meat and drink, though they are here beside me, by reason
of longing for you. There is nothing worse than this I could suffer,
not even if I were to hear of the death of my father
who now, I think, in Phthia somewhere lets fall a soft tear
for bereavement of such a son, for me, who now in a strange land
make war upon the Trojans for the sake of accursed Helen;
or the death of my dear son, who is raised for my sake in Skyros

now, if godlike Neoptolemos is still one of the living.
Before now the spirit inside my breast was hopeful
that I alone should die far away from horse-pasturing Argos
here in Troy; I hoped you would win back again to Phthia
so that in a fast black ship you could take my son back
from Skyros to Phthia, and show him all my possessions,
my property, my serving men, my great high-roofed house.
For by this time I think that Peleus must altogether
have perished, or still keeps a little scant life in sorrow
for the hatefulness of old age and because he waits ever from me
the evil message, for the day he hears I have been killed."
    So he spoke, mourning, and the elders lamented around him
remembering each those he had left behind in his own halls.

                                                    [Book 19, ll. 303–39]

    But now the kings of the Achaians brought the swift-footed
lord, the son of Peleus, to great Agamemnon, hardly
persuading him, since his heart was still angered for his companion.
When these had made their way to the shelter of Agamemnon
straightway they gave orders to the heralds, the clear crying,
to set a great cauldron over the fire, if so they might persuade
the son of Peleus to wash away the filth of the bloodstains,
but he denied them stubbornly and swore an oath on it:
"No, before Zeus, who is greatest of gods and the highest,
there is no right in letting water come near my head, until
I have laid Patroklos on the burning pyre, and heaped the mound over
    him,
and cut my hair for him, since there will come no second sorrow
like this to my heart again while I am still one of the living.
Then let us now give way to the gloomy feast; and with the dawn
cause your people to rise, o lord of men Agamemnon,
and bring in timber and lay it by, with all that is fitting
for the dead man to have when he goes down under the gloom and the
    darkness,
so that with the more speed the unwearying fire may burn him
away from our eyes, and the people turn back to that which they must
    do."
    So he spoke, and they listened well to him and obeyed him,
and in speed and haste they got the dinner ready, and each man
feasted, nor was any man's hunger denied a fair portion.
But when they had put aside their desire for eating and drinking,
they went away to sleep, each man into his own shelter,
but along the beach of the thunderous sea the son of Peleus

lay down, groaning heavily, among the Myrmidon numbers
in a clear place where the waves washed over the beach; and at that
    time
sleep caught him and was drifted sweetly about him, washing
the sorrows out of his mind, for his shining limbs were grown weary
indeed, from running in chase of Hektor toward windy Ilion;
and there appeared to him the ghost of unhappy Patroklos
all in his likeness for stature, and the lovely eyes, and voice,
and wore such clothing as Patroklos had worn on his body.
The ghost came and stood over his head and spoke a word to him:
"You sleep, Achilleus; you have forgotten me; but you were not
careless of me when I lived, but only in death. Bury me
as quickly as may be, let me pass through the gates of Hades.
The souls, the images of dead men, hold me at a distance,
and will not let me cross the river and mingle among them,
but I wander as I am by Hades' house of the wide gates.
And I call upon you in sorrow, give me your hand; no longer
shall I come back from death, once you give me my rite of burning.
No longer shall you and I, alive, sit apart from our other
beloved companions and make our plans, since the bitter destiny
that was given me when I was born has opened its jaws to take me.
And you, Achilleus like the gods, have your own destiny;
to be killed under the wall of the prospering Trojans. There is one
more thing I will say, and ask of you, if you will obey me:
do not have my bones laid apart from yours, Achilleus,
but with them, just as we grew up together in your house,
when Menoitios brought me there from Opous, when I was little,
and into your house, by reason of a baneful manslaying,
on that day when I killed the son of Amphidamas. I was
a child only, nor intended it, but was angered over a dice game.
There the rider Peleus took me into his own house,
and brought me carefully up, and named me to be your henchman.
Therefore, let one single vessel, the golden two-handled
urn the lady your mother gave you, hold both our ashes."
    Then in answer to him spoke swift-footed Achilleus:
"How is it, o hallowed head of my brother, you have come back to me
here, and tell me all these several things? Yet surely
I am accomplishing all, and I shall do as you tell me.
But stand closer to me, and let us, if only for a little,
embrace, and take full satisfaction from the dirge of sorrow."
    So he spoke, and with his own arms reached for him, but could not
take him, but the spirit went underground, like vapour,
with a thin cry, and Achilleus started awake, staring,

and drove his hands together, and spoke, and his words were sorrowful:
"Oh, wonder! Even in the house of Hades there is left something,
a soul and an image, but there is no real heart of life in it.
For all night long the phantom of unhappy Patroklos
stood over me in lamentation and mourning, and the likeness
to him was wonderful, and it told me each thing I should do."

[Book 23, ll. 35–107]

Translated by Richmond Lattimore

HORACE

Epistle 1.3

Julius Florus, tell me on what distant shores of this world
Tiberius, the Emperor's stepson, leads his armies.
Are you surrounded by Thrace and the River Hebrus, with its icy
Chains, or at the Hellespont, between Sestos and Abydos,
Or crossing Asia's fertile fields and mountains?
What are you learned officers writing? This too interests me.
The Emperor's great battles: who shapes them in words fit
For eternity to read? His wars—and also the peace
He has fought for. And Titus, meant to be a name in every mouth,
And soon, what has he done—unafraid of the pure Pindaric fountain,
Brave enough to turn his back on artificial pools?
Is he well? Does he think of me? Is he courting the Muse,
Coaxing Theban melodies into our Latin song?
Or has he roared and puffed to a tragic tune?
And my Celsus? I've warned him—and he needs to be warned—
To hunt in himself, to be careful of those great treasures
Stored in Apollo's library, on the Palatine hill:
Some day those beautifully colored birds might claim
Their plumage—and he, poor crow, stripped to his skin,
Would make the world laugh. And you, what are you writing?
What lovely flowers are you fluttering around? Your gift
Is a real one, you've trimmed it well, groomed it with care.

Whether you sharpen your tongue for the law, or shape
Charming poems, you'll earn yourself laurel wreaths.
And yet, if only you could give up more, put aside
Worry—that ice pack that ruins inspiration!—Heaven's
Wisdom would lead you as far as your genius could go.
Noble and commoner alike, we owe that task
To our country, if we want it to love us—and we owe it to ourselves.
    And tell me, when you write, if you love Muntius as much
As you should—or if the friendship you patched together
Has ripped apart? Remember, my friend: driven
Across the world by your ignorance of the world, propelled
By rash young blood, both of you wild, unbroken stallions,
You're both too virtuous to break that brotherhood: wherever
You are, I'm fattening a heifer for the day you return.

Translated by Burton Raffel

MARTIAL

Epigram 5.42

Deft thieves can break your locks and carry off
    your savings, fire consume your home,
debtors default on principal and interest, failed crops
    return not even the seed you'd sown,
cheating women run up your charge accounts,
    storm overwhelm ships freighted with all your goods—
fortune can't take away what you give friends:
    that wealth stays yours forever.

Translated by Jim Powell

Epigram 1.32

I do not love thee, Doctor Fell;
The reason why I cannot tell.
But this I'm sure I know full well,
I do not love thee, Doctor Fell.

Translated by Tom Brown

WANG CHIEN

Hearing That His Friend Was Coming Back from the War

In old days those who went to fight
In three years had one year's leave.
But in *this* war the soldiers are never changed;
They must go on fighting till they die on the battle-field.
I thought of you, so weak and indolent,
Hopelessly trying to learn to march and drill.
That a young man should ever come home again
Seemed about as likely as that the sky should fall.
Since I got the news that you were coming back,
Twice I have mounted to the high hall of your home.
I found your brother mending your horse's stall;
I found your mother sewing your new clothes.
I am half afraid; perhaps it is not true;
Yet I never weary of watching for you on the road.
Each day I go out at the City Gate
With a flask of wine, lest you should come thirsty.
Oh that I could shrink the surface of the World,
So that suddenly I might find you standing at my side.

Translated by Arthur Waley

PO CHÜ-I

OLD AGE

*Addressed to Liu Yü-*hsi, who was born in the same year

We are growing old together, you and I,
Let us ask ourselves, what is age like?
The dull eye is closed ere night comes;
The idle head, still uncombed at noon.
Propped on a staff, sometimes a walk abroad;
Or all day sitting with closed doors.
One dares not look in the mirror's polished face;
One cannot read small-letter books.
Deeper and deeper, one's love of old friends;
Fewer and fewer, one's dealings with young men.
One thing only, the pleasure of idle talk
Is great as ever, when you and I meet.

Translated by Arthur Waley

THE LETTER

Preface: After I parted with Yüan Chēn, I suddenly dreamt one
night that I saw him. When I awoke, I found that a letter from
him had just arrived and, enclosed in it, a poem on the *paulovnia*
flower.

We talked together in the Yung-shou Temple;
We parted to the north of the Hsin-ch'ang dyke.
Going home—I shed a few tears,
Grieving about things,—not sorry for you.

Long, long the road to Lan-t'ien;
You said yourself you would not be able to write.
Reckoning up your halts for eating and sleeping—
By this time you've crossed the Shang mountains.
Last night the clouds scattered away;
A thousand leagues, the same moonlight scene.
When dawn came, I dreamt I saw your face;
It must have been that you were thinking of me.
In my dream, I thought I held your hand
And asked you to tell me what your thoughts were.
And *you* said: "I miss you bitterly,
But there's no one here to send to you with a letter."
When I awoke, before I had time to speak,
A knocking on the door sounded "Doong, doong!"
They came and told me a messenger from Shang-chou
Had brought a letter,—a single scroll from you!
Up from my pillow I suddenly sprang out of bed,
And threw on my clothes, all topsy-turvy.
I undid the knot and saw the letter within;
A single sheet with thirteen lines of writing.
At the top it told the sorrows of an exile's heart;
At the bottom it described the pains of separation.
The sorrows and pains took up so much space
There was no room left to talk about the weather!
         But you said that when you wrote
You were staying for the night to the east of Shang-chou;
Sitting alone, lighted by a solitary candle
Lodging in the mountain hostel of Yang-Ch'ēng.
         Night was late when you finished writing,
The mountain moon was slanting towards the west.
What is it lies aslant across the moon?
A single tree of purple *paulovnia* flowers,
Paulovnia flowers just on the point of falling
Are a symbol to express "thinking of an absent friend."
Lovingly—you wrote on the back side,
To send in the letter, your "Poem of the Paulovnia Flower."
The "Poem of the Paulovnia Flower" has eight rhymes;
Yet these eight couplets have cast a spell on my heart.
They have taken hold of this morning's thoughts
And carried them to yours, the night you wrote your letter.
The whole poem I read three times;
Each verse ten times I recite.

So precious to me are the fourscore words
That each letter changes into a bar of gold!

Translated by Arthur Waley

To Liu Yu-Hsi

In length of days and soundness of limb you and I are one;
Our eyes are not wholly blind, nor our ears quite deaf.
Deep drinking we lie together, fellows of a spring day;
Or gay-hearted boldly break into gatherings of young men.
When, seeking flowers, we borrowed his horse, the river-keeper was
    vexed;
When, to play on the water, we stole his boat, the Duke Ling was sore.
I hear it said that in Lo-yang, people are all shocked,
And call us by the name of "Liu and Po, those two mad old men."

Translated by Arthur Waley

Dreaming That I Went with Lu and Yu
to Visit Yüan Chēn

(Written in exile)

At night I dreamt I was back in Ch'ang-an;
I saw again the faces of old friends.
And in my dreams, under an April sky,
They led me by the hand to wander in the spring winds.
Together we came to the village of Peace and Quiet;
We stopped our horses at the gate of Yüan Chēn.
Yüan Chēn was sitting all alone;
When he saw me coming, a smile came to his face.
He pointed back at the flowers in the western court;
Then opened wine in the northern summer-house.
He seemed to be saying that neither of us had changed;
He seemed to be regretting that joy will not stay;
That our souls had met only for a little while,
To part again with hardly time for greeting.

I woke up and thought him still at my side;
I put out my hand; there was nothing there at all.

Translated by Arthur Waley

DANTE ALIGHIERI

From THE DIVINE COMEDY

By now we were so distant from the wood
that I should not have made out where it was—
not even if I'd turned around to look—
    when we came on a company of spirits
who made their way along the bank; and each
stared steadily at us, as in the dusk,
    beneath the new moon, men look at each other.
They knit their brows and squinted at us—just
as an old tailor at his needle's eye.
    And when that family looked harder, I
was recognized by one, who took me by
the hem and cried out: "This is marvelous!"
    That spirit having stretched his arm toward me,
I fixed my eyes upon his baked, brown features,
so that the scorching of his face could not
    prevent my mind from recognizing him;
and lowering my face to meet his face,
I answered him: "Are you here, Ser Brunetto?"
    And he: "My son, do not mind if Brunetto
Latino* lingers for a while with you
and lets the file he's with pass on ahead."
    I said: "With all my strength I pray you, stay;
and if you'd have me rest awhile with you,
I shall, if that please him with whom I go."
    "O son," he said, "whoever of this flock
stops but a moment, stays a hundred years
and cannot shield himself when fire strikes.

*Brunetto Latino, Dante's friend, condemned to hell for pederasty.

Therefore move on; below—but close—I'll follow;
and then I shall rejoin my company,
who go lamenting their eternal sorrows."
    I did not dare to leave my path for his
own level; but I walked with head bent low
as does a man who goes in reverence.
    And he began: "What destiny or chance
has led you here below before your last
day came, and who is he who shows the way?"
    "There, in the sunlit life above," I answered,
"before my years were full, I went astray
within a valley. Only yesterday
    at dawn I turned my back upon it—but
when I was newly lost, he here appeared,
to guide me home again along this path."
    And he to me: "If you pursue your star,
you cannot fail to reach a splendid harbor,
if in fair life, I judged you properly;
    and if I had not died too soon for this,
on seeing Heaven was so kind to you,
I should have helped sustain you in your work. . . ."

. . . .

    "If my desire were answered totally,"
I said to Ser Brunetto, "you'd still be
among, not banished from, humanity.
    Within my memory is fixed—and now
moves me—your dear, your kind paternal image
when, in the world above, from time to time
    you taught me how man makes himself eternal;
and while I live, my gratitude for that
must always be apparent in my words.
            [*Inferno*, Canto 15, ll. 13–60, 79–87]

Translated by Allen Mandelbaum

DANTE ALIGHIERI TO GUIDO CAVALCANTI

Guido, I would that Lapo, thou, and I,
Led by some strong enchantment, might ascend
A magic ship, whose charmèd sails should fly
With winds at will where'er our thoughts might wend,

So that no change, nor any evil chance
Should mar our joyous voyage; but it might be,
That even satiety should still enhance
Between our hearts their strict community:
And that the bounteous wizard then would place
Vanna and Bice and my gentle love
Companions of our wandering, and would grace
With passionate talk, wherever we might rove,
Our time, and each were as content and free
As I believe that thou and I should be.

                              Translated by Percy Bysshe Shelley

MICHELANGELO BUONARROTI

To Giovanni da Pistoja on the Painting
of the Sistine Chapel

I've grown a goitre by dwelling in this den—
    As cats from stagnant streams in Lombardy,
    Or in what other land they hap to be—
Which drives the belly close beneath the chin:
My beard turns up to heaven; my nape falls in,
    Fixed on my spine: my breast-bone visibly
    Grows like a harp: a rich embroidery
Bedews my face from brush-drops thick and thin.
My loins into my paunch like levers grind:
    My buttock like a crupper bears my weight;
    My feet unguided wander to and fro;
In front my skin grows loose and long; behind,
    By bending it becomes more taut and strait;
    Crosswise I strain me like a Syrian bow:
        Whence false and quaint, I know,
Must be the fruit of squinting brain and eye;
For ill can aim the gun that bends awry.

Come then, Giovanni, try
To succour my dead pictures and my fame,
Since foul I fare and painting is my shame.

Translated by John Addington Symonds

To Tommaso Cavalieri

With your bright eyes I see the living light
which my blind eyes alone can never see;
and your sure feet take up that load for me
which my lame gait would let fall helplessly.
Wingless, but with your plumes, here I'm in flight;
in your strong mind are my weak thoughts set free
and as it pleases you I'm pale or bright,
cold in the sun, hot in the winter's night.
In what you wish is all that I would want,
my very thoughts are framed within your heart,
my words are uttered with the air you breathe.
Thus, like the moon, a lonely suppliant,
invisible myself, I sail apart
until the sun reveals me with its beams.

Translated by George Bull and Peter Porter

EDMUND SPENSER

From The Faerie Queene

It often fals, (as here it earst befell)
    That mortall foes doe turne to faithfull frends,
    And friends profest are chaungd to foemen fell:
    The cause of both, of both their minds depends,
    And th'end of both likewise of both their ends.
    For enmitie, that of no ill proceeds,

But of occasion, with th'occasion ends;
And friendship, which a faint affection breeds
Without regard of good, dyes like ill grounded seeds.
[Book 4, Canto 4.1]

Hard is the doubt, and difficult to deeme,
  When all three kinds of loue together meet,
  And doe dispart the hart with powre extreme,
  Whether shall weigh the balance downe; to weet
  The deare affection into kindred sweet,
  Or raging fire of loue to woman kind,   .
  Or zeale of friends combynd with vertues meet.
  But of them all the band of vertuous mind
Me seemes the gentle hart should most assured bind.

For naturall affection soone doth cesse,
  And quenched is with *Cupids* greater flame:
  But faithfull friendship doth them both suppresse,
  And them with maystring discipline doth tame,
  Through thoughts aspyring to eternall fame.
  For as the soule doth rule the earthly masse,
  And all the seruice of the bodie frame,
  So loue of soule doth loue of bodie passe,
No lesse then perfect gold surmounts the meanest brasse. . . .
[Book 4, Canto 9.1–2]

(The following passage is set in the gardens of the fortified island where the temple of Venus is located. In one section of the gardens thousands of lovers are walking; in another section, true friends are conversing.)

All these together by themselves did sport
    Their spotlesse pleasures, and sweet loues content.
    But farre away from these, another sort
    Of louers lincked in true harts consent;
    Which loued not as these, for like intent,
    But on chast vertue grounded their desire,
    Farre from all fraud, or fayned blandishment;
    Which in their spirits kindling zealous fire,
Braue thoughts and noble deedes did euermore aspire.

Such were great *Hercules,* and *Hylas* deare;
    Trew *Ionathan,* and *Dauid* trustie tryde;
    Stout *Theseus,* and *Pirithous* his feare;

Pylades and *Orestes* by his syde;
Myld *Titus* and *Gesippus* without pryde;
Damon and *Pythias* whom death could not seuer:
All these and all that euer had bene tyde
In bands of friendship, there did liue for euer,
Whose liues although decay'd, yet loues decayed neuer.

Which when as I, that neuer tasted blis,
   Nor happie howre, beheld with gazefull eye,
   I thought there was none other heauen then this;
   And gan their endlesse happinesse enuye,
   That being free from feare and gealosye,
   Might frankely there their loues desire possesse;
   Whilest I through paines and perlous ieopardie,
   Was forst to seeke my lifes deare patronesse:
Much dearer be the things, which come through hard distresse.
                              [Book 4, Canto 10.26–28]

BEN JONSON

From TO THE IMMORTAL MEMORY AND FRIENDSHIP OF
THAT NOBLE PAIR, SIR LUCIUS CARY AND SIR H. MORISON

THE TURN

   It is not growing like a tree
   In bulk, doth make man better be;
   Or standing long an oak, three hundred year,
   To fall a log at last, dry, bald, and sere:
      A lily of a day
      Is fairer far, in May,
   Although it fall and die that night;
   It was the plant and flower of light.
   In small proportions we just beauty see,
   And in short measures life may perfect be.

THE COUNTER-TURN

Call, noble Lucius, then for wine,
And let thy looks with gladness shine;
Accept this garland, plant it on thy head;
And think, nay know, thy Morison's not dead.
He leaped the present age,
Possessed with holy rage
To see that bright eternal day,
Of which we priests and poets say
Such truths as we expect for happy men;
And there he lives with memory, and Ben

THE STAND

Jonson, who sung this of him, ere he went
Himself to rest,
Or taste a part of that full joy he meant
To have expressed
In this bright asterism;
Where it were friendship's schism
(Were not his Lucius long with us to tarry)
To separate these twi-
Lights, the Dioscuri;
And keep the one half from his Harry.
But fate doth so alternate the design,
Whilst that in heaven, this light on earth must shine.

THE TURN

And shine as you exalted are;
Two names of friendship, but one star:
Of hearts the union. And those not by chance
Made, or indentured, or leased out to advance
The profits for a time.
No pleasures vain did chime,
Of rhymes, or riots, at your feasts,
Orgies of drink, or feigned protests:
But simple love of greatness, and of good;
That knits brave minds and manners, more than blood.

THE COUNTER-TURN

This made you first to know the why
You liked; then after to apply

That liking; and approach so one the t'other,
Till either grew a portion of the other:
Each stylèd, by his end,
The copy of his friend.
You lived to be the great surnames
And titles by which all made claims
Unto the virtue. Nothing perfect done
But as a Cary, or a Morison.

THE STAND

And such a force the fair example had,
As they that saw
The good and durst not practise it, were glad
That such a law
Was left yet to mankind;
Where they might read and find
Friendship in deed was written, not in words;
And with the heart, not pen,
Of two so early men
Whose lines her rolls were, and records.
Who, ere the first down bloomèd on the chin,
Had sowed these fruits, and got the harvest in.

To the Memory of My Beloved, the Author, Mr. William Shakespeare, And What He Hath Left Us

To draw no envy, Shakespeare, on thy name,
    Am I thus ample to thy book and fame;
While I confess thy writings to be such
    As neither man nor muse can praise too much:
'Tis true, and all men's suffrage. But these ways
    Were not the paths I meant unto thy praise:
For silliest ignorance on these may light,
    Which, when it sounds at best, but echoes right;
Or blind affection, which doth ne'er advance
    The truth, but gropes, and urgeth all by chance;
Or crafty malice might pretend this praise,
    And think to ruin where it seemed to raise.
These are as some infamous bawd or whore
    Should praise a matron: what could hurt her more?

But thou art proof against them, and indeed
   Above the ill fortune of them, or the need.
I therefore will begin. Soul of the age!
   The applause, delight, the wonder of our stage!
My Shakespeare, rise: I will not lodge thee by
   Chaucer or Spenser, or bid Beaumont lie
A little further, to make thee a room;
   Thou art a monument without a tomb,
And art alive still while thy book doth live,
   And we have wits to read, and praise to give.
That I not mix thee so, my brain excuses:
   I mean with great, but disproportioned, muses;
For if I thought my judgement were of years
   I should commit thee surely with thy peers:
And tell how far thou didst our Lyly outshine,
   Or sporting Kyd, or Marlowe's mighty line.
And though thou hadst small Latin, and less Greek,
   From thence to honour thee I would not seek
For names, but call forth thundering Aeschylus,
   Euripides, and Sophocles to us,
Pacuvius, Accius, him of Cordova dead,
   To life again, to hear thy buskin tread
And shake a stage; or, when thy socks were on,
   Leave thee alone for the comparison
Of all that insolent Greece or haughty Rome
   Sent forth, or since did from their ashes come.
Triumph, my Britain, thou hast one to show
   To whom all scenes of Europe homage owe.
He was not of an age, but for all time!
   And all the muses still were in their prime
When like Apollo he came forth to warm
   Our ears, or like a Mercury to charm!
Nature herself was proud of his designs,
   And joyed to wear the dressing of his lines,
Which were so richly spun and woven so fit
   As, since, she will vouchsafe no other wit.
The merry Greek, tart Aristophanes,
   Neat Terence, witty Plautus, now not please,
But antiquated and deserted lie
   As they were not of nature's family.
Yet must I not give nature all: thy art,
   My gentle Shakespeare, must enjoy a part.

For though the poet's matter nature be,
  His art doth give the fashion. And that he
Who casts to write a living line must sweat
  (Such as thine are) and strike the second heat
Upon the muses' anvil: turn the same
  (And himself with it) that he thinks to frame;
Or for the laurel he may gain a scorn:
  For a good poet's made, as well as born;
And such wert thou. Look how the father's face
  Lives in his issue: even so, the race
Of Shakespeare's mind and manners brightly shines
  In his well-turnèd and true-filèd lines:
In each of which he seems to shake a lance,
  As brandished at the eyes of ignorance.
Sweet swan of Avon! What a sight it were
  To see thee in our waters yet appear,
And make those flights upon the banks of Thames
  That so did take Eliza, and our James!
But stay, I see thee in the hemisphere
  Advanced, and made a constellation there!
Shine forth, thou star of poets, and with rage
  Or influence chide or cheer the drooping stage;
Which, since thy flight from hence, hath mourned like night,
  And despairs day, but for thy volume's light.

JOHN DONNE

To Mr T. W.

Pregnant again with th' old twins Hope, and Feare,
Oft have I askt for thee, both how and where
Thou wert, and what my hopes of letters were;

As in the streets sly beggers narrowly
Watch motions of the givers hand and eye,
And evermore conceive some hope thereby.

And now thy Almes is given, thy letter'is read,
The body risen againe, the which was dead,
And thy poore starveling bountifully fed.

After this banquet my Soule doth say grace,
And praise thee for'it, and zealously imbrace
Thy love, though I thinke thy love in this case
  To be as gluttons, which say 'midst their meat,
  They love that best of which they most do eat.

KATHERINE PHILIPS

To Mrs. Mary Awbrey

Soul of my soul, my Joy, my Crown, my Friend,
A name which all the rest doth comprehend;
How happy are we now, whose souls are grown,
By an incomparable mixture, one:
Whose well-acquainted minds are now as near
As Love, or Vows, or Friendship can endear?
I have no thought but what's to thee reveal'd,
Nor thou desire that is from me conceal'd.
Thy heart locks up my secrets richly set,
And my breast is thy private cabinet.
Thou shed'st no tear but what my moisture lent,
And if I sigh, it is thy breath is spent.
United thus, what horror can appear
Worthy our sorrow, anger, or our fear?
Let the dull World alone to talk and fight,
And with their vast ambitions Nature fright;
Let them despise so innocent a flame,
While Envy, Pride, and Faction play their game:
But we by Love sublim'd so high shall rise,
To pity Kings, and Conquerors despise,
Since we that sacred union have engrost,
Which they and all the factious World have lost.

From FRIENDSHIP

For Love, like earthly fires (which will decay
If the material fuel be away)
Is with offensive smoke accompanied,
And by resistance only is supplied:
But Friendship, like the fiery element,
With its own heat and nourishment content,
Where neither hurt, nor smoke, nor noise is made,
Scorns the assistance of a foreign aid.
Friendship (like Heraldry) is hereby known,
Richest when plainest, bravest when alone;
Calm as a virgin, and more innocent
Than sleeping doves are, and as much content
As Saints in visions; quiet as the night,
But clear and open as the summer's light;
United more than spirits' faculties,
Higher in thoughts than are the eagle's eyes;
What shall I say? when we true friends are grown,
W' are like—Alas, w' are like ourselves alone.

ANNE FINCH

FRIENDSHIP BETWEEN EPHELIA AND ARDELIA

EPH.   What *Friendship* is, ARDELIA shew.
ARD.   'Tis to love, as I love You.
EPH.   This Account, so short (tho' kind)
       Suits not my enquiring Mind.
       Therefore farther now repeat;
       What is *Friendship* when compleat?
ARD.   'Tis to share all Joy and Grief;
       'Tis to lend all due Relief
       From the Tongue, the Heart, the Hand;
       'Tis to mortgage House and Land;

For a Friend be sold a Slave;
'Tis to die upon a Grave,
If a Friend therein do lie.
EPH.   This indeed, tho' carry'd high,
This, tho' more than e'er was done
Underneath the rolling Sun,
This has all been said before.
Can ARDELIA say no more?
ARD.   Words indeed no more can shew:
But 'tis to love, as I love you.

TO A FRIEND

In Praise of the Invention of Writing Letters

Blest be the Man! his Memory at least,
Who found the Art, thus to unfold his Breast,
And taught succeeding Times an easy way
Their secret Thoughts by *Letters* to convey;
To baffle Absence, and secure Delight,
Which, till that Time, was limited to Sight.
The parting Farewel spoke, the last Adieu,
The less'ning Distance past, then loss of View,
The Friend was gone, which some kind Moments gave,
And Absence separated, like the Grave.
The Wings of Love were tender too, till then
No Quill, thence pull'd, was shap'd into a Pen,
To send in Paper-sheets, from Town to Town,
Words smooth as they, and softer than his Down.
O'er such he reign'd, whom Neighbourhood had join'd,
And hopt, from Bough to Bough, supported by the Wind.
When for a Wife the youthful *Patriarch* sent,
The Camels, Jewels, and the Steward went,
A wealthy Equipage, tho' grave and slow;
But not a Line, that might the Lover shew.
The Rings and Bracelets woo'd her Hands and Arms;
But had she known of melting Words, the Charms
That under secret Seals in Ambush lie,
To catch the Soul, when drawn into the Eye,
The Fair *Assyrian* had not took this Guide,
Nor her soft Heart in Chains of Pearl been ty'd.

Had these Conveyances been then in Date,
Joseph had known his wretched Father's State,
Before a Famine, which his Life pursues,
Had sent his other Sons, to tell the News.

Oh! might I live to see an Art arise,
As this to Thoughts, indulgent to the Eyes;
That the dark Pow'rs of distance cou'd subdue,
And make me *See,* as well as *Talk* to You;
That tedious Miles, nor Tracts of Air might prove
Bars to my Sight, and shadows to my Love!
Yet were it granted, such unbounded Things
Are wand'ring Wishes, born on Phancy's Wings,
They'd stretch themselves beyond this happy Case,
And ask an Art, to help us to Embrace.

JONATHAN SWIFT

From VERSES ON THE DEATH OF DR. SWIFT, D.S.P.D.

Occasioned By Reading a Maxim in Rochefoulcault

Dans l'adversité de nos meilleurs amis nous trouvons quelque
chose, qui ne nous deplaist pas.
In the Adversity of our best Friends, we find something that
doth not displease us.

As *Rochefoucault* his Maxims drew
From Nature, I believe 'em true:
They argue no corrupted Mind
In him; the Fault is in Mankind.

This Maxim more than all the rest
Is thought too base for human Breast;
"In all Distresses of our Friends
"We first consult our private Ends.

"While Nature kindly bent to ease us,
"Points out some Circumstance to please us.

If this perhaps your Patience move
Let Reason and Experience prove.

We all behold with envious Eyes,
Our *Equal* rais'd above our *Size;*
Who wou'd not at a crowded Show,
Stand high himself, keep others low?
I love my Friend as well as you,
But would not have him stop my View;
Then let him have the higher Post;
I ask but for an Inch at most.

If in a Battle you should find,
One, whom you love of all Mankind,
Had some heroick Action done,
A Champion kill'd, or Trophy won;
Rather than thus be over-topt,
Would you not wish his Lawrels cropt?

Dear honest *Ned* is in the Gout,
Lies rackt with Pain, and you without:
How patiently you hear him groan!
How glad the Case is not your own!

What Poet would not grieve to see,
His Brethren write as well as he?
But rather than they should excel,
He'd wish his Rivals all in Hell.

Her End when Emulation misses,
She turns to Envy, Stings and Hisses:
The strongest Friendship yields to Pride,
Unless the Odds be on our Side.

Vain human Kind! Fantastick Race!
Thy various Follies, who can trace?
Self-love, Ambition, Envy, Pride,
Their Empire in our Hearts divide:
Give others Riches, Power, and Station,
'Tis all on me an Usurpation.

I have no Title to aspire;
Yet, when you sink, I seem the higher.
In POPE, I cannot read a Line,
But with a Sigh, I wish it mine:
When he can in one Couplet fix
More Sense than I can do in Six:
It gives me such a jealous Fit,
I cry, Pox take him, and his Wit.

Why must I be outdone by GAY,
In my own hum'rous biting Way?

ARBUTHNOT is no more my Friend,
Who dares to Irony pretend;
Which I was born to introduce,
Refin'd it first, and shew'd its Use.

ST. JOHN, as well as PULTNEY knows,
That I had some repute for Prose;
And till they drove me out of Date,
Could maul a Minister of State:
If they have mortify'd my Pride,
And made me throw my Pen aside;
If with such Talents Heav'n hath blest 'em
Have I not Reason to detest 'em?

To all my Foes, dear Fortune, send
Thy Gifts, but never to my Friend:
I tamely can endure the first,
But, this with Envy makes me burst.

WILLIAM COWPER

From RETIREMENT

I praise the Frenchman, his remark was shrew'd—
How sweet, how passing sweet is solitude!
But grant me still a friend in my retreat,
Whom I may whisper, solitude is sweet.

WILLIAM BLAKE

A POISON TREE

I was angry with my friend:
I told my wrath, my wrath did end.
I was angry with my foe:
I told it not, my wrath did grow.

And I water'd it in fears,
Night & morning with my tears;
And I sunned it with smiles,
And with soft deceitful wiles.

And it grew both day and night,
Till it bore an apple bright;
And my foe beheld it shine,
And he knew that it was mine,

And into my garden stole
When the night had veil'd the pole:

In the morning glad I see
My foe outstretch'd beneath the tree.

To Hayley

Thy Friendship oft has made my heart to ake:
Do be my Enemy for Friendship's sake.

(Blake also commented on Hayley in an untitled couplet.)

To forgive Enemies Hayley does pretend,
Who never in his Life forgave a friend.

JOHN KEATS

To J. R.

O that a week could be an age, and we
    Felt parting and warm meeting every week;
Then one poor year a thousand years would be,
    The flush of welcome ever on the cheek.
So could we live long life in little space;
    So time itself would be annihilate;
So a day's journey, in oblivious haze
    To serve our joys, would lengthen and dilate.
O to arrive each Monday morn from Ind,
    To land each Tuesday from the rich Levant,
In little time a host of joys to bind,
    And keep our souls in one eternal pant!
This morn, my friend, and yester evening taught
Me how to harbour such a happy thought.

ROBERT BROWNING

May and Death

I.

I wish that when you died last May,
   Charles, there had died along with you
Three parts of spring's delightful things;
   Ay, and, for me, the fourth part too.

II.

A foolish thought, and worse, perhaps!
   There must be many a pair of friends
Who, arm in arm, deserve the warm
   Moon-births and the long evening-ends.

III.

So, for their sake, be May still May!
   Let their new time, as mine of old,
Do all it did for me: I bid
   Sweet sights and sounds throng manifold.

IV.

Only, one little sight, one plant,
   Woods have in May, that starts up green
Save a sole streak which, so to speak,
   Is spring's blood, split its leaves between,—

V.

That, they might spare; a certain wood
   Might miss the plant; their loss were small:
But I,—whene'er the leaf grows there,
   Its drop comes from my heart, that's all.

WALT WHITMAN

We Two, How Long We Were Fool'd

We two, how long we were fool'd,
Now transmuted, we swiftly escape as Nature escapes,
We are Nature, long have we been absent, but now we return,
We become plants, trunks, foliage, roots, bark,
We are bedded in the ground, we are rocks,
We are oaks, we grow in the openings side by side,
We browse, we are two among the wild herds spontaneous as any,
We are two fishes swimming in the sea together,
We are what locust blossoms are, we drop scent around lanes mornings
    and evenings,
We are also the coarse smut of beasts, vegetables, minerals,
We are two predatory hawks, we soar above and look down,
We are two resplendent suns, we it is who balance ourselves orbic and
    stellar, we are as two comets,
We prowl fang'd and four-footed in the woods, we spring on prey,
We are two clouds forenoons and afternoons driving overhead,
We are seas mingling, we are two of those cheerful waves rolling over
    each other and interwetting each other,
We are what the atmosphere is, transparent, receptive, pervious,
    impervious,
We are snow, rain, cold, darkness, we are each product and influence of
    the globe,
We have circled and circled till we have arrived home again, we two,
We have voided all but freedom and all but our own joy.

As Toilsome I Wander'd Virginia's Woods

As toilsome I wander'd Virginia's woods,
To the music of rustling leaves kick'd by my feet, (for 'twas autumn,)
I mark'd at the foot of a tree the grave of a soldier;

Mortally wounded he and buried on the retreat, (easily all could I
    understand,)
The halt of a mid-day hour, when up! no time to lose—yet this sign
    left,
On a tablet scrawl'd and nail'd on the tree by the grave,
Bold, cautious, true, and my loving comrade.

Long, long I muse, then on my way go wandering,
Many a changeful season to follow, and many a scene of life,
Yet at times through changeful season and scene, abrupt, alone, or in
    the crowded street,
Comes before me the unknown soldier's grave, comes the inscription
    rude in Virginia's woods,
Bold, cautious, true, and my loving comrade.

I Saw in Louisiana a Live-Oak Growing

I saw in Louisiana a live-oak growing,
All alone stood it and the moss hung down from the branches,
Without any companion it grew there uttering joyous leaves of dark
    green,
And its look, rude, unbending, lusty, made me think of myself,
But I wonder'd how it could utter joyous leaves standing alone there
    without its friend near, for I knew I could not,
And I broke off a twig with a certain number of leaves upon it, and
    twined around it a little moss,
And brought it away, and I have placed it in sight in my room,
It is not needed to remind me as of my own dear friends,
(For I believe lately I think of little else than of them,)
Yet it remains to me a curious token, it makes me think of manly love;
For all that, and though the live-oak glistens there in Louisiana solitary
    in a wide flat space,
Uttering joyous leaves all its life without a friend a lover near,
I know very well I could not.

EMILY DICKINSON

I'M NOBODY! WHO ARE YOU?

I'm Nobody! Who are you?
Are you—Nobody—too?
Then there's a pair of us!
Dont tell! they'd banish us—you know!

How dreary—to be—Somebody!
How public—like a Frog—
To tell your name—the livelong June—
To an admiring Bog!

I SHOWED HER HIGHTS SHE NEVER SAW

I showed her Hights she never saw—
"Would'st Climb," I said?
She said—"Not so"—
"With *me*—" I said—With *me*?
I showed her Secrets—Morning's Nest—
The Rope the Nights were put across—
And *now*—"Would'st have me for a Guest?"
She could not find her Yes—
And then, I brake my life—And Lo,
A Light, for her, did solemn glow,
The larger, as her face withdrew—
And *could* she, further, "No"?

WE TALKED AS GIRLS DO

We talked as Girls do—
Fond, and late—

We speculated fair, on every subject, but the Grave—
Of our's, none affair—

We handled Destinies, as cool—
As we—Disposers—be—
And God, a Quiet Party
To our Authority—

But fondest, dwelt upon Ourself
As we eventual—be—
When Girls to Women, softly raised
We—occupy—Degree—

We parted with a contract
To cherish, and to write
But Heaven made both, impossible
Before another night.

ELYSIUM IS AS FAR

Elysium is as far as to
The very nearest Room
If in that Room a Friend await
Felicity or Doom—

What fortitude the Soul contains,
That it can so endure
The accent of a coming Foot—
The opening of a Door—

GIOSUÈ CARDUCCI

A SNOW-STORM

Large, slow snowflakes fall from an ashen heaven: the noisy
Hum and hubbub of life no more go up from the town.

Hushed is the cry of the vendor of herbs, the rumble of waggons,
Hushed are the voices that sang blithely of youth and of love.

Harsh thro' the throbbing air the chimes from the tower o'er the
   market
Moan, like the sigh of a world far from the daylight withdrawn.

Tap on the frosted panes, birdlike, forlorn, the belovèd
Ghosts of old friends who return, calling on me to depart.

Soon, dear ones, very soon—O strong heart, calm thyself—I too
Shall to the silence descend, lay me to rest in the gloom.

Translated by G.L. Bickersteth

ANONYMOUS

THE RAKES OF MALLOW

Beauing, belling, dancing, drinking,
Breaking windows, damning, sinking,
Ever raking, never thinking,
   Live the rakes of Mallow.

Spending faster than it comes,
Beating waiters, bailiffs, duns,
Bacchus' true-begotten sons,
   Live the rakes of Mallow.

One time naught but claret drinking,
Then like politicians thinking
To raise the sinking funds when sinking,
   Live the rakes of Mallow.

When at home with dadda dying
Still for Mallow water crying;
But where there's good claret plying,
   Live the rakes of Mallow.

Living short, but merry lives;
Going where the devil drives;
Having sweethearts, but no wives,
    Live the rakes of Mallow.

Racking tenants, stewards teasing,
Swiftly spending, slowly raising,
Wishing to spend all their lives in
    Raking as in Mallow.

Then to end this raking life,
They get sober, take a wife,
Ever after live in strife,
    And wish again for Mallow.

THOMAS HARDY

A Confession to a Friend in Trouble

Your troubles shrink not, though I feel them less
Here, far away, than when I tarried near;
I even smile old smiles—with listlessness—
Yet smiles they are, not ghastly mockeries mere.

A thought too strange to house within my brain
Haunting its outer precincts I discern:
—*That I will not show zeal again to learn
Your griefs, and, sharing them, renew my pain.* . . .

It goes, like murky bird or buccaneer
That shapes its lawless figure on the main,
And staunchness tends to banish utterly
The unseemly instinct that had lodgment here;
Yet, comrade old, can bitterer knowledge be
Than that, though banned, such instinct was in me!

The Man He Killed

"Had he and I but met
By some old ancient inn,
We should have sat us down to wet
Right many a nipperkin!

"But ranged as infantry,
And staring face to face,
I shot at him as he at me,
And killed him in his place.

"I shot him dead because—
Because he was my foe,
Just so: my foe of course he was;
That's clear enough; although

"He thought he'd 'list, perhaps,
Off-hand like—just as I—
Was out of work—had sold his traps—
No other reason why.

"Yes; quaint and curious war is!
You shoot a fellow down
You'd treat if met where any bar is,
Or help to half-a-crown."

A. E. HOUSMAN

A Shropshire Lad

LIV

With rue my heart is laden
For golden friends I had,
For many a rose-lipt maiden
And many a lightfoot lad.

By brooks too broad for leaping
The lightfoot boys are laid;
The rose-lipt girls are sleeping
In fields where roses fade.

WILLIAM BUTLER YEATS

THE MUNICIPAL GALLERY RE-VISITED

I

Around me the images of thirty years;
An ambush; pilgrims at the water-side;
Casement upon trial, half hidden by the bars,
Guarded; Griffith staring in hysterical pride;
Kevin O'Higgins' countenance that wears
A gentle questioning look that cannot hide
A soul incapable of remorse or rest;
A revolutionary soldier kneeling to be blessed.

II

An Abbot or Archbishop with an upraised hand
Blessing the Tricolour. "This is not" I say
"The dead Ireland of my youth, but an Ireland
The poets have imagined, terrible and gay."
Before a woman's portrait suddenly I stand;
Beautiful and gentle in her Venetian way.
I met her all but fifty years ago
For twenty minutes in some studio.

III

Heart smitten with emotion I sink down
My heart recovering with covered eyes;
Wherever I had looked I had looked upon

My permanent or impermanent images;
Augusta Gregory's son; her sister's son,
Hugh Lane, "onlie begetter" of all these;
Hazel Lavery living and dying, that tale
As though some ballad singer had sung it all.

IV

Mancini's portrait of Augusta Gregory,
"Greatest since Rembrandt," according to John Synge,
A great ebullient portrait certainly;
But where is the brush that could show anything
Of all that pride and that humility,
And I am in despair that time may bring
Approved patterns of women or of men
But not that selfsame excellence again.

V

My mediaeval knees lack health until they bend,
But in that woman, in that household where
Honour had lived so long, all lacking found.
Childless I thought "my children may find here
Deep-rooted things," but never foresaw its end,
And now that end has come I have not wept;
No fox can foul the lair the badger swept.

VI

(An image out of Spenser and the common tongue)
John Synge, I and Augusta Gregory, thought
All that we did, all that we said or sang
Must come from contact with the soil, from that
Contact everything Antaeus-like grew strong.
We three alone in modern times had brought
Everything down to that sole test again,
Dream of the noble and the beggarman.

VII

And here's John Synge himself, that rooted man
"Forgetting human words," a grave deep face.
You that would judge me do not judge alone
This book or that, come to this hallowed place

Where my friends' portraits hang and look thereon;
Ireland's history in their lineaments trace;
Think where man's glory most begins and ends
And say my glory was I had such friends.

FRIENDS

Now must I these three praise—
Three women that have wrought
What joy is in my days:
One because no thought,
Nor those unpassing cares,
No, not in these fifteen
Many-times-troubled years,
Could ever come between
Mind and delighted mind;
And one because her hand
Had strength that could unbind
What none can understand,
What none can have and thrive,
Youth's dreamy load, till she
So changed me that I live
Labouring in ecstasy.
And what of her that took
All till my youth was gone
With scarce a pitying look?
How could I praise that one?
When day begins to break
I count my good and bad,
Being wakeful for her sake,
Remembering what she had,
What eagle look still shows,
While up from my heart's root
So great a sweetness flows
I shake from head to foot.

The Lover pleads with His Friend for Old Friends

Though you are in your shining days,
Voices among the crowd
And new friends busy with your praise,
Be not unkind or proud,
But think about old friends the most:
Time's bitter flood will rise,
Your beauty perish and be lost
For all eyes but these eyes.

A Deep-sworn Vow

Others because you did not keep
That deep-sworn vow have been friends of mine;
Yet always when I look death in the face,
When I clamber to the heights of sleep,
Or when I grow excited with wine,
Suddenly I meet your face.

To a Friend Whose Work Has Come to Nothing

Now all the truth is out,
Be secret and take defeat
From any brazen throat,
For how can you compete,
Being honour bred, with one
Who, were it proved he lies,
Were neither shamed in his own
Nor in his neighbours' eyes?
Bred to a harder thing
Than Triumph, turn away
And like a laughing string
Whereon mad fingers play
Amid a place of stone,
Be secret and exult,
Because of all things known
That is most difficult.

EDWIN ARLINGTON ROBINSON

Mr. Flood's Party

Old Eben Flood, climbing alone one night
Over the hill between the town below
And the forsaken upland hermitage
That held as much as he should ever know
On earth again of home, paused warily.
The road was his with not a native near;
And Eben, having leisure, said aloud,
For no man else in Tilbury Town to hear:

"Well, Mr. Flood, we have the harvest moon
Again, and we may not have many more;
The bird is on the wing, the poet says,
And you and I have said it here before.
Drink to the bird." He raised up to the light
The jug that he had gone so far to fill,
And answered huskily: "Well, Mr. Flood,
Since you propose it, I believe I will."

Alone, as if enduring to the end
A valiant armor of scarred hopes outworn,
He stood there in the middle of the road
Like Roland's ghost winding a silent horn.
Below him, in the town among the trees,
Where friends of other days had honored him,
A phantom salutation of the dead
Rang thinly till old Eben's eyes were dim.

Then, as a mother lays her sleeping child
Down tenderly, fearing it may awake,
He set the jug down slowly at his feet
With trembling care, knowing that most things break;
And only when assured that on firm earth

It stood, as the uncertain lives of men
Assuredly did not, he paced away,
And with his hand extended paused again:

"Well, Mr. Flood, we have not met like this
In a long time; and many a change has come
To both of us, I fear, since last it was
We had a drop together. Welcome home!"
Convivially returning with himself,
Again he raised the jug up to the light:
And with an acquiescent quaver said:
"Well, Mr. Flood, if you insist, I might.

"Only a very little, Mr. Flood—
For auld lang syne. No more, sir; that will do."
So, for the time, apparently it did,
And Eben evidently thought so too;
For soon amid the silver loneliness
Of night he lifted up his voice and sang,
Secure, with only two moons listening,
Until the whole harmonious landscape rang—

"For auld lang syne." The weary throat gave out,
The last word wavered, and the song was done.
He raised again the jug regretfully
And shook his head, and was again alone.
There was not much that was ahead of him.
And there was nothing in the town below—
Where strangers would have shut the many doors
That many friends had opened long ago.

WALTER DE LA MARE

The Listeners

"Is there anybody there?" said the Traveller,
    Knocking on the moonlit door;
And his horse in the silence champed the grasses
    Of the forest's ferny floor:
And a bird flew up out of the turret,
    Above the Traveller's head:
And he smote upon the door again a second time;
    "Is there anybody there?" he said.
But no one descended to the Traveller;
    No head from the leaf-fringed sill
Leaned over and looked into his grey eyes,
    Where he stood perplexed and still.
But only a host of phantom listeners
    That dwelt in the lone house then
Stood listening in the quiet of the moonlight
    To that voice from the world of men:
Stood thronging the faint moonbeams on the dark stair,
    That goes down to the empty hall,
Hearkening in an air stirred and shaken
    By the lonely Traveller's call.
And he felt in his heart their strangeness,
    Their stillness answering his cry,
While his horse moved, cropping the dark turf,
    'Neath the starred and leafy sky;
For he suddenly smote on the door, even
    Louder, and lifted his head:—
"Tell them I came, and no one answered,
    That I kept my word," he said.
Never the least stir made the listeners,
    Though every word he spake
Fell echoing through the shadowiness of the still house
    From the one man left awake:

Ay, they heard his foot upon the stirrup,
And the sound of iron on stone,
And how the silence surged softly backward,
When the plunging hoofs were gone.

RAINER MARIA RILKE

Sonnets to Orpheus

1.24

Shall we reject our primordial friendship, the sublime
unwooing gods, because the steel that we keep
harshly bringing to hardness has never known them—
or shall we suddenly look for them on a map?

All these powerful friends, who withdraw the dead
from the reach of the senses, touch nowhere against our wheels.
We have moved our banquets, our baths and our festivals,
far away. And their messengers, long since outstripped by our speed,

have vanished. Lonelier now, dependent on one another
utterly, though not knowing one another at all,
we no longer lay out each path as a lovely meander,

but straight ahead. Only in factories do the once-consecrate flames still
burn and lift up the always heavier hammers.
We, though, keep losing what small strength we have, like swimmers.

Translated by Stephen Mitchell

2.8

(IN MEMORIAM EGON VON RILKE)

You playmates of mine in the scattered parks of the city,
small friends from a childhood of long ago:

how we found and liked one another, hesitantly,
and, like the lamb with the talking scroll,

spoke with our silence. When we were filled with joy,
it belonged to no one: it was simply there.
And how it dissolved among all the adults who passed by
and in the fears of the endless year.

Wheels rolled past us, we stood and stared at the carriages;
houses surrounded us, solid but untrue—and none
of them ever knew us. *What* in that world was real?

Nothing. Only the balls. Their magnificent arches.
Not even the children . . . But sometimes one,
oh a vanishing one, stepped under the plummeting ball.

Translated by Stephen Mitchell

ANNA AKHMATOVA

BORIS PASTERNAK

He who compared himself to the eye of a horse,
Peers, looks, sees, recognizes,
And instantly puddles shine, ice
Pines away, like a melting of diamonds.

Backyards drowse in lilac haze. Branch-
Line platforms, logs, clouds, leaves . . .
The engine's whistle, watermelon's crunch,
A timid hand in a fragrant kid glove. He's

Ringing, thundering, grinding, up to his breast
In breakers . . . and suddenly is quiet . . . This means
He is tiptoeing over pine needles, fearful lest
He should startle space awake from its light sleep.

It means he counts the grains in the empty ears,
And it means he has come back
From another funeral, back to Darya's
Gorge, the tombstone, cursed and black.

And burns again, the Moscow tedium,
In the distance death's sleigh-bell rings . . .
Who has got lost two steps from home,
Where the snow is waist-deep, an end to everything?

Because he compared smoke with Laocoön,
Made songs out of graveyard thistles,
Because he filled the world with a sound no-one
Has heard before, in a new space of mirrored

Verses, he has been rewarded with a form
Of eternal childhood, with the stars' vigilant love,
The whole earth has been passed down to him,
And he has shared it with everyone.

Translated by D. M. Thomas

There are Four of Us

O Muse of Weeping. . . .
—M. Tsvetaeva

I have turned aside from everything,
From the whole earthly store.
The spirit and guardian of this place
Is an old tree-stump in water.

We are brief guests of the earth, as it were,
And life is a habit we put on.
On paths of air I seem to overhear
Two friendly voices, talking in turn.

Did I say two? . . . There
By the east wall's tangle of raspberry,

Is a branch of elder, dark and fresh.
Why! it's a letter from Marina.

Translated by D. M. Thomas

IF ALL WHO HAVE BEGGED HELP

If all who have begged help
From me in this world,
All the holy innocents,
Broken wives, and cripples,
The imprisoned, the suicidal—
If they had sent me one kopeck
I should have become 'richer
Than all Egypt' . . .
But they did not send me kopecks,
Instead they shared with me their strength,
And so nothing in the world
Is stronger than I,
And I can bear anything, even this.

Translated by D. M. Thomas

GIUSEPPE UNGARETTI

IN MEMORIAM

His name was
Mohammed Sceab

A descendant
of the emirs of the nomads
he killed himself
because he no longer had
a homeland

He loved France
and changed his name

He became Marcel
but he was not French
and he forgot
how to live
in the tents of his people
where they listen to choruses
of the Koran
and sip coffee

And he forgot
how to set loose
the song
of his abandonment

I went with him
and the woman who owned the hotel
where we lived
in Paris
from number 5, rue des Carmes
a faded descending alley

He rests
in the graveyard at Ivry
a suburb which
always
seems like the last day
of a broken-down carnival

And perhaps I alone
still know
that he lived

Translated by Henry Taylor

WILFRED OWEN

To My Friend

(With an Identity Disc)

If ever I had dreamed of my dead name
   High in the heart of London, unsurpassed
By Time for ever, and the Fugitive, Fame,
   There seeking a long sanctuary at last,—

Or if I onetime hoped to hide its shame,
—Shame of success, and sorrow of defeats,—
Under those holy cypresses, the same
   That shade always the quiet place of Keats,

Now rather thank I God there is no risk
   Of gravers scoring it with florid screed.
Let my inscription be this soldier's disc. . . .
   Wear it, sweet friend. Inscribe no date nor deed.
But may thy heart-beat kiss it, night and day,
Until the name grow blurred and fade away.

BERTOLT BRECHT

The Friends

The war separated
Me, the writer of plays, from my friend the stage designer.

The cities where we worked are no longer there.
When I walk through the cities that still are
At times I say: that blue piece of washing
My friend would have placed it better.

Translated by Michael Hamburger

FEDERICO GARCÍA LORCA

LAMENT FOR IGNACIO SÁNCHEZ MEJIAS

1. COGIDA* AND DEATH

At five in the afternoon.
It was exactly five in the afternoon.
A boy brought the white sheet
at five in the afternoon.
A frail of lime ready prepared
at five in the afternoon.
The rest was death, and death alone
at five in the afternoon.

The wind carried away the cottonwool
at five in the afternoon.
And the oxide scattered crystal and nickel
at five in the afternoon.
Now the dove and the leopard wrestle
at five in the afternoon.
And a thigh with a desolate horn
at five in the afternoon.
The bass-string struck up
at five in the afternoon.
Arsenic bells and smoke
at five in the afternoon.

*Cogida is the catching and tossing of the bullfighter by the bull. Ignacio Sánchez Mejias, Lorca's friend, was a bullfighter.

Groups of silence in the corners
at five in the afternoon.
And the bull alone with a high heart!
At five in the afternoon.
When the sweat of snow was coming
at five in the afternoon,
when the bull ring was covered in iodine
at five in the afternoon.
death laid eggs in the wound
at five in the afternoon.
At five in the afternoon.
Exactly at five o'clock in the afternoon.

A coffin on wheels is his bed
at five in the afternoon.
Bones and flutes resound in his ears
at five in the afternoon.

Now the bull was bellowing through his forehead
at five in the afternoon.
The room was iridescent with agony
at five in the afternoon.
In the distance the gangrene now comes
at five in the afternoon.
Horn of the lily through green groins
at five in the afternoon.
The wounds were burning like suns
at five in the afternoon,
and the crowd was breaking the windows
at five in the afternoon.
At five in the afternoon.
Ah, that fatal five in the afternoon!
It was five by all the clocks!
It was five in the shade of the afternoon!

2. THE SPILLED BLOOD

I will not see it!

Tell the moon to come
for I do not want to see the blood
of Ignacio on the sand.

I will not see it!

The moon wide open.
Horse of still clouds,
and the grey bull ring of dreams
with willows in the barreras.

I will not see it!

Let my memory kindle!
Warn the jasmines
of such minute whiteness!

I will not see it!

The cow of the ancient world
passed her sad tongue
over a snout of blood
spilled on the sand,
and the bulls of Guisando,
partly death and partly stone,
bellowed like two centuries
sated with treading the earth.
No.
I do not want to see it!
I will not see it!

Ignacio goes up the tiers
with all his death on his shoulders.
He sought for the dawn
but the dawn was no more.
He seeks for his confident profile
and the dream bewilders him.
He sought for his beautiful body
and encountered his opened blood.
I will not see it!
I do not want to hear it spurt
each time with less strength:
that spurt that illuminates
the tiers of seats, and spills
over the corduroy and the leather
of a thirsty multitude.

Who shouts that I should come near!
Do not ask me to see it!

His eyes did not close
when he saw the horns near,
but the terrible mothers
lifted their heads.
And across the ranches,
an air of secret voices rose,
shouting to celestial bulls,
herdsmen of pale mist.
There was no prince in Seville
who could compare with him,
nor sword like his sword
nor heart so true.
Like a river of lions
was his marvellous strength,
and like a marble torso
his firm drawn moderation.
The air of Andalusian Rome
gilded his head
where his smile was a spikenard
of wit and intelligence.
What a great torero in the ring!
What a good peasant in the sierra!
How gentle with the sheaves!
How hard with the spurs!
How tender with the dew!
How dazzling in the fiesta!
How tremendous with the final
banderillas of darkness!

But now he sleeps without end.
Now the moss and the grass
open with sure fingers
the flower of his skull.
And now his blood comes out singing;
singing along marshes and meadows,
sliding on frozen horns,
faltering soulless in the mist,
stumbling over a thousand hoofs
like a long, dark, sad tongue,
to form a pool of agony

close to the starry Guadalquivir.
Oh, white wall of Spain!
Oh, black bull of sorrow!
Oh, hard blood of Ignacio!
Oh, nightingale of his veins!
No.
I will not see it!
No chalice can contain it,
no swallows can drink it,
no frost of light can cool it,
nor song nor deluge of white lilies,
no glass can cover it with silver.
No.
I will not see it!

3. THE LAID OUT BODY

Stone is a forehead where dreams grieve
without curving waters and frozen cypresses.
Stone is a shoulder on which to bear Time
with trees formed of tears and ribbons and planets.

I have seen grey showers move towards the waves
raising their tender riddled arms,
to avoid being caught by the lying stone
which loosens their limbs without soaking the blood.

For stone gathers seed and clouds,
skeleton larks and wolves of penumbra:
but yields not sounds nor crystals nor fire,
only bull rings and bull rings and more bull rings without walls.

Now, Ignacio the well born lies on the stone.
All is finished. What is happening? Contemplate his face:
death has covered him with pale sulphur
and has placed on him the head of a dark minotaur.

All is finished. The rain penetrates his mouth.
The air, as if mad, leaves his sunken chest,
and Love, soaked through with tears of snow,
warms itself on the peak of the herd.

What are they saying? A stenching silence settles down.
We are here with a body laid out which fades away,

with a pure shape which had nightingales
and we see it being filled with depthless holes.

Who creases the shroud? What he says is not true!
Nobody sings here, nobody weeps in the corner,
nobody pricks the spurs, nor terrifies the serpent.
Here I want nothing else but the round eyes
to see this body without a chance of rest.

Here I want to see those men of hard voice.
Those that break horses and dominate rivers;
those men of sonorous skeleton who sing
with a mouth full of sun and flint.

Here I want to see them. Before the stone.
Before this body with broken reins.
I want to know from them the way out
for this captain strapped down by death.

I want them to show me a lament like a river
which will have sweet mists and deep shores,
to take the body of Ignacio where it loses itself
without hearing the double panting of the bulls.

Loses itself in the round bull ring of the moon
which feigns in its youth a sad quiet bull:
loses itself in the night without song of fishes
and in the white thicket of frozen smoke.

I don't want them to cover his face with handkerchiefs
that he may get used to the death he carries.
Go, Ignacio; feel not the hot bellowing.
Sleep, fly, rest: even the sea dies!

4. ABSENT SOUL

The bull does not know you, nor the fig tree,
nor the horses, nor the ants in your own house.
The child and the afternoon do not know you
because you have died for ever.

The back of the stone does not know you,
nor the black satin in which you crumble.

Your silent memory does not know you
because you have died for ever.

The autumn will come with small white snails,
misty grapes and with clustered hills,
but no one will look into your eyes
because you have died for ever.

Because you have died for ever,
like all the dead of the Earth,
like all the dead who are forgotten
in a heap of lifeless dogs.

Nobody knows you. No. But I sing of you.
For posterity I sing of your profile and grace.
Of the signal maturity of your understanding.
Of your appetite for death and the taste of its mouth.
Of the sadness of your once valiant gaiety.

It will be a long time, if ever, before there is born
an Andalusian so true, so rich in adventure.
I sing of his elegance with words that groan,
and I remember a sad breeze through the olive trees.

Translated by Stephen Spender and J. L. Gili

JORGE LUIS BORGES

To Francisco López Merino

If, by your own hand, you brought death on yourself,
if it was your wish to reject all the mornings of this world,
these contradictory words summon you now to no purpose,
doomed as they are to impossibility and failure.

Then all that is left us
is to speak of the roses' dishonor that found no way of detaining you,
the opprobrious day that gave you the gunshot and the end.

How can our voices
gainsay what dissolution, the tear-drop, the marble confirmed for us?
For surely something is left of our tenderness no death can diminish—
the indecipherable, intimate news that music confides to us,
a country pared down to its essence: a fig tree and a patio well,
the burning gravitation of love to which our souls bear witness—
the weighted minutes
by which reality's honor is salvaged again.

I think of them now, my recondite friend, I think that
perhaps we contrive our own deaths with images of our choosing,
that you knew it already, full of bells, childlike and graceful,
a sister of your schoolboy's painstaking hand,
that you might even have thought to humor yourself with your death,
   like a dream
that brings forgetfulness of the world, but in a comradely way,
where all oblivion blesses us.

If that is the sense of it, and if when time leaves us behind
a grain of eternity clings to us, an aftertaste of the world,
then your death weighs more lightly,
light as the verse wherein you still wait for us always,
and the comradeship that calls to you now
no longer profanes your shadow.

                                        Translated by Ben Belitt

To a Minor Poet of the Greek Anthology

Where now is the memory
of the days that were yours on earth, and wove
joy with sorrow, and made a universe that was your own?

The river of years has lost them
from its numbered current; you are a word in an index.

To others the gods gave glory that has no end:
inscriptions, names on coins, monuments, conscientious historians;
all that we know of you, eclipsed friend,
is that you heard the nightingale one evening.

Among the asphodels of the Shadow, your shade, in its vanity,
must consider the gods ungenerous.

But the days are a web of small troubles,
and is there a greater blessing
than to be the ash of which oblivion is made?

Above other heads the gods kindled
the inexorable light of glory, which peers into the secret parts and
    discovers each separate fault;
glory, that at last shrivels the rose it reveres;
they were more considerate with you, brother.

In the rapt evening that will never be night
you listen without end to Theocritus' nightingale.

Translated by W. S. Merwin

LANGSTON HUGHES

POEM

I loved my friend.
He went away from me.
There's nothing more to say.
The poem ends,
Soft as it began—
I loved my friend.

OGDEN NASH

From HEARTS OF GOLD

or A Good Excuse is Worse Than None

There are some people who are very resourceful
At being remorseful.
And who apparently feel that the best way to make friends
Is to do something terrible and then make amends.

W. H. AUDEN

FOR FRIENDS ONLY

(for John and Teckla Clark)

Ours yet not ours, being set apart
As a shrine to friendship,
Empty and silent most of the year,
This room awaits from you
What you alone, as visitor, can bring,
A weekend of personal life.

In a house backed by orderly woods,
Facing a tractored sugar-beet country,
Your working hosts engaged to their stint,
You are unlike to encounter
Dragons or romance: were drama a craving,
You would not have come.

Books we do have for almost any
Literate mood, and notepaper, envelopes,
For a writing one (to "borrow" stamps
Is a mark of ill-breeding):
Between lunch and tea, perhaps a drive;
After dinner, music or gossip.

Should you have troubles (pets will die,
Lovers are always behaving badly)
And confession helps, we will hear it,
Examine and give our counsel:
If to mention them hurts too much,
We shall not be nosey.

Easy at first, the language of friendship
Is, as we soon discover,
Very difficult to speak well, a tongue
With no cognates, no resemblance
To the galimatias of nursery and bedroom,
Court rhyme or shepherd's prose,

And, unless often spoken, soon goes rusty.
Distance and duties divide us,
But absence will not seem an evil
If it make our re-meeting
A real occasion. Come when you can:
Your room will be ready.

In Tum-Tum's reign a tin of biscuits
On the bedside table provided
For nocturnal munching. Now weapons have changed,
And the fashion in appetites:
There, for sunbathers who count their calories,
A bottle of mineral water.

Felicissima notte! May you fall at once
Into a cordial dream, assured
That whoever slept in this bed before
Was also someone we like,
That within the circle of our affection
Also you have no double.

THE COMMON LIFE

(for Chester Kallman)

A living room, the catholic area you
   (Thou, rather) and I may enter
without knocking, leave without a bow, confronts
   each visitor with a style,

a secular faith: he compares its dogmas
   with his, and decides whether
he would like to see more of us. (Spotless rooms
   where nothing's left lying about

chill me, so do cups used for ashtrays or smeared
   with lipstick: the homes I warm to,
though seldom wealthy, always convey a feeling
   of bills being promptly settled

with checks that don't bounce.) There's no *We* at an instant,
   only *Thou* and *I*, two regions
of protestant being which nowhere overlap:
   a room is too small, therefore,

if its occupants cannot forget at will
   that they are not alone, too big
if it gives them any excuse in a quarrel
   for raising their voices. What,

quizzing ours, would Sherlock Holmes infer? Plainly,
   ours is a sitting culture
in a generation which prefers comfort
   (or is forced to prefer it)

to command, would rather incline its buttocks
   on a well-upholstered chair
than the burly back of a slave: a quick glance
   at book titles would tell him

that we belong to the clerisy and spend much
   on our food. But could he read
what our prayers and jokes are about, what creatures
   frighten us most, or what names

head our roll call of persons we would least like
    to go to bed with? What draws
singular lives together in the first place,
    loneliness, lust, ambition,

or mere convenience, is obvious, why they drop
    or murder one another
clear enough: how they create, though, a common world
    between them, like Bombelli's

impossible yet useful numbers, no one
    has yet explained. Still, they do
manage to forgive impossible behavior,
    to endure by some miracle

conversational tics and larval habits
    without wincing (were you to die,
I should miss yours). It's a wonder that neither
    has been butchered by accident,

or, as lots have, silently vanished into
    History's criminal noise
unmourned for, but that, after twenty-four years,
    we should sit here in Austria

as cater-cousins, under the glassy look
    of a Naples Bambino,
the portrayed regards of Strauss and Stravinsky,
    doing British crossword puzzles,

is very odd indeed. I'm glad the builder gave
    our common-room small windows
through which no observed outsider can observe us:
    every home should be a fortress,

equipped with all the very latest engines
    for keeping Nature at bay,
versed in all ancient magic, the arts of quelling
    the Dark Lord and his hungry

animivorous chimeras. (Any brute
    can buy a machine in a shop,

but the sacred spells are secret to the kind,
    and if power is what we wish

they won't work.) *The ogre will come in any case:*
    so Joyce has warned us. Howbeit,
fasting or feasting, we both know this: without
    the Spirit we die, but life

without the Letter is in the worst of taste,
    and always, though truth and love
can never really differ, when they seem to,
    the subaltern should be truth.

THEODORE ROETHKE

Elegy for Jane

My Student, Thrown by a Horse

I remember the neckcurls, limp and damp as tendrils;
And her quick look, a sidelong pickerel smile;
And how, once startled into talk, the light syllables leaped for her,
And she balanced in the delight of her thought,
A wren, happy, tail into the wind,
Her song trembling the twigs and small branches.
The shade sang with her;
The leaves, their whispers turned to kissing;
And the mold sang in the bleached valleys under the rose.

Oh, when she was sad, she cast herself down into such a pure depth,
Even a father could not find her:
Scraping her cheek against straw;
Stirring the clearest water.

My sparrow, you are not here,
Waiting like a fern, making a spiny shadow.

The sides of wet stones cannot console me,
Nor the moss, wound with the last light.

If only I could nudge you from this sleep,
My maimed darling, my skittery pigeon.
Over this damp grave I speak the words of my love:
I, with no rights in this matter,
Neither father nor lover.

DELMORE SCHWARTZ

DO THE OTHERS SPEAK OF ME MOCKINGLY, MALICIOUSLY?

"As in water face answereth to face, so the heart of man to man."

Do they whisper behind my back? Do they speak
Of my clumsiness? Do they laugh at me,
Mimicking my gestures, retailing my shame?
I'll whirl about, denounce them, saying
That they are shameless, they are treacherous,
No more my friends, nor will I once again
Never, amid a thousand meetings in the street,
Recognize their faces, take their hands,
Not for our common love or old times' sake:
They whispered behind my back, they mimicked me.

I know the reason why, I too have done this,
Cruel for wit's sake, behind my dear friend's back,
And to amuse betrayed his private love,
His nervous shame, her habit, and their weaknesses;
I have mimicked them, I have been treacherous,
For wit's sake, to amuse, because their being weighed
Too grossly for a time, to be superior,
To flatter the listeners by this, the intimate,
Betraying the intimate, but for the intimate,

To free myself of friendship's necessity,
Fearing from time to time that they would hear,
Denounce me and reject me, say once for all
That they would never meet me, take my hands,
Speaking for old times' sake and our common love.

What an unheard-of thing it is, in fine,
To love another and equally be loved!
What sadness and what joy! How cruel it is
That pride and wit distort the heart of man,
How vain, how sad, what cruelty, what need,
For this is true and sad, that I need them
And they need me. What can we do? We need
Each other's clumsiness, each other's wit,
Each other's company and our own pride. I need
My face unshamed, I need my wit, I cannot
Turn away. We know our clumsiness,
Our weakness, our necessities, we cannot
Forget our pride, our faces, our common love.

RICHARD WILBUR

WHAT IS THE OPPOSITE OF *Two?*

What is the opposite of *two?*
A lonely me, a lonely you.

ANNE SEXTON

WITH MERCY FOR THE GREEDY

For my friend, Ruth, who urges me to make an
appointment for the Sacrament of Confession

Concerning your letter in which you ask
me to call a priest and in which you ask
me to wear The Cross that you enclose;
your own cross,
your dog-bitten cross,
no larger than a thumb,
small and wooden, no thorns, this rose—

I pray to its shadow,
that gray place
where it lies on your letter . . . deep, deep.
I detest my sins and I try to believe
in The Cross. I touch its tender hips, its dark jawed face,
its solid neck, its brown sleep.

True. There is
a beautiful Jesus.
He is frozen to his bones like a chunk of beef.
How desperately he wanted to pull his arms in!
How desperately I touch his vertical and horizontal axes!
But I can't. Need is not quite belief.

All morning long
I have worn
your cross, hung with package string around my throat.
It tapped me lightly as a child's heart might,
tapping secondhand, softly waiting to be born.
Ruth, I cherish the letter you wrote.

My friend, my friend, I was born
doing reference work in sin, and born
confessing it. This is what poems are:
with mercy
for the greedy,
they are the tongue's wrangle,
the world's pottage, the rat's star.

URSULA K. LE GUIN

Vita Amicae

When you were rain you fell
when you were cup you held
when you were whole you broke
    loud, loud you spoke
      when you were bell

When you were way you led
homeward until the end
when you were life you died
    live, live, you cried
      when you were dead

ADRIENNE RICH

PAULA BECKER TO CLARA WESTHOFF

Paula Becker 1876–1907
Clara Westhoff 1878–1954

became friends at Worpswede, an artists' colony near
Bremen, Germany, summer 1899. In January 1900, spent
a half-year together in Paris, where Paula painted and Clara
studied sculpture with Rodin. In August they returned to
Worpswede, and spent the next winter together in Berlin.
In 1901, Clara married the poet Rainer Maria Rilke; soon
after, Paula married the painter Otto Modersohn. She died in a
hemmorrhage after childbirth, murmuring, *What a pity!*

The autumn feels slowed down,
summer still holds on here, even the light
seems to last longer than it should
or maybe I'm using it to the thin edge.
The moon rolls in the air. I didn't want this child.
You're the only one I've told.
I want a child maybe, someday, but not now.
Otto has a calm, complacent way
of following me with his eyes, as if to say
Soon you'll have your hands full!
And yes, I will; this child will be mine
not his, the failures, if I fail
will be all mine. We're not good, Clara,
at learning to prevent these things,
and once we have a child, it *is* ours.
But lately, I feel beyond Otto or anyone.
I know now the kind of work I have to do.
It takes such energy! I have the feeling I'm
moving somewhere, patiently, impatiently,
in my loneliness. I'm looking everywhere in nature

for new forms, old forms in new places,
the planes of an antique mouth, let's say, among the
     leaves.
I know and do not know
what I am searching for.
Remember those months in the studio together,
you up to your strong forearms in wet clay,
I trying to make something of the strange impressions
assailing me—the Japanese
flowers and birds on silk, the drunks
sheltering in the Louvre, that river-light,
those faces. . . . Did we know exactly
why we were there? Paris unnerved you,
you found it too much, yet you went on
with your work . . . and later we met there again,
both married then, and I thought you and Rilke
both seemed unnerved. I felt a kind of joylessness
between you. Of course he and I
have had our difficulties. Maybe I was jealous
of him, to begin with, taking you from me,
maybe I married Otto to fill up
my loneliness for you.
Rainer, of course, *knows* more than Otto knows,
he believes in women. But he feeds on us,
like all of them. His whole life, his art
is protected by women. Which of us could say that?
Which of us, Clara, hasn't had to take that leap
out beyond our being women
to save our work? or is it to save ourselves?
Marriage is lonelier than solitude.
Do you know: I was dreaming I had died
giving birth to the child.
I couldn't paint or speak or even move.
My child—I think—survived me. But what was funny
in the dream was, Rainer had written my requiem—
a long, beautiful poem, and calling me his friend.
I was *your* friend
but in the dream you didn't say a word.
In the dream his poem was like a letter
to someone who has no right
to be there but must be treated gently, like a guest
who comes on the wrong day. Clara, why don't I dream of you?
That photo of the two of us—I have it still,

you and I looking hard into each other
and my painting behind us. How we used to work
side by side! And how I've worked since then
trying to create according to our plan
that we'd bring, against all odds, our full power
to every subject. Hold back nothing
because we were women. Clara, our strength still lies
in the things we used to talk about:
how life and death take one another's hands,
the struggle for truth, our old pledge against guilt.
And now I feel dawn and the coming day.
I love waking in my studio, seeing my pictures
come alive in the light. Sometimes I feel
it is myself that kicks inside me,
myself I must give suck to, love . . .
I wish we could have done this for each other
all our lives, but we can't . . .
They say a pregnant woman
dreams of her own death. But life and death
take one another's hands. Clara, I feel so full
of work, the life I see ahead, and love
for you, who of all people
however badly I say this
will hear all I say and cannot say.

DEREK WALCOTT

FOREST OF EUROPE

For Joseph Brodsky

The last leaves fell like notes from a piano
and left their ovals echoing in the ear;
with gawky music stands, the winter forest
looks like an empty orchestra, its lines
ruled on these scattered manuscripts of snow.

The inlaid copper laurel of an oak
shines through the brown-bricked glass above your head
as bright as whiskey, while the wintry breath
of lines from Mandelstam, which you recite,
uncoils as visibly as cigarette smoke.

"The rustling of ruble notes by the lemon Neva."
Under your exile's tongue, crisp under heel,
the gutturals crackle like decaying leaves,
the phrase from Mandelstam circles with light
in a brown room, in barren Oklahoma.

There is a Gulag Archipelago
under this ice, where the salt, mineral spring
of the long Trail of Tears runnels these plains
as hard and open as a herdsman's face
sun-cracked and stubbled with unshaven snow.

Growing in whispers from the Writers' Congress,
the snow circles like cossacks round the corpse
of a tired Choctaw till it is a blizzard
of treaties and white papers as we lose
sight of the single human through the cause.

So every spring these branches load their shelves,
like libraries with newly published leaves,
till waste recycles them—paper to snow—
but, at zero of suffering, one mind
lasts like this oak with a few brazen leaves.

As the train passed the forest's tortured icons,
the floes clanging like freight yards, then the spires
of frozen tears, the stations screeching steam,
he drew them in a single winter's breath
whose freezing consonants turned into stones.

He saw the poetry in forlorn stations
under clouds vast as Asia, through districts
that could gulp Oklahoma like a grape,
not these tree-shaped prairie halts but space
so desolate it mocked destinations.

Who is that dark child on the parapets
of Europe, watching the evening river mint

its sovereigns stamped with power, not with poets,
the Thames and the Neva rustling like banknotes,
then, black on gold, the Hudson's silhouettes?

From frozen Neva to the Hudson pours,
under the airport domes, the echoing stations,
the tributary of emigrants whom exile
has made as classless as the common cold,
citizens of a language that is now yours,

and every February, every "last autumn,"
you write far from the threshing harvesters
folding wheat like a girl plaiting her hair,
far from Russia's canals quivering with sunstroke,
a man living with English in one room.

The tourist archipelagoes of my South
are prisons too, corruptible, and though
there is no harder prison than writing verse,
what's poetry, if it is worth its salt,
but a phrase men can pass from hand to mouth?

From hand to mouth, across the centuries,
the bread that lasts when systems have decayed,
when, in his forest of barbed-wire branches,
a prisoner circles, chewing the one phrase
whose music will last longer than the leaves,

whose condensation is the marble sweat
of angels' foreheads, which will never dry
till Borealis shuts the peacock lights
of its slow fan from L.A. to Archangel,
and memory needs nothing to repeat.

Frightened and starved, with divine fever
Osip Mandelstam shook, and every
metaphor shuddered him with ague,
each vowel heavier than a boundary stone,
"to the rustling of ruble notes by the lemon Neva,"

but now that fever is a fire whose glow
warms our hands, Joseph, as we grunt like primates
exchanging gutturals in this winter cave

of a brown cottage, while in drifts outside
mastodons force their systems through the snow.

MICHAEL S. HARPER

The View from Mount Saint Helens

We picnicked on the Columbia River Gorge
on a splendid table of leaves,
olives, cheese, Rioja wine,
and talked of Ethiopia,
which Du Bois called Abyssinia
as a blessed namesake's child
is called "snowball,"
which is the word I name
as I look up at the mountain.

This was years ago, when I could
look down on the faces of the dead
above; I dream your son, Kevin,
looks down on us from his perch
above us, his face up to the ancestors
he could paint or collect
if he could leave the side of his mother,
in this life and in the life of Ethiopia.

The flying African would leap from the shores
of the continent called America,
though it was really only an island
in the Caribbean:
the text demanded the casirenas
be called cedars,
what a great poet called
the insulted landscape,
which is the breast of your forehead

now, so dense with frenesy
and greasepaint.

There is little comfort in the words
of a mountain: the Nez Perce would
climb Mount Saint Helens for vectors of meditation
and what they saw was what they lived.

I see you now in the busywork of healing
an old scar, perhaps in bed for a year
in paralysis, or painting in a mulch
for the cure to radiation, the bacteria
of the mind without vision.
                Once you knit
for hours over my second living son,
Patrice, smoother than a seal or an orchid:
take him now into your heart for the mountain,
and the face looking up for us
who cannot see down, and touch the river
of the flying African in your bosom
for the husbanding of Abyssinia
to wash your wings.

AUGUST KLEINZAHLER

FRIENDS THROUGH AT NEW YEAR'S

The old year's calendars flutter down
in the mist,
                countless sheets
of dated memoranda escorting them like pilot fish
to the street below

as friends pass through, alone and with kids:
the one down from Juneau
headed south to Belize for the diving;

and the clan from Vancouver, two little girls now
and a grubstake to buy a boat with, sail
the islands off of Crete, Turkey maybe, just way
the hell away from housepainting and rain.

We watch cartoons as front after front
sweeps through,
                worse than Vancouver. —*This is worse
than Vancouver,* she says,
but they all go to the carousel in the park anyhow
and catch cold
because the big one remembers from last time.

The other friend is drinking, talking
about the woman back up in Sitka, how the last letter
was strange;
                and her youngest boy, Tom,
the way the two of them got along.

When old friends speak of the past
after the years apart, lives so different,
                            how well

they seem to know us, still,
after such a long time, better than our families,
our lovers.
                So much of ourselves that we had forgotten
alive in them still

whose children fall asleep in our arms.

PART V

AFFINITIES: GROUP 1

Flowers are lovely; Love is flower-like;
Friendship is a sheltering tree.

—*Samuel Taylor Coleridge*

SAMUEL TAYLOR COLERIDGE

THIS LIME-TREE BOWER MY PRISON

(Addressed to Charles Lamb, of the India House, London)

In the June of 1797 some long-expected friends paid a visit to
the author's cottage; and on the morning of their arrival, he met
with an accident, which disabled him from walking during the
whole time of their stay. One evening, when they had left him
for a few hours, he composed the following lines in the garden-
bower. [Coleridge's note]

Well, they are gone, and here must I remain,
This lime-tree bower my prison! I have lost
Beauties and feelings, such as would have been
Most sweet to my remembrance even when age
Had dimm'd mine eyes to blindness! They, meanwhile,
Friends, whom I never more may meet again,
On springy heath, along the hill-top edge,
Wander in gladness, and wind down, perchance,
To that still roaring dell, of which I told,
The roaring dell, o'erwooded, narrow, deep,
And only speckled by the mid-day sun;
Where its slim trunk the ash from rock to rock
Flings arching like a bridge;—that branchless ash,
Unsunn'd and damp, whose few poor yellow leaves
Ne'er tremble in the gale, yet tremble still,
Fann'd by the water-fall! and there my friends
Behold the dark green file of long lank weeds,
That all at once (a most fantastic sight!)
Still nod and drip beneath the dripping edge
Of the blue clay-stone.

              Now, my friends emerge
Beneath the wide wide Heaven—and view again

The many-steepled tract magnificent
Of hilly fields and meadows, and the sea,
With some fair bark, perhaps, whose sails light up
The slip of smooth clear blue betwixt two Isles
Of purple shadow! Yes! they wander on
In gladness all; but thou, methinks, most glad,
My gentle-hearted Charles! for thou hast pined
And hunger'd after Nature, many a year,
In the great City pent, winning thy way
With sad yet patient soul, through evil and pain
And strange calamity! Ah! slowly sink
Behind the western ridge, thou glorious Sun!
Shine in the slant beams of the sinking orb,
Ye purple heath-flowers! richlier burn, ye clouds!
Live in the yellow light, ye distant groves!
And kindle, thou blue Ocean! So my friend
Struck with deep joy may stand, as I have stood,
Silent with swimming sense; yea, gazing round
On the wide landscape, gaze till all doth seem
Less gross than bodily; and of such hues
As veil the Almighty Spirit, when yet he makes
Spirits perceive his presence.

                       A delight
Comes sudden on my heart, and I am glad
As I myself were there! Nor in this bower,
This little lime-tree bower, have I not mark'd
Much that has sooth'd me. Pale beneath the blaze
Hung the transparent foliage; and I watch'd
Some broad and sunny leaf, and lov'd to see
The shadow of the leaf and stem above
Dappling its sunshine! And that walnut-tree
Was richly ting'd, and a deep radiance lay
Full on the ancient ivy, which usurps
Those fronting elms, and now, with blackest mass
Makes their dark branches gleam a lighter hue
Through the late twilight: and though now the bat
Wheels silent by, and not a swallow twitters,
Yet still the solitary humble-bee
Sings in the bean-flower! Henceforth I shall know
That Nature ne'er deserts the wise and pure;
No plot so narrow, be but Nature there,
No waste so vacant, but may well employ

Each faculty of sense, and keep the heart
Awake to Love and Beauty! and sometimes
'Tis well to be bereft of promis'd good,
That we may lift the soul, and contemplate
With lively joy the joys we cannot share.
My gentle-hearted Charles! when the last rook
Beat its straight path along the dusky air
Homewards, I blest it! deeming its black wing
(Now a dim speck, now vanishing in light)
Had cross'd the mighty Orb's dilated glory,
While thou stood'st gazing; or, when all was still,
Flew creeking o'er thy head, and had a charm
For thee, my gentle-hearted Charles, to whom
No sound is dissonant which tells of Life.

DOROTHY WORDSWORTH

From THE GRASMERE JOURNALS

[*November 9th, 1801, Monday.*] Walked with Coleridge to Keswick ... the mountains for ever varying, now hid in the Clouds, and now with their tops visible while perhaps they were half concealed below—Legberthwaite beautiful. We ate Bread and Cheese at John Stanley's, and reached Keswick without fatigue just before Dark. We enjoyed ourselves in the study and were *at home.* Supped at Mr. Jackson's. Mary and I sate in C.'s room a while.

[*November*] 10th, 1801, Tuesday. Poor C. left us, and we came home together. We left Keswick at 2 o'clock and did not arrive at G. till 9 o'clock. Drank tea at John Stanley's very comfortably. I burnt myself with Coleridge's Aquafortis. Mary's feet sore. C. had a sweet day for his ride. Every sight and every sound reminded me of him—dear, dear fellow, of his many walks to us by day and by night, of all dear things. I was melancholy, and could not talk, but at last I eased my heart by weeping—nervous blubbering, says William. It is not so. O! how many, many reasons have I to be anxious for him. . . .

[*November*] 11th, 1801, Wednesday. Baked bread and giblet pie—

put books in order—mended stockings. Put aside dearest C.'s letters, and now at about 7 o'clock we are all sitting by a nice fire. Wm. with his book and a candle, and Mary writing to Sara. . . .

[*December*] 12th, 1801, *Saturday.* A fine frosty morning—Snow upon the ground. I made bread and pies. We walked with Mrs. Luff to Rydale and came home the other side of the Lake, met Townley with his dogs. All looked chearful and bright. Helm Crag rose very bold and craggy, a being by itself, and behind it was the large Ridge of mountain, smooth as marble and snow white. All the mountains looked like solid stone, on our left, going from Grasmere, *i.e.* White Moss and Nab Scar. The snow hid all the grass, and all signs of vegetation, and the Rocks showed themselves boldly everywhere, and seemed more stony than Rock or stone. The Birches on the crags beautiful, red brown and glittering. The ashes glittering spears with their upright stems. The hips very beautiful, and so good!! and, dear Coleridge! I ate twenty for thee, when I was by myself! I came home first—they walked too slow for me. William went to look at Langdale Pikes. We had a sweet invigorating walk. Mr. Clarkson came in before tea. We played at cards—sate up late. The moon shone upon the water below Silver-How, and above it hung, combining with Silver-How on one side, a Bowl-shaped moon, the curve downwards; the white fields, glittering Roof of Thomas Ashburner's house, the dark yew tree, the white fields gay and beautiful. William lay with his curtains open that he might see it. . . .

[*April*] *29th, 1802, Thursday.* A beautiful morning—the sun shone and all was pleasant. We sent off our parcel to Coleridge by the waggon. Mr. Simpson heard the Cuckow to-day. Before we went out, after I had written down *The Tinker,* which William finished this morning, Luff called—he was very lame, limped into the kitchen. He came on a little pony. We then went to John's Grove, sate a while at first. Afterwards William lay, and I lay, in the trench under the fence—he with his eyes shut, and listening to the waterfalls and the Birds. There was no one waterfall above another—it was a sound of waters in the air—the voice of the air. William heard me breathing and rustling now and then, but we both lay still, and unseen by one another; he thought that it would be as sweet thus to lie so in the grave, to hear the *peaceful* sounds of the earth, and just to know that our dear friends were near. . . .

May 4th, 1802, Tuesday. William had slept pretty well and though he went to bed nervous, and jaded in the extreme, he rose refreshed. I wrote *The Leech Gatherer* for him, which he had begun the night before, and of which he wrote several stanzas in bed this morning. It was very hot; we called at Mr. Simpson's door as we passed, but did not go in. We rested several times by the way, read, and repeated *The Leech Gatherer.* We were almost melted before we were at the top of the hill. We saw

Coleridge on the Wytheburn side of the water; he crossed the Beck to us. Mr. Simpson was fishing there. William and I ate a luncheon, then went on towards the waterfall. It is a glorious wild solitude under that lofty purple crag. It stood upright by itself. Its own self, and its shadow below, one mass—all else was sunshine. We went on further. A Bird at the top of the crags was flying round and round, and looked in thinness and transparency, shape and motion like a moth. We climbed the hill, but looked in vain for a shade, except at the foot of the great waterfall, and there we did not like to stay on account of the loose stones above our heads. We came down, and rested upon a moss-covered rock, rising out of the bed of the river. There we lay, ate our dinner, and stayed there till about 4 o'clock or later. William and C. repeated and read verses. I drank a little Brandy and water, and was in Heaven. The Stag's horn is very beautiful and fresh, springing upon the fells. Mountain ashes, green. We drank tea at a farm house. The woman had not a pleasant countenance, but was civil enough. She had a pretty Boy, a year old, whom she suckled. We parted from Coleridge at Sara's crag, after having looked at the letters which C. carved in the morning. I kissed them all. Wm. deepened the T with C.'s pen-knife. We sate afterwards on the wall, seeing the sun go down, and the reflections in the still water. C. looked well, and parted from us chearfully, hopping up upon the side stones.

SAMUEL TAYLOR COLERIDGE

From CHRISTABEL

Alas! they had been friends in youth;
But whispering tongues can poison truth;
And constancy lives in realms above;
And life is thorny; and youth is vain;
And to be wroth with one we love
Doth work like madness in the brain.
And thus it chanced, as I divine,
With Roland and Sir Leoline.
Each spake words of high disdain

And insult to his heart's best brother:
They parted—ne'er to meet again!
But never either found another
To free the hollow heart from paining—
They stood aloof, the scars remaining,
Like cliffs which had been rent asunder;
A dreary sea now flows between;—
But neither heat, nor frost, nor thunder,
Shall wholly do away, I ween,
The marks of that which once hath been.

To William Wordsworth

(This letter was written seven months after Wordsworth and Coleridge had been reconciled, following their quarrel two years earlier. Two of Wordsworth's children died in 1812—the second, a week before this letter was written.)

71, Berners' Street.
Monday Noon, 7 Decr. 1812

Write? My dearest Friend! O that it were in my power to be with you myself instead of my Letter. The Lectures I could give up; but the Rehearsal of my Play commences this week—& upon this depends my best Hopes of leaving Town after Christmas & living among you as long as I live.—Strange, strange are the Coincidences of Things! Yesterday Martha Fricker dined here—and after Tea I had asked question after question respecting your children, first one, then the other; but more than all, concerning Thomas—till at length Mrs Morgan said, What ails you, Coleridge? Why don't you talk about Hartley, Derwent, & Sara? And not two hours ago (for the whole Family were late from bed) I was asked what was the matter with my eyes?—I told the fact—that I had awoke three times during the Night & Morning, & at each time found my face & part of the pillow wet with Tears—"Were you dreaming of the Wordsworths?" she asked.—Of the children?—I said, No! not so much of them—but of Mrs W. & Miss Hutchinson, & yourself & Sister—.

Mrs Morgan and her Sister are come in—& I have been relieved by Tears. The sharp, sharp Pang at the heart needed it, when they reminded me of my words the very yester night—"It is not possible, that I should do other than love Wordsworth's children, all of them; but Tom is nearest my heart—I so often have him before my eyes sitting on the little stool by my side, while I was writing my Essays—& how quiet & happy the affectionate little fellow would be, if he could but touch me, & now and then be looked at!"—

O dearest Friend! what comfort can I afford you? What comfort ought I not to afford, who have given you so much pain?—Sympathy deep, of my whole being, & a necessity of my Being—that, so help me God at my last hour! has never been other than what it is, substantially! In Grief, and in joy, in the anguish of perplexity & in the fullness & overflow of Confidence, it has been ever what it is.—There is a sense of the word, Love, in which I never felt it but to you & one of your Household—! I am distant from you some hundred miles, but glad I am, that I am no longer distant in spirit, & have faith, that as it has happened *but once,* so it never can happen again. An aweful Truth it seems to me, & prophetic of our future, as well as declarative of our present *real,* nature, that one mere Thought, one feeling of Suspicion or Jealousy or resentment can remove two human Beings farther from each other, than winds or seas can separate their Bodies.

The words *"religious* fortitude" occasion me to add, that my Faith in our progressive nature, and in all the *doctrinal* parts of Christianity is become habitual in my understanding no less than in my feelings. More cheering illustrations of our survival I have never received, than from a recent Study of the *instincts* of animals, their clear heterogeneity from the reason & moral essence of Man, & yet the beautiful analogy.— Especially, on the death of Children, & of the *mind* in childhood, altogether, many thoughts have accumulated—from which I hope to derive consolation from that most oppressive feeling, which hurries in upon the first anguish of such Tidings, as I have received—the sense of uncertainty, the fear in enjoyment, the pale & deathy Gleam thrown over the countenances of the Living, whom we love—As I saw bef[ore] me the dear little Boy in his Coffin, it *dim* [*med?*] (suddenly & wholly involuntarily & without any conscious connection of Thought preceding) & I beheld Derwent lying beside him!—

But this is bad comforting. Your own virtues, your own Love itself, must give it.— . . .

Dear Mary! dear Dorothy! dearest Sarah!—O be assured, no thought relative to myself has half the influence in inspiring the wish & effort to *appear* & to *act* what I always in my will & heart have been, as the knowledge that few things could more console you than to see me healthy & worthy of myself!—Again & again, my dearest Wordsworth!!

I am affectionately, & truly your
S.T. Coleridge

CHARLES LAMB

POPULAR FALLACIES, XVI—THAT A SULKY TEMPER IS A MISFORTUNE

We grant that it is, and a very serious one—to a man's friends, and to all that have to do with him; but whether the condition of the man himself is so much to be deplored, may admit of a question. We can speak a little to it, being ourself but lately recovered—we whisper it in confidence, reader—out of a long and desperate fit of the sullens. Was the cure a blessing? The conviction which wrought it, came too clearly to leave a scruple of the fanciful injuries—for they were mere fancies—which had provoked the humour. But the humour itself was too self-pleasing, while it lasted—we know how bare we lay ourself in the confession—to be abandoned all at once with the grounds of it. We still brood over wrongs which we know to have been imaginary; and for our old acquaintance, N—, whom we find to have been a truer friend than we took him for, we substitute some phantom—a Caius or a Titius—as like him as we dare to form it, to wreak our yet unsatisfied resentments on. It is mortifying to fall at once from the pinnacle of neglect; to forego the idea of having been ill-used and contumaciously treated by an old friend. The first thing to aggrandise a man in his own conceit, is to conceive of himself as neglected. There let him fix if he can. To undeceive him is to deprive him of the most tickling morsel within the range of self-complacency. No flattery can come near it. Happy is he who suspects his friend of an injustice; but supremely blest, who thinks all his friends in a conspiracy to depress and undervalue him. There is a pleasure (we sing not to the profane) far beyond the reach of all that the world counts joy—a deep, enduring satisfaction in the depths, where the superficial seek it not, of discontent. Were we to recite one half of this mystery, which we were let into by our late dissatisfaction, all the world would be in love with disrespect; we should wear a slight for a bracelet, and neglects and con-tumacies would be the only matter for courtship. Unlike to that mysteri-ous book in the Apocalypse, the study of this mystery is unpalatable only in the commencement. The first sting of a suspicion is grievous; but wait—out of that wound, which to flesh and blood seemed so difficult, there is balm and honey to be extracted. Your friend passed you on such or such a day,—having in his company one that you conceived worse than ambiguously disposed towards you,—passed you in the street without notice. To be sure he is something short-sighted; and it was in your power to have accosted *him*. But facts and sane inferences are trifles to a true adept in the science of dissatisfaction. He must have seen you; and S——, who was with him, must have been the cause of the contempt. It galls you, and well it may. But have patience. Go home, and make the worst of it, and you are a made man from this time. Shut yourself up, and—rejecting, as an enemy to your peace, every whispering suggestion that but insinuates there may be a mistake—reflect seriously upon the many lesser instances which you had begun to perceive, in proof of your friend's disaffection towards you. None of them singly was much to the purpose, but the aggregate weight is positive; and you have this last affront to clench them. Thus far the process is any thing but agreeable. But now to your relief comes in the comparative faculty. You conjure up all the kind feelings you have had for your friend; what you have been to him, and what you would have been to him, if he would have suffered you; how you defended him in this or that place; and his good name—his literary reputation, and so forth, was always dearer to you than your own! Your heart, spite of itself, yearns towards him. You could weep tears of blood but for a restraining pride. How say you? do you not yet begin to apprehend a comfort? some allay of sweetness in the bitter waters? Stop not here, nor penuriously cheat yourself of your reversions. You are on vantage ground. Enlarge your speculations, and take in the rest of your friends, as a spark kindles more sparks. Was there one among them, who has not to you proved hollow, false, slippery as water? Begin to think that the relation itself is inconsistent with mortality. That the very idea of friendship, with its component parts, as honour, fidelity, steadiness, exists but in your single bosom. Image yourself to yourself, as the only possible friend in a world incapable of that communion. Now the gloom thickens. The little star of self-love twinkles, that is to encourage you through deeper glooms than this. You are not yet at the half point of your elevation. You are not yet, believe me, half sulky enough. Adverting to the world in general, (as these circles in the mind will spread to infinity) reflect with what strange injustice you have been treated in quarters where, (setting gratitude and the expectation of friendly returns aside as chimeras,) you pretended no claim beyond justice, the naked due of all men. Think the very idea of right and fit fled from the earth, or your breast the solitary receptacle of it, till you have swelled yourself into at least one hemisphere; the other being the vast Arabia Stony of your friends and the world aforesaid. To grow bigger every moment in your own conceit, and the world to lessen: to deify yourself at the expense of your species; to judge the world—this is the acme and supreme point of your mystery—these the true PLEASURES of SULKINESS. We profess no more of this grand secret than what ourself experimented on one rainy afternoon in the last week, sulking in our study. We had proceeded to the penultimate point, at which the true adept seldom stops, where the consideration of benefit forgot is about to merge in the meditation of general injustice—when a knock at the door was followed by the entrance of the very friend, whose not seeing of us in the morning, (for we will now confess the case our own), an accidental oversight, had given rise to so much agreeable generalization! To mortify us still more, and take down the whole flattering superstructure which pride had piled upon neglect, he had brought in his hand the identical S———, in whose favour we had suspected him of the contumacy. Asserverations were needless, where the frank manner of them both was convictive of the injurious nature of the suspicion. We fancied that they perceived our embarrassment; but were too proud, or something else, to confess to the secret of it. . . .

THE OLD FAMILIAR FACES

Where are they gone, the old familiar faces?

I had a mother, but she died, and left me,
Died prematurely in a day of horrors—
All, all are gone, the old familiar faces.

I have had playmates, I have had companions,
In my days of childhood, in my joyful school-days—
All, all are gone, the old familiar faces.

I have been laughing, I have been carousing,
Drinking late, sitting late, with my bosom cronies—
All, all are gone, the old familiar faces.

I loved a love once, fairest among women.
Closed are her doors on me, I must not see her—
All, all are gone, the old familiar faces.

I have a friend, a kinder friend has no man.
Like an ingrate, I left my friend abruptly;
Left him, to muse on the old familiar faces.

Ghost-like, I paced round the haunts of my childhood.
Earth seem'd a desert I was bound to traverse,
Seeking to find the old familiar faces.

Friend of my bosom, thou more than a brother!
Why wert not thou born in my father's dwelling?
So might we talk of the old familiar faces.

For some they have died, and some they have left me,
And some are taken from me; all are departed;
All, all are gone, the old familiar faces.

PART VI

THE BIBLE

Greater love hath no man than this,
that a man lay down his life for his friends.

—John 15:13

THE BOOK OF RUTH

Chapter 1

Now it came to pass in the days when the judges ruled, that there was a famine in the land. And a certain man of Beth-lehem-judah went to sojourn in the country of Moab, he, and his wife, and his two sons. And the name of the man was Elimelech, and the name of his wife Naomi, and the name of his two sons Mahlon and Chilion, Ephrathites of Beth-lehem-judah. And they came into the country of Moab, and continued there. And Elimelech Naomi's husband died; and she was left, and her two sons. And they took them wives of the women of Moab; the name of the one was Orpah, and the name of the other Ruth: and they dwelled there about ten years. And Mahlon and Chilion died also both of them; and the woman was left of her two sons and her husband.

Then she arose with her daughters-in-law, that she might return from the country of Moab: for she had heard in the country of Moab how that the LORD had visited his people in giving them bread. Wherefore she went forth out of the place where she was, and her two daughters-in-law with her; and they went on the way to return unto the land of Judah. And Naomi said unto her two daughters-in-law, "Go, return each to her mother's house: the LORD deal kindly with you, as ye have dealt with the dead, and with me. The LORD grant you that ye may find rest, each of you in the house of her husband." Then she kissed them; and they lifted up their voice, and wept.

And they said unto her, "Surely we will return with thee unto thy people." And Naomi said, "Turn again, my daughters: why will ye go with me? are there yet any more sons in my womb, that they may be your husbands? Turn again, my daughters, go your way; for I am too old to have an husband. If I should say, I have hope, if I should have an husband also to night, and should also bear sons; would ye tarry for them till they were grown? would ye stay for them from having husbands? nay, my daughters; for it grieveth me much for your sakes that the hand of the LORD is gone out against me."

And they lifted up their voice, and wept again: and Orpah kissed her mother-in-law; but Ruth clave unto her. And she said, "Behold, thy sister-in-law-is gone back unto her people, and unto her gods: return thou after thy sister-in-law." And Ruth said, "Intreat me not to leave thee, or to return from following after thee: for whither thou goest, I will go; and where thou lodgest, I will lodge: thy people shall be my people, and thy God my God: where thou diest, will I die, and there will I be buried: the LORD do so to me, and more also, if aught but death part thee and me." When she saw that she was steadfastly minded to go with her, then she left speaking unto her.

So they two went until they came to Beth-lehem. And it came to pass, when they were come to Beth-lehem, that all the city was moved about them, and they said, "Is this Naomi?" And she said unto them, "Call me not Naomi, call me Mara: for the Almighty hath dealt very bitterly with me. I went out full, and the LORD hath brought me home again empty: why then call ye me Naomi, seeing the LORD hath testified against me, and the Almighty hath afflicted me?" So Naomi returned, and Ruth the Moabitess, her daughter-in-law, with her, which returned out of the country of Moab: and they came to Beth-lehem in the beginning of barley harvest.

Chapter 2

And Naomi had a kinsman of her husband's, a mighty man of wealth, of the family of Elimelech; and his name was Boaz.

And Ruth the Moabitess said unto Naomi, "Let me now go to the field, and glean ears of corn after him in whose sight I shall find grace." And she said unto her, "Go, my daughter." And she went, and came, and gleaned in the field after the reapers: and her hap was to light on a part of the field belonging unto Boaz, who was of the kindred of Elimelech.

And, behold, Boaz came from Beth-lehem, and said unto the reapers, "The LORD be with you." And they answered him, "The LORD bless thee." Then said Boaz unto his servant that was set over the reapers, "Whose damsel is this?" And the servant that was set over the reapers answered and said, "It is the Moabitish damsel that came back with Naomi out of the country of Moab: and she said, 'I pray you, let me glean and gather after the reapers among the sheaves': so she came, and hath continued even from the morning until now, that she tarried a little in the house." Then said Boaz unto Ruth, "Hearest thou not, my daughter? Go not to glean in another field, neither go from hence, but abide here fast by my maidens: let thine eyes be on the field that they do reap, and go thou after them: have I not charged the young men that they shall not touch thee? and when thou art athirst, go unto the vessels, and drink of that which the young men have drawn." Then she fell on her face, and bowed herself to the ground, and said unto him, "Why have I found grace in thine eyes, that thou shouldest take knowledge of me, seeing I am a stranger?"

And Boaz answered and said unto her, "It hath fully been shewed me, all that thou hast done unto thy mother-in-law since the death of thine husband: and how thou hast left thy father and thy mother, and the land of thy nativity, and art come unto a people which thou knewest not heretofore. The LORD recompense thy work, and a full reward be given thee of the LORD God of Israel, under whose wings thou art come to trust." Then she said, "Let me find favour in thy sight, my lord; for that thou hast comforted me, and for that thou hast spoken friendly unto thine handmaid, though I be not like unto one of thine handmaidens." And Boaz said unto her, "At mealtime come thou hither, and eat of the bread, and dip thy morsel in the vinegar." And she sat beside the reapers: and he reached her parched corn, and she did eat, and was sufficed, and left. And when she was risen up to glean, Boaz commanded his young men, saying, "Let her glean even among the sheaves, and reproach her not: and let fall also some of the handfuls of purpose for her, and leave them, that she may glean them, and rebuke her not." So she gleaned in the field until even, and beat out that she had gleaned: and it was about an ephah of barley. And she took it up, and went into the city: and her mother-in-law saw what she had gleaned: and she brought forth, and gave to her that she had reserved after she was sufficed. And her mother-in-law said unto her, "Where hast thou gleaned to day? and where wroughtest thou? blessed be he that did take knowledge of thee." And she shewed her mother-in-law with whom she had wrought, and said, "The man's name with whom I wrought to day is Boaz." And Naomi said unto her daughter-in-law, "Blessed be he of the LORD, who hath not left off his kindness to the living and to the dead." And Naomi said unto her, "The man is near of kin unto us, one of our next kinsmen." And Ruth the Moabitess said, "He said unto me also, 'Thou shalt keep fast by my young men, until they have ended all my harvest.' " And Naomi said unto Ruth her daughter-in-law, "It is good, my daughter, that thou go out with his maidens, that they meet thee not in any other field." So she kept fast by the maidens of Boaz to glean unto the end of barley harvest and of wheat harvest; and dwelt with her mother-in-law.

Chapter 3

Then Naomi her mother-in-law said unto her, "My daughter, shall I not seek rest for thee, that it may be well with thee? And now is not Boaz of our kindred, with whose maidens thou wast? Behold, he winnoweth barley to night in the threshing floor. Wash thyself therefore, and anoint thee, and put thy raiment upon thee, and get thee down to the floor: but make not thyself known unto the man, until he shall have done eating and drinking. And it shall be, when he lieth down, that thou shalt mark the place where he shall lie, and thou shalt go in, and uncover his feet, and lay thee down; and he will tell thee what thou shalt do." And she said unto her, "All that thou sayest unto me I will do."

And she went down unto the floor, and did according to all that her mother-in-law bade her. And when Boaz had eaten and drunk, and his heart was merry, he went to lie down at the end of the heap of corn: and she came softly, and uncovered his feet, and laid her down. And it came to pass at midnight, that the man was afraid, and turned himself: and, behold, a woman lay at his feet. And he said, "Who art thou?" And she answered, "I am Ruth thine handmaid: spread therefore thy skirt over thine handmaid; for thou art a near kinsman."

And he said, "Blessed be thou of the LORD, my daughter: for thou hast shewed more kindness in the latter end than at the beginning, inasmuch as thou followedst not young men, whether poor or rich. And now, my daughter, fear not; I will do to thee all that thou requirest: for all the city of my people doth know that thou art a virtuous woman. And now it is true that I am thy near kinsman: howbeit there is a kinsman nearer than I. Tarry this night, and it shall be in the morning, that if he will perform unto thee the part of a kinsman, well; let him do the kinsman's part: but if he will not do the part of a kinsman to thee, then will I do the part of a kinsman to thee, as the LORD liveth: lie down until the morning."

And she lay at his feet until the morning: and she rose up before one could know another. And he said, "Let it not be known that a woman came into the floor." Also he said, "Bring the veil that thou hast upon thee, and hold it." And when she held it, he measured six measures of barley, and laid it on her: and she went into the city. And when she came to her mother-in-law, she said, "Who art thou, my daughter?" And she told her all that the man had done to her. And she said, "These six measures of barley gave he me; for he said to me, 'Go not empty unto thy mother-in-law.' " Then said she, "Sit still, my daughter, until thou know how the matter will fall: for the man will not be in rest, until he have finished the thing this day."

Chapter 4

Then went Boaz up to the gate, and sat him down there: and, behold, the kinsman of whom Boaz spake came by; unto whom he said, "Ho, such a one! turn aside, sit down here." And he turned aside, and sat down. And he took ten men of the elders of the city, and said, "Sit ye down here." And they sat down. And he said unto the kinsman, "Naomi, that is come again out of the country of Moab, selleth a parcel of land, which was our brother Elimelech's: and I thought to advertise thee, saying, Buy it before the inhabitants, and before the elders of my people. If thou wilt redeem it, redeem it: but if thou wilt not redeem it, then tell me, that I may know: for there is none to redeem it beside thee; and I am after thee." And he said, "I will redeem it."

Then said Boaz, "What day thou buyest the field of the hand of Naomi, thou must buy it also of Ruth the Moabitess, the wife of the dead, to raise up the name of the dead upon his inheritance." And the kinsman said, "I cannot redeem it for myself, lest I mar mine own inheritance: redeem thou my right to thyself; for I cannot redeem it." Now this was the manner in former time in Israel concerning redeeming and concerning changing, for to confirm all things; a man plucked off his shoe, and gave it to his neighbour: and this was a testimony in Israel. Therefore the kinsman said unto Boaz, "Buy it for thee." So he drew off his shoe.

And Boaz said unto the elders, and unto all the people, "Ye are witnesses this day, that I have bought all that was Elimelech's, and all that was Chilion's and Mahlon's, of the hand of Naomi. Moreover Ruth the Moabitess, the wife of Mahlon, have I purchased to be my wife, to raise up the name of the dead upon his inheritance, that the name of the dead be not cut off from among his brethren, and from the gate of his place: ye are witnesses this day." And all the people that were in the gate, and the elders, said, "We are witnesses. The LORD make the woman that is come into thine house like Rachel and like Leah, which two did build the house of Israel: and do thou worthily in Ephratah, and be famous in Beth-lehem: and let thy house be like the house of Pharez, whom Tamar bare unto Judah, of the seed which the LORD shall give thee of this young woman." So Boaz took Ruth, and she was his wife: and when he went in unto her, the LORD gave her conception, and she bare a son. And the women said unto Naomi, "Blessed be the LORD, which hath not left thee this day without a kinsman, that his name may be famous in Israel. And he shall be unto thee a restorer of thy life, and a nourisher of thine old age: for thy daughter-in-law, which loveth thee, which is better to thee than seven sons, hath borne him." And Naomi took the child, and laid it in her bosom, and became nurse unto it. And the women her neighbours gave it a name, saying, "There is a son born to Naomi"; and they called his name Obed: he is the father of Jesse, the father of David.

Now these are the generations of Pharez: Pharez begat Hezron, and Hezron begat Ram, and Ram begat Amminadab, and Amminadab begat Nahshon, and Nahshon begat Salmon, and Salmon begat Boaz, and Boaz begat Obed, and Obed begat Jesse, and Jesse begat David.

THE BOOK OF SAMUEL

BOOK 1

Chapter 18

And it came to pass, when he had made an end of speaking unto Saul, that the soul of Jonathan was knit with the soul of David, and Jonathan loved him as his own soul. And Saul took him that day, and would let him go no more home to his father's house. Then Jonathan and David made a covenant, because he loved him as his own soul. And Jonathan stripped himself of the robe that was upon him, and gave it to David, and his garments, even to his sword, and to his bow, and to his girdle. And David went out whithersoever Saul sent him, and behaved himself wisely: and Saul set him over the men of war, and he was accepted in the sight of all the people, and also in the sight of Saul's servants.

And it came to pass as they came, when David was returned from the slaughter of the Philistine, that the women came out of all cities of Israel, singing and dancing, to meet king Saul, with tabrets, with joy, and with instruments of musick. And the women answered one another as they played, and said,

> "Saul hath slain his thousands,
> And David his ten thousands."

And Saul was very wroth, and the saying displeased him; and he said, "They have ascribed unto David ten thousands, and to me they have ascribed but thousands: and what can he have more but the kingdom?" And Saul eyed David from that day and forward.

And it came to pass on the morrow, that the evil spirit from God came upon Saul, and he prophesied in the midst of the house: and David played with his hand, as at other times: and there was a javelin in Saul's hand. And Saul cast the javelin; for he said, "I will smite David even to the wall with it." And David avoided out of his presence twice. And Saul was afraid of David, because the LORD was with him, and was departed from Saul.

. . . And Saul was yet the more afraid of David; and Saul became David's enemy continually.

Then the princes of the Philistines went forth: and it came to pass, after they went forth, that David behaved himself more wisely than all the servants of Saul; so that his name was much set by.

Chapter 19

And Saul spake to Jonathan his son, and to all his servants, that they should kill David. But Jonathan Saul's son delighted much in David: and Jonathan told David, saying, "Saul my father seeketh to kill thee: now therefore, I pray thee, take heed to thyself until the morning, and abide in a secret place, and hide thyself: and I will go out and stand beside my father in the field where thou art, and I will commune with my father of thee; and what I see, that I will tell thee." And Jonathan spake good of David unto Saul his father, and said unto him, "Let not the king sin against his servant, against David; because he hath not sinned against thee, and because his works have been to thee-ward very good: for he did put his life in his hand, and slew the Philistine, and the LORD wrought a great salvation for all Israel: thou sawest it, and didst rejoice: wherefore then wilt thou sin against innocent blood, to slay David without a cause?" And Saul hearkened unto the voice of Jonathan: and Saul sware, "As the LORD liveth, he shall not be slain." And Jonathan called David, and Jonathan shewed him all those things. And Jonathan brought David to Saul, and he was in his presence, as in times past.

And there was war again: and David went out, and fought with the Philistines, and slew them with a great slaughter; and they fled from him. And the evil spirit from the LORD was upon Saul, as he sat in his house with his javelin in his hand: and David played with his hand. And Saul sought to smite David even to the wall with the javelin; but he slipped away out of Saul's presence, and he smote the javelin into the wall: and David fled, and escaped that night. Saul also sent messengers unto David's house, to watch him, and to slay him in the morning: and Michal David's wife told him, saying, "If thou save not thy life to night, to morrow thou shalt be slain." So Michal let David down through a window: and he went, and fled, and escaped.

Chapter 20

And David fled from Naioth in Ramah, and came and said before Jonathan, "What have I done? what is mine iniquity? and what is my sin before thy father, that he seeketh my life?" And he said unto him, "God forbid; thou shalt not die: behold, my father will do nothing either great or small, but that he will shew it me: and why should my father hide this thing from me? it is not so." And David sware moreover, and said, "Thy father certainly knoweth that I have found grace in thine eyes; and he saith, 'Let not Jonathan know this, lest he be grieved': but truly as the LORD liveth, and as thy soul liveth, there is but a step between me and death." Then said Jonathan unto David, "Whatsoever thy soul desireth, I will even do it for thee." And David said unto Jonathan, "Behold, to morrow is the new moon, and I should not fail to sit with the king at meat: but let me go, that I may hide myself in the field unto the third day at even. If thy father at all miss me, then say, 'David earnestly asked leave of me that he might run to Beth-lehem his city: for there is a yearly sacrifice there for all the family.' If he say thus, 'It is well'; thy servant shall have peace: but if he be very wroth, then be sure that evil is determined by him. Therefore thou shalt deal kindly with thy servant; for thou hast brought thy servant into a covenant of the LORD with thee: notwithstanding, if there be in me iniquity, slay me thyself; for why shouldest thou bring me to thy father?" And Jonathan said, "Far be it from thee: for if I knew certainly that evil were determined by my father to come upon thee, then would not I tell it thee?" Then said David to Jonathan, "Who shall tell me? or what if thy father answer thee roughly?" And Jonathan said unto David, "Come, and let us go out into the field." And they went out both of them into the field.

And Jonathan said unto David, "O LORD God of Israel, when I have sounded my father about to morrow any time, or the third day, and, behold, if there be good toward David, and I then send not unto thee, and shew it thee; the LORD do so and much more to Jonathan: but if it please my father to do thee evil, then I will shew it thee, and send thee away, that thou mayest go in peace: and the LORD be with thee, as he hath been with my father. And thou shalt not only while yet I live shew me the kindness of the LORD, that I die not: but also thou shalt not cut off thy kindness from my house for ever: no, not when the LORD hath cut off the enemies of David every one from the face of the earth." So Jonathan made a covenant with the house of David, saying, "Let the LORD even require it at the hand of David's enemies." And Jonathan caused David to swear again, because he loved him: for he loved him as he loved his own soul. Then Jonathan said to David, "To morrow is the new moon: and thou shalt be missed, because thy seat will be empty. And when thou hast stayed three days, then thou shalt go down quickly, and come to the place where thou didst hide thyself when the business was in hand, and shalt remain by the stone Ezel. And I will shoot three arrows on the side thereof, as though I shot at a mark. And, behold, I will send a lad, saying, 'Go, find out the arrows.' If I expressly say unto the lad, 'Behold, the arrows are on this side of thee, take them'; then come thou: for there is peace to thee, and no hurt; as the LORD liveth. But if I say thus unto the young man, 'Behold, the arrows are beyond thee'; go thy way: for the LORD hath sent thee away. And as touching the matter which thou and I have spoken of, behold, the LORD be between thee and me for ever."

So David hid himself in the field: and when the new moon was come, the king sat him down to eat meat. And the king sat upon his seat, as at other times, even upon a seat by the wall: and Jonathan arose, and Abner sat by Saul's side, and David's place was empty. Nevertheless Saul spake not any thing that day: for he thought, "Something hath befallen him, he is not clean; surely he is not clean." And it came to pass on the morrow, which was the second day of the month, that David's place was empty: and Saul said unto Jonathan his son, "Wherefore cometh not the son of Jesse to meat, neither yesterday, nor to day?" And Jonathan answered Saul, "David earnestly asked leave of me to go to Beth-lehem: and he said, 'Let me go, I pray thee; for our family hath a sacrifice in the city; and my brother, he hath commanded me to be there: and now, if I have found favour in thine eyes, let me get away, I pray thee, and see my brethren.' Therefore he cometh not unto the king's table." Then Saul's anger was kindled against Jonathan, and he said unto him, "Thou son of the perverse rebellious woman, do not I know that thou hast chosen the son of Jesse to thine own confusion, and unto the confusion of thy mother's nakedness? For as long as the son of Jesse liveth upon the ground, thou shalt not be established, nor thy kingdom. Wherefore now send and fetch him unto me, for he shall surely die." And Jonathan answered Saul his father, and said unto him, "Wherefore shall he be slain? what hath he done?" And Saul cast a javelin at him to smite him: whereby Jonathan knew that it was determined of his father to slay David. So Jonathan arose from the table in fierce anger, and did eat no meat the second day of the month: for he was grieved for David, because his father had done him shame.

And it came to pass in the morning, that Jonathan went out into the field at the time appointed with David, and a little lad with him. And he said unto his lad, "Run, find out now the arrows which I shoot." And as the lad ran, he shot an arrow beyond him. And when the lad was come to the place of the arrow which Jonathan had shot, Jonathan cried after the lad, and said, "Is not the arrow beyond thee?" And Jonathan cried after the lad, "Make speed, haste, stay not." And Jonathan's lad gathered up the arrows, and came to his master. But the lad knew not any thing: only Jonathan and David knew the matter. And Jonathan gave his artillery unto his lad, and said unto him, "Go, carry them to the city." And as soon as the lad was gone, David arose out of a place toward the south, and fell on his face to the ground, and bowed himself three times: and they kissed one another, and wept one with another, until David exceeded. And Jonathan said to David, "Go in peace, forasmuch as we have sworn both of us in the name of the LORD, saying, 'The LORD be between me and thee, and between my seed and thy seed for ever.' " And he arose and departed: and Jonathan went into the city. . . .

Chapter 23

. . . And David abode in the wilderness in strong holds, and remained in a mountain in the wilderness of Ziph. And Saul sought him every day, but God delivered him not into his hand. And David saw that Saul was come out to seek his life: and David was in the wilderness of Ziph in a wood. And Jonathan Saul's son arose, and went to David into the wood, and strengthened his hand in God. And he said unto him, "Fear not: for the hand of Saul my father shall not find thee; and thou shalt be king over Israel, and I shall be next unto thee; and that also Saul my father knoweth." And they two made a covenant before the LORD: and David abode in the wood, and Jonathan went to his house. . . .

Chapter 31

Now the Philistines fought against Israel: and the men of Israel fled from before the Philistines, and fell down slain in mount Gilboa. And the Philistines followed hard upon Saul and upon his sons; and the Philistines slew Jonathan, and Abinadab, and Malchishua, Saul's sons. And the battle went sore against Saul, and the archers hit him; and he was sore wounded of the archers. Then said Saul unto his armourbearer, "Draw thy sword, and thrust me through therewith; lest these uncircumcised come and thrust me through, and abuse me." But his armourbearer would not; for he was sore afraid. Therefore Saul took a sword, and fell upon it. And when his armourbearer saw that Saul was dead, he fell likewise upon his sword, and died with him. So Saul died, and his three sons, and his armourbearer, and all his men, that same day together. . . .

BOOK 2

Chapter 1

Now it came to pass after the death of Saul, when David was returned from the slaughter of the Amalekites, and David had abode two days in Ziklag; it came even to pass on the third day, that, behold, a man came out of the camp from Saul with his clothes rent, and earth upon his head:

and so it was, when he came to David, that he fell to the earth, and did obeisance. And David said unto him, "From whence comest thou?" And he said unto him, "Out of the camp of Israel am I escaped." And David said unto him, "How went the matter? I pray thee, tell me." And he answered, "That the people are fled from the battle, and many of the people also are fallen and dead; and Saul and Jonathan his son are dead also." And David said unto the young man that told him, "How knowest thou that Saul and Jonathan his son be dead?" And the young man that told him said, "As I happened by chance upon mount Gilboa, behold, Saul leaned upon his spear; and, lo, the chariots and horsemen followed hard after him. And when he looked behind him, he saw me, and called unto me. And I answered, Here am I. And he said unto me, 'Who art thou?' And I answered him, I am an Amalekite. He said unto me again, 'Stand, I pray thee, upon me, and slay me: for anguish is come upon me, because my life is yet whole in me.' So I stood upon him, and slew him, because I was sure that he could not live after that he was fallen: and I took the crown that was upon his head, and the bracelet that was on his arm, and have brought them hither unto my lord." Then David took hold on his clothes, and rent them; and likewise all the men that were with him: and they mourned, and wept, and fasted until even, for Saul, and for Jonathan his son, and for the people of the Lord, and for the house of Israel; because they were fallen by the sword. And David said unto the young man that told him, "Whence art thou?" And he answered, "I am the son of a stranger, an Amalekite." And David said unto him, "How wast thou not afraid to stretch forth thine hand to destroy the Lord's anointed?" And David called one of the young men, and said, "Go near, and fall upon him." And he smote him that he died. And David said unto him, "Thy blood be upon thy head; for thy mouth hath testified against thee, saying, 'I have slain the Lord's anointed.' "

And David lamented with this lamentation over Saul and over Jonathan his son: (also he bade them teach the children of Judah the use of the bow: behold, it is written in the book of Jasher).

"The beauty of Israel is slain upon thy high places:
How are the mighty fallen!
Tell it not in Gath,
Publish it not in the streets of Askelon;
Lest the daughters of the Philistines rejoice,
Lest the daughters of the uncircumcised triumph.
Ye mountains of Gilboa, let there be no dew,
Neither let there be rain, upon you, nor fields of offerings:
For there the shield of the mighty is vilely cast away,
The shield of Saul, as though he had not been anointed with oil.

From the blood of the slain,
From the fat of the mighty,
The bow of Jonathan turned not back,
And the sword of Saul returned not empty.
Saul and Jonathan were lovely and pleasant in their lives,
And in their death they were not divided:
They were swifter than eagles,
They were stronger than lions.
Ye daughters of Israel, weep over Saul,
Who clothed you in scarlet, with other delights,
Who put on ornaments of gold upon your apparel.
How are the mighty fallen in the midst of the battle!
O Jonathan, thou wast slain in thine high places.
I am distressed for thee, my brother Jonathan:
Very pleasant hast thou been unto me:
Thy love to me was wonderful,
Passing the love of women.
How are the mighty fallen,
And the weapons of war perished!"

Chapter 4

. . . And Jonathan, Saul's son, had a son that was lame of his feet. He was five years old when the tidings came of Saul and Jonathan out of Jezreel, and his nurse took him up, and fled: and it came to pass, as she made haste to flee, that he fell, and became lame. And his name was Mephibosheth. . . .

Chapter 9

And David said, "Is there yet any that is left of the house of Saul, that I may shew him kindness for Jonathan's sake?" And there was of the house of Saul a servant whose name was Ziba. And when they had called him unto David, the king said unto him. . . , "Is there not yet any of the house of Saul, that I may shew the kindness of God unto him?" And Ziba said unto the king, "Jonathan hath yet a son, which is lame on his feet." And the king said unto him, "Where is he?" And Ziba said unto the king, "Behold, he is in the house of Machir, the son of Ammiel, in Lo-debar." Then king David sent, and fetched him out of the house of Machir, the son of Ammiel, from Lo-debar. Now when Mephibosheth, the son of Jonathan, the son of Saul, was come unto David, he fell on his face, and did reverence. And David said, "Mephibosheth." And he answered, "Behold thy servant!" And David said unto him, "Fear not: for I will surely shew thee kindness for Jonathan thy father's sake, and will restore thee all the land of Saul thy father; and thou shalt eat bread at my table continually." And he bowed himself, and said, "What is thy servant, that thou shouldest look upon such a dead dog as I am?" Then the king called to Ziba, Saul's servant, and said unto him, "I have given unto thy master's son all that pertained to Saul and to all his house. Thou therefore, and thy sons, and thy servants, shall till the land for him, and thou shalt bring in the fruits, that thy master's son may have food to eat: but Mephibosheth thy master's son shall eat bread alway at my table." Now Ziba had fifteen sons and twenty servants. Then said Ziba unto the king, "According to all that my lord the king hath commanded his servant, so shall thy servant do." "As for Mephibosheth," said the king, "he shall eat at my table, as one of the king's sons." And Mephibosheth had a young son, whose name was Micha. And all that dwelt in the house of Ziba were servants unto Mephibosheth. So Mephibosheth dwelt in Jerusalem: for he did eat continually at the king's table; and was lame on both his feet.

PART VII

SHAKESPEARE

Two lovely berries moulded on one stem:
So with two seeming bodies, but one heart.

—*A Midsummer Night's Dream*

WILLIAM SHAKESPEARE

Sonnet 29

When in disgrace with Fortune and men's eyes,
I all alone beweep my outcast state,
And trouble deaf heav'n with my bootless cries,
And look upon myself and curse my fate,
Wishing me like to one more rich in hope,
Featured like him, like him with friends possessed,
Desiring this man's art, and that man's scope,
With what I most enjoy contented least;
Yet in these thoughts myself almost despising,
Haply I think on thee, and then my state,
Like to the lark at break of day arising
From sullen earth, sings hymns at heaven's gate;
    For thy sweet love rememb'red such wealth brings,
    That then I scorn to change my state with kings.

Sonnet 30

When to the sessions of sweet silent thought
I summon up remembrance of things past,
I sigh the lack of many a thing I sought,
And with old woes new wail my dear time's waste.
Then can I drown an eye, unused to flow,
For precious friends hid in death's dateless night,
And weep afresh love's long since cancelled woe,
And moan th' expense of many a vanished sight.
Then can I grieve at grievances foregone,
And heavily from woe to woe tell o'er
The sad account of fore-bemoanèd moan,

Which I new pay as if not paid before.
But if the while I think on thee, dear friend,
All losses are restored, and sorrows end.

SONNET 32

If thou survive my well-contented day,
When that churl death my bones with dust shall cover,
And shalt by fortune once more re-survey
These poor rude lines of thy deceasèd lover,
Compare them with the bett'ring of the time,
And though they be outstripped by every pen
Reserve them for my love, not for their rhyme,
Exceeded by the height of happier men.
O then vouchsafe me but this loving thought:
Had my friend's muse grown with this growing age,
A dearer birth than this his love had brought
To march in ranks of better equipage.
    But since he died, and poets better prove,
    Theirs for their style I'll read, his for his love.

SONNET 37

As a decrepit father takes delight
To see his active child do deeds of youth,
So I, made lame by fortune's dearest spite,
Take all my comfort of thy worth and truth.
For whether beauty, birth, or wealth, or wit,
Or any of these all, or all, or more,
Entitled in thy parts do crownèd sit,
I make my love engrafted to this store.
So then I am not lame, poor, nor despised,
Whilst that this shadow doth such substance give,
That I in thy abundance am sufficed,
And by a part of all thy glory live.
    Look what is best, that best I wish in thee.
    This wish I have, then ten times happy me.

SONNET 71

No longer mourn for me when I am dead
Than you shall hear the surly sullen bell
Give warning to the world that I am fled
From this vile world with vildest worms to dwell.
Nay, if you read this line, remember not
The hand that writ it, for I love you so,
That I in your sweet thoughts would be forgot,
If thinking on me then should make you woe.
O if, I say, you look upon this verse,
When I, perhaps, compounded am with clay,
Do not so much as my poor name rehearse,
But let your love ev'n with my life decay,
    Lest the wise world should look into your moan,
    And mock you with me after I am gone.

SONNET 104

To me, fair friend, you never can be old,
For as you were when first your eye I eyed,
Such seems your beauty still. Three winters cold
Have from the forests shook three summers' pride,
Three beauteous springs to yellow autumn turned
In process of the seasons have I seen,
Three April pérfumes in three hot Junes burncd,
Since first I saw you fresh, which yet are green.
Ah yet doth beauty, like a dial hand,
Steal from his figure, and no pace perceived;
So your sweet hue, which methinks still doth stand,
Hath motion, and mine eye may be deceived:
    For fear of which, hear this, thou age unbred,
    Ere you were born was beauty's summer dead.

SONNET 116

Let me not to the marriage of true minds
Admit impediments. Love is not love

Which alters when it alteration finds,
Or bends with the remover to remove.
O no, it is an ever-fixèd mark
That looks on tempests and is never shaken;
It is the star to every wand'ring bark,
Whose worth's unknown, although his height be taken.
Love's not time's fool, though rosy lips and cheeks
Within his bending sickle's compass come.
Love alters not with his brief hours and weeks,
But bears it out ev'n to the edge of doom.
    If this be error and upon me proved,
    I never writ, nor no man ever loved.

From A Midsummer Night's Dream

(Helena and Hermia have been friends since childhood and are now apparently
in competition for the same husband.)

HELENA.   Lo! She is one of this confederacy.
    Now I perceive, they have conjoin'd all three
    To fashion this false sport, in spite of me.
    Injurious Hermia, most ungrateful maid!
    Have you conspir'd, have you with these contriv'd
    To bait me with this foul derision?
    Is all the counsel that we two have shar'd,
    The sisters' vows, the hours that we have spent,
    When we have chid the hasty-footed time
    For parting us—O, is all forgot?
    All school-days friendship, childhood innocence?
    We, Hermia, like two artificial gods,
    Have with our needles created both one flower,
    Both on one sampler, sitting on one cushion,
    Both warbling of one song, both in one key,
    As if our hands, our sides, voices, and minds
    Had been incorporate. So we grew together,
    Like to a double cherry, seeming parted,
    But yet an union in partition,
    Two lovely berries moulded on one stem;
    So with two seeming bodies, but one heart,
    Two of the first, [like] coats in heraldry,
    Due but to one, and crowned with one crest.

And will you rent our ancient love asunder,
To join with men in scorning your poor friend?
It is not friendly, 'tis not maidenly.
Our sex, as well as I, may chide you for it,
Though I alone do feel the injury.

[3.2, ll. 192–219]

From THE MERCHANT OF VENICE

(Portia is the newly married wife of Bassanio, whose friend is Antonio.)

PORTIA.   . . . for in companions
That do converse and waste the time together,
Whose souls do bear an egall yoke of love,
There must be needs a like proportion
Of lineaments, of manners, and of spirit;
Which makes me think that this Antonio,
Being the bosom lover of my lord,
Must needs be like my lord.

[3.4., ll. 11–18]

(Though he is eventually rescued, Antonio believes he is about to have a pound
of his own flesh removed by Shylock the Jew as a penalty for defaulting on a loan
that he took out for Bassanio.)

ANTONIO.   But little; I am arm'd and well prepar'd.
Give me your hand, Bassanio, fare you well.
Grieve not that I am fall'n to this for you;
For herein Fortune shows herself more kind
Than is her custom. It is still her use
To let the wretched man outlive his wealth,
To view with hollow eye and wrinkled brow
An age of poverty; from which ling'ring penance
Of such misery doth she cut me off.
Commend me to your honorable wife,
Tell her the process of Antonio's end,
Say how I lov'd you, speak me fair in death;
And when the tale is told, bid her be judge
Whether Bassanio had not once a love.
Repent but you that you shall lose your friend.
And he repents not that he pays your debt;

For if the Jew do cut but deep enough,
I'll pay it instantly with all my heart.
BASS.   Antonio, I am married to a wife
Which is as dear to me as life itself,
But life itself, my wife, and all the world,
Are not with me esteem'd above thy life.
I would lose all, ay, sacrifice them all
Here to this devil, to deliver you.

[4.1, ll. 264–87]

From 1 HENRY IV

(Hal, Prince of Wales, is heir to the throne; Falstaff is his bawdy and—despite
his title—emphatically unaristocratic drinking buddy.)

Enter PRINCE OF WALES *and* SIR JOHN FALSTAFF.
FAL.   Now, Hal, what time of day is it, lad?
PRINCE.   Thou art so fat-witted with drinking of old sack, and unbut-
toning thee after supper, and sleeping upon benches after noon,
that thou hast forgotten to demand that truly which thou wouldest
truly know. What a devil hast thou to do with the time of the day?
unless hours were cups of sack, and minutes capons, and clocks the
tongues of bawds, and dials the signs of leaping-houses, and the
blessed sun himself a fair hot wench in flame-color'd taffata; I see
no reason why thou shouldst be so superfluous to demand the time
of the day. . . .
FAL.   Thou hast the most unsavory [similes] and art indeed the most
comparative, rascalliest, sweet young prince.

[1.2, ll. 1–12, 79–81]

FAL.   I would your Grace would take me with you. Whom means your
Grace?
PRINCE.   That villainous abominable misleader of youth, Falstaff, that
old white-bearded Sathan.
FAL.   My lord, the man I know.
PRINCE.   I know thou dost.
FAL.   But to say I know more harm in him than in myself, were to say
more than I know. That he is old, the more the pity, his white hairs
do witness it, but that he is, saving your reverence, a whoremaster,
that I utterly deny. If sack and sugar be a fault, God help the
wicked! If to be old and merry be a sin, then many an old host that

I know is damn'd. If to be fat be to be hated, then Pharaoh's [lean] kine are to be lov'd. No, my good lord, banish Peto, banish Bardolph, banish Poins, but for sweet Jack Falstaff, kind Jack Falstaff, true Jack Falstaff, valiant Jack Falstaff, and therefore more valiant, being as he is old Jack Falstaff, banish not him thy Harry's company, banish not him thy Harry's company—banish plump Jack, and banish all the world.

PRINCE.   I do, I will.

                                                          [2.4, ll. 460–81]

From 2 HENRY IV

(Robert Shallow and Silence, friends and country justices of peace, reminisce about the old days.)

Enter JUSTICE SHALLOW *and* JUSTICE SILENCE, [*meeting;* MOULDY, SHADOW, WART, FEEBLE, BULLCALF, *and* SERVANTS *behind*].

SHAL.   Come on, come on, come on, give me your hand, sir, give me your hand, sir. An early stirrer, by the rood! And how doth my good cousin Silence?

SIL.   Good morrow, good cousin Shallow.

SHAL.   And how doth my cousin, your bedfellow? and your fairest daughter and mine, my goddaughter Ellen?

SIL.   Alas, a black woosel, cousin Shallow!

SHAL.   By yea and no, sir. I dare say my cousin William is become a good scholar. He is at Oxford still, is he not?

SIL.   Indeed, sir, to my cost.

SHAL.   'A must then to the Inns a' Court shortly. I was once of Clement's Inn, where I think they will talk of mad Shallow yet.

SIL.   You were call'd lusty Shallow then, cousin.

SHAL.   By the mass, I was call'd any thing, and I would have done any thing indeed too, and roundly too. There was I, and little John Doit of Staffordshire, and black George Barnes, and Francis Pickbone, and Will Squele, a Cotsole man. You had not four such swingebucklers in all the Inns a' Court again; and I may say to you, we knew where the bona [robas] were and had the best of them all at commandment. Then was Jack Falstaff, now Sir John, a boy, and page to Thomas Mowbray, Duke of Norfolk.

SIL.   This Sir John, cousin, that comes hither anon about soldiers?

SHAL.   The same Sir John, the very same. I see him break Scoggin's head at the court-gate, when 'a was a crack not thus high; and the very same day did I fight with one Samson Stockfish, a fruiterer, behind Gray's Inn. Jesu, Jesu, the mad days that I have spent! And to see how many of my old acquaintance are dead!

SIL. We shall all follow, cousin.

SHAL. Certain, 'tis certain, very sure, very sure. Death, as the Psalmist saith, is certain to all, all shall die. How a good yoke of bullocks at [Stamford] fair?

SIL. By my troth, I was not there.

SHAL. Death is certain. Is old Double of your town living yet?

SIL. Dead, sir.

SHAL. Jesu, Jesu, dead! 'A drew a good bow, and dead! 'A shot a fine shoot. John a' Gaunt lov'd him well, and betted much money on his head. Dead! 'a would have clapp'd i' th' clout at twelvescore, and carried you a forehand shaft a fourteen and fourteen and a half, that it would have done a man's heart good to see. How a score of ewes now?

SIL. Thereafter as they be, a score of good ewes may be worth ten pounds.

SHAL. And is old Double dead?

[3.2, ll. 1–52]

From JULIUS CAESAR

(Caesar's friend and political ally Mark Antony speaks at Caesar's funeral. Caesar was assassinated by Brutus, Cassius, and their followers.)

ANTONY. That I did love thee, Caesar, O, 'tis true;
If then thy spirit look upon us now,
Shall it not grieve thee dearer than thy death,
To see thy Antony making his peace,
Shaking the bloody fingers of thy foes,
Most noble! in the presence of thy corse?
Had I as many eyes as thou hast wounds,
Weeping as fast as they stream forth thy blood,
It would become me better than to close
In terms of friendship with thine enemies.
Pardon me, Julius! Here wast thou bay'd, brave hart,
Here didst thou fall, and here thy hunters stand,
Sign'd in thy spoil, and crimson'd in thy lethe.
O world! thou wast the forest to this hart,
And this indeed, O world, the heart of thee.

How like a deer, strooken by many princes,
Dost thou here lie!

[3.1, ll. 194–210]

(Brutus, who is also speaking at Caesar's funeral, explains why he was persuaded by Cassius to help assassinate his longtime friend.)

BRUTUS.   Be patient till the last. Romans, countrymen, and lovers, hear
me for my cause, and be silent, that you may hear. Believe me for
mine honor, and have respect to mine honor, that you may believe.
Censure me in your wisdom, and awake your senses, that you may
the better judge. If there be any in this assembly, any dear friend
of Caesar's, to him I say, that Brutus' love to Caesar was no less
than his. If then that friend demand why Brutus rose against
Caesar, this is my answer: Not that I love'd Caesar less, but that
I lov'd Rome more. Had you rather Caesar were living, and die all
slaves, than that Caesar were dead, to live all freemen? As Caesar
lov'd me, I weep for him; as he was fortunate, I rejoice at it; as he
was valiant, I honor him; but, as he was ambitious, I slew him.
There is tears for his love; joy for his fortune; honor for his valor;
and death for his ambition. Who is here so base that would be a
bondman? If any, speak, for him have I offended. Who is here so
rude that would not be a Roman? If any, speak, for him have I
offended. Who is here so vile that will not love his country? If any,
speak, for him have I offended. I pause for a reply.

[3.2, ll. 13–34]

(Realizing that their side is losing the battle to consolidate power, Brutus and Cassius quarrel.)

BRUTUS.   You have done that you should be sorry for.
There is no terror, Cassius, in your threats;
For I am arm'd so strong in honesty
That they pass by me as the idle wind,
Which I respect not. I did send to you
For certain sums of gold, which you denied me;
For I can raise no money by vile means.
By heaven, I had rather coin my heart
And drop my blood for drachmaes than to wring
From the hard hands of peasants their vile trash
By any indirection. I did send
To you for gold to pay my legions,
Which you denied me. Was that done like Cassius?

Should I have answer'd Caius Cassius so?
When Marcus Brutus grows so covetous
To lock such rascal counters from his friends,
Be ready, gods, with all your thunderbolts,
Dash him to pieces!

CASSIUS.   I denied you not.

BRU.   You did.

CAS.   I did not. He was but a fool that brought
My answer back. Brutus hath riv'd my heart.
A friend should bear his friend's infirmities;
But Brutus makes mine greater than they are.

BRU.   I do not, till you practice them on me.

CAS.   You love me not.

BRU.   I do not like your faults.

CAS.   A friendly eye could never see such faults.

BRU.   A flatterer's would not, though they do appear
As huge as high Olympus.

CAS.   Come, Antony, and young Octavius, come,
Revenge yourselves alone on Cassius,
For Cassius is a-weary of the world;
Hated by one he loves, brav'd by his brother,
Check'd like a bondman, all his faults observ'd,
Set in a note-book, learn'd, and conn'd by rote,
To cast into my teeth. O, I could weep
My spirit from mine eyes! There is my dagger,
And here my naked breast; within, a heart
Dearer than Pluto's mine, richer than gold:
If that thou be'st a Roman, take it forth.
I, that denied thee gold, will give my heart:
Strike as thou didst at Caesar; for I know,
When thou didst hate him worst, thou lovedst him better
Than ever thou lovedst Cassius.

BRU.   Sheathe your dagger.
Be angry when you will, it shall have scope;
Do what you will, dishonor shall be humor.
O Cassius, you are yoked with a lamb
That carries anger as the flint bears fire,
Who, much enforced, shows a hasty spark,
And straight is cold again.

CAS.   Hath Cassius liv'd
To be but mirth and laughter to his Brutus,
When grief and blood ill-temper'd vexeth him?

BRU.   When I spoke that, I was ill-temper'd too.

CAS.   Do you confess so much? Give me your hand.

BRU.   And my heart too.

CAS.   O Brutus!

BRU.   What's the matter?

CAS.   Have not you love enough to bear with me,
      When that rash humor which my mother gave me
      Makes me forgetful?

BRU.   Yes, Cassius, and from henceforth,
      When you are over-earnest with your Brutus,
      He'll think your mother chides, and leave you so.

                                    [4.3, ll. 65–123]

From AS YOU LIKE IT

(Celia defends her cousin Rosalind against Celia's father, Duke Frederick, who has conspired to banish Rosalind's father and now Rosalind.)

Enter ROSALIND *and* CELIA.

CEL.   I pray thee, Rosalind, sweet my coz, be merry.

ROS.   Dear Celia—I show more mirth than I am mistress of, and would you yet [I] were merrier? Unless you could teach me to forget a banish'd father, you must not learn me how to remember any extraordinary pleasure.

CEL.   Herein I see thou lov'st me not with the full weight that I love thee. If my uncle, thy banish'd father, had banish'd thy uncle, the Duke my father, so thou hadst been still with me, I could have taught my love to take thy father for mine; so wouldst thou, if the truth of thy love to me were so righteously temper'd as mine is to thee.

ROS.   Well, I will forget the condition of my estate, to rejoice in yours.

CEL.   You know my father hath no child but I, nor none is like to have; and truly when he dies, thou shalt be his heir; for what he hath taken away from thy father perforce, I will render thee again in affection. By mine honor, I will, and when I break that oath, let me turn monster. Therefore, my sweet Rose, my dear Rose, be merry.

ROS.   From henceforth I will, coz, and devise sports. Let me see—what think you of falling in love?

                                    [1.2, ll. 1–25]

CEL.   I did not then entreat to have her stay,
      It was your pleasure and your own remorse.

I was too young that time to value her,
But now I know her. If she be a traitor,
Why, so am I. We still have slept together,
Rose at an instant, learn'd, play'd, eat together,
And wheresoe'er we went, like Juno's swans,
Still we went coupled and inseparable.

DUKE F.   She is too subtile for thee, and her smoothness,
Her very silence, and her patience
Speak to the people, and they pity her.
Thou art a fool; she robs thee of thy name,
And thou wilt show more bright and seem more virtuous
When she is gone. Then open not thy lips:
Firm and irrevocable is my doom
Which I have pass'd upon her; she is banish'd.

CEL.   Pronounce that sentence then on me, my liege,
I cannot live out of her company.

DUKE F.   You are a fool. You, niece, provide yourself;
If you outstay the time, upon mine honor,
And in the greatness of my word, you die.

                            Exit Duke [with Lords].

CEL.   O my poor Rosalind, whither wilt thou go?
Wilt thou change fathers? I will give thee mine.
I charge thee be not thou more griev'd than I am.

ROS.   I have more cause.

CEL.   Thou hast not, cousin,
Prithee be cheerful. Know'st thou not the Duke
Hath banish'd me, his daughter?

ROS.   That he hath not.

CEL.   No, hath not? Rosalind lacks then the love
Which teacheth thee that thou and I am one.
Shall we be sund'red? shall we part, sweet girl?
No, let my father seek another heir.
Therefore devise with me how we may fly,
Whither to go, and what to bear with us,
And do not seek to take your change upon you,
To bear your griefs yourself, and leave me out;
For by this heaven, now at our sorrows pale,
Say what thou canst, I'll go along with thee.

                                        [1.3, ll. 69–105]

(Amiens entertains Duke Senior and Orlando in the Forest of Arden.)

[*Amiens*]:   Blow, blow, thou winter wind,
                    Thou art not so unkind
                    As man's ingratitude;
                    Thy tooth is not so keen,
                    Because thou art not seen,
                    Although thy breath be rude.
Heigh-ho, sing heigh-ho! unto the green holly,
Most friendship is feigning, most loving mere folly.
              [Then] heigh-ho, the holly!
              This life is most jolly.

              Freeze, freeze, thou bitter sky,
              That dost not bite so nigh
              As benefits forgot;
              Though thou the waters warp,

              Thy sting is not so sharp
              As friend rememb'red not.
Heigh-ho, sing, etc.

                                                    [2.7, ll. 174–90]

From HAMLET

(Polonius gives advice to his son Laertes as he goes off to college.)

POLONIUS.   Those friends thou hast, and their adoption tried,
        Grapple them unto thy soul with hoops of steel,
        But do not dull thy palm with entertainment
        Of each new-hatch'd, unfledg'd courage.

                                                    [1.3, ll. 62–65]

(Horatio, Hamlet's old friend, remains true while the rest of the court—including his friends Rosencrantz and Guildenstern, who flatter and betray him—turn against him.)

Enter HORATIO.
HOR.   Here, sweet lord, at your service.
HAMLET.   Horatio, thou art e'en as just a man
        As e'er my conversation cop'd withal.

HOR.   O my dear lord—

HAM.   Nay, do not think I flatter,
        For what advancement may I hope from thee
        That no revenue hast but thy good spirits
        To feed and clothe thee? Why should the poor be flatter'd?
        No, let the candied tongue lick absurd pomp,
        And crook the pregnant hinges of the knee
        Where thrift may follow fawning. Dost thou hear?
        Since my dear soul was mistress of her choice
        And could of men distinguish her election,
        Sh' hath seal'd thee for herself, for thou hast been
        As one in suff'ring all that suffers nothing,
        A man that Fortune's buffets and rewards
        Hast ta'en with equal thanks; and blest are those
        Whose blood and judgment are so well co-meddled,
        That they are not a pipe for Fortune's finger
        To sound what stop she please. Give me that man
        That is not passion's slave, and I will wear him
        In my heart's core, ay, in my heart of heart,
        As I do thee. Something too much of this.

                                                [3.2, ll. 57–74]

(In deep melancholy, Hamlet enters the graveyard and comes upon the skull of
his former friend the court jester Yorick.)

1. CLOWN.   A pestilence on him for a mad rogue! 'a pour'd a flagon of
        Rhenish on my head once. This same skull, sir, was, sir, Yorick's
        skull, the King's jester.

HAM.   This?   [*Takes the skull.*]

1. CLO.   E'en that.

HAM.   Alas, poor Yorick! I knew him, Horatio, a fellow of infinite jest,
        of most excellent fancy. He hath bore me on his back a thousand
        times, and now how abhorr'd in my imagination it is! my gorge rises
        at it. Here hung those lips that I have kiss'd I know not how oft.
        Where be your gibes now, your gambols, your songs, your flashes
        of merriment, that were wont to set the table on a roar? Not one
        now to mock your own grinning—quite chop-fall'n.

                                                [5.1, ll. 180–92]

(Hamlet speaks these words as he is dying.)

HAM.   As th' art a man,
        Give me the cup. Let go! By heaven, I'll ha't!

O God, Horatio, what a wounded name,
Things standing thus unknown, shall I leave behind me!
If thou didst ever hold me in thy heart,
Absent thee from felicity a while,
And in this harsh world draw thy breath in pain
To tell my story. *A march afar off* [*and a shot within*].
                What warlike noise is this?
          [*Osric goes to the door and returns.*]

OSRIC.   Young Fortinbras, with conquest come from Poland,
To th' embassadors of England gives
This warlike volley.

HAM.   O, I die, Horatio,
The potent poison quite o'er-crows my spirit.
I cannot live to hear the news from England,
But I do prophesy th' election lights
On Fortinbras, he has my dying voice.
So tell him, with th' occurrents more and less
Which have solicited—the rest is silence.   [*Dies.*]

HOR.   Now cracks a noble heart. Good night, sweet prince,
And flights of angels sing thee to thy rest!

                              [5.2, ll. 344–60]

From TIMON OF ATHENS

(Timon, a paragon of generosity whose friends turn on him when he loses his money, becomes a misanthrope by the end of the play.)

APEMANTUS.   Friendship's full of dregs;
                            [1.2, l. 233]

FLAMINIUS.   May these add to the number that may scald thee!
Let molten coin be thy damnation,
Thou disease of a friend, and not himself!
Has friendship such a faint and milky heart,
It turns in less than two nights? O you gods!
I feel my master's passion. This slave
Unto his honor has my lord's meat in him;
Why should it thrive and turn to nutriment
When he is turn'd to poison?
O, may diseases only work upon't!
And when he's sick to death, let not that part of nature

Which my lord paid for, be of any power
To expel sickness, but prolong his hour!

[3.1, ll. 52–63]

ALCIBIADES   *(Reads the epitaph.)* "Here lies a wretched corse, of
wretched soul bereft;
Seek not my name: a plague consume you, wicked caitiffs left!
Here lie I, Timon, who, alive, all living men did hate;
Pass by and curse thy fill, but pass and stay not here thy gait."

[5.4, ll. 70–73]

From THE WINTER'S TALE

(Hermione, wife of Leontes, King of Sicily, speaks with Leontes' old friend
Polixenes, King of Bohemia, who is visiting the Sicilian court. Leontes will soon
become insanely jealous of Polixenes.)

HERMIONE.   Come, I'll question you
Of my lord's tricks and yours when you were boys.
You were pretty lordings then?
POLIXENES.   We were, fair queen,
Two lads that thought there was no more behind
But such a day to-morrow as to-day,
And to be boy eternal.
HER.   Was not my lord
The verier wag o' th' two?
POL.   We were as twinn'd lambs that did frisk i' th' sun,
And bleat the one at th' other. What we chang'd
Was innocence for innocence; we knew not
The doctrine of ill-doing, nor dream'd
That any did. Had we pursu'd that life,
And our weak spirits ne'er been higher rear'd
With stronger blood, we should have answer'd heaven
Boldly, "Not guilty"; the imposition clear'd,
Hereditary ours.

[1.2, ll. 60–74]

From The Two Noble Kinsmen

(Hippolyta, Queen of the Amazons, speaks of the friendship of Palamon and Arcite, who are contending for the hand of her sister Emilia, who speaks of her friend Flavina. Pirithous and Theseus are both in love with Hippolyta.)

HIPPOLYTA. They two have cabin'd
    In many as dangerous as poor a corner,
    Peril and want contending, they have skiff'd
    Torrents whose roaring tyranny and power
    I' th' least of these was dreadful, and they have
    Fought out together where death's self was lodg'd;
    Yet fate hath brought them off. Their knot of love
    Tied, weav'd, entangled, with so true, so long,
    And with a finger of so deep a cunning,
    May be outworn, never undone. I think
    Theseus cannot be umpire to himself,
    Cleaving his conscience into twain and doing
    Each side like justice, which he loves best.
EMILIA.   Doubtless
    There is a best, and reason has no manners
    To say it is not you. I was acquainted
    Once with a time when I enjoy'd a playfellow;
    You were at wars when she the grave enrich'd,
    Who made too proud the bed, took leave o' th' moon
    (Which then look'd pale at parting) when our count
    Was each aleven.
HIP.   'Twas [Flavina].
EMIL.   Yes.
    You talk of Pirithous' and Theseus' love:
    Theirs has more ground, is more maturely season'd,
    More buckled with strong judgment, and their needs
    The one of th' other may be said to water
    Their intertangled roots of love, but I
    And she (I sigh and spoke of) were things innocent,
    Lov'd for we did, and like the elements
    That know not what nor why, yet do effect
    Rare issues by their operance, our souls
    Did so to one another. What she lik'd
    Was then of me approv'd, what not, condemn'd,
    No more arraignment. The flow'r that I would pluck
    And put between my breasts (O then but beginning
    To swell about the blossom), she would long

Till she had such another, and commit it
To the like innocent cradle, where phoenix-like
They died in perfume. On my head no toy
But was her pattern, her affections (pretty,
Though happily her careless [wear]) I followed
For my most serious decking. Had mine ear
Stol'n some new air, or at adventure humm'd [one]
From musical coinage, why, it was a note
Whereon her spirits would sojourn (rather dwell on)
And sing it in her slumbers. This rehearsal
(Which, [ev'ry] innocent wots well, comes in
Like old importment's bastard) has this end,
That the true love 'tween maid and maid may be
More than in sex [dividual].

[1.3, ll. 35–82]

PART VIII

LETTERS: GROUP 2

*[Friends] cherish each other's hopes. They
are kind to each other's dreams.*

—*Henry David Thoreau*

HERMAN MELVILLE

To Nathaniel Hawthorne

1 [?] June 1851

. . . I'm rather sore, perhaps, in this letter; but see my hand!—four blisters on this palm, made by hoes and hammers within the last few days. It is a rainy morning; so I am indoors, and all work suspended. I feel cheerfully disposed, and therefore I write a little bluely. Would the Gin were here! If ever, my dear Hawthorne, in the eternal times that are to come, you and I shall sit down in Paradise, in some little shady corner by ourselves; and if we shall by any means be able to smuggle a basket of champagne there (I won't believe in a Temperance Heaven), and if we shall then cross our celestial legs in the celestial grass that is forever tropical, and strike our glasses and our heads together, till both musically ring in concert,—then, O my dear fellow-mortal, how shall we pleasantly discourse of all the things manifold which now so distress us,—when all the earth shall be but a reminiscence, yea, its final dissolution an antiquity. Then shall songs be composed as when wars are over; humorous, comic songs,—"Oh, when I lived in that queer little hole called the world," or, "Oh, when I toiled and sweated below," or, "Oh, when I knocked and was knocked in the fight"—yes, let us look forward to such things. Let us swear that, though now we sweat, yet it is because of the dry heat which is indispensable to the nourishment of the vine which is to bear the grapes that are to give us the champagne hereafter. . . .

[22 July 1851]
Tuesday afternoon.

My dear Hawthorne:
    This is not a letter, or even a note—but only a passing word said to you over your garden gate. I thank you for your easy-flowing long letter (received yesterday) which flowed through me, and refreshed all my meadows, as the Housatonic—opposite me—does in reality. I am now busy with various things—not incessantly though; but enough to require

my frequent tinkerings; and this is the height of the haying season, and my nag is dragging me home his winter's dinners all the time. And so, one way and another, I am not yet a disengaged man; but shall be, very soon. Meantime, the earliest good chance I get, I shall roll down to you, my good fellow, seeing we—that is, you and I—must hit upon some little bit of vagabondism, before Autumn comes. Graylock—we must go and vagabondize there. But ere we start, we must dig a deep hole, and bury all Blue Devils, there to abide till the Last Day.

> Goodbye,
> his x mark.

> *[17 ? November 1851]*
> *Pittsfield, Monday afternoon.*

My Dear Hawthorne,—People think that if a man has undergone any hardship, he should have a reward; but for my part, if I have done the hardest possible day's work, and then come to sit down in a corner and eat my supper comfortably—why, then I don't think I deserve any reward for my hard day's work—for am I not now at peace? Is not my supper good? My peace and my supper are my reward, my dear Hawthorne. So your joy-giving and exultation-breeding letter is not my reward for my ditcher's work with that book, but is the good goddess's bonus over and above what was stipulated for—for not one man in five cycles, who is wise, will expect appreciative recognition from his fellows, or any one of them. Appreciation! Recognition! Is love appreciated? Why, ever since Adam, who has got to the meaning of this great allegory—the world? Then we pygmies must be content to have our paper allegories but ill comprehended. I say your appreciation is my glorious gratuity. In my proud, humble way,—a shepherd-king,—I was lord of a little vale in the solitary Crimea; but you have now given me the crown of India. But on trying it on my head, I found it fell down on my ears, notwithstanding their asinine length—for it's only such ears that sustain such crowns.

Your letter was handed me last night on the road going to Mr. Morewood's, and I read it there. Had I been at home, I would have sat down at once and answered it. In me divine magnanimities are spontaneous and instantaneous—catch them while you can. The world goes round, and the other side comes up. So now I can't write what I felt. But I felt pantheistic then—your heart beat in my ribs and mine in yours, and both in God's. A sense of unspeakable security is in me this moment, on account of your having understood the book. I have written a wicked book, and feel spotless as the lamb. Ineffable socialities are in me. I

would sit down and dine with you and all the gods in old Rome's Pantheon. It is a strange feeling—no hopefulness is in it, no despair. Content—that is it; and irresponsibility; but without licentious inclination. I
speak now of my profoundest sense of being, not of an incidental feeling.

Whence come you, Hawthorne? By what right do you drink from my
flagon of life? And when I put it to my lips—lo, they are yours and not
mine. I feel that the Godhead is broken up like the bread at the Supper,
and that we are the pieces. Hence this infinite fraternity of feeling. Now,
sympathizing with the paper, my angel turns over another page. You did
not care a penny for the book. But, now and then as you read, you
understood the pervading thought that impelled the book—and that you
praised. Was it not so? You were archangel enough to despise the imperfect body, and embrace the soul. Once you hugged the ugly Socrates
because you saw the flame in the mouth, and heard the rushing of the
demon,—the familiar,—and recognized the sound; for you have heard it
in your own solitudes.

My dear Hawthorne, the atmospheric skepticisms steal into me now,
and make me doubtful of my sanity in writing you thus. But, believe me,
I am not mad, most noble Festus! But truth is ever incoherent, and when
the big hearts strike together, the concussion is a little stunning. Farewell. Don't write a word about the book. That would be robbing me of
my miserly delight. I am heartily sorry I ever wrote anything about
you—it was paltry. Lord, when shall we be done growing? As long as we
have anything more to do, we have done nothing. So, now, let us add
Moby Dick to our blessing, and step from that. Leviathan is not the
biggest fish;—I have heard of Krakens.

This is a long letter, but you are not at all bound to answer it. Possibly,
if you do answer it, and direct it to Herman Melville, you will missend
it—for the very fingers that now guide this pen are not precisely the
same that just took it up and put it on this paper. Lord, when shall we be
done changing? Ah! It's a long stage, and no inn in sight, and night
coming, and the body cold. But with you for a passenger, I am content
and can be happy. I shall leave the world, I feel, with more satisfaction
for having come to know you. Knowing you persuades me more than the
Bible of our immortality.

What a pity, that, for your plain, bluff letter, you should get such
gibberish! Mention me to Mrs. Hawthorne and to the children, and so,
good-by to you, with my blessing.

Herman.

P.S. I can't stop yet. If the world was entirely made up of Magians, I'll
tell you what I should do. I should have a paper-mill established at one

end of the house, and so have an endless riband of foolscap rolling in upon my desk; and upon that endless riband I should write a thousand—a million—billion thoughts, all under the form of a letter to you. The divine magnet is on you, and my magnet responds. Which is the biggest? A foolish question—they are *One*.

H.

P.P.S. Don't think that by writing me a letter, you shall always be bored with an immediate reply to it—and so keep both of us delving over a writing-desk eternally. No such thing! I sh'n't always answer your letters, and you may do just as you please.

EMILY DICKINSON

To Susan Gilbert (Dickinson)

[About February 1852]

Thank the dear little snow flakes, because they fall *today* rather than some vain *weekday,* when the world and the cares of the world try so hard to keep me from my departed friend—and thank you, too, dear Susie, that you never weary of me, or never *tell* me so, and that when the world is cold, and the storm sighs e'er so piteously, I am sure of one sweet shelter, *one* covert from the storm! The bells are ringing, Susie, north, and east, and south, and *your own* village bell, and the people who love God, are expecting to go to meeting; dont *you* go Susie, not to *their* meeting, but come with me this morning to the church within our hearts, where the bells are always ringing, and the preacher whose name is Love—shall intercede there for us!

They will all go but me, to the usual meetinghouse, to hear the usual sermon; the inclemency of the storm so kindly detaining me; and as I sit here Susie, alone with the winds and you, I have the old *king feeling* even more than before, for I know not even the *cracker man* will invade *this* solitude, this sweet Sabbath of our's. And thank you for my dear letter, which came on Saturday night, when all the world was still; thank you for the love it bore me, and for it's golden thoughts, and feelings so like gems, that I was sure I *gathered* them in whole baskets of pearls! I mourn this morning, Susie, that I have no sweet sunset to gild a page for *you*, nor any bay so blue—not even a little chamber way up in the sky, as your's is, to give me thoughts of heaven, which *I* would give to you. You know how I must write you, down, down, in the terrestrial; no sunset here, no stars; not even a bit of *twilight* which I may poetize—and send you! Yet Susie, there will be romance in the letter's ride to you—think of the hills and the dales, and the rivers it will pass over, and the drivers and conductors who will hurry it on to you; and wont that make a poem such as can ne'er be written? I think of you dear Susie, *now*, I dont know how or why, but more dearly as every day goes by, and that sweet month of promise draws nearer and nearer; and I view July so differently from what I used to—once it seemed parched, and dry—and I hardly loved it *any* on account of it's heat and dust; but *now* Susie, month of all the year the best; I skip the violets—and the dew, and the early Rose and the Robins; I will exchange them *all* for that angry and hot noonday, when I can count the hours and the *minutes* before you come—Oh Susie, I often think that I will try to tell you how very dear you are, and how I'm watching for you, but the words wont come, tho' the *tears* will, and I sit down disappointed—yet darling, you know it all—then why do I seek to tell you? I do not know; in thinking of those I love, my reason is all gone from me, and I do fear sometimes that I must make a hospital for the hopelessly insane, and chain me up there such times, so I wont injure you. . . .

GEORGE S. HILLARD AND
NATHANIEL HAWTHORNE

CORRESPONDENCE

Hillard to Hawthorne

Boston, *January 17, 1850*

It occurred to me, and some other of your friends that, in consideration of the events of the last year, you might at this time be in need of a little pecuniary aid. I have therefore collected, from some of those who admire your genius and respect your character, the enclosed sum of money, which I send you with my warmest wishes for your health and happiness. I know the sensitive edge of your temperament; but do not speak or think of obligation. It is only paying, in a very imperfect measure, the debt we owe you for what you have done for American literature. Could you know the readiness with which every one to whom I applied contributed to this little offering, and could you have heard the warm expressions with which some accompanied their gift, you would have felt that the bread you had cast on the waters had indeed come back to you. Let no shadow of despondency, my dear friend, steal over you. Your friends do not and will not forget you. You shall be protected against "eating cares," which, I take it, mean cares lest we should not have enough to eat.

Hawthorne to Hillard

Salem, January 20th. 1850.

My dear Hillard,

I read your letter in the entry of the Post-Office; and it drew—what my troubles never have—the water to my eyes; so that I was glad of the sharply cold west wind that blew into them as I came homeward, and gave them an excuse for being red and bleared.

There was much that was very sweet—and something too that was very bitter—mingled with that same moisture. It is sweet to be remembered and cared for by one's friends—some of whom know me for what I am, while others, perhaps, know me only through a generous faith—sweet to think that they deem me worth upholding in my poor walk through life. And it is bitter, nevertheless, to need their support. It is something else besides pride that teaches me that ill-success in life is really and justly a matter of shame. I am ashamed of it, and I ought to be. The fault of a failure is attributable—in a great degree, at least—to the man who fails. I should apply this truth in judging of other men; and it behoves me not to shun its point or edge in taking it home to my own heart. Nobody has a right to live in this world, unless he be strong and able, and applies his ability to good purpose.

The money, dear Hillard, will smooth my path for a long time to come. The only way in which a man can retain his self-respect, while availing himself of the generosity of his friends, is, by making it an incitement to his utmost exertions, so that he may not need their help again. I shall look upon it so—nor will shun any drudgery that my hand shall find to do, if thereby I may win bread.

Your friend,
Nath[1] Hawthorne.

Liverpool, Dec[r] 9th. 1853.

Dear Hillard,

I herewith send you a draft on Ticknor for the sum (with interest included) which was so kindly given me by unknown friends, through you, about four years ago.

I have always hoped and intended to do this, from the first moment when I made up my mind to accept the money. It could not have been right to speak of this purpose, before it was in my power to accomplish it; but it has never been out of my mind for a single day, nor hardly, I think, for a single waking hour. I am most happy that this loan, (as I may fairly call it, at this moment) can now be repaid, without the risk on my part of leaving my wife and children utterly destitute. I should have done it sooner; but I felt that it would be selfish to purchase this great satisfaction for myself, at any such risk to them. We are not rich, nor are ever likely to be; but the miserable pinch is over.

The friends, who were so generous to me, must not suppose that I have not felt deeply grateful, nor that my delight at relieving myself from this pecuniary obligation is of any ungracious kind. I have been grateful all along, and am more so now than ever. This act of kindness did me an unspeakable amount of good; for it came when I most needed to be assured that anybody thought it worth while to keep me from sinking. And it did me even greater good than this, in making me sensible of the necessity of sterner efforts than my former ones, in order to establish a right for myself to live and be comfortable. For it is my creed (and was so, even at that wretched time) that a man has no claim upon his fellow creatures, beyond bread and water, and a grave, unless he can win it by his own strength or skill. But so much the kinder were those unknown friends—whom I thank again with all my heart.

Their generosity, I believe, was never made known to the public; and I trust that nothing may be said of this conclusion of the affair, beyond the circle of those immediately concerned.

Most Sincerely Yours,
Nath[l] Hawthorne.

PART IX

SHORT STORIES

The things they did well and in which each was most interested, they could not do together, and yet they were a pair, meeting in a euphoric third state each alone conjured up in the other.

—Nadine Gordimer

V. S. PRITCHETT

The Voice

A message came from the rescue party, who straightened up and leaned on their spades in the rubble. The policeman said to the crowd: "Everyone keep quiet for five minutes. No talking, please. They're trying to hear where he is."

The silent crowd raised their faces and looked across the ropes to the church which, now it was destroyed, broke the line of the street like a decayed tooth. The bomb had brought down the front wall and the roof, the balcony had capsized. Freakishly untouched, the hymnboard still announced the previous Sunday's hymns.

A small wind blew a smell of smouldering cloth across people's noses from another street where there was another scene like this. A bus roared by and heads turned in passive anger until the sound of the engine had gone. People blinked as a pigeon flew from a roof and crossed the building like an omen of release. There was dead quietness again. Presently a murmuring sound was heard by the rescue party. The man buried under the debris was singing again.

At first difficult to hear, soon a tune became definite. Two of the rescuers took up their shovels and shouted down to encourage the buried man, and the voice became stronger and louder. Words became clear. The leader of the rescue party held back the others, and those who were near strained to hear. Then the words were unmistakable:

> "Oh Thou whose Voice the waters heard,
> And hushed their raging at Thy Word."

The buried man was singing a hymn.

A clergyman was standing with the warden in the middle of the ruined church.

"That's Mr. Morgan all right," the warden said. "He could sing. He got silver medals for it."

The Reverend Frank Lewis frowned.

"Gold, I shouldn't wonder," said Mr. Lewis, dryly. Now he knew
Morgan was alive he said: "What the devil's he doing in there? How did
he get in? I locked up at eight o'clock last night myself."

Lewis was a wiry, middle-aged man, but the white dust on his hair and
his eye-lashes, and the way he kept licking the dust off his dry lips,
moving his jaws all the time, gave him the monkeyish, testy, and suspicious air of an old man. He had been up all night on rescue work in the
raid and he was tired out. The last straw was to find the church had gone
and that Morgan, the so-called Rev. Morgan, was buried under it.

The rescue workers were digging again. There was a wide hole now
and a man was down in it filling a basket with his hands. The dust rose
like smoke from the hole as he worked.

The voice had not stopped singing. It went on, rich, virile, masculine,
from verse to verse of the hymn. Shooting up like a stem through the
rubbish, the voice seemed to rise and branch out powerfully, luxuriantly,
and even theatrically, like a tree, until everything was in its shade. It was
a shade that came towards one like dark arms.

"All the Welsh can sing," the warden said. Then he remembered that
Lewis was Welsh also. "Not that I've got anything against the Welsh,"
the warden said.

"The scandal of it," Lewis was thinking. "Must he sing so loud, must
he advertise himself? I locked up myself last night. How the devil did he
get in?" And he really meant: "How did the devil get in?"

To Lewis, Morgan was the nearest human thing to the devil. He could
never pass that purple-gowned figure, sauntering like a cardinal in his
skull cap on the sunny side of the street, without a shudder of distaste
and derision. An unfrocked priest, his predecessor in the church, Morgan ought in strict justice to have been in prison, and would have been
but for the indulgence of the bishop. But this did not prevent the old
man with the saintly white head and the eyes half-closed by the worldly
juices of food and wine from walking about dressed in his vestments, like
an actor walking in the sun of his own vanity, a hook-nosed satyr, a
he-goat significant to servant girls, the crony of the public-house, the
chaser of bookmakers, the smoker of cigars. It was terrible, but it was just
that the bomb had buried him; only the malice of the Evil One would
have thought of bringing the punishment of the sinner upon the church
as well. And now, from the ruins, the voice of the wicked man rose up in
all the elaborate pride of art and evil.

Suddenly there was a moan from the sloping timber, slates began to
skate down.

"Get out. It's going," shouted the warden.

The man who was digging struggled out of the hole as it bulged under
the landslide. There was a dull crumble, the crashing and splitting of

wood, and then the sound of brick and dust tearing down below the water. Thick dust clouded over and choked them all. The rubble rocked like a cakewalk. Everyone rushed back and looked behind at the wreckage as if it were still alive. It remained still. They all stood there, frightened and suspicious. Presently one of the men with the shovel said: "The bloke's shut up."

Everyone stared stupidly. It was true. The man had stopped singing. The clergyman was the first to move. Gingerly he went to what was left of the hole and got down on his knees.

"Morgan!" he said in a low voice.

Then he called out more loudly: "Morgan!"

Getting no reply, Lewis began to scramble the rubble away with his hands.

"Morgan!" he shouted. "Can you hear?" He snatched a shovel from one of the men and began digging and shovelling the stuff away. He had stopped chewing and muttering. His expression had entirely changed. "Morgan!" he called. He dug for two feet and no one stopped him. They looked with bewilderment at the sudden frenzy of the small man grubbing like a monkey, spitting out the dust, filing down his nails. They saw the spade at last shoot through the old hole. He was down the hole widening it at once, letting himself down as he worked. He disappeared under a ledge made by the fallen timber.

The party above could do nothing. "Morgan," they heard him call. "It's Lewis. We're coming. Can you hear?" He shouted for an axe and presently they heard him smashing with it. He was scratching like a dog or a rabbit.

A voice like that to have stopped, to have gone! Lewis was thinking. How unbearable this silence was. A beautiful proud voice, the voice of a man, a voice like a tree, the soul of a man spreading in the air like the cedars of Lebanon. "Only one man I have heard with a bass like that. Owen the Bank, at Newtown before the war. Morgan!" he shouted. "Sing! God will forgive you everything, only sing!"

One of the rescue party following behind the clergyman in the tunnel shouted back to his mates.

"I can't do nothing. This bleeder's blocking the gangway."

Half an hour Lewis worked in the tunnel. Then an extraordinary thing happened to him. The tunnel grew damp and its floor went as soft as clay to the touch. Suddenly his knees went through. There was a gap with a yard of cloth, the vestry curtain or the carpet at the communion rail was unwound and hanging through it. Lewis found himself looking down into the blackness of the crypt. He lay down and put his head and shoulders through the hole and felt about him until he found something solid again. The beams of the floor were tilted down into the crypt.

"Morgan. Are you there, man?" he called.

He listened to the echo of his voice. He was reminded of the time he had talked into a cistern when he was a boy. Then his heart jumped. A voice answered him out of the darkness from under the fallen floor. It was like the voice of a man lying comfortably and waking up from a snooze, a voice thick and sleepy.

"Who's that?" asked the voice.

"Morgan, man. It's Lewis. Are you hurt?" Tears pricked the dust in Lewis's eyes, and his throat ached with anxiety as he spoke. Forgiveness and love were flowing out of him. From below, the deep thick voice of Morgan came back.

"You've been a hell of a long time," it said. "I've damn near finished my whisky."

"Hell" was the word which changed Mr. Lewis's mind. Hell was a real thing, a real place for him. He believed in it. When he read out the word "Hell" in the Scriptures he could see the flames rising as they rise out of the furnaces at Swansea. "Hell" was a professional and poetic word for Mr. Lewis. A man who had been turned out of the church had no right to use it. Strong language and strong drink, Mr. Lewis hated both of them. The idea of whisky being in his church made his soul rise like an angered stomach. There was Morgan, insolent and comfortable, lying (so he said) under the old altar-table, which was propping up the fallen floor, drinking a bottle of whisky.

"How did you get in?" Lewis said, sharply, from the hole."Were you in the church last night when I locked up?"

The old man sounded not as bold as he had been. He even sounded shifty when he replied: "I've got my key."

"*Your* key. I have the only key of the church. Where did you get a key?"

"My old key. I always had a key."

The man in the tunnel behind the clergyman crawled back up the tunnel to the daylight.

"O.K.," the man said. "He's got him. They're having a ruddy row."

"Reminds me of ferreting. I used to go ferreting with my old dad," said the policeman.

"You should have given that key up," said Mr. Lewis. "Have you been in here before?"

"Yes, but I shan't come here again," said the old man.

There was the dribble of powdered rubble, pouring down like sand in an hour-glass, the ticking of the strained timber like the loud ticking of a clock.

Mr. Lewis felt that at last after years he was face to face with the devil, and the devil was trapped and caught. The tick-tock of the wood went on.

"Men have been risking their lives, working and digging for hours because of this," said Lewis. "I've ruined a suit of . . ."

The tick-tock had grown louder in the middle of the words. There was a sudden lurching and groaning of the floor, followed by a big heaving and splitting sound.

"It's going," said Morgan with detachment from below. "The table leg." The floor crashed down. The hole in the tunnel was torn wide and Lewis grabbed at the darkness until he caught a board. It swung him out and in a second he found himself hanging by both hands over the pit.

"I'm falling. Help me," shouted Lewis in terror. "Help me." There was no answer.

"Oh, God," shouted Lewis, kicking for a foothold. "Morgan, are you there? Catch me. I'm going."

Then a groan like a snore came out of Lewis. He could hold no longer. He fell. He fell exactly two feet.

The sweat ran down his legs and caked on his face. He was as wet as a rat. He was on his hands and knees gasping. When he got his breath again, he was afraid to raise his voice.

"Morgan," he said quietly, panting.

"Only one leg went," the old man said in a quiet grating voice. "The other three are all right."

Lewis lay panting on the floor. There was a long silence. "Haven't you ever been afraid before, Lewis?" Morgan said. Lewis had no breath to reply. "Haven't you ever felt rotten with fear," said the old man, calmly, "like an old tree, infested and worm-eaten with it, soft as a rotten orange? You were a fool to come down here after me. I wouldn't have done the same for you," Morgan said.

"You would," Lewis managed to say.

"I wouldn't," said the old man. "I'm afraid. I'm an old man, Lewis, and I can't stand it. I've been down here every night since the raids got bad."

Lewis listened to the voice. It was low with shame, it had the roughness of the earth, the kicked and trodden choking dust of Adam. The earth of Mr. Lewis listened for the first time to the earth of Morgan. Coarsened and sordid and unlike the singing voice, the voice of Morgan was also gentle and fragmentary.

"When you stop feeling shaky," Morgan said, "you'd better sing. I'll do a bar, but I can't do much. The whisky's gone. Sing, Lewis. Even if they don't hear, it does you good. Take the tenor, Lewis."

Above in the daylight the look of pain went from the mouths of the rescue party, a grin came on the dusty lips of the warden.

"Hear it?" he said. "A ruddy Welsh choir!"

LEO TOLSTOY

THE THREE HERMITS

An Old Legend Current in the Volga District

And in praying use not vain repetitions as the Gentiles do: for they think that they shall be heard for their much speaking. Be not therefore like them; for your Father knoweth what things ye have need of, before ye ask Him.

—Matthew vi: 7, 8.

A bishop was sailing from Archangel to the Solovétsk Monastery, and on the same vessel were a number of pilgrims on their way to visit the shrines at that place. The voyage was a smooth one. The wind favorable and the weather fair. The pilgrims lay on deck, eating, or sat in groups talking to one another. The Bishop, too, came on deck, and as he was pacing up and down he noticed a group of men standing near the prow and listening to a fisherman, who was pointing to the sea and telling them something. The Bishop stopped, and looked in the direction in which the man was pointing. He could see nothing, however, but the sea glistening in the sunshine. He drew nearer to listen, but when the man saw him, he took off his cap and was silent. The rest of the people also took off their caps and bowed.

"Do not let me disturb you, friends," said the Bishop. "I came to hear what this good man was saying."

"The fisherman was telling us about the hermits," replied one, a tradesman, rather bolder than the rest.

"What hermits?" asked the Bishop, going to the side of the vessel and seating himself on a box. "Tell me about them. I should like to hear. What were you pointing at?"

"Why, that little island you can just see over there," answered the man, pointing to a spot ahead and a little to the right. "That is the island where the hermits live for the salvation of their souls."

"Where is the island?" asked the Bishop. "I see nothing."

"There, in the distance, if you will please look along my hand. Do you see that little cloud? Below it, and a bit to the left, there is just a faint streak. That is the island."

The Bishop looked carefully, but his unaccustomed eyes could make out nothing but the water shimmering in the sun.

"I cannot see it," he said. "But who are the hermits that live there?"

"They are holy men," answered the fisherman. "I had long heard tell of them, but never chanced to see them myself till the year before last."

And the fisherman related how once, when he was out fishing, he had been stranded at night upon that island, not knowing where he was. In the morning, as he wandered about the island, he came across an earth hut, and an old man standing near it. Presently two others came out, and after having fed him and dried his things, they helped him mend his boat.

"And what are they like?" asked the Bishop.

"One is a small man and his back is bent. He wears a priest's cassock and is very old; he must be more than a hundred, I should say. He is so old that the white of his beard is taking a greenish tinge, but he is always smiling, and his face is as bright as an angel's from heaven. The second is taller, but he also is very old. He wears a tattered peasant coat. His beard is broad, and of a yellowish grey color. He is a strong man. Before I had time to help him, he turned my boat over as if it were only a pail. He too is kindly and cheerful. The third is tall, and has a beard as white as snow and reaching to his knees. He is stern, with overhanging eyebrows; and he wears nothing but a piece of matting tied round his waist."

"And did they speak to you?" asked the Bishop.

"For the most part they did everything in silence, and spoke but little even to one another. One of them would just give a glance, and the others would understand him. I asked the tallest whether they had lived there long. He frowned, and muttered something as if he were angry; but the oldest one took his hand and smiled, and then the tall one was quiet. The oldest one only said: 'Have mercy upon us,' and smiled."

While the fisherman was talking, the ship had drawn nearer to the island.

"There, now you can see it plainly, if your Lordship will please to look," said the tradesman, pointing with his hand.

The Bishop looked, and now he really saw a dark streak—which was the island. Having looked at it a while, he left the prow of the vessel, and going to the stern, asked the helmsman:

"What island is that?"

"That one," replied the man, "has no name. There are many such in this sea."

"Is it true that there are hermits who live there for the salvation of their souls?"

"So it is said, your Lordship, but I don't know if it's true. Fishermen say they have seen them; but of course they may only be spinning yarns."

"I should like to land on the island and see these men," said the Bishop. "How could I manage it?"

"The ship cannot get close to the island," replied the helmsman, "but you might be rowed there in a boat. You had better speak to the captain."

The captain was sent for and came.

"I should like to see these hermits," said the Bishop. "Could I not be rowed ashore?"

The captain tried to dissuade him.

"Of course it could be done," said he, "but we should lose much time. And if I might venture to say so to your Lordship, the old men are not worth your pains. I have heard say that they are foolish old fellows, who understand nothing, and never speak a word, any more than the fish in the sea."

"I wish to see them," said the Bishop, "and I will pay you for your trouble and loss of time. Please let me have a boat."

There was no help for it; so the order was given. The sailors trimmed the sails, the steersman put up the helm, and the ship's course was set for the island. A chair was placed at the prow for the Bishop, and he sat there, looking ahead. The passengers all collected at the prow, and gazed at the island. Those who had the sharpest eyes could presently make out the rocks on it, and then a mud hut was seen. At last one man saw the hermits themselves. The captain brought a telescope and, after looking through it, handed it to the Bishop.

"It's right enough. There are three men standing on the shore. There, a little to the right of that big rock."

The Bishop took the telescope, got it into position, and he saw the three men: a tall one, a shorter one, and one very small and bent, standing on the shore and holding each other by the hand.

The captain turned to the Bishop.

"The vessel can get no nearer in than this, your Lordship. If you wish to go ashore, we must ask you to go in the boat, while we anchor here."

The cable was quickly let out; the anchor cast, and the sails furled. There was a jerk, and the vessel shook. Then, a boat having been lowered, the oarsmen jumped in, and the Bishop descended the ladder and took his seat. The men pulled at their oars and the boat moved rapidly towards the island. When they came within a stone's throw, they saw three old men: a tall one with only a piece of matting tied round his waist, a shorter one in a tattered peasant coat, and a very old one bent with age and wearing an old cassock—all three standing hand in hand.

The oarsmen pulled in to the shore, and held on with the boathook while the Bishop got out.

The old men bowed to him, and he gave them his blessing, at which they bowed still lower. Then the Bishop began to speak to them.

"I have heard," he said, "that you, godly men, live here saving your own souls and praying to our Lord Christ for your fellow men. I, an unworthy servant of Christ, am called, by God's mercy, to keep and teach His flock. I wished to see you, servants of God, and to do what I can to teach you, also."

The old men looked at each other smiling, but remained silent.

"Tell me," said the Bishop, "what you are doing to save your souls, and how you serve God on this island."

The second hermit sighed, and looked at the oldest, the very ancient one. The latter smiled, and said:

"We do not know how to serve God. We only serve and support ourselves, servant of God."

"But how do you pray to God?" asked the Bishop.

"We pray in this way," replied the hermit. "Three are ye, three are we, have mercy upon us."

And when the old man said this, all three raised their eyes to heaven, and repeated:

"Three are ye, three are we, have mercy upon us!"

The Bishop smiled.

"You have evidently heard something about the Holy Trinity," said he. "But you do not pray aright. You have won my affection, godly men. I see you wish to please the Lord, but you do not know how to serve Him. That is not the way to pray; but listen to me, and I will teach you. I will teach you, not a way of my own, but the way in which God in the Holy Scriptures has commanded all men to pray to Him."

And the Bishop began explaining to the hermits how God had revealed Himself to men; telling them of God the Father, and God the Son, and God the Holy Ghost.

"God the Son came down on earth," said he, "to save men, and this is how He taught us all to pray. Listen, and repeat after me: 'Our Father.' "

And the first old man repeated after him, "Our Father," and the second said, "Our Father," and the third said, "Our Father."

"Which art in heaven," continued the Bishop.

The first hermit repeated, "Which art in heaven," but the second blundered over the words, and the tall hermit could not say them properly. His hair had grown over his mouth so that he could not speak plainly. The very old hermit, having no teeth, also mumbled indistinctly.

The Bishop repeated the words again, and the old men repeated them after him. The Bishop sat down on a stone, and the old men stood before him, watching his mouth, and repeating the words as he uttered them. And all day long the Bishop labored, saying a word twenty, thirty, a hundred times over, and the old men repeated it after him. They blundered, and he corrected them, and made them begin again.

The Bishop did not leave off till he had taught them the whole of the Lord's Prayer so that they could not only repeat it after him, but could say it by themselves. The middle one was the first to know it, and to repeat the whole of it alone. The Bishop made him say it again and again, and at last the others could say it too.

It was getting dark and the moon was appearing over the water, before the Bishop rose to return to the vessel. When he took leave of the old men they all bowed down to the ground before him. He raised them, and kissed each of them, telling them to pray as he had taught them. Then he got into the boat and returned to the ship.

And as he sat in the boat and was rowed to the ship he could hear the three voices of the hermits loudly repeating the Lord's Prayer. As the boat drew near the vessel their voices could no longer be heard, but they could still be seen in the moonlight, standing as he had left them on the shore, the shortest in the middle, the tallest on the right, the middle one on the left. As soon as the Bishop had reached the vessel and got on board, the anchor was weighed and the sails unfurled. The wind filled them and the ship sailed away, and the Bishop took a seat in the stern and watched the island they had left. For a time he could still see the hermits, but presently they disappeared from sight, though the island was still visible. At last it too vanished, and only the sea was to be seen, rippling in the moonlight.

The pilgrims lay down to sleep, and all was quiet on deck. The Bishop did not wish to sleep, but sat alone at the stern, gazing at the sea where the island was no longer visible, and thinking of the good old men. He thought how pleased they had been to learn the Lord's Prayer; and he thanked God for having sent him to teach and help such godly men.

So the Bishop sat, thinking, and gazing at the sea where the island had disappeared. And the moonlight flickered before his eyes, sparkling, now here, now there, upon the waves. Suddenly he saw something white and shining, on the bright path which the moon cast across the sea. Was it a seagull, or the little gleaming sail of some small boat? The Bishop fixed his eyes on it, wondering.

"It must be a boat sailing after us," thought he, "but it is overtaking us very rapidly. It was far, far away a minute ago, but now it is much nearer. It cannot be a boat, for I can see no sail; but whatever it may be, it is following us and catching us up."

And he could not make out what it was. Not a boat, nor a bird, nor a fish! It was too large for a man, and besides a man could not be out there in the midst of the sea. The Bishop rose, and said to the helmsman:

"Look there, what is that, my friend? What is it?" the Bishop repeated, though he could now see plainly what it was—the three hermits running upon the water, all gleaming white, their grey beards shining, and approaching the ship as quickly as though it were not moving.

The steersman looked, and let go the helm in terror.

"Oh, Lord! The hermits are running after us on the water as though it were dry land!"

The passengers, hearing him, jumped up and crowded to the stern. They saw the hermits coming along hand in hand, and the two outer ones beckoning the ship to stop. All three were gliding along upon the water without moving their feet. Before the ship could be stopped, the hermits had reached it, and raising their heads, all three as with one voice, began to say:

"We have forgotten your teaching, servant of God. As long as we kept repeating it we remembered, but when we stopped saying it for a time, a word dropped out, and now it has all gone to pieces. We can remember nothing of it. Teach us again."

The Bishop crossed himself, and leaning over the ship's side, said:

"Your own prayer will reach the Lord, men of God. It is not for me to teach you. Pray for us sinners."

And the Bishop bowed low before the old men; and they turned and went back across the sea. And a light shone until daybreak on the spot where they were lost to sight.

Translated by Louise and Aylmer Maude

GUY DAVENPORT

Ithaka

There was, as Ezra Pound remarked, a mouse in the tree. We sat under the *pergola di trattoria* above San Pantaleone in Sant' Ambrogio di Rapallo. His panama on the table, his stick across his lap, Pound leaned back in his chair. In the congenial mat of vine and fig above him there was, as he said, a mouse.

—So there is, Miss Rudge said. What eyes you have, Ezra.

We had been moving Pound's and Miss Rudge's effects from a *dependenza* in an olive grove above Rapallo to the little house that Miss Rudge had lived in before the war and only now had managed to regain. The heavier pieces had gone on the day before. We loaded our Renault named Hephaistiskos with crockery, Max Ernst's *Blue,* the photograph of the Schifanoia *freschi* Yeats writes about in *A Vision,* books, and baskets of household linen.

Pound's cot would not fit into the car and I carried it on my head along the *salita.*

Then we drove down to the harbor, to meet Massimo for a swim. We changed in a *cameretta di spiaggia* that belonged to Massimo's family, Pound into bathing drawers of some black clerical cloth that sheathed him from chest to knee, so that alongside our *piccole mutandine* he seemed to be the nineteenth century, bearded, doctoral, and titled, going swimming with the twentieth. A fierce pink scar, obviously the incision of an operation, curved across the old man's lower back.

—He's going out much too far! Miss Rudge called to me once we were in the water.

She sat under a fetching floppy hat on the terrace of the beach house. It was a while before I saw that she was genuinely anxious.

—Do tell him to come in closer!

I swam out and signaled Steve.

—You and Massimo, I said, swim around the old boy in circles. Don't let him out of your sight.

We had taken the measure of his stubbornness in the last few days. It was phenomenal. He strode ahead of us all up the *salita,* swung himself onto the yacht like a sailor, walked the streets of Rapallo as soldierly as a major general on parade.

They swam around him like dolphins. Miss Rudge kept hailing me back to the pier.

—He won't listen to us, I said. He keeps swimming farther out. I've told the boys not to leave him for a second.

—Tell him to come back!

I didn't want to say I might as well command the Mediterranean to turn to lemonade for all the good it would do, so I raised my eyebrows and looked hopeless. She nodded her understanding but insisted again that I make the attempt.

Meanwhile he was well out into the offing, going great guns, straight out, flanked by Steve and Massimo. I had the awful feeling that their presence merely egged him on.

And at lunch he had been stubborner. We went to a place he had eaten in for years. The waiters made on over him. The proprietor came and shook hands. But when it came to giving an order, Pound fell into his silence. Miss Rudge cajoled. The waiters understood. We kept up a screen of talk to fill in for the silence after the repeated question as to what Pound would fancy for lunch. He would neither say, nor answer yes or no to suggestions.

—Well, then, Miss Rudge said cheerfully, you do without your lunch, don't you, Ezra?

He was anguished, terrified, caught. Then we all became helplessly silent. His head sank deeper between his shoulders. His tongue moved across his lips. He spoke in a plaintive whisper.

—*Gnocchi,* he said.

When I first knew him, years before, at St. Elizabeths Hospital for the Criminally Insane in Washington, he was not yet the immensely old man that I would eventually have to remember, old as Titian, old as Walter Savage Landor, glaring and silent, standing in gondolas in Venice like some ineffably old Chinese court poet in exile, flowing in cape and wide poet's hat along the red walls of the Giudecca.

But in those days his beard and hair were already white. He wore an editor's eyeshade, giving him the air of a man who had just come off a tennis court. He had come instead from a cell. He would have letters from Marianne Moore in a string bag, letters from Tom Eliot, Kumrad Cummings, Achilles Fang, together with a battered and much-scribbled copy of *The Cantos,* and food for the squirrels, who knew him, and ventured close, their necks long with hope, their tails making rolling whisks.

And in those days he talked.

—Billy Yeats, he closed his eyes to say, is most decidedly *not* buried under bare Ben Bulben's head, did you know?

We did not know. He gave us a look that implied that we did not know anything.

—The story goes this way. WBY was parked temporarily beside Aubrey Beardsley in the cemetery for Prots at Roquebrune, up above Mentone, in which place there resided a certain exile from the old sod, her name escapes me if I ever knew it. *When,* therefore, the only naval vessel ever to leave Hibernian territorial waters, a destroyer which I think constitutes the entire Irish Navy, made its way after the war to reclaim Willy's mortal remains, it was met by whatever French protocol and then by the lady exile, who asked the commander if he had an extra drop on board of the real whisky a mere taste of which would make up for centuries of longing for the peat fires in the shebeens, and for the Liffey swans.

—Most naturally he did. Moreover, the captain and crew accepted the lively lady's invitation to her quarters somewhere up the hill between Mentone and Roquebrune, bringing along with them a case of the specified booze.

—Dawn, I believe, found them draining the last bottles. The full litany of Irish martyrs and poets had been toasted at this *festum hilarilissimum,* Lady Circe had danced the fling, the Charleston, and a fandango native to the Connemara tinkers, and the honor guard that was to dig up Willy and bring him with military pomp down the old Roman tesselated steps, presumably with pibrachs squealing and the drum rolling solemnly and without *cease,* and a flag displaying the shamrock and harp whipping nobly in the breeze, were distributed about the lair of the lady like so many ragdolls spilt from a basket.

—Well, and well, some deputation of frog officials turned up, the press had wetted its pencils, and there was nothing for it but that the gallant crew shake a leg, *exhume* Billy Yeats, and mount the distinguished coffin on the prow of the destroyer, where, flanked by handsome Irish guardsmen, it would sail to old Ireland to rest forever, or at least until Resurrection Day, in Drumcliffe churchyard.

—They did, shall we imagine, the best they could. If the ceremony lacked *steadiness,* nothing untoward happened until they had the stiff in the jollyboat headed across the bay. The French Navy boomed a salute and the local *filarmonica* tootled an Irish tune, and well out in the offing but far short of the Irish Navy, the jollyboat, Willy Yeats, and the convivial crew capsized.

—They sank.

—The French, well, the French were *étonnés,* and made haste to fish them *out.*

—But they couldn't find Willy. The Irish were beyond trying, having been drowned two ways, as it were, and the frogs shrugged their shoulders.

—Never mind, they decided. The coffin of state into which they were to put Billy was on board, so they simply moved it up to the prow, hoisted the flag, rolled the drum, and steamed away.

—Billy being still there, at the bottom of the Mediterranean.

Mischief had danced in his eyes. He tied a peanut to a string and dangled it at arm's length. A squirrel ventured toward it, hop a bit, run a bit, stood, and got the peanut loose.

—It's all in knowing how to tie the knot, he had said.

And now the awful silence had found him. Aside from the word *gnocchi* and the observation that there was a mouse in the tree, he had said nothing all day.

The evening was coming on cool and sweet. Our meal was set out on a long table. Pound sat at the head, Steve and I along one side facing Olga Rudge and Massimo. The conversation was about certain experimental film makers, in whom Massimo was interested, Stan Brakhage, Jonas Mekas, Gregory Markopoulas, Smith, Baille, Anger. Pound plucked the back of a hand already raw. Suddenly he looked up, glared, and
spoke.

—There is a magpie in China, he said, can turn a hedgehog over and do it in.

His rusted hand lifted his wine to his frizzled beard but he did not sip. Massimo shot a glance my way.

—Where in the world did you learn that, Ezra? Miss Rudge asked.

He put his wine back on the table. He sighed. One hand clawed at the knuckles of the other.

—I found it, he said, in Gile's dictionary.

Miss Rudge smiled at me.

—We've been reading your Archilochos. Ezra says that you drew the decorations as well.

The conversation changed over to translation. I tried an anecdote about Wilamowitz-Moellendorff and his stout refusal to believe that Sappho was anything but a sound wife and mother of good family.

—Wilamowitz! Miss Rudge said. He was the handsomest man in Europe in his day.

—There's a restaurant down in Rapallo, Pound said, where Nietzsche inscribed the guest book. The *padrone* knew who he was and asked him to write his name. They still show it. It says: *Beware the beefsteak.*

—Ezra, Miss Rudge said, taking a bottle from her purse, it's time for your pill.

His face fell. She handed him a small tablet.

—Take it with your wine. Right now, so I'll know if you've had it.

Pound closed his hand around the pill, tight.

—Please, Ezra. What will these young men think? They adore you. They'll remember these days as long as they live. Do you want them to remember that you refused to take your medicine?

She did not say that Massimo's father was Pound's doctor, and that there would be criticism from another quarter if he didn't take his pill.

Massimo asked about Jack Smith. Pound talked about a profile of Natalie Clifford Barney that some artist had made with a single hair pasted onto paper. He had found it among his plundered possessions after returning to Italy.

—But it had come unstuck in places and didn't look like her anymore.

—Ezra, have you taken your pill?

He glared at her.

We talked about Sartre's *Les Mots,* which Pound had said he was reading.

—The very beginning is like a page of Flaubert, I said.

—Perhaps, Pound said.

We talked about William Carlos Williams, the Biennale, Greece, Hugh Kenner (*such an entertaining raconteur,* Miss Rudge said), words (*Ezra has been trying to remember the Spanish for* romance), scholars *(It's their wives who are such a trial),* Tino Trova, John Cournos, photographers from *Life* who had run wires all over the apartment in Venice until the furniture looked like the Laocoön, the olive crop, Michael Ventris.

—Ezra, you really must take your pill.

His fist tightened.

It was fully night, and we had had a long day. I asked to be allowed to pay for the meal.

—Never, said Miss Rudge.

No waiter was in sight and I got up to go in search of one.

—No, Miss Rudge said. This is our treat.

She was up and away into the *trattoria* before I could see any sign of a waiter.

As soon as she was out of sight, Pound uncurled his fist and popped the pill into his mouth, washing it down with a swallow of wine.

—Time to hit the hay, he said.

Miss Rudge returned with the *padrone* and his wife. There were handshakes and farewells.

—Ezra, have you taken your pill?
He did not answer. He glared at us all. Both his hands were obviously
empty.
We exchanged knowing glances, Massimo, Steve, and I. Miss Rudge
graciously did not ask us if he had taken his pill. We did not offer to say
that he had. It was a trying moment.
We drove them to the house where Miss Rudge had lived twenty
years before, to which she was now returning. We said our goodbyes in a
room where Pound's cot was neatly made with an American Indian
blanket. The pillowcase was of unbleached linen. Ernst's *Blue* stood
against the wall.
—*Addio!* he used to say. Now, anguish in his eyes, he said nothing at
all.

ANTON CHEKHOV

Kashtanka

I

MISBEHAVIOUR

A young dog, a reddish mongrel, between a dachshund and a "yard-
dog," very like a fox in face, was running up and down the pavement
looking uneasily from side to side. From time to time she stopped and,
whining and lifting first one chilled paw and then another, tried to make
up her mind how it could have happened that she was lost.

She remembered very well how she had passed the day, and how, in
the end, she had found herself on this unfamiliar pavement.

The day had begun by her master Luka Alexandritch's putting on his
hat, taking something wooden under his arm wrapped up in a red handkerchief, and calling: "Kashtanka, come along!"

Hearing her name the mongrel had come out from under the work-
table, where she slept on the shavings, stretched herself voluptuously
and run after her master. The people Luka Alexandritch worked for lived
a very long way off, so that, before he could get to any one of them, the
carpenter had several times to step into a tavern to fortify himself. Kash-

tanka remembered that on the way she had behaved extremely improperly. In her delight that she was being taken for a walk she jumped about, dashed barking after the trams, ran into yards, and chased other dogs. The carpenter was continually losing sight of her, stopping, and angrily shouting at her. Once he had even, with an expression of fury in his face, taken her fox-like ear in his fist, smacked her, and said emphatically: "Pla-a-ague take you, you pest!"

After having left the work where it had been bespoken, Luka Alexandritch went into his sister's and there had something to eat and drink; from his sister's he had gone to see a bookbinder he knew; from the bookbinder's to a tavern, from the tavern to another crony's, and so on. In short, by the time Kashtanka found herself on the unfamiliar pavement, it was getting dusk, and the carpenter was as drunk as a cobbler. He was waving his arms and, breathing heavily, muttered:

"In sin my mother bore me! Ah, sins, sins! Here now we are walking along the street and looking at the street lamps, but when we die, we shall burn in a fiery Gehenna. . . ."

Or he fell into a good-natured tone, called Kashtanka to him, and said to her: "You, Kashtanka, are an insect of a creature, and nothing else. Beside a man, you are much the same as a joiner beside a cabinet-maker. . . ."

While he talked to her in that way, there was suddenly a burst of music. Kashtanka looked round and saw that a regiment of soldiers was coming straight towards her. Unable to endure the music, which unhinged her nerves, she turned round and round and wailed. To her great surprise, the carpenter, instead of being frightened, whining and barking, gave a broad grin, drew himself up to attention, and saluted with all his five fingers. Seeing that her master did not protest, Kashtanka whined louder than ever, and dashed across the road to the opposite pavement.

When she recovered herself, the band was not playing and the regiment was no longer there. She ran across the road to the spot where she had left her master, but alas, the carpenter was no longer there. She dashed forward, then back again and ran across the road once more, but the carpenter seemed to have vanished into the earth. Kashtanka began sniffing the pavement, hoping to find her master by the scent of his tracks, but some wretch had been that way just before in new rubber goloshes, and now all delicate scents were mixed with an acute stench of india-rubber, so that it was impossible to make out anything.

Kashtanka ran up and down and did not find her master, and meanwhile it had got dark. The street lamps were lighted on both sides of the road, and lights appeared in the windows. Big, fluffy snowflakes were falling and painting white the pavement, the horses' backs and the cabmen's caps, and the darker the evening grew the whiter were all these objects. Unknown customers kept walking incessantly to and fro, obstructing her field of vision and shoving against her with their feet. (All mankind Kashtanka divided into two uneven parts: masters and customers; between them there was an essential difference: the first had the right to beat her, and the second she had the right to nip by the calves of their legs.) These customers were hurrying off somewhere and paid no attention to her.

When it got quite dark, Kashtanka was overcome by despair and horror. She huddled up in an entrance and began whining piteously. The long day's journeying with Luka Alexandritch had exhausted her, her ears and her paws were freezing, and, what was more, she was terribly hungry. Only twice in the whole day had she tasted a morsel: she had eaten a little paste at the bookbinder's, and in one of the taverns she had found a sausage skin on the floor, near the counter—that was all. If she had been a human being she would have certainly thought: "No, it is impossible to live like this! I must shoot myself!"

II

A MYSTERIOUS STRANGER

But she thought of nothing, she simply whined. When her head and back were entirely plastered over with the soft feathery snow, and she had sunk into a painful doze of exhaustion, all at once the door of the entrance clicked, creaked, and struck her on the side. She jumped up. A man belonging to the class of customers came out. As Kashtanka whined and got under his feet, he could not help noticing her. He bent down to her and asked:

"Doggy, where do you come from? Have I hurt you? Oh, poor thing, poor thing. . . . Come, don't be cross, don't be cross. . . . I am sorry."

Kashtanka looked at the stranger through the snow-flakes that hung on her eyelashes, and saw before her a short, fat little man, with a plump, shaven face wearing a top hat and a fur coat that swung open.

"What are you whining for?" he went on, knocking the snow off her back with his fingers. "Where is your master? I suppose you are lost? Ah, poor doggy! What are we going to do now?"

Catching in the stranger's voice a warm, cordial note, Kashtanka licked his hand, and whined still more pitifully.

"Oh, you nice funny thing!" said the stranger. "A regular fox! Well, there's nothing for it, you must come along with me! Perhaps you will be of use for something. . . . Well!"

He clicked with his lips, and made a sign to Kashtanka with his hand, which could only mean one thing: "Come along!" Kashtanka went.

Not more than half an hour later she was sitting on the floor in a big, light room, and, leaning her head against her side, was looking with tenderness and curiosity at the stranger who was sitting at the table, dining. He ate and threw pieces to her. . . . At first he gave her bread and the green rind of cheese, then a piece of meat, half a pie and chicken bones, while through hunger she ate so quickly that she had not time to distinguish the taste, and the more she ate the more acute was the feeling of hunger.

"Your master don't feed you properly," said the stranger, seeing with what ferocious greediness she swallowed the morsels without munching them. "And how thin you are! Nothing but skin and bones. . . ."

Kashtanka ate a great deal and yet did not satisfy her hunger, but was simply stupefied with eating. After dinner she lay down in the middle of the room, stretched her legs and, conscious of an agreeable weariness all over her body, wagged her tail. While her new master, lounging in an easy-chair, smoked a cigar, she wagged her tail and considered the question, whether it was better at the stranger's or at the carpenter's. The stranger's surroundings were poor and ugly; besides the easy-chairs, the sofa, the lamps and the rugs, there was nothing, and the room seemed empty. At the carpenter's the whole place was stuffed full of things: he had a table, a bench, a heap of shavings, planes, chisels, saws, a cage with a goldfinch, a basin. . . . The stranger's room smelt of nothing, while there was always a thick fog in the carpenter's room, and a glorious smell of glue, varnish, and shavings. On the other hand, the stranger had one great superiority—he gave her a great deal to eat and, to do him full justice, when Kashtanka sat facing the table and looking wistfully at him, he did not once hit or kick her, and did not once shout: "Go away, damned brute!"

When he had finished his cigar her new master went out, and a minute later came back holding a little mattress in his hands.

"Hey, you dog, come here!" he said, laying the mattress in the corner near the dog. "Lie down here, go to sleep!"

Then he put out the lamp and went away. Kashtanka lay down on the mattress and shut her eyes; the sound of a bark rose from the street, and she would have liked to answer it, but all at once she was overcome with unexpected melancholy. She thought of Luka Alexandritch, of his son Fedyushka, and her snug little place under the bench. . . . She remembered on the long winter evenings, when the carpenter was planing or reading the paper aloud, Fedyushka usually played with her. . . . He used to pull her from under the bench by her hind legs, and play such tricks with her, that she saw green before her eyes, and ached in every joint. He would make her walk on her hind legs, use her as a bell, that is, shake her violently by the tail so that she squealed and barked, and give her to-

bacco to sniff. . . . The following trick was particularly agonising: Fedyushka would tie a piece of meat to a thread and give it to Kashtanka,
and then, when she had swallowed it he would, with a loud laugh, pull it
back again from her stomach, and the more lurid were her memories the
more loudly and miserably Kashtanka whined.

But soon exhaustion and warmth prevailed over melancholy. She
began to fall asleep. Dogs ran by in her imagination: among them a
shaggy old poodle, whom she had seen that day in the street with a white
patch on his eye and tufts of wool by his nose. Fedyushka ran after the
poodle with a chisel in his hand, then all at once he too was covered with
shaggy wool, and began merrily barking beside Kashtanka. Kashtanka
and he good-naturedly sniffed each other's noses and merrily ran down
the street. . . .

III

NEW AND VERY AGREEABLE ACQUAINTANCES

When Kashtanka woke up it was already light, and a sound rose from the
street, such as only comes in the daytime. There was not a soul in the
room. Kashtanka stretched, yawned and, cross and ill-humoured, walked
about the room. She sniffed the corners and the furniture, looked into
the passage and found nothing of interest there. Besides the door that
led into the passage there was another door. After thinking a little Kashtanka scratched on it with both paws, opened it, and went into the
adjoining room. Here on the bed, covered with a rug, a customer, in
whom she recognised the stranger of yesterday, lay asleep.

"Rrrrr . . ." she growled, but recollecting yesterday's dinner, wagged
her tail, and began sniffing.

She sniffed the stranger's clothes and boots and thought they smelt of
horses. In the bedroom was another door, also closed. Kashtanka
scratched at the door, leaned her chest against it, opened it, and was
instantly aware of a strange and very suspicious smell. Foreseeing an
unpleasant encounter, growling and looking about her, Kashtanka
walked into a little room with a dirty wall-paper and drew back in alarm.
She saw something surprising and terrible. A grey gander came straight
towards her, hissing, with its neck bowed down to the floor and its wings
outspread. Not far from him, on a little mattress, lay a white tom-cat;
seeing Kashtanka, he jumped up, arched his back, wagged his tail with
his hair standing on end and he, too, hissed at her. The dog was frightened in earnest, but not caring to betray her alarm, began barking loudly
and dashed at the cat. . . . The cat arched his back more than ever,
mewed and gave Kashtanka a smack on the head with his paw. Kashtanka jumped back, squatted on all four paws, and craning her nose

towards the cat, went off into loud, shrill barks; meanwhile the gander came up behind and gave her a painful peck in the back. Kashtanka leapt up and dashed at the gander.

"What's this?" They heard a loud angry voice, and the stranger came into the room in his dressing-gown, with a cigar between his teeth. "What's the meaning of this? To your places!"

He went up to the cat, flicked him on his arched back, and said:

"Fyodor Timofeyitch, what's the meaning of this? Have you got up a fight? Ah, you old rascal! Lie down!"

And turning to the gander he shouted: "Ivan Ivanitch, go home!"

The cat obediently lay down on his mattress and closed his eyes. Judging from the expression of his face and whiskers, he was displeased with himself for having lost his temper and got into a fight. Kashtanka began whining resentfully, while the gander craned his neck and began saying something rapidly, excitedly, distinctly, but quite unintelligibly.

"All right, all right," said his master, yawning. "You must live in peace and friendship." He stroked Kashtanka and went on: "And you, red-hair, don't be frightened. . . . They are capital company, they won't annoy you. Stay, what are we to call you? You can't go on without a name, my dear."

The stranger thought a moment and said, "I tell you what . . . you shall be Auntie. . . . Do you understand? Auntie!"

And repeating the word "Auntie" several times he went out. Kashtanka sat down and began watching. The cat sat motionless on his little mattress, and pretended to be asleep. The gander, craning his neck and stamping, went on talking rapidly and excitedly about something. Apparently it was a very clever gander; after every long tirade, he always stepped back with an air of wonder and made a show of being highly delighted with his own speech. . . . Listening to him and answering "R-r-r-r," Kashtanka fell to sniffing the corners. In one of the corners she found a little trough in which she saw some soaked peas and a sop of rye crusts. She tried the peas; they were not nice; she tried the sopped bread and began eating it. The gander was not at all offended that the strange dog was eating his food, but, on the contrary, talked even more excitedly, and to show his confidence went to the trough and ate a few peas himself.

IV

MARVELS ON A HURDLE

A little while afterwards the stranger came in again, and brought a strange thing with him like a hurdle, or like the figure II. On the cross-piece on the top of this roughly made wooden frame hung a bell, and a pistol was also tied to it; there were strings from the tongue of the bell, and the trigger of the pistol. The stranger put the frame in the middle of the room, spent a long time tying and untying something, then looked at the gander and said: "Ivan Ivanitch, if you please!"

The gander went up to him and stood in an expectant attitude.

"Now then," said the stranger, "let us begin at the very beginning. First of all, bow and make a curtsey! Look sharp!"

Ivan Ivanitch craned his neck, nodded in all directions, and scraped with his foot.

"Right. Bravo. . . . Now die!"

The gander lay on his back and stuck his legs in the air. After performing a few more similar, unimportant tricks, the stranger suddenly clutched at his head, and assuming an expression of horror, shouted: "Help! Fire! We are burning!"

Ivan Ivanitch ran to the frame, took the string in his beak, and set the bell ringing.

The stranger was very much pleased. He stroked the gander's neck and said:

"Bravo, Ivan Ivanitch! Now pretend that you are a jeweller selling gold and diamonds. Imagine now that you go to your shop and find thieves there. What would you do in that case?"

The gander took the other string in his beak and pulled it, and at once a deafening report was heard. Kashtanka was highly delighted with the bell ringing, and the shot threw her into so much ecstasy that she ran round the frame barking.

"Auntie, lie down!" cried the stranger; "be quiet!"

Ivan Ivanitch's task was not ended with the shooting. For a whole hour afterwards the stranger drove the gander round him on a cord, cracking a whip, and the gander had to jump over barriers and through hoops; he had to rear, that is, sit on his tail and wave his legs in the air. Kashtanka could not take her eyes off Ivanitch, wriggled with delight, and several times fell to running after him with shrill barks. After exhausting the gander and himself, the stranger wiped the sweat from his brow and cried:

"Marya, fetch Havronya Ivanovna here!"

A minute later there was the sound of grunting. . . . Kashtanka growled, assumed a very valiant air, and to be on the safe side, went nearer to the stranger. The door opened, an old woman looked in, and, saying something, led in a black and very ugly sow. Paying no attention to Kashtanka's growls, the sow lifted up her little hoof and grunted good-humouredly. Apparently it was very agreeable to her to see her master, the cat, and Ivan Ivanitch. When she went up to the cat and gave him a light tap on the stomach with her hoof, and then made some remark to the gander, a great deal of good-nature was expressed in her movements, and the quivering of her tail. Kashtanka realised at once that to growl and bark at such a character was useless.

The master took away the frame and cried: "Fyodor Timofeyitch, if you please!"

The cat stretched lazily, and reluctantly, as though performing a duty, went up to the sow.

"Come, let us begin with the Egyptian pyramid," began the master.

He spent a long time explaining something, then gave the word of command, "One . . . two . . . three!" At the word "three" Ivan Ivanitch flapped his wings and jumped on to the sow's back. . . . When, balancing himself with his wings and his neck, he got a firm foothold on the bristly back, Fyodor Timofeyitch listlessly and lazily, with manifest disdain, and with an air of scorning his art and not caring a pin for it, climbed on to the sow's back, then reluctantly mounted on to the gander, and stood on his hind legs. The result was what the stranger called the Egyptian pyramid. Kashtanka yapped with delight, but at that moment the old cat yawned and, losing his balance, rolled off the gander. Ivan Ivanitch lurched and fell off too. The stranger shouted, waved his hands, and began explaining something again. After spending an hour over the pyramid their indefatigable master proceeded to teach Ivan Ivanitch to ride on the cat, then began to teach the cat to smoke, and so on.

The lesson ended in the stranger's wiping the sweat off his brow and going away. Fyodor Timofeyitch gave a disdainful sniff, lay down on his mattress, and closed his eyes; Ivan Ivanitch went to the trough, and the pig was taken away by the old woman. Thanks to the number of her new impressions, Kashtanka hardly noticed how the day passed, and in the evening she was installed with her mattress in the room with the dirty wall-paper, and spent the night in the society of Fyodor Timofeyitch and the gander.

V

TALENT! TALENT!

A month passed.

Kashtanka had grown used to having a nice dinner every evening, and being called Auntie. She had grown used to the stranger too, and to her new companions. Life was comfortable and easy.

Every day began in the same way. As a rule, Ivan Ivanitch was the first to wake up, and at once went up to Auntie or to the cat, twisting his neck, and beginning to talk excitedly and persuasively, but, as before, unintelligibly. Sometimes he would crane up his head in the air and utter a long monologue. At first Kashtanka thought he talked so much because he was very clever, but after a little time had passed, she lost all her respect for him; when he went up to her with his long speeches she no longer wagged her tail, but treated him as a tiresome chatterbox, who would not let anyone sleep and, without the slightest ceremony, answered him with "R-r-r-r!"

Fyodor Timofeyitch was a gentleman of a very different sort. When he woke he did not utter a sound, did not stir, and did not even open his eyes. He would have been glad not to wake, for, as was evident, he was not greatly in love with life. Nothing interested him, he showed an apathetic and nonchalant attitude to everything, he disdained everything and, even while eating his delicious dinner, sniffed contemptuously.

When she woke Kashtanka began walking about the room and sniffing the corners. She and the cat were the only ones allowed to go all over the flat; the gander had not the right to cross the threshold of the room with the dirty wall-paper, and Havronya Ivanovna lived somewhere in a little outhouse in the yard and made her appearance only during the lessons. Their master got up late, and immediately after drinking his tea began teaching them their tricks. Every day the frame, the whip, and the hoop were brought in, and every day almost the same performance took place. The lesson lasted three or four hours, so that sometimes Fyodor Timofeyitch was so tired that he staggered about like a drunken man, and Ivan Ivanitch opened his beak and breathed heavily, while their master became red in the face and could not mop the sweat from his brow fast enough.

The lesson and the dinner made the day very interesting, but the evenings were tedious. As a rule, their master went off somewhere in the evening and took the cat and the gander with him. Left alone, Auntie lay down on her little mattress and began to feel sad. . . .

Melancholy crept on her imperceptibly and took possession of her by degrees, as darkness does of a room. It began with the dog's losing every inclination to bark, to eat, to run about the rooms, and even to look at things; then vague figures, half dogs, half human beings, with countenances attractive, pleasant, but incomprehensible, would appear in her imagination; when they came Auntie wagged her tail, and it seemed to her that she had somewhere, at some time, seen them and loved them. . . . And as she dropped asleep, she always felt that those figures smelt of glue, shavings, and varnish.

When she had grown quite used to her new life, and from a thin, long mongrel, had changed into a sleek, well-groomed dog, her master looked at her one day before the lesson and said:

"It's high time, Auntie, to get to business. You have kicked up your heels in idleness long enough. I want to make an artiste of you. . . . Do you want to be an artiste?"

And he began teaching her various accomplishments. At the first lesson he taught her to stand and walk on her hind legs, which she liked extremely. At the second lesson she had to jump on her hind legs and catch some sugar, which her teacher held high above her head. After that, in the following lessons she danced, ran tied to a cord, howled to music, rang the bell, and fired the pistol, and in a month could successfully replace Fyodor Timofeyitch in the "Egyptian Pyramid." She learned very eagerly and was pleased with her own success; running with her tongue out on the cord, leaping through the hoop, and riding on old Fyodor Timofeyitch, gave her the greatest enjoyment. She accompanied every successful trick with a shrill, delighted bark, while her teacher wondered, was also delighted, and rubbed his hands.

"It's talent! It's talent!" he said. "Unquestionable talent! You will certainly be successful!"

And Auntie grew so used to the word talent, that every time her master pronounced it, she jumped up as if it had been her name.

VI

AN UNEASY NIGHT

Auntie had a doggy dream that a porter ran after her with a broom, and she woke up in a fright.

It was quite dark and very stuffy in the room. The fleas were biting. Auntie had never been afraid of darkness before, but now, for some reason, she felt frightened and inclined to bark.

Her master heaved a loud sigh in the next room, then soon afterwards the sow grunted in her sty, and then all was still again. When one thinks about eating one's heart grows lighter, and Auntie began thinking how that day she had stolen the leg of chicken from Fyodor Timofeyitch, and had hidden it in the drawing-room, between the cupboard and the wall, where there were a great many spiders' webs and a great deal of dust. Would it not be as well to go now and look whether the chicken leg were still there or not? It was very possible that her master had found it and eaten it. But she must not go out of the room before morning, that was the rule. Auntie shut her eyes to go to sleep as quickly as possible, for she knew by experience that the sooner you go to sleep the sooner the morning comes. But all at once there was a strange scream not far from her which made her start and jump up on all four legs. It was Ivan Ivanitch, and his cry was not babbling and persuasive as usual, but a wild, shrill, unnatural scream, like the squeak of a door opening. Unable to distinguish anything in the darkness, and not understanding what was wrong, Auntie felt still more frightened and growled: "R-r-r-r. . . ."

Some time passed, as long as it takes to eat a good bone; the scream was not repeated. Little by little Auntie's uneasiness passed off and she began to doze. She dreamed of two big black dogs with tufts of last year's coat left on their haunches and sides; they were eating out of a big basin some swill, from which there came a white steam and a most appetising smell; from time to time they looked round at Auntie, showed their teeth and growled: "We are not going to give you any!" But a peasant in a fur-coat ran out of the house and drove them away with a whip; then Auntie went up to the basin and began eating, but as soon as the peasant went out of the gate, the two black dogs rushed at her growling, and all at once there was again a shrill scream.

"K-gee! K-gee-gee!" cried Ivan Ivanitch.

Auntie woke, jumped up and, without leaving her mattress, went off into a yelping bark. It seemed to her that it was not Ivan Ivanitch that was screaming but someone else, and for some reason the sow again grunted in her sty.

Then there was the sound of shuffling slippers, and the master came into the room in his dressing-gown with a candle in his hand. The flickering light danced over the dirty wall-paper and the ceiling, and chased away the darkness. Auntie saw that there was no stranger in the room. Ivan Ivanitch was sitting on the floor and was not asleep. His wings were spread out and his beak was open, and altogether he looked as though he were very tired and thirsty. Old Fyodor Timofeyitch was not asleep either. He, too, must have been awakened by the scream.

"Ivan Ivanitch, what's the matter with you?" the master asked the gander. "Why are you screaming? Are you ill?"

The gander did not answer. The master touched him on the neck, stroked his back, and said: "You are a queer chap. You don't sleep yourself, and you don't let other people. . . ."

When the master went out, carrying the candle with him, there was darkness again. Auntie felt frightened. The gander did not scream, but again she fancied that there was some stranger in the room. What was most dreadful was that this stranger could not be bitten, as he was unseen and had no shape. And for some reason she thought that something very bad would certainly happen that night. Fyodor Timofeyitch was uneasy too. Auntie could hear him shifting on his mattress, yawning and shaking his head.

Somewhere in the street there was a knocking at a gate and the sow grunted in her sty. Auntie began to whine, stretched out her front-paws and laid her head down upon them. She fancied that in the knocking at the gate, in the grunting of the sow, who was for some reason awake, in the darkness and the stillness, there was something as miserable and dreadful as in Ivan Ivanitch's scream. Everything was in agitation and anxiety, but why? Who was the stranger who could not be seen? Then two dim flashes of green gleamed for a minute near Auntie. It was Fyodor Timofeyitch, for the first time of their whole acquaintance coming up to her. What did he want? Auntie licked his paw, and not asking why he had come, howled softly and on various notes.

"K-gee!" cried Ivan Ivanitch, "K-g-ee!"

The door opened again and the master came in with a candle.

The gander was sitting in the same attitude as before, with his beak open, and his wings spread out, his eyes were closed.

"Ivan Ivanitch!" his master called him.

The gander did not stir. His master sat down before him on the floor, looked at him in silence for a minute, and said:

"Ivan Ivanitch, what is it? Are you dying? Oh, I remember now, I remember!" he cried out, and clutched at his head. "I know why it is! It's because the horse stepped on you to-day! My God! My God!"

Auntie did not understand what her master was saying, but she saw from his face that he, too, was expecting something dreadful. She stretched out her head towards the dark window, where it seemed to her some stranger was looking in, and howled.

"He is dying, Auntie!" said her master, and wrung his hands. "Yes, yes, he is dying! Death has come into your room. What are we to do?"

Pale and agitated, the master went back into his room, sighing and shaking his head. Auntie was afraid to remain in the darkness, and followed her master into his bedroom. He sat down on the bed and repeated several times: "My God, what's to be done?"

Auntie walked about round his feet, and not understanding why she was wretched and why they were all so uneasy, and trying to understand, watched every movement he made. Fyodor Timofeyitch, who rarely left his little mattress, came into the master's bedroom too, and began rubbing himself against his feet. He shook his head as though he wanted to shake painful thoughts out of it, and kept peeping suspiciously under the bed.

The master took a saucer, poured some water from his wash-stand into it, and went to the gander again.

"Drink, Ivan Ivanitch!" he said tenderly, setting the saucer before him: "drink, darling."

But Ivan Ivanitch did not stir and did not open his eyes. His master bent his head down to the saucer and dipped his beak into the water, but the gander did not drink, he spread his wings wider than ever, and his head remained lying in the saucer.

"No, there's nothing to be done now," sighed his master. "It's all over. Ivan Ivanitch is gone!"

And shining drops, such as one sees on the window-pane when it rains, trickled down his cheeks. Not understanding what was the matter, Auntie and Fyodor Timofeyitch snuggled up to him and looked with horror at the gander.

"Poor Ivan Ivanitch!" said the master, sighing mournfully. "And I was dreaming I would take you in the spring into the country, and would walk with you on the green grass. Dear creature, my good comrade, you are no more! How shall I do without you now?"

It seemed to Auntie that the same thing would happen to her, that is, that she too, there was no knowing why, would close her eyes, stretch out her paws, open her mouth, and everyone would look at her with horror. Apparently the same reflections were passing through the brain of Fyodor Timofeyitch. Never before had the old cat been so morose and gloomy.

It began to get light, and the unseen stranger who had so frightened Auntie was no longer in the room. When it was quite daylight, the porter came in, took the gander, and carried him away. And soon afterwards the old woman came in and took away the trough.

Auntie went into the drawing-room and looked behind the cupboard: her master had not eaten the chicken bone, it was lying in its place among the dust and spiders' webs. But Auntie felt sad and dreary and wanted to cry. She did not even sniff at the bone, but went under the sofa, sat down there, and began softly whining in a thin voice.

VII

AN UNSUCCESSFUL DÉBUT

One fine evening the master came into the room with the dirty wall-paper, and, rubbing his hands, said:

"Well. . . ."

He meant to say something more, but went away without saying it. Auntie, who during her lessons had thoroughly studied his face and intonations, divined that he was agitated, anxious and, she fancied, angry. Soon afterwards he came back and said:

"To-day I shall take with me Auntie and Fyodor Timofeyitch. To-day, Auntie, you will take the place of poor Ivan Ivanitch in the 'Egyptian Pyramid.' Goodness knows how it will be! Nothing is ready, nothing has been thoroughly studied, there have been few rehearsals! We shall be disgraced, we shall come to grief!"

Then he went out again, and a minute later, came back in his fur-coat and top hat. Going up to the cat he took him by the fore-paws and put him inside the front of his coat, while Fyodor Timofeyitch appeared completely unconcerned, and did not even trouble to open his eyes. To him it was apparently a matter of absolute indifference whether he remained lying down, or were lifted up by his paws, whether he rested on his mattress or under his master's fur-coat. . . .

"Come along, Auntie," said her master.

Wagging her tail, and understanding nothing, Auntie followed him. A minute later she was sitting in a sledge by her master's feet and heard him, shrinking with cold and anxiety, mutter to himself:

"We shall be disgraced! We shall come to grief!"

The sledge stopped at a big strange-looking house, like a soup-ladle turned upside down. The long entrance to this house, with its three glass doors, was lighted up with a dozen brilliant lamps. The doors opened with a resounding noise and, like jaws, swallowed up the people who were moving to and fro at the entrance. There were a great many people, horses, too, often ran up to the entrance, but no dogs were to be seen.

The master took Auntie in his arms and thrust her in his coat, where Fyodor Timofeyitch already was. It was dark and stuffy there, but warm. For an instant two green sparks flashed at her; it was the cat, who opened his eyes on being disturbed by his neighbour's cold rough paws. Auntie licked his ear, and, trying to settle herself as comfortably as possible, moved uneasily, crushed him under her cold paws, and casually poked her head out from under the coat, but at once growled angrily, and tucked it in again. It seemed to her that she had seen a huge, badly lighted room, full of monsters; from behind screens and gratings, which stretched on both sides of the room, horrible faces looked out: faces of horses with horns, with long ears, and one fat, huge countenance with a tail instead of a nose, and two long gnawed bones sticking out of his mouth.

The cat mewed huskily under Auntie's paws, but at that moment the coat was flung open, the master said, "Hop!" and Fyodor Timofeyitch and Auntie jumped to the floor. They were now in a little room with grey plank walls; there was no other furniture in it but a little table with a looking-glass on it, a stool, and some rags hung about the corners, and instead of a lamp or candles, there was a bright fan-shaped light attached to a little pipe fixed in the wall. Fyodor Timofeyitch licked his coat which had been ruffled by Auntie, went under the stool, and lay down. Their master, still agitated and rubbing his hands, began undressing. . . . He undressed as he usually did at home when he was preparing to get under the rug, that is, took off everything but his underlinen, then he sat down on the stool, and, looking in the looking-glass, began playing the most surprising tricks with himself. . . . First of all he put on his head a wig, with a parting and with two tufts of hair standing up like horns, then he smeared his face thickly with something white, and over the white colour painted his eyebrows, his moustaches, and red on his cheeks. His antics did not end with that. After smearing his face and neck, he began putting himself into an extraordinary and incongruous costume, such as Auntie had never seen before, either in houses or in the street. Imagine very full trousers, made of chintz covered with big flowers, such as is used in working-class houses for curtains and covering furniture, trousers which buttoned up just under his armpits. One trouser leg was made of brown chintz, the other of bright yellow. Almost lost in these, he then put on a short chintz jacket, with a big scalloped collar, and a gold star on the back, stockings of different colours, and green slippers.

Everything seemed going round before Auntie's eyes and in her soul. The white-faced, sack-like figure smelt like her master, its voice, too, was the familiar master's voice, but there were moments when Auntie was tortured by doubts, and then she was ready to run away from the particoloured figure and to bark. The new place, the fan-shaped light, the smell, the transformation that had taken place in her master—all this aroused in her a vague dread and a foreboding that she would certainly meet with some horror such as the big face with the tail instead of a nose. And then, somewhere through the wall, some hateful band was playing, and from time to time she heard an incomprehensible roar. Only one thing reassured her—that was the imperturbability of Fyodor Timofeyitch. He dozed with the utmost tranquillity under the stool, and did not open his eyes even when it was moved.

A man in a dress coat and a white waistcoat peeped into the little room and said:

"Miss Arabella has just gone on. After her—you."

Their master made no answer. He drew a small box from under the table, sat down, and waited. From his lips and his hands it could be seen that he was agitated, and Auntie could hear how his breathing came in gasps.

"Monsieur George, come on!" someone shouted behind the door. Their master got up and crossed himself three times, then took the cat from under the stool and put him in the box.

"Come, Auntie," he said softly.

Auntie, who could make nothing out of it, went up to his hands, he kissed her on the head, and put her beside Fyodor Timofeyitch. Then followed darkness. . . . Auntie trampled on the cat, scratched at the walls of the box, and was so frightened that she could not utter a sound, while the box swayed and quivered, as though it were on the waves. . . .

"Here we are again!" her master shouted aloud: "here we are again!"

Auntie felt that after that shout the box struck against something hard and left off swaying. There was a loud deep roar, someone was being slapped, and that someone, probably the monster with the tail instead of a nose, roared and laughed so loud that the locks of the box trembled. In response to the roar, there came a shrill, squeaky laugh from her master, such as he never laughed at home.

"Ha!" he shouted, trying to shout above the roar. "Honoured friends! I have only just come from the station! My granny's kicked the bucket and left me a fortune! There is something very heavy in the box, it must be gold, ha! ha! I bet there's a million here! We'll open it and look. . . ."

The lock of the box clicked. The bright light dazzled Auntie's eyes, she jumped out of the box, and, deafened by the roar, ran quickly round her master, and broke into a shrill bark.

"Ha!" exclaimed her master. "Uncle Fyodor Timofeyitch! Beloved Aunt, dear relations! The devil take you!"

He fell on his stomach on the sand, seized the cat and Auntie, and fell to embracing them. While he held Auntie tight in his arms, she glanced round into the world into which fate had brought her and, impressed by its immensity, was for a minute dumfounded with amazement and delight, then jumped out of her master's arms, and to express the intensity of her emotions, whirled round and round on one spot like a top. This new world was big and full of bright light; wherever she looked, on all sides, from floor to ceiling there were faces, faces, faces, and nothing else.

"Auntie, I beg you to sit down!" shouted her master. Remembering what that meant, Auntie jumped on to a chair, and sat down. She looked at her master. His eyes looked at her gravely and kindly as always, but his face, especially his mouth and teeth, were made grotesque by a broad immovable grin. He laughed, skipped about, twitched his shoulders, and made a show of being very merry in the presence of the thousands of faces. Auntie believed in his merriment, all at once felt all over her that those thousands of faces were looking at her, lifted up her fox-like head, and howled joyously.

"You sit there, Auntie," her master said to her, "while Uncle and I will dance the Kamarinsky."

Fyodor Timofeyitch stood looking about him indifferently, waiting to be made to do something silly. He danced listlessly, carelessly, sullenly, and one could see from his movements, his tail and his ears, that he had a profound contempt for the crowd, the bright light, his master and himself. When he had performed his allotted task, he gave a yawn and sat down.

"Now, Auntie!" said her master, "we'll have first a song, and then a dance, shall we?"

He took a pipe out of his pocket, and began playing. Auntie, who could not endure music, began moving uneasily in her chair and howled. A roar of applause rose from all sides. Her master bowed, and when all was still again, went on playing. . . . Just as he took one very high note, someone high up among the audience uttered a loud exclamation:

"Auntie!" cried a child's voice, "why, it's Kashtanka!"

"Kashtanka it is!" declared a cracked drunken tenor. "Kashtanka! Strike me dead, Fedyushka, it is Kashtanka. Kashtanka! here!"

Someone in the gallery gave a whistle, and two voices, one a boy's and one a man's, called loudly: "Kashtanka! Kashtanka!"

Auntie started, and looked where the shouting came from. Two faces, one hairy, drunken and grinning, the other chubby, rosy-cheeked and frightened-looking, dazed her eyes as the bright light had dazed them before. . . . She remembered, fell off the chair, struggled on the sand, then jumped up, and with a delighted yap dashed towards those faces. There was a deafening roar, interspersed with whistles and a shrill childish shout: "Kashtanka! Kashtanka!"

Auntie leaped over the barrier, then across someone's shoulders. She found herself in a box: to get into the next tier she had to leap over a high wall. Auntie jumped, but did not jump high enough, and slipped back down the wall. Then she was passed from hand to hand, licked hands and faces, kept mounting higher and higher, and at last got into the gallery. . . .

Half an hour afterwards, Kashtanka was in the street, following the people who smelt of glue and varnish. Luka Alexandritch staggered and instinctively, taught by experience, tried to keep as far from the gutter as possible.

"In sin my mother bore me," he muttered. "And you, Kashtanka, are a thing of little understanding. Beside a man, you are like a joiner beside a cabinetmaker."

Fedyushka walked beside him, wearing his father's cap. Kashtanka looked at their backs, and it seemed to her that she had been following them for ages, and was glad that there had not been a break for a minute in her life.

She remembered the little room with dirty wall-paper, the gander, Fyodor Timofeyitch, the delicious dinners, the lessons, the circus, but all that seemed to her now like a long, tangled oppressive dream.

Translated by Constance Garnett

NADINE GORDIMER

Otherwise Birds Fly In

Toni and Kate still saw each other regularly once or twice a year.

One would have quite expected Toni to be out of sight, by now; Kate would have accepted this as inevitable, if it had happened, and have looked up with affection at the bright passage of the little satellite among other worlds. Yet since Toni's extraordinary marriage, their alliance had survived their slummy bachelor-girlhood together, just as it had survived school. Perhaps it was because both had had no family to speak of, and had thought of themselves as independent rather than as good as orphaned. Certainly nothing else clung to either from the school in the Bernese Oberland where they had been part of an international community of five- to eighteen-year-olds displaced by war and divorce—their parents' war, and the wars between their parents. Kate was born in 1934, in Malta, where her father was an English naval officer. He was blown up in a submarine in the early forties, and her mother married an American major and went to live in St. Louis; somehow Kate was ceded to Europe, got left behind at the *Ecole Internationale,* and spent her holidays with her grandmother in Hertfordshire. Toni had a father somewhere—at school, when her mail arrived, she used to tear off the beautiful stamps from Brazil, for the collection of a boy she was keen on: days would go by before she would take her father's letter from the mutilated envelope. As she grew old enough to be knowing, she gathered that her English mother had gone off with someone her family loathed; though what sort of man that would be, Toni could not imagine, because her mother's family were English socialists of the most peace-proselytizing sort— indeed, this made them choose to let her grow up in an international school in a neutral country, their hostage to one world.

At the school, Toni and Kate were "friends" in the real, giggly, perfectly exclusive, richly schoolgirl sense of the word. Kate played the flute and was top in maths. Toni was the best skier in the school and too busy keeping up with her passionate pen-friend correspondence in four languages to do much work. The things they did well and in which each was most interested, they could not do together, and yet they were a pair, meeting in a euphoric third state each alone conjured up in the other. In their last year their room was decorated with a packing-case bar with empty vermouth bottles that Toni thought looked crazily homely. *Mutti* (Frau Professor) Sperber used to come and sniff at them, just to make sure; now and then, as women, Toni and Kate were reminded of things like this, but they were not dependent upon "amusing" memories for contact.

When Kate left school her grandmother paid for her to study music in Geneva. The two girls had always talked of Toni going off to ride about vast haciendas in Brazil, but as she grew up letters from her father came more and more irregularly—finally, one didn't know for certain whether he was still in Brazil, never mind the haciendas. She tried England for a few months; the English relatives thought she ought to take up nursing or work on a Quaker self-help project among the poor of Glasgow. She got back to Switzerland on a free air trip won by composing a jingle at a trade fair, and moved in with Kate, imitating for her the speech, mannerisms, and impossible kindness of the English relatives. In Geneva she seemed to attract offers of all kinds of jobs without much effort on her part. She met Kate several times a day to report, over coffee.

"To India? But who's this man?"

"Something to do with the UN delegation. His beard's trained up under his turban at the sides, like a creeper. He says I'd spend six months a year in Delhi and six here."

She and Kate shared a flat in Geneva for five years; at least, Kate was there all the time, and Toni came and went. She spent three months in Warsaw typing material for a Frenchman who was bringing out a book on the Polish cinema. Another time she accompanied an old Australian lady home to Brisbane, and came back to Europe by way of Tokyo and Hong Kong, eking out funds by working as a hotel receptionist. An Italian film director noticed her at an exhibition and asked her what she did; she replied in her good Italian accent, with her pretty, capable grin, "I live." He and his mistress invited her to join a party of friends for a week in Corsica. Toni met people as others pick up food poisoning or fleas—although she was without money or position, soon a network of friends-of-friends was there across the world for her to balance on.

Between times, life was never dull at home in the tiny Geneva flat; Toni took a job as a local tourist guide and the two girls entertained their friends on beer and sausage, and, coming home late at night, used to wake up one another to talk about their love affairs. Kate had dragged on a long and dreary one with a middle-aged professor who taught composition and had an asthmatic wife. They discussed him for hours, arranging and rearranging the triangle of wife, asthma, and Kate. They could not find a satisfactory pattern. Although this was never formulated in so many words, they had plumbed (but perhaps it had been there always, instinctive basis of their being "friends" against other indications of temperament) a touchstone in common: what finally mattered wasn't the graph of an event or human relationship in its *progress*, but the casual or insignificant sign or moment you secretly took away from it. So that they knew nothing would come of recomposing the triangle. Just as Kate understood when Toni said of the disastrous end of an affair in England with a bad poet—"But there *was* that day in Suffolk, when we went to see the old church at the sea and he read out just as he ducked his head under the door, 'Please close behind you otherwise birds fly in.' That was his one good line."

Kate had been the intellectual with talent and opportunity, when they left school. Yet it was Toni who moved on the fringe of the world of fashionable thinkers, painters, writers and politicians. Kate passed exams at the conservatoire, all right, but she was away down in the anonymous crowd when it came to scholarships and honours. Long after her days at the conservatoire were over she still dressed like a student, going happily about Geneva with her long, thick blond hair parting on the shoulders of her old suède jacket. She was content to teach, and to continue experiments with electronic music with a young man she was, at last, in love with. Egon was living in the flat with her when the cable came: "Arriving Sunday with friend. Take a deep breath." At the time, Toni had her best job yet—away commuting between Paris and New York as something called personal assistant to an elderly oil man with a collection of modern paintings. That Sunday night, she stood in the doorway, a carrier smelling of truffles balanced on her hip. Next to her, holding lilies and a bottle of *Poire William*, was a prematurely bald young man with a dark, withdrawn face that was instantly familiar. "Where're your things?" Egon said, making to go downstairs for the luggage. "We came as we were," said Toni, dumping her burden and hugging him, laughing.

Food, drink, and flowers lay on the old ottoman. That was to be Toni's luggage, in future. The young man's face was familiar because he was Marcus Kelp, a second-generation shipping magnate badgered by picture magazine photographers not only because his yacht and houses were frequented by actresses, but also because he conceived and financed social rehabilitation and land reclamation schemes in countries where he had no "interests." He and Toni were blazingly in love with each other. She was proud that he was not a playboy; she would have married him if he had been one of his own deck-hands. Yet her childlike pleasure in the things she could, suddenly, do and buy and give away, was intoxicating. When first Kate and Egon were married, Toni used to telephone Geneva at odd hours from all over the world; but in time she no longer needed to find ways to demonstrate to herself that she could do whatever she wanted, she grew used to the conveniences of being a rich woman. She was drawn into the preoccupations of life on Marcus's scale; she went with him on his business about the world (they had houses and apartments everywhere) not allowing even the birth of her daughter to keep her at home. Later, of course, she was sometimes persuaded to accept some invitation that he had to forgo because of the necessity to be somewhere dull, and gradually, since her responsibilities towards her child and various households were taken care of by servants, she acquired a rich woman's life of her own. Yet once or twice a year, always, she arrived at Kate's for a night or a day or two, with *Poire William* and flowers. Egon was still at the institute for musical research; he and Kate had a car, a daily cleaning-woman, and one of those Swiss houses withdrawn behind green in summer, shutters in winter.

Kate had owed Toni a letter for months when she wrote, mentioning in a general round-up of personal news that she and Egon hoped to go to France in the spring. She was surprised when at once a letter came back from London saying wouldn't it be fun to meet somewhere and spend part of the holiday together?

It was years since Kate had spent any length of time with Toni. "Toni and Marcus want to come with us!" she told Egon; they were very fond of Marcus, with his dry honesty and his rich man's conscience. But Toni drove alone up to the villa near Pont du Loup with her little daughter, Emma, standing beside her on the nanny's lap. "Oh Marcus can't leave the Nagas," Toni said. At once she went enthusiastically through the small rented house.

Later, in the content of lunch outdoors, Egon said, "What was that about Nagaland? Since when?"

"You know how Marcus takes the whole world on his shoulders. He went to Pakistan in July, that's how it started. Now they're absolutely depending on him. Well, he doesn't know what he's missing"—Toni was already in her bikini, and the strong muscles of her belly, browned all winter in Barbados and Tunisia, contracted energetically as she thrust out her glass at arm's length for some more wine, and Kate and Egon laughed. Emma ran about, tripping on the uneven flagstones and landing hard on her frilly bottom—something she found very funny. She spoke French and only a few words of English, because the nanny was French. "And what an accent!" Toni didn't bother for the woman to be out of earshot. "It wouldn't have done at the *Ecole Internationale*, I can tell you." And she picked up the child and wouldn't let her go, so that they could hear her furious protests in provincial French as she struggled to get down.

Toni wanted to go to the beach right away, that afternoon. They drove down the steep roads of the river gorge to the sea they knew, from the house's terrace, as a misty borderland between horizon and sky. Sitting or standing on the stony beach was putting one's weight on a bag of marbles, but Toni carried Emma astride her neck into the water, and the two of them floundered and ducked and gasped with joy. "I must teach her to swim. Perhaps I'll take her along to Yugoslavia this summer, after all." Toni came out of the sea looking like a beautiful little blond seal, the shiny brown flesh of her legs shuddering sturdily as she mano-euvred the stones. They were in their early thirties, she and Kate, and Toni was at the perfection of her feminine rounding-out. There was no slack, and there were no wrinkles; she had the physical assurance of a woman who has been attractive so long that she cannot imagine a change ahead. Kate's body had gone soft and would pass unnoticeably into middle-age; the deep concentration of her blue eyes was already a contrast to her faded face and freckled lips.

Kate and Egon were stimulated—and touched—that first afternoon, by the fun of having Toni there, so quick to enjoyment, so full of attack, a presence like a spot-light bringing out colour and detail. It was exciting to find that this quality of hers was, if anything, stronger than ever; hectic, almost. They were slightly ashamed to discover how quiet-living they had become, and pleased to find that they could still break out of this with zest. They left the beach late, lingered at the fishing-harbour where Toni and Emma got into conversation with a fisherman and were given a newspaper full of fresh sardines, and half-way home in the dark they decided to have dinner at a restaurant they liked the look of. The food was remarkable, they drank a lot of pastis and wine, and Emma chased moths until she fell asleep in a chair. The nanny was disapproving when they got home and they all apologized rather more profusely than they would have thought necessary had they been sober.

In the days that followed they went to another beach, and another—they would never have been so energetic if it had not been for Toni. She anointed them with some marvellous unguent everyone used in Jamaica, and they turned the colour of a nicotine stain, in the sun. But after three days, when Kate and Egon were beginning to feel particularly drugged and well, Toni began to talk about places farther away, inland. There was a Polish painter living near Albi—it might be fun to look him up? Well, what about Arles then—had they ever eaten sausage or seen the lovely Roman theatre at Arles? And the Camargue? One must see the white horses there, eh? But even Arles was a long way, Egon said; one couldn't do it in a day. "Why a day?" Toni said. "Let's just get in the car and go." And the baby? "Emma and Mathilde will stay here, Mathilde will love to have the place to herself, to be in charge—you know how they are."

They went off in the morning, in the spring sun with the hood of

Toni's car down. It had rained and the air smelled of herbs when they stopped to eat Kate's picnic lunch. They stood and looked down the valley where peasants were spraying the vines in new leaf, so thin, tender, and so brilliant a green that the sun struck through them, casting a shivering yellow light on hands and bare arms moving there. A long, chalky-mauve mountain rode the distance as a ship comes over an horizon. "Is it Sainte-Victoire?" said Kate. If so, it didn't seem to be in quite the right place; she and Egon argued eagerly. Toni sat on a rock between the rosemary bushes with a glass of wine in one hand and a chunk of crust thick with cheese in the other, and grinned at them between large, sharp bites.

Egon was, as Toni said delightedly, "quite corrupted" by the Jaguar and couldn't resist taking her up to ninety on the auto-route. Kate and Toni called him Toad and laughed to themselves at the solemn expression on his face as he crouched his tall body in the seat. They reached Arles in the middle of the afternoon and found a little hotel up in the old town. There was time to have a look at the theatre and the medieval cloister. In the Roman arena, as they walked past at dusk, a team of small boys was playing soccer. Toni stood watching the moon come up while Egon and Kate climbed to the stone roof of the church. Her back was quite still, jaunty, as she stood; she turned to smile, watching them come down out of the dark doorway. "I can't explain," Kate was saying, "It seems to me the most satisfying old town I've ever been in. The way when you're in the theatre you can see the pimply spires of the medieval buildings . . . and that figure on top of the church, rising up over everything, peering over the Roman walls. The boys yelling down in the arena . . ." "Kate darling!" Toni smiled. "Well, we'll see it all properly tomorrow," Kate said. And over dinner, Egon was earnestly ecstatic: "What I can't believe is the way the farm buildings have that perfect rectilinear relationship with the size and perspective of the fields—and the trees, yes. I thought that was simply Van Gogh's vision that did it—?" He had driven very slowly indeed along the road beneath the plane trees that led from Aix to Arles. Late that night Kate leant on the window in her nightgown, looking out into the splotchy moon-and-dark of the little courtyard garden and could not come to bed.

But they left next morning straight after coffee, after all.

"We buy a *saucisson d'Arles* and we're on our way, eh? Don't you think so?" Toni drew deeply on her first cigarette and pulled the sympathetic, intimate face of accord over something that didn't have to be discussed.

Egon said, "Whatever you girls want to do"; and Kate wouldn't have dreamt of getting them to hang on a second day in Arles just because she wanted another look at things they'd already seen. It wasn't all that important. They drove rather dreamily through the Camargue and didn't talk much—the watery landscape was conducive to contemplation rather than communication. A salt wind parted the pelt of grasses this way and that and the hackles of the grey waters rose to it. Egon said he could make out floating dark dots as waterfowl, but there was no sign of the white horses Toni wanted to see, except in the riding stables around Les Saintes-Maries-de-la-Mer. Toni disappeared into one of the village shops there and came out in a pair of skin-tight cowboy pants and a brilliant shirt, to make them laugh. The sun strengthened and they sat and drank wine; Kate wandered off and when she came back remarked that she had had a look at the ancient Norman church. Toni, with her legs sprawled before her in classic Western style, looked dashing by no other effort than her charming indolence. "Should we see it, too?" Egon asked. "Oh I don't think . . . there's nothing much," Kate said with sudden shyness.

"It's nice, nice, nice, here," Toni chanted to herself, turning her face up to the sun.

"I'm going to take a picture of you for Marcus," said Kate.

"Shall we have some more wine?" Egon said to Toni.

She nodded her head vehemently, and beamed at her friends.

When the wine came and they were all three drinking, Egon said— "Then let's spend the night. Stay here. We can look at the church. I suppose there's some sort of hotel."

Kate broke the moment's pause. "Oh I don't think we'd want to. I mean the church is nothing."

They crossed the Rhone at Bac de Bacarin early in the afternoon. "We should go back to Saintes-Maries in the autumn, there's something between a religious procession and a rodeo, then—let's do that," said Toni; and Egon, just as if he could leave the institute whenever he felt like it and he and Kate had money to travel whenever they pleased, agreed—"The four of us."

"Yes let's. Only Marcus hates Europe. We're supposed to be going to North Africa in October. Oh, we can eat in Marseilles tonight," Toni had taken out the road map. "Must eat a bouillabaisse in Marseilles. But we don't want to sleep there, mm?"

After she had bought them a wonderful dinner they lost their way in the dark making, as she suggested, for "some little place" along the coast. They ended up at Bandol, in a hotel that was just taking the dust covers off in preparation for the season. Before morning, they saw nothing of the place but the glitter of black water and the nudging and nodding of masts under the window. In the room Kate and Egon slept in, last season's cockroaches ran out from under the outsize whore of a bed behind whose padded head were the cigarette butts of many occupants. Kate woke early in the musty room and got Egon up to come out and walk. The ugly glass restaurants along the sea-front were closed and the palms rustled dryly as they do when the air is cold. Fishermen had spread a huge length of net along the broad walk where, in a month's time, hundreds of tourists would crowd up and down. Without them the place was dead, as a person who has taken to drink comes to life only when he gets the stuff that has destroyed him. When they walked back through the remains of the hotel garden—it had almost all been built upon in the course of additions and alterations in various styles—Egon pointed out a plaque at the entrance. *Il est trois heures. Je viens d'achever "Félicité"* . . . *Dieu sait que j'ai été heureuse en l'écrivant.—Katherine Mansfield. Jeudi 28 Févier 1918.* "My God yes, of course, I'd forgotten," Kate said. "It was Bandol. She wrote 'Bliss' here. This place." Kate and Toni as young girls had felt the peculiar affinity that young girls feel for Katherine Mansfield—dead before they were born—with her meticulously chronicled passions, her use of pet-names, her genius and her suffering. Somewhere within this barracks of thick carpets and air-conditioned bars were buried the old rooms of the hotel in a garden, in a village, where she had lain in exile, coughing, waiting for letters from Bogey, and fiercely struggling to work. "We must show Toni," Egon said.

"No don't. Don't say anything."

Egon looked at Kate. Her face was anxious, curiously ashamed; as it had been the day before, in Les Saintes-Maries-de-la-Mer.

"I don't think she's enjoying . . . it all . . . everything, the way we are."

"But you're the one who said we shouldn't stay, in the Camargue. You were the one—"

"I have the feeling it's not the same for her, Egon. She can't help it. She can go everywhere she likes whenever she likes. The South Seas or Corinthia—or Zanzibar. She could be there now. Couldn't she? Why here rather than there?" Her voice slowed to a stop.

Egon made as if to speak, and the impulse was crossed by counterimpulses of objection, confusion.

"The world's beautiful," said Kate.

"You're embarrassed to be enjoying yourself!" Egon accused.

The whole exchange was hurried, parenthetic as they walked along the hotel corridors, and then suddenly suppressed as they reached their rooms and Toni herself appeared, banging her door behind her, calling out to them.

Kate said quickly, "No, for *her.* I mean if she were to find out . . . about herself."

They were back at the villa by evening, and all shared the good mood of being "home" again. For the next few days, Kate and Egon were not inclined to leave the terrace; they read and wrote letters and went no farther than the shops in the village, while Toni drove up and down to the beaches with Emma and the nurse. But on the day before Toni was to leave, Kate went along with her to the beach. She and Toni ate lobster in a beach restaurant, very much at ease; all their lives, there would always be this level at which they were more at ease with each other than they would ever be with anyone else. The child and the nanny had something sent down to them on the beach. Mathilde had been promised that she would be taken into Nice to buy a souvenir for her sister, but Toni couldn't face the idea of the town, after lunch, and with the wheedling charm disguising command that Kate noticed she had learnt in the past few years asked the nanny to take the bus: she would be picked up later, and could leave the child behind.

Wherever Toni went she bought a pile of magazines in several languages; the wind turned their pages, while the two women dozed and smoked. At one stage Kate realized that Toni was gone, and Emma. Being alone somehow woke her up; on her rubber mattress, she rolled onto her stomach and began to read antique and picture dealers' advertisements. Then the position in which she was lying brought on a muscular pain in the shoulder-blade that she was beginning to be plagued with, the last few years, and she got up and took a little walk towards the harbour. She was rotating the shoulder gently as the masseuse had told her and quite suddenly—it was as if she had thought of the child and she had materialized—there was Emma, lying in the water between two fishing boats. She was face-down, like a fallen doll. Kate half-stumbled, half-jumped into the oily water a-wash with fruit-skins—she actually caught her left foot in a rope as she landed in the water, and, in panic for the child, threshed wildly to free herself. She reached the child easily and hauled her up the side of one of the boats, letting her roll over onto the deck, while she herself climbed aboard. All the things that ought to be done came back to her shaking hands. She thrust her forefinger like a hook into the little mouth and pulled the tongue forward. She snatched a bit of old awning and crammed it tight under the stomach so that the body would be at an angle to have the water expelled from the lungs. She was kneeling, shaking, working frantically among stinking gut and fins, and the water and vomit that poured from the child. She pressed her mouth to the small, slimy blue lips and tried to remember exactly, exactly, how it was done, how she had read about it, making a casual mental note, in the newspapers. She didn't scream for help; there was no time, she didn't even know if anyone passed on the quay—afterwards she knew there had been the sound of strolling footsteps, but the greatest concentration she had ever summoned in all her life had cut her off from everything and everyone: she and the child were alone between life and death. And in a little while, the child began to breathe, time came back again, the existence of other people, the possibility of help. She picked her up and carried her, a vessel full of priceless breath, out of the mess of the boat and onto the quay, and then broke into a wild run, running, running, for the beach restaurant.

And that had been all there was to it; as she kept telling Toni. In twenty-fours Emma was falling hard on her bottom on the terrace again, and laughing, but Toni had to be told about it, over and over, and to tell over and over how one moment Emma was playing with Birgit Sorenson's dachshund (Toni had just that minute run into the Sorensons, she hadn't known their yacht was in the harbour) and the next moment child and dog were gone. "Then we saw the dog up the quay toward the boathouse end—" and of course the child had gone the other way, and they didn't know it. Marcus was flying back from Pakistan; but what Toni could not face was Mathilde: "She never looks at me, never, without thinking that it could not have happened with her; I see it in her face."

They were sitting on the terrace in the evening, letting Toni talk it out. "Then get rid of her," said Kate.

"Yes, let her go," Egon urged. "It could have happened with anybody, remember that."

Toni said to Kate in the dark, "But it was you. *That* couldn't have been anyone else."

This idea persisted. Toni believed that because it was her child who lay in the water, Kate had woken up and walked to the spot. No one else would have known, no one else could have given her child back to her. The idea became a question that demanded some sort of answer. She had to do something. She wanted to give Kate—a present. What else? As time went by the need became more pressing. She had to give Kate a present. But what? "Why shouldn't I give them the little house in Spain?" As she said this to her husband Marcus, she instantly felt light and relieved.

"By all means. If you imagine that they would strike such a bargain." He had listened to her account of that day, many times, in silence, but she did not know what he would say if she wanted to take Emma away with her anywhere, again.

She thought of a new car; Egon had so enjoyed driving the Jaguar. Yet the idea of simply arriving with the deed of a house or a new car filled her with a kind of shyness; she was afraid of a certain look passing between Kate and Egon, the look of people who know something about you that you don't know yourself. At last one day she felt impatiently determined to have done with it, to forget it once and for all, and she went once again through her jewellery, looking for a piece—something—something worthy—for Kate. She arrived unannounced in Geneva with a little suède pouch containing a narrow emerald-and-diamond collar. "I've smuggled this bauble in, Kate, you do just as you like with it—sell it if you can't stand the sight of such things. But I thought it might look nice around your long neck."

It lay on the table among the coffee cups, and Kate and Egon looked at it but did not touch it. Toni thought: as if it might bite.

Kate said kindly, "It's from Marcus's family, Toni, you must keep it."

"Sell the damn thing!"

They laughed.

"Surely I'm entitled to give you something!"

They did not look at each other; Toni was watching them very carefully.

"Toni," Kate said, "you've forgotten my *Poire William* and the flowers."

HENRY JAMES

Brooksmith

We are scattered now, the friends of the late Mr Oliver Offord; but whenever we chance to meet I think we are conscious of a certain esoteric respect for each other. "Yes, you too have been in Arcadia," we seem not too grumpily to allow. When I pass the house in Mansfield Street I remember that Arcadia was there. I don't know who has it now, and I don't want to know; it's enough to be so sure that if I should ring the bell there would be no such luck for me as that Brooksmith should open the door. Mr Offord, the most agreeable, the most lovable of bachelors, was a retired diplomatist, living on his pension, confined by his infirmities to his fireside and delighted to be found there any afternoon in the year by such visitors as Brooksmith allowed to come up. Brooksmith was his butler and his most intimate friend, to whom we all stood, or I should say sat, in the same relation in which the subject of the sovereign finds himself to the prime minister. By having been for years, in foreign lands, the most delightful Englishman any one had ever known, Mr Offord had, in my opinion, rendered signal service to his country. But I suppose he had been too much liked—liked even by those who didn't like *it*—so that as people of that sort never get titles or dotations for the horrid things they have *not* done, his principal reward was simply that we went to see him.

Oh, we went perpetually, and it was not our fault if he was not overwhelmed with this particular honour. Any visitor who came once came again—to come merely once was a slight which nobody, I am sure, had ever put upon him. His circle, therefore, was essentially composed of *habitués*, who were *habitués* for each other as well as for him, as those of a happy *salon* should be. I remember vividly every element of the place, down to the intensely Londonish look of the grey opposite houses, in the gap of the white curtains of the high windows, and the exact spot where, on a particular afternoon, I put down my tea-cup for Brooksmith, lingering an instant, to gather it up as if he were plucking a flower. Mr Offord's drawing-room was indeed Brooksmith's garden, his pruned and tended human *parterre*, and if we all flourished there and grew well in our places it was largely owing to his supervision.

Many persons have heard much, though most have doubtless seen little, of the famous institution of the *salon*, and many are born to the depression of knowing that this finest flower of social life refuses to bloom where the English tongue is spoken. The explanation is usually that our women have not the skill to cultivate it—the art to direct, between suggestive shores, the course of the stream of talk. My affectionate, my pious memory of Mr Offord contradicts this induction only, I fear, more insidiously to confirm it. The very sallow and slightly smoked drawing-room in which he spent so large a portion of the last years of his life certainly deserved the distinguished name; but on the other hand it could not be said at all to owe its stamp to the soft pressure of the indispensable sex. The dear man had indeed been capable of one of those sacrifices to which women are deemed peculiarly apt; he had recognised (under the influence, in some degree, it is true, of physical infirmity), that if you wished people to find you at home you must manage not to be out. He had in short accepted the fact which many dabblers in the social art are slow to learn, that you must really, as they say, take a line and that the only way to be at home is to stay at home. Finally his own fireside had become a summary of his habits. Why should he ever have left it?—since this would have been leaving what was notoriously pleasantest in London, the compact charmed cluster (thinning away indeed into casual couples), round the fine old last century chimney-piece which, with the exception of the remarkable collection of miniatures, was the best thing the place contained. Mr Offord was not rich; he had nothing but his pension and the use for life of the somewhat super-annuated house.

When I am reminded by some uncomfortable contrast of to-day how perfectly we were all handled there I ask myself once more what had been the secret of such perfection. One had taken it for granted at the time, for anything that is supremely good produces more acceptance than surprise. I felt we were all happy, but I didn't consider how our happiness was managed. And yet there were questions to be asked, questions that strike me as singularly obvious now that there is nobody to answer them. Mr Offord had solved the insoluble; he had, without feminine help (save in the sense that ladies were dying to come to him and he saved the lives of several), established a *salon;* but I might have guessed that there was a method in his madness—a law in his success. He had not hit it off by a mere fluke. There was an art in it all, and how was the art so hidden? Who, indeed, if it came to that, was the occult artist? Launching this inquiry the other day, I had already got hold of the tail of my reply. I was helped by the very wonder of some of the conditions that came back to me—those that used to seem as natural as sunshine in a fine climate.

How was it, for instance, that we never were a crowd, never either too many or too few, always the right people *with* the right people (there must really have been no wrong people at all), always coming and going, never sticking fast nor overstaying, yet never popping in or out with an indecorous familiarity? How was it that we all sat where we wanted and moved when we wanted and met whom we wanted and escaped whom we wanted; joining, according to the accident of inclination, the general circle or falling in with a single talker on a convenient sofa? Why were all the sofas so convenient, the accidents so happy, the talkers so ready, the listeners so willing, the subjects presented to you in a rotation as quickly fore-ordained as the courses at dinner? A dearth of topics would have been as unheard of as a lapse in the service. These speculations couldn't fail to lead me to the fundamental truth that Brooksmith had been somehow at the bottom of the mystery. If he had not established the *salon* at least he had carried it on. Brooksmith, in short, was the artist!

We felt this, covertly, at the time, without formulating it, and were conscious, as an ordered and prosperous community, of his evenhanded justice, untainted with flunkeyism. He had none of that vulgarity—his touch was infinitely fine. The delicacy of it was clear to me on the first occasion my eyes rested, as they were so often to rest again, on the domestic revealed, in the turbid light of the street, by the opening of the house-door. I saw on the spot that though he had plenty of school he carried it without arrogance—he had remained articulate and human. *L'Ecole Anglaise,* Mr Offord used to call him, laughing, when, later, it happened more than once that we had some conversation about him. But I remember accusing Mr Offord of not doing him quite ideal justice.

That he was not one of the giants of the school, however, my old friend, who really understood him perfectly and was devoted to him, as I shall show, quite admitted; which doubtless poor Brooksmith had himself felt, to his cost, when his value in the market was originally determined. The utility of his class in general is estimated by the foot and the inch, and poor Brooksmith had only about five feet two to put into circulation. He acknowledged the inadequacy of this provision, and I am sure was penetrated with the everlasting fitness of the relation between service and stature. If *he* had been Mr Offord he certainly would have found Brooksmith wanting, and indeed the laxity of his employer on this score was one of many things which he had had to condone and to which he had at last indulgently adapted himself.

I remember the old man's saying to me: "Oh, my servants, if they can live with me a fortnight they can live with me for ever. But it's the first fortnight that tries 'em." It was in the first fortnight, for instance, that Brooksmith had had to learn that he was exposed to being addressed as "my dear fellow" and "my poor child." Strange and deep must such a probation have been to him, and he doubtless emerged from it tempered and purified. This was written to a certain extent in his appearance; in his spare, brisk little person, in his cloistered white face and extraordinarily polished hair, which told of responsibility, looked as if it were kept up to the same high standard as the plate; in his small, clear, anxious eyes, even in the permitted, though not exactly encouraged tuft on his chin. "He thinks me rather mad, but I've broken him in, and now he likes the place, he likes the company," said the old man. I embraced this fully after I had become aware that Brooksmith's main characteristic was a deep and shy refinement, though I remember I was rather puzzled when, on another occasion, Mr Offord remarked: "What he likes is the talk—mingling in the conversation." I was conscious that I had never seen Brooksmith permit himself this freedom, but I guessed in a moment that what Mr Offord alluded to was a participation more intense than any speech could have represented—that of being perpetually present on a hundred legitimate pretexts, errands, necessities, and breathing the very atmosphere of criticism, the famous criticism of life. "Quite an education, sir, isn't it, sir?" he said to me one day at the foot of the stairs, when he was letting me out; and I have always remembered the words and the tone as the first sign of the quickening drama of poor Brooksmith's fate. It was indeed an education, but to what was this sensitive young man of thirty-five, of the servile class, being educated?

Practically and inevitably, for the time, to companionship, to the perpetual, the even exaggerated reference and appeal of a person brought to dependence by his time of life and his infirmities and always addicted moreover (this was the exaggeration) to the art of giving you pleasure by letting you do things for him. There were certain things Mr Offord was capable of pretending he liked you to do, even when he didn't, if he thought *you* liked them. If it happened that you didn't either (this was rare, but it might be), of course there were cross-purposes; but Brooksmith was there to prevent their going very far. This was precisely the way he acted as moderator: he averted misunderstandings or cleared them up. He had been capable, strange as it may appear, of acquiring for this purpose an insight into the French tongue, which was often used at Mr Offord's; for besides being habitual to most of the foreigners, and they were many, who haunted the place or arrived with letters (letters often requiring a little worried consideration, of which Brooksmith always had cognisance), it had really become the primary language of the master of the house. I don't know if all the *malentendus* were in French, but almost all the explanations were, and this didn't a bit prevent Brooksmith from following them. I know Mr Offord used to read passages to him from Montaigne and Saint-Simon, for he read perpetually when he was alone—when they were alone, I should say— and Brooksmith was always about. Perhaps you'll say no wonder Mr Offord's butler regarded him as "rather mad." However, if I'm not sure what he thought about Montaigne I'm convinced he admired Saint-Simon. A certain feeling for letters must have rubbed off on him from the mere handling of his master's books, which he was always carrying to and fro and putting back in their places.

I often noticed that if an anecdote or a quotation, much more a lively discussion, was going forward, he would, if busy with the fire or the curtains, the lamp or the tea, find a pretext for remaining in the room till the point should be reached. If his purpose was to catch it you were not discreet to call him off, and I shall never forget a look, a hard, stony stare (I caught it in its passage), which, one day when there were a good many people in the room, he fastened upon the footman who was helping him in the service and who, in an undertone, had asked him some irrelevant question. It was the only manifestation of harshness that I ever observed on Brooksmith's part, and at first I wondered what was the matter. Then I became conscious that Mr Offord was relating a very curious anecdote, never before perhaps made so public, and imparted to the narrator by an eye-witness of the fact, bearing upon Lord Byron's life in Italy. Nothing would induce me to reproduce it here; but Brooksmith had been in danger of losing it. If I ever should venture to reproduce it I shall feel how much I lose in not having my fellow-auditor to refer to.

The first day Mr Offord's door was closed was therefore a dark date in contemporary history. It was raining hard and my umbrella was wet, but Brooksmith took it from me exactly as if this were a preliminary for going upstairs. I observed however that instead of putting it away he held it poised and trickling over the rug, and then I became aware that he was looking at me with deep, acknowledging eyes—his air of universal responsibility. I immediately understood; there was scarcely need of the question and the answer that passed between us. When I did understand that the old man had given up, for the first time, though only for the occasion, I exclaimed dolefully: "What a difference it will make—and to how many people!"

"I shall be one of them, sir!" said Brooksmith; and that was the beginning of the end.

Mr Offord came down again, but the spell was broken, and the great sign of it was that the conversation was, for the first time, not directed. It wandered and stumbled, a little frightened, like a lost child—it had let go the nurse's hand. "The worst of it is that now we shall talk about my health—*c'est la fin de tout,*" Mr Offord said, when he reappeared; and then I recognised what a sign of change that would be—for he had never tolerated anything so provincial. The talk became ours, in a word—not his; and as ours, even when *he* talked, it could only be inferior. In this form it was a distress to Brooksmith, whose attention now wandered from it altogether: he had so much closer a vision of his master's intimate conditions than our superficialities represented. There were better hours, and he was more in and out of the room, but I could see that he was conscious that the great institution was falling to pieces. He seemed to wish to take counsel with me about it, to feel responsible for its going on in some form or other. When for the second period—the first had lasted several days—he had to tell me that our old friend didn't receive, I half expected to hear him say after a moment: "Do you think I ought to, sir, in his place?"—as he might have asked me, with the return of autumn, if I thought he had better light the drawing-room fire.

He had a resigned philosophic sense of what his guests—our guests, as I came to regard them in our colloquies—would expect. His feeling was that he wouldn't absolutely have approved of himself as a substitute for the host; but he was so saturated with the religion of habit that he would have made, for our friends, the necessary sacrifice to the divinity. He would take them on a little further, till they could look about them. I think I saw him also mentally confronted with the opportunity to deal—for once in his life—with some of his own dumb preferences, his limitations of sympathy, *weeding* a little, in prospect, and returning to a purer tradition. It was not unknown to me that he considered that toward the end of Mr Offord's career a certain laxity of selection had crept in.

At last it came to be the case that we all found the closed door more often than the open one; but even when it was closed Brooksmith managed a crack for me to squeeze through; so that practically I never turned away without having paid a visit. The difference simply came to be that the visit was to Brooksmith. It took place in the hall, at the familiar foot of the stairs, and we didn't sit down—at least Brooksmith didn't; moreover it was devoted wholly to one topic and always had the air of being already over—beginning, as it were, at the end. But it was always interesting—it always gave me something to think about. It is true that the subject of my meditation was ever the same—ever "It's all very well, but what *will* become of Brooksmith?" Even my private answer to this question left me still unsatisfied. No doubt Mr Offord would provide for him, but *what* would he provide? that was the great point. He couldn't provide society; and society had become a necessity of Brooksmith's nature. I must add that he never showed a symptom of what I may call sordid solicitude—anxiety on his own account. He was rather livid and intensely grave, as befitted a man before whose eyes the "shade of that which once was great" was passing away. He had the solemnity of a person winding up, under depressing circumstances, a long established and celebrated business; he was a kind of social executor or liquidator. But his manner seemed to testify exclusively to the uncertainty of *our* future. I couldn't in those days have afforded it—I lived in two rooms in Jermyn Street and didn't "keep a man;" but even if my income had permitted I shouldn't have ventured to say to Brooksmith (emulating Mr Offord), "My dear fellow, I'll take you on." The whole tone of our intercourse was so much more an implication that it was *I* who should now want a lift. Indeed there was a tacit assurance in Brooksmith's whole attitude that he would have me on his mind.

One of the most assiduous members of our circle had been Lady Kenyon, and I remember his telling me one day that her ladyship had, in spite of her own infirmities, lately much aggravated, been in person to inquire. In answer to this I remarked that she would feel it more than any one. Brooksmith was silent a moment; at the end of which he said, in a certain tone (there is no reproducing some of his tones), "I'll go and see her." I went to see her myself, and I learned that he had waited upon her; but when I said to her, in the form of a joke but with a core of earnest, that when all was over some of us ought to combine, to club together to set Brooksmith up on his own account, she replied a trifle disappointingly: "Do you mean in a public-house?" I looked at her in a way that I think Brooksmith himself would have approved, and then I answered: "Yes, the Offord Arms." What I had meant, of course, was that, for the love of art itself, we ought to look to it that such a peculiar faculty and so much acquired experience should not be wasted. I really think that if we had caused a few black-edged cards to be struck off and circulated—"Mr Brooksmith will continue to receive on the old premises from four to seven; business carried on as usual during the alterations"—the majority of us would have rallied.

Several times he took me upstairs—always by his own proposal—and our dear old friend, in bed, in a curious flowered and brocaded *casaque* which made him, especially as his head was tied up in a handkerchief to match, look, to my imagination, like the dying Voltaire, held for ten minutes a sadly shrunken little *salon*. I felt indeed each time, as if I were attending the last *coucher* of some social sovereign. He was royally whimsical about his sufferings and not at all concerned—quite as if the Constitution provided for the case—about his successor. He glided over *our* sufferings charmingly, and none of his jokes—it was a gallant abstention, some of them would have been so easy—were at our expense. Now and again, I confess, there was one at Brooksmith's, but so pathetically sociable as to make the excellent man look at me in a way that seemed to say: "Do exchange a glance with me, or I sha'n't be able to stand it." What he was not able to stand was not what Mr Offord said about him, but what he wasn't able to say in return. His notion of conversation, for himself, was giving you the convenience of speaking to him; and when he went to "see" Lady Kenyon, for instance, it was to carry her the tribute of his receptive silence. Where would the speech of his betters have been if proper service had been a manifestation of sound? In that case the fundamental difference would have had to be shown by *their* dumbness, and many of them, poor things, were dumb enough without that provision. Brooksmith took an unfailing interest in the preservation of the fundamental difference; it was the thing he had most on his conscience.

What had become of it, however, when Mr Offord passed away like any inferior person—was relegated to eternal stillness like a butler upstairs? His aspect for several days after the expected event may be imagined, and the multiplication by funereal observance of the things he didn't say. When everything was over—it was late the same day—I knocked at the door of the house of mourning as I so often had done before. I could never call on Mr Offord again, but I had come, literally, to call on Brooksmith. I wanted to ask him if there was anything I could do for him, tainted with vagueness as this inquiry could only be. My wild dream of taking him into my own service had died away: my service was not worth his being taken into. My offer to him could only be to help him to find another place, and yet there was an indelicacy, as it were, in taking for granted that his thoughts would immediately be fixed on another. I had a hope that he would be able to give his life a different form—though certainly not the form, the frequent result of such bereavements, of his setting up a little shop. That would have been dreadful; for I should have wished to further any enterprise that he might embark in, yet how could I have brought myself to go and pay him shillings and take back coppers over a counter? My visit then was simply an intended compliment. He took it as such, gratefully and with all the tact in the world. He knew I really couldn't help him and that I knew he knew I couldn't; but we discussed the situation—with a good deal of elegant generality—at the foot of the stairs, in the hall already dismantled, where I had so often discussed other situations with him. The executors were in possession, as was still more apparent when he made me pass for a few minutes into the dining-room, where various objects were muffled up for removal.

Two definite facts, however, he had to communicate; one being that he was to leave the house for ever that night (servants, for some mysterious reason, seem always to depart by night), and the other—he mentioned it only at the last, with hesitation—that he had already been informed his late master had left him a legacy of eighty pounds. "I'm very glad," I said, and Brooksmith rejoined: "It was so like him to think of me." This was all that passed between us on the subject, and I know nothing of his judgment of Mr Offord's memento. Eighty pounds are always eighty pounds, and no one has ever left *me* an equal sum; but, all the same, for Brooksmith, I was disappointed. I don't know what I had expected—in short I was disappointed. Eighty pounds might stock a little shop—a *very* little shop; but, I repeat, I couldn't bear to think of that. I asked my friend if he had been able to save a little, and he replied: "No, sir; I have had to do things." I didn't inquire what things he had had to do; they were his own affair, and I took his word for them as assentingly as if he had had the greatness of an ancient house to keep up; especially as there was something in his manner that seemed to convey a prospect of further sacrifice.

"I shall have to turn round a bit, sir—I shall have to look about me," he said; and then he added, indulgently, magnanimously: "If you should happen to hear of anything for me—"

I couldn't let him finish; this was, in its essence, too much in the really grand manner. It would be a help to my getting him off my mind to be able to pretend I *could* find the right place, and that help he wished to give me, for it was doubtless painful to him to see me in so false a position. I interposed with a few words to the effect that I was well aware that wherever he should go, whatever he should do, he would miss our old friend terribly—miss him even more than I should, having been with him so much more. This led him to make the speech that I have always remembered as the very text of the whole episode.

"Oh, sir, it's sad for *you*, very sad, indeed, and for a great many gentlemen and ladies; that it is, sir. But for me, sir, it is, if I may say so, still graver even than that: it's just the loss of something that was everything. For me, sir," he went on, with rising tears, "he was just *all*, if you know what I mean, sir. You have others, sir, I daresay—not that I would have you understand me to speak of them as in any way tantamount. But you have the pleasures of society, sir; if it's only in talking about him, sir, as I daresay you do freely—for all his blessed memory has to fear from it—with gentlemen and ladies who have had the same honour. That's not for me, sir, and I have to keep my associations to myself. Mr Offord was *my* society, and now I have no more. You go back to conversation, sir, after all, and I go back to my place," Brooksmith stammered, without exaggerated irony or dramatic bitterness, but with a flat, unstudied veracity and his hand on the knob of the street-door. He turned it to let me out and then he added: "I just go downstairs, sir, again, and I stay there."

"My poor child," I replied, in my emotion, quite as Mr Offord used to speak, "my dear fellow, leave it to me; we'll look after you, we'll all do something for you."

"Ah, if you could give me some one *like* him! But there ain't two in the world," said Brooksmith as we parted.

He had given me his address—the place where he would be to be heard of. For a long time I had no occasion to make use of the information; for he proved indeed, on trial, a very difficult case. In a word the people who knew him and had known Mr Offord, didn't want to take him, and yet I couldn't bear to try to thrust him among people who didn't know him. I spoke to many of our old friends about him, and I found them all governed by the odd mixture of feelings of which I myself was conscious, and disposed, further, to entertain a suspicion that he was "spoiled," with which I then would have nothing to do. In plain terms a certain embarrassment, a sensible awkwardness, when they thought of it, attached to the idea of using him as a menial: they had met him so often in society. Many of them would have asked him, and did ask him, or rather did ask me to ask him, to come and see them; but a mere visiting-list was not what I wanted for him. He was too short for people who were very particular; nevertheless I heard of an opening in a diplomatic household which led me to write him a note, though I was looking much less for something grand than for something human. Five days later I heard from him. The secretary's wife had decided, after keeping him waiting till then, that she couldn't take a servant out of a house in which there had not been a lady. The note had a P.S.: "It's a good job there wasn't, sir, such a lady as some."

A week later he came to see me and told me he was "suited"— committed to some highly respectable people (they were something very large in the City), who lived on the Bayswater side of the Park. "I daresay it will be rather poor, sir," he admitted; "but I've seen the fireworks, haven't I, sir?—it can't be fireworks *every* night. After Mansfield Street there ain't much choice." There was a certain amount, however, it seemed; for the following year, going one day to call on a country cousin, a lady of a certain age who was spending a fortnight in town with some friends of her own, a family unknown to me and resident in Chester Square, the door of the house was opened, to my surprise and gratification, by Brooksmith in person. When I came out I had some conversation with him, from which I gathered that he had found the large City people too dull for endurance, and I guessed, though he didn't say it, that he had found them vulgar as well. I don't know what judgment he would have passed on his actual patrons if my relative had not been their friend; but under the circumstances he abstained from comment.

None was necessary, however, for before the lady in question brought her visit to a close they honoured me with an invitation to dinner, which I accepted. There was a largeish party on the occasion, but I confess I thought of Brooksmith rather more than of the seated company. They required no depth of attention—they were all referable to usual, irredeemable, inevitable types. It was the world of cheerful commonplace and conscious gentility and prosperous density, a full-fed, material, insular world, a world of hideous florid plate and ponderous order and thin conversation. There was not a word said about Byron. Nothing would have induced me to look at Brooksmith in the course of the repast, and I felt sure that not even my overturning the wine would have induced him to meet my eye. We were in intellectual sympathy—we felt, as regards each other, a kind of social responsibility. In short we had been in Arcadia together, and we had both come to *this!* No wonder we were ashamed to be confronted. When he helped on my overcoat, as I was going away, we parted, for the first time since the earliest days in Mansfield Street, in silence. I thought he looked lean and wasted, and I guessed that his new place was not more "human" than his previous one. There was plenty of beef and beer, but there was no reciprocity. The question for him to have asked before accepting the position would have been not "How many footmen are kept?" but "How much imagination?"

The next time I went to the house—I confess it was not very soon—I encountered his successor, a personage who evidently enjoyed the good fortune of never having quitted his natural level. Could any be higher? he seemed to ask—over the heads of three footmen and even of some visitors. He made me feel as if Brooksmith were dead; but I didn't dare to inquire—I couldn't have borne his "I haven't the least idea, sir." I despatched a note to the address Brooksmith had given me after Mr Offord's death, but I received no answer. Six months later, however, I was favoured with a visit from an elderly, dreary, dingy person, who introduced herself to me as Mr Brooksmith's aunt and from whom I learned that he was out of place and out of health and had allowed her to come and say to me that if I could spare half-an-hour to look in at him he would take it as a rare honour.

I went the next day—his messenger had given me a new address—and found my friend lodged in a short sordid street in Marylebone, one of those corners of London that wear the last expression of sickly meanness. The room into which I was shown was above the small establishment of a dyer and cleaner who had inflated kid gloves and discoloured shawls in his shop-front. There was a great deal of grimy infant life up and down the place, and there was a hot, moist smell within, as of the "boiling" of dirty linen. Brooksmith sat with a blanket over his legs at a clean little window, where, from behind stiff bluish-white curtains, he could look across at a huckster's and a tinsmith's and a small greasy public-house. He had passed through an illness and was convalescent, and his mother, as well as his aunt, was in attendance on him. I liked the mother, who was bland and intensely humble, but I didn't much fancy the aunt, whom I connected, perhaps unjustly, with the opposite public-house (she seemed somehow to be greasy with the same grease), and whose furtive eye followed every movement of my hand, as if to see if it were not going into my pocket. It didn't take this direction—I couldn't, unsolicited, put myself at that sort of ease with Brooksmith. Several times the door of the room opened, and mysterious old women peeped in and shuffled back again. I don't know who they were; poor Brooksmith seemed encompassed with vague, prying, beery females.

He was vague himself, and evidently weak, and much embarrassed, and not an allusion was made between us to Mansfield Street. The vision of the *salon* of which he had been an ornament hovered before me, however, by contrast, sufficiently. He assured me that he was really getting better, and his mother remarked that he would come round if he could only get his spirits up. The aunt echoed this opinion, and I became more sure that in her own case she knew where to go for such a purpose. I'm afraid I was rather weak with my old friend, for I neglected the opportunity, so exceptionally good, to rebuke the levity which had led him to throw up honourable positions—fine, stiff, steady berths, with morning prayers, as I knew, attached to one of them—in Bayswater and Belgravia. Very likely his reasons had been profane and sentimental; he didn't want morning prayers, he wanted to be somebody's dear fellow; but I couldn't be the person to rebuke him. He shuffled these episodes out of sight—I saw that he had no wish to discuss them. I perceived further, strangely enough, that it would probably be a questionable pleasure for him to see me again: he doubted now even of my power to condone his aberrations. He didn't wish to have to explain; and his behaviour, in future, was likely to need explanation. When I bade him

farewell he looked at me a moment with eyes that said everything: "How
can I talk about those exquisite years in this place, before these people,
with the old women poking their heads in? It was very good of you to
come to see me—it wasn't my idea; *she* brought you. We've said everything; it's over; you'll lose all patience with me, and I'd rather you
shouldn't see the rest." I sent him some money, in a letter, the next day,
but I saw the rest only in the light of a barren sequel.

A whole year after my visit to him I became aware once, in dining out,
that Brooksmith was one of the several servants who hovered behind our
chairs. He had not opened the door of the house to me, and I had not
recognised him in the cluster of retainers in the hall. This time I tried to
catch his eye, but he never gave me a chance, and when he handed me a
dish I could only be careful to thank him audibly. Indeed I partook of
two *entrées* of which I had my doubts, subsequently converted into
certainties, in order not to snub him. He looked well enough in health,
but much older, and wore, in an exceptionally marked degree, the glazed
and expressionless mask of the British domestic *de race*. I saw with
dismay that if I had not known him I should have taken him, on the
showing of his countenance, for an extravagant illustration of irrespon-
sive servile gloom. I said to myself that he had become a reactionary,
gone over to the Philistines, thrown himself into religion, the religion of
his "place," like a foreign lady *sur le retour*. I divined moreover that he
was only engaged for the evening—he had become a mere waiter, had
joined the band of the white-waistcoated who "go out." There was something pathetic in this fact, and it was a terrible vulgarisation of Brooksmith. It was the mercenary prose of butlerhood; he had given up the
struggle for the poetry. If reciprocity was what he had missed, where was
the reciprocity now? Only in the bottoms of the wine-glasses and the five
shillings (or whatever they get), clapped into his hand by the permanent
man. However, I supposed he had taken up a precarious branch of his
profession because after all it sent him less downstairs. His relations with
London society were more superficial, but they were of course more
various. As I went away, on this occasion, I looked out for him eagerly
among the four or five attendants whose perpendicular persons, fluting
the walls of London passages, are supposed to lubricate the process of
departure; but he was not on duty. I asked one of the others if he were
not in the house, and received the prompt answer: "Just left, sir. Anything I can do for you, sir?" I wanted to say "Please give him my kind
regards;" but I abstained; I didn't want to compromise him, and I never
came across him again.

Often and often, in dining out, I looked for him, sometimes accepting
invitations on purpose to multiply the chances of my meeting him. But
always in vain; so that as I met many other members of the casual class

over and over again, I at last adopted the theory that he always procured a list of expected guests beforehand and kept away from the banquets which he thus learned I was to grace. At last I gave up hope, and one day, at the end of three years, I received another visit from his aunt. She was drearier and dingier, almost squalid, and she was in great tribulation and want. Her sister, Mrs Brooksmith, had been dead a year, and three months later her nephew had disappeared. He had always looked after her a bit—since her troubles; I never knew what her troubles had been—and now she hadn't so much as a petticoat to pawn. She had also a niece, to whom she had been everything, before her troubles, but the niece had treated her most shameful. These were details; the great and romantic fact was Brooksmith's final evasion of his fate. He had gone out to wait one evening, as usual, in a white waistcoat she had done up for him with her own hands, being due at a large party up Kensington way. But he had never come home again, and had never arrived at the large party, or at any party that any one could make out. No trace of him had come to light—no gleam of the white waistcoat had pierced the obscurity of his doom. This news was a sharp shock to me, for I had my ideas about his real destination. His aged relative had promptly, as she said, guessed the worst. Somehow and somewhere he had got out of the way altogether, and now I trust that, with characteristic deliberation, he is changing the plates of the immortal gods. As my depressing visitant also said, he never *had* got his spirits up. I was fortunately able to dismiss her with her own somewhat improved. But the dim ghost of poor Brooksmith is one of those that I see. He had indeed been spoiled.

SARAH ORNE JEWETT

Miss Tempy's Watchers

The time of year was April; the place was a small farming town in New Hampshire, remote from any railroad. One by one the lights had been blown out in the scattered houses near Miss Tempy Dent's; but as her neighbors took a last look out of doors, their eyes turned with instinctive curiosity toward the old house where a lamp burned steadily. They gave a little sigh. "Poor Miss Tempy!" said more than one bereft acquaintance; for the good woman lay dead in her north chamber, and the lamp was a watcher's light. The funeral was set for the next day, at one o'clock.

The watchers were two of the oldest friends, Mrs. Crowe and Sarah Ann Binson. They were sitting in the kitchen, because it seemed less awesome than the unused best room, and they beguiled the long hours by steady conversation. One would think that neither topics nor opinions would hold out, at that rate, all through the long spring night; but there was a certain degree of excitement just then, and the two women had risen to an unusual level of expressiveness and confidence. Each had already told the other more than one fact that she had determined to keep secret; they were again and again tempted into statements that either would have found impossible by daylight. Mrs. Crowe was knitting a blue yarn stocking for her husband; the foot was already so long that it seemed as if she must have forgotten to narrow it at the proper time. Mrs. Crowe knew exactly what she was about, however; she was of a much cooler disposition than Sister Binson, who made futile attempts at some sewing, only to drop her work into her lap whenever the talk was most engaging.

Their faces were interesting,—of the dry, shrewd, quick-witted New England type, with thin hair twisted neatly back out of the way. Mrs. Crowe could look vague and benignant, and Miss Binson was, to quote her neighbors, a little too sharp-set; but the world knew that she had need to be, with the load she must carry of supporting an inefficient widowed sister and six unpromising and unwilling nieces and nephews. The eldest boy was at last placed with a good man to learn the mason's trade. Sarah Ann Binson, for all her sharp, anxious aspect, never defended herself, when her sister whined and fretted. She was told every week of her life that the poor children never would have had to lift a finger if their father had lived, and yet she had kept her steadfast way with the little farm, and patiently taught the young people many useful things, for which, as everybody said, they would live to thank her. However pleasureless her life appeared to outward view, it was brimful of pleasure to herself.

Mrs. Crowe, on the contrary, was well-to-do, her husband being a rich farmer and an easy-going man. She was a stingy woman, but for all that she looked kindly; and when she gave away anything, or lifted a finger to help anybody, it was thought a great piece of beneficence, and a compliment, indeed, which the recipient accepted with twice as much gratitude as double the gift that came from a poorer and more generous acquaintance. Everybody liked to be on good terms with Mrs. Crowe. Socially she stood much higher than Sarah Ann Binson.

They were both old schoolmates and friends of Temperance Dent, who had asked them, one day, not long before she died, if they would not come together and look after the house, and manage everything, when she was gone. She may have had some hope that they might become closer friends in this period of intimate partnership, and that the richer woman might better understand the burdens of the poorer. They had not kept the house the night before; they were too weary with their care of their old friend, whom they had not left until all was over.

There was a brook which ran down the hillside very near the house, and the sound of it was much louder than usual. When there was silence in the kitchen, the busy stream had a strange insistence in its wild voice, as if it tried to make the watchers understand something that related to the past.

"I declare, I can't begin to sorrow for Tempy yet. I am so glad to have her at rest," whispered Mrs. Crowe. "It is strange to set here without her, but I can't make it clear that she has gone. I feel as if she had got easy and dropped off to sleep, and I'm more scared about waking her up than knowing any other feeling."

"Yes," said Sarah Ann, "it's just like that, ain't it? But I tell you we are goin' to miss her worse than we expect. She's helped me through with many a trial, has Temperance. I ain't the only one who says the same, neither."

These words were spoken as if there were a third person listening; somebody beside Mrs. Crowe. The watchers could not rid their minds of the feeling that they were being watched themselves. The spring wind whistled in the window crack, now and then, and buffeted the little house in a gusty way that had a sort of companionable effect. Yet, on the whole, it was a very still night, and the watchers spoke in a half whisper.

"She was the freest-handed woman that ever I knew," said Mrs. Crowe, decidedly. "According to her means, she gave away more than anybody. I used to tell her 'twa'nt right. I used really to be afraid that she went without too much, for we have a duty to ourselves."

Sister Binson looked up in a half-amused, unconscious way, and then recollected herself.

Mrs. Crowe met her look with a serious face. "It ain't so easy for me to give as it is for some," she said simply, but with an effort which was made possible only by the occasion. "I should like to say, while Tempy is laying here yet in her own house, that she has been a constant lesson to me. Folks are too kind, and shame me with thanks for what I do. I ain't such a generous woman as poor Tempy was, for all she had nothin' to do with, as one may say."

Sarah Binson was much moved at this confession, and was even pained and touched by the unexpected humility. "You have a good many calls on you"—she began, and then left her kind little compliment half finished.

"Yes, yes, but I've got means enough. My disposition's more of a cross to me as I grow older, and I made up my mind this morning that Tempy's example should be my pattern henceforth." She began to knit faster than ever.

" 'Tain't no use to get morbid: that's what Tempy used to say herself," said Sarah Ann, after a minute's silence. "Ain't it strange to say 'used to say'?" and her own voice choked a little. "She never did like to hear folks git goin' about themselves."

" 'Twas only because they're apt to do it so as other folks say 'twan't so, an' praise 'em up," humbly replied Mrs. Crowe, "and that ain't my object. There wa'n't a child but what Tempy set herself to work to see what she could do to please it. One time my brother's folks had been stopping here in the summer, from Massachusetts. The children was all little, and they broke up a sight of toys, and left 'em when they were going away. Tempy come right up after they rode by, to see if she couldn't help me set the house to rights, and she caught me just as I was going to fling some of the clutter into the stove. I was kind of tired out, starting 'em off in season. 'Oh, give me them!' says she, real pleading; and she wropped 'em up and took 'em home with her when she went, and she mended 'em up and stuck 'em together, and made some young one or other happy with every blessed one. You'd thought I'd done her the biggest favor. 'No thanks to me. I should ha' burnt 'em, Tempy,' says I."

"Some of 'em came to our house, I know," said Miss Binson. "She'd take a lot o' trouble to please a child, 'stead o' shoving of it out o' the way, like the rest of us when we're drove."

"I can tell you the biggest thing she ever gave, and I don't know's there's anybody left but me to tell it. I don't want it forgot," Sarah Binson went on, looking up at the clock to see how the night was going. "It was that pretty-faced Trevor girl, who taught the Corners school, and married so well afterward, out in New York State. You remember her, I dare say?"

"Certain," said Mrs. Crowe, with an air of interest.

"She was a splendid scholar, folks said, and give the school a great start; but she'd overdone herself getting her education, and working to pay for it, and she all broke down one spring, and Tempy made her come and stop with her awhile,—you remember that? Well, she had an uncle, her mother's brother, out in Chicago, who was well off and friendly, and used to write to Lizzie Trevor, and I dare say make her some presents; but he was a lively, driving man, and didn't take time to stop and think about his folks. He hadn't seen her since she was a little girl. Poor Lizzie was so pale and weakly that she just got through the term o' school. She looked as if she was just going straight off in a decline. Tempy, she cosseted her up awhile, and then, next thing folks knew, she was tellin' round how Miss Trevor had gone to see her uncle, and meant to visit Niagary Falls on the way, and stop over night. Now I happened to know, in ways I won't dwell on to explain, that the poor girl was in debt for her schoolin' when she come here, and her last quarter's pay had just squared it off at last, and left her without a cent ahead, hardly; but it had fretted her thinking of it, so she paid it all; they might have dunned her that she owed it to. An' I taxed Tempy about the girl's goin' off on such a journey till she owned up, rather 'n have Lizzie blamed, that she'd given her sixty dollars, same's if she was rolling in riches, and sent her off to have a good rest and vacation."

"Sixty dollars!" exclaimed Mrs. Crowe. "Tempy only had ninety dollars a year that came in to her; rest of her livin' she got by helpin' about, with what she raised off this little piece o' ground, sand one side an' clay the other. An' how often I've heard her tell, years ago, that she'd rather see Niagary than any other sight in the world!"

The women looked at each other in silence; the magnitude of the generous sacrifice was almost too great for their comprehension.

"She was just poor enough to do that!" declared Mrs. Crowe at last, in an abandonment of feeling. "Say what you may, I feel humbled to the dust," and her companion ventured to say nothing. She never had given away sixty dollars at once, but it was simply because she never had it to give. It came to her very lips to say in explanation, "Tempy was so situated"; but she checked herself in time, for she would not break in upon her own loyal guarding of her dependent household.

"Folks say a great deal of generosity, and this one's being public sperited, and that one freehanded about giving," said Mrs. Crowe, who was a little nervous in the silence. "I suppose we can't tell the sorrow it would be to some folks not to give, same's 'twould be to me not to save. I seem kind of made for that, as if 'twas what I'd got to do. I should feel sights better about it if I could make it evident what I was savin' for. If I had a child, now, Sarah Ann," and her voice was a little husky,—"if I had a child, I should think I was heapin' of it up because he was the one trained by the Lord to scatter it again for good. But here's Crowe and me, we can't do anything with money, and both of us like to keep things same's they've always been. Now Priscilla Dance was talking away like a mill clapper, week before last. She'd think I would go right off and get one o' them new-fashioned gilt-and-white papers for the best room, and some new furniture, an' a marble-top table. And I looked at her, all stuck up. 'Why,' says I, 'Priscilla, that nice old velvet paper ain't hurt a mite. I shouldn't feel 'twas my best room without it. Dan'el says 'tis the first thing he can remember rubbin' his little baby fingers on to it, and how splendid he thought them red roses was.' I maintain," continued Mrs.

Crowe stoutly, "that folks wastes sights o' good money doin' just such foolish things. Tearin' out the insides o' meetin'houses, and fixin' the pews different; 'twas good enough as 'twas with mendin'; then times come, an' they want to put it all back same's 'twas before."

This touched upon an exciting subject to active members of that parish. Miss Binson and Mrs. Crowe belonged to opposite parties, and had at one time come as near hard feelings as they could, and yet escape them. Each hastened to speak of other things, and to show her untouched friendliness.

"I do agree with you," said Sister Binson, "that few of us know what use to make of money, beyond everyday necessities. You've seen more o' the world than I have, and know what's expected. When it comes to taste and judgment about such things, I ought to defer to others"; and with this modest avowal the critical moment passed when there might have been an improper discussion.

In the silence that followed, the fact of their presence in a house of death grew more clear than before. There was something disturbing in the noise of a mouse gnawing at the dry boards of a closet wall near by. Both the watchers looked up anxiously at the clock; it was almost the middle of the night, and the whole world seemed to have left them alone with their solemn duty. Only the brook was awake.

"Perhaps we might give a look upstairs now," whispered Mrs. Crowe, as if she hoped to hear some reason against their going just then to the chamber of death; but Sister Binson rose, with a serious and yet satisfied countenance, and lifted the small lamp from the table. She was much more used to watching than Mrs. Crowe, and much less affected by it. They opened the door into a small entry with a steep stairway; they climbed the creaking stairs, and entered the cold upper room on tiptoe. Mrs. Crowe's heart began to beat very fast as the lamp was put on a high bureau, and made long, fixed shadows about the walls. She went hesitatingly toward the solemn shape under its white drapery, and felt a sense of remonstrance as Sarah Ann gently, but in a business-like way, turned back the thin sheet.

"Seems to me she looks pleasanter and pleasanter," whispered Sarah Ann Binson impulsively, as they gazed at the white face with its wonderful smile. "Tomorrow 'twill all have faded out. I do believe they kind of wake up a day or two after they die, and it's then they go." She replaced the light covering, and they both turned quickly away; there was a chill in this upper room.

" 'Tis a great thing for anybody to have got through, ain't it?" said Mrs. Crowe softly, as she began to go down the stairs on tiptoe. The warm air from the kitchen beneath met them with a sense of welcome and shelter.

"I don't know why it is, but I feel as near again to Tempy down here as I do up there," replied Sister Binson. "I feel as if the air was full of her, kind of. I can sense things, now and then, that she seems to say. Now I never was one to take up with no nonsense of sperits and such, but I declare I felt as if she told me just now to put some more wood into the stove."

Mrs. Crowe preserved a gloomy silence. She had suspected before this that her companion was of a weaker and more credulous disposition than herself. " 'Tis a great thing to have got through," she repeated, ignoring definitely all that had last been said. "I suppose you know as well as I that Tempy was one that always feared death. Well, it's all put behind her now; she knows what 'tis." Mrs. Crowe gave a little sigh, and Sister Binson's quick sympathies were stirred toward this other old friend, who also dreaded the great change.

"I'd never like to forgit almost those last words Tempy spoke plain to me," she said gently, like the comforter she truly was. "She looked up at me once or twice, that last afternoon after I come to set by her, and let Mis' Owen go home; and I says, 'Can I do anything to ease you, Tempy?' and the tears come into my eyes so I couldn't see what kind of a nod she give me. 'No, Sarah Ann, you can't, dear,' says she; and then she got her breath again, and says she, looking at me real meanin', 'I'm only a-gettin' sleepier and sleepier; that's all there is,' says she, and smiled up at me kind of wishful, and shut her eyes. I knew well enough all she meant. She'd been lookin' out for a chance to tell me, and I don' know's she ever said much afterwards."

Mrs. Crowe was not knitting; she had been listening too eagerly. "Yes, 'twill be a comfort to think of that sometimes," she said, in acknowledgment.

"I know that old Dr. Prince said once, in evenin' meetin', that he'd watched by many a dyin' bed, as we well knew, and enough o' his sick folks had been scared o' dyin' their whole lives through; but when they come to the last, he'd never seen one but was willin', and most were glad, to go. ' 'Tis as natural as bein' born or livin' on,' he said. I don't know what had moved him to speak that night. You know he wa'n't in the habit of it, and 'twas the monthly concert of prayer for foreign missions anyways," said Sarah Ann; "but 'twas a great stay to the mind to listen to his words of experience."

"There never was a better man," responded Mrs. Crowe, in a really cheerful tone. She had recovered from her feeling of nervous dread, the kitchen was so comfortable with lamplight and firelight; and just then the old clock began to tell the hour of twelve with leisurely whirring strokes.

Sister Binson laid aside her work, and rose quickly and went to the cupboard. "We'd better take a little to eat," she explained. "The night will go fast after this. I want to know if you went and made some o' your nice cupcake, while you was home today?" she asked, in a pleased tone; and Mrs. Crowe acknowledged such a gratifying piece of thoughtfulness for this humble friend who denied herself all luxuries. Sarah Ann brewed a generous cup of tea, and the watchers drew their chairs up to the table presently, and quelled their hunger with good country appetites. Sister Binson put a spoon into a small, old-fashioned glass of preserved quince, and passed it to her friend. She was almost familiar with the house, and played the part of hostess. "Spread some o' this on your bread and butter," she said to Mrs. Crowe. "Tempy wanted me to use some three or four times, but I never felt to. I know she'd like to have us comfortable now, and would urge us to make a good supper, poor dear."

"What excellent preserves she did make!" mourned Mrs. Crowe. "None of us has got her light hand at doin' things tasty. She made the most o' everything, too. Now, she only had that one old quince tree down in the far corner of the piece, but she'd go out in the spring and tend to it, and look at it so pleasant, and kind of expect the old thorny thing into bloomin'."

"She was just the same with folks," said Sarah Ann. "And she'd never git more'n a little apernful o' quinces, but she'd have every mite o' goodness out o' those, and set the glasses up onto her best-room closet shelf, *so* pleased. 'Twa'n't but a week ago tomorrow mornin' I fetched her a little taste o' jelly in a teaspoon; and she says 'Thank ye,' and took it, an' the minute she tasted it she looked up at me as worried as could be. 'Oh, I don't want to eat that,' says she. 'I always keep that in case o' sickness.' 'You're goin' to have the good o' one tumbler yourself,' says I. 'I'd just like to know who's sick now, if you ain't t!' An' she couldn't help laughin', I spoke up so smart. Oh, dear me, how I shall miss talkin' over things with her! She always sensed things, and got just the p'int you meant."

"She didn't begin to age until two or three years ago, did she?" asked Mrs. Crowe. "I never saw anybody keep her looks as Tempy did. She looked young long after I begun to feel like an old woman. The doctor used to say 'twas her young heart, and I don't know but what he was right. How she did do for other folks! There was one spell she wasn't at home a day to a fort-night. She got most of her livin' so, and that made her own potatoes and things last her through. None o' the young folks could get married without her, and all the old ones was disappointed if she wa'n't round when they was down with sickness and had to go. An' cleanin', or tailorin' for boys, or rug hookin',—there was nothin' but what she could do as handy as most. 'I do love to work,'—ain't you heard her say that twenty times a week?"

Sarah Ann Binson nodded, and began to clear away the empty plates. 'We may want a taste o' somethin' more towards mornin'," she said. "There's plenty in the closet here; and in case some comes from a distance to the funeral, we'll have a little table spread after we get back to the house."

"Yes, I was busy all the mornin'. I've cooked up a sight o' things to bring over," said Mrs. Crowe. "I felt 'twas the last I could do for her."

They drew their chairs near the stove again, and took up their work. Sister Binson's rocking chair creaked as she rocked; the brook sounded louder than ever. It was more lonely when nobody spoke, and presently Mrs. Crowe returned to her thoughts of growing old.

"Yes, Tempy aged all of a sudden. I remember I asked her if she felt as well as common, one day, and she laughed at me good. There, when Dan'el begun to look old, I couldn't help feeling as if somethin' ailed him, and like as not 'twas somethin' he was goin' to git right over, and I dosed him for it stiddy, half of one summer."

"How many things we shall be wanting to ask Tempy!" exclaimed Sarah Ann Binson, after a long pause. "I can't make up my mind to doin' without her. I wish folks could come back just once, and tell us how 'tis where they've gone. Seems then we could do without 'em better."

The brook hurried on, the wind blew about the house now and then; the house itself was a silent place, and the supper, the warm fire, and an absence of any new topics for conversation made the watchers drowsy. Sister Binson closed her eyes first, to rest them for a minute; and Mrs. Crowe glanced at her compassionately, with a new sympathy for the hard-worked little woman. She made up her mind to let Sarah Ann have a good rest, while she kept watch alone; but in a few minutes her own knitting was dropped, and she, too, fell asleep.

Overhead, the pale shape of Tempy Dent, the outworn body of that generous, loving-hearted, simple soul, slept on also in its white raiment. Perhaps Tempy herself stood near, and saw her own life and its surroundings with new understanding. Perhaps she herself was the only watcher.

Later, by some hours, Sarah Ann Binson woke with a start. There was a pale light of dawn outside the small windows. Inside the kitchen, the lamp burned dim. Mrs. Crowe awoke, too.

"I think Tempy'd be the first to say 'twas just as well we both had some rest," she said, not without a guilty feeling.

Her companion went to the outer door, and opened it wide. The fresh air was none too cold, and the brook's voice was not nearly so loud as it had been in the midnight darkness. She could see the shapes of the hills, and the great shadows that lay across the lower country. The east was fast growing bright.

" 'Twill be a beautiful day for the funeral," she said, and turned again, with a sigh, to follow Mrs. Crowe up the stairs. The world seemed more and more empty without the kind face and helpful hands of Tempy Dent.

FRANK O'CONNOR

GUESTS OF THE NATION

I

At dusk the big Englishman Belcher would shift his long legs out of the ashes and ask, "Well, chums, what about it?" and Noble or me would say, "As you please, chum" (for we had picked up some of their curious expressions), and the little Englishman 'Awkins would light the lamp and produce the cards. Sometimes Jeremiah Donovan would come up of an evening and supervise the play, and grow excited over 'Awkins's cards (which he always played badly), and shout at him as if he was one of our own, "Ach, you divil you, why didn't you play the tray?" But, ordinarily, Jeremiah was a sober and contented poor devil like the big Englishman Belcher, and was looked up to at all only because he was a fair hand at documents, though slow enough at these, I vow. He wore a small cloth hat and big gaiters over his long pants, and seldom did I perceive his hands outside the pockets of that pants. He reddened when you talked to him, tilting from toe to heel and back and looking down all the while at his big farmer's feet. His uncommon broad accent was a great source of jest to me, I being from the town as you may recognise.

I couldn't at the time see the point of me and Noble being with Belcher and 'Awkins at all, for it was and is my fixed belief you could have planted that pair in any untended spot from this to Claregalway and they'd have stayed put and flourished like a native weed. I never seen in my short experience two men that took to the country as they did.

They were handed on to us by the Second Battalion to keep when the search for them became too hot, and Noble and myself, being young, took charge with a natural feeling of responsibility. But little 'Awkins made us look right fools when he displayed he knew the countryside as well as we did and something more. "You're the bloke they calls Bonaparte?" he said to me. "Well, Bonaparte, Mary Brigid Ho'Connell was arskin abaout you and said 'ow you'd a pair of socks belonging to 'er young brother." For it seemed, as they explained it, that the Second used to have little evenings of their own, and some of the girls of the neighbourhood would turn in, and, seeing they were such decent fellows, our lads couldn't well ignore the two Englishmen, but invited them in and were hail-fellow-well-met with them. 'Awkins told me he learned to dance "The Walls of Limerick" and "The Siege of Ennis" and "The Waves of Tory" in a night or two, though naturally he could not return the compliment, because our lads at that time did not dance foreign dances on principle.

So whatever privileges and favours Belcher and 'Awkins had with the Second they duly took with us, and after the first evening we gave up all pretence of keeping a close eye on their behaviour. Not that they could have got far, for they had a notable accent and wore khaki tunics and overcoats with civilian pants and boots. But it's my belief they never had an idea of escaping and were quite contented with their lot.

Now, it was a treat to see how Belcher got off with the old woman of the house we were staying in. She was a great warrant to scold, and crotchety even with us, but before ever she had a chance of giving our guests, as I may call them, a lick of her tongue, Belcher had made her his friend for life. She was breaking sticks at the time, and Belcher, who hadn't been in the house for more than ten minutes, jumped up out of his seat and went across to her.

"Allow me, madam," he says, smiling his queer little smile; "please allow me," and takes the hatchet from her hand. She was struck too parlatic to speak, and ever after Belcher would be at her heels carrying a bucket, or basket, or load of turf, as the case might be. As Noble wittily remarked, he got into looking before she lept, and hot water or any little thing she wanted Belcher would have it ready before her. For such a huge man (and though I am five foot ten myself I had to look up to him) he had an uncommon shortness—or should I say lack—of speech. It took us some time to get used to him walking in and out like a ghost, without a syllable out of him. Especially because 'Awkins talked enough for a platoon, it was strange to hear big Belcher with his toes in the ashes come out with a solitary "Excuse me, chum," or "That's right, chum." His one and only abiding passion was cards, and I will say for him he was a good card-player. He could have fleeced me and Noble many a time; only if we lost to him, 'Awkins lost to us, and 'Awkins played with the money Belcher gave him.

'Awkins lost to us because he talked too much, and I think now we lost to Belcher for the same reason. 'Awkins and Noble would spit at one another about religion into the early hours of the morning; the little Englishman as you could see worrying the soul out of young Noble (whose brother was a priest) with a string of questions that would puzzle a cardinal. And to make it worse, even in treating of these holy subjects, 'Awkins had a deplorable tongue; I never in all my career struck across a man who could mix such a variety of cursing and bad language into the simplest topic. Oh, a terrible man was little 'Awkins, and a fright to argue! He never did a stroke of work, and when he had no one else to talk to he fixed his claws into the old woman.

I am glad to say that in her he met his match, for one day when he tried to get her to complain profanely of the drought she gave him a great comedown by blaming the drought upon Jupiter Pluvius (a deity neither 'Awkins nor I had ever even heard of, though Noble said among the pagans he was held to have something to do with rain). And another day the same 'Awkins was swearing at the capitalists for starting the German war, when the old dame laid down her iron, puckered up her little crab's mouth and said, "Mr. 'Awkins, you can say what you please about the war, thinking to deceive me because I'm an ignorant old woman, but I know well what started the war. It was that Italian count that stole the heathen divinity out of the temple in Japan, for believe me, Mr. 'Awkins, nothing but sorrow and want follows them that disturbs the hidden powers!" Oh, a queer old dame, as you remark!

II

So one evening we had our tea together, and 'Awkins lit the lamp and we all sat in to cards. Jeremiah Donovan came in too, and sat down and watched us for a while. Though he was a shy man and didn't speak much, it was easy to see he had no great love for the two Englishmen, and I was surprised it hadn't struck me so clearly before. Well, like that in the story, a terrible dispute blew up late in the evening between 'Awkins and Noble, about capitalists and priests and love for your own country.

"The capitalists," says 'Awkins, with an angry gulp, "the capitalists pays the priests to tell you all abaout the next world, so's you waon't notice what they do in this!"

"Nonsense, man," says Noble, losing his temper, "before ever a capitalist was thought of people believed in the next world."

'Awkins stood up as if he was preaching a sermon. "Oh, they did, did they?" he says with a sneer. "They believed all the things you believe, that's what you mean? And you believe that God created Hadam and Hadam created Shem and Shem created Jehoshophat? You believe all the silly hold fairy-tale abaout Heve and Heden and the happle? Well, listen to me, chum. If you're entitled to 'old to a silly belief like that, I'm entitled to 'old to my own silly belief—which is, that the fust thing your God created was a bleedin' capitalist with mirality and Rolls Royce complete. Am I right, chum?" he says then to Belcher.

"You're right, chum," says Belcher, with his queer smile, and gets up from the table to stretch his long legs into the fire and stroke his moustache. So, seeing that Jeremiah Donovan was going, and there was no knowing when the conversation about religion would be over, I took my hat and went out with him. We strolled down towards the village together, and then he suddenly stopped, and blushing and mumbling, and shifting, as his way was, from toe to heel, he said I ought to be behind keeping guard on the prisoners. And I, having it put to me so suddenly, asked him what the hell he wanted a guard on the prisoners at all for, and said that so far as Noble and me were concerned we had talked it over and would rather be out with a column. "What use is that pair to us?" I asked him.

He looked at me for a spell and said, "I thought you knew we were keeping them as hostages." "Hostages—?" says I, not quite understanding. "The enemy," he says in his heavy way, "have prisoners belong' to us, and now they talk of shooting them. If they shoot our prisoners we'll shoot theirs, and serve them right." "Shoot them?" said I, the possibility just beginning to dawn on me. "Shoot them, exactly," said he. "Now," said I, "wasn't it very unforeseen of you not to tell me and Noble that?" "How so?" he asks. "Seeing that we were acting as guards upon them, of course." "And hadn't you reason enough to guess that much?" "We had not, Jeremiah Donovan, we had not. How were we to know when the men were on our hands so long?" "And what difference does it make? The enemy have our prisoners as long or longer, haven't they?" "It makes a great difference," said I. "How so?" said he sharply; but I couldn't tell him the difference it made, for I was struck too silly to speak. "And when may we expect to be released from this anyway?" said I. "You may expect it to-night," says he. "Or to-morrow or the next day at latest. So if it's hanging round here that worries you, you'll be free soon enough."

I cannot explain it even now, how sad I felt, but I went back to the cottage, a miserable man. When I arrived the discussion was still on, 'Awkins holding forth to all and sundry that there was no next world at all and Noble answering in his best canonical style that there was. But I saw 'Awkins was after having the best of it. "Do you know what, chum?" he was saying, with his saucy smile, "I think you're jest as big a bleedin' hunbeliever as I am. You say you believe in the next world and you know jest as much abaout the next world as I do, which is sweet damn-all. What's 'Eaven? You dunno. Where's 'Eaven? You dunno. Who's in

'Eaven? You dunno. You know sweet dámn-all! I arsk you again, do they wear wings?"

"Very well then," says Noble, "they do; is that enough for you? They do wear wings." "Where do they get them then? Who makes them? 'Ave they a fact'ry for wings? 'Ave they a sort of store where you 'ands in your chit and tikes your bleedin' wings? Answer me that."

"Oh, you're an impossible man to argue with," says Noble. "Now listen to me—." And off the pair of them went again.

It was long after midnight when we locked up the Englishmen and went to bed ourselves. As I blew out the candle I told Noble what Jeremiah Donovan had told me. Noble took it very quietly. After we had been in bed about an hour he asked me did I think we ought to tell the Englishmen. I having thought of the same thing myself (among many others) said no, because it was more than likely the English wouldn't shoot our men, and anyhow it wasn't to be supposed the Brigade who were always up and down with the second battalion and knew the Englishmen well would be likely to want them bumped off. "I think so," says Noble. "It would be sort of cruelty to put the wind up them now." "It was very unforeseen of Jeremiah Donovan anyhow," says I, and by Noble's silence I realised he took my meaning.

So I lay there half the night, and thought and thought, and picturing myself and young Noble trying to prevent the Brigade from shooting 'Awkins and Belcher sent a cold sweat out through me. Because there were men on the Brigade you daren't let nor hinder without a gun in your hand, and at any rate, in those days disunion between brothers seemed to me an awful crime. I knew better after.

It was next morning we found it so hard to face Belcher and 'Awkins with a smile. We went about the house all day scarcely saying a word. Belcher didn't mind us much; he was stretched into the ashes as usual with his usual look of waiting in quietness for something unforeseen to happen, but little 'Awkins gave us a bad time with his audacious gibing and questioning. He was disgusted at Noble's not answering him back. "Why can't you tike your beating like a man, chum?" he says. "You with your Hadam and Heve! I'm a Communist—or an Anarchist. An Anarchist, that's what I am." And for hours after he went round the house, mumbling when the fit took him "Hadam and Heve! Hadam and Heve!"

III

I don't know clearly how we got over that day, but get over it we did, and a great relief it was when the tea-things were cleared away and Belcher said in his peaceable manner, "Well, chums, what about it?" So we all sat round the table and 'Awkins produced the cards, and at that moment I heard Jeremiah Donovan's footsteps up the path, and a dark presentiment crossed my mind. I rose quietly from the table and laid my hand on him before he reached the door. "What do you want?" I asked him. "I want those two soldier friends of yours," he says reddening. "Is that the way it is, Jeremiah Donovan?" I ask. "That's the way. There were four of our lads went west this morning, one of them a boy of sixteen." "That's bad, Jeremiah," says I.

At that moment Noble came out, and we walked down the path together talking in whispers. Feeney, the local intelligence officer, was standing by the gate. "What are you going to do about it?" I asked Jeremiah Donovan. "I want you and Noble to bring them out: you can tell them they're being shifted again; that'll be the quietest way." "Leave me out of that," says Noble suddenly. Jeremiah Donovan looked at him hard for a minute or two. "All right so," he said peaceably. "You and Feeney collect a few tools from the shed and dig a hole by the far end of the bog. Bonaparte and I'll be after you in about twenty minutes. But whatever else you do, don't let anyone see you with the tools. No one must know but the four of ourselves."

We saw Feeney and Noble go round to the houseen where the tools were kept, and sidled in. Everything if I can so express myself was tottering before my eyes, and I left Jeremiah Donovan to do the explaining as best he could, while I took a seat and said nothing. He told them they were to go back to the Second. 'Awkins let a mouthful of curses out of him at that, and it was plain that Belcher, though he said nothing, was duly perturbed. The old woman was for having them stay in spite of us, and she did not shut her mouth until Jeremiah Donovan lost his temper and said some nasty things to her. Within the house by this time it was pitch dark, but no one thought of lighting the lamp, and in the darkness the two Englishmen fetched their khaki topcoats and said good-bye to the woman of the house. "Just as a man mikes a 'ome of a bleedin' place," mumbles 'Awkins shaking her by the hand, "some bastard at headquarters thinks you're too cushy and shunts you off." Belcher shakes her hand very hearty. "A thousand thanks, madam," he says, "a thousand thanks for everything . . ." as though he'd made it all up.

We go round to the back of the house and down towards the fatal bog. Then Jeremiah Donovan comes out with what is in his mind. "There were four of our lads shot by your fellows this morning so now you're to be bumped off." "Cut that stuff out," says 'Awkins flaring up. "It's bad enough to be mucked about such as we are without you plying at soldiers." "It's true," says Jeremiah Donovan, "I'm sorry, 'Awkins, but 'tis true," and comes out with the usual rigmarole about doing our duty and obeying our superiors. "Cut it out," says 'Awkins irritably, "Cut it out!"

Then, when Donovan sees he is not being believed he turns to me. "Ask Bonaparte here," he says. "I don't need to arsk Bonaparte. Me and Bonaparte are chums." "Isn't it true, Bonaparte?" says Jeremiah Donovan solemnly to me. "It is," I say sadly, "it is." 'Awkins stops. "Now, for Christ's sike. . . ." "I mean it, chum," I say. "You daon't saound as if you mean it. You knaow well you don't mean it." "Well, if he don't I do," says Jeremiah Donovan. "Why the 'ell sh'd you want to shoot me, Jeremiah Donovan?" "Why the hell should your people take out four prisoners and shoot them in cold blood upon a barrack square?" I perceive Jeremiah Donovan is trying to encourage himself with hot words.

Anyway, he took little 'Awkins by the arm and dragged him on, but it was impossible to make him understand that we were in earnest. From which you will perceive how difficult it was for me, as I kept feeling my Smith and Wesson and thinking what I would do if they happened to put up a fight or ran for it, and wishing in my heart they would. I knew if only they ran I would never fire on them. "Was Noble in this?" 'Awkins wanted to know, and we said yes. He laughed. But why should Noble want to shoot him? Why should we want to shoot him? What had he done to us? Weren't we chums (the word lingers painfully in my memory)? Weren't we? Didn't we understand him and didn't he understand us? Did either of us imagine for an instant that he'd shoot us for all the so-and-so brigadiers in the so-and-so British Army? By this time I began to perceive in the dusk the desolate edges of the bog that was to be their last earthly bed, and, so great a sadness overtook my mind, I could not answer him. We walked along the edge of it in the darkness, and every now and then 'Awkins would call a halt and begin again, just as if he was wound up, about us being chums, and I was in despair that nothing but the cold and open grave made ready for his presence would convince him that we meant it all. But all the same, if you can understand, I didn't want him to be bumped off.

IV

At last we saw the unsteady glint of a lantern in the distance and made towards it. Noble was carrying it, and Feeney stood somewhere in the darkness behind, and somehow the picture of the two of them so silent in the boglands was like the pain of death in my heart. Belcher, on recognising Noble, said " 'Allo, chum" in his usual peaceable way, but 'Awkins flew at the poor boy immediately, and the dispute began all over again, only that Noble hadn't a word to say for himself, and stood there with the swaying lantern between his gaitered legs.

It was Jeremiah Donovan who did the answering. 'Awkins asked for the twentieth time (for it seemed to haunt his mind) if anybody thought he'd shoot Noble. "You would," says Jeremiah Donovan shortly. "I wouldn't, damn you!" "You would if you knew you'd be shot for not doing it." "I wouldn't, not if I was to be shot twenty times over; he's my chum. And Belcher wouldn't—isn't that right, Belcher?" "That's right, chum," says Belcher peaceably. "Damned if I would. Anyway, who says Noble'd be shot if I wasn't bumped off? What d'you think I'd do if I was in Noble's place and we were out in the middle of a blasted bog?" "What would you do?" "I'd go with him wherever he was going. I'd share my last bob with him and stick by 'im through thick and thin."

"We've had enough of this," says Jeremiah Donovan, cocking his revolver. "Is there any message you want to send before I fire?" "No, there isn't, but . . ." "Do you want to say your prayers?" 'Awkins came out with a cold-blooded remark that shocked even me and turned to Noble again. "Listen to me, Noble," he said. "You and me are chums. You won't come over to my side, so I'll come over to your side. Is that fair? Just you give me a rifle and I'll go with you wherever you want."

Nobody answered him.

"Do you understand?" he said. "I'm through with it all. I'm a deserter or anything else you like, but from this on I'm one of you. Does that prove to you that I mean what I say?" Noble raised his head, but as Donovan began to speak he lowered it again without answering. "For the last time have you any messages to send?" says Donovan in a cold and excited voice.

"Ah, shut up, you, Donovan; you don't understand me, but these fellows do. They're my chums; they stand by me and I stand by them. We're not the capitalist tools you seem to think us."

I alone of the crowd saw Donovan raise his Webley to the back of 'Awkins's neck, and as he did so I shut my eyes and tried to say a prayer. 'Awkins had begun to say something else when Donovan let fly, and, as I opened my eyes at the bang, I saw him stagger at the knees and lie out flat at Noble's feet, slowly, and as quiet as a child, with the lantern-light falling sadly upon his lean legs and bright farmer's boots. We all stood very still for a while watching him settle out in the last agony.

Then Belcher quietly takes out a handkerchief, and begins to tie it about his own eyes (for in our excitement we had forgotten to offer the same to 'Awkins), and, seeing it is not big enough, turns and asks for a loan of mine. I give it to him and as he knots the two together he points with his foot at 'Awkins. " 'E's not quite dead," he says, "better give 'im another." Sure enough 'Awkins's left knee as we see it under the lantern is rising again. I bend down and put my gun to his ear; then, recollecting myself and the company of Belcher, I stand up again with a few hasty words. Belcher understands what is in my mind. "Give 'im 'is first," he says. "I don't mind. Poor bastard, we dunno what's 'appening to 'im now." As by this time I am beyond all feeling I kneel down again and skilfully give 'Awkins the last shot so as to put him for ever out of pain.

Belcher who is fumbling a bit awkwardly with the handkerchiefs comes out with a laugh when he hears the shot. It is the first time I have heard him laugh, and it sends a shiver down my spine, coming as it does so inappropriately upon the tragic death of his old friend. "Poor blighter," he says quietly, "and last night he was so curious abaout it all. It's very queer, chums, I always think. Naow, 'e knows as much abaout it as they'll ever let 'im know, and last night 'e was all in the dark."

Donovan helps him to tie the handkerchiefs about his eyes. "Thanks, chum," he says. Donovan asks him if there are any messages he would like to send. "Naow, chum," he says, "none for me. If any of you likes to write to 'Awkins's mother you'll find a letter from 'er in 'is pocket. But my missus left me eight years ago. Went away with another fellow and took the kid with her. I likes the feelin' of a 'ome (as you may 'ave noticed) but I couldn't start again after that."

We stand around like fools now that he can no longer see us. Donovan looks at Noble and Noble shakes his head. Then Donovan raises his Webley again and just at that moment Belcher laughs his queer nervous laugh again. He must think we are talking of him; anyway, Donovan lowers his gun. " 'Scuse me, chums," says Belcher, "I feel I'm talking the 'ell of a lot . . . and so silly . . . abaout me being so 'andy abaout a 'ouse. But this thing come on me so sudden. You'll forgive me, I'm sure." "You don't want to say a prayer?" asks Jeremiah Donovan. "No, chum," he replies, "I don't think that'd 'elp. I'm ready if you want to get it over." "You understand," says Jeremiah Donovan, "it's not so much our doing. It's our duty, so to speak." Belcher's head is raised like a real blind man's, so that you can only see his nose and chin in the lamplight. "I never could make out what duty was myself," he said, "but I think you're all good lads, if that's what you mean. I'm not complaining." Noble, with a look of desperation, signals to Donovan, and in a flash Donovan raises his gun and fires. The big man goes over like a sack of meal, and this time there is no need of a second shot.

I don't remember much about the burying, but that it was worse than all the rest, because we had to carry the warm corpses a few yards before we sunk them in the windy bog. It was all mad lonely, with only a bit of lantern between ourselves and the pitch-blackness, and birds hooting and screeching all round disturbed by the guns. Noble had to search 'Awkins first to get the letter from his mother. Then having smoothed all signs of the grave away, Noble and I collected our tools, said good-bye to the others, and went back along the desolate edge of the treacherous bog without a word. We put the tools in the houseen and went into the house. The kitchen was pitch-black and cold, just as we left it, and the old woman was sitting over the hearth telling her beads. We walked past her into the room, and Noble struck a match to light the lamp. Just then she rose quietly and came to the doorway, being not at all so bold or crabbed as usual.

"What did ye do with them?" she says in a sort of whisper, and Noble took such a mortal start the match quenched in his trembling hand. "What's that?" he asks without turning round. "I heard ye," she said. "What did you hear?" asks Noble, but sure he wouldn't deceive a child the way he said it. "I heard ye. Do you think I wasn't listening to ye putting the things back in the houseen?" Noble struck another match and this time the lamp lit for him. "Was that what ye did with them?" she said, and Noble said nothing—after all what could he say?

So then, by God, she fell on her two knees by the door, and began telling her beads, and after a minute or two Noble went on his knees by the fireplace, so I pushed my way out past her, and stood at the door, watching the stars and listening to the damned shrieking of the birds. It is so strange what you feel at such moments, and not to be written afterwards. Noble says he felt he seen everything ten times as big, perceiving nothing around him but the little patch of black bog with the two Englishmen stiffening into it; but with me it was the other way, as though the patch of bog where the two Englishmen were was a thousand miles away from me, and even Noble mumbling just behind me and the old woman and the birds and the bloody stars were all far away, and I was somehow very small and very lonely. And anything that ever happened me after I never felt the same about again.

WILLIAM MAXWELL

The Fisherman Who Had No One to Go Out in His Boat with Him

Once upon a time there was a poor fisherman who had no one to go out in his boat with him. The man he started going out with when he was still a boy was now crippled with rheumatism and sat all day by the fire. The other fishermen were all paired off, and there was nobody for him. Out on the water, without a soul to talk to, the hours between daybreak and late afternoon were very long, and to pass the time he sang. He sang the songs that other people sang, whatever he had heard, and this was of course a good deal in the way of music, because in the olden times people sang more than they do now. But eventually he came to the end of all the songs he knew or had ever heard and wanted to learn some new songs. He knew that they were written down and published, but this was no help to him because he had never been to school and didn't know how to read words, let alone the musical staff. You might as well have presented him with a clay tablet of Egyptian hieroglyphics. But there were ways, and he took advantage of them. At a certain time, on certain days of the week, the children in the schoolhouse had singing, and he managed to be in the vicinity. He brought his boat in earlier those days, on one pretext or another, and stood outside the school building. At first the teacher was mystified, but he saw that the poor fisherman always went away as soon as the singing lesson was over, and putting two and two together he realized why the man was there. So, one day, he went to the door and invited the fisherman in. The fisherman backed away, and then he turned and hurried off down the road to the beach. But the next time they had singing, there he was. The schoolteacher opened a window so the fisherman could hear better and went on with the lesson. While the children were singing "There were three sisters fair and bright," the door opened slowly. The teacher pointed to a desk in the back row, and the fisherman squeezed himself into it, though it was a child's desk and much too small for him. The children waved their hands in the air and asked silly questions and giggled, but, never having been to school, the fisherman thought this was customary and did not realize that he was creating a disturbance. He came again, and again.

People manage to believe in magic—of one kind or another. And ghosts. And the influence of the stars. And reincarnation. And a life everlasting. But not enough room is allowed for strangeness: that birds and animals know the way home; that a blind man, having sensed the presence of a wall, knows as well where to walk as you or I; that there have been many recorded instances of conversations between two persons who did not speak the same language but, each speaking his own, nevertheless understood each other perfectly. When the teacher passed out the songbooks, he gave one to the fisherman, well aware that his only contact with the printed page was through his huge, calloused hands. And time after time the fisherman knew, before the children opened their mouths and began to sing, what the first phrase would be, and where the song would go from there.

Naturally, he did not catch as many fish as he had when he was attending to his proper work, and sometimes there was nothing in the house to eat. His wife could not complain, because she was a deaf-mute.

She was not ugly, but no one else would have her. Though she had never heard the sound of her own voice, or indeed any sound whatever, she could have made him feel her dissatisfaction, but she saw that what he was doing was important to him, and did not interfere. What the fisherman would have liked would have been to sing with the children when they sang, but his voice was so deep there was no possibility of its blending unnoticeably with theirs, so he sat in silence, and only when he was out in his boat did the songs burst forth from his throat. What with the wind and the sea birds' crying, he had to sing openly or he would not have known he was singing at all. If he had been on shore, in a quiet room, the sound would have seemed tremendous. Out under the sky, it merely seemed like a man singing.

He often thought that if there had only been a child in the house he could have sung the child to sleep, and that would have been pleasant. He would have sung to his wife if she could have heard him, and he did try, on his fingers, to convey the sound of music—the way the sounds fell together, the rising and descending, the sudden changes in tempo, and the pleasure of expecting to hear this note and hearing, instead, a different one, but she only smiled at him uncomprehendingly.

The schoolteacher knew that if it had been curiosity alone that drew the fisherman to the schoolhouse at the time of singing lessons, he would have stopped coming as soon as his curiosity was satisfied, and he didn't stop coming, which must mean that there was a possibility that he was innately musical. So he stopped the fisherman one day when they met by accident, and asked him to sing the scale. The fisherman opened his mouth and no sound came. He and the schoolteacher looked at each other, and then the fisherman colored, and hung his head. The schoolteacher clapped him on the shoulder and walked on, satisfied that what there was here was the love of music rather than a talent for it, and even that seemed to him something hardly short of a miracle.

IN those islands, storms were not uncommon and they were full of peril. Even large sailing ships were washed on the rocks and broken to pieces. As for the little boats the fishermen went out in, one moment they would be bobbing on the waves like a cork, now on the crest and now out of sight in a trough, and then suddenly there wasn't any boat. The sea would have swallowed it, and the men in it, in the blinking of an eye. It was a terrible fact that the islanders had learned to live with. If they had not been fishermen, they would have starved, so they continued to go out in their boats, and to read the sky for warnings, which were usually dependable, but every now and then a storm—and usually the very worst kind—would come up without any warning, or with only a short time between the first alarming change in the odor of the air, the first wisps of storm clouds, and the sudden lashing of the waters. When this happened, the women gathered on the shore and prayed. Sometimes they waited all night, and sometimes they waited in vain.

One evening, the fisherman didn't come home at the usual time. His wife could not hear the wind or the shutters banging, but when the wind blew puffs of smoke down the chimney, she knew that a storm had come up. She put on her cloak, and wrapped a heavy scarf around her head, and started for the strand, to see if the boats were drawn up there. Instead, she found the other women waiting with their faces all stamped with the same frightened look. Usually the sea birds circled above the beach, waiting for the fishing boats to come in and the fishermen to cut open their fish and throw them the guts, but this evening there were no gulls or cormorants. The air was empty. The wind had blown them all inland, just as, by a freak, it had blown the boats all together, out on the water, so close that it took great skill to keep them from knocking against each other and capsizing in the dark. The fishermen called back and forth for a time, and then they fell silent. The wind had grown higher and higher, and the words were blown right out of their mouths, and they could not even hear themselves what they were saying. The wind was so high and the sound so loud that it was like a silence, and out of this silence, suddenly, came the sound of singing. Being poor ignorant fishermen, they did the first thing that occurred to them—they fell on their knees and prayed. The singing went on and on, in a voice that none of them had ever heard, and so powerful and rich and deep it seemed to come from the same place that the storm came from. A flash of lightning revealed that it was not an angel, as they thought, but the fisherman who was married to the deaf-mute. He was standing in his boat, with his head bared, singing, and in their minds this was no stranger or less miraculous than an angel would have been. They crossed themselves and went on praying, and the fisherman went on singing, and in a little while the waves began to grow smaller and the wind to abate, and the storm, which should have taken days to blow itself out, suddenly turned into an intense calm. As suddenly as it had begun, the singing stopped. The boats drew apart as in one boat after another the men took up their oars again, and in a silvery brightness, all in a cluster, the fishing fleet came safely in to shore.

S. Y. AGNON

Friendship

My wife had returned from a journey, and I was very happy. But a tinge of sadness mingled with my joy, for the neighbors might come and bother us. "Let us go and visit Mr. So-and-so, or Mrs. Such-and-such," I said to my wife, "for if they come to us we shall not get rid of them in a hurry, but if we go to them we can get up and be rid of them whenever we like."

So we lost no time and went to visit Mrs. Klingel. Because Mrs. Klingel was in the habit of coming to us, we went to her first.

Mrs. Klingel was a famous woman and had been principal of a school before the war. When the world went topsy-turvy, she fell from her high estate and became an ordinary teacher. But she was still very conscious of her own importance and talked to people in her characteristic patronizing tone. If anyone acquired a reputation, she would seek his acquaintance and become a frequent visitor in his house. My wife had known her when she was a principal, and she clung to my wife as she clung to anyone who had seen her in her prime. She was extremely friendly to my wife and used to call her by her first name. I too had known Mrs. Klingel in her prime, but I doubt whether I had talked to her. Before the war, when people were not yet hostile to each other, a man could meet his neighbor and regard him as his friend even if he did not talk to him.

Mrs. Klingel was lying in bed. Not far away, on a velvet-covered couch, sat three of her woman friends whom I did not know.

When I came in I greeted each of them, but I did not tell them my name or trouble myself to listen to theirs.

Mrs. Klingel smiled at us affectionately and went on chattering as usual. I held my tongue and said to myself: I have really nothing against her, but she is a nuisance. I shall be walking in the street one day, not wanting anyone to notice me, when suddenly this woman will come up to me and I will ask her how she is and be distracted from my thoughts. Because I knew her several years ago, does that mean that I belong to her all my life? I was smouldering with anger, and I did not tell myself: If you come across someone and you do not know what connection there is between you, you should realize that you have not done your duty to him previously and you have both been brought back into the world to put right the wrong you did to your neighbor in another incarnation.

As I sat nursing my anger, Mrs. Klingel said to my wife, "You were away, my dear, and in the meantime your husband spent his nights in pleasure." As she spoke, she shook her finger at me and said, laughingly, "I am not telling your wife that pretty girls came to visit you."

Nothing had been further from my thoughts in those days than pleasure. Even in my dreams there was nothing to give me pleasure, and now this woman tells my wife, "Your husband had visits from pretty girls, your husband took his pleasure with them." I was so furious that my very bones trembled. I jumped up and showered her with abuse. Every opprobrious word I knew I threw in her face. My wife and she looked at me in wonderment. And I wondered at myself too, for after all Mrs. Klingel had only been joking, and why should I flare up and insult her in this way? But I was boiling with anger, and every word I uttered was either a curse or an insult. Finally I took my wife by the arm and left without a farewell.

On my way out I brushed past Mrs. Klingel's three friends, and I believe I heard one saying to the other, "That was a strange joke of Mrs. Klingel's."

My wife trailed along behind me. From her silence it was obvious that she was distressed, not so much because I had shamed Mrs. Klingel but because I had fallen into a rage. But she was silent out of love, and said nothing at all.

So we walked on without uttering a word. We ran into three men. I knew one of them, but not the other two. The one I knew had been a Hebrew teacher, who had gone abroad and come back rich; now he spent his time stuffing the periodicals with his verbiage. These teachers, even if their pupils have grown up, still treat them as schoolmasters do and teach them things of no importance. But in one of his articles I had found a good thing, and now we had met I paid him a compliment. His face lit up and he presented me to his companions, one of whom had been a senator in Poland, while the other was the brother of one of Mrs. Klingel's three friends—or perhaps I am mistaken and she has no brother.

I should have asked the distinguished visitors if they liked the city, and so forth, but my wife was tired from the journey and still distressed, and it was hard to stop. So I cut the conversation short and took my leave.

My wife had already gone off, without waiting for me. I was not angry at her for not waiting. It is hard for a young woman to stand and show herself to people when she is sad and weary.

While I was walking, I put my hand in my pocket and took out an envelope or a letter, and stopped to read: "The main trial of Job was not that of Job, but of the Holy One, blessed be He, as it were, because He had handed over His servant Job to Satan's power. That is, God's trial was greater than Job's: He had a perfect and upright man, and He placed him in the power of Satan." After reading what I had written, I tore up the envelope and the letter, and scattered the pieces to the wind, as I usually do to every letter, sometimes before I read it and sometimes at the time of reading.

After I had done this, I said to myself: I must find my wife. My thoughts had distracted me and I had strayed from the road; I now found myself suddenly standing in a street where I had never been before. It was no different from all the other streets in the city, but I knew I had strayed to a place I did not know. By this time all the shops were locked up, and little lamps shone in the windows among all kinds of commodities. I saw that I had strayed far from home, and I knew I must go by a different road, but I did not know which. I looked at a stairway bounded on both sides by an iron fence and went up until I reached a flower shop. There I found a small group of men standing with their backs to the flowers, and Dr. Rischel standing among them, offering them his new ideas on grammar and language.

I greeted him and asked: "Which way to . . ." but before I could say the name of the street I started to stammer. I had not forgotten the name of the street, but I could not get the words out of my mouth.

It is easy to understand a man's feelings when he is looking for the place where he lives but, when he is about to ask, cannot pronounce the name. However, I took heart and pretended I was joking. Suddenly I was covered in a cold sweat. What I wanted to conceal I was compelled to reveal. When I asked again where the street was, the same thing happened again.

Dr. Rischel stood there amazed: he was in the midst of expounding his new ideas, and I had come along and interrupted him. Meanwhile, his companions had gone away, looking at me mockingly as they left. I looked this way and that. I tried to remember the name of my street, but could not. Sometimes I thought the name of the street was Humboldt and sometimes that it was West Street. But as soon as I opened my mouth to ask I knew that its name was neither Humboldt nor West. I put my hand in my pocket, hoping to find a letter on which I would see my address. I found two letters I had not yet torn up, but one had been sent to my old home, which I had left, and another was addressed *poste restante*. I had received only one letter in this house where I was living, and I had torn it up a short time before. I started reciting aloud names of towns and villages, kings and nobles, sages and poets, trees and flowers, every kind of street name: perhaps I would remember the name of my street—but I could not recall it.

Dr. Rischel's patience had worn out, and he started scraping the ground with his feet. I am in trouble and he wants to leave me, I said to myself. We are friends, we are human beings, aren't we? How can you leave a man in such distress? Today my wife came back from a journey and I cannot reach her, for the trivial reason that I have forgotten where I live. "Get into a streetcar and come with me," said Dr. Rischel. I wondered why he was giving me such unsuitable advice. He took me by the arm and got in with me.

I rode on against my will, wondering why Rischel had seen fit to drag me into this tramcar. Not only was it not bringing me home, but it was taking me further away from my own street. I remembered that I had seen Rischel in a dream wrestling with me. I jumped off the tramcar and left him.

When I jumped off the car I found myself standing by the post office. An idea came into my head: to ask for my address there. But my head replied: Be careful, the clerk may think you are crazy, for a sane man usually knows where he lives. So I asked a man I found there to ask the clerk.

In came a fat, well-dressed man, an insurance agent, rubbing his hands in pleasure and satisfaction, who buttonholed him and interrupted him with his talk. My blood boiled with indignation. "Have you no manners?" I said to him. "When two people are talking, what right have you to interrupt them?" I knew I was not behaving well, but I was in a temper and completely forgot my manners. The agent looked at me in surprise, as if saying: What have I done to you? Why should you insult me? I knew that if I was silent he would have the best of the argument, so I started shouting again, "I've got to go home, I'm looking for my house, I've forgotten the name of my street, and I don't know how to get to my wife!" He began to snigger, and so did the others who had gathered at the sound of my voice. Meanwhile, the clerk had closed his window and gone away, without my knowing my address.

Opposite the post office stood a coffeehouse. There I saw Mr. Jacob Tzorev. Mr. Jacob Tzorev had been a banker in another city; I had known him before the war. When I went abroad, and he heard I was in difficulties, he had sent me money. Since paying the debt I had never written to him. I used to say: Any day now I will return to the Land of Israel and make it up with him. Meanwhile, twenty years had passed and we had not met. Now that I saw him I rushed into the coffeehouse and gripped both his arms from behind, clinging to them joyfully and calling him by name. He turned his head toward me but said nothing. I wondered why he was silent and showed me no sign of friendship. Didn't he see how much I liked him, how much I loved him?

A young man whispered to me, "Father is blind." I looked and saw that he was blind in both his eyes. It was hard for me not to rejoice in my friend, and hard to rejoice in him, for when I had left him and gone abroad there had been light in his eyes, but now they were blind.

I wanted to ask how he was, and how his wife was. But when I started to speak I spoke about my home. Two wrinkles appeared under his eyes, and it looked as if he were peeping out of them. Suddenly he groped with his hands, turned toward his son, and said, "This gentleman was my friend." I nodded and said, "Yes, that's right, I was your friend and I am your friend." But neither his father's words nor my own made any impression on the son, and he paid no attention to me. After a brief pause, Mr. Tzorev said to his son, "Go and help him find his home."

The young man stood still for a while. It was obvious that he found it hard to leave his father alone. Finally the father opened his eyes and gazed at me. His two beautiful eyes shone, and I saw myself standing beside my home.

Translated by Misha Louvish

JAMES JOYCE

A LITTLE CLOUD

Eight years before he had seen his friend off at the North Wall and wished him godspeed. Gallaher had got on. You could tell that at once by his travelled air, his well-cut tweed suit and fearless accent. Few fellows had talents like his and fewer still could remain unspoiled by such success. Gallaher's heart was in the right place and he had deserved to win. It was something to have a friend like that.

Little Chandler's thoughts ever since lunch-time had been of his meeting with Gallaher, of Gallaher's invitation and of the great city London where Gallaher lived. He was called Little Chandler because, though he was but slightly under the average stature, he gave one the idea of being a little man. His hands were white and small, his frame was fragile, his voice was quiet and his manners were refined. He took the greatest care of his fair silken hair and moustache and used perfume discreetly on his handkerchief. The half-moons of his nails were perfect and when he smiled you caught a glimpse of a row of childish white teeth.

As he sat at his desk in the King's Inns he thought what changes those eight years had brought. The friend whom he had known under a shabby and necessitous guise had become a brilliant figure on the London Press. He turned often from his tiresome writing to gaze out of the office window. The glow of a late autumn sunset covered the grass plots and walks. It cast a shower of kindly golden dust on the untidy nurses and decrepit old men who drowsed on the benches; it flickered upon all the moving figures—on the children who ran screaming along the gravel paths and on everyone who passed through the gardens. He watched the scene and thought of life; and (as always happened when he thought of life) he became sad. A gentle melancholy took possession of him. He felt how useless it was to struggle against fortune, this being the burden of wisdom which the ages had bequeathed to him.

He remembered the books of poetry upon his shelves at home. He had bought them in his bachelor days and many an evening, as he sat in the little room off the hall, he had been tempted to take one down from the bookshelf and read out something to his wife. But shyness had always held him back; and so the books had remained on their shelves. At times he repeated lines to himself and this consoled him.

When his hour had struck he stood up and took leave of his desk and of his fellow-clerks punctiliously. He emerged from under the feudal arch of the King's Inns, a neat modest figure, and walked swiftly down Henrietta Street. The golden sunset was waning and the air had grown sharp. A horde of grimy children populated the street. They stood or ran in the roadway or crawled up the steps before the gaping doors or squatted like mice upon the thresholds. Little Chandler gave them no thought. He picked his way deftly through all that minute vermin-like life and under the shadow of the gaunt spectral mansions in which the old nobility of Dublin had roistered. No memory of the past touched him, for his mind was full of a present joy.

He had never been in Corless's but he knew the value of the name. He knew that people went there after the theatre to eat oysters and drink liqueurs; and he had heard that the waiters there spoke French and German. Walking swiftly by at night he had seen cabs drawn up before the door and richly dressed ladies, escorted by cavaliers, alight and enter quickly. They wore noisy dresses and many wraps. Their faces were powdered and they caught up their dresses, when they touched earth, like alarmed Atalantas. He had always passed without turning his head to look. It was his habit to walk swiftly in the street even by day and whenever he found himself in the city late at night he hurried on his way apprehensively and excitedly. Sometimes, however, he courted the causes of his fear. He chose the darkest and narrowest streets and, as he walked boldly forward, the silence that was spread about his footsteps troubled him, the wandering silent figures troubled him; and at times a sound of low fugitive laughter made him tremble like a leaf.

He turned to the right towards Capel Street. Ignatius Gallaher on the London Press! Who would have thought it possible eight years before? Still, now that he reviewed the past, Little Chandler could remember many signs of future greatness in his friend. People used to say that Ignatius Gallaher was wild. Of course, he did mix with a rakish set of fellows at that time, drank freely and borrowed money on all sides. In the end he had got mixed up in some shady affair, some money transaction: at least, that was one version of his flight. But nobody denied him talent. There was always a certain . . . something in Ignatius Gallaher that impressed you in spite of yourself. Even when he was out at elbows and at his wits' end for money he kept up a bold face. Little Chandler remembered (and the remembrance brought a slight flush of pride to his cheek) one of Ignatius Gallaher's sayings when he was in a tight corner:

—Half time, now, boys, he used to say light-heartedly. Where's my considering cap?

That was Ignatius Gallaher all out; and, damn it, you couldn't but admire him for it.

Little Chandler quickened his pace. For the first time in his life he felt himself superior to the people he passed. For the first time his soul revolted against the dull inelegance of Capel Street. There was no doubt about it: if you wanted to succeed you had to go away. You could do nothing in Dublin. As he crossed Grattan Bridge he looked down the river towards the lower quays and pitied the poor stunted houses. They seemed to him a band of tramps, huddled together along the river-banks, their old coats covered with dust and soot, stupefied by the panorama of sunset and waiting for the first chill of night to bid them arise, shake themselves and begone. He wondered whether he could write a poem to express his idea. Perhaps Gallaher might be able to get it into some London paper for him. Could he write something original? He was not sure what idea he wished to express but the thought that a poetic moment had touched him took life within him like an infant hope. He stepped onward bravely.

Every step brought him nearer to London, farther from his own sober inartistic life. A light began to tremble on the horizon of his mind. He was not so old—thirty-two. His temperament might be said to be just at the point of maturity. There were so many different moods and impressions that he wished to express in verse. He felt them within him. He tried to weigh his soul to see if it was a poet's soul. Melancholy was the dominant note of his temperament, he thought, but it was a melancholy tempered by recurrences of faith and resignation and simple joy. If he could give expression to it in a book of poems perhaps men would listen. He would never be popular: he saw that. He could not sway the crowd but he might appeal to a little circle of kindred minds. The English critics, perhaps, would recognise him as one of the Celtic school by reason of the melancholy tone of his poems; besides that, he would put in allusions. He began to invent sentences and phrases from the notices which his book would get. *Mr Chandler has the gift of easy and graceful verse. . . . A wistful sadness pervades these poems. . . . The Celtic note.* It was a pity his name was not more Irish-looking. Perhaps it would be better to insert his mother's name before the surname: Thomas Malone Chandler, or better still: T. Malone Chandler. He would speak to Gallaher about it.

He pursued his revery so ardently that he passed his street and had to turn back. As he came near Corless's his former agitation began to overmaster him and he halted before the door in indecision. Finally he opened the door and entered.

The light and noise of the bar held him at the doorway for a few moments. He looked about him, but his sight was confused by the shining of many red and green wine-glasses. The bar seemed to him to be full of people and he felt that the people were observing him curiously. He glanced quickly to right and left (frowning slightly to make his errand appear serious), but when his sight cleared a little he saw that nobody had turned to look at him: and there, sure enough, was Ignatius Gallaher leaning with his back against the counter and his feet planted far apart.

—Hallo, Tommy, old hero, here you are! What is it to be? What will you have? I'm taking whisky: better stuff than we get across the water. Soda? Lithia? No mineral? I'm the same. Spoils the flavour. . . . Here, *garçon,* bring us two halves of malt whisky, like a good fellow. . . . Well, and how have you been pulling along since I saw you last? Dear God, how old we're getting! Do you see any signs of aging in me—eh, what? A little grey and thin on the top—what?

Ignatius Gallaher took off his hat and displayed a large closely cropped head. His face was heavy, pale and clean-shaven. His eyes, which were of bluish slate-colour, relieved his unhealthy pallor and shone out plainly above the vivid orange tie he wore. Between these rival features the lips appeared very long and shapeless and colourless. He bent his head and felt with two sympathetic fingers the thin hair at the crown. Little Chandler shook his head as a denial. Ignatious Gallaher put on his hat again.

—It pulls you down, he said, Press life. Always hurry and scurry,

looking for copy and sometimes not finding it: and then, always to have
something new in your stuff. Damn proofs and printers, I say, for a few
days. I'm deuced glad, I can tell you, to get back to the old country. Does
a fellow good, a bit of a holiday. I feel a ton better since I landed again in
dear dirty Dublin. . . . Here you are, Tommy. Water? Say when.

Little Chandler allowed his whisky to be very much diluted.

—You don't know what's good for you, my boy, said Ignatius Gallaher. I drink mine neat.

—I drink very little as a rule, said Little Chandler modestly. An odd
half-one or so when I meet any of the old crowd: that's all.

—Ah, well, said Ignatius Gallaher, cheerfully, here's to us and to old
times and old acquaintance.

They clinked glasses and drank the toast.

—I met some of the old gang to-day, said Ignatious Gallaher. O'Hara
seems to be in a bad way. What's he doing?

—Nothing, said Little Chandler. He's gone to the dogs.

—But Hogan has a good sit, hasn't he?

—Yes; he's in the Land Commission.

—I met him one night in London and he seemed to be very flush.
. . . Poor O'Hara! Boose, I suppose?

—Other things, too, said Little Chandler shortly.

Ignatius Gallaher laughed.

—Tommy, he said, I see you haven't changed an atom. You're the
very same serious person that used to lecture me on Sunday mornings
when I had a sore head and a fur on my tongue. You'd want to knock
about a bit in the world. Have you never been anywhere, even for a trip?

—I've been to the Isle of Man, said Little Chandler.

Ignatius Gallaher laughed.

—The Isle of Man! he said. Go to London or Paris: Paris, for choice.
That'd do you good.

—Have you seen Paris?

—I should think I have! I've knocked about there a little.

—And is it really so beautiful as they say? asked Little Chandler.

He sipped a little of his drink while Ignatius Gallaher finished his
boldly.

—Beautiful? said Ignatius Gallaher, pausing on the word and on the
flavour of his drink. It's not so beautiful, you know. Of course, it is
beautiful. . . . But it's the life of Paris; that's the thing. Ah, there's no city
like Paris for gaiety, movement, excitement. . . .

Little Chandler finished his whisky and, after some trouble, succeeded
in catching the barman's eye. He ordered the same again.

—I've been to the Moulin Rouge, Ignatius Gallaher continued when
the barman had removed their glasses, and I've been to all the Bohemian

cafés. Hot stuff! Not for a pious chap like you, Tommy.

Little Chandler said nothing until the barman returned with the two glasses: then he touched his friend's glass lightly and reciprocated the former toast. He was beginning to feel somewhat disillusioned. Gallaher's accent and way of expressing himself did not please him. There was something vulgar in his friend which he had not observed before. But perhaps it was only the result of living in London amid the bustle and competition of the Press. The old personal charm was still there under this new gaudy manner. And, after all, Gallaher had lived, he had seen the world. Little Chandler looked at his friend enviously.

—Everything in Paris is gay, said Ignatius Gallaher. They believe in enjoying life—and don't you think they're right? If you want to enjoy yourself properly you must go to Paris. And, mind you, they've a great feeling for the Irish there. When they heard I was from Ireland they were ready to eat me, man.

Little Chandler took four or five sips from his glass.

—Tell me, he said, is it true that Paris is so . . . immoral as they say?

Ignatius Gallaher made a catholic gesture with his right arm.

—Every place is immoral, he said. Of course you do find spicy bits in Paris. Go to one of the students' balls, for instance. That's lively, if you like, when the *cocottes* begin to let themselves loose. You know what they are, I suppose?

—I've heard of them, said Little Chandler.

Ignatius Gallaher drank off his whisky and shook his head.

—Ah, he said, you may say what you like. There's no woman like the Parisienne—for style, for go.

—Then it is an immoral city, said Little Chandler, with timid insistence—I mean, compared with London or Dublin?

—London! said Ignatius Gallaher. It's six of one and half-a-dozen of the other. You ask Hogan, my boy. I showed him a bit about London when he was over there. He'd open your eye. . . . I say, Tommy, don't make punch of that whisky: liquor up.

—No, really. . . .

—O, come on, another one won't do you any harm. What is it? The same again, I suppose?

—Well . . . all right.

—*François*, the same again. . . . Will you smoke, Tommy?

Ignatius Gallaher produced his cigar-case. The two friends lit their cigars and puffed at them in silence until their drinks were served.

—I'll tell you my opinion, said Ignatius Gallaher, emerging after some time from the clouds of smoke in which he had taken refuge, it's a rum world. Talk of immorality! I've heard of cases—what am I saying?—I've known them: cases of . . . immorality. . . .

Ignatius Gallaher puffed thoughtfully at his cigar and then, in a calm historian's tone, he proceeded to sketch for his friend some pictures of the corruption which was rife abroad. He summarised the vices of many capitals and seemed inclined to award the palm to Berlin. Some things he could not vouch for (his friends had told him), but of others he had had personal experience. He spared neither rank nor caste. He revealed many of the secrets of religious houses on the Continent and described some of the practices which were fashionable in high society and ended by telling, with details, a story about an English duchess—a story which he knew to be true. Little Chandler was astonished.

—Ah, well, said Ignatius Gallaher, here we are in old jog-along Dublin where nothing is known of such things.

—How dull you must find it, said Little Chandler, after all the other places you've seen!

—Well, said Ignatius Gallaher, it's a relaxation to come over here, you know. And, after all, it's the old country, as they say, isn't it? You can't help having a certain feeling for it. That's human nature. . . . But tell me something about yourself. Hogan told me you had . . . tasted the joys of connubial bliss. Two years ago, wasn't it?

Little Chandler blushed and smiled.

—Yes, he said. I was married last May twelve months.

—I hope it's not too late in the day to offer my best wishes, said Ignatius Gallaher. I didn't know your address or I'd have done so at the time.

He extended his hand, which Little Chandler took.

—Well, Tommy, he said, I wish you and yours every joy in life, old chap, and tons of money, and may you never die till I shoot you. And that's the wish of a sincere friend, an old friend. You know that?

—I know that, said Little Chandler.

—Any youngsters? said Ignatius Gallaher.

Little Chandler blushed again.

—We have one child, he said.

—Son or daughter?

—A little boy.

Ignatius Gallaher slapped his friend sonorously on the back.

—Bravo, he said, I wouldn't doubt you, Tommy.

Little Chandler smiled, looked confusedly at his glass and bit his lower lip with three childishly white front teeth.

—I hope you'll spend an evening with us, he said, before you go back. My wife will be delighted to meet you. We can have a little music and—

—Thanks awfully, old chap, said Ignatius Gallaher, I'm sorry we didn't meet earlier. But I must leave to-morrow night.

—To-night, perhaps . . . ?

—I'm awfully sorry, old man. You see I'm over here with another fellow, clever young chap he is too, and we arranged to go to a little card-party. Only for that . . .

—O, in that case. . . .

—But who knows? said Ignatius Gallaher considerately. Next year I may take a little skip over here now that I've broken the ice. It's only a pleasure deferred.

—Very well, said Little Chandler, the next time you come we must have an evening together. That's agreed now, isn't it?

—Yes, that's agreed, said Ignatius Gallaher. Next year if I come, *parole d'honneur*.

—And to clinch the bargain, said Little Chandler, we'll just have one more now.

Ignatius Gallaher took out a large gold watch and looked at it.

—Is it to be the last? he said. Because you know, I have an a.p.

—O, yes, positively, said Little Chandler.

—Very well, then, said Ignatius Gallaher, let us have another one as a *deoc an doruis*—that's good vernacular for a small whisky, I believe.

Little Chandler ordered the drinks. The blush which had risen to his face a few moments before was establishing itself. A trifle made him blush at any time: and now he felt warm and excited. Three small whiskies had gone to his head and Gallaher's strong cigar had confused his mind, for he was a delicate and abstinent person. The adventure of meeting Gallaher after eight years, of finding himself with Gallaher in Corless's surrounded by lights and noise, of listening to Gallaher's stories and of sharing for a brief space Gallaher's vagrant and triumphant life, upset the equipoise of his sensitive nature. He felt acutely the contrast between his own life and his friend's, and it seemed to him unjust. Gallaher was his inferior in birth and education. He was sure that he could do something better than his friend had ever done, or could ever do, something higher than mere tawdry journalism if he only got the chance. What was it that stood in his way? His unfortunate timidity! He wished to vindicate himself in some way, to assert his manhood. He saw behind Gallaher's refusal of his invitation. Gallaher was only patronising him by his friendliness just as he was patronising Ireland by his visit.

The barman brought their drinks. Little Chandler pushed one glass towards his friend and took up the other boldly.

—Who knows? he said, as they lifted their glasses. When you come next year I may have the pleasure of wishing long life and happiness to Mr and Mrs Ignatius Gallaher.

Ignatius Gallaher in the act of drinking closed one eye expressively over the rim of his glass. When he had drunk he smacked his lips decisively, set down his glass and said:

—No blooming fear of that, my boy. I'm going to have my fling first
and see a bit of life and the world before I put my head in the sack—if I
ever do.

—Some day you will, said Little Chandler calmly.

Ignatius Gallaher turned his orange tie and slate-blue eyes full upon
his friend.

—You think so? he said.

—You'll put your head in the sack, repeated Little Chandler stoutly,
like everyone else if you can find the girl.

He had slightly emphasised his tone and he was aware that he had
betrayed himself; but, though the colour had heightened in his cheek, he
did not flinch from his friend's gaze. Ignatius Gallaher watched him for
a few moments and then said:

—If ever it occurs, you may bet your bottom dollar there'll be no
mooning and spooning about it. I mean to marry money. She'll have a
good fat account at the bank or she won't do for me.

Little Chandler shook his head.

—Why, man alive, said Ignatius Gallaher, vehemently, do you know
what it is? I've only to say the word and to-morrow I can have the woman
and the cash. You don't believe it? Well, I know it. There are hundreds—what am I saying?—thousands of rich Germans and Jews, rotten
with money, that'd only be too glad. . . . You wait a while, my boy. See if
I don't play my cards properly. When I go about a thing I mean business,
I tell you. You just wait.

He tossed his glass to his mouth, finished his drink and laughed loudly.
Then he looked thoughtfully before him and said in a calmer tone:

—But I'm in no hurry. They can wait. I don't fancy tying myself up to
one woman, you know.

He imitated with his mouth the act of tasting and made a wry face.

—Must get a bit stale, I should think, he said.

Little Chandler sat in the room off the hall, holding a child in his
arms. To save money they kept no servant but Annie's young sister
Monica came for an hour or so in the morning and an hour or so in the
evening to help. But Monica had gone home long ago. It was a quarter to
nine. Little Chandler had come home late for tea and, moreover, he had
forgotten to bring Annie home the parcel of coffee from Bewley's. Of
course she was in a bad humour and gave him short answers. She said she
would do without any tea but when it came near the time at which the
shop at the corner closed she decided to go out herself for a quarter of a
pound of tea and two pounds of sugar. She put the sleeping child deftly
in his arms and said:

—Here. Don't waken him.

A little lamp with a white china shade stood upon the table and its light fell over a photograph which was enclosed in a frame of crumpled horn. It was Annie's photograph. Little Chandler looked at it, pausing at the thin tight lips. She wore the pale blue summer blouse which he had brought her home as a present one Saturday. It had cost him ten and elevenpence; but what an agony of nervousness it had cost him! How he had suffered that day, waiting at the shop door until the shop was empty, standing at the counter and trying to appear at his ease while the girl piled ladies' blouses before him, paying at the desk and forgetting to take up the odd penny of his change, being called back by the cashier, and, finally, striving to hide his blushes as he left the shop by examining the parcel to see if it was securely tied. When he brought the blouse home Annie kissed him and said it was very pretty and stylish; but when she heard the price she threw the blouse on the table and said it was a regular swindle to charge ten and elevenpence for that. At first she wanted to take it back but when she tried it on she was delighted with it, especially with the make of the sleeves, and kissed him and said he was very good to think of her.

Hm! . . .

He looked coldly into the eyes of the photograph and they answered coldly. Certainly they were pretty and the face itself was pretty. But he found something mean in it. Why was it so unconscious and lady-like? The composure of the eyes irritated him. They repelled him and defied him: there was no passion in them, no rapture. He thought of what Gallaher had said about rich Jewesses. Those dark Oriental eyes, he thought, how full they are of passion, of voluptuous longing! . . . Why had he married the eyes in the photograph?

He caught himself up at the question and glanced nervously round the room. He found something mean in the pretty furniture which he had bought for his house on the hire system. Annie had chosen it herself and it reminded him of her. It too was prim and pretty. A dull resentment against his life awoke within him. Could he not escape from his little house? Was it too late for him to try to live bravely like Gallaher? Could he go to London? There was the furniture still to be paid for. If he could only write a book and get it published, that might open the way for him.

A volume of Byron's poems lay before him on the table. He opened it cautiously with his left hand lest he should waken the child and began to read the first poem in the book:

> Hushed are the winds and still the evening gloom,
> Not e'en a Zephyr wanders through the grove,
> Whilst I return to view my Margaret's tomb
> And scatter flowers on the dust I love.

He paused. He felt the rhythm of the verse about him in the room. How melancholy it was! Could he, too, write like that, express the melancholy of his soul in verse? There were so many things he wanted to describe: his sensation of a few hours before on Grattan Bridge, for example. If he could get back again into that mood. . . .

The child awoke and began to cry. He turned from the page and tried to hush it: but it would not be hushed. He began to rock it to and fro in his arms but its wailing cry grew keener. He rocked it faster while his eyes began to read the second stanza:

> Within this narrow cell reclines her clay,
>   That clay where once . . .

It was useless. He couldn't read. He couldn't do anything. The wailing of the child pierced the drum of his ear. It was useless, useless! He was a prisoner for life. His arms trembled with anger and suddenly bending to the child's face he shouted:

—Stop!

The child stopped for an instant, had a spasm of fright and began to scream. He jumped up from his chair and walked hastily up and down the room with the child in his arms. It began to sob piteously, losing its breath for four or five seconds, and then bursting out anew. The thin walls of the room echoed the sound. He tried to soothe it but it sobbed more convulsively. He looked at the contracted and quivering face of the child and began to be alarmed. He counted seven sobs without a break between them and caught the child to his breast in fright. If it died! . . .

The door was burst open and a young woman ran in, panting.

—What is it? What is it? she cried.

The child, hearing its mother's voice, broke out into a paroxysm of sobbing.

—It's nothing, Annie . . . it's nothing. . . . He began to cry . . .

She flung her parcels on the floor and snatched the child from him.

—What have you done to him? she cried, glaring into his face.

Little Chandler sustained for one moment the gaze of her eyes and his heart closed together as he met the hatred in them. He began to stammer:

—It's nothing. . . . He . . . he began to cry. . . . I couldn't . . . I didn't do anything. . . . What?

Giving no heed to him she began to walk up and down the room, clasping the child tightly in her arms and murmuring:

—My little man! My little mannie! Was 'ou frightened, love? . . .

There now, love! There now! . . . Lambabaun! Mamma's little lamb of the world! . . . There now!

Little Chandler felt his cheeks suffused with shame and he stood back out of the lamplight. He listened while the paroxysm of the child's sobbing grew less and less; and tears of remorse started to his eyes.

PART X

LETTERS: GROUP 3

Believe me, my Wendly boy, what poor possibility of friendship abides in the crazy frame of W. J. meanders about thy neighborhood.

—William James to Oliver Wendell Holmes, Jr.

GUSTAVE FLAUBERT
AND IVAN TURGENEV

CORRESPONDENCE

Flaubert to Turgenev

Bagnères-de-Luchon
Monday, 5 August [1872]

My dear Turgenev,

I shall be back in Paris next Friday; and three or four days later, I shall be back at Croisset *where I expect you.* I have to be away during the first few days of September. So don't come after the 25th at the latest.

I have the end of *Saint Anthony* to read to you. I'm afraid of having skimped on it, and there are so many things to talk to you about. I don't feel in very good form either. I am in a "state of dryness" as the mystics say. I am without "grace."

It's hard to talk in Paris. The noise from the street and the nearness of Other People deprive one of any peace. Come to my old homestead then. We shall be completely alone, and we'll have a good chat.

Will you please give my respects to Mme Viardot? As for you, I embrace you.

Your
G. Flaubert

Don't think of treating your gout, poor dear friend. All remedies are dangerous. There's only one that I trust, and it's atrocious. I'll tell you about it. My blessings on the head of mademoiselle Jeanne.

[Croisset]
[8 November 1879]

My old darling,

Send me, or better bring me your work when you like. Don't make any promises, don't tell me you're coming. Warn me twenty-four hours in advance, and *come,* that's all I ask you. *B. and P.,* who send you their respects, are now about their devotions. They are going "to approach the altar"; I think this chapter on Religion will make the Ecclesiastical gentlemen take a dim view of me? I have stuffed myself with pious literature! At last on New Year's Day I hope to embark on the last chapter, and when that's finished, I shall have six months more to go.

My niece is leaving me in a week's time, and I shall be alone until the spring. This evening I shall have a visit from young Maupassant. That's all, my good fellow.

I have only read five or six episodes of *Nana:* consequently I can't talk about it. But I have delighted in Renan's new volume; what a jewel of erudition!

Say nice things to everyone, beginning with Mme Viardot and ending with the new-born baby.

I embrace you very tenderly.

Your old
G. Flaubert

You don't mention the gout. It's left you then? So much the better.

I also feel very old sometimes, weary, exhausted in my bones. Never mind! I carry on, and would like not to die before having emptied a few more buckets of sh— on the heads of my fellow men.

That's the only thing that keeps me going.

Turgenev to Flaubert

Les Frenes Bougival
Sunday 23 November 79

My good old fellow,

Certainly I'll come to Croisset on the 12th—with two bottles of champagne under my arm, to celebrate the howmanyeth year of your existence? Just two weeks ago—on 9 November—I was 61!

You will have the proofs of my thing for "La Nouvelle Revue" in the first days of December, and correct them harshly, if you find something that's not quite right.

I am, like you, a patron of the reception in aid of the flood victims of Murcia. (The date of the reception is set for 11 November [*sic*].) All that we shall have to do (for I assume you'll accept) is to put on a suit, a white tie, and *honour* the party with our presence, with a little badge in our buttonhole. You see it's not difficult. You would have to send your acceptance and then come to Paris on the 11th or the evening of the 10th—and we would leave together for Croisset on the evening of the 11th or the 12th first thing in the morning. There you are!

We are continuing to read "Sentimental Education" *en famille* and still with the same pleasure.

No, "Nana" has had no success. There were, however, two quite fine chapters a few days ago. But on the whole, it's boring—and what would displease Zola especially, it is as naive as can be, and tendancious (Is that the right spelling?) to the devil!

I have an engagement with your niece tomorrow. I'm leaving the country at the end of this week.

I shall see you again soon—I embrace you.

Your
Iv. Turgenev

Flaubert to Turgenev

[Croisset]
Wednesday 5 o'clock [3 December 1879]

You will receive your *parcel* at the same time as this. Included is a little note of explanation.

No, I shan't go to Paris for the Spaniards, it would be too silly. But I expect you on the 12th.

B. and P. are not coming on very well. The weather is making me sad, and I'm worn out by my reading. But thank God that's finished!

I embrace you.

Your old
G. Flaubert

[Croisset]
Friday 26 December [1879]

Generous man,

I have not yet received the caviar or the salmon. By what means did you dispatch these two boxes? My stomach is ravaged with anxiety.

Your journey to Russia upsets me extraordinarily, my poor old fellow. It seems to me that this departure is more significant than the others. Why? Do you really need to go, is it unavoidable? Arrange things so as to avoid a long absence, and come back quickly to France where your friends and loved ones are.

I am now preparing the last eight pages of my Religion. I am afraid that that chapter will be rather dry.

I embrace you strongly.

Your
G. Flaubert

Turgenev to Flaubert

> *50 rue de Douai Paris*
> *Saturday morning [27 December 1879]*

My good old fellow,

The caviar and the salmon were sent *4 days* ago "care of *M. Pilon*, quai du Havre, Rouen—to be handed to M. G.F." (This address was given to me by Commanville.) Find out what you can. I should be particularly sorry if the salmon were to be lost, it was splendid.

This cold spell is freezing me—and reducing me to stupidity. However I have started preparations for my departure. "The wine (what a wine!!) has been opened—it must be drunk."

I shall send you shortly a novel in 3 vols by Count Leo Tolstoy, whom I consider to be the foremost contemporary writer. You know who in my opinion could challenge him in that position. Unfortunately it has been translated by a Russian lady . . . and in general I am apprehensive about lady translators, especially when it's such a vigorous writer as Tolstoy is.

In the meantime I embrace you.

> Your
> I.T.

Flaubert to Turgenev

> *[Croisset]*
> *Sunday evening [28 December 1879]*

I received the box yesterday evening. The salmon is magnificent, but the caviar makes me cry out in ecstasy. When shall we eat such things together? I wish you were gone and come back. Write to me at least from over there.

It looks like thawing this evening. Can it be true?

As for Tolstoy's novel, have it sent to my niece's. Commanville will bring it to me.

All the best, my dear old fellow. Your old fellow embraces you.

> G. Flaubert

> *[Croisset]*
> *Tuesday evening [30 December 1879]*

Thank you! Many, many thanks, oh Saint Vincent de Paul of gastronomy! My word, you are treating me like a kept man! Too many delicacies! Well I must tell you that I'm eating the caviar almost without bread, like jam.

As for the novel, its three volumes frighten me. Three volumes unconnected with my work are hard going now. Never mind, I shall tackle it. As I expect to have finished my chapter towards the end of next week (!!!!) it will be a relaxation before starting the next.

When are you leaving, or rather when are you coming back? It's stupid to love one another as we do and to see so little of each other.

I embrace you.

Your old
G. Flaubert

[Croisset]
Wednesday evening [21 January 1880]

Just two lines, my good dear old fellow. i) When are you leaving, or rather no: when are you coming back? Are you less worried about the consequences of your journey? ii) Thank you for making me read Tolstoy's novel. It's first rate. What a painter and what a psychologist! The first two are sublime; but the third goes terribly to pieces. He repeats himself and he philosophises! In fact the man, the author, the Russian are visible, whereas up until then one had seen only Nature and Humanity. It seems to me that in places he has some elements of Shakespeare. I uttered cries of admiration during my reading of it . . . and it's long! Tell me about the *author.* Is it his first book? In any case he has his head *well screwed on!* Yes! It's very good! Very good!

I've finished my *Religion* and I'm working on the plan of my last chapter: *Education.*

My niece came to spend three full days here. She left this morning, and she bemoans that fact that our dear friend the great Turgenev is abandoning us. I embrace you tenderly.

Your old
G. Flaubert

Turgenev to Flaubert

50 rue de Douai Paris
Saturday 24 January 80

My good old fellow,

You cannot imagine the pleasure your letter gave me and what you say about Tolstoy's novel. Your approval confirms my own ideas about him. Yes, he is a man of great talent, and yet you put your finger on the weak spot: he also has built himself a philosophical system, which is at one and the same time mystical, childish and presumptuous, and which has spoilt his third volume dreadfully, and the second novel that he wrote after "War and Peace"—and where there are also things of the first order. I don't know what the critics will say. (I have sent "War and Peace" to Daudet and Zola as well.) But for me the matter is settled: *Flaubertus dixit.* The rest is of no significance.

I am pleased to see that your old fellows are coming along.

I'll be leaving Paris in the course of next week, but I'll write you a note before I go. In the meantime I embrace you.

Your
Iv. Turgenev

Flaubert to Turgenev

Croisset near Deville (Seine-Inférieure)
Thursday 4 March [1880]

My old darling,

As you no longer write to me once you are in Russia, the correspondence between me and Mme Viardot has started up again.

A letter from her informs me that you have sciatica, that you are sad, that you are fed up etc. and she exhorts me to write to you to cheer you up. Why can I not, my poor old fellow, send you all the flowers of the world and of life?

What can I tell you? That Du Camp has been elected to the Académie Française! That you surely knew? It makes me giddy . . . Why "court this honour"? How ridiculous men are!

I have started my last chapter and I've got to page seven. There will be forty. When shall I have finished it? God only knows. Whatever happens, I plan to spend the months of May and June in Paris, then I shall return by [September] and will not budge for a long time. So we shall see each other! ?

I've read *Nana* in volume form, in one sitting, and I think you're a bit hard on it. There are some fine things, superb cries of passion and two or three characters (that of Mignon amongst others) that delighted me.

Young Maupassant narrowly escaped a libel suit. I say escaped, as the proceedings, which had barely begun, were dropped. I published a letter on the subject in *Le Gaulois* (the last Saturday of February) and I didn't even have time to read through my piece! Consequently it's quite badly put together. I've never made such a concession to any one, but the poor young devil moved me to pity. I must say (strictly *between you and me*) that my disciple's health worries me. His *heart* will play a nasty trick on him one of these days, I fear.

Have you thought about Commanville's business, seeing a lawyer about the woods of Prince Solloouh? (That can't be the spelling? Never mind.)

In your friendship for me, you'll be pleased to learn that there is now some blue sky on my financial horizon. Commanville has got a sawmill going again, he has found some funds. The contract should be signed, perhaps, this evening? Once that's done, Commanville is leaving for Odessa immediately.

My niece, alone in Paris, is hastening to finish a portrait for the Exhibition. You know she is not at all pleased with you, and I'm sure she'll speak ill of you this evening at Mme Viardot's.

What else? A pile of little books sent to me by young writers that it's not worth naming. *Conscience* makes me read them, and that makes me waste time, and so I get cross! I already have so much to read for *B. and P.* now I am lost in education systems, including ways of preventing masturbation! Important issue! The further I get, the more ridiculous I find the significance attached to the uro-genital organs. It's time we laughed at them—not at the organs, but at those people who want to base the whole of human morality on them.

Today the weather is splendid, the shrubs are in bud, and the violets are poking through the lawn. So you can imagine your friend in his setting. Yours is misty and uncertain for me . . .

So come back to us, and write me as long a letter as you can.

From the bottom of my heart and with arms outstretched,

your old
G. Flaubert

ANGUS DAVIDSON

From EDWARD LEAR: LANDSCAPE PAINTER
AND NONSENSE POET

In 1850 Tennyson—whom Lear had admired, as a poet, long before he met him—was made Laureate: in the same year he married Emily Selwood, and the friendship between him and Lear was strengthened by the affection and sympathy which quickly grew up between his friend and his wife. When Lear was in England he never failed to pay them a visit; and he wrote frequently to Emily Tennyson, for whom he entertained a devoted admiration all the rest of his life. "I should think," he told Fortescue, "computing moderately, that 15 angels, several hundreds of ordinary women, many philosophers, a heap of truly wise and kind mothers, 3 or 4 minor prophets, and a lot of doctors and schoolmistresses, might be boiled down, and yet their combined essence fall short of what Emily Tennyson really is." She had the gift of true sympathy, and became, for him, an angel of consolation to whom he poured out his troubles. Illness, financial worries, grief for the death of a friend, depths of melancholy and loneliness—all brought a ready response from one who herself suffered much from ill-health and who had her own difficulties and sorrows; for to be married to Alfred Tennyson was no sinecure, and the early death of her son Lionel was a grief from which she never fully recovered. She understood Lear's character better, perhaps, than anyone: she understood, also, the bitter loneliness that often beset him, and the difficulties of his relationship with Lushington. "You are not alone, Mr. Lear," she wrote to him at a time when depression seemed to have vanquished him; "you cannot be while you can be so much to those so very dear to you, to those to whom so few are anything but the mere outside world. . . ."

When his Greek and Albanian journals were published, Lear sent a copy of the book to Tennyson, who expressed his appreciation of it in a poem:

To E. L. on His Travels in Greece

Illyrian woodlands, echoing falls
Of water, sheets of summer glass,
The long divine Peneïan pass,
The vast Akrokeraunian walls,

Tomohrit, Athos, all things fair,
With such a pencil, such a pen,
You shadow forth to distant men,
I read and felt that I was there:

And trust me while I turn'd the page,
And track'd you still on classic ground,
I grew in gladness till I found
My spirits in the golden age.

For me the torrent ever pour'd
And glisten'd—here and there alone
The broad-limb'd gods at random thrown
By fountain-urns;—and Naiads oar'd

A glimmering shoulder under gloom
Of cavern pillars; on the swell

The silver lily heav'd and fell;
And many a slope was rich in bloom

From him that on the mountain lea
By dancing rivulets fed his flocks,
To him who sat upon the rocks,
And fluted to the morning sea.

. . . It was while he was at Clivevale Farm with Holman Hunt that he first conceived the project of illustrating Tennyson's poems—a project to which he clung with the greatest pertinacity, which was to occupy him on and off during the remaining thirty-five years of his life and was only to be partially realized, and that after his death. It was to be a complete edition of the poems, with one hundred and twenty-four landscape illustrations: he had worked out the whole scheme in detail, and wrote to Emily Tennyson asking her to obtain the approval of the Laureate. He spoke of Tennyson's "genius for the perception of the beautiful in landscape," which "I am possibly more than most in my profession able to illustrate, not—pray understand me—from any other reason than that I possess a very remarkable collection of sketches from nature in such widely separated districts of Europe, not to say Asia and Africa. But," he added, "my powers of execution do not at all equal my wishes, or my understanding of the passages I have alluded to." Permission was given, and Lear, delighted, set to work. "I don't want to be a sort of pictorial Boswell," he wrote, "but to be able to reproduce certain lines of poetry in form and colour." . . .

[Ill at San Remo, Lear] returned to the plan, first proposed to Emily Tennyson twenty years before, of carrying out his landscape illustrations to Tennyson's poems. It had never been wholly forgotten: many of the scenes that he had painted in the intervening years, in many different countries, had been chosen for that ultimate purpose; and, now that at last he had a prospect of uninterrupted quiet, he returned to the task with enthusiasm. There were to be one hundred and twelve illustrations. "Don't laugh !" he wrote to Fortescue: "not that I'm such a fool as to suppose that I can ever live to finish them (seven more years at farthest I think will conclude this child), but I believe it wiser to create and go on with new objects of interest as the course of nature washes and sweeps the old ones away." In his heart of hearts, however, he believed that he would finish them. They became the chief occupation of his old age, when constant ill-health made work a labour. . . .

Keeping to his principle of "Always have ten years' work mapped out before you, if you wish to be happy," Lear had planned a vast programme—in his work, at any rate, a determined optimist—that would take many more years to complete than he expected to live. He was busy with the "penning out" of his Indian sketches; he had the large picture of Kinchinjunga to paint for Lord Northbrook; plans for an even larger "Enoch Arden," and for the finishing of a "big Athos" and a "Bavella"; and, above all, he had returned to his work on the Tennyson illustrations. During the remaining ten years of his life this last project absorbed him more and more: the more his strength and his eyesight failed (he had already lost, almost completely, the sight of one eye), the more obstinately he clung to a labour which brought him little satisfaction and which he knew he could never finish. His dealings with publishers, printers and lithographers exhausted and exasperated him: he spent far more money than he could afford on experiments in reproduction, none of which satisfied him; and so the dream of his life, his tribute of admiration and love to his friend Tennyson, gradually turned into a nightmare that served only to hasten him into his grave. . . .

EDWARD LEAR

To Emily Tennyson

17. Stratford Place. Oxford Street.
December. 2. 1851.

My dear Madam,

It seems rather late in the day to beg you & Tennyson to accept a small "wedding present"——but on the grounds of the proverb— "never to [*sic*] late to do right"—I shall run the risk of doing so.

I intended long ago to have done a series of little landscapes illustrative of some of the Poems—but a thousand things have stepped in between me & my wishes,—so that, (though I hope to do them someday,) my poetic illustrations are for the present laid aside—& the matter of fact ones I shall send you to day must do duty for them in the mean time.

The two volumes (which I will forward by rail—) are my own drawings & letterpress relating to some of the Neapolitan provinces, & if you will give them a place on your drawing room table I shall be very much gratified.

There have been but few weeks or days within the last 8 years, that I have not been more or less in the habit of remembering or reading Tennyson's poetry, & the amount of pleasure derived by me from them has been quite beyond reckoning.—And feeling this I have often thought how ungrateful one habitually becomes, if one does not seek to thank—in some way, however insignificant—the writer from whose mind such daily pleasure has been mixed with our existence.—

When these superabominable (or infraabominable) fogs and cold are gone by—I shall hope to call at Twickenham, with or without Frank Lushington;—but at present the winter-world of England seems so horrible to me, that I resort to a kind of hybernating tortoise-ship as much as possible.

Begging you will give my best remembrances to Tennyson,

Believe me,
My dear Madam,
Your's sincerely,
Edward Lear.

Clive Vale Farm,
Fairlight
Hastings.
Tuesday 5th. Oct. 1852.

My dear Mrs. Tennyson,

It was very kind of you to think of asking me for today's festivity, and had I been within reach, I should have come with great pleasure. But I only received your note 5 minutes ago—& even *could* I have rushed up to Twickenham in time, a friend being here by appointment would have prevented me. I have often thought of writing to you lately—& *nearly* came down to Twickenham last Thursday—: but with all these neglects of mine I can assure you I was most sincerely glad to hear of your little boy's birth, and that you and Alfred Tennyson must be so very happy. I hope he may live to make you both more & more so every year.—

I was about to write to you as soon as I thought you could think of any matters beyond the baby, and have been thinking of a long letter to you on a subject that from time to time has occupied me for a long while past.

Whereupon I proceed to explain, & if Master Tennyson disapproves of your attention being taken up by reading—why—you can easily throw the letter on one side.

I think I once said something about illustrating Tennysons poems—so far as the Landscape therein set forth admits of.——Many of the subjects I have arranged——though none as yet have I thoroughly carried out—which indeed it would require great time & labour thoroughly to do.—But I have latterly extracted & placed in a sort of order all the lines which convey to me in the most decided manner his genius for the perception of the beautiful in Landscape, & I have divided them into "suggestive" and "Positive": & altogether there are 124 subjects in the 2 volumes. (I have not included the Princess or In Memoriam.) By "suggestive" I mean such lines as

> "vast images in glittering dawn"—————————
> "Hateful is the dark blue sky["]—————————

&c&c&c—which are adaptable to any country or a wide scope of scenery.

> By "positive"—————such as———
> ———"The lonely *moated grange* ["]———
> ———"They cut away my tallest *pines* ["]—————
> ———"A huge *crag platform* ["]—
> ———"The balmy moon of blessed *Israel* ["]———

&c&c—which indicate perforce certain limits of landscape & wh: I am possibly more than most in my profession able to illustrate————— —not—pray understand me—from any other reason than that I possess a very remarkable collection of sketches from Nature in such widely separated districts of Europe—not to say Asia & Africa.

It may seem rather impertinent that I can't help thinking "no one could illustrate Tennysons landscape lines & feelings more aptly than I could do"—————————but this very modest assertion may after all turn out to be groundless inasmuch as my powers of execution do not at all equal my wishes, or my understanding of the passages I have alluded to.

My desire has been to shew that Alfred Tennyson's poetry (with regard to scenes—) is as real & exquisite as it is relatively to higher & deeper matters:—that his descriptions of certain spots are as positively true as if drawn from the places themselves, & that his words have the power of calling up images as distinct & correct as if they were written from those images, instead of giving rise to them. If I could prove this at all, it would be a pleasant carrying out & sealing of his own words—————————

> "Cleaving—took root & | springing forth anew,
>   Whereer they fell, behold
> Like to the mother plant in semblance grew
>   A flower all gold"—————————

—a quotation wh: if my illustrations ever "come to anything" I would willingly see at the head.—

If you wish, I will send you a list of the quotations I have made—& I should very much like to hear your & his opinion about them. I should not like anything of the sort to be done hastily, & I am sure they had better not be done at all if not *well done,* for if badly executed or ill conceived they will

> "*Un*like the mother plant in semblance grow
>   A flower all mud["]—or all cold—or all anything else totally
> disagreeable.—

If I carry out 2 or 3—& could have Tennyson's permission to fill up the whole—I cannot but think that the Engravings from such would make a beautiful edition—& thereby to parody the lines above once more———"might grow

> "a flower all *tin.*"

But of that there is time enough to think:—nor, if there be any chance of this thought being embodied, should it as yet be buzzed forth—since I should like to produce some actually *good* work before it is noised abroad.

> "Only to hear were sweet
>   Stretched out beneath the pine,"

& 3 or 4 more, are the subjects I am at all advanced in, but owing to the obvious necessity of working for bread I cannot devote much time to the idea, tho' I should do so were it possible to realize it, as the chance of doing so would give me a spur.

Will you kindly write to me—& tell me if I shall transcribe & send you a list of the quotations, and the subjects I have already chosen?

Now I will make an end at once of this fearful Epistle———————& with best regards to Tennyson, & best wishes for your little boy,

> believe me,
> Dear Mrs. Tennyson
> Your's very sincerely,
> Edward Lear.

please excuse this mistakeful letter.
I am becoming a Pre-Raphælite.

Woodbury House. Stoke Newington.
28. October. 1855.

My dear Mrs. Tennyson,

At times, ever since last Sunday,—I have had reproachful twinges for never having written to you: but I have never had real leisure, or, if I had any, I was all jarry & out of tune & you would not have thanked me for scribbling ever so little. Not but what I have thought of Faringford [*sic*] at all times & seasons ever since I left. In the morning I see everything— even to the plate of Mushrooms: then Hallam & Lionel come in,—& when they are gone, you, Alfred & Frank begin to talk like Gods to-gether careless of mankind:—& so on, all through the day. According to the morbid nature of the animal, I even complain sometimes that such rare flashes of light as such visits are to me, make the path darker after they are over:—a bright blue & green landscape with purple hills, & winding rivers, & unexplored forests, and airy downs, & trees & birds, & all sorts of calm repose,—————exchanged for a dull dark plain horizonless, pathless, & covered with cloud above, while beneath are brambles & weariness.

I really do believe that I enjoy hardly any one thing on earth while it is present:—always looking back, or frettingly peering into the dim beyond.—With all this, I may say to you & Alfred, that the 3 or 4 days of the 16th–20th. October/55,—were the best I have passed for many a long day.—If I live to grow old, & can hope to exist in England, I *should* like to be somewhere near you in one's later days.—I wish sometimes you could settle near Park House. Then I might have a room in Boxley, & moon cripply cripply about those hills, & sometimes see by turns Hallam & Lionel's children, & Frank's grandchildren, & so slide pleasantly out of life. Alfred, by that time would have written endlessly, & there would be 6 or 8 thick green volumes of poems. I—possibly,—should be in the workhouse, but I know you would all come & see me. . . .

Kind love to Alfred, & believe me,

Dear Mrs. Tennyson,
Yours very sincerely,
Edward Lear.

Corfu. 16. Feby. 1862.

My dear Mrs. Tennyson,

The ducklike benevolence with which you have sent me another letter, before I had answered your last!!—and in this one—the dedication verses by Alfred—which are doubtless among the loveliest & grandest of all he has ever written. As for me, I copied them out at once for Mrs.

Decie,—& go about reading them to all who will hear me. They are exquisite.

Do you know, just as you were writing,—I have been going through every one of [Tennyson's] poems—Princess, Maud Idylls, & all—— having lost my former list of Landscape Illustrations,——in order to get up my ideas on the subject of the Landscapes once more. In all, I have put down 250. In the Poems 153—Princess 24. Tithonus 1, Maud 32. In Memoriam. 23.—Idylls—17.—Shall I ever live to paint them? It is to be doubted. Meanwhile I am working very drudgefully at various necessities, & wish I were a chimneysweeper or a teapot. . . .

I had intended to write you a very long letter, but I have written two, Mammothian in size: & cannot write well any longer. This house too is unquiet—for there is a family named Maud above me—which I wish I could send "into the Garden" if there were one:—& although one of the twins is dead, yet the other, having I firmly believe swallowed the violin (which has been mute of late,—)—hath a hoarser & catguttier voice than in aforetime. . . .

Thank you extremely for the letters & the Dedication. My love to Alfred & the boys: Why are they unwell?

Your's affectionately,
Edward Lear.

To Ruth Decie

15. Stratford Place. Oxfd St.
9. Sept. 1862

My dear little tiny child,

You will excuse my familiar mode of addressing you, because, you know,—you have as yet got no Christian name—;—& to say—"my dear Miss Decie" would be as much too formal, as "my dear Decie" would be too rude. But as your Grandmamma has written to me that you are just born I will write to congratulate you, & possibly this is one of the first letters you have as yet received. One of the old Greek Tragedians says—

——and I am sure you will not think me impertinent in translating what he says—(μὴ φῦναι & c) [not to have been born &c] because there has not been time hitherto to buy you a Greek Dictionary, (& I am sure you cannot read Sophocles without,——besides, the Dictionaries are so fat & heavy I am certain you could not use them comfortably to yourself & your nurse,)—μὴ φῦναι &c—which means "it is better never to have [been] born at all, or if born,—to die as soon as possible."

But this I wholly dissent from: & on the contrary I congratulate you heartily on coming into a world where if we look for it there is far more good & pleasure than we can use up—even in the longest life. And you in particular will find that you have—all quite without any of your own exertions—a mother & a father,—a grandmother & a grandfather,—some uncles,—an extremely merry brother (who propels himself along the floor like a compasses,) a conservatory & a croquet ground, & a respectable old cove who is very fond of small children & will give you an Alphabet bye & bye.—I therefore advise you to live & laugh as long as you can for your own pleasure, & that of all your belongings.

Please tell your Grandmama that I also wished to stop when the carriage passed but couldn't—& say also, that I will write to her again shortly. And now my dear you have read enough for the present. Good night, & believe me,

> Your affte. old friend
> Edward Lear.

Give my love to your Papa & Mama.

To John Ruskin

> *Villa Tennyson*
> *Sanremo.*
> *19. Feby. 1886*

Dear Mr. Ruskin,

Several friends have sent me by this last post—(cut from the Pall Mall of Feby. 15—) your letter about the "Choice of Books." And I cannot help writing a line to thank you for your most kind mention of my "Nonsense"——& to say how proud & gratified I am by your praise.

I am now (æt 74) nearly always in bed—but can sit up now & then,—& even go on working at my 200 Tennyson illustrations begun in 1849 in Sussex in the days of old Holman Hunt—& Tennyson. I suppose perseverance is a virtue, even if in a foolish cause—: only one can't be sure whether the sequel will be foolishness or not. Most probably I shall die before the 200 are ready to Autotype.

> With many & sincere thanks,
> believe me Your's,
> Edward Lear.

Villa Tennyson.
Sanremo.
16 Feby. 1883

My dear Sir,

Although I hesitate to take up any of your time, which is that of the public,—I cannot help sending a few lines to thank you for your kindness to a young Artist, whom at times I have tried to help————F. T. Underhill,—who writes to me in a great state of delight at having had a letter from you about his Seppia Copies. I do not think,—if I may be excused saying so, that public writers however they may praise your works & writings, have ever paid sufficient attention to the great readiness you have ever shown to assist beginners,—for the present instance is by no means the first that has come to my notice.

Underhill, (who has at times made several good copies of Turner for me,—also one of a large painting by myself of Damascus, with a vast crowd of "penning out" work,—)—is a most deserving fellow, with a fund of perseverance that has stood him in good stead in many difficulties. His having been employed by Lord Northbrook latterly, & last of all having been encouraged by you, will however I trust place him henceforward in a good path towards success.

The last time I was in England (1880) I saw at Oxford (by means of a friend at one of the Colleges—R. W. Roper,) the wonderful Turners, in the Taylor(?) Institution. A treat for which I may also take this opportunity of thanking you, as I often do mentally for having by your books caused me to use my own eyes in looking at Landscape, from a period dating many years back.

I have also often wished that you could have seen some of the tropical Vegetation I saw in Malabar Ceylon & Elsewhere, which for 2 Years I tried to draw when in India by Lord Northbrook's kindness. I thought some of the river scenery about Calicut & Maheè more lovely than any I had before imagined, & some of the Darjeeling & Kinchinjunga scenes among the grandest conceivable.

Believe me,
My dear Sir,
Your's very truly,
Edward Lear.

HENRY JAMES

To Hugh Walpole

Lamb House, Rye
May 13th 1910

Dearest, Dearest Hugh.

I have been utterly, but necessarily, silent—so much of the time lately quite too ill to write. Deeply your note touches me, as I needn't tell you—and I would give anything to be able to have the free use of your "visible and tangible" affection—no touch of its tangibility but would be dear and helpful to me. But, alas, I am utterly unfit for visits—with the black devils of Nervousness, direst, damnedest demons, that ride me so cruelly and that I have perpetually to reckon with. I am mustering a colossal courage to try—even tomorrow—in my blest sister-in-law's company (without whom and my brother, just now in Paris, I couldn't have struggled on at all) to get away for some days by going to see a kind friend in the country—in Epping Forest. I feel it a most precarious and dangerous undertaking—but my desire and need for change of air, scene and circumstance, after so fearfully overmuch of these imprisoning objects, is so fiercely intense that I am making the push—as to save my life—at any cost. It *may* help me—even much, and the doctor intensely urges it— and if I am able, afterwards (that is if the experiment isn't disastrous), I shall try to go to 105 Pall Mall for a little instead of coming abjectly back here. Then I shall be able to see you—but all this is fearfully contingent. Meanwhile the sense of your personal tenderness to me, dearest Hugh, is far from not doing much for me. I adore it.

I "read," in a manner, "Maradick"—but there's too much to say about it, and even my weakness doesn't alter me from the grim and battered old *critical* critic—no *other* such creature among all the "reviewers" do I meanwhile behold. Your book has a great sense and love of life—but seems to me very nearly as irreflectively juvenile as the Trojans, and to have the prime defect of your having gone into a subject—i.e. the marital, sexual, bedroom relations of M. and his wife—the literary man and his wife—since these *are* the key to the whole situation—which have to be tackled and faced to mean anything. You don't tackle and face them—you *can't*. Also the whole thing is a monument to the abuse of voluminous dialogue, the absence of a plan of composition, alternation, distribution, structure, and other phases of presentation than the dialogue—so that *line* (the only thing *I* value in a fiction etc.) is replaced by a vast formless featherbediness—billows in which one sinks and is lost. And yet it's all so loveable—though not so *written*. It isn't written *at all*, darling Hugh—by which I mean you have—or, truly, only in a few places, as in Maradick's dive—never got expression *tight* and in close quarters (of discrimination, of specification) with its subject. It remains loose and far. And you have never made out, recognized, nor stuck to, *the centre of your subject*. But can you forgive all this to your fondest old reaching-out-his-arms-to you

H.J.

To William Dean Howells

(This letter appeared in the *North American Review* in April 1912.)

It is made known to me that they are soon to feast in New York the newest and freshest of the splendid birthdays to which you keep treating us, and that your many friends will meet round you to rejoice in it and reaffirm their allegiance. I shall not be there, to my sorrow; and, though this is inevitable, I yet want to be missed, peculiarly and monstrously missed, so that these words shall be a public apology for my absence: read by you, if you like and can stand it, but, better still, read *to* you and, in fact, straight *at* you by whoever will be so kind and so loud and so distinct. For I doubt, you see, whether any of your toasters and acclaimers have anything like my ground and title for being with you at such an hour. There can scarce be one, I think, to-day who has known you from so far back, who has kept so close to you for so long, and who has such fine old reasons—so old, yet so well preserved—to feel your virtue and sound your praise. My debt to you began well-nigh half a century ago in the most personal way possible, and then kept growing and growing with your own admirable growth—but always rooted in the early intimate benefit. This benefit was that you held out your open editorial hand to me at the time I began to write—and I allude especially to the summer of 1866—with a frankness and sweetness of hospitality that was really the making of me, the making of the confidence that required help and sympathy and that I should otherwise, I think, have strayed and stum-

bled about a long time without acquiring. You showed me the way and
opened me the door; you wrote to me and confessed yourself struck with
me—I have never forgotten the beautiful thrill of *that.* You published
me at once—and paid me, above all, with a dazzling promptitude; magnificently, I felt, and so that nothing since has ever quite come up to it.
More than this even, you cheered me on with a sympathy that was in
itself an inspiration. I mean that you talked to me and listened to me—
ever so patiently and genially and suggestively conversed and consorted
with me. This won me to you irresistibly and made you the most interesting person I knew—lost as I was in the charming sense that my best
friend was an editor, and an almost insatiable editor, and that such a
delicious being as that was a kind of property of my own. Yet how didn't
that interest still quicken and spread when I became aware that—with
such attention as you could spare from us, for I recognized my fellow-
beneficiaries—you had started to cultivate *your* great garden as well; the
tract of virgin soil that, beginning as a cluster of bright, fresh, sunny, and
savory patches close about the house, as it were, was to become that vast
goodly pleasaunce of art and observation, of appreciation and creation,
in which you have labored, without a break or a lapse, to this day, and in
which you have grown so grand a show of—well, really of everything.
Your liberal visits to *my* plot and your free-handed purchases there were
still greater events when I began to see you handle yourself with such
ease the key to our rich and inexhaustible mystery. Then the question of
what you would make of your own powers began to be even more interesting than the question of what you would make of mine—all the more,
I confess, as you had ended by settling this one so happily. My confidence in myself, which you had so helped me to, gave way to a fascinated
impression of your own spread and growth, for you broke out so insis-
tently and variously that it was a charm to watch and an excitement to
follow you. The only drawback that I remember suffering from was that
I, your original debtor, couldn't print or publish or pay you—which
would have been a sort of ideal of *re*payment and of enhanced credit;
you could take care of yourself so beautifully, and I could (unless by some
occasional happy chance or rare favor) scarce so much as glance at your
proofs or have a glimpse of your "endings." I could only read you, full-
blown and finished, always so beautifully finished—and see, with the rest
of the world, how you were doing it again and again.

That, then, was what I had with time to settle down to—the common
attitude of seeing you do it again and again; keep on doing it, with your
heroic consistency and your noble, genial abundance, during all the years
that have seen so many apparitions come and go, so many vain flourishes
attempted and achieved, so many little fortunes made and unmade, so

many weaker inspirations betrayed and spent. Having myself to practise meaner economies, I have admired from period to period your so ample and liberal flow; wondered at your secret for doing positively a little—what do I say, a little? I mean a magnificent deal!—of Everything. I seem to myself to have faltered and languished, to have missed more occasions than I have grasped, while you have piled up your monument just by remaining at your post. For you have had the advantage, after all, of breathing an air that has suited and nourished you; of sitting up to your neck, as I may say—or at least up to your waist—amid the sources of your inspiration. There and so you were at your post; there and so the spell could ever work for you, there and so your relation to all your material grow closer and stronger, your perception penetrate, your authority accumulate. They make a great array, a literature in themselves, your studies of American life so acute, so direct, so disinterested, so preoccupied but with the fine truth of the case; and the more attaching to me always for their referring themselves to a time and an order when we knew together what American life *was*—or thought we did, deluded though we may have been! I don't pretend to measure the effect or to sound the depths, if they be not the shallows, of the huge wholesale importations and so-called assimilations of this later time; I only feel and speak for those conditions in which, as "quiet observers," as careful painters, as sincere artists, we could still in our native, our human and social element, know more or less where we were and feel more or less what we had hold of. You knew and felt these things better than I; you had learned them earlier and more intimately, and it was impossible, I think, to be in more instinctive and more informed possession of the general truth of your subject than you happily found yourself. The *real* affair of the American case and character, as it met your view and brushed your sensibility, that was what inspired and attached you, and, heedless of foolish flurries from other quarters, of all wild or weak slashings of the air and wavings in the void, you gave yourself to it with an incorruptible faith. You saw your field with a rare lucidity: you saw all it had to give in the way of the romance of the real and the interest and the thrill and the charm of the common, as one may put it; the character and the comedy, the point, the pathos, the tragedy, the particular home-grown humanity under your eyes and your hand and with which the life all about you was closely interknitted. Your hand reached out to these things with a fondness that was in itself a literary gift and played with them as the artist only and always can play: freely, quaintly, incalculably, with all the assurance of his fancy and his irony, and yet with that fine taste for the truth and the pity and the meaning of the matter which keeps the temper of observation both sharp and sweet. To observe by such an instinct and by such reflection is to find work to one's hands and a challenge in every bush; and as the familiar American scene thus bristled about you, so year by year your vision more and more justly responded and swarmed. You put forth *A Modern Instance,* and *The Rise of Silas Lapham,* and *A Hazard of New Fortunes,* and *The Landlord at Lion's Head,* and *The Kentons* (that perfectly classic illustration of your spirit and your form) after having put forth in perhaps lighter-fingered prelude *A Foregone Conclusion,* and *The Undiscovered Country,* and *The Lady of the Aroostook,* and *The Minister's Charge*—to make of a long list too short a one; with the effect again and again of a feeling for the human relation, as the social climate of our country qualifies, intensifies, generally conditions and colors it, which, married in perfect felicity to the expression you found for its service, constituted the originality that we want to fasten upon you as with silver nails to-night. Stroke by stroke and book by book your work was to become for this exquisite notation of our whole democratic light and shade and give and take in the highest degree *documentary,* so that none other, through all your fine long season, could approach it in value and amplitude. None, let me say, too, was to approach it in essential distinction; for you had grown master, by insidious practices best known to yourself, of a method so easy and so natural, so marked with the personal element of your humor and the play, not less personal, of your sympathy, that the critic kept coming on its secret connection with the grace of letters much as Fenimore Cooper's Leatherstocking—so knowing to be able to do it!—comes in the forest on the subtle tracks of Indian braves. However, these things take us far, and what I wished mainly to put on record is my sense of that unfailing, testifying truth in you which will keep you from ever being neglected. The critical intelligence—if any such fitful and discredited light may still be conceived as within our sphere—has not at all begun to render you its tribute. The more inquiringly and perceivingly it shall still be projected upon the American life we used to know, the more it shall be moved by the analytic and historic spirit, the more indispensable, the more a vessel of light, will you be found. It's a great thing to have used one's genius and done one's work with such quiet and robust consistency that they fall by their own weight into that happy service. You may remember perhaps, and I like to recall, how the great and admirable Taine, in one of the fine excursions of his French curiosity, greeted you as a precious painter and a sovereign witness. But his appreciation, I want you to believe with me, will yet be carried much further, and then—though you may have argued yourself happy, in your generous way and with your incurable optimism, even while noting yourself not understood—your really beautiful time will come. Nothing so much as feeling that he may himself perhaps help a little to bring it on can give pleasure to yours all faithfully,

Henry James

WILLIAM JAMES

To O. W. Holmes, Jr.

Berlin, Jan. 3, 1868.

My dear Wendle,—

Ich weiss nicht was soll es bedeuten, dass ich so traurig bin,* tonight. The ghosts of the past all start from their unquiet graves and keep dancing a senseless whirligig around me so that, after trying in vain to read three books, to sleep, or to think, I clutch the pen and ink and resolve to work off the fit by a few lines to one of the most obtrusive ghosts of all—namely the tall and lank one of Charles Street. Good golly! how I would prefer to have about twenty-four hours talk with you up in that whitely lit-up room—without the sun rising or the firmament revolving so as to put the gas out, without sleep, food, clothing or shelter except your whiskey bottle, of which, or the like of which, I have not partaken since I have been in these longitudes! I should like to have you opposite me in any mood, whether the facetiously excursive, the metaphysically discursive, the personally confidential, or the jadedly *cursive* and argumentative—so that the oyster-shells which enclose my being might slowly turn open on their rigid hinges under the radiation, and the critter within loll out his dried-up gills into the circumfused ichor of life, till they grew so fat as not to know themselves again. I feel as if a talk with you of any kind could not fail to set me on my legs again for three weeks at least. I have been chewing on two or three dried-up old cuds of ideas I brought from America with me, till they have disappeared, and the nudity of the Kosmos has got beyond anything I have as yet experi-

---

*"I feel sad and I do not know why." James is quoting the opening of Heinrich Heine's song about Lorelei.

enced. I have not succeeded in finding any companion yet, and I feel the want of some outward stimulus to my Soul. There is a man named Grimm here whom my soul loves, but in the way Emerson speaks of, *i.e.* like those people we meet on staircases, etc., and who always ignore our feelings towards them. I don't think we shall ever be able to establish a straight line of communication between us.

I don't know how it is I am able to take so little interest in reading this winter. I marked out a number of books when I first came here, to finish. What with their heaviness and the damnable slowness with which the Dutch still goes, they weigh on me like a haystack. I loathe the thought of them; and yet they have poisoned my slave of a conscience so that I can't enjoy anything else. I have reached an age when practical work of some kind clamors to be done—and I must still wait!

There! Having worked off that pent-up gall of six weeks' accumulation I feel more genial. I wish I could have some news of you—now that the postage is lowered to such a ridiculous figure (and no letter is double) there remains no *shadow* of an excuse for not writing—but, still, I don't expect anything from you. I suppose you are sinking ever deeper into the sloughs of the law—yet I ween the Eternal Mystery still from time to time gives her goad another turn in the raw she once established between your ribs. Don't let it heal over yet. When I get home let's establish a philosophical society to have regular meetings and discuss none but the very tallest and broadest questions—to be composed of none but the very topmost cream of Boston manhood. It will give each one a chance to air his own opinion in a grammatical form, and to sneer and chuckle when he goes home at what damned fools all the other members are— and may grow into something very important after a sufficient number of years. . . .

I'll now pull up. I don't know whether you take it as a compliment that I should only write to you when in the dismalest of dumps—perhaps you ought to—you, the one emergent peak, to which I cling when all the rest of the world has sunk beneath the wave. Believe me, my Wendly boy, what poor possibility of friendship abides in the crazy frame of W. J. meanders about thy neighborhood. Goodbye! Keep the same bold front as ever to the Common Enemy—and don't forget your ally,

W. J.

To His Class at Radcliffe College

which had sent a potted azalea to him at Easter

Cambridge, Apr. 6, 1896.

Dear Young Ladies,—

I am deeply touched by your remembrance. It is the first time anyone ever treated me so kindly, so you may well believe that the impression on the heart of the lonely sufferer will be even more durable than the impression on your minds of all the teachings of Philosophy 2A. I now perceive one immense omission in my Psychology,—the deepest principle of Human Nature is the *craving to be appreciated,* and I left it out altogether from the book, because I had never had it gratified till now. I fear you have let loose a demon in me, and that all my actions will now be for the sake of such rewards. However, I will try to be faithful to this one unique and beautiful azalea tree, the pride of my life and delight of my existence. Winter and summer will I tend and water it—even with my tears. Mrs. James shall never go near it or touch it. If it dies, I will die too; and if I die, it shall be planted on my grave.

Don't take all this too jocosely, but believe in the extreme pleasure you have caused me, and in the affectionate feelings with which I am and shall always be faithfully your friend,

Wm. James

EDWARD FITZGERALD

To William Makepeace Thackeray

(Geldestone Hall)
Pmk., Beecles
October 10, 1831

My dear Thackeray,

. . . You are a genuine lover of the theater. When we are in London we must go to the pit. Now, Thackeray, I lay you ten thousand pounds that you will be thoroughly disappointed when we come together—our letters have been so warm, that we shall expect each minute to contain a sentence like those in our letters. But in letters we are not always together: there are no blue devilish moments: one of us isn't kept waiting for the other: and above all in letters there is Expectation! I am thus foreboding because I have felt it—and put you on your guard very seriously about it, for the disappointment of such hopes has caused a flatness, then a disgust, and then a coldness betwixt many friends, I'll be bound. So think of meeting me not as I am in my letters (for they being written when in a good humour, and read when you have nothing better to do, make all seem alert and agreeable) but as you used to see me in London, Cambridge, etc. If you come to think, you will see there is a great difference. Do not think I speak thus in a light hearted way about the tenacity of our friendship, but with a very serious heart anxious lest we should disappoint each other, and so lessen our love a little. I hate this subject and to the devil with it.

PART XI

AFFINITIES: GROUP 2

Friendship . . . does not abolish distance between human beings but brings that distance to life.

—*Walter Benjamin*

H. L. MENCKEN

To Theodore Dreiser

1524 Hollins St.
Baltimore
April 23rd [1911]

Dear Dreiser:—

When "Jennie Gerhardt" is printed it is probable that more than one reviewer will object to its length, its microscopic detail, its enormous painstaking—but rest assured that Heinrich Ludwig von Mencken will not be in that gang. I have just finished reading the ms.—every word of it, from first to last—and I put it down with a clear notion that it should remain as it stands. The story comes upon me with great force; it touches my own experience of life in a hundred places; it preaches (or perhaps I had better say exhibits) a philosophy of life that seems to me to be sound; altogether I get a powerful effect of reality, stark and unashamed. It is drab and gloomy, but so is the struggle for existence. It is without humor, but so are the jests of that great comedian who shoots at our heels and makes us do our grotesque dancing.

I needn't say that it seems to me an advance above "Sister Carrie." Its obvious superiority lies in its better form. You strained (or perhaps even broke) the back of "Sister Carrie" when you let Hurstwood lead you away from Carrie. In "Jennie Gerhardt" there is no such running amuck. The two currents of interest, of spiritual unfolding, are very deftly managed. Even when they do not actually coalesce, they are parallel and close together. Jennie is never out of Kane's life, and after their first meeting, she is never out of his. The reaction of will upon will, of character upon character, is splendidly worked out and indicated. In brief, the story hangs together; it is a complete whole; consciously or unconsciously, you have avoided the chief defect of "Sister Carrie."

It is difficult, just rising from the book, to describe the impression I bring away. That impression is of a living whole, not of a fabric that may be unravelled and examined in detail. In brief, you have painted so smoothly and yet so vigorously that I have no memory of brush strokes. But for one thing, the great naturalness of the dialogue sticks in mind. In particular, you have been extremely successful with Gerhardt. His speeches are perfect: nothing could be nearer to truth. I am well aware that certain persons are impatient of this photographic accuracy. Well, let them choose their poison. As for me, I prefer the fact to the fancy. You have tried to depict a German of a given type—a type with which I, by chance, happen to be very familiar. You have made him as thoroughly alive as Huck Finn.

These are random, disordered notes. When the time comes, I'll reduce my thoughts to order and write a formal, intelligible review. At the moment I am too near the book. I rather distrust my own enthusiasm for it. Perhaps I read my own prejudices and ideas into it. My interest is always in the subjective event, seldom or never in the objective event. That is why I like "Lord Jim." Here you have got very close to the very well-springs of action. The march of episodes is nothing: the slow unfolding of character is everything.

If anyone urges you to cut down the book bid that one be damned. And if anyone argues that it is over-gloomy call the police. Let it stand as it is. Its bald, forthright style; its scientific, unemotional piling up of detail; the incisive truthfulness of its dialogue; the stark straightforwardness of it all—these are merits that need no praise. It is at once an accurate picture of life and a searching criticism of life. And that is my definition of a good novel.

Here and there I noted minor weaknesses. For one thing, it is doubtful that Jennie would have been able to conceal from so sophisticated a man as Kane the fact that she had had a child. Child-bearing leaves physical marks, and those marks commonly persist for five or six years. But there are, of course, exceptions to this rule. Not many readers, I suppose, will raise the point. Again, if I remember correctly, you speak of L. S. & M. S. "shares" as being worth $1,000 par. Don't you mean bonds? If bonds, the income would be fixed and could not fluctuate. Again you give Kane $5,000 income from $75,000 at 6 percent. A small thing—but everywhere else you are so utterly careful that small errors stick out.

A final word: the least satisfactory personage in the book is Jennie herself. Not that you do not account for her, from head to heels—but I would have preferred, had I the choice, a more typical kept woman. She is, in brief, uncompromisingly exceptional, almost unique, in several important details. Her connection with her mother and father and with the facts of her life grows, at times, very fragile. But I can well understand how her essential plausibility must have reacted upon you—how your own creation must have dragged you on. There is always Letty Pace to show Jennie's limitations. In her class she is a miracle, and yet she never quite steps out of that class.

But I go back to the effect of the book as a whole. That effect, believe me, is very powerful. I must go to Hardy and Conrad to find its like. David Phillips, I believe, might have done such a story had he lived, but the best that he actually wrote, to wit, "The Hungry Heart," goes to pieces beside "Jennie." I mean this in all seriousness. You have written a novel that no other American of the time could have written, and even in England there are not six men who, with your material, could have reached so high a level of reality. My earnest congratulations. By all means let me see that third book. "Jennie" shows immense progress in craftsmanship. As a work of art it is decidedly superior to "Sister Carrie."

I'll return the ms. by express tomorrow morning. Maybe chance will throw us together soon and we'll have a session over "Jennie." At the moment I am rather too full of the story as a human document to sit down in cold blood and discourse upon its merits and defects as a work of art. I know that it is immensely good, but I have still to get my reasons reduced to fluent words.

God keep you. As for me, I lately enjoyed the first of the season's rashers of crab à la creole. With genuine Muenchener to flush the esophagus afterward.

Yours,
H. L. M.

Reading this over it seems damned cold. [What] I really want to say is just—"Hurrah!" You have put over a truly *big* thing.

1524 Hollins St.
Baltimore
December 25th [1915]

Dear Dreiser:—

This is the impression the group of poems makes on me: the first three are hopelessly commonplace, and two of them open with intolerable banalities, but the last four are truly excellent. "Wood Note" is genuinely superb; I am enthusiastic over it. "For a Moment the Wind Died" is almost as good. "Ye Ages, Ye Tribes" is a fine statement of your philosophy. Even "They Shall Fall as Stripped Garments," despite the obviousness of the thought, is a sound poem. But why hook up these with such obvious and hollow stuff as "Life is so beautiful" and "How pleasant is the waterside"? I am wholly unable to understand the idea beneath the grouping. My recommendation is that the first three be dropped entirely and the last four be made into a group. The former will hurt you; the latter will be sure to do you good. . . .

1524 Hollins St.
Baltimore
March 27th [1921]

Dear Dreiser:—

. . . I have a notion that you are unduly sensitive to criticism. Van Doren's article was certainly in the best of humor. What if he did call you a peasant? In a sense you are. I see nothing opprobrious in the charge. It is like saying that a man is a Swede or an Italian or an American. I am myself partly a peasant, and glad of it. If it were not for my peasant blood, the Mencken element would have made a professor of me. I always tremble on the brink of pedantry, even as it is. This heritage from the Gelehrten is my worst internal enemy. Thank God that my mother's grandfather was a Bauer, with all of a Bauer's capacity for believing in the romantic. Without him I'd have been a mere intellectual machine.

It seems plain to me that the most valuable baggage that you carry is your capacity for seeing the world from a sort of proletarian standpoint. It is responsible for all your talent for evoking feeling. Imagine Sister Carrie written by a man without that capacity, say Nietzsche. It would have been a mess. You say you are not striking at me when you complain of Van Doren. Well, why in hell *shouldn't* you strike at me, if the spirit moves you? When I write about you as an author I put aside all friendship and try to consider you objectively. When, as an author, you discuss me as a critic, you are free to do the same thing, and ought to do it. In this department I am a maniacal advocate of free speech. Politeness is the worst curse of the world. . . .

To James Joyce

Smart Set
456 Fourth Avenue,
New York
April 20th [1915]

Dear Mr. Joyce:—

Two of your stories, "The Boarding-House" and "A Little Cloud" are in the May Smart Set; I am having two copies of the number sent to you by this post. We were unable to take more because the American publisher of "Dubliners," Mr. B. W. Huebsch, of 225 Fifth Avenue, New York, planned to bring out the book at about this time. Apparently it has been delayed a bit, but I assume that Mr. Huebsch still proposes to do it during the Spring. The publishing business in the United States has been hard hit by the war, and there are constant changes of plans among the publishers. I think you are fortunate to get into the hands of Mr. Huebsch in this country. He is one of the few intelligent publishers in New York.

Mr. Pound sent me cuttings of the first 15 or 20 instalments of "A Portrait of the Artist as a Young Man," and I read them with much interest, but the story, unfortunately, is too long and diffuse for The Smart Set. We do not publish serials, but do a whole novel, or rather novelette, in each number. Sometimes it is possible to carve a novelette out of a novel of the usual length, but, as I wrote to Mr. Pound, I felt that it would do unpardonable violence to your story to attempt anything of the sort. If you ever have a plan for a novelette, say of 30,000 words, I surely hope that you let us hear of it. As you may know, we also publish an English edition, and so we desire both the English and the American rights whenever it is possible to get them. In the case of your two short stories we had to send other stories to England, thus, of course, doubling our expense.

Please don't hesitate to ask if I can do anything for you here in America. And keep The Smart Set in mind! Mr. Nathan and I took charge of it just as the war began, and we have had an uphill battle, but it is now, I am glad to say, in good financial condition, paying cash for everything and with both circulation and advertising increasing. We have to go slowly, but it is our aim ultimately to make it the best magazine in America. In particular, we want to print all the good novelties that the other editors baulk at. Curiously enough, our most successful novelty so far has been an omission: we have not printed a line about the war, not even a war poem!

Sincerely yours,
H. L. Mencken

To Jim Tully

Baltimore
May 4th, 1927

Dear Tully:—

. . . I am credited with discovering many writers who actually discovered themselves. Among those I whooped for in their earliest days are James Joyce, Ruth Suckow, James Stevens, Eugene O'Neill and Dreiser. I also did a lot of writing about Joseph Conrad and Lord Dunsany when

they were new to this country. But what I did for all these, and the rest
likewise, was really very little. I was looking for good copy, not for or-
phans to rescue. . . .

Yours,
H. L. Mencken

JAMES THURBER

My Friend McNulty

The angel that writes names in a book of gold must long ago have put
McNulty down as one who delighted in his fellow man. His delight in
human beings was warm and deep and, though he deserved to be called a
social critic, he was concerned mainly with men, not Man, with persons,
not People. McNulty's love of humanity was not expressed at a distance,
from a platform, but in pieces that have the lasting pulse of life in every
sentence. He moved among men, shoulder to shoulder, from morning
till night until the end of his too brief sixty years on earth.

American writing in our time has developed few men with so keen an
eye and so sharp an ear. Nothing, however commonplace, that he
touched with words remained commonplace, but was magnified and
enlivened by his intense and endless fascination with the stranger in the
street, the drinker at the bar and the bartender behind it, the horse
player, the cab driver, the guy at the ball game, the fellow across the
room, the patient in the next hospital bed. John McNulty, city man and
newspaperman, self-assigned in his mature years to human-interest stories of the world about him, left not only a body of work that throbs with
his love of life but a vast and equally durable legacy of spoken words that
remain vivid in the memory of his friends. The only person who could
get McNulty down in words was McNulty himself, but those of us who
knew and loved him like to sit around at night in Tim and Joe Costello's
Bar and Restaurant on Third Avenue and talk about him. This is the
only real way to bring McNulty to life. Cold type could never do justice
to such a man.

After John McNulty died, I wrote a short piece about him for the
crowded pages of *The New Yorker,* and I reproduce it here in part:

"Nobody who knew McNulty as man or writer could ever have confused him for a moment with anybody else. His presence in a room—or in a town, for that matter—was as special as the way he put words down on paper. His death darkened the skies for literally countless friends and acquaintances, for he seemed to know everybody. He came back to New York in the early thirties from a long sojourn in the Middle West, and in 1937 he began writing pieces for *The New Yorker*. They were the reports of a true and eager eye and ear that found high excitement in both the unusual and the common phrases and postures of men, and turned them into the sparkle of his unique idiom.

"The days didn't go by for John McNulty; they happened to him. He was up and out at six every morning, wandering the beloved streets and 'avenyas' of his city, stopping to talk and listen to everybody. His week was a seven-day circus that never lost its savor. He was not merely an amusing companion; he was one of the funniest of men. When he told a tale of people or places, it had a color and vitality that faded in the retelling by anyone else. The name McNulty, for us, meant 'Inimitable,' and at the same time something in lower case, familiar and cherished—a kind of synonym for laughter. We grieve that such a man cannot be replaced, in our hearts or on our pages."

The pages of *The New Yorker* sparkled with his pieces from the first one, which appeared on Christmas Day, 1937, until the last one, which was printed on New Year's Eve, 1955.

McNulty and I were reporters together on Columbus, Ohio, newspapers in the early 1920's. He did general assignments for a morning paper while I covered City Hall for an afternoon paper, but our offices were just a few blocks apart, in the center of town, and I bumped into him almost every day, often at the corner of Broad and High streets, the city's main intersection. He was invariably excited about something, the cabin lights of the Shenandoah which he had seen twinkling in the sky the night before, a girl at the James Theatre who sang "Roses Are Shining in Picardy," Donn Byrne's novel *The Changelings*, which he demanded that I begin reading right away, there on that crowded corner, or a song called "Last Night on the Back Porch" which he insisted on playing for me, then and almost there. Actually, he took me around the corner to a music store and began beating out the song on the first piano he came to, to the astonishment of the store's staff. "It's McNulty," I explained to them in a whisper and they all nodded and breathed his name in unison, obviously believing that he was a great pianist, come to play at Memorial Hall, who had suddenly been seized by a rare moment of relaxation and frivolity. He had once played the piano in a movie theatre in the days of silent films and, within his range, there wasn't anything he couldn't make the keys do. While playing "My Gal Sal" he used to recite the succession to the presidency, and it was upon the conclusion of that bravura performance that we left the music shop and its startled and transfigured staff. Once he got me up before breakfast to play on my Victrola two records that had entranced him—"Singin' Sam from Alabam' " and a bright arrangement of "Everybody Calls Me Honey," in which piano, trumpet, and banjo alternately took over the solo.

McNulty was a widely experienced newspaperman at twenty-five, when he arrived in Columbus from the East, to work for the *Ohio State Journal* at sixty dollars a week, higher pay than any reporter in town had been getting. I have forgotten, if I ever knew, what whim or compulsion had sent him into the Middle West. It was probably an impulse peculiar to his volatile spirit, such as that which sent him one day, years later, to New Iberia, Louisiana, to visit the tabasco factory there. In Columbus he lingered for a dozen years. Before the first of these had passed he knew more people in the city than I did, although I had been born and brought up there. They included everybody from taxi drivers, cops, prizefighters, and bellboys to the mayor of the city and the governor of the state. He wrote speeches for one successful candidate for governor, and in that, as in everything else, he had the time of his life.

John once explained to me, "Two thirds of the Irish blood is grease paint," and he was a fine offhand actor and raconteur rampant, who would jump from his chair in a living room and theatrically bring to life one of the characters he had so fondly collected during his wanderings. I think he did as much as anyone, with his acting, to ridicule the Ku Klux Klan out of existence in Columbus. He had arranged for me to accost him whenever I saw him at Broad and High in the company of a group of men—he was always surrounded by men—and loudly try to enroll him in the Klan. "We are looking for likely one hundred percent Americans," I would say, "so we can build up in this city the biggest Kleagle in the country."

"Klavern," he would correct me, and while his companions stared at me in disbelief, he would take off his hat, present to me the shining map of Ireland that was his face, and say proudly, "The name is John Aloysius McNulty." At this I would slink away, muttering, while his friends stared after me. "Them guys must be crazy!" I heard a boxer named Sully exclaim after one of these rituals, and the word got around town that the local Klan was made up of imbeciles. It didn't last long.

Trying to describe McNulty is a little like trying to describe Ed Wynn or George M. Cohan. "A small, jaunty man, best described as Irish of face and manner" is the way the *New York Times* went about it in that paper's appreciative obituary. He was small, I guess, measured by physical height and weight, but I have a tendency to look up when I think of him, for to me he was nine feet tall. This was the stature, at any rate, of his unflagging comic spirit. The dictionary has no exact words for the face and voice of the man, or for the shape and color of the moods he put on every morning with his clothes. There was nothing of the literary elf about McNulty, who once said to me, "Only people with Vincent for a middle name write about leprechauns." It is true that the world of John McNulty bordered on Oz and Wonderland, but it consisted mainly of Ireland, New York's Third Avenue, the city rooms of American newspapers, and the race tracks of the world, with many an odd and unexpected nook and corner. From the border states came curious and wondrous figures, attracted to McNulty, not magically, but naturally. This gave his world, and his comments on it, a strange truth, undreamed of in ordinary philosophies. When he said, of 1885, "That was the year the owls were so bad," or when he told a lady trying to think of her hairdresser's name, "Girls named Dolores become hairdressers," or when he tracked down a bookie in a jewelry shop by suddenly remembering "All watch repairers are named Schneider," the listener felt that this was not mere whimsy but McNulty fact. There was always, faint or sharp, in what he said or did a critical comment on our tangled civilization, a sound parody of the ways of men. Walking about the streets of any city with McNulty was to be taken on a guided tour of what William James called, in another context, unexplored experience. Two men would pass by you, one of them saying, "It's the biggest gorilla in the world. They call it Garganetta," or a waiter in a café would tell him, "We get stranglers come in here at all hours." Through the ears of many of us such things pass unregistered, but McNulty's sensitized mind recorded everything. "The lady was a Bostonian, they call them" rang like a bell in his consciousness. To a man whose awareness was always on the lookout for the unusual, as well as the typical, the world was a book he was reading with intense concentration. He loved sentiment, being Irish, and he came right out with it. Of a pretty young bride he once wrote about in the *Daily News* he said, "She was as cute as a little red wagon." He once called me long distance to tell me he had just read something lovely which I had to hear. It was the four words of a lover: "My eyes desire you." My phone brought me often, but not often enough, phrases, sentences, or paragraphs from an enthusiastic McNulty who had just stumbled upon them. Sometimes he read me a whole piece.

There were a dozen shops of all kinds on New York's East Side with whose proprietors McNulty, making his daily rounds, kept up some kind of running gag. Once when I lived on East Fifty-seventh Street, a region he knew well, he took me into a small corner store after explaining, "There's a wonderful guy runs this place." He was a wonderful guy, too, in the McNulty tradition, perfectly suited to their particular running gag, which was managed deadpan, as if the two had never met before.

"What can I do for you, sir?" the man said. McNulty consulted the back
of an envelope. "Elephant goad," he said finally. An amateur actor of
McNulty's stripe, the man began snapping his fingers, humming, and
searching his shelves and opening doors underneath the shelves, at
length turning around to report, "Sorry, seem to be fresh out of elephant
goads. Anything else?" McNulty shook his head sorrowfully and out we
went. I found out later, dropping into the shop, some of the other things
McNulty had asked for in vain—fetlock cleaners, beagle harness, and
noiseless dice. "He says he supplies dice to a couple of fugitives holed up
in this house with marble floors," the proprietor said. This is the thinnest
ice of comedy and it takes experts to skate on it without falling in. You
had to behold such performances yourself to understand the skill of
McNulty and his stooges. I have never read a critic who captured the
subtle essence of Beatrice Lillie's comic art, and none of them could do
justice to McNulty's, either, on flat paper. His timing was perfect, and so
were the tricks of his tones of voice. One day a few years ago I phoned
him to ask if he remembered the year he had interviewed Donald Ogden
Stewart (a great McNulty admirer) for the *Ohio State Journal.*
McNulty's answer was prompt, and in the tone of a professional quiz
panelist. "It was the year Black Gold won the Derby," he said, and
having given me all the help a true horseplayer should need, he hung up.
I had to look up in the World Almanac the year Black Gold won the
Derby. Checking later with the *Journal* files, I found out, of course, that
the answer was correct.

John Augustine McNulty (Aloysius had been invented for effect) was
capable of a fine anger that could rise to fury. Like my own temper, his
was sometimes as unreasonable as it was quick, but our occasional disagreements, as sudden as summer storms, passed just as quickly. After
one loud hour of argument over the play *Shadow and Substance,* about
which I think we were both right, we parted like men who would never
see each other again. But we had a running-gag manner of making up,
during which the cause of the trouble was never mentioned or even
hinted at. Spotting him in a bar, I would present myself, politely, as a
man just in from Columbus, Ohio, with a letter to him from Sully. "Let
me see the letter," he would say, and there ensued a search through all
my pockets, in which he helped. "Let me have another go at your coat,"
he would say grimly, but the letter was never there. "Well, when you
find it," he would say, "bring it around. If I'm not here, I'll probably be
somewhere else. Meanwhile, let's have a drink to old Sully." His gallery
of persons he disliked was not large, but it included the right figures, the
phony, or "wax banana," the snob, the show-off, the blow-hard, the
bigot, the unfriendly, the humorless, and all their cold ilk.

I happened to be in Columbus in 1933 when McNulty decided to return to the New York he hadn't seen for more than a decade, and I came back on the train with him. We hadn't ridden in a taxi more than three blocks from Pennsylvania Station before he began waving at guys he knew. "You're obvious New York born and bred, Mac," the taxi driver told him, adding that he was studying "human psychology." He picked me as a stranger "from the outlands" and said to my companion, "Better look after your friend. You don't know your way around, it's a tough town." In the next few years McNulty worked on the *Mirror,* the *Daily News,* and the *Herald Tribune* under its great city editor Stanley Walker, who once told me, "There is a kind of story that only McNulty could write, and it was a pleasure to have him around." He meant the kind of feature story that calls for the use of the heart as well as the mind.

McNulty was a fast writer, but before he reached his typewriter his alert photographic mind, backed up by an amazing memory, had worked the story out in all but a few details. He was temperamental if the thing didn't come out right, but he discarded his temperament like an over-coat when he set out to explore his fascinating world. His first assign-ment on *The New Yorker* was a "Reporter at Large" piece and he went out, got the facts, came back, and batted out the story within a couple of hours. "He can't get over writing for a newspaper deadline," said the late Harold Ross, but McNulty learned to slow down. When he left for a stint in Hollywood, Ross was genuinely reluctant to see him go. "Well, God bless you, McNulty, goddam it," said Ross. As John told me later, "Ross has two gods, Upper Case and lower case." Through Ross and the rest of us McNulty met a few people he hadn't known before. I remem-ber his delight, one night in "21," when Marc Connelly told him some of Lloyd Lewis's anecdotes about the Southwest, one of which involved a rancher whose cat had been missing for three weeks. "Then one day I turned over my mattress," said the rancher, "and there, between the mat-tress and the springs, was Boss, pressed as pretty as a flower." The next day McNulty said to me, "The cat's name wasn't Boss. The cat's name was Pete. All ranchers' cats are named Pete." I'm sure Connelly would have lost money betting against this intuitive bit of McNulty truth.

McNulty was not New York born, for he first saw the enchanting light of his world in Lawrence, Massachusetts, where his mother ran a little store after the death of his father. Her son has done some justice to these early scenes, but not as much as I wish he had, for his mother is one of the vivid memories of my life. I first met her in Columbus when she visited him there, and he and I went to the train together to see her off, both of us, by coincidence, carrying identical boxes of candy. He knew what to do about that. "If you cry," he told her affectionately, "you get the box of candy that's poisoned. If you're good, you get the other one." The leave-taking was as jolly as it could be when two McNultys parted.

Years later in New York, Mrs. McNulty was knocked down by a taxi on Park Avenue, and my wife and I went with John to call on her. Before we could tiptoe into the bedroom, where she was supposed to be lying wrapped in bandages from head to foot, we heard a small clatter in the kitchen and her son went out to investigate. It was Mama, of course. "And did you think I'd let the Thurbers call on me," she said indignantly, "and not fix them a cup o' tea?" It took more than a New York taxi to finish off a McNulty. John himself, although he never talked about it, and wrote about it only sparingly and obliquely, had gone through some of the toughest battles of the First World War, in the Infantry. He got a leg full of shrapnel at Fère-en-Tardenois, and he was made a sergeant when the company's sergeants were killed in battle. After the war, he spent a year in hospital, and his wounds gave him trouble from then on. He was once a pet patient for three weeks in a hospital in Columbus, but none of us knew for a long time that Fère-en-Tardenois had sent him there. He made lasting friendships, of course, with doctors, nurses, and orderlies.

A few years before he died he gave me his precious copy of Mencken's *The American Language,* saying, "This is the book I love the most." Mencken once spoke to me, in the Algonquin lobby, in praise of McNulty and his handling of the people and the parlance of Third Avenue, and I remember how McNulty's face lighted up when I told him about it. He had a lot of favorite books, including the Oxford English Dictionary, which he read as if it were a novel filled with wonders and suspense. There must be many of us who have books that McNulty once owned. "He couldn't keep a book he loved," Faith McNulty told me once. "He wasn't happy until he had given it to some friend."

In the last ten years of his life, alas, we ran into each other only occasionally, but we talked a lot on the phone and exchanged letters. His letters were invariably carefully thought out single sentences, each relating some highlight of his city adventures. The last one I ever got was different, though, and puzzled me. It began, as always, "Dear Jimmy," and went on to say, "I think that maybe threescore years and ten is subject to change without notice." I searched it for the laugh, and realized there weren't going to be any more laughs. One night shortly afterward my phone rang in the country and I was told that he was dead. I had been planning to write him suggesting that he read certain poems and pieces by Dylan Thomas, particularly the poem that ends: "They shall have stars at elbow and foot . . . and death shall have no dominion. And death shall have no dominion." But I was too late. If Thomas was right about these bright eternal ornaments, John Augustine McNulty has his stars, and never you mind about that.

F. SCOTT FITZGERALD

RING

October, 1933

For a year and a half, the writer of this appreciation was Ring Lardner's most familiar companion; after that, geography made separations and our contacts were rare. When my wife and I last saw him in 1931, he looked already like a man on his deathbed—it was terribly sad to see that six feet three inches of kindness stretched out ineffectual in the hospital room. His fingers trembled with a match, the tight skin on his handsome skull was marked as a mask of misery and nervous pain.

He gave a very different impression when we first saw him in 1921— he seemed to have an abundance of quiet vitality that would enable him to outlast anyone, to take himself for long spurts of work or play that would ruin any ordinary constitution. He had recently convulsed the country with the famous kitten-and-coat saga (it had to do with a world's series bet and with the impending conversion of some kittens into fur), and the evidence of the betting, a beautiful sable, was worn by his wife at the time. In those days he was interested in people, sports, bridge, music, the stage, the newspapers, the magazines, the books. But though I did not know it, the change in him had already begun—the impenetrable despair that dogged him for a dozen years to his death.

He had practically given up sleeping, save on short vacations deliberately consecrated to simple pleasures, most frequently golf with his friends, Grantland Rice or John Wheeler. Many a night we talked over a case of Canadian ale until bright dawn, when Ring would rise and yawn: "Well, I guess the children have left for school by this time—I might as well go home."

The woes of many people haunted him—for example, the doctor's death sentence pronounced upon Tad, the cartoonist, (who, in fact, nearly outlived Ring)—it was as if he believed he could and ought to do something about such things. And as he struggled to fulfill his contracts, one of which, a comic strip based on the character of "the busher," was a terror, indeed, it was obvious that he felt his work to be directionless, merely "copy." So he was inclined to turn his cosmic sense of responsibility into the channel of solving other people's problems—finding someone an introduction to a theatrical manager, placing a friend in a job, maneuvering a man into a golf club. The effort made was often out of proportion to the situation; the truth back of it was that Ring was getting off—he was a faithful and conscientious workman to the end, but he had stopped finding any fun in his work ten years before he died.

About that time (1922) a publisher undertook to reissue his old books and collect his recent stories and this gave him a sense of existing in the literary world as well as with the public, and he got some satisfaction from the reiterated statements of Mencken and F. P. A. as to his true stature as a writer. But I don't think he cared then—it is hard to understand but I don't think he really gave a damn about anything except his personal relations with a few people. A case in point was his attitude to those imitators who lifted everything except the shirt off his back—only Hemingway has been so thoroughly frisked—it worried the imitators more than it worried Ring. His attitude was that if they got stuck in the process he'd help them over any tough place.

Throughout this period of huge earnings and an increasingly solid reputation on top and beneath, there were two ambitions more important to Ring than the work by which he will be remembered; he wanted to be a musician—sometimes he dramatized himself ironically as a thwarted composer—and he wanted to write shows. His dealings with managers would make a whole story: they were always commissioning him to do work which they promptly forgot they had ordered, and accepting librettos that they never produced. (Ring left a short ironic record of Ziegfeld.) Only with the aid of the practical George Kaufman did he achieve his ambition, and by then he was too far gone in illness to get a proper satisfaction from it.

The point of these paragraphs is that, whatever Ring's achievement was, it fell short of the achievement he was capable of, and this because of a cynical attitude toward his work. How far back did that attitude go?—back to his youth in a Michigan village? Certainly back to his days with the Cubs. During those years, when most men of promise achieve an adult education, if only in the school of war, Ring moved in the company of a few dozen illiterates playing a boy's game. A boy's game, with no more possibilities in it than a boy could master, a game bounded by walls which kept out novelty or danger, change or adventure. This material, the observation of it under such circumstances, was the text of Ring's schooling during the most formative period of the mind. A writer can spin on about his adventures after thirty, after forty, after fifty, but the criteria by which these adventures are weighed and valued are irrevocably settled at the age of twenty-five. However deeply Ring might cut into it, his cake had exactly the diameter of Frank Chance's diamond.

Here was his artistic problem, and it promised future trouble. So long as he wrote within that enclosure the result was magnificent: within it he heard and recorded the voice of a continent. But when, inevitably, he outgrew his interest in it, what was Ring left with?

He was left with his fine linguistic technique—and he was left rather helpless in those few acres. He had been formed by the very world on which his hilarious irony had released itself. He had fought his way through to knowing what people's motives are and what means they are likely to resort to in order to attain their goals. But now he had a new problem—what to do about it. He went on seeing, and the sights traveled back to the optic nerve, but no longer to be thrown off in fiction, because they were no longer sights that could be weighed and valued by the old criteria. It was never that he was completely sold on athletic virtuosity as the be-all and end-all of problems; the trouble was that he could find nothing finer. Imagine life conceived as a business of beautiful muscular organization—an arising, an effort, a good break, a sweat, a bath, a meal, a love, a sleep—imagine it achieved; then imagine trying to apply that standard to the horribly complicated mess of living, where nothing, even the greatest conceptions and workings and achievements, is else but messy, spotty, tortuous—and then one can imagine the confusion that Ring faced on coming out of the ball park.

He kept on recording but he no longer projected, and this accumulation, which he has taken with him to the grave, crippled his spirit in the latter years. It was not the fear of Niles, Michigan, that hampered him— it was the habit of silence, formed in the presence of the "ivory" with which he lived and worked. Remember it was not humble ivory—Ring has demonstrated that—it was arrogant, imperative, often megalomaniacal ivory. He got the habit of silence, then the habit of repression that finally took the form of his odd little crusade in the *New Yorker* against pornographic songs. He had agreed with himself to speak only a small portion of his mind.

The present writer once suggested to him that he organize some *cadre* within which he could adequately display his talents, suggesting that it should be something deeply personal, and something on which Ring could take his time, but he dismissed the idea lightly; he was a disillusioned idealist but he had served his Fates well, and no other ones could be casually created for him—"This is something that can be printed," he reasoned; "this, however, belongs with that bunch of stuff that can never be written."

He covered himself in such cases with protests of his inability to bring off anything big, but this was specious, for he was a proud man and had no reason to rate his abilities cheaply. He refused to "tell all" because in a crucial period of his life he had formed the habit of not doing it—and this he had elevated gradually into a standard of taste. It never satisfied him by a damn sight.

So one is haunted not only by a sense of personal loss but by a conviction that Ring got less percentage of himself on paper than any other American of the first flight. There is *"You Know Me, Al,"* and there are about a dozen wonderful short stories (my God, he hadn't even saved them—the material of *How to Write Short Stories* was obtained by photographing old issues in the public library!), and there is some of the most uproarious and inspired nonsense since Lewis Carroll. Most of the rest is mediocre stuff, with flashes, and I would do Ring a disservice to suggest it should be set upon an altar and worshipped, as have been the most casual relics of Mark Twain. Those three volumes should seem enough—to everyone who didn't know Ring. But I venture that no one who knew him but will agree that the personality of the man overlapped it. Proud, shy, solemn, shrewd, polite, brave, kind, merciful, honorable— with the affection these qualities aroused he created in addition a certain awe in people. His intentions, his will, once in motion, were formidable factors in dealing with him—he always did every single thing he said he would do. Frequently he was the melancholy Jaques, and sad company indeed, but under any conditions a noble dignity flowed from him, so that time in his presence always seemed well spent.

On my desk, at the moment, I have the letters Ring wrote to us; here is a letter one thousand words long, here is one of two thousand words— theatrical gossip, literary shop talk, flashes of wit but not much wit, for he was feeling thin and saving the best of that for his work, anecdotes of his activities. I reprint the most typical one I can find:

"The Dutch Treat show was a week ago Friday night. Grant Rice and I had reserved a table, and a table holds ten people and no more. Well, I had invited, as one guest, Jerry Kern, but he telephoned at the last moment that he couldn't come. I then consulted with Grant Rice, who said he had no substitute in mind, but that it was a shame to waste our extra ticket when tickets were at a premium. So I called up Jones, and Jones said yes, and would it be all right for him to bring along a former Senator who was a pal of his and had been good to him in Washington. I said I was sorry, but our table was filled and, besides, we didn't have an extra ticket. "Maybe I could dig up another ticket somewhere," said Jones. "I don't believe so," I said, "but anyway the point is that we haven't room at our table." "Well," said Jones, "I could have the Senator eat somewhere else and join us in time for the show." "Yes," I said, "but we have no ticket for him." "Well, I'll think up something," he said. Well, what he thought up was to bring himself and the Senator and I had a hell of a time getting an extra ticket and shoving the Senator in at another table where he wasn't wanted, and later in the evening, the Senator thanked Jones and said he was the greatest fella in the world and all I got was goodnight.

"Well, I must close and nibble on a carrot. R.W.L."

Even in a telegram Ring could compress a lot of himself. Here is one:

WHEN ARE YOU COMING BACK AND WHY PLEASE ANSWER   RING LARD-
NER

This is not the moment to recollect Ring's convivial aspects, especially as he had, long before his death, ceased to find amusement in dissipation, or indeed in the whole range of what is called entertainment—save for his perennial interest in songs. By grace of the radio and of the many musicians who, drawn by his enormous magnetism, made pilgrimages to his bedside, he had a consolation in the last days, and he made the most of it, hilariously rewriting Cole Porter's lyrics in the *New Yorker.* But it would be an evasion for the present writer not to say that when he was Ring's neighbor a decade ago, they tucked a lot under their belts in many weathers, and spent many words on many men and things. At no time did I feel that I had known him enough, or that anyone knew him—it was not the feeling that there was more stuff in him and that it should come out, it was rather a qualitative difference, it was rather as though, due to some inadequacy in one's self, one had not penetrated to something unsolved, new and unsaid. That is why one wishes that Ring had written down a larger proportion of what was in his mind and heart. It would have saved him longer for us, and that in itself would be something. But I would like to know what it was, and now I will go on wishing—what did Ring want, how did he want things to be, how did he think things were?

A great and good American is dead. Let us not obscure him by the flowers, but walk up and look at that fine medallion, all abraded by sorrows that perhaps we are not equipped to understand. Ring made no enemies, because he was kind, and to many millions he gave release and delight.

To Ernest Hemingway

Villa St. Louis
Juan-les-Pins
[December, 1926]

Dear Ernest:

We leave this house Tuesday for Genoa and New York. I hope everything's going better for you. If there is anything you need done here as in America—anything about your work, or money, or human help under any head—remember you can always call on

Your devoted friend,
Scott

S.S. Conte Biancamano
[En route New York]
[postmarked December 23, 1926]

Dear Ernest:

Your letter depressed me—illogically because I knew more or less what was coming. I wish I could have seen you and heard you, if you wished, give some sort of version of what happened to you. Anyhow I'm sorry for you and for Hadley and for Bumby and I hope some way you'll all be content and things will not seem so hard and bad.

I can't tell you how much your friendship has meant to me during this year and a half—it is the brightest thing in our trip to Europe for me. I will try to look out for your interests with Scribners in America, but I gather that the need of that is past now and that soon you'll be financially more than on your feet.

I'm sorry you didn't come to Marseille. I go back with my novel still unfinished and with less health and not much more money than when I came, but somehow content, for the moment, with motion and New York ahead and Zelda's entire recovery—and happy about the amount of my book that I've already written.

I'm delighted with what press I've already seen of *The Sun, etc.* Did not realize that you had stolen it from me but am prepared to believe that it's true and shall tell everyone. By the way I liked it in print even better than in manuscript.

1st printing was probably 5000. 2nd printing may mean that they've sold 4500 so have ordered up 3000 more. It may mean any sale from 2500 to 5000, tho.

College Humor pays fine. No movie in *Sun Also* unless book is big success of scandal. That's just a guess.

We all enjoyed *"La vie est beau avec Papa."* We agree with Bumby.

Always yours affectionately,
Scott

Write me care of Scribners.

Hotel Roosevelt
Washington, D.C.
[March, 1927]

Dear Ernest:

A line in terrible haste. Lunched with Mencken in Baltimore yesterday. He is just starting reading *The Sun, etc.*—has no recollection of having seen "Big Two-Hearted River" and admits confusion about two *In Our Times.* Got him to say he'd pay you $250.00 for anything of yours he could use. So there's another market.

Told him about how you were going to beat him up. He's a "peach of a fellow" (no irony; just a slip of the pen). He's thoroughly interested and utterly incapable of malice. Whole thing was simply rather sloppy, as he's one of the busiest men in America.

"The Killers" was fine.

Your devoted friend,
Scott

[Ellerslie]
[Edgemoor, Delaware]
[Postmarked April 18, 1927]

Dear Ernest:

Your stories were great (in April *Scribner's*). But like me you must beware Conrad rhythms in direct quotation from characters, especially if you're pointing a single phrase and making a man live by it.

"In the fall the war was always there but we did not go to it any more" is one of the most beautiful prose sentences I've ever read.

So much has happened to me lately that I despair of ever assimilating it—or forgetting it, which is the same thing.

I hate to think of your being hard up. Please use this if it would help. *The Atlantic* will pay about $200.00, I suppose. I'll get in touch with Perkins about it when he returns from vacation (1 week). Won't they advance you all you need on the book of stories? Your title is fine by the way. What chance of your crossing this summer?

My novel to be finished July 1st.

> With eager and anxious good wishes,
> Scott

Address for a year—Ellerslie Mansion, Edgemoor, Delaware. Huge old house on Delaware River. Pillars, etc. I am called "Colonel." Zelda "de old Missus."

> *Ellerslie*
> *Edgemoor, Delaware*
> *[November, 1927]*

Dear Ernest:

Thousands will send you this clipping. I should think it would make you quite conscious of your public existence. It's well meant—he praised your book a few days before.

The book is fine. I like it quite as well as *The Sun,* which doesn't begin to express my enthusiasm. In spite of all its geographical and emotional rambling, it's a unit, as much as Conrad's books of Contes were. Zelda read it with fascination, liking it better than anything you've written. Her favorite was "Hills Like White Elephants," mine, barring "The Killers," was "Now I Lay Me." The one about the Indians was the only one that left me cold and I'm glad you left out "Up in Michigan." They probably belong to an earlier and almost exhausted vein.

"In the fall the war was always there but we did not go to it any more." God, what a beautiful line. And the waking dreams in "Now I Lay Me" and the whole mood of "Hills Like."

Did you see the pre-review by that. . . . Rascoe who obviously had only read three stories but wanted to be up to the minute?

Max says it's almost exhausted 7500—however that was five days ago. I like your title—*All the Sad Young Men Without Women*—and I feel my influence is beginning to tell. Manuel Garcia is obviously Gatsby. What you haven't learned from me you'll get from Good Woman Bromfield and soon you'll be Marching in the Van of the Younger Generation.

No work this summer but lots this fall. Hope to finish the novel by 1st December. Have got nervous as hell lately—purely physical but scared me somewhat—to the point of putting me on the wagon and smoking denicotinized cigarettes. Zelda is ballet dancing three times a week with the Phila Symphony—painting also. I think you were wise not jumping at *Hearst's* offer. I had a contract with them that, as it turned out, did me unspeakable damage in one way or another. Long is a sentimental scavenger with no ghost of taste or individuality, not nearly so much as Lorimer for example. However, why not send your stories to Paul Reynolds? He'll be glad to handle them and will get you good prices. The *Post* now pays me $3500—this detail so you'll be sure who's writing this letter.

I can't tell you how I miss you. May cross for 6 weeks in March or April. *The Grandmothers* was respectable but undistinguished, and are you coming home? Best to Pauline. With good wishes and affection,

Scott

1307 Park Avenue
Baltimore, Maryland
June 1, 1934

Dear Ernest:

Your letter crossed, or almost crossed, one of mine which I am glad now I didn't send, because the old charming frankness of your letter cleared up the foggy atmosphere through which I felt it was difficult for us to talk any more. . . .

I think it is obvious that my respect for your artistic life is absolutely unqualified, that save for a few of the dead or dying old men you are the only man writing fiction in America that I look up to very much. There are pieces and paragraphs of your work that I read over and over—in fact, I stopped myself doing it for a year and a half because I was afraid that your particular rhythms were going to creep in on mine by process of infiltration. Perhaps you will recognize some of your remarks in *Tender*, but I did every damn thing I could to avoid that. . . .

Thanks again for your letter which was damned nice, and my absolute best wishes to all of you. (By the way, where did you ever get the idea that I didn't like Pauline, or that I didn't like her as much as I should?) Of all that time of life the only temperamental coolness that I ever felt toward any of the people we ran around with was toward——, and even in that case it was never any more than that. I have honestly never gone in for hating. My temporary bitternesses toward people have all been ended by what Freud called an inferiority complex and Christ called "Let him without sin"—I remember the day he said it. We were just-likethat then; we tossed up for who was going to go through with it—and he lost.

I am now asking only $5000 for letters. Make out the check to Malcolm Republic, *c/o The New Cowlick.*

Ever your friend,
[Scott]

P.S. Did you ever see my piece about Ring in *The New Cowlick*—I think you'd have liked it.

P.S.S. This letter and questions require no answers. You are "write" that I no longer listen, but my case histories seem to go in largely for the same magazines, and with simple people I get polite. But I listen to you and would like damn well to hear your voice again.

> *[Grove Park Inn]*
> *[Asheville, North Carolina]*
> *[August, 1936]*

Dear Ernest:

Please lay off me in print. If I choose to write *de profundis* sometimes it doesn't mean I want friends praying aloud over my corpse. No doubt you meant it kindly but it cost me a night's sleep. And when you incorporate it (the story) in a book would you mind cutting my name?

It's a fine story—one of your best—even though the "Poor Scott Fitzgerald, etc." rather spoiled it for me.

> Ever your friend,
> Scott

Riches have *never* fascinated me, unless combined with the greatest charm or distinction.

> *[On the train, traveling to some point in the South]*
> *June 5, 1937*

It was fine to see you so well and full of life, Ernest. I hope you'll make your book fat—I know some of that *Esquire* work is too good to leave out. All best wishes to your Spanish trip—I wish we could meet more often. I don't feel I know you at all.

> Ever yours,
> Scott

Going South always seems to me rather desolate and fatal and uneasy. This is no exception. Going North is a safe dull feeling.

To Maxwell Perkins

c/o Phil Berg Agency
9484 Wilshire Blvd.
Beverly Hills, Calif.
May 20, 1940

Dear Max:—

I've owed you a decent letter for some months. First—the above is my best address though at the moment I'm hunting for a small apartment. I am in the last week of an eight week movie job for which I will receive $2300. I couldn't pay you anything from it, nor the government, but it was something, because it was my own picture *Babylon Revisited* and may lead to a new line up here. I just couldn't make the grade as a hack—that, like everything else, requires a certain practised excellence—

The radio has just announced the fall of St. Quentin! My God! What was the use of my wiring you that Andre Chamson has a hit when the war has now passed into a new stage making his book a chestnut of a bygone quiet era.

I wish I was in print. It will be odd a year or so from now when Scottie assures her friends I was an author and finds that no book is procurable. It is certainly no fault of yours. You (and one other man, Gerald Murphy) have been a friend through every dark time in these five years. It's funny what a friend is—Ernest's crack in *The Snows,* poor John Bishop's article in the Virginia Quarterly (a nice return for ten years of trying to set him up in a literary way) and Harold's sudden desertion at the wrong time, have made them something less than friends. Once I believed in friendship, believed I *could* (if I didn't always) make people happy and it was more fun than anything. Now even that seems like a vaudevillian's cheap dream of heaven, a vast minstrel show in which one is the perpetual Bones.

Professionally, I know, the next move must come from me. Would the 25 cent press keep *Gatsby* in the public eye—or *is the book unpopular.* Has it *had* its chance? Would a popular reissue in that series with a preface *not* by me but by one of its admirers—I can maybe pick one— make it a favorite with class rooms, profs, lovers of English prose— anybody. But to die, so completely and unjustly after having given so much. Even now there is little published in American fiction that doesn't slightly bare my stamp—in a *small* way I was an original. I remember we had one of our few and trifling disagreements because I said that to anyone who loved "When Lilacs last—" Tom Wolfe couldn't be such a *great* original. Since then I have changed about him. I like "Only the Dead" and "Arthur, Garfield etc.," right up with the tops. And where are Tom and I and the rest whcn psychological Robespierres parade through American letters elevating such melo as "Christ in Concrete" to the top, and the boys read Steinbeck like they once read Mencken! I have not lost faith. People will *buy* my new book and I hope I shan't again make the many mistakes of *Tender.*

Tell me news if you have time. Where is Ernest and what doing? . . .

Love to all of you, of all generations.

A. SCOTT BERG

From MAX PERKINS: EDITOR OF GENIUS

On the eve of Perkins's departure for Key West, the second week in January, only two parts of Tom Wolfe's book remained to be agreed upon. The first was a foreword. . . . The other part of the book to be discussed was the dedication page, which Wolfe had been drafting in the back of his mind since he had first begun the manuscript. In recent weeks John Hall Wheelock had been helping him polish it. Max knew little about it but had suspicions. Now, about to leave for Florida, he decided to speak his mind. "Nothing could give me greater pleasure or greater pride as an editor," he wrote Tom, "than that the book of the writer whom I have most greatly admired should be dedicated to me if it were sincerely done.

> But you cannot, and should not try to change your conviction that I have deformed your book, or at least prevented it from coming to perfection. It is therefore impossible for you sincerely to dedicate it to me and it ought not to be done. I know we are truly friends and have gone through much in company and this matter, for my part, can have nothing to do with that, or ever shall. But this is another matter. I would have said this sooner, but for some fear that you would misinterpret me. But the plain truth is that working on your writing, however it has turned out, for good or bad, has been the greatest pleasure, for all its pain, and the most interesting episode of my editorial life. The way in which we are presenting this book must

prove our (and my) belief in it. But what I have done has destroyed your belief in it and you must not act inconsistently with that fact. . . .

When Perkins returned from his vacation he found that he had succeeded in getting Wolfe to leave out his long foreword, but he had failed to keep Wolfe from dedicating the novel to him. *Of Time and the River* was entirely in print—including Wolfe's lavish inscription. "I fought with Tom to keep it at a minimum," Wheelock said later, "to a level of propriety that would not embarrass Max altogether." The dedication read:

TO

MAXWELL EVARTS PERKINS

A great editor and a brave and honest man, who stuck to the writer of this book through times of bitter hopelessness and doubt and would not let him give in to his own despair, a work to be known as "Of Time and the River" is dedicated with the hope that all of it may be in some way worthy of the loyal devotion and the patient care which a dauntless and unshaken friend has given to each part of it, and without which none of it could have been written.

Once Perkins saw it he wrote Wolfe, "Whatever the degree of justice in what it implied, I can think of nothing that could have made me more happy. I won't go further into what I feel about it: I'm a Yankee and cannot speak what I feel most strongly, well, but I do wish to say that I think it a most generous and noble utterance. Certainly for one who could say that of me I ought to have done all that it says I did do."

Of Time and the River sprang from the symbiotic union of two artistic forces—Wolfe's passion and Perkins's judgment. The two men had been at frequent odds, but together they both had accomplished the greatest work of their careers.

Max wrote Tom on February 8, 1935, "I swear, I believe that in truth the whole episode was a most happy one for me. I like to think we may go through another such war together."

A torn fragment in Wolfe's journals, never sent to Perkins, states: "In all my life, until I met you, I never had a friend."

ROBERT FROST

To Sidney Cox

[c. 17] September 1917 Franconia, N.H.

Dear Sidney:

Here it is, then, in all its sympathy, understanding and devotion. Do you remember the misunderstanding we began in that night when we watched the normal school dance from among the empty chairs along the wall? I didn't suspect then that we were to live to owe each other so much. You do owe me something, too, I think. Not much, but a little. Not enough to make your wife jealous of me, because it is nothing in comparison with what you owe her for being what she is. It made us happy to see you so happy on your way with her. Keep her my friend as I shall remain

Always friend of both of you
Robert Frost.

8 August 1942

. . . I am expecting you to write a book on and for me some day—and a deep one. You may not have noticed anything, but I have been taking measures steadily to put off the day till you should assume the toga as a man and my equal. You made a bad start with the note of inferiority you struck in your first chapter, long ago. You were afraid people would think you had sought my society rather than I yours. I was ashamed for you. I probably did seek your society. I administer this with benevolent malice. I remember seeking you in Plymouth at least once for the pleasure of teasing the young fellow I had found so easy to tease on our first meeting at that dance at the Normal School. What added to the wicked pleasure was revenge for your having asked Silver or someone if drink was the explanation of my not having got anywhere at my age. After I came to like you, I can't tell how it was, whether you sought me or I you. I naturally live above or below such considerations with my friends. I am almost morbid in my avoidance of the subtler forms of rivalry and strife. Take this matter of biography between us for instance. Why should you be writing mine and not I yours. You are just as much of a character as I am. Why has it never occurred to me before? I know a lot of good stories about you. I am not going to have it said of me that I let people write biographies of me without returning the compliment.

Ever yours
Robert

WILLIAM FAULKNER

To Malcolm Cowley

Hollywood
Sunday, 7 May [1944]

Dear Mr. Cowley:
   I just found your letter of last Feb. by idle chance today. Please excuse this. During the last several years my correspondence has assumed a tone a divination of which your letter implies. My mail consists of two sorts: from people who dont write, asking me for something, usually money, which being a serious writer trying to be an artist, I naturally dont have; and from people who do write telling me I cant. So, since I have already agreed to answer No to the first and All right to the second, I open the envelopes to get the return postage stamps (if any) and dump the letters into a desk drawer, to be read when (usually twice a year) the drawer overflows.
   I would like very much to have the piece done. I think (at 46) that I have worked too hard at my (elected or doomed, I dont know which) trade, with pride but I believe not vanity, with plenty of ego but with humility too (being a poet, of course I give no fart for glory) to leave no better mark on this our pointless chronicle than I seem to be about to leave.
   As you can see from above, I am at the salt mines again. It would cost more to come here than to come to Miss. This town is crowded with war

factory workers and troops, is unpleasant. But I have a cubbyhole which you are welcome to share until June 1, when my family is coming out. In the fall I will go back home. I dont know when I will come East, I mean to New York. I would like to, but I never seem to have that much money anymore, as I try to save what I earn here to stay at home as long as possible on.

I would like the piece, except the biography part. You are welcome to it privately, of course. But I think that if what one has thought and hoped and endeavored and failed at is not enough, if it must be explained and excused by what he has experienced, done or suffered, while he was not being an artist, then he and the one making the evaluation have both failed.

Thank you for your letter, and again excuse the time lapse.

William Faulkner

Oxford
Saturday [early November 1944]

Dear Maitre:

I saw the piece in Times Book R. It was all right. If that is a fair sample, I dont think I need to see the rest of it before publication because I might want to collaborate and you're doing all right. But if you want comments from me before you release it, that's another horse. So I'll leave it to you whether I see it beforehand or not.

Vide the paragraph you quoted: As regards any specific book, I'm trying primarily to tell a story, in the most effective way I can think of, the most moving, the most exhaustive. But I think even that is incidental to what I am trying to do, taking my output (the course of it) as a whole. I am telling the same story over and over, which is myself and the world. Tom Wolfe was trying to say everything, get everything, the world plus "I" or filtered through "I" or the effort of "I" to embrace the world in which he was born and walked a little while and then lay down again, into one volume. I am trying to go a step further. This I think accounts for what people call the obscurity, the involved formless "style," endless sentences. I'm trying to say it all in one sentence, between one Cap and one period. I'm still trying, to put it all, if possible, on one pinhead. I dont know how to do it. All I know to do is to keep on trying in a new way. I'm inclined to think that my material, the South, is not very important to me. I just happen to know it, and dont have time in one life to learn another one and write at the same time. Though the one I know is probably as good as another, life is a phenomenon but not a novelty, the same frantic steeplechase toward nothing everywhere and man stinks the same stink no matter where in time.

Your divination (vide paragraph) is correct. I didn't intend it, but afterward I dimly saw myself what you put into words. I think though you went a step further than I (unconsciously, I repeat) intended. I think Quentin, not Faulkner, is the correct yardstick here. I was writing the story, but he not I was brooding over a situation. I mean, I was creating him as a character, as well as Sutpen et al. He grieved and regretted the passing of an order the dispossessor of which he was not tough enough to withstand. But more he grieved the fact (because he hated and feared the portentous symptom) that a man like Sutpen, who to Quentin was trash, origin-less, could not only have dreamed so high but have had the force and strength to have failed so grandly. Quentin probably contemplated Sutpen as the hyper-sensitive, already self-crucified cadet of an old long-time Republican Philistine house contemplated the ruin of Samson's portico. He grieved and was moved by it but he was still saying "I told you so" even while he hated himself for saying it.

You are correct; I was first of all (I still think) telling what I thought was a good story, and I believed Quentin could do it better than I in this case. But I accept gratefully all your implications, even though I didn't carry them consciously and simultaneously in the writing of it. In principle I'd like to think I could have. But I dont believe it would have been necessary to carry them or even to have known their analogous derivation, to have had them in the story. Art is simpler than people think because there is so little to write about. All the moving things are eternal in man's history and have been written before, and if a man writes hard enough, sincerely enough, humbly enough, [and, with the unalterable determination never never never to be quite satisfied with it] he will repeat them, because art like poverty takes care of its own, shares its bread.

I am free of Hollywood for 6 months, must go back then for the reason that when I was broke in '42 and the air force didn't want me again, I had to sign a seven year contract with Warner to get a job. Re the book offer. I wrote Harold Ober, who forwarded it to me, that I would not undertake it right now. I can work at Hollywood 6 months, stay home 6, am used to it now and have movie work locked off into another room. I dont want to undertake a book of the nature suggested because I'm like the old mare who has been bred and dropped foals 15-16 times, and she has a feeling that she has only 3 or 4 more in her, and cant afford to spend one on something from outside. I am working on something now. Random House has about 70 pages of it. I will write them to let you see it, if you would like to. It's not Yoknapatawpha this time, though I explained above that I'm still trying to put all mankind's history in one sentence.

Thank you for letter,
William Faulkner

My best to Hal Smith when you see him.

[Oxford]
Tuesday [23 April 1946]

Dear Cowley:

The job is splendid.* Damn you to hell anyway. But even if I had beat you to the idea, mine wouldn't have been this good. By God, I didn't know myself what I had tried to do, and how much I had succeeded.

I am asking Viking to send me more copies (I had just one) and I want to sign one for you, if you are inclined. Spotted Horses is pretty funny, after a few years.

Random House and Ober lit a fire under Warner, I dont know how, and I am here until September anyway, on a dole from Random House, working on what seems now to me to be my magnum o.

Faulkner

To Robert K. Haas

(The *Memphis Commercial Appeal* had recorded Faulkner's brief remarks at the service for Mammy Callie.)

Oxford
Wednesday [7 February 1940]

Dear Bob:

Thank you for note and clipping. This is what I said, and when I got it on paper afterward, it turned out to be pretty good prose:

"Caroline has known me all my life. It was my privilege to see her out of hers. After my father's death, to Mammy I came to represent the head of that family to which she had given a half century of fidelity and devotion. But the relationship between us never became that of master and servant. She still remained one of my earliest recollections, not only as a person, but as a fount of authority over my conduct and of security

*The Portable Faulkner, edited by Malcolm Cowley (New York, 1954), in the Viking Portable Library series.

for my physical welfare, and of active and constant affection and love. She was an active and constant precept for decent behavior. From her I learned to tell the truth, to refrain from waste, to be considerate of the weak and respectful to age. I saw fidelity to a family which was not hers, devotion and love for people she had not borne.

"She was born in bondage and with a dark skin and most of her early maturity was passed in a dark and tragic time for the land of her birth. She went through vicissitudes which she had not caused; she assumed cares and griefs which were not even her cares and griefs. She was paid wages for this, but pay is still just money. And she never received very much of that, so that she never laid up anything of this world's goods. Yet she accepted that too without cavil or calculation or complaint, so that by that very failure she earned the gratitude and affection of the family she had conferred the fidelity and devotion upon, and gained the grief and regret of the aliens who loved and lost her.

"She was born and lived and served, and died and now is mourned; if there is a heaven, she has gone there."

Bill

To Erik Boheman

Oxford, Miss.
27 Dec. 1950

Your Excellency:

Please accept my thanks for your kindness in making even more pleasant my daughter's and my most pleasant visit to your country in December.

I hope that it was within my power, and that mine and my daughter's conduct was such, to leave as high an opinion of Americans in Sweden as the regard and respect for Sweden which we brought away.

Respectfully,
William Faulkner

To Mrs. Robert K. Haas

[Oxford]
Wednesday, 27 [December 1950]

Dear Merle:

This is belated, though the sincere wishes are not, were in existence long before the day to offer them.

We are at home again, lots of family, plenty of Xmas. Missy is still trying to adjust herself to her experience, get things sifted into order so she can tell people all she saw and did.

I dont at all regret going to Stockholm now; I realise it was the only thing to do; you can commit mistake and only feel regret, but when you commit bad taste, what you feel is shame. Anyway, I went, and did the best I knew to behave like a Swedish gentleman, and leave the best taste possible on the Swedish palate for Americans and Random House. I hope to see you soon, and tell you all about it.

My best to Bob and the children, and please accept the seasonal wishes which are not seasonal from me to you, because seasons dont have anything to do with them; they are constant.

Bill

To Robert K. Haas

[Oxford]
Monday [1 January 1951]

Dear Bob:

Thank you for your note. The piece* was what I believe and wanted to say, though I might have said it better with more time to compose it. But then, maybe not; I might have lost its thread in trying to make literature out of it. . . .

Bill

*Faulkner's Noble Prize acceptance speech.

TO PHILLIP E. MULLEN*

[Oxford]
[probably January 1951]

Dear Phil:

Thank you for letter and pictures. Enclosed is a clipping from Ben Wasson, Greenville, and a letter. The letter is interesting. I fear that some of my fellow Mississippians will never forgive that 30,000$ that durn foreign country gave me for just sitting on my ass and writing stuff that makes my own state ashamed to own me.

Yours
Bill

*Associate editor, the Oxford *Eagle*.

PART XII

MEMOIRS AND HISTORIES

*Make the attempt if you want to, but you will find
that trying to go through life without friendship
is like milking a bear to get cream for your morning
coffee. It is a whole lot of trouble, and then not
worth much after you get it.*

—*Zora Neale Hurston*

FANNY BURNEY

From JUVENILE JOURNAL

ADDRESSED TO A CERTAIN MISS NOBODY

Poland Street, London, March 27, 1768

To have some account of my thoughts, manners, acquaintance and actions, when the hour arrives in which time is more nimble than memory, is the reason which induces me to keep a Journal. A Journal in which I must confess my *every* thought, must open my whole heart! But a thing of this kind ought to be addressed to somebody—I must imagion myself to be talking—talking to the most intimate of friends—to one in whom I should take delight in confiding, and remorse in concealment:—but who must this friend be? to make choice of one in whom I can but *half* rely, would be to frustrate entirely the intention of my plan. The only one I could wholly, totally confide in, lives in the same house with me, and not only never *has*, but never *will*, leave me one secret to tell her. To *whom*, then, *must* I dedicate my wonderful, surprising and interesting Adventures?—to *whom* dare I reveal my private opinion of my nearest relations? My secret thoughts of my dearest friends? my own hopes, fears, reflections, and dislikes?——Nobody!

To Nobody, then, will I write my Journal! since to Nobody can I be wholly unreserved—to Nobody can I reveal every thought, every wish of my heart, with the most unlimited confidence, the most unremitting sincerity to the end of my life! For what chance, what accident can end my connections with Nobody? No secret *can* I conceal from Nobody, and to Nobody can I be *ever* unreserved. Disagreement cannot stop our affection, Time itself has no power to end our friendship. The love, the esteem I entertain for Nobody, Nobody's self has not power to destroy. From Nobody I have nothing to fear, the secrets sacred to friendship Nobody will not reveal when the affair is doubtful, Nobody will not look towards the side least favourable.

I will suppose you, then, to be my best friend, (tho' God forbid you ever should!) my dearest companion—and a romantick girl, for mere oddity may perhaps be more sincere—more tender—than if you were a friend in propria persona—in as much as imagionation often exceeds reality. In your breast my errors may create pity without exciting contempt; may raise your compassion, without eradicating your love. From this moment, then, my dear girl—but why, permit me to ask, must a *female* be made Nobody? Ah! my dear, what were this world good for, *were* Nobody a female? And now I have done with preambulation.

JANET FLANNER

From PARIS WAS YESTERDAY

Miss Sylvia Beach, who is Shakespeare and Company, the most famous American bookshop and young authors' fireside in Europe, is shortly to sell in manuscript important modern writings which she, along with the world's other booksellers, has been selling only in print. As first publisher of James Joyce's complete *Ulysses,* Miss Beach has unique Joyceiana, comprising collector's items that no one else on earth has, not even Mr. Joyce. To bibliophiles, the sale's finest item will be her first edition of *Ulysses,* 1922, blue-morocco binding, printed on white Dutch paper, the second volume off the press in the rare edition of two hundred, and containing a poem Joyce wrote her, his inscription, and, bound in the back, his original plan of the book. Item two will be *Ulysses* proofs and various typescript versions not included in the final book, plus marginal notes and pen corrections. Item three will be a manuscript version of *Portrait of the Artist as a Young Man*—about six hundred pages, being what was left after Joyce threw it in the fire in despair at publishers' refusals. This MS is written in ink on white copybook paper, unlined, with very wide margins. Further rarities will be a partial MS of *Dubliners,* "A Painful Case" and "Grace" complete, "The Dead" incomplete. Also the MS of *Chamber Music* from which Joyce read the poems to Yeats, the MS of *Pomes Penyeach,* and the MS of a lecture in Italian on Defoe given by Joyce at the Universita del Popolo, Trieste, in 1913. Also pamphlets published by Joyce, including that by Skeffington, murdered in the Irish revolution, and Joyce's own *Day of Rabblement,* both in original pink covers; as well as (a great rarity, since most pious people destroyed it) a blasphemous broadside Joyce wrote and left at leading Dublin citizens' doorsteps on quitting the town. For autograph-hunters, the hundred and fifty signatures, some with letters attached, to the "Protest Against the Pirating of *Ulysses*" is an unusually complete selection of modern literary lights from A to Y, there being no Z; just from Aldington to Maeterlinck to Wells to Yeats. Non-Joyceian items in the sale will include two original drawings by Blake, a first edition of *Lady Chatterley's Lover,* a MS of Walt Whitman, etc. Miss Beach's sale will be the first first-water Joyceiana marketing since the Quinn sale. It will probably take place in her Rue de l'Odéon Shakespeare shop.

[*Sylvia had told me at this time, with sadness, with grief, that her bookshop and personal finances were at a low ebb and she would have to sell some of her treasures. She asked if I had any American friends who were collectors and might be interested. Because her coming sale was important if melancholy international news, I suggested that I ought to announce it in the Paris Letter in* The New Yorker, *optimistically assuring her it would surely attract the eye of some useful bibliophiles. To my humiliation no Americans who later attended her sale and made purchases seemed to have been brought there by my Paris Letter announcement, a mortification intensified when Sylvia insisted upon giving me, for my effort at least, a numbered uncut first edition of* Ulysses *on vergé d' Arches paper, which carried with it an original page of the manuscript, which Joyce had overwritten with his typical extra entangling sentences, dealing with the so-called Circe incident. This concerned the music-hall actress Fay Arthur and the "non political concupiscence" caused by "Fay Arthur's revelation of white articles of underclothing while she [Fay Arthur] was in the articles."*

It was not until after the second war, in 1950, when Paris was still chill and expensive, that I decided to sell my Ulysses, *which she had given me, for her benefit, without informing her until it was a* fait accompli. *A Boston bibliophile friend of mine, in France for a visit, had happened to say he wished to give a fine modern book to the Morgan Library, one not already included in its collection, his gift to be made in memory of Miss Belle da Costa Greene, a friend of his during her post as the library's first director. What would I suggest as a suitable book? I said that if the library contained no* Ulysses *I myself could furnish one with a rather special history, which I related to him, which I would cede to him at the going market price for such a rarity, adding optimistically (once more!) that it would probably be around five hundred dollars—I hoped. It turned out that the current price at this time was exactly one hundred dollars. This still seems to me shockingly little for a first edition of a book which had in 1922 created such a stir that even pirated copies sold for far more. My only satisfaction was that Sylvia accepted the sum, perhaps because it was so niggardly, without demur and was actually delighted that her volume, and in a way mine, would now belong forever to a great and glorious third party, the Pierpont Morgan Library. In consequence the 1950 Report to the Fellows of the Library announced the acquisition of "a first edition of one of the most famous contemporary novels, James Joyce's Ulysses. This volume is a presentation copy from the publisher, Miss Sylvia Beach, and is in mint condition in its original printed wrappers. Accompanying it is an early draft of the manuscript, a portion of the controversial Circe episode." The card catalogue on the acquisition further noted that it was accompanied by Miss Beach's engraved calling card, pasted on the book's front lining, and bearing her autographed inscription, "For Janet Flanner with Sylvia Beach's love and gratitude."*

She always gave more than she received. Publishing Ulysses was her greatest act of generosity. *

FRÉDÉRIC MISTRAL

From Memoirs

(Frédéric Mistral (1830–1914) was the guiding spirit of a group of Provençal poets—the Félibres, latter-day troubadours who revived and refined their native language as a literary medium.)

And Glaup poured into our crystal glasses a bottle of Châteauneuf-du-Pape that had been aging for seven years, saying solemnly, "To the health of the Félibres! And while we are christening our Renaissance, let us adapt the name to all the shoots that are bound to sprout. First I propose *Félibrarié* as a name for every school of Félibres that includes at least seven members in memory, gentlemen, of the *Pléiade* of Avignon."

"I," said Roumanille, "propose the nice word *Félibreja,* meaning 'to hold a gathering of Félibres,' as we are doing here."

"I," said Mathieu, "contribute the word *Félibrejado,* meaning 'a fellowship of Provençal poets.' "

*From a memorial volume, *Sylvia Beach* (1887–1962) published 1963 in Paris by The Mercure de France and containing reminiscences by various of her friends.

"I," said Tavan, "believe that the adjective *Félibren* would not be a bad way of describing whatever concerns the Félibres."

"I," said Aubanel, "confer the name of *Félibresso* on the ladies who will sing in the Provençal tongue."

"And I," said Brunet, "find that the word *Félibrihoun* would suit the children of the Félibres."

"And I," said Mistral, "conclude with this patriotic cry to designate the work of our association: *'Félibrige, 'Félibrige!'* "

Then Glaup spoke again: "That's not all, my fellow poets. We are the Félibres of the Law. But who is going to establish the Law?"

"I will," said I, "and I swear to you that if it takes me twenty years to demonstrate that our language is a language, I will draw up the articles of law that govern it."

How funny! It sounds like a story, and yet that pledge made on a holiday, a day of poetry and intoxication, resulted in the enormous, absorbing task of my *Tresor dóu Felibrige* or dictionary of the Provençal tongue, which consumed twenty years of a poet's career. . . .

At that truly memorable and now legendary meeting we decided to publish a small annual anthology in the form of an almanac which was to be the ensign of our poetry, the battle flag of our ideas, the link among Félibres, and their means of communicating with the people.

When all that was settled, we noticed that the date of our meeting, the 21st of May, was the feast of Saint Estelle, and like the Magi recognizing the mysterious influence of some conjunction of the spheres, we hailed the Star that presided over the cradle of our redemption.

The Provençal Almanac for the Fine Year of Our Lord 1855 appeared the same year, 112 pages long. At the very front, like a frame for athletic prizes, our "Song of the Félibres" announced the program of that vigorous popular revival. . . .

> We are all friends, all brothers,
> We are the singers of the land!
> As all children love their mothers,
> And all nestlings love their nests,
> So we love our blue sky and our land,
> To us they are a paradise.
>
> We are all friends, joyful and free,
> All enamored of Provence;
> We are the Félibres,
> The merry Félibres of Provence!
>
> In Provençal your thoughts
> Come readily to your lips.

Oh, sweet tongue of Provence,
That's why we love you!
On the pebbles of Durance
We swear this oath today!

We are all friends, etc.

Warblers do not forget
The warbling of their father;
Nightingales do not forget
What their father sang to them;
So how could we forget
The language of our mothers?

We are all friends, etc.

On Sundays while the girls are dancing
To the beat of the little drum,
We like to sit in the shade
Of a fig tree or a pine
And have ourselves a snack
And swig wine from the flask.

We are all friends, etc.

Then as the new wine sparkles,
Bubbles, and laughs in the glass,
If a Félibre utters a word
Of a song he has heard,
All burst into song at once
And all together we sing.

We are all friends, etc.

We love the innocent laughter
Of bright and sprightly girls;
And if we find one pleasing,
We sing her again and again
In our love poems
With the prettiest words we know.

We are all friends, etc.

When the harvest season comes
And the frying pan is busy,
When you're pressing out the vintage

And the grapes are in a ferment,
And you need a little help,
Count on us to all come running.

We are all friends, etc.

We always lead the dance;
To Saint Eloi we raise a toast;
At a wrestling match, we strip;
On Saint John's we leap the fire;
And for the great feast of Christmas
We bring in the Yule log together.

We are all friends, etc.

When you open the sacks in the olive mill
And find you need help with the pressing,
Some fellows to push that heavy bar,
Call us, we're always ready;
You will find us jolly fellows—
There aren't ten like us in the world.

We are all friends, etc.

When it's time for roasting chestnuts
In the season of Saint Martin,
If you want to hear good stories,
Call us, neighbors, for the evening,
And we'll tell you such an earful
It will make you laugh till morning.

We are all friends, etc.

If you need us for your saint's day,
Here we are, no matter when.
And you, newlyweds,
Would a jolly couplet please you?
Invite us, sweethearts, and we'll have
Hundreds for you to choose from.

We are all friends, etc.

When you slaughter the hog,
Don't fail to call on us!
Even on a rainy day,
Count on us to hold the tail:

Nothing's so tasty for dinner
As a morsel of liver or lights.

We are all friends, etc.

People need to work like slaves;
Alas, it's always been that way.
But if you could never speak,
It would be enough to kill you!
You need someone to make you laugh,
You need someone to make you sing!

We are all friends, joyful and free,
All enamored of Provence:
We are the Félibres,
The merry Félibres of Provence!

As you can see, the Félibres did not spawn melancholy or pessimism. Everything was done in high spirits, without any thought of profit or fame. Those who contributed to the first *Almanac* had all taken pseudonyms: the Félibre of the Gardens (Roumanille), the Félibre of the Pomegranate (Aubanel), the Félibre of Kisses (Mathieu), the Playful Félibre (Glaup), the Félibre of the Farm or of Belle-Viste (Mistral), the Félibre of the Army (Tavan, who had drawn an unlucky number), the Félibre of the Rainbow (J. Brunet, who was a painter).

Translated by George Wickes

E. M. FORSTER

From Marianne Thornton: A Domestic Biography

... Marianne adored her. There is an extensive passage in the "Recollections."

But I have yet said nothing of the friend par excellence of my mother, the woman who held that rare place of having been my father's nearest associate and most confidential counsellor before his marriage, and then become the nearest and dearest tie she had out of her own family, to my mother. I mean Mrs Hannah More. I should add Hannah More and her sisters for my parents loved them all, and though Hannah More was the most celebrated, they always thought Patty her equal in talent and goodness. "May is coming and then Hannah will be with us," was one of the earliest hopes of my childhood, and when she did arrive I always felt I had a fresh companion just my own age, and ready to sympathize with all my pleasures and troubles. Her health was always very bad and often prevented her going out for weeks together, and when this was the case and I was too young to go to Church, I was delighted at being left under her care on a Sunday. How well I remember sitting on her bed whilst she discoursed to me about Joseph and his brethren, and all the wonderful adventures of the children of Israel with such eloquence and force that I fancied she must have lived amongst them herself. She was in many ways a charming companion for children, but she had very little power of resisting either persuasion or fun, and I early found I had much more influence over her than I had over my mother. As I grew older I learnt not to take advantage of this. I have this year [1857] revisited that Paradise of my childhood, Barley Wood, and fancied I could once more see the venerable forms, and hear the kind greetings of the 5 hospitable sisters.

Surely there never was such a house, so full of intellect and piety and active benevolence. They lived in such uninterrupted harmony with each other, were so full of their separate pursuits, enjoyed with such interest and vivacity all the pleasures of their beautiful home, or wholly laid aside all the forms of society that were irksome, that young or old one felt oneself in a brighter and happier world, alloyed indeed by the most fearful attacks of illness occasionally, but even when these occurred the patience and cheerfulness of both patient and nurses never failed. I can now imagine our arrival at the door covered with roses, and "the ladies" as they were always called, rushing out to cover us with kisses, and then take us into the kitchen to exhibit us to Mary and Charles, the housemaid and coachman, then running themselves to fetch the tea things, Mrs Patty allowing no one but herself to fry the eggs for "the darling," the brown loaf brought out, the colour of a mahogany table, baked only once a week, of enormous size but excellent taste. Then the 2 cats called "Non-resistance" and "Passive obedience" who were fed by us all day long, and then the next day crowns of flowers were made for ourselves, garlands for the sheep; the peas we were set to pick, and then shell, perched upon the kitchen dresser, while Sally made the room resound with some of her merry stories of the cottagers round, and then we were sent off by ourselves or with some village child to buy chickens at the next farm, and when we returned dragging along our purchases, how we were fed with strawberries and cream, and told to lie down in the hay whilst Charles the coachman, gardener bailiff and carpenter, made us a syllabub under the cow. Then came Sunday—when they were younger "the ladies" rode behind Charles on horseback to the school they meant to visit, but in my time they always went in some odd conveyance on wheels. In those small parishes the service was seldom performed twice in the day and after going with the children to church we dined at some farmer's who was proud to take us in, and then proceeded to the school.

How Bell and Lancaster [educationists] were unknown then, and to read their Bible was the highest summit of knowledge to which they aspired. I chiefly recollect Mrs Hannah's or Mrs Patty's eloquent exhortations made to the whole school in the most familiar homely language, full of anecdotes of the people round them, as well as of the good people who lived in old times, and full of practical piety brought down to such minute details one never hears now. I particularly remember how she explained the fifth commandment, enjoined us to "do errands for mother not saucily or lazily or stupidly" amongst many other small duties that she enumerated. Hannah More was always ready to talk about the literary set with whom she passed her youth. Many an evening has she amused me by describing Johnson and Burke, Horace Walpole, Mrs Montagu and the many personages I had read of in Boswell, and for this reason I suppose no period in history interests me so much. . . .

FORD MADOX FORD

From YOUR MIRROR TO MY TIMES

(Joseph Conrad and Ford Madox Ford collaborated on the novel *Romance*, which was published in 1903.)

I may as well dispose, once and for all, of the legend that I had any part in teaching Conrad English, though, on the face of it, it may well look plausible enough since he was a foreigner who never till the end of his life spoke English other than as a foreigner. But when it came to writing, it was at once quite a different matter. As I said elsewhere a little time ago, the moment he got a pen in his hand and had no eye to publication, Conrad could write English with a speed, a volubility and a banal correctness that used to amaze me. So you have his immense volume of letters. On the other hand, when, as it were, he was going before the public, a species of stage-fright would almost completely paralyse him so that his constructions were frequently very un-English.

In his letters, that is to say, he just let himself go without precision of phrase as without *arrière-pensée,* pouring out supplications, abuse of third parties, eternal and unvarying complaints, so that in the end the impression is left of a weak, rather whining personality. But no impression could be more false. Conrad was a man, a He-man if you like, who fought against enormous odds with undying—with almost unfaltering—courage. And his courage was all the more impressive in that by birth, race and temperament he was an unshakable pessimist. Life for him was predestined to end tragically, or, if not, in banality; literature was foredoomed to failure. These were his *choses données,* his only certain truths. In face of that creed, his struggles were unceasing.

And it was astonishing what small things could call down to his underlying buoyancy. I remember once we had been struggling with *Romance* for hours and hours, and he had been in complete despair, and everything that I had suggested had called forth his bitterest gibes, and he was sick, and over ears in debt, and penniless. And we had come to a blank full-stop—one of those intervals when the soul *must* pause to breathe, and love itself have rest. And Mrs. Conrad came in and said that the mare had trotted from Postling Vents to Sandling in five minutes—say, twelve miles an hour! At once, there in the room was Conrad-Jack-ashore! The world was splendid; hope nodded from every rosebud that looked over the window-sill of the low room. We were going to get a car and go to Canterbury; the mare should have a brand new breeching strap. And in an incredibly short space of time—say, three hours—at least half a page of *Romance* got itself written.

That was how it went, day in day out, for years—the despair, the lamentations continuing for hours and then the sudden desperate attack on the work—the attack that would become the fabulous engrossment. We would write for whole days, for half nights, for half the day, or all the night. We would jot down passages on scraps of paper or on the margins of books, handing them one to the other or exchanging them. We would roar with laughter over passages that would have struck no other soul as humorous; Conrad would howl with rage and I would almost sigh over others that no other soul perhaps would have found as bad as we considered them. We would recoil one from the other and go each to our own cottage—our cottages at that period never being further the one from the other than an old mare could take us in an afternoon. In those

cottages we would prepare other drafts and so drive backwards and forwards with packages of manuscript under the dog-cart seats. We drove
in the heat of summer, through the deluges of autumn, with the winter
snows blinding our eyes—always, always with manuscripts. Heavens,
don't my fingers still tingle with the feeling of undoing the stiff buckles,
long past midnight, of a horse streaming with rain—and the rubbing
down in the stable and the backing the cart into the coach-house. And
with always at the back of the mind, the consideration of some unfinished passage, the puzzledom to avoid some too-used phrase that yet
seemed hypnotically inevitable.

There was an occasion when the whole of the manuscript of the last
instalment of *The End of the Tether* for *Blackwood's* was burnt shortly
before it was due for publication. That sounds a small thing. But the
instalments of *Blackwood's* are pretty long and the idea of letting *Maga*
miss an instalment appalled: it was the almost unthinkable crime. . . .
The manuscript had been lying on the round, Madox Brown table,
under a paraffin-lamp with a glass reservoir, no doubt also an 1840 con-
trivance: the reservoir had burst. . . . For a day or so it was like a funeral;
then for moral support or because his writing-room was burnt out, Conrad drove over to Winchelsea, to which Ancient Town the writer had
removed. Then you should have seen Romance! It became a matter of
days; then of hours. Conrad wrote; I corrected the manuscript behind
him or wrote in a sentence—I in my study on the street, Conrad in a
two-roomed cottage that we had hired immediately opposite. The household sat up all night keeping soups warm. In the middle of the night
Conrad would open his window and shout, "For heaven's sake give me
something for *sale pochard;* it's been holding me up for an hour." I
called back, "Confounded swilling pig!" across the dead-still, grass-
grown street.

Telegrams went back and forth between ancient Winchelsea and the
ancient house of Blackwood in Edinburgh. So ancient was that house
that it was said to send its proofs from London to Edinburgh and back by
horse-messenger. We started the manuscript like that. Our telegrams
would ask what was the latest day, the latest hour, the latest half minute
that would do if *The End of the Tether* was to catch the presses. *Blackwood's* answered, at first Wednesday morning, then Thursday. Then
Friday night would be just possible. . . . At two in the morning the
mare—another mare by then—was saddled by the writer and the stable-
boy. The stable boy was to ride to the junction with the manuscript and
catch the six-in-the-morning mail-train. The soup kept hot; the writers
wrote. By three I had done all that I could in my room. I went across the
road to where Conrad was still at it. Conrad said, "For God's sake. . . .
Another half-hour; just finishing. . . ." At four I looked over Conrad's

shoulder. He was writing, "The blow had come, softened by the spaces of the earth, by the years of absence." I said, "You must finish now." To Ashford Junction was eighteen miles. Conrad muttered, "Just two paragraphs more." He wrote, "There had been whole days when she had not thought of him at all—had no time." I said, "You absolutely must stop!" Conrad wrote on, "But she loved him, she felt that she loved him after all," and muttered, "Two paragraphs. . . ." I shouted—it had come to me as an inspiration—"In the name of God, don't you know you can write those two paragraphs into the proofs when you get them back? . . ."

The occupation of writing to such a nature as Conrad's is terribly engrossing. To be suddenly disturbed is apt to cause a second's real madness. . . . We were once going up to town in order to take some proofs to a publisher, and half-way between Sandling and Charing Cross Conrad remembered some phrase that he had forgotten to attend to in the proofs. He tried to correct them with a pencil, but the train jolted so badly that writing, sitting on a seat, was impossible. Conrad got down on the floor of the carriage and lying on his stomach went on writing. Naturally when the one phrase was corrected twenty other necessities for correction stuck out of the page. We were alone in the carriage. The train passed Paddock Wood, passed Orpington, rushed through the suburbs. I said, "We're getting into town!" Conrad never moved except to write. The houseroofs of London whirled in perspective round us; the shadow of Cannon Street Station was over us. Conrad wrote. The final shadow of Charing Cross was over us. It must have been very difficult to see down there. He never moved. . . . Mildly shocked at the idea that a porter might open the carriage door and think us peculiar, I touched Conrad on the shoulder and said, "We're there!" Conrad's face was most extraordinary—suffused and madly vicious. He sprang to his feet and straight at my throat. . . .

OSCAR WILDE

From DE PROFUNDIS

Three more months go over. The calendar of my daily conduct and labour that hangs on the outside of my cell-door, with my name and sentence written upon it, tells me that it is Maytime. My friends come to see me again. I enquire, as I always do, after you. I am told that you are in your villa at Naples, and are bringing out a volume of poems. At the close of the interview it is mentioned casually that you are dedicating them to me. The tidings seemed to give me a sort of nausea of life. I said nothing, but silently went back to my cell with contempt and scorn in my heart. How could you dream of dedicating a volume of poems to me without first asking my permission? Dream, do I say? How could you dare to do such a thing? . . .

Where there is Sorrow there is holy ground. Some day you will realise what that means. You will know nothing of life till you do. Robbie, and natures like his, can realise it. When I was brought down from my prison to the Court of Bankruptcy between two policemen, Robbie waited in the long dreary corridor, that before the whole crowd, whom an action so sweet and simple hushed into silence, he might gravely raise his hat to me, as handcuffed and with bowed head I passed him by. Men have gone to heaven for smaller things than that. It was in this spirit, and with this mode of love that the saints knelt down to wash the feet of the poor, or stooped to kiss the leper on the cheek. I have never said one single word to him about what he did. I do not know to the present moment whether he is aware that I was even conscious of his action. It is not a thing for which one can render formal thanks in formal words. I store it in the treasury-house of my heart. I keep it there as a secret debt that I am glad to think I can never possibly repay. It is embalmed and kept sweet by the myrrh and cassia of many tears. When Wisdom has been profitless to me, and Philosophy barren, and the proverbs and phrases of those who have sought to give me consolation as dust and ashes in my mouth, the memory of that little lowly silent act of Love has unsealed for me all the wells of pity, made the desert blossom like a rose, and brought me out of the bitterness of lonely exile into harmony with the wounded, broken and great heart of the world. When you are able to understand, not merely how beautiful Robbie's action was, but why it meant so much to me, and always will mean so much, then, perhaps, you will realise how and in what spirit you should have approached me for permission to dedicate to me your verses. . . .

While I was in Wandsworth Prison I longed to die. It was my one desire. When after two months in the Infirmary I was transferred here, and found myself growing gradually better in physical health, I was filled with rage. I determined to commit suicide on the very day on which I left prison. After a time that evil mood passed away, and I made up my mind to live, but to wear gloom as a King wears purple: never to smile again: to turn whatever house I entered into a house of mourning: to make my friends walk slowly in sadness with me: to teach them that melancholy is the true secret of life: to maim them with an alien sorrow: to mar them with my own pain. Now I feel quite differently. I see it would be both ungrateful and unkind of me to pull so long a face that when my friends came to see me they would have to make their faces still longer in order to show their sympathy, or, if I desired to entertain them, to invite them to sit down silently to bitter herbs and funeral backed meats. I must learn how to be cheerful and happy.

The last two occasions on which I was allowed to see my friends here I tried to be as cheerful as possible, and to show my cheerfulness in order to make them some slight return for their trouble in coming all the way from town to visit me. It is only a slight return, I know, but it is the one, I feel certain, that pleases them most. I saw Robbie for an hour on Saturday week, and I tried to give the fullest possible expression to the delight I really felt at our meeting. And that, in the views and ideas I am here shaping for myself, I am quite right is shown to me by the fact that now for the first time since my imprisonment I have a real desire to live. . . .

If after I go out a friend of mine gave a feast, and did not invite me to it, I shouldn't mind a bit. I can be perfectly happy by myself. With freedom, books, flowers, and the moon, who could not be happy? Besides, feasts are not for me any more. I have given too many to care about them. That side of life is over for me, very fortunately I dare say. But if, after I go out, a friend of mine had a sorrow, and refused to allow me to share it, I should feel it most bitterly. If he shut the doors of the house of mourning against me I would come back again and again and beg to be admitted, so that I might share in what I was entitled to share in. If he thought me unworthy, unfit to weep with him, I should feel it as the most poignant humiliation, as the most terrible mode in which disgrace could be inflicted on me. But that could not be. I have a right to share in Sorrow, and he who can look at the loveliness of the world, and share its sorrow, and realise something of the wonder of both, is in immediate contact with divine things, and has got as near to God's secret as anyone can get.

FREDERICK DOUGLASS

From NARRATIVE OF THE LIFE OF FREDERICK DOUGLASS, AN AMERICAN SLAVE

. . .For the ease with which I passed the year, I was, however, somewhat indebted to the society of my fellow-slaves. They were noble souls; they not only possessed loving hearts, but brave ones. We were linked and interlinked with each other. I loved them with a love stronger than any thing I have experienced since. It is sometimes said that we slaves do not love and confide in each other. In answer to this assertion, I can say, I never loved any or confided in any people more than my fellow-slaves, and especially those with whom I lived at Mr. Freeland's. I believe we would have died for each other. We never undertook to do any thing, of any importance, without a mutual consultation. We never moved separately. We were one; and as much so by our tempers and dispositions, as by the mutual hardships to which we were necessarily subjected by our condition as slaves. . . .

(In the passage that follows Douglass describes the eve of his second—and successful—attempt to escape North from slavery.)

. . . It is impossible for me to describe my feelings as the time of my contemplated start drew near. I had a number of warm-hearted friends in Baltimore,—friends that I loved almost as I did my life,—and the thought of being separated from them forever was painful beyond expression. It is my opinion that thousands would escape from slavery, who now remain, but for the strong cords of affection that bind them to their friends. The thought of leaving my friends was decidedly the most painful thought with which I had to contend. The love of them was my tender point, and shook my decision more than all things else. Besides the pain of separation, the dread and apprehension of a failure exceeded what I had experienced at my first attempt. The appalling defeat I then sustained returned to torment me. I felt assured that, if I failed in this attempt, my case would be a hopeless one—it would seal my fate as a slave forever. I could not hope to get off with any thing less than the severest punishment, and being placed beyond the means of escape. It required no very vivid imagination to depict the most frightful scenes through which I should have to pass, in case I failed. The wretchedness of slavery, and the blessedness of freedom, were perpetually before me. It was life and death with me. But I remained firm, and, according to my resolution, on the third day of September, 1838, I left my chains, and succeeded in reaching New York without the slightest interruption of any kind. . . .

FRANCIS PARKMAN

From PIONEERS OF FRANCE IN THE NEW WORLD

On the twenty-fifth of June, 1564, a French squadron anchored a second time off the mouth of the River of May. There were three vessels, the smallest of sixty tons, the largest of one hundred and twenty, all crowded with men. René de Laudonnière held command. . . . Adventurous gentlemen, reckless soldiers, discontented tradesmen, all keen for novelty and heated with dreams of wealth,—these were they who would build for their country and their religion an empire beyond the sea.

On Thursday, the twenty-second of June, Laudonnière saw the low coast line of Florida, and entered the harbor of St. Augustine, which he named the River of Dolphins, "because that at mine arrival I saw there a great number of Dolphins which were playing in the mouth thereof." Then he bore northward, following the coast till, on the twenty-fifth, he reached the mouth of the St. John's or River of May. The vessels anchored, the boats were lowered, and he landed with his principal followers on the south shore, near the present village of Mayport. It was the very spot where he had landed with Ribaut two years before. They were scarcely on shore when they saw an Indian chief, "which having espied us cryed very far off, *Antipola, Antipola,* and being so joyful that he could not containe himselfe, he came to meet us accompanied with two of his sonnes, as faire and mightie persons as might be found in al the world. There was in their trayne a great number of men and women which stil made very much of us, and by signes made us understand how glad they were of our arrivall. This good entertainment past, the Paracoussy [chief] prayed me to goe see the pillar which we had erected in the voyage of John Ribault." The Indians, regarding it with mysterious awe, had crowned it with evergreens, and placed baskets full of maize before it as an offering.

The chief then took Laudonnière by the hand, telling him that he was named Satouriona, and pointed out the extent of his dominions, far up the river and along the adjacent coasts. One of his sons, a man "perfect in beautie, wisedome, and honest sobrietie," then gave the French commander a wedge of silver, and received some trifles in return, after which the voyagers went back to their ships. "I prayse God continually," says Laudonnière, "for the great love I have found in these savages."

In the morning the French landed again, and found their new friends on the same spot, to the number of eighty or more, seated under a shelter of boughs, in festal attire of smoke-tanned deer-skins, painted in many colors. The party then rowed up the river, the Indians following them along the shore. As they advanced, coasting the borders of a great marsh that lay upon their left, the St. John's spread before them in vast sheets of glistening water, almost level with its flat, sedgy shores, the haunt of alligators, and the resort of innumerable birds. Beyond the marsh, some five miles from the mouth of the river, they saw a ridge of high ground abutting on the water, which, flowing beneath in a deep, strong current, had undermined it, and left a steep front of yellowish sand. This was the hill now called St. John's Bluff. Here they landed and entered the woods, where Laudonnière stopped to rest while his lieutenant, Ottigny, with a sergeant and a few soldiers, went to explore the country.

They pushed their way through the thickets till they were stopped by a marsh choked with reeds, at the edge of which, under a great laurel tree, they had seated themselves to rest, overcome with the summer heat, when five Indians suddenly appeared, peering timidly at them from among the bushes. Some of the men went towards them with signs of friendship, on which, taking heart, they drew near, and one of them, who was evidently a chief, made a long speech, inviting the strangers to their dwellings. The way was across the marsh, through which they carried the lieutenant and two or three of the soldiers on their backs, while the rest circled by a narrow path through the woods. When they reached the lodges, a crowd of Indians came out "to receive our men gallantly, and feast them after their manner." One of them brought a large earthen vessel full of spring water, which was served out to each in turn in a wooden cup. But what most astonished the French was a venerable chief, who assured them that he was the father of five successive generations, and that he had lived two hundred and fifty years. Opposite sat a still more ancient veteran, the father of the first, shrunken to a mere anatomy, and "seeming to be rather a dead carkeis than a living body." "Also," pursues the history, "his age was so great that the good man had lost his sight, and could not speak one onely word but with exceeding great paine." In spite of his dismal condition, the visitors were told that he might expect to live, in the course of nature, thirty or forty years more. As the two patriarchs sat face to face, half hidden with their streaming white hair, Ottigny and his credulous soldiers looked from one to the other, lost in speechless admiration.

One of these veterans made a parting present to his guests of two young eagles, and Ottigny and his followers returned to report what they had seen. Laudonnière was waiting for them on the side of the hill, and now, he says, "I went right to the toppe thereof, where we found nothing else but Cedars, Palme, and Baytrees of so sovereigne odour that Baulme smelleth nothing like in comparison." From this high standpoint they surveyed their Canaan. The unruffled river lay before them, with its marshy islands overgrown with sedge and bulrushes, while on the farther side the flat, green meadows spread mile on mile, veined with countless creeks and belts of torpid water, and bounded leagues away by the verge of the dim pine forest. On the right, the sea glistened along the horizon, and on the left, the St. John's stretched westward between verdant shores, a highway to their fancied Eldorado. . . .

ELIZABETH BISHOP

Gwendolyn

My Aunt Mary was eighteen years old and away in "the States," in Boston, training to be a nurse. In the bottom bureau drawer in her room, well wrapped in soft pink tissue paper, lay her best doll. That winter, I had been sick with bronchitis for a long time, and my grandmother finally produced it for me to play with, to my amazement and delight, because I had never even known of its existence before. It was a girl doll, but my grandmother had forgotten her name.

She had a large wardrobe, which my Aunt Mary had made, packed in a toy steamer trunk of green tin embossed with all the proper boards, locks, and nailheads. The clothes were wonderful garments, beautifully sewn, looking old-fashioned even to me. There were long drawers trimmed with tiny lace, and a corset cover, and a corset with little bones. These were exciting, but best of all was the skating costume. There was a red velvet coat, and a turban and muff of some sort of moth-eaten brown fur, and, to make it almost unbearably thrilling, there was a pair of laced white glacé-kid boots, which had scalloped tops and a pair of too small, dull-edged, but very shiny skates loosely attached to their soles by my Aunt Mary with stitches of coarse white thread.

The looseness of the skates didn't bother me. It went very well with the doll's personality, which in turn was well suited to the role of companion to an invalid. She had lain in her drawer so long that the elastic in her joints had become weakened; when you held her up, her head fell gently to one side, and her outstretched hand would rest on yours for a moment and then slip wearily off. She made the family of dolls I usually played with seem rugged and childish: the Campbell Kid doll, with a childlike scar on her forehead where she had fallen against the fender; the two crudely felt-dressed Indians, Hiawatha and Nokomis; and the stocky "baby doll," always holding out his arms to be picked up.

My grandmother was very nice to me when I was sick. During this same illness, she had already given me her button basket to play with, and her scrap bag, and the crazy quilt was put over my bed in the afternoons. The button basket was large and squashed and must have weighed ten pounds, filled with everything from the metal snaps for men's overalls to a set of large cut-steel buttons with deer heads with green glass eyes on them. The scrap bag was interesting because in it I could find pieces of my grandmother's house dresses that she was wearing right then, and pieces of my grandfather's Sunday shirts. But the crazy quilt was the best entertainment. My grandmother had made it long before, when such quilts had been a fad in the little Nova Scotian village where we lived. She had collected small, irregularly shaped pieces of silk or velvet of all colors and got all her lady and gentleman friends to write their names on them in pencil—their names, and sometimes a date or word or two as well. Then she had gone over the writing in chain stitch with silks of different colors, and then put the whole thing together on maroon flannel, with feather-stitching joining the pieces. I could read well enough to make out the names of people I knew, and then my grandmother would sometimes tell me that that particular piece of silk came from Mrs. So-and-So's "going-away" dress, forty years ago, or that that was from a necktie of one of her brothers, since dead and buried in London, or that that was from India, brought back by another brother, who was a missionary.

When it grew dark—and this, of course, was very early—she would take me out of bed, wrap me in a blanket, and, holding me on her knees, rock me vigorously in the rocking chair. I think she enjoyed this exercise as much as I did, because she would sing me hymns, in her rather affectedly lugubrious voice, which suddenly thinned out to half its ordinary volume on the higher notes. She sang me "There is a green hill far away," "Will there be any stars in my crown?" and "In the sweet bye-and-bye." Then there were more specifically children's hymns, such as:

> Little children, little children,
> Who love their Redeemer,
> Are the jewels, precious jewels,
> Bright gems for his crown
> . . .

And then, perhaps because we were Baptists—nice watery ones—all the saints casting down their crowns (in what kind of a tantrum?) "around the glassy sea"; "Shall we gather at the river?"; and her favorite, "Happy day, happy day, when Jesus washed my sins away."

This is preliminary. The story of Gwendolyn did not begin until the following summer, when I was in my usual summer state of good health and had forgotten about the bronchitis, the realistic cat-and-kitten family in my chest, and the doctor's cold stethoscope.

Gwendolyn Appletree was the youngest child and only daughter of a large, widely spaced family that lived away out, four or five miles, on a lonely farm among the fir trees. She was a year or so older than I—that is, about eight—and her five or six brothers, I suppose in their teens, seemed like grown men to me. But Gwendolyn and I, although we didn't see each other very often, were friends, and to me she stood for everything that the slightly repellent but fascinating words "little girl" should mean. In the first place, her beautiful name. Its dactyl trisyllables could have gone on forever as far as I was concerned. And then, although older, she was as small as I was, and blond, and pink and white, exactly like a blossoming apple tree. And she was "delicate," which, in spite of the bronchitis, I was not. She had diabetes. I had been told this much and had some vague idea that it was because of "too much sugar," and that in itself made Gwendolyn even more attractive, as if she would prove to be solid candy if you bit her, and her pure-tinted complexion would taste exactly like the icing-sugar Easter eggs or birthday-candle holders, held to be inedible, except that I knew better.

I don't know what the treatment for diabetes was at that time—whether, for example, Gwendolyn was given insulin or not, but I rather think not. My grandparents, however, often spoke disapprovingly of the way her parents would not obey the doctor's orders and gave her whatever she wanted to eat, including two pieces of cake for tea, and of how, if they weren't more sensible, they would never keep her. Every once in a while, she would have a mysterious attack of some sort, "convulsions" or a "coma," but a day or two later I would see her driving with her father to the store right next door to our house, looking the same as ever and waving to me. Occasionally, she would be brought to spend the day or afternoon with me while her parents drove down the shore to visit relatives.

These were wonderful occasions. She would arrive carrying a doll or some other toy; her mother would bring a cake or a jar of preserves for my grandmother. Then I would have the opportunity of showing her all my possessions all over again. Quite often, what she brought was a set of small blocks that exactly fitted in a shallow cardboard box. These blocks were squares cut diagonally across, in clear reds, yellows, and blues, and we arranged them snugly together in geometric designs. Then, if we were careful, the whole thing could be lifted up and turned over, revealing a similar brilliant design in different colors on the other side. These designs were completely satisfying in their forthrightness, like the Union Jack. We played quietly together and did not quarrel.

Before her mother and father drove off in their buggy, Gwendolyn was embraced over and over, her face was washed one last time, her stockings were pulled up, her nose was wiped, she was hoisted up and down and swung around and around by her father and given some white pills by her mother. This sometimes went on so long that my grandfather would leave abruptly for the barn and my grandmother would busy herself at the sink and start singing a hymn under her breath, but it was nothing to the scenes of tenderness when they returned a few hours later. Then her parents almost ate her up, alternately, as if she really were made of sugar, as I half suspected. I watched these exciting scenes with envy until Mr. and Mrs. Appletree drove away, with Gwendolyn standing between them in her white dress, her pale-gold hair blowing, still being kissed from either side. Although I received many demonstrations of affection from my grandparents, they were nothing like this. My grandmother was disgusted. "They'll kiss that child to death if they're not careful," she said. "Oh, lallygagging, lallygagging!" said my grandfather, going on about his business.

I remember clearly three episodes of that summer in which Gwendolyn played the role of beautiful heroine—the role that grew and grew until finally it had grown far beyond the slight but convincing talents she had for acting it.

Once, my grandparents and I went to a church picnic. As I said, we were Baptists, but most of the village, including the Appletrees, were Presbyterians. However, on social occasions I think the two sects sometimes joined forces, or else we were broad-minded enough to go to a Presbyterian picnic—I'm not sure. Anyway, the three of us, dressed in our second-best, took a huge picnic supper and drove behind Nimble II to the picnic grounds beside the river. It was a beautiful spot; there were large spruce and pine trees right to the edge of the clear brown water and mossy terra-cotta-colored rocks; the ground was slippery with brown pine needles. Pans of beans and biscuits and scalloped potatoes were set out on long tables, and all our varieties of pickles and relishes (chowchows and piccalillis), conserves and preserves, cakes and pies, parkins and hermits—all glistening and gleaming in the late sunshine—and water for tea was being brought to the boil over two fires. My grandmother settled herself on a log to talk to her friends, and I went wading in the river with mine. My cousin Billy was there, and Seth Hill, and the little McNeil twins, but Gwendolyn was missing. Later, I joined my family for supper, or as all Nova Scotians call their suppers, "tea." My grandmother spoke to one of the Appletree boys, filling his plate beside us, and asked him where his father and mother were, and how Gwendolyn was.

"Pretty poorly," he answered, with an imitative elderly-man shake of his head. "Ma thought we'd lost her yesterday morning. I drove down and got the doctor. She's resting better today, though."

We went on drinking our tea and eating in silence, and after a while my grandfather started talking about something else. But just before we finished, when it was beginning to get gray, and a sweet, dank, freshwater smell had suddenly started to come up off the river, a horse and buggy turned rapidly in to the picnic grounds and pulled up beside us. In it were Mr. and Mrs. Appletree, and Gwendolyn—standing between them, as usual—wearing one of her white dresses, with a little black-and-white-checked coat over it. A great fuss was made over them and her, and my grandfather lifted her down and held her on his knee, sitting on one of the rough benches beside the picnic tables. I leaned against him, but Gwendolyn wouldn't speak to me; she just smiled as if very pleased with everything. She looked prettier and more delicate than ever, and her cheeks were bright pink. Her mother made her a cup of weak tea, and I could see my grandmother's look as the sugar went into it. Gwendolyn had wanted to come so badly, her mother said, so they thought they'd bring her just for a little while.

Some time after this, Gwendolyn was brought to visit me again, but this time she was to spend the whole day and night and part of the next day. I was very excited, and consulted with my grandmother endlessly as to how we should pass the time—if I could jump with her in the barn or take her swimming in the river. No, both those sports were too strenuous for Gwendolyn, but we could play at filling bottles with colored water (made from the paints in my paintbox), my favorite game at the moment, and in the afternoon we could have a dolls' tea party.

Everything went off very well. After dinner, Gwendolyn went and lay on the sofa in the parlor, and my grandmother put a shawl over her. I wanted to pretend to play the piano to her, but I was made to stop and go outside by myself. After a while, Gwendolyn joined me in the flower garden and we had the tea party. After that, I showed her how to trap bumblebees in the foxgloves, but that was also put a stop to by my grandmother as too strenuous and dangerous. Our play was not without a touch of rustic corruption, either. I can't remember what happened, if anything, but I do remember being ordered out of the whitewashed privy in the barn after we had locked ourselves in and climbed on the seats and hung out the little window, with its beautiful view of the elm-studded "interval" in back of us. It was just getting dark; my grandmother was very stern with me and said we must never lock ourselves in there, but she was objectionably kind to Gwendolyn, who looked more angelic than ever.

After tea, we sat at the table with the oil lamp hanging over it for a while, playing with the wonderful blocks, and then it was bedtime. Gwendolyn was going to sleep in my bed with me. I was so overwrought with the novelty of this that it took me a long time to get ready for bed, but Gwendolyn was ready in a jiffy and lay on the far side of the bed with her eyes shut, trying to make me think she was asleep, with the lamplight shining on her blond, blond hair. I asked her if she didn't say her prayers before she got into bed and she said no, her mother let her say them in bed, "because I'm going to die."

At least, that was what I thought she said. I couldn't quite believe I had really heard her say it and I certainly couldn't ask her if she had said it. My heart pounding, I brushed my teeth with the icy well water, and spat in the china pot. Then I got down on my knees and said my own prayers, half aloud, completely mechanically, while the pounding went on and on. I couldn't seem to make myself get into my side of the bed, so I went around and picked up Gwendolyn's clothes. She had thrown them on the floor. I put them over the back of a chair—the blue-and-white-striped dress, the waist, the long brown stockings. Her drawers had lace around the legs, but they were very dirty. This fact shocked me so deeply that I recovered my voice and started asking her more questions.

"I'm asleep," said Gwendolyn, without opening her eyes.

But after my grandmother had turned out the lamp, Gwendolyn began to talk to me again. We told each other which colors we liked best together, and I remember the feeling of profound originality I experienced when I insisted, although it had just occurred to me, that I had always liked black and brown together best. I saw them floating in little patches of velvet, like the crazy quilt, or smooth little rectangles of enamel, like the paint-sample cards I was always begging for at the general store.

Two days after this visit, Gwendolyn did die. One of her brothers came in to tell my grandmother—and I was there in the kitchen when he told her—with more of the elderly-man headshakes and some sad and ancient phrases. My grandmother wept and wiped her eyes with her apron, answering him with phrases equally sad and ancient. The funeral was to be two days later, but I was not going to be allowed to go.

My grandfather went, but not my grandmother. I wasn't even supposed to know what was taking place, but since the Presbyterian church was right across the village green from our house, and I could hear the buggies driving up over the gravel, and then the bell beginning to ring, I knew quite well, and my heart began to pound again, apparently as loudly as the bell was ringing. I was sent out to play in the yard at the far side of the house, away from the church. But through one of the kitchen windows—the kitchen was an ell that had windows on both sides—I could see my curious grandmother drawing up her rocking chair, as she did every Sunday morning, just behind a window on the other side of the ell, to watch the Presbyterians going to church. This was the unacknowledged practice of the Baptists who lived within sight of the church, and later, when they met at their own afternoon service, they would innocently say to each other things like "They had a good turnout this morning" and "Is Mrs. Peppard still laid up? I missed her this morning."

But today it was quite different, and when I peeked in at my grandmother at one side of the ell, she was crying and crying between her own peeks at the mourners out the other side. She had a handkerchief already very wet, and was rocking gently.

It was too much for me. I sneaked back into the house by the side door and into the shut-up parlor, where I could look across at the church, too. There were long lace curtains at the window and the foxgloves and bees were just outside, but I had a perfectly clear, although lace-patterned, view of everything. The church was quite large—a Gothic structure made of white clapboards, with non-flying buttresses, and a tall wooden steeple—and I was as familiar with it as I was with my grandmother. I used to play hide-and-seek among the buttresses with my friends. The buggy sheds, now all filled, were at the back, and around the large grass plot were white wooden pillars with double chains slung slackly between them, on which my cousin Billy, who lived right next door to the church, and I liked to clamber and swing.

At last, everyone seemed to have gone inside, and an inner door shut. No, two men in black stood talking together in the open outside door-way. The bell suddenly stopped ringing and the two men vanished, and I was afraid of being in the parlor alone, but couldn't leave now. Hours seemed to go by. There was some singing, but I didn't recognize the hymns, either because I was too nervous or because, as they sometimes did, the Presbyterians sang hymns unfamiliar to me.

I had seen many funerals like this before, of course, and I loved to go with my grandfather when he went to the graveyard with a scythe and a sickle to cut the grass on our family's graves. The graveyard belonging to the village was surely one of the prettiest in the world. It was on the bank of the river, two miles below us, but where the bank was high. It lay small and green and white, with its firs and cedars and gravestones balancing against the dreaming lavender-red Bay of Fundy. The headstones were mostly rather thin, coarse white marble slabs, frequently leaning slightly, but there was a scattering of small urns and obelisks and broken columns. A few plots were lightly chained in, like the Presbyterian church, or fenced in with wood or iron, like little gardens, and wild rosebushes grew in the grass. Blueberries grew there, too, but I didn't eat them, because I felt I "never knew," as people said, but once when I went there, my grandmother had given me a teacup without a handle and requested me to bring her back some teaberries, which "grew good" on the graves, and I had.

And so I used to play while my grandfather, wearing a straw hat, scythed away, and talked to me haphazardly about the people lying there. I was, of course, particularly interested in the children's graves, their names, what ages they had died at—whether they were older than I or younger. The favorite memorial for small children was a low rectangle of the same coarse white marble as the larger stones, but with a little lamb recumbent on top. I adored these lambs, and counted them and caressed them and sat on them. Some were almost covered by dry, bright-gold lichen, some with green and gold and gray mixed together, some were almost lost among the long grass and roses and blueberries and teaberries.

But now, suddenly, as I watched through the window, something happened at the church across the way. Something that could not possibly have happened, so that I must, in reality, have seen something like it and imagined the rest; or my concentration on the one thing was so intense that I could see nothing else.

The two men in black appeared again, carrying Gwendolyn's small white coffin between them. Then—this was the impossibility—they put it down just outside the church door, one end on the grass and the other lifted up a little, to lean at a slight angle against the wall. Then they disappeared inside again. For a minute, I stared straight through my lace curtain at Gwendolyn's coffin, with Gwendolyn shut invisibly inside it forever, there, completely alone on the grass by the church door.

Then I ran howling to the back door, out among the startled white hens, with my grandmother, still weeping, after me.

If I care to, I can bring back the exact sensation of that moment today, but then, it is also one of those that from time to time are terrifyingly thrust upon us. I was familiar with it and recognized it; I had already experienced it once, shortly before the bronchitis attack of the previous winter. One evening, we were all sitting around the table with the lamp hanging above it; my grandfather was dozing in the Morris chair, my grandmother was crocheting, and my Aunt Mary, who had not yet gone away to Boston, was reading *Maclean's Magazine.* I was drawing pictures when suddenly I remembered something, a present that had been given to me months before and that I had forgotten all about. It was a strawberry basket half filled with new marbles—clay ones, in the usual mottled shades of red, brown, purple, and green. However, in among them were several of a sort I had never seen before: fine, unglazed, cream-colored clay, with purple and pink lines around them. One or two of the larger ones of this sort even had little sprigs of flowers on them. But the most beautiful of all, I thought, was a really big one, probably an inch and a half in diameter, of a roughly shiny glazed pink, like crockery. It moved me almost to tears to look at it; it "went right through me."

Anyway, I started thinking about these marbles—wondering where they had been all this time, where I had put them, if they had got lost—until at last it became unbearable and I had to go and find them. I went out to the kitchen in the dark and groped around on the floor of a cupboard where I kept some of my belongings. I felt the edges of riffled old books and sharp mechanical toys, and then, at the back, I did feel the strawberry basket. I dragged it out and carried it into the sitting room.

My relatives paid no attention. I stared into the basket and took out a few of the marbles. But what could have happened? They were covered with dirt and dust, nails were lying mixed in with them, bits of string, cobwebs, old horse chestnuts blue with mildew, their polish gone. The big pink marble was there, but I hardly recognized it, all covered with dirt. (Later, when my grandmother washed it off, it was as good as new, of course.) The broad lamp flame started to blur; my aunt's fair hair started to blur; I put my head down on top of the marbles and cried aloud. My grandfather woke up with a jerk and said, "Heavens, what ails the child now?" Everyone tried to comfort me—for what, they had no idea.

A month or so after the funeral—it was still summer—my grandparents went away for the day to visit Cousin Sophy, "over the mountain." I was supposed to stay with another aunt, the mother of my cousin Billy, and to play with him while they were gone. But we soon left his yard and wandered back to mine, which was larger and more interesting, and where we felt the additional charm of being all alone and unwatched. Various diversions, quarrels, and reconcilations made up the long, sunny afternoon. We sucked water from jelly glasses through chive straws until we reeked of them, and fought for the possession of insects in matchboxes. To tease me, Billy deliberately stepped on one of the boxes and crushed its inhabitant flat. When we had made up after this violence, we sat and talked for a while, desultorily, about death in general, and going to heaven, but we were growing a little bored and reckless, and finally I did something really bad: I went in the house and upstairs to my Aunt Mary's bedroom and brought down the tissue-paper-wrapped, retired doll. Billy had never seen her before and was as impressed with her as I had been.

We handled her carefully. We took off her hat and shoes and stockings, and examined every stitch of her underclothes. Then we played vaguely at "operating" on her stomach, but we were rather too much in awe of her for that to be a success. Then we had the idea of adorning her with flowers. There was a clump of Johnny-jump-ups that I thought belonged to me; we picked them and made a wreath for the nameless doll. We laid her out in the garden path and outlined her body with Johnny-jump-ups and babies'-breath and put a pink cosmos in one limp hand. She looked perfectly beautiful. The game was more exciting than "operation." I don't know which one of us said it first, but one of us did, with wild joy—that it was Gwendolyn's funeral, and that the doll's real name, all this time, was Gwendolyn.

But then my grandparents drove into the yard and found us, and my grandmother was furious that I had dared to touch Aunt Mary's doll. Billy was sent straight home and I don't remember now what awful thing happened to me.

REYNOLDS PRICE

From CLEAR PICTURES

When I was eleven and had just completed five grades in the same good public school in Asheboro, Will was offered a better job. This time he'd manage the sale of appliances in all of eastern North Carolina for the Farmers Cooperative Exchange, a young but thriving co-op centered in Raleigh. We would finally begin to be solvent. And what was even more attractive for him and Elizabeth, it would let us reel in the hundred miles of navel string between themselves and the family homes we trekked to visit over such long roads—we could live once more in Warren County.

With the big exceptions of Ida and Mac, I liked my country relatives in varying degrees. But I hated the thought of leaving Asheboro, the town where I'd lived for as long as I had substantial memory. I was prospering at school, and I relished the work. I had dozens of friends with whom I played everything from football to King Arthur model-dolls, and I had no enemies. There were three first-run picture shows, and I was midway through a sweep of the possible Cub Scout ranks and eager for the Boy Scouts. No part of town was foreign to me and my friends on our bikes; and far as I could see, I was in firm control of a long clear future. In addition, my body had lately begun to notice itself with sensuous care—my own best irreplaceable, and apparently inexhaustible, toy. It, like all my other contentments, was socketed deeply in this one place—the only home I really remembered. Any move would ruin or scatter it all. No Russian prince ever faced exile with stronger fears.

When Will's offer came, school had just turned out for the summer. So I had long hot days for dread and hope. And I took to my knees in fervent prayer—let him not take the job; let us stay on here. But in early July I met with my first bitter No from the sky. Will took the job, he and Elizabeth went up to scout a likely house, we'd leave in early August. My sadness tainted my parents' relieved delight—prosperity at last, in the bosom of home—but the coming change lay on me with a heaviness that proved prophetic. In the last weeks before moving, I avoided sight of all my friends. Loneliness was better than a frenzied last bout of company.

David Sumner, Harry Anderson, Chisholm Story—the names are still a
little hard to say, the first of a lifetime's casualty lists. Will and Elizabeth
said I could come back and visit anytime, but I knew I'd lost them for
good and I had. This was America; no look back. I've never seen one of
them, that day to this.

It was more than a year before Will and Elizabeth realized their error.
"Home" was no longer home but a set of changed houses full of edgy
kin. Most of their old school friends were gone or sunk in their own
domestic bogs, and their other contemporaries had already woven complex social webs that had no room for one new couple. But oblivious at
first, they swam and dived in a crowded bath of familiarity. Bill, at age
three, rolled easily with the change; he'd left only one playmate behind.
And in a matter of weeks, even I was considering eating my tears. My
age-mates in town, all dozen of them, welcomed me in. I was biking,
swimming and—as summer ended—playing touch football. Though I
didn't feel weaned enough from Asheboro to accompany Mother and
Bill back for a first fall visit, I'd begun signaling to the family that this
new place might not be the disaster I'd foretold. And by the time school
opened, Will and Elizabeth's guilt at uprooting me was almost allayed.
    I had a good sixth-grade teacher; and to the roll of my new town
friends, I added a number of children bused in from farms in the country. By the start of cool weather in mid-October, I seemed rooted in a life
as rewarding as the one I'd left. The only hitch was a temporary annoyance. Stable and old-line as it was, Warrenton had almost no rental
property; so while we waited for a vacant house, we packed into a four-
room second-floor hot apartment at the Hotel Warren.

Then came a crucial afternoon, two weeks before Halloween, one of
those days on which a whole life is rudely bent but which starts with
nothing more special than sunlight. Late October but the late afternoon
was still so warm I'd pulled off my sweater and tied it around my waist in
a manner that always felt jaunty. Three of my new town friends and I
had biked away from school together and were aimlessly cruising the
back streets of town. One of them was my first friend here, a distant
cousin small enough to be called Midget. One was the myopic but
powerfully magnetic, mouth-breathing son of my father's second-best
boyhood friend.
    The other had no close connection with my family, though Will had
known his mother forever. Aryan blond and blue-eyed, the boy was a
third-generation son of wealthy English stock and poor German immi-
grant farmers. His father had made good, moved to town and married.
The Second War had six months to run; so of course we called our friend

"the German," which he seemed not to mind. I still suspect the German caused what happened next. All my life I'd had my instinct for slicing a way into tight-sealed bonds—Will and Elizabeth, Ida and Marvin, some Asheboro boys. Now I'd sliced into dangerous ground; I'd got too close to the myopic friend—too close, too fast—and the German wouldn't have it.

By four o'clock we were down near the jail. I thought we'd stopped to hear the prisoner sing. For more than a week, there'd been a black prisoner who stood at his barred window, singing hymns. But that afternoon he didn't appear, and the German said his bike tires were low. Everybody's tires are always low, so we rolled a few yards downhill for air at Shorty Gillam's garage and bus station. The air pump was on the jail side of the building, behind a five-foot pile of coal. It was my turn next. I was off my bike and squatting by the tire; my school books were strapped to the red back-fender. The German said one clear word, "Ready?" I thought he meant me—was I ready to go?—but when I looked up, he was facing the myopic.

With no further sound, they came down on me. First they knocked me back into the coal; my bike fell too and my books hit the coal. Then as I scrambled up, more shoves and kicks—no blood or cuts and still no words. My midget cousin only watched, still as they. Thirty seconds' pummeling spent their purpose on my actual body; but for his climax, the German found a pointed stick and pounded deep holes in the lid of a box of watercolor pencils I prized and had kept in perfect condition. Still silent, they mounted their bikes and left. Midget had watched without protest, and he rode off with them.

From the first grade on, instead of renting my textbooks from the school, Will had bought me new copies at my request (I liked to color the illustrations and have them to keep when the school year ended). But now as I gathered the coal-grimed books and the pierced pencil-box, they seemed the real victims. And at once they shared the victim's curse. They were ruined past my power to forgive; at every glimpse, they'd revive my shame. I'd already copied Will's fastidious respect for useful objects—keep them clean and orderly; they'll serve you all the better. At once I knew I'd throw these away.

A man's voice said "Son, are you all right?" I looked toward a grown man ten yards away. He was a friend of Elizabeth's, named Johnny Adcock; and he worked at the garage. He'd stood there smoking a cigarette and watching the scene.

I said I was fine, but silently I hoped he would die or disappear. I didn't resent his passive witness; I only felt that he knew too much. So I hoped I'd never see him again, alive in this world or dead in the next.

I was only a single long block from our hotel, up a back street where nobody much but blacks ever walked; and they wouldn't know me. Not that I was crying or bleeding. A genuine Rodwell, all my life I've misted over readily for minor emotions, mostly small delights; but at big events, I'm desert dry. And not till I'd turned in at the hotel parking lot, leaned my bike on the wall and thrown the pencils in a garbage can, did I realize that the target was me and would always be till I left this ingrown, sealed and hateful town. If I'd trusted my foresight back in Asheboro, I'd have fought for a way to stay behind.

A moppet melodrama? A standard heartbreak suffered by billions of new children in whatever town and easily mended by vigorous reaction the next day at school? *Hit the bastards back, throw their books down the coal chute (not that they give a damn about their books). In another week you'll have won your spurs and be safe again.* Right?—in Newark maybe or South Philadelphia. This was small-town North Carolina in the forties; the total white population was under a thousand. Those were literally the main white boys of my exact age and class (and class was a power, in my parents' eyes). What was worse, till the moment of that word "Ready," all three boys had convinced me of their friendship. Now they'd not only ruined my books and pencils, they'd revealed me as a whey-faced fool to trust them. I hadn't understood that, while children can generally spot deceit in adults, they're blind to their age-mates.

I was neither a pacifist, a coward nor a bloodless boy-saint; but telling me to hit back was as useful as telling me to vaporize. I understood the purpose and technique of fist-fighting about as well as your dog understands algebra. Aside from mild switchings, I'd never felt an angry hand; and though I enjoyed healthy tussles and pillow fights and had watched playground scuffles, I'd never had the least occasion to strike out at anyone. And cowboy movies, along with family drunks, had shown me enough of the pain of hateful acts to convince me that fighting was a skill I didn't mean to learn. Finally I saw no future in another dust-up. Like my books and watercolor pencils, these friends were ruined. I'd never want them again.

The only treacheries I'd ever suspected lay well behind me and had proved imaginary—the thought that my parents might someday remove their masks of love to show other faces or that they might call me in one evening and, far from announcing their own divorce, reveal that they'd adopted me, that I hadn't worked out and was being sent back. So I was unprepared for one of the worst human discoveries—that friends you trusted have plotted your ruin. If that word "Ready" hadn't hung in the air, I might have waded back in the next day. But "Ready" was nailed up in those few yards between Shorty Gillam's and the jailed black singer like a red roadsign. That certain proof stopped me—the German and the myopic planned the attack. I already knew their lock-jawed natures; they'd never relent.

When I got to our apartment, Elizabeth and Bill were out. Will was there; he looked me over for bruises, heard my story and responded kindly but with no understanding of my sense of permanent disaster. Next time, fight back. And Mother agreed. In an hour she served my favorite supper, country-style steak; but with my afternoon and their effortless air of conduct-as-normal, it stuck in my throat.

Given their big-family knockabout childhoods, it probably never occurred to Will and Elizabeth to contact the lead-boys' parents, lifelong friends that they were, and tactfully suggest a pullback. That brand of intervention was so foreign to the parent-child thought of those days that I doubt I even thought of asking for it. I'd like to think my refusal to fight back came from a naturally gentle nature. Of course it didn't. If I could have eliminated the German from the landscape, bloodlessly, with the press of a button, I'd likely have pressed. But lacking such dream technology, I was mired like my parents in an ancient code of meaningless honor. I'd accepted shame; there was no way back.

LILLIAN HELLMAN

From JULIA

Now, so many years later, I could climb the steps without a light, move in the night through the crowded rooms of her grandparents' great Fifth Avenue house with the endless chic-shabby rooms, their walls covered with pictures, their tables crowded with objects whose value I didn't know. True, I cannot remember anything said or done in that house except for the first night I was allowed to sleep there. Julia and I were both twelve years old that New Year's Eve night, sitting at a late dinner, with courses of fish and meats, and sherbets in between to change the tastes, "clear the palate" is what her grandmother said, with watered wine for us, and red and white wine and champagne for the two old people. (Were they old? I don't know: they were her grandparents.) I cannot remember any talk at the table, but after dinner we were allowed to go with them to the music room. A servant had already set the phonograph for "So Sheep May Safely Graze," and all four of us listened until Julia rose, kissed the hand of her grandmother, the brow of her grandfather, and left the room, motioning for me to follow. It was an odd ritual, the whole thing, I thought, the life of the very rich, and beyond my understanding.

Each New Year's Eve of my life has brought back the memory of that night. Julia and I lay in twin beds and she recited odds and ends of poetry—every once in a while she would stop and ask me to recite, but I didn't know anything—Dante in Italian, Heine in German, and even though I could not understand either language, the sounds were so lovely that I felt a sweet sadness as if much was ahead in the world, much that was going to be fine and fulfilling if I could ever find my way. I did recite Mother Goose and she did Donne's "Julia," and laughed with pleasure "at his tribute to me." I was ashamed to ask if it was a joke.

Very late she turned her head away for sleep, but I said, "More, Julia, please. Do you know more?" And she turned on the light again and recited from Ovid and Catullus, names to me without countries.

I don't know when I stopped listening to look at the lovely face propped against the pillow—the lamp throwing fine lights on the thick dark hair. I cannot say now that I knew or had ever used the words gentle or delicate or strong, but I did think that night that it was the most beautiful face I had ever seen. In later years I never thought about how she looked, although when we were grown other people often said she was a "strange beauty," she "looked like nobody else," and one show-off said a "Burne-Jones face" when, of course, her face had nothing to do with Burne-Jones or fake spirituality.

There were many years, almost twenty, between that New Year's Eve and the train moving into Germany. In those years, and the years after Julia's death, I have had plenty of time to think about the love I had for her, too strong and too complicated to be defined as only the sexual yearnings of one girl for another. And yet certainly that was there. I don't know, I never cared, and it is now an aimless guessing game. It doesn't prove much that we never kissed each other; even when I leaned down in a London funeral parlor to kiss the battered face that had been so hideously put back together, it was not the awful scars that worried me: because I had never kissed her I thought perhaps she would not want it and so I touched the face instead. . . .

(Before Julia was killed by the Fascists, Lillian visited her in Europe and agreed to smuggle money on Julia's behalf to rescue some of the victims. In the following excerpt the two friends meet at a restaurant and make the clandestine exchange.)

I didn't like being in the station so I crossed the street to Albert's. I went through a revolving door and was so shocked at the sight of Julia at a table that I stopped at the door. She half rose, called softly, and I went toward her with tears that I couldn't stop because I saw two crutches lying next to her and now knew what I had never wanted to know before. Half out of her seat, holding to the table, she said, "Fine, fine. I have ordered caviar for us to celebrate, Albert had to send for it, it won't be long."

She held my hand for several minutes, and said, "Fine. Everything has gone fine. Nothing will happen now. Let's eat and drink and see each other. So many years."

I said, "How long have we got? How far is the other station, the one where I get the train to Moscow?"

"You have two hours, but we haven't that long together because you have to be followed to the station and the ones who follow you must have time to find the man who will be with you on the train until Warsaw in the morning."

I said, "You look like nobody else. You are more beautiful now."

She said, "Stop crying about my leg. It was amputated and the false leg is clumsily made so I am coming to New York in the next few months, as soon as I can, and get a good one. Lilly, don't cry for me. *Stop the tears*. We must finish the work now. Take off the hat the way you would if it was too hot for this place. Comb your hair, and put the hat on the seat between us."

Her coat was open, and the minute I put the hat on the bench she pinned it deep inside her coat with a safety pin that was ready for it.

She said, "Now I am going to the toilet. If the waiter tries to help me up, wave him aside and come with me. The toilet locks. If anybody should try to open it, knock on the door and call to me, but I don't think that will happen."

She got up, picked up one of the crutches, and waved me to the other arm. She spoke in German to a man I guess was Albert as we moved down the long room. She pulled the crutch too quickly into the toilet door, it caught at a wrong angle, and she made a gesture with the crutch, tearing at it in irritation.

When she came out of the toilet, she smiled at me. As we walked back to the table, she spoke in a loud voice, saying something in German about the toilet and then, in English, "I forget you don't know German. I was saying that German public toilets are always clean, much cleaner than ours, particularly under the new regime. The bastards, the murderers."

Caviar and wine were on the table when we sat down again and she was cheerful with the waiter. When he had gone away she said, "Ah, Lilly. Fine, fine. Nothing will happen now. But it is your right to know that it is my money you brought in and we can save five hundred, and maybe, if we can bargain right, a thousand people with it. So believe that you have been better than a good friend to me, you have done something important."

"Jews?"

"About half. And political people. Socialists, Communists, plain old Catholic dissenters. Jews aren't the only people who have suffered here." She sighed. "That's enough of that. We can only do today what we can do today and today you did it for us. Do you need something stronger than wine?"

I said I didn't and she said to talk fast now, there wasn't much time, to tell her as much as possible. I told her about my divorce, about the years with Hammett. She said she had read *The Children's Hour,* she was pleased with me, and what was I going to do next?

I said, "I did it. A second play, a failure. Tell me about your baby."

"She's fat and handsome. I've got over minding that she looks like my mother."

"I want very much to see her."

"You will," she said, "I'll bring her when I come home for the new leg and she can live with you, if you like."

I said, meaning no harm, "Couldn't I see her now?"

"Are you crazy? Do you think I would bring her here? Isn't it enough I took chances with your safety? I will pay for that tonight and tomorrow and . . ." Then she smiled. "The baby lives in Mulhouse, with some nice folks. I see her that way whenever I cross the border. Maybe, when I come back for the leg, I'll leave her with you. She shouldn't be in Europe. It ain't for babies now."

"I haven't a house or even an apartment of any permanence," I said, "but I'll get one if you bring the baby."

"Sure. But it wouldn't matter. You'd be good to her." Then she laughed. . . .

She smiled and patted my hand. "Someday I will take you to meet Freud. What am I saying? I will probably never see him again—I have only so much longer to last in Europe. The crutches make me too noticeable. The man who will take care of you has just come into the street. Do you see him outside the window? Get up and go now. Walk across the street, get a taxi, take it to Bahnhof 200. Another man will be waiting there. He will make sure you get safely on the train and will stay with you until Warsaw tomorrow morning. He is in car A, compartment 13. Let me see your ticket."

I gave it to her. "I think that will be in the car to your left." She laughed. *"Left,* Lilly, *left.* Have you ever learned to tell left from right, south from north?"

"No. I don't want to leave you. The train doesn't go for over an hour. I want to stay with you a few more minutes."

"No," she said. "Something could still go wrong and we must have time to get help if that should happen. I'll be coming to New York in a few months. Write from Moscow to American Express in Paris. I have stuff picked up every few weeks." She took my hand and raised it to her lips. "My beloved friend."

Then she pushed me and I was on my feet. When I got to the door I turned and must have taken a step back because she shook her head and moved her face to look at another part of the room.

ELIE WIESEL

From NIGHT

(The following excerpt from Elie Wiesel's memoir of his childhood in the Nazi death camps describes events during the forty-mile forced march of Jewish prisoners from Buna to Gleiwitz and ultimately to Buchenwald. Juliek is a young Pole whom Elie befriended at Buna.)

On the way it snowed, snowed, snowed endlessly. We were marching more slowly. The guards themselves seemed tired. My wounded foot no longer hurt me. It must have been completely frozen. The foot was lost to me. It had detached itself from my body like the wheel of a car. Too bad. I should have to resign myself; I could live with only one leg. The main thing was not to think about it. Above all, not at this moment. Leave thoughts for later.

Our march had lost all semblance of discipline. We went as we wanted, as we could. We heard no more shots. Our guards must have been tired.

But death scarcely needed any help from them. The cold was conscientiously doing its work. At every step someone fell and suffered no more.

From time to time, SS officers on motorcycles would go down the length of the column to try and shake us out of our growing apathy:

"Keep going! We are getting there!"

"Courage! Only a few more hours!"

"We're reaching Gleiwitz."

These words of encouragement, even though they came from the mouths of our assassins, did us a great deal of good. No one wanted to give up now, just before the end, so near to the goal. Our eyes searched the horizon for the barbed wire of Gleiwitz. Our only desire was to reach it as quickly as possible.

The night had now set in. The snow had ceased to fall. We walked for several more hours before arriving.

We did not notice the camp until we were just in front of the gate.

Some Kapos rapidly installed us in the barracks. We pushed and jostled one another as if this were the supreme refuge, the gateway to life. We walked over pain-racked bodies. We trod on wounded faces. No cries. A few groans. My father and I were ourselves thrown to the ground by this rolling tide. Beneath our feet someone let out a rattling cry:

"You're crushing me . . . mercy!"

A voice that was not unknown to me.

"You're crushing me . . . mercy! mercy!"

The same faint voice, the same rattle, heard somewhere before. That voice had spoken to me one day. Where? When? Years ago? No, it could only have been at the camp.

"Mercy!"

I felt that I was crushing him. I was stopping his breath. I wanted to get up. I struggled to disengage myself, so that he could breathe. But I was crushed myself beneath the weight of other bodies. I could hardly breathe. I dug my nails into unknown faces. I was biting all round me, in order to get air. No one cried out.

Suddenly I remembered. Juliek! The boy from Warsaw who played the violin in the band at Buna. . . .

"Juliek, is it you?"

"Eliezer . . . the twenty-five strokes of the whip. Yes . . . I remember."

He was silent. A long moment elapsed.

"Juliek! Can you hear me, Juliek?"

"Yes . . . ," he said, in a feeble voice. "What do you want?"

He was not dead.

"How do you feel, Juliek?" I asked, less to know the answer than to hear that he could speak, that he was alive.

"All right, Eliezer. . . . I'm getting on all right . . . hardly any air . . . worn out. My feet are swollen. It's good to rest, but my violin. . . ."

I thought he had gone out of his mind. What use was the violin here?

"What, your violin?"

He gasped.

"I'm afraid . . . I'm afraid . . . that they'll break my violin. . . . I've brought it with me."

I could not answer him. Someone was lying full length on top of me, covering my face. I was unable to breathe, through either mouth or nose. Sweat beaded my brow, ran down my spine. This was the end—the end of the road. A silent death, suffocation. No way of crying out, of calling for help.

I tried to get rid of my invisible assassin. My whole will to live was centered in my nails. I scratched. I battled for a mouthful of air. I tore at decaying flesh which did not respond. I could not free myself from this mass weighing down my chest. Was it a dead man I was struggling against? Who knows?

I shall never know. All I can say is that I won. I succeeded in digging a hole through this wall of dying people, a little hole through which I could drink in a small quantity of air.

"Father, how are you?" I asked, as soon as I could utter a word.

I knew he could not be far from me.

"Well!" answered a distant voice, which seemed to come from another world. I tried to sleep.

He tried to sleep. Was he right or wrong? Could one sleep here? Was it not dangerous to allow your vigilance to fail, even for a moment, when at any minute death could pounce upon you?

I was thinking of this when I heard the sound of a violin. The sound of a violin, in this dark shed, where the dead were heaped on the living. What madman could be playing the violin here, at the brink of his own grave? Or was it really an hallucination?

It must have been Juliek.

He played a fragment from Beethoven's concerto. I had never heard sounds so pure. In such a silence.

How had he managed to free himself? To draw his body from under mine without my being aware of it?

It was pitch dark. I could hear only the violin, and it was as though Juliek's soul were the bow. He was playing his life. The whole of his life was gliding on the strings—his lost hopes, his charred past, his extinguished future. He played as he would never play again.

I shall never forget Juliek. How could I forget that concert, given to an audience of dying and dead men! To this day, whenever I hear Beethoven played my eyes close and out of the dark rises the sad, pale face of my Polish friend, as he said farewell on his violin to an audience of dying men.

I do not know for how long he played. I was overcome by sleep. When I awoke, in the daylight, I could see Juliek, opposite me, slumped over, dead. Near him lay his violin, smashed, trampled, a strange overwhelming little corpse.

Translated by Stella Rodway

GEORGE F. KENNAN

From SKETCHES FROM A LIFE

December 9, 1987
Washington

I have been back in Washington for these past three days—not *my* Washington, of course, but let us say, the Washington that might have appeared to anyone else who was born in 1904, who had seen something of that city in the days of his maturity, had then died at a normal age, but had been permitted, by some extraordinary indulgence of Providence, to be resurrected from the dead and to revisit this, together with other, scenes of his brief passage across the face of history.

I, on this occasion, found the city cowering under a faint, cold December sunshine, but roaring more than ever with surface and airplane traffic; and I viewed it, resurrected as I was from the past, with a slight shudder, and an offer of thanks to Providence that I was absolved from contributing further to its active life.

Ten days ago I reiterated, in these notes, my periodic complaints about the endless series of visits I seemed to have to make, for one reason or another, outside Princeton; and I described them as "empty formality: nothing accomplished, nothing to show for it." Today's events—or one of them, at least—put those self-pitying words in their place as the over-dramatization they were.

These events were both connected with the historic visit to Washington of Mikhail Sergeyevich Gorbachev. The first of them contained, to be sure, no surprises. It was a great luncheon tendered by Secretary of State and Mrs. Schultz for Gorbachev and his wife—an affair (as we used to say in the old diplomatic service) of some two hundred and fifty "plates." I shall not go into the political aspects of this affair or the speeches given by the principals; all that will take its place in the overabundant historical record, to enjoy there the privacy of a deep oblivion. I recall only that we waited an interminable time for those principals to make their appearance, and that I sat next to a lady from somewhere in the Southwest, the wife of some prominent politician, I believe, whose ignorance of my identity was as great as mine of hers, and, since neither of us was particularly interested in enlightening the other on this matter, remained that way to the end.

The afternoon appointment was another matter. It was a reception for Gorbachev at the Soviet embassy, to which I, in company with one or two hundred other Americans, had been invited by the Russians. (How these persons were chosen by the Soviet hosts, I do not know. The press, always anxious to make a story out of it, alleged afterward that we were "the intellectuals," although I saw there a number of eminent Republicans, including a couple of former secretaries of state, who would probably resent being thus described—and in some instances, perhaps not without reason.)

The function took place at the old Russian embassy building on Sixteenth Street, right next to what was then the Racquet Club, where I sometimes went to swim on the dark winter afternoons of 1926. After penetrating the successive lines of security guards deployed for several blocks around the place, we guests had our credentials carefully but politely examined at the entrance of the building and were then taken upstairs and shown into a large and beautiful chamber, of ballroom ambiance, already densely packed with people.

Remembering my wife's admonishments not to stand uncomfortably in the background as I normally do on such occasions but to insist on meeting the guest of honor and adding my particular set of banalities to the others he was condemned to endure, I decided to make the effort. So I pushed through the crowd and eventually squeezed myself into the small circle of photographers, journalists, and other pushy guests surrounding the distinguished visitor. The latter, whom I was meeting for the first time, appeared to recognize me, and amazed me by throwing out his arms and treating me to what has now become the standard statesman's embrace. Then, still holding on to my elbows, he looked me seriously in the eye and said: "Mr. Kennan. We in our country believe that a man may be the friend of another country and remain, at the same time, a loyal and devoted citizen of his own; and that is the way we view you."

I cannot recall what I said in response to this statement. Whatever it was, it was wholly inadequate.

We sooned moved to another room, filled with small tables. Gorbachev, seated at one of these tables, delivered himself of a lengthy (too lengthy for American tastes, short by Russian standards) impromptu address. The table to which I was assigned included, as I recall it, Ken Galbraith, McGeorge Bundy, and a lady of most striking appearance, who chain-smoked Danish cigars and appeared to be rather bored with the whole performance, and of whom I was later told that I should have recognized her—as the widow of a famous rock singer.

My ears failed me badly during Gorbachev's long talk, and I amused myself by fidgeting with the earphones and trying to figure out which was harder to catch: the speaker's Russian or the plodding artificialities of the simultaneous translation. But actually, I could not concentrate on what he was saying. His words to me still rang in my ears. And as I reflected on them, the whole sixty years of my involvement with Soviet affairs (which included, at one point, being banned from Russia as an "enemy of the Soviet people") revolved before the mind's eye; and I could think of no better conclusion to this entire chapter of activity—at least none from the Soviet side—than this extraordinarily gracious and tactful statement, worthy, when you think of it, of the finest standards of royal courtesy. I reflected that if you cannot have this sort of recognition from your own government to ring down your involvement in such a relationship, it is nice to have it at least from the one-time adversary.

PART XIII

LETTERS: GROUP 4

*To be capable of steady friendship or lasting
love, are the two greatest proofs, not only of
goodness of heart, but of strength of mind.*

—*William Hazlitt*

DIETRICH BONHOEFFER

To Eberhard Bethge

(These letters were written from Tegel Military Prison in Berlin, to which Bonhoeffer had been sentenced for his involvement with the German underground's efforts to overthrow Hitler. Renate Bethge, Bonhoeffer's niece, is married to Eberhard.)

[Tegel] Friday, 26 November 1943

Dear Eberhard,
So it really came off! Only for a moment, but that doesn't matter so much; even a few hours would be far too little, and when we are isolated here we can take in so much that even a few minutes gives us something to think about for a long time afterwards. It will be with me for a long time now—the memory of having the four people who are nearest and dearest to me with me for a brief moment. When I got back to my cell afterwards, I paced up and down for a whole hour, while my dinner stood there and got cold, so that at last I couldn't help laughing at myself when I found myself repeating over and over again, "That was really great!" I always hesitate to use the word "indescribable" about anything, because if you take enough trouble to make a thing clear, I think there is very little that is something really "indescribable"—but at the moment that it is just what this morning seems to be. Karl's cigar is on the table in front of me, and that is something really indescribable—was he nice? and understanding? and V. too? How grand it was that you saw them. And the good old favourite "Wolf" cigar from Hamburg, which I used to be so fond of in better times. Just by me, standing on a box, is Maria's Advent garland, and on the shelf there are (among other things) your gigantic eggs, waiting for breakfasts still to come. (It's no use my saying that you oughtn't to have deprived yourselves of them; but that's what I think, though I am glad of them all the same.) . . .

Now you've been able to convince yourself that I'm my old self in every respect and that all is well. I believe that a moment was enough to make clear to both of us that everything that has happened in the last seven and a half months has left both of us essentially unchanged; I never doubted it for a moment, and you certainly didn't either. That's the advantage of having spent almost every day and having experienced almost every event and discussed every thought together for eight years. One needs only a second to know about each other, and now one doesn't really need even that second any more. I can remember that my first visit to a prison (I went to see Fritz O., and you were with me) took it out of me terribly, although Fritz was very cheerful and nice. I hope you didn't feel like that when you were here today. You see, it would be wrong to suppose that prison life is uninterrupted torture. It certainly is not, and visits like yours relieve it for days on end, even though they do, of course, awaken feelings that have fortunately lain dormant for a while. But that doesn't matter either. I realize again in thankfulness how well off I was, and feel new hope and energy. Thank you *very* much, you yourself and all the others. When and where will I be able to visit you? Make sure that you spend a long time in Lissa! We really must see each other as quickly as possible after my release. It's truly horrible that they refuse a soldier who wants to visit his closest friend. Damned bureaucrats! But one learns from everything—and for later on!

Christmas Eve 1943

Dear Renate and Eberhard,
It's half past nine in the evening; I've been spending a few lovely peaceful hours, and thinking very thankfully about your being able to spend the day together. . . .

One of my greatest joys this Christmas is that we have again been able to exchange the *Losungen** for the coming year. I had already thought of it and hoped for it, though I hardly expected that it would be possible. And now this book, which has meant so much to me in the past months, will be with us throughout next year too, and when we read it in the morning we shall think especially of each other. Many, many thanks. It was a particularly nice idea of yours to look for the beautiful book of poetry; I keep reading it and find much joy and gain in it. I was at first rather sad that I can't give you anything nice this time; but my thoughts and wishes have been closer than ever to you, if that is possible.

I should like to say something to help you in the time of separation that lies ahead. There is no need to say how hard any such separation is for us; but as I've now been separated for nine months from all the people that I'm devoted to, I should like to pass on to you something of what I have learnt. So far, Eberhard and I have exchanged all the experi-

---

*Daily texts, published yearly since 1731.

ences that have been important to us, and this has been a great help to us; now you, Renate, will have some part in this. You must try to forget your "uncle" and think more of your husband's friend.

First: nothing can make up for the absence of someone whom we love, and it would be wrong to try to find a substitute; we must simply hold out and see it through. That sounds very hard at first, but at the same time it is a great consolation, for the gap, as long as it remains unfilled, preserves the bonds between us. It is nonsense to say that God fills the gap; he doesn't fill it, but on the contrary, he keeps it empty and so helps us to keep alive our former communion with each other, even at the cost of pain.

Secondly: the dearer and richer our memories, the more difficult the separation. But gratitude changes the pangs of memory into a tranquil joy. The beauties of the past are borne, not as a thorn in the flesh, but as a precious gift in themselves. We must take care not to wallow in our memories or hand ourselves over to them, just as we do not gaze all the time at a valuable present, but only at special times, and apart from these keep it simply as a hidden treasure that is ours for certain. In this way the past gives us lasting joy and strength.

Thirdly: times of separation are not a total loss or unprofitable for our companionship, or at any rate they need not be so. In spite of all the difficulties that they bring, they can be the means of strengthening fellowship quite remarkably. . . .

[Tegel] 9 May 1944

Dear Renate and Eberhard,
Your hope that leave may be near is also a great piece of good news for me. If you really manage to be together again in a few days—though in all these hopes one must always keep the joyful anticipation damped down a bit until the last minute—and if you can also have your child baptized then, I shouldn't like the thought of my absence to cast the least shadow on your happiness and particularly on you personally, Eberhard. I shall try to write you something for the occasion, and you know that I shall be with you in spirit. It's painful to me, to be sure, that the improbable has happened, and that I shall not be able to celebrate the day with you; but I've quite reconciled myself to it. I believe that nothing that happens to me is meaningless, and that it is good for us all that it should be so, even if it runs counter to our own wishes. As I see it, I'm here for some purpose, and I only hope I may fulfil it. In the light of the great purpose all our privations and disappointments are trivial. Nothing would be more unworthy and wrong-headed than to turn one of those rare occasions of joy, such as you're now experiencing, into a calamity

because of my present situation. That would go entirely against the grain, and would undermine my optimism with regard to my case. However thankful we may be for all our personal pleasures, we mustn't for a moment lose sight of the great things that we're living for, and they must shed light rather than gloom on your joy. I couldn't bear to think that your few weeks of happiness, which you've had difficulty enough in getting, should be in the very least clouded by my present circumstances. That would be a real calamity, and the other is not. My only concern is to help you, as far as I can, to keep the lustre of these spring days—I expect you're celebrating your first wedding anniversary together—as radiant as may be. Please don't think for a moment that you're missing something through my not being with you—far from it! And above all, please don't think I'm finding it difficult to get these words out for your sake; on the contrary, they are my most earnest request to you, and its fulfilment would simply make me pleased and happy. If we did manage to meet while you're on leave, I should be only too delighted; but please don't put yourself out over it—I still have vivid memories of 23 December! And please don't lose a single day for the sake of spending a little time with me here. I know you would willingly do so, but it would only distress me. Of course, if your father could arrange for you to visit me, as he did in December, I should be extremely grateful. Anyway, I know we shall be thinking of each other every morning as we read the daily texts.

. . .

I don't want to bother you with too long a letter just at the beginning of your reunion; all I wanted to do was to send you my good wishes and tell you that I'm sharing your pleasure. Mind you have plenty of good music!

I wish you all imaginable good things with all my heart.

Your Dietrich.

Translated by Reginald H. Fuller, Frank Clarke, and John Bowden

THOMAS MANN
AND ERICH KAHLER

CORRESPONDENCE

Mann to Kahler

441 *North Rockingham*
Los Angeles-Brentwood
July 8, 1940

Dear Friend:

I feel the need to say how much we wish that we had you here together with us during this period of agonizing and numbing expectation. It is painful and constricting that we should be so far apart now of all times. The hour of decision is almost upon us, and there is little hope that the brainless fanatics will not succeed in attaining their every end. The world and the times show a distinct disposition to let them succeed, perhaps not only out of weakness and affinity to evil, but also out of the instinct to view these desperate fanatics, who nevertheless have a talent for victory, as an instrument for still unknown but necessary aims and purposes. The situation is ghastly, a torture to the mind and the emotions. Everything depends on England's capacity for resistance, which no one can estimate. If she falls in one way or another, the gates are thrown open to hell itself *everywhere*. We must prepare to face total defenselessness and homelessness, with eternity the only refuge. I have always believed that maintaining a kind of personal serenity can bring one safely through the darkest circumstances, and I have trusted to my capacity for adaptation. But these days I often feel hopelessly trapped. . . .

Kahler to Mann

Woodstock, N.Y.
July 20, 1940

My dear Friend:

Your news was already eagerly awaited, and your letter, troubled through it sounds, was still comforting and warming in its confirmation of our closeness. I need not tell you how hard it has been for *me* to be separated from you for so long at this particular time. What remains to us in this ghastly world except the few people we are attached to? Together with them it is somewhat easier to bear what has to be borne! It moves me to hear you speaking in a way I have not been accustomed to hear from you. For as you know, I've always let you carry me along into more sanguine views; I've always been so grateful for your faith, and often enough I've blamed myself for my skepticism, which I was unable to silence. Deep down I have *never,* since Munich, in fact since Spain, since Baldwin and Blum and more than ever since the first days of Chamberlain and Daladier, believed in a victory of the Allies. The way things have turned out seems to me nothing but consistent. I have felt too keenly the way the wind was blowing, have been too conscious of the magnitude of the transformation we are involved in. If I look back now, everything I have undertaken seems to me nothing but an attempt to save, to preserve, to transport what was dear to us, to try to impose some intellectual control on this transformation so that it achieves the goal it will have to reach anyhow. It was a childish endeavor, for upheavals of such dimensions necessarily take the elemental course, setting in motion avalanches of earth and crap. Forgive me for talking this way, although I am well aware that you too have striven toward the same end, both within and outside your writing. Of course it is of no use; we have to face up to that. Yet in spite of everything and no matter what is taking place, I still do believe that it will not have been in vain, some day, beyond our personal selves. Only we cannot spare mankind anything. There was not enough time for preparation and education; there was not enough human room for the urge toward goodness to unfold. The pressure of circumstances and of instincts has been faster and mightier. . . .

Mann to Kahler

Pacific Palisades
June 14, 1942

Dear friend Kahler:

At last I get around to saying hello to you and to thanking you. There is always so much to do, and the letter-writing hours are often taken from me by those who worry very little about the time of people like us, and they are usually the same persons who in all innocence wonder *when* we manage to do "all that."

How kindly you have again remembered my birthday, and your dear mother too. I must include a page for her. The sweets and cigars have arrived in good condition. The good old Optimos! It was a clever thought on your part. They are very hard to get here, and smoking them,

I feel keenly and nostalgically transported back to the old times when we lived in the same place. I wonder whether we did right to leave those days behind us? It remains a question that we answer one way or the other at different times. . . .

Kahler to Mann

June 2, 1944

Do you know what is hardest to bear in the era that is advancing upon us, and especially in this country? It is this omnipresent, terrifying feeling of futility! Not only are natural law, the elements, absolute truth all gone—the same thing is taking place in the purely physical, animal condition. We've known all that for a long time, thought and written about it, but we haven't entirely believed it physically, believed it with the naïve base of the body. We've counted on saving ourselves romantically somewhere, in the existence of nature, in the primeval forests somewhere in the world. But that hope is being thoroughly crushed. There is not going to be any way out. Nothing for it; back to the human mess, politics, economy, Big Three, Standard Oil, State Dept., Churchill, the pope, and all that follows. What is good old Nature, what are the primeval forest? Bomb fodder. And what primeval forests are left? In the South Sea Islands, where not so long ago the subtle psychological fables of Joseph Conrad were still possible, the Rockette girls are kicking up their legs; and Frank Sinatra will soon be teaching the parrots to sing. No, nature has no permanence; people have won, are continuing to win, and it is becoming impossible to see what for.

Forgive me, my friend, this is hardly in the birthday spirit, and I shouldn't be letting it spill out. But this is me at the moment—if I am to communicate anything truthful from myself, this is what it must be.

Please write again, a few comforting words. Is it true you are doing a film? The newspapers say so. I also read what you published in the *Atlantic* on Germany . . . I have likewise had to comment on this dismal theme, more elaborately than I liked.

I shall think of you on June 6 with the most heartfelt good wishes. The whole household sends regards to you and Katia.

Ever yours,
E. K.

Mann to Kahler

Pacific Palisades
October 7, 1945

Dear Kahler:

Your sixtieth is impending; it's the fourteenth of this month; you cannot deceive me, so let me congratulate you very heartily, dear friend, and thank you for all the good and fine things you have given us and for your many years of constancy, your intelligent sympathy with my own trying and laborious work. I must also congratulate you, and with sincere respect, for the way you have withstood the crass vicissitudes of life, have adapted to entirely changed conditions, to a foreign land, to a different language, and through it all have held your own in a manly and engaging fashion. That is admirable, impressive and moving; I cannot forbear to say it. The rest, or a little of the rest, is set down in the little congratulatory article, the manuscript and copy of which I am enclosing as a modest birthday gift. . . .

Kahler to Mann

Princeton
October 14, 1945

My dear Friend:

I preferred not to know that I am sixty, and should like to forget it again as quickly as possible. This day seems to have come upon me overnight; but it could not have been brought to my awareness in any gentler, more comforting fashion than by the truly touching tributes my friends and others close to me have been offering. And most especially the wonderful, overwhelmingly good and honored words you have bestowed on me, publicly and privately, have cast a golden glow upon this otherwise rather dreary day. My deepest and sincerest thanks for that— although all this, it seems to me, lies beyond anything that one can express thanks for, and therefore puts all thanks to shame. I take you at your words and receive it all as a pledge of your friendship, which is one of the most precious good things in my life. . . .

Princeton
May 24, 1953

Dear Friend:

Once again I should have written long ago and meant to, and now the final push is given to me by this handsome gift of the essay volume; with pride and joy I see myself figuring in it. Many and special thanks! What a wonderful volume it is. How freely and surprisingly it is yourself, in person, from all sides, in all facets: the grand, far-reaching, earnestly concerned aspects alongside lightness, gracefulness, casualness, into which suddenly, unexpectedly, a total surprise within the context itself, slips something deeply stirring! The richness, the superabundance of the collection is tossed off with the ease that a writer attains only from the summit of a great opus. And a whole generation—how much of my own life also!—moves with you through the book. I have been strolling in it evenings and at night, full of memories, deeply moved, recollecting, with you and with myself. And sometimes I must pause in amazement: To think of all the things we have been through, and what a miracle that we have survived it all up to this point! . . .

Translated by Richard and Clara Winston

ALBERT CAMUS AND
BORIS PASTERNAK

CORRESPONDENCE

June 9, 1958

Dear Boris Pasternak,

René Char, who is my best friend, gave me your address because he knows the friendship and admiration that I have long felt for your work and the man whom one feels living within. I just wanted to send you a small text whose only importance is that of a far-off, but faithful, sign with regards to you. There are a few of us in France who know you, who share your life, in a certain way. I, who would be nothing without the Russian nineteenth century. I find in you once more the Russia that nourished me and gave me strength. It is false to say that frontiers do not exist. They do exist, temporarily. But at the same time there exists a force of creativity and truth uniting us all, in humility and pride at the same time. I never felt this more than while reading you and that is why I would like to express my gratitude and my solidarity. I send warm wishes to you and yours, for your work and your great country. I shake your hand.

Albert Camus

Translated by Emily Tall and Linda Orr

June 28, 1958

Dear Mr. Camus,

I can hardly believe my eyes, writing to you, Camus. A new page has opened in my life, that of having acquired the pretext, the right, the chance to tell you my delight and my gratitude for the special nuance in the play of today's universal thought, [to tell you] that it is owing to you. A man without principles, whose tip of the hat I returned only because of the dark glasses which made him unrecognizable, who, having taken them off and staggered me with regrets when I recognized him, told me, if one wants to believe him, that he was lucky enough to make your acquaintance and to speak to you, among others, of me. Oh how I regret it! I prefer to be the victim of baseness openly than to seem to be its ally.

I rarely have the time to read what I like and what interests me. Kafka, Faulkner, still not read, wait for me to take them from the library shelf. "Remembrance of Things Past" is broken off at the end of "Sodom and Gomorrah." I exult. I congratulate you for writing a prose whose reading becomes a true journey: one visits the places you describe, one experiences the situations related, one feels them for the main characters. In "The Stranger," above and beyond all the rest, one idea struck me. How, in a naked and unlimited sensualism, sensuality itself becomes obtuse and weak! As if in the interests of its own strength it needed its opposite, that which is the eternal presence of the soul: *pity.* I have your "Fall." I shall read it. My new friendship, if I dare say so, with you, with R.C., A. de B., his wife, with P.S., is an unspeakable happiness, an enchantment, a fairy tale. I catch the inconceivable breath of the garden at dawn. I want to surprise the mystery of the green eclipse of the dense foliage, and I think of René Char, who is all that. Or else I meditate on the absolute originality of art and on what is the task of art, rather than philosophy—seizing the essence of life and saying it palpably, and I think of du Bouchet and the domain of his unfathomable perspicacity. And the state of mind of his wife, magical, enchanted! And you are anxious about what can happen to me and you forget that no price is enough for this new kinship which is infinitely worth being lived and even suffered for. Thank you, thank you for everything.

(Pasternak did not sign his letters to Camus because of Soviet censorship.)

Translated by Maurice Friedberg

PART XIV

AFFINITIES: GROUP 3

Each friend represents a world in us, a world
possibly not born until they arrive, and it is
only by this meeting that a new world is born.

—*Anaïs Nin*

T. S. ELIOT

To Marianne Moore

9 Clarence Gate Gardens,
London, N.W.I.
3 April 1921

Dear Miss Moore,

I am writing to thank you for your review of my essays in the *Dial.* It gave me pleasure, and still more pleasure to be reviewed by you, as I have long delayed writing to you, in fact since the 1917 *Others,* to tell you how much I admire your verse. It interests me, I think, more than that of anyone now writing in America. I wish that you would make a book of it, and I should like to try to get it published here. I wish you would let me try.

Sincerely yours
T. S. Eliot

I have just met McAlmon, who spoke of you, and whom I liked.

VIVIEN ELIOT

To *Ezra Pound*

9 Clarence Gate Gardens, N.W.I.
2 November [1922]

Dear Ezra,

1) T. is running down again. He keeps trying to write to you I know but in the meanwhile I am writing and this letter is PRIVATE.

2)—*and most important*—the Rothermere woman has been and is being offense to T. about the *Criterion.* She has written 3 offensive letters and I am afraid this is going to bring about an awful crisis unless someone can be clever about it—*in time.* She is coming to London about the 15th and if when she sees T. she behaves in the same way as her letters I don't see that he can do anything but throw up the *Criterion—and I believe that is what she wants.* She is unhinged—one of those beastly raving women who are the most dangerous. She is now in that asylum for the insane called La Prieure where she does religious dances naked with Katherine Mansfield. "K..M.", she says in every letter—"is *the most intelligent* woman I have *ever* met." K.M. is pouring poison in her ear (of course) for K.M. hates T. more than anyone.

3) Can you get for T. this money (Bel Esp.) which you speak of in your letter, without the condition that he leaves the Bank *immediately?* If so—could he not buy the *Criterion* from Rothermere? Not using his own name in the transaction. I am sure a few people here would help in *that,* with small sums. She *might* be glad to sell it, *now,* for it may be that she is just furious at having promised the money for something she now hates and is bored with.

She would *not sell it later on* if it began to *pay.* Do you think this is a *possible* idea? If so, how shall we do it—and *can you get that money?* T. would of course leave the Bank ultimately—and I know he could make the *Criterion* a success. I could provide £500 (it would halve my income)—and would gladly. Write at once.

V E

It could not be run *at all* under £400 a year.

T. S. ELIOT AND EZRA POUND

CORRESPONDENCE

[London, 3 November 1922]

Cher Ezra

Vivien wrote to you yesterday about the position I am in. Lady Rothermere has been getting increasingly offensive ever since the *Criterion* came out, and especially since she entered her retreat for maniacs. I wish you could see her before she leaves Paris and tell her bluntly that the *Criterion* is a SUCCESS. I have had nothing but good notices. Nearly all the copies are sold (600 printed). But this woman will shipwreck it.

V's idea is to get the money somehow and buy the paper from her—*before* she has time or opportunity to make my position such that I must throw it up, on her hands. V. thinks she would take £500 for it *now*, especially if my name was kept out of it, and we could find some American who would allow us to use his name in the purchase.

Can you not come over to London for a weekend and see me, as you *know* I cannot come to you.

If you and I could get the *Criterion* into our own hands and could only find the money to run it for a couple of years, it would be the thing of our lives.

Try to get over here to see me, and meanwhile *don't let a soul suspect that* everything is not absolutely right between me and Rothermere.

T.

70 bis, N.D. des Champs,
Paris VIe.
4 November [1922]

Cher T:

This shd. reach you on the anniversary of the Guy Fawks plot.

I answered V's note last night, but had no means of knowing whether her letter was a familial consortium or her own impressions.

I have this A.M. written to Lady R. asking for an interview. Last time I saw her she was affable, and said she was coming to tea, whereafter she vanished, and I did not know she was still in Paris.

I wish you'd be specific. What is she trying to force into the Crit.

Of course if she says it looks like a corpse, she's right, mon POSSUM, do you expect her to see what is scarce discernable to the naked eye, that it is *supposed* to be PLAYIN' POSSUM I think both you and V. are in delirium, thinking of payin £500 for the privilege of having worked six months. Bring out another number. Put in all our own stuff. IF, ever IF the bills have been and are being paid.

£500 for a review that has run one issue?? Gees she'd be SOME financier if she cd. work that dimereena

Dear ole SON. You jess set and hev a quiet draw at youh cawn-kob.

The only asset of the Crit. is YOU, youh-sellf. If you quit, *it* quits. You'll have been euchred for a free start that is the common fate of all mankind, them as boosts periodicals they dont own.

Run one more number . at least . Announce your resignation therein, if necessary. Pay your patient friends. and announce the opening of the "New Effigy", "The Golden Vanity" (there's fine title for for a really sumptuous work). (dont give this one away)

But sink money into a liability, that wd. stay a liability for some years. *Nevairrrrrrrrr!* For the privilige of disguising oneself to look like a member of the Athenaeum Club . Mon gibletts . Mon Gosh , Mon chienggggg.

If you can trust my discretion, send me the correspondence between you and L.R. and I'll try to get a clear idea of the matter.

£500 is bunk. If she is scared of the prospect of expenses she'll give the damn thing away. Chrissssttttt cant you see that *you are* the Criterion. If you go it collapses. Have you . . . got a contract? Not that English contracts are worth a damn, but on the chance that she may not know that no english contract is binding.

I dont see that one story by Katherine M. wd. queer the review. Print the Adams in the next number, and the Mansfie[l]d in the third. That will hold things calm over the interval. Tell her you had already accepted the Obsequies for the 2nd number. I dare say K. M. IS the most intelligent female she has ever met. So long as she dont include Middleton M[urry]., I dont mind. Personally I find it no worse to conciliate the K. M. faction than to conciliate the Binyon faction. When I first met Lady R. she seemed rather more ready to burn the Bastile than you are.

Air yew sure, mon cher, that she is being *intentionally* offensive. Remember that she is not one who has started at the social apex and descended. People of a slightly lower social order than we are . . . . . apt to be offensive when they are only, in their own eye, being frank, hearty and outspoken.

especially in your present exhausted and enerve condition. . . . perhaps a slight magnification takes place.

At any rate, consider hanging on for another three months. Let us get our own money back out of it. At least divide what spoils there are, IF there are any. I hope you haven't undertaken printing expenses on yr. own???

IF you're going to chuck it, you at least have the chance of launching a few explosives, or a few new authors before you abandon the deck. Print my article, and blame the demise on me.

et tu exageres. NO periodical cd. be the "thing of our lives"

As I said in note to V. Bill Bird who is doing the 3 Mts Press is ready to print a review . at his expense.

IF you cant stick the Crit. let it go out in glory and seek then the southern shore. more anon. must keep an appointment.

E

ELIZABETH BISHOP

From EFFORTS OF AFFECTION:
A MEMOIR OF MARIANNE MOORE

. . . The day came when Miss Borden told me that she had heard from Miss Moore and that Miss Moore was willing to meet me in New York, on a Saturday afternoon. Years later I discovered that Marianne had agreed to do this with reluctance; in the past, it seems, dear Miss Borden had sent several Vassar girls to meet Miss Moore and sometimes her mother as well, and every one had somehow failed to please. This probably accounted for the conditions laid down for our first rendezvous: I was to find Miss Moore seated on the bench at the right of the door leading to the reading room of the New York Public Library. They might have been even more strict. I learned later that if Miss Moore really expected *not* to like would-be acquaintances, she arranged to meet them at the Information Booth in Grand Central Station—no place to sit down, and, if necessary, an instant getaway was possible. In the meantime, I had been told a little more about her by Miss Borden, who described her

as a child, a strange and appealing little creature with bright red hair—
playful, and, as might have been expected, fond of calling her family and
friends by the names of animals.

I was very frightened, but I put on my new spring suit and took the
train to New York. I had never seen a picture of Miss Moore; all I knew
was that she had red hair and usually wore a wide-brimmed hat. I expected the hair to be bright red and for her to be tall and intimidating. I
was right on time, even a bit early, but she was there before me (no
matter how early one arrived, Marianne was always there first) and, I saw
at once, not very tall and not in the least intimidating. She was forty-
seven, an age that seemed old to me then, and her hair was mixed with
white to a faint rust pink, and her rust-pink eyebrows were frosted with
white. The large flat black hat was as I'd expected it to be. She wore a
blue tweed suit that day and, as she usually did then, a man's "polo
shirt," as they were called, with a black bow at the neck. The effect was
quaint, vaguely Bryn Mawr 1909, but stylish at the same time. I sat
down and she began to talk.

It seems to me that Marianne talked to me steadily for the next
thirty-five years, but of course that is nonsensical. I was living far from
New York many of those years and saw her at long intervals. She must
have been one of the world's greatest talkers: entertaining, enlightening,
fascinating, and memorable; her talk, like her poetry, was quite different
from anyone else's in the world. I don't know what she talked about at
that first meeting; I wish I had kept a diary. Happily ignorant of the poor
Vassar girls before me who hadn't passed muster, I began to feel less
nervous and even spoke some myself. I had what may have been an
inspiration, I don't know—at any rate, I attribute my great good fortune
in having known Marianne as a friend in part to it. Ringling Bros. and
Barnum & Bailey Circus was making its spring visit to New York and I
asked Miss Moore (we called each other "Miss" for over two years) if she
would care to go to the circus with me the Saturday after next. I didn't
know that she *always* went to the circus, wouldn't have missed it for
anything, and when she accepted, I went back to Poughkeepsie in the
grimy day coach extremely happy.

THE CIRCUS

I got to Madison Square Garden very early—we had settled on the hour
because we wanted to see the animals before the show began—but Marianne was there ahead of me. She was loaded down: two blue cloth bags,
one on each arm, and two huge brown paper bags, full of something. I
was given one of these. They contained, she told me, stale brown bread

for the elephants, because stale brown bread was one of the things they liked best to eat. (I later suspected that they might like stale white bread just as much but that Marianne had been thinking of their health.) As we went in and down to the lower level, where we could hear (and smell) the animals, she told me her preliminary plan for the circus. Her brother, Warner, had given her an elephant-hair bracelet, of which she was very fond, two or three strands of black hairs held together with gold clasps. One of the elephant hairs had fallen out and been lost. As I probably knew, elephant hairs grow only on the tops of the heads of very young elephants. In her bag, Marianne had a pair of strong nail scissors. I was to divert the adult elephants with the bread, and, if we were lucky, the guards wouldn't observe her at the end of the line where the babies were, and she could take out her scissors and snip a few hairs from a baby's head, to repair her bracelet.

She was quite right; the elephants adored stale brown bread and started trumpeting and pushing up against each other to get it. I stayed at one end of the line, putting slices of bread into the trunks of the older elephants, and Miss Moore went rapidly down to the other end, where the babies were. The large elephants were making such a to-do that a keeper did come up my way, and out of the corner of my eye I saw Miss Moore leaning forward over the rope on tiptoe, scissors in hand. Elephant hairs are tough; I thought she would never finish her haircutting. But she did, and triumphantly we handed out the rest of the bread and set off to see the other animals. She opened her bag and showed me three or four coarse, grayish hairs in a piece of Kleenex.

I hate seeing animals in cages, especially small cages, and especially circus animals, but I think that Marianne, while probably feeling the same way, was so passionately interested in them, and knew so much about them, that she could put aside any pain or outrage for the time being. That day I remember that one handsomely patterned snake, writhing about in a glass-walled cage, seemed to raise his head on purpose to look at us. "See, he knows me!" said Miss Moore. "He remembers me from last year." This was a joke, I decided, but perhaps not altogether a joke. Then we went upstairs and the six-ring affair began. The blue bags held our refreshments: thermos jugs of orange juice, hard-boiled eggs (the yolks only), and more brown bread, but fresh this time, and buttered. I also remember of this first visit to the circus (there were to be others) that in front of us sat a father with three young children, two boys and a girl. A big circus goes on for a long time and the children began to grow restless. Marianne leaned over with the abruptness that characterized all her movements and said to the father that if the little girl wanted to go to the bathroom, she'd be glad to take her. . . .

She had a way of laughing at what she or someone else had just said if she meant to show outrage or mock disapproval—an *oh-ho* kind of sound, rough, that went with a backwards and sidewise toss of the head toward the left shoulder. She accepted compliments with this laugh too, without words; it disparaged and made light of them, and implied that she and her audience were both far above such absurdities. I believe she was the only person I have ever known who "bridled" at praise, while turning pink with pleasure. These gestures of her head were more pronounced in the presence of gentlemen because Marianne was innately flirtatious.

The Moore *chinoiserie* of manners made giving presents complicated. All of her friends seemed to share the desire of giving her presents, and it must sometimes have been, as she would have said, a "burden." One never knew what would succeed, but one learned that if a gift did not succeed it would be given back, unobtrusively, but somehow or other, a year or two later. My most successful gift was a pair of gloves. I don't know why they made such a hit, but they did; they weren't actually worn for a long time, but they appear in a few of her photographs, held in one hand. Marianne brought them to the photographer wrapped in the original tissue paper. Another very successful gift was a paper nautilus, which became the subject of her poem "The Paper Nautilus":

> . . . its wasp-nest flaws
> of white on white, and close-
>
> laid Ionic chiton-folds
> like the lines in the mane of
> a Parthenon horse . . .

Fruit or flowers were acclaimed and examined but never, I felt, really welcomed. But a very unbeautiful bracelet from Morocco, alternate round beads of amber and black ambergris on a soiled string, was very well received. I was flattered to see this worn at a poetry reading, and afterwards learned that, as it was too loose for Marianne's wrist, Mother had carefully sewn it onto the edge of her sleeve. But another friend's attempt to give her a good gramophone was a disaster, a drama that went on for months. Eventually (it was portable but very heavy) it was carried back by Marianne to the shop in New York.

She liked to show her collection of jewelry, which had a few beautiful and valuable pieces. I once gave her a modest brooch of the semi-precious stones of Brazil, red and green tourmalines and amethysts; this she seemed to like so much that I gave her a matching bracelet. A few years later I wrote her from Brazil asking what I could bring her on my return to New York, and she wrote back, "I like *jewels.*"

Knowing her fondness for snakes, I got for her when I was in Florida a beautiful specimen of the deadly coral snake with inch-wide rose-red and black stripes separated by narrow white stripes, a bright new snake coiled in liquid in a squat glass bottle. This bottle sat on her hall bookcase, at the other end from the bowl of nickels, for many years. The colors gradually faded, and the formaldehyde grew cloudy, and finally I said I thought she could dispense with the coral snake. A mutual friend told me that Marianne was relieved; she had always hated it. Perhaps it had only been brought out for my visits. . . .

The atmosphere of 260 Cumberland Street was of course "old-fashioned," but even more, otherworldly—as if one were living in a diving bell from a different world, let down through the crass atmosphere of the twentieth century. Leaving the diving bell with one's nickel, during the walk to the subway and the forty-five-minute ride back to Manhattan, one was apt to have a slight case of mental or moral bends—so many things to be remembered: stories, phrases, the unaccustomed deference, the exquisitely prolonged etiquette—these were hard to reconcile with the New Lots Avenue express and the awful, jolting ride facing a row of indifferent faces. Yet I never left Cumberland Street without feeling happier: uplifted, even inspired, determined to be good, to work harder, not to worry about what other people thought, never to try to publish anything until I thought I'd done my best with it, no matter how many years it took—or never to publish at all.

To change the image from air to water: somehow, under all the subaqueous pressure at 260 Cumberland Street—admonitions, reserves, principles, simple stoicism—Marianne rose triumphant, or rather her voice did, in a lively, unceasing jet of shining bubbles. I had "taken" chemistry at preparatory school; I also could imagine that in this water, or heavy water glass, I saw forming the elaborate, logical structures that became her poems. . . .

Her scrupulous and strict honesty could be carried to extremes of Protestant, Presbyterian, Scotch-Irish literalness that amazed me. We went together to see an exceptionally beautiful film, a documentary in color about Africa, with herds of gazelles and giraffes moving across the plains, and we loved it. Then a herd of elephants appeared, close up and clear, and the narrator commented on their feet and tread. I whispered to Marianne that they looked as if their feet were being lifted up off the ground by invisible threads. The next day she phoned and quoted my remark about the elephants' walk, and suddenly came out with, "Elizabeth, I'll give you ten dollars for that." There was often no telling how serious she was. I said something like "For heaven's sake, Marianne, please take it," but I don't believe it ever made an appearance in a poem.

I confess to one very slight grudge: she *did* use a phrase of mine once without a note. This may be childish of me, but I want to reclaim it. I had been asked by a friend to bring her three glass buoy-balls in nets, sometimes called "witch balls," from Cape Cod. When I arrived at the old hotel where I lived, a very old porter took them with my bag, and as I watched him precede me down the corridor, I said to myself, "The bellboy with the buoy-balls." I liked the sound of this so much that in my vanity I repeated the phrase to Marianne a day or so later. You will find "The sea- / side burden should not embarrass / the bell-boy with the buoy-ball / endeavoring to pass / hotel patronesses" in the fifth stanza of "Four Quartz Crystal Clocks." It was so thoroughly out of character for her to do this that I have never understood it. I am sometimes appalled to think how much I may have unconsciously stolen from her. Perhaps we are all magpies.

> The deepest feeling always shows
> itself in silence;
> not in silence, but restraint.

These lines from her early poem "Silence" are simply another one of Marianne's convictions. Like Auden, whom she admired, she believed that graceful behavior—and writing, as well—demands a certain reticence. She told me, "Ezra says all dedications are *dowdy,*" but it was surely more than to avoid dowdiness that caused her to write this postscript in *Selected Poems* (1935): "Dedications imply giving, and we do not care to make a gift of what is insufficient; but in my immediate family there is one 'who thinks in a particular way' and I should like to add that where there is an effect of thought or pith in these pages, the thinking and often the actual phrases are hers." This postscript was obviously meant for Mrs. Moore, and after her mother's death in 1947, Marianne became more outspoken about dedications; however, when she wrote an acrostic on the name of one of her oldest and closest friends, it too was semi-concealed, by being written upside down. . . .

It was because of Marianne that in 1935 my poems first appeared in a book, an anthology called *Trial Balances.* Each of the poets in this anthology had an older mentor, who wrote a short preface or introduction to the poems, and Marianne, hearing of this project, had offered to be mine. I was much too shy to dream of asking her. I had two or three feeble pastiches of late seventeenth-century poetry called "Valentines," in one of which I had rhymed "even the English sparrows in the dust" with "lust." She did not like those English sparrows very much, and said so ("Miss Bishop's sparrows are not revolting, merely disaffecting"), but her sponsorship brought about this first appearance in a book. . . .

Two friends of Marianne's, two elderly Boston ladies, shared an exquisitely neat white clapboard house in northern Maine. I once spent a day there, and they teased Marianne about her habit of secreting food. She laughed, blushed, and tossed her head, and did not seem to mind when one of them told of going into Marianne's room for a book only to discover two boiled potatoes lying on the dresser. Some years later the older lady phoned Marianne from Boston and told her she was dying of cancer. She was perfectly stoical about it, and said she was in a hospital and knew she could not last very long. She asked Marianne to come and stay near her until she died, and Marianne went. At the hospital, she told Marianne that while she would be grateful to her if she came to see her every day, she knew that Marianne couldn't possibly spend all her time with her, so she had arranged for her to take driving lessons. Marianne, who must have been nearly seventy at the time, agreed that this was a good idea; she had always wanted to learn to drive, and she did, with a lesson at the driving school every day and a visit to the hospital. A day or so after her friend died, Marianne passed her driving test. She said she had a little trouble with the lights in Copley Square and confessed she thought the "policeman" giving her the test had been a little overlenient. I said I hoped she hadn't driven too fast, and she replied, "A steady forty-five, Elizabeth!" . . .

Sometimes we went to movies together, to *Kon-Tiki* twice, I recall. I never attempted to lure her to any dramatic or "artistic" films. Since Dr. and Mrs. Sibley Watson were her dearest friends, she must have seen his early experimental films, such as *Lot in Sodom.* I heard the sad story of two young men, however, who when they discovered that she had never seen Eisenstein's *Potemkin* insisted on taking her. There was a short before *Potemkin,* a Walt Disney film; this was when the Disney films still had charm and humor. After the movies they went to tea and Marianne talked at length and in detail about the ingenuity of the Disney film, and nothing more. Finally they asked her what she had thought of *Potemkin.* Her opinion was brief but conclusive: "Life," she said, "is not like that." . . .

There was something about her good friend T. S. Eliot that seemed to amuse Marianne. On Eliot's first visit to Brooklyn after his marriage to Valerie, his young wife asked them to pose together for her for a snapshot. Valerie said, "Tom, put your arm around Marianne." I asked if he had. Marianne gave that short deprecatory laugh and said, "Yes, he did, but very *gingerly.*" Toward the last, Marianne entrusted her Eliot letters for safekeeping with Robert Giroux, who told me that with each letter of the poet's she had preserved the envelope in which it had come. One envelope bore Marianne's Brooklyn address in Eliot's handwriting, but no return address or other identification. Within, there was a sheet of

yellow pad paper on which was drawn a large heart pierced by an arrow,
with the words "from an anonymous and grateful admirer." . . .

CRUSOE IN ENGLAND

A new volcano has erupted,
the papers say, and last week I was reading
where some ship saw an island being born:
at first a breath of steam, ten miles away;
and then a black fleck—basalt, probably—
rose in the mate's binoculars
and caught on the horizon like a fly.
They named it. But my poor old island's still
un-rediscovered, un-renamable.
None of the books has ever got it right.

Well, I had fifty-two
miserable, small volcanoes I could climb
with a few slithery strides—
volcanoes dead as ash heaps.
I used to sit on the edge of the highest one
and count the others standing up,
naked and leaden, with their heads blown off.
I'd think that if they were the size
I thought volcanoes should be, then I had
become a giant;
and if I had become a giant,
I couldn't bear to think what size
the goats and turtles were,
or the gulls, or the overlapping rollers
—a glittering hexagon of rollers
closing and closing in, but never quite,
glittering and glittering, though the sky
was mostly overcast.

My island seemed to be
a sort of cloud-dump. All the hemisphere's
left-over clouds arrived and hung
above the craters—their parched throats
were hot to touch.
Was that why it rained so much?

And why sometimes the whole place hissed?
The turtles lumbered by, high-domed,
hissing like teakettles.
(And I'd have given years, or taken a few,
for any sort of kettle, of course.)
The folds of lava, running out to sea,
would hiss. I'd turn. And then they'd prove
to be more turtles.
The beaches were all lava, variegated,
black, red, and white, and gray;
the marbled colors made a fine display.
And I had waterspouts. Oh,
half a dozen at a time, far out,
they'd come and go, advancing and retreating,
their heads in cloud, their feet in moving patches
of scuffed-up white.
Glass chimneys, flexible, attenuated,
sacerdotal beings of glass . . . I watched
the water spiral up in them like smoke.
Beautiful, yes, but not much company.

I often gave way to self-pity.
"Do I deserve this? I suppose I must.
I wouldn't be here otherwise. Was there
a moment when I actually chose this?
I don't remember, but there could have been."
What's wrong about self-pity, anyway?
With my legs dangling down familiarly
over a crater's edge, I told myself
"Pity should begin at home." So the more
pity I felt, the more I felt at home.

The sun set in the sea; the same odd sun
rose from the sea,
and there was one of it and one of me.
The island had one kind of everything:
one tree snail, a bright violet-blue
with a thin shell, crept over everything,
over the one variety of tree,
a sooty, scrub affair.
Snail shells lay under these in drifts
and, at a distance,
you'd swear that they were beds of irises.

There was one kind of berry, a dark red.
I tried it, one by one, and hours apart.
Sub-acid, and not bad, no ill effects;
and so I made home-brew. I'd drink
the awful, fizzy, stinging stuff
that went straight to my head
and play my home-made flute
(I think it had the weirdest scale on earth)
and, dizzy, whoop and dance among the goats.
Home-made, home-made! But aren't we all?
I felt a deep affection for
the smallest of my island industries.
No, not exactly, since the smallest was
a miserable philosophy.

Because I didn't know enough.
Why didn't I know enough of something?
Greek drama or astronomy? The books
I'd read were full of blanks;
the poems—well, I tried
reciting to my iris-beds,
"They flash upon that inward eye,
which is the bliss . . ." The bliss of what?
One of the first things that I did
when I got back was look it up.

The island smelled of goat and guano.
The goats were white, so were the gulls,
and both too tame, or else they thought
I was a goat, too, or a gull.
Baa, baa, baa and *shriek, shriek, shriek,*
baa . . . shriek . . . baa . . . I still can't shake
them from my ears; they're hurting now.
The questioning shrieks, the equivocal replies
over a ground of hissing rain
and hissing, ambulating turtles
got on my nerves.

When all the gulls flew up at once, they sounded
like a big tree in a strong wind, its leaves.
I'd shut my eyes and think about a tree,
an oak, say, with real shade, somewhere.
I'd heard of cattle getting island-sick.

I thought the goats were.
One billy-goat would stand on the volcano
I'd christened *Mont d'Espoir* or *Mount Despair*
(I'd time enough to play with names),
and bleat and bleat, and sniff the air.
I'd grab his beard and look at him.
His pupils, horizontal, narrowed up
and expressed nothing, or a little malice.
I got so tired of the very colors!
One day I dyed a baby goat bright red
with my red berries, just to see
something a little different.
And then his mother wouldn't recognize him.

Dreams were the worst. Of course I dreamed of food
and love, but they were pleasant rather
than otherwise. But then I'd dream of things
like slitting a baby's throat, mistaking it
for a baby goat. I'd have
nightmares of other islands
stretching away from mine, infinities
of islands, islands spawning islands,
like frogs' eggs turning into polliwogs
of islands, knowing that I had to live
on each and every one, eventually,
for ages, registering their flora,
their fauna, their geography.

Just when I thought I couldn't stand it
another minute longer, Friday came.
(Accounts of that have everything all wrong.)
Friday was nice.
Friday was nice, and we were friends.
If only he had been a woman!
I wanted to propagate my kind,
and so did he, I think, poor boy.
He'd pet the baby goats sometimes,
and race with them, or carry one around.
—Pretty to watch; he had a pretty body.

And then one day they came and took us off.

Now I live here, another island,
that doesn't seem like one, but who decides?

My blood was full of them; my brain
bred islands. But that archipelago
has petered out. I'm old.
I'm bored, too, drinking my real tea,
surrounded by uninteresting lumber.
The knife there on the shelf—
it reeked of meaning, like a crucifix.
It lived. How many years did I
beg it, implore it, not to break?
I knew each nick and scratch by heart,
the bluish blade, the broken tip,
the lines of wood-grain on the handle . . .
Now it won't look at me at all.
The living soul has dribbled away.
My eyes rest on it and pass on.

The local museum's asked me to
leave everything to them:
the flute, the knife, the shrivelled shoes,
my shedding goatskin trousers
(moths have got in the fur),
the parasol that took me such a time
remembering the way the ribs should go.
It still will work but, folded up,
looks like a plucked and skinny fowl.
How can anyone want such things?
—And Friday, my dear Friday, died of measles
seventeen years ago come March.

ROBERT LOWELL

From Four Poems for Elizabeth Bishop

3 LETTER WITH POEMS FOR A LETTER WITH POEMS

'You're right to worry about me, only please DON'T,
though I'm pretty worried myself. I've somehow got
into the worst situation I've ever
had to cope with. I can't see the way out.
Cal . . . have you ever gone through caves?
I did once . . . Mexico, and hated it—
I've never done the famous ones near here.
Finally after hours of stumbling along,
one sees daylight ahead, a faint blue glimmer.
Air never looked so beautiful before.
That's what I feel I'm waiting for now:
a faintest glimmer I am going to get out
somehow alive from this. Your last letter helped,
like being handed a lantern or a spiked stick.'

T. S. ELIOT AND GROUCHO MARX

CORRESPONDENCE

Eliot to Marx

26th April, 1961

Dear Groucho Marx,
    This is to let you know that your portrait has arrived and has given me
great joy and will soon appear in its frame on my wall with other famous

friends such as W. B. Yeats and Paul Valery. Whether you really want a
photograph of me or whether you merely asked for it out of politeness, you
are going to get one anyway. I am ordering a copy of one of my better
ones and I shall certainly inscribe it with my gratitude and assurance
of admiration. You will have learned that you are my most coveted pin-
up. I shall be happy to occupy a much humbler place in your collection.

And incidentally, if and when you and Mrs. Marx are in London, my
wife and I hope that you will dine with us.

Yours very sincerely,
T. S. Eliot

P.S. I like cigars too but there isn't any cigar in my portrait either.

Marx to Eliot

June 19, 1961

Dear T. S.:

Your photograph arrived in good shape and I hope this note of thanks
finds you in the same condition.

I had no idea you were so handsome. Why you haven't been offered
the lead in some sexy movies I can only attribute to the stupidity of the
casting directors.

Should I come to London I will certainly take advantage of your kind
invitation and if you come to California I hope you will allow me to do
the same.

Cordially,
Groucho Marx

January 25, 1963

Dear Mr. Eliot:

I read in the current Time Magazine that you are ill. I just want you to
know that I am rooting for your quick recovery. First because of your
contributions to literature and, then, the fact that under the most trying
conditions you never stopped smoking cigars.

Hurry up and get well.

Regards,
Groucho Marx

Eliot to Marx

23rd February, 1963

Dear Groucho Marx,

It seems more of an impertinence to address Groucho Marx as "Dear
Mr. Marx" than it would be to address any other celebrity by his first

name. It is out of respect, my dear Groucho, that I address you as I do. I should only be too happy to have a letter from Groucho Marx beginning "Dear T.S.E." However, this is to thank you for your letter and to say that I am convalescing as fast as the awful winter weather permits, that my wife and I hope to get to Bermuda later next month for warmth and fresh air and to be back in London in time to greet you in the spring. So come, let us say, about the beginning of May.

Will Mrs. Groucho be with you? (We think we saw you both in Jamaica early in 1961, about to embark in that glass-bottomed boat from which we had just escaped.) You ought to bring a secretary, a public relations official and a couple of private detectives, to protect you from the London press; but however numerous your engagements, we hope you will give us the honour of taking a meal with us.

Yours very sincerely,
T. S. Eliot

P.S. Your portrait is framed on my office mantelpiece, but I have to point you out to my visitors as nobody recognises you without the cigar and rolling eyes. I shall try to provide a cigar worthy of you.

16th May, 1963

Dear Groucho,

I ought to have written at once on my return from Bermuda to thank you for the second beautiful photograph of Groucho, but after being in hospital for five weeks at the end of the year, and then at home for as many under my wife's care, I was shipped off to Bermuda in the hope of getting warmer weather and have only just returned. Still not quite normal activity, but hope to be about when you and Mrs. Groucho turn up. Is there any date known? We shall be away in Yorkshire at the end of June and the early part of July, but are here all the rest of the summer.

Meanwhile, your splendid new portrait is at the framers. I like them both very much and I cannot make up my mind which one to take home and which one to put on my office wall. The new one would impress visitors more, especially those I want to impress, as it is unmistakably Groucho. The only solution may be to carry them both with me every day.

Whether I can produce as good a cigar for you as the one in the portrait appears to be, I do not know, but I will do my best.

Gratefully,
Your admirer,
T.S.

Marx to Eliot

June 11, 1963

Dear Mr. Eliot:

I am a pretty shabby correspondent. I have your letter of May 16th in front of me and I am just getting around to it.

The fact is, the best laid plans of mice and men, etc. Soon after your letter arrived I was struck down by a mild infection. I'm still not over it, but all plans of getting away this summer have gone by the board.

My plan now is to visit Israel the first part of October when all the tourists are back from their various journeys. Then, on my way back from Israel, I will stop off in London to see you.

I hope you have fully recovered from your illness, and don't let anything else happen to you. In October, remember you and I will get drunk together.

Cordially,
Groucho

Eliot to Marx

24th June, 1963

Dear Groucho,

This is not altogether bad news because I shall be in better condition for drinking in October than I am now. I envy you going to Israel and I wish I could go there too if the winter climate is good as I have a keen admiration for that country. I hope to hear about your visit when I see you and I hope that, meanwhile, we shall both be in the best of health.

One of your portraits is on the wall of my office room and the other one on my desk at home.

Salutations,
T. S.

Marx to Eliot

October 1, 1963

Dear Tom:

If this isn't your first name, I'm in a hell of a fix! But I think I read somewhere that your first name is the same as Tom Gibbons', a prizefighter who once lived in St. Paul.

I had no idea you were seventy-five. There's a magnificent tribute to you in the New York Times Book Review Section of the September 29th issue. If you don't get the New York Times let me know and I'll send you my copy. There is an excellent photograph of you by a Mr. Gerald Kelly.

I would say, judging from this picture, that you are about sixty and two weeks.

There was also a paragraph mentioning the many portraits that are housed in your study. One name was conspicuous by its absence. I trust this was an oversight on the part of Stephen Spender.

My illness which, three months ago, my three doctors described as trivial, is having quite a run in my system. The three medics, I regret to say, are living on the fat of the land. So far, they've hooked me for eight thousand bucks. I only mention this to explain why I can't get over there in October. However, by next May or thereabouts, I hope to be well enough to eat that free meal you've been promising me for the past two years.

My best to you and your lovely wife, whoever she may be.

I hope you are well again.

Kindest regards,
Groucho

Eliot to Marx

16th October, 1963

Dear Groucho,

Yours of October 1st to hand. I cannot recall the name of Tom Gibbons at present, but if he helps you to remember my name that is all right with me.

I think that Stephen Spender was only attempting to enumerate oil and water colour pictures and not photographs—I trust so. But, there are a good many photographs of relatives and friends in my study, although I do not recall Stephen going in there. He sent me what he wrote for the New York Times and I helped him a bit and reminded him that I had a good many books, as he might have seen if he had looked about him.

There is also a conspicuous and important portrait in my office room which has been identified by many of my visitors together with other friends of both sexes.

I am sorry that you are not coming over here this year, and still sorrier for the reason for it. I hope, however, that you will turn up in the spring if your doctors leave you a few nickels to pay your way. If you do not turn up, I am afraid all the people to whom I have boasted of knowing you (and on being on first name terms at that) will take me for a four flusher. There will be a free meal and free drinks for you by next May. Meanwhile, we shall be in New York for the month of December and if you should happen to be passing through there at that time of year, I hope you will take a free meal there on me. I would be delighted to see you wherever we are and proud to be seen in your company. My lovely wife joins me in sending you our best, but she didn't add "whoever he may be"—she knows. It was I who introduced her in the first place to the Marx Brothers films and she is now as keen a fan as I am. Not long ago we went to see a revival of "The Marx Brothers Go West," which I had never seen before. It was certainly worth it.

Ever yours,
Tom

P.S. The photograph is on an oil portrait, done 2 years ago, not a photograph direct from life. It is very good-looking and my wife thinks it is a very accurate representation of me.

Marx to Eliot

November 1, 1963

Dear Tom:

Since you are actually an early American, (I don't mean that you are an old piece of furniture, but you are a fugitive from St. Louis), you should have heard of Tom Gibbons. For your edification, Tom Gibbons was a native of St. Paul, Minnesota, which is only a stone's throw from Missouri. That is, if the stone is encased in a missile. Tom was, at one time, the light-heavyweight champion of the world, and, although out-weighed by twenty pounds by Jack Dempsey, he fought him to a stand-still in Shelby, Montana.

The name Tom fits many things. There was once a famous Jewish actor named Thomashevsky. All male cats are named Tom—unless they have been fixed. In that case they are just neutral and, as the upheaval in Saigon has just proved, there is no place any more for neutrals.

There is an old nursery rhyme that begins "Tom, Tom, the piper's son," etc. The third President of the United States first name was Tom . . . in case you've forgotten Jefferson.

So, when I call you Tom, this means you are a mixture of a heavy-weight prizefighter, a male alley cat and the third President of the United States.

I have just finished my latest opus, "Memoirs of a Mangy Lover." Most of it is autobiographical and very little of it is fiction. I doubt whether it will live through the ages, but if you are in a sexy mood the night you read it, it may stimulate you beyond recognition and rekindle memories that you haven't recalled in years.

Sex, as an industry, is big business in this country, as it is in England. It's something everyone is deeply interested in even if only theoretically. I suppose it's always been this way, but I believe that in the old days it was discussed and practiced in a more surreptitious manner. However, the new school of writers have finally brought the bedroom and the lavatory out into the open for everyone to see. You can blame the whole thing on Havelock Ellis, Krafft-Ebing and Brill, Jung and Freud. (Now there's a trio for you!) Plus, of course, the late Mr. Kinsey who, not satisfied with hearsay, trundled from house to house, sticking his nose in where angels have always feared to tread.

However I would be interested in reading your views on sex, so don't hesitate. Confide in me. Though admittedly unreliable, I can be trusted with matters as important as that.

If there is a possibility of my being in New York in December, I will certainly try to make it and will let you know in time.

My best to you and Mrs. Tom.

Yours,
Groucho

Eliot to Marx

3rd June, 1964

Dear Groucho,

This is to let you know that we have arranged for a car from International Car Hire (a firm of whom we make a good deal of use) to collect you and Mrs. Groucho at 6:40 P.M. on Saturday from the Savoy, and to bring you to us for dinner and take you home again at the end of the evening. You are, of course, our guests entirely, and we look forward to seeing you both with great pleasure.

The picture of you in the newspapers saying that, amongst other reasons, you have come to London to see me has greatly enhanced my credit in the neighbourhood, and particularly with the greengrocer across the street. Obviously I am now someone of importance.

Ever yours,
Tom

GROUCHO MARX

To Gummo Marx

June, 1964

Dear Gummo:

Last night Eden and I had dinner with my celebrated pen pal, T. S. Eliot. It was a memorable evening.

The poet met us at the door with Mrs. Eliot, a good-looking, middle-aged blonde whose eyes seemed to fill up with adoration every time she looked at her husband. He, by the way, is tall, lean and rather stooped over; but whether this is from age, illness or both, I don't know.

At any rate, your correspondent arrived at the Eliots' fully prepared for a literary evening. During the week I had read "Murder in the Cathedral" twice; "The Waste Land" three times, and just in case of a conversational bottleneck, I brushed up on "King Lear."

Well, sir, as cocktails were served, there was a momentary lull—the kind that is more or less inevitable when strangers meet for the first time. So, apropos of practically nothing (and "not with a bang but a whimper") I tossed in a quotation from "The Waste Land." That, I thought, will show him I've read a thing or two besides my press notices from vaudeville.

Eliot smiled faintly—as though to say he was thoroughly familiar with his poems and didn't need me to recite them. So I took a whack at "King Lear." I said the king was an incredibly foolish old man, which God knows he _was;_ and that if he'd been _my_ father I would have run away from home at the age of eight—instead of waiting until I was ten.

That, too, failed to bowl over the poet. He seemed more interested in discussing "Animal Crackers" and "A Night at the Opera." He quoted a joke—one of mine—that I had long since forgotten. Now it was my turn to smile faintly. I was not going to let anyone—not even the British poet from St. Louis—spoil my Literary Evening. I pointed out that King Lear's opening speech was the height of idiocy. Imagine (I said) a father asking his three children: Which of you kids loves me the most? And then disowning the youngest—the sweet, honest Cordelia—because, unlike her wicked sister, she couldn't bring herself to gush out insincere flattery. And Cordelia, mind you, had been her father's favorite!

The Eliots listened politely. Mrs. Eliot then defended Shakespeare; and Eden, too, I regret to say, was on King Lear's side, even though I am the one who supports her. (In all fairness to my wife, I must say that, having played the Princess in a high school production of "The Swan," she has retained a rather warm feeling for all royalty.)

As for Eliot, he asked if I remembered the courtroom scene in "Duck Soup." Fortunately I'd forgotten every word. It was obviously the end of the Literary Evening, but very pleasant none the less. I discovered that Eliot and I had three things in common: (1) an affection for good cigars and (2) cats; and (3) a weakness for making puns—a weakness that for many years I have tried to overcome. T. S., on the other hand, is an unashamed—even proud—punster. For example, there's his Gus, the Theater Cat, whose "real name was Asparagus."

Speaking of asparagus, the dinner included good, solid English beef, very well prepared. And, although they had a semi-butler serving, Eliot insisted on pouring the wine himself. It was an excellent wine and no maitre d' could have served it more graciously. He is a dear man and a charming host.

When I told him that my daughter Melinda was studying his poetry at Beverly High, he said he regretted that, because he had no wish to become compulsory reading.

We didn't stay late, for we both felt that he wasn't up to a long evening of conversation—especially mine.

Did I tell you we called him Tom?—possibly because that's his name. I, of course, asked him to call me Tom too, but only because I loathe the name Julius.

Yours,
Tom Marx

To Russell Baker

January 21, 1965

. . . I was saddened by the death of T. S. Eliot. My wife and I had dinner at his home a few months ago and I realized then that he was not long for this world. He was a nice man, the best epitaph any man can have. . . .

Part XV

Further Essays

Friendship is a miracle by which a person consents to view from a certain distance, and without coming any nearer, the very being who is necessary to him as food.

— Simone Weil

HENRY DAVID THOREAU

From A WEEK ON THE CONCORD AND MERRIMACK RIVERS

. . . After years of vain familiarity, some distant gesture or unconscious behavior, which we remember, speaks to us with more emphasis than the wisest or kindest words. We are sometimes made aware of a kindness long passed, and realize that there have been times when our Friends' thoughts of us were of so pure and lofty a character that they passed over us like the winds of heaven unnoticed; when they treated us not as what we were, but as what we aspired to be. There has just reached us, it may be, the nobleness of some such silent behavior, not to be forgotten, not to be remembered, and we shudder to think how it fell on us cold, though in some true but tardy hour we endeavor to wipe off these scores. . . .

Friendship is evanescent in every man's experience, and remembered like heat lightning in past summers. Fair and flitting like a summer cloud—there is always some vapor in the air, no matter how long the drought; there are even April showers. Surely from time to time, for its vestiges never depart, it floats through our atmosphere. It takes place, like vegetation in so many materials, because there is such a law, but always without permanent form, though ancient and familiar as the sun and moon, and as sure to come again. The heart is forever inexperienced. They silently gather as by magic, these never failing, never quite deceiving visions, like the bright and fleecy clouds in the calmest and clearest days. The Friend is some fair floating isle of palms eluding the mariner in Pacific seas. Many are the dangers to be encountered, equinoctial gales and coral reefs, ere he may sail before the constant trades. But who would not sail through mutiny and storm, even over Atlantic waves, to reach the fabulous retreating shores of some continent man? . . .

No word is oftener on the lips of men than Friendship, and indeed no thought is more familiar to their aspirations. All men are dreaming of it, and its drama, which is always a tragedy, is enacted daily. It is the secret of the universe. You may thread the town, you may wander the country, and none shall ever speak of it, yet thought is everywhere busy about it, and the idea of what is possible in this respect affects our behavior toward all new men and women, and a great many old ones. Nevertheless, I can remember only two or three essays on this subject in all literature. No wonder that the mythology, and Arabian Nights, and Shakespeare, and Scott's novels entertain us—we are poets and fablers and dramatists and novelists ourselves. We are continually acting a part in a more interesting drama than any written. We are dreaming that our Friends are our *Friends,* and that we are our Friends' *Friends.* Our actual Friends are but distant relations of those to whom we are pledged. We never exchange more than three words with a Friend in our lives on that level to which our thoughts and feelings almost habitually rise. One goes forth prepared to say, "Sweet Friends!" and the salutation is, "Damn your eyes!" But never mind; faint heart never won true Friend. O my Friend, may it come to pass once, that when you are my Friend I may be yours.

Of what use the friendliest dispositions even, if there are no hours given to Friendship, if it is forever postponed to unimportant duties and relations? Friendship is first, Friendship last. But it is equally impossible to forget our Friends, and to make them answer to our ideal. When they say farewell, then indeed we begin to keep them company. How often we find ourselves turning our backs on our actual Friends, that we may go and meet their ideal cousins. I would that I were worthy to be any man's Friend.

What is commonly honored with the name of Friendship is no very profound or powerful instinct. Men do not, after all, *love* their Friends greatly. I do not often see the farmers made seers and wise to the verge of insanity by their Friendship for one another. They are not often transfigured and translated by love in each other's presence. I do not observe them purified, refined, and elevated by the love of a man. If one abates a little the price of his wood, or gives a neighbor his vote at town meeting, or a barrel of apples, or lends him his wagon frequently, it is esteemed a rare instance of Friendship. Nor do the farmers' wives lead lives consecrated to Friendship. I do not see the pair of farmer Friends of either sex prepared to stand against the world. There are only two or three couples in history. To say that a man is your Friend means commonly no more than this, that he is not your enemy. Most contemplate only what would be the accidental and trifling advantages of Friendship, so that the Friend can assist in time of need, by his substance, or his influence, or his counsel; but he who foresees such advantages in this relation proves himself blind to its real advantage, or indeed wholly inexperienced in the relation itself. Such services are particular and menial, compared with the perpetual and all-embracing service which it is. Even the utmost good will and harmony and practical kindness are not sufficient for

Friendship, for Friends do not live in harmony merely, as some say, but in melody. We do not wish for Friends to feed and clothe our bodies—neighbors are kind enough for that—but to do the like office to our spirits. For this few are rich enough, however well disposed they may be. For the most part we stupidly confound one man with another. The dull distinguish only races or nations, or at most classes, but the wise man, individuals. To his Friend a man's peculiar character appears in every feature and in every action, and it is thus drawn out and improved by him. . . .

All the abuses which are the object of reform with the philanthropist, the statesman, and the housekeeper are unconsciously amended in the intercourse of Friends. A Friend is one who incessantly pays us the compliment of expecting from us all the virtues, and who can appreciate them in us. It takes two to speak the truth—one to speak, and another to hear. How can one treat with magnanimity mere wood and stone? If we dealt only with the false and dishonest, we should at last forget how to speak truth. Only lovers know the value and magnanimity of truth, while traders prize a cheap honesty, and neighbors and acquaintance a cheap civility. In our daily intercourse with men, our nobler faculties are dormant and suffered to rust. None will pay us the compliment to expect nobleness from us. Though we have gold to give, they demand only copper. We ask our neighbor to suffer himself to be dealt with truly, sincerely, nobly; but he answers no by his deafness. He does not even hear this prayer. He says practically, I will be content if you treat me as "no better than I should be," as deceitful, mean, dishonest, and selfish. For the most part, we are contented so to deal and to be dealt with, and we do not think that for the mass of men there is any truer and nobler relation possible. A man may have *good* neighbors, so called, and acquaintances, and even companions, wife, parents, brothers, sisters, children, who meet himself and one another on this ground only. The State does not demand justice of its members, but thinks that it succeeds very well with the least degree of it, hardly more than rogues practice; and so do the neighborhood and the family. What is commonly called Friendship even is only a little more honor among rogues.

But sometimes we are said to *love* another, that is, to stand in a true relation to him, so that we give the best to, and receive the best from, him. Between whom there is hearty truth, there is love; and in proportion to our truthfulness and confidence in one another, our lives are divine and miraculous, and answer to our ideal. There are passages of affection in our intercourse with mortal men and women, such as no prophecy had taught us to expect, which transcend our earthly life, and anticipate Heaven for us. What is this Love that may come right into the middle of a prosaic Goffstown day, equal to any of the gods? that discovers a new world, fair and fresh and eternal, occupying the place of the old one, when to the common eye a dust has settled on the universe?—which world cannot else be reached, and does not exist. What other words, we may almost ask, are memorable and worthy to be repeated than those which love has inspired? . . .

. . . Friendship takes place between those who have an affinity for one another, and is a perfectly natural and inevitable result. No professions nor advances will avail. Even speech, at first, necessarily has nothing to do with it; but it follows after silence, as the buds in the graft do not put forth into leaves till long after the graft has taken. It is a drama in which the parties have no part to act. We are all Mussulmans and fatalists in this respect. Impatient and uncertain lovers think that they must say or do something kind whenever they meet; they must never be cold. But they who are Friends do not do what they *think* they must, but what they *must.* Even their Friendship is to some extent but a sublime phenomenon to them.

The true and not despairing Friend will address his Friend in some such terms as these. . . .

"You are the fact in a fiction, you are the truth more strange and admirable than fiction. Consent only to be what you are. I alone will never stand in your way. . . ."

The Friend asks no return but that his Friend will religiously accept and wear and not disgrace his apotheosis of him. They cherish each other's hopes. They are kind to each other's dreams.

Though the poet says, " 'Tis the pre-eminence of Friendship to impute excellence," yet we can never praise our Friend, nor esteem him praiseworthy, nor let him think that he can please us by any *behavior,* or ever *treat* us well enough. That kindness which has so good a reputation elsewhere can least of all consist with this relation, and no such affront can be offered to a Friend, as a conscious goodwill, a friendliness which is not a necessity of the Friend's nature. . . .

Confucius said, "Never contract Friendship with a man who is no better than thyself." It is the merit and preservation of Friendship that it takes place on a level higher than the actual characters of the parties would seem to warrant. The rays of light come to us in such a curve that every man whom we meet appears to be taller than he actually is. Such foundation has civility. My Friend is that one whom I can associate with my choicest thought. . . .

. . . There are times when we have had enough even of our Friends, when we begin inevitably to profane one another, and must withdraw religiously into solitude and silence, the better to prepare ourselves for a loftier intimacy. Silence is the ambrosial night in the intercourse of Friends, in which their sincerity is recruited and takes deeper root.

Friendship is never established as an understood relation. Do you demand that I be less your Friend that you may know it? Yet what right have I to think that another cherishes so rare a sentiment for me? It is a miracle which requires constant proofs. It is an exercise of the purest imagination and the rarest faith. It says by a silent but eloquent behavior, "I will be so related to thee as thou canst imagine; even so thou mayest believe. I will spend truth, all my wealth on thee,"—and the Friend responds silently through his nature and life, and treats his Friend with the same divine courtesy. He knows us literally through thick and thin. He never asks for a sign of love, but can distinguish it by the features which it naturally wears. We never need to stand upon ceremony with him with regard to his visits. Wait not till I invite thee, but observe that I am glad to see thee when thou comest. It would be paying too dear for thy visit to ask for it. Where my Friend lives there are all riches and every attraction, and no slight obstacle can keep me from him. . . .

The language of Friendship is not words, but meanings. It is an intelligence above language. One imagines endless conversations with his Friend, in which the tongue shall be loosed, and thoughts be spoken without hesitancy or end; but the experience is commonly far otherwise. Acquaintances may come and go, and have a word ready for every occasion; but what puny word shall he utter whose very breath is thought and meaning? . . .

. . . Their relation implies such qualities as the warrior prizes; for it takes a valor to open the hearts of men as well as the gates of castles. It is not an idle sympathy and mutual consolation merely, but a heroic sympathy of aspiration and endeavor. . . .

. . . A base Friendship is of a narrowing and exclusive tendency, but a noble one is not exclusive; its very superfluity and dispersed love is the humanity which sweetens society, and sympathizes with foreign nations; for though its foundations are private, it is, in effect, a public affair and a public advantage, and the Friend, more than the father of a family, deserves well of the state.

The only danger in Friendship is that it will end. It is a delicate plant, though a native. The least unworthiness, even if it be unknown to one's self, vitiates it. Let the Friend know that those faults which he observes in his Friend his own faults attract. There is no rule more invariable than that we are paid for our suspicions by finding what we suspected. By our narrowness and prejudices we say, I will have so much and such of you, my Friend, no more. Perhaps there are none charitable, none disinterested, none wise, noble, and heroic enough, for a true and lasting Friendship.

I sometimes hear my Friends complain finely that I do not appreciate their fineness. I shall not tell them whether I do or not. As if they expected a vote of thanks for every fine thing which they uttered or did. Who knows but it was finely appreciated. It may be that your silence was the finest thing of the two. There are some things which a man never speaks of, which are much finer kept silent about. To the highest communications we only lend a silent ear. Our finest relations are not simply kept silent about, but buried under a positive depth of silence never to be revealed. It may be that we are not even yet acquainted. In human intercourse the tragedy begins, not when there is misunderstanding about words, but when silence is not understood. Then there can never be an explanation. What avails it that another loves you, if he does not understand you? Such love is a curse. What sort of companions are they who are presuming always that their silence is more expressive than yours? How foolish, and inconsiderate, and unjust, to conduct as if you were the only party aggrieved! Has not your Friend always equal ground of complaint? No doubt my Friends sometimes speak to me in vain, but they do not know what things I hear which they are not aware that they have spoken. I know that I have frequently disappointed them by not giving them words when they expected them, or such as they expected. Whenever I see my Friend I speak to him; but the expecter, the man with the ears, is not he. They will complain too that you are hard. O ye that would have the cocoanut wrong side outwards, when next I weep I will let you know. They ask for words and deeds, when a true relation is word and deed. If they know not of these things, how can they be informed? We often forbear to confess our feelings, not from pride, but for fear that we could not continue to love the one who required us to give such proof of our affection. . . .

For a companion, I require one who will make an equal demand on me with my own genius. Such a one will always be rightly tolerant. It is suicide, and corrupts good manners, to welcome any less than this. I value and trust those who love and praise my aspiration rather than my performance. If you would not stop to look at me, but look whither I am looking, and farther, then my education could not dispense with your company. . . .

Ignorance and bungling with love are better than wisdom and skill without. There may be courtesy, there may be even temper, and wit, and talent, and sparkling conversation, there may be good will even—and yet the humanest and divinest faculties pine for exercise. Our life without love is like coke and ashes. Men may be pure as alabaster and Parian marble, elegant as a Tuscan villa, sublime as Niagara, and yet if there is no milk mingled with the wine at their entertainments, better is the hospitality of Goths and Vandals.

My Friend is not of some other race or family of men, but flesh of my flesh, bone of my bone. He is my real brother. I see his nature groping yonder so like mine. We do not live far apart. Have not the fates associated us in many ways? It says, in the *Vishnu Purana:* "Seven paces together is sufficient for the friendship of the virtuous, but thou and I have dwelt together." Is it of no significance that we have so long partaken of the same loaf, drunk at the same fountain, breathed the same air summer and winter, felt the same heat and cold; that the same fruits have been pleased to refresh us both, and we have never had a thought of different fiber the one from the other! . . .

But all that can be said of Friendship is like botany to flowers. How can the understanding take account of its friendliness?

RALPH WALDO EMERSON

From FRIENDSHIP

. . . The moment we indulge our affections, the earth is metamorphosed: there is no winter, and no night: all tragedies, all ennuis vanish,—all duties even; nothing fills the proceeding eternity but the forms all radiant of beloved persons. Let the soul be assured that somewhere in the universe it should rejoin its friend, and it would be content and cheerful alone for a thousand years.

I awoke this morning with devout thanksgiving for my friends, the old and the new. . . .

. . . My friends have come to me unsought. The great God gave them to me. By oldest right, by the divine affinity of virtue with itself, I find them, or rather, not I, but the Deity in me and in them derides and cancels the thick walls of individual character, relation, age, sex, circumstance, at which he usually connives, and now makes many one. High thanks I owe you, excellent lovers, who carry out the world for me to new and noble depths, and enlarge the meaning of all my thoughts. . . .

I do not wish to treat friendships daintily, but with roughest courage. When they are real, they are not glass threads or frostwork, but the solidest thing we know. For now, after so many ages of experience, what do we know of nature, or of ourselves? Not one step has man taken toward the solution of the problem of his destiny. In one condemnation of folly stand the whole universe of men. But the sweet sincerity of joy and peace, which I draw from this alliance with my brother's soul, is the nut itself whereof all nature and all thought is but the husk and shell. Happy is the house that shelters a friend! . . .

. . . There are two elements that go to the composition of friendship, each so sovereign, that I can detect no superiority in either, no reason why either should be first named. One is Truth. A friend is a person with whom I may be sincere. . . .

The other element of friendship is Tenderness. We are holden to men by every sort of tie, by blood, by pride, by fear, by hope, by lucre, by lust, by hate, by admiration, by every circumstance and badge and trifle, but we can scarce believe that so much character can subsist in another as to draw us by love. Can another be so blessed, and we so pure, that we can offer him tenderness? When a man becomes dear to me, I have touched the goal of fortune. . . .

E. M. FORSTER

From NOTES ON ENGLISH CHARACTER

Once upon a time (this is an anecdote) I went for a week's holiday on the Continent with an Indian friend. We both enjoyed ourselves and were sorry when the week was over, but on parting our behaviour was absolutely different. He was plunged in despair. He felt that because the holiday was over all happiness was over until the world ended. He could not express his sorrow too much. But in me the Englishman came out strong. I reflected that we should meet again in a month or two, and could write in the interval if we had anything to say; and under these circumstances I could not see what there was to make a fuss about. It wasn't as if we were parting forever or dying. "Buck up," I said, "do buck up." He refused to buck up, and I left him plunged in gloom.

The conclusion of the anecdote is even more instructive. For when we met the next month our conversation threw a good deal of light on the English character. I began by scolding my friend. I told him that he had been wrong to feel and display so much emotion upon so slight an occasion; that it was inappropriate. The word "inappropriate" roused him to fury. "What?" he cried. "Do you measure out your emotions as if they were potatoes?" I did not like the simile of the potatoes, but after a moment's reflection I said, "Yes, I do; and what's more, I think I ought to. A small occasion demands a little emotion, just as a large occasion demands a great one. I would like my emotions to be appropriate. This may be measuring them like potatoes, but it is better than slopping them about like water from a pail, which is what you did." He did not like the simile of the pail. "If those are your opinions, they part us forever," he cried, and left the room. Returning immediately, he added: "No—but your whole attitude toward emotion is wrong. Emotion has nothing to do with appropriateness. It matters only that it shall be sincere. I happened to feel deeply. I showed it. It doesn't matter whether I ought to have felt deeply or not."

This remark impressed me very much. Yet I could not agree with it, and said that I valued emotion as much as he did, but used it differently; if I poured it out on small occasions I was afraid of having none left for the great ones, and of being bankrupt at the crises of life. Note the word "bankrupt." I spoke as a member of a prudent middle-class nation, always anxious to meet my liabilities. But my friend spoke as an Oriental, and the Oriental has behind him a tradition, not of middle-class prudence, but of kingly munificence and splendour. He feels his resources are endless, just as John Bull feels his are finite. As regards material resources, the Oriental is clearly unwise. Money isn't endless. If we spend or give away all the money we have, we haven't any more, and must take the consequences, which are frequently unpleasant. But, as regards the resources of the spirit, he may be right. The emotions may be endless. The more we express them, the more we may have to express.

From WHAT I BELIEVE

I do not believe in Belief. But this is an age of faith, and there are so many militant creeds that, in self-defence, one has to formulate a creed of one's own. Tolerance, good temper and sympathy are no longer enough in a world which is rent by religious and racial persecution, in a world where ignorance rules, and science, who ought to have ruled, plays the subservient pimp. Tolerance, good temper and sympathy—they are what matter really, and if the human race is not to collapse they must come to the front before long. But for the moment they are not enough, their action is no stronger than a flower, battered beneath a military jack-boot. They want stiffening, even if the process coarsens them. Faith, to my mind, is a stiffening process, a sort of mental starch, which ought to be applied as sparingly as possible. I dislike the stuff. I do not believe in it, for its own sake, at all. Herein I probably differ from most people, who believe in Belief, and are only sorry they cannot swallow even more than they do. My law-givers are Erasmus and Montaigne, not Moses and St. Paul. My temple stands not upon Mount Moriah but in that Elysian Field where even the immoral are admitted. My motto is: "Lord, I disbelieve—help thou my unbelief."

I have, however, to live in an Age of Faith—the sort of epoch I used to hear praised when I was a boy. It is extremely unpleasant really. It is bloody in every sense of the word. And I have to keep my end up in it. Where do I start?

With personal relationships. Here is something comparatively solid in a world full of violence and cruelty. Not absolutely solid, for Psychology has split and shattered the idea of a "Person," and has shown that there is something incalculable in each of us, which may at any moment rise to the surface and destroy our normal balance. We don't know what we are like. We can't know what other people are like. How, then, can we put any trust in personal relationships, or cling to them in the gathering political storm? In theory we cannot. But in practice we can and do. Though A is not unchangeably A or B unchangeably B, there can still be love and loyalty between the two. For the purpose of living one has to assume that the personality is solid, and the "self" is an entity, and to ignore all contrary evidence. And since to ignore evidence is one of the characteristics of faith, I certainly can proclaim that I believe in personal relationships.

Starting from them, I get a little order into the contemporary chaos. One must be fond of people and trust them if one is not to make a mess of life, and it is therefore essential that they should not let one down. They often do. The moral of which is that I must, myself, be as reliable as possible, and this I try to be. But reliability is not a matter of contract—that is the main difference between the world of personal relationships and the world of business relationships. It is a matter for the heart, which signs no documents. In other words, reliability is impossible unless there is a natural warmth. Most men possess this warmth, though they often have bad luck and get chilled. Most of them, even when they are politicians, *want* to keep faith. And one can, at all events, show one's own little light here, one's own poor little trembling flame, with the knowledge that it is not the only light that is shining in the darkness, and not the only one which the darkness does not comprehend. Personal relations are despised today. They are regarded as bourgeois luxuries, as products of a time of fair weather which is now past, and we are urged to get rid of them, and to dedicate ourselves to some movement or cause instead. I hate the idea of causes, and if I had to choose between betraying my country and betraying my friend, I hope I should have the guts to betray my country. Such a choice may scandalise the modern reader, and he may stretch out his patriotic hand to the telephone at once and ring up the police. It would not have shocked Dante, though. Dante places Brutus and Cassius in the lowest circle of Hell because they had chosen to betray their friend Julius Caesar rather than their country Rome. Probably one will not be asked to make such an agonising choice. Still, there lies at the back of every creed something terrible and hard for which the worshipper may one day be required to suffer, and there is even a terror and a hardness in this creed of personal relationships, urbane and mild though it sounds. Love and loyalty to an individual can run counter to the claims of the State. When they do—down with the State, say I, which means that the State would down me.

HANNAH ARENDT

From MEN IN DARK TIMES

. . . As is well known, the ancients thought friends indispensable to human life, indeed that a life without friends was not really worth living. In holding this view they gave little consideration to the idea that we need the help of friends in misfortune; on the contrary, they rather thought that there can be no happiness or good fortune for anyone unless a friend shares in the joy of it. Of course there is something to the maxim that only in misfortune do we find out who our true friends are; but those whom we regard as our true friends without such proof are usually those to whom we unhesitatingly reveal happiness and whom we count on to share our rejoicing.

We are wont to see friendship solely as a phenomenon of intimacy, in which the friends open their hearts to each other unmolested by the world and its demands. Rousseau, not Lessing, is the best advocate of this view, which conforms so well to the basic attitude of the modern individual, who in his alienation from the world can truly reveal himself only in privacy and in the intimacy of face-to-face encounters. Thus it is hard for us to understand the political relevance of friendship. When, for example, we read in Aristotle that *philia,* friendship among citizens, is one of the fundamental requirements for the well-being of the City, we tend to think that he was speaking of no more than the absence of factions and civil war within it. But for the Greeks the essence of friendship consisted in discourse. They held that only the constant interchange of talk united citizens in a *polis*. In discourse the political importance of friendship, and the humanness peculiar to it, were made manifest. This converse (in contrast to the intimate talk in which individuals speak about themselves), permeated though it may be by pleasure in the friend's presence, is concerned with the common world, which remains "inhuman" in a very literal sense unless it is constantly talked about by human beings. For the world is not humane just because it is made by human beings, and it does not become humane just because the human voice sounds in it, but only when it has become the object of discourse. However much we are affected by the things of the world, however deeply they may stir and stimulate us, they become human for us only when we can discuss them with our fellows. Whatever cannot become the object of discourse—the truly sublime, the truly horrible or the uncanny—may find a human voice through which to sound into the world, but it is not exactly human. We humanize what is going on in the world and in ourselves only by speaking of it, and in the course of speaking of it we learn to be human.

The Greeks called this humanness which is achieved in the discourse of friendship *philanthropia,* "love of man," since it manifests itself in a readiness to share the world with other men. Its opposite, misanthropy, means simply that the misanthrope finds no one with whom he cares to share the world, that he regards nobody as worthy of rejoicing with him in the world and nature and the cosmos.

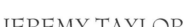

JEREMY TAYLOR

From A DISCOURSE OF THE NATURE, OFFICES, AND MEASURES, OF FRIENDSHIP

(Taylor concludes his essay, which is dedicated to Katherine Philips, with a series of ten final points, some of which we reprint here.)

3. There are two things which a friend can never pardon, a treacherous blow and the revealing of a secret, because these are against the

nature of friendship; they are the adulteries of it, and dissolve the union; and in the matters of friendship, which is the marriage of souls, these are the proper causes of divorce: and therefore I shall add this only, that secrecy is the chastity of friendship, and the publication of it is a prostitution and direct debauchery; but a secret, treacherous wound is a perfect and unpardonable apostasy. I remember a pretty apologue that Bromiard tells,—A fowler in a sharp frosty morning having taken many little birds for which he had long watched, began to take up his nets; and nipping the birds on the head laid them down. A young thrush, espying the tears trickling down his cheeks by reason of the extreme cold, said to her mother, that certainly the man was very merciful and compassionate that wept so bitterly over the calamity of the poor birds: but her mother told her more wisely, that she might better judge of the man's disposition by his hand than by his eye;—and if the hands do strike treacherously, he can never be admitted to friendship, who speaks fairly and weeps pitifully. Friendship is the greatest honesty and ingenuity in the world.

4. Never accuse thy friend, nor believe him that does; if thou dost, thou hast broken the skin: but he that is angry with every little fault, breaks the bones of friendship. . . .

5. Give thy friend counsel wisely and charitably, but leave him to his liberty whether he will follow thee or no: and be not angry if thy counsel be rejected: for advice is no empire, and he is not my friend that will be my judge whether I will or no. Neoptolemus had never been honoured with the victory and spoils of Troy, if he had attended to the tears and counsel of Lycomedes, who being afraid to venture the young man, fain would have had him sleep at home safe in his little island. He that gives advice to his friend and exacts obedience to it, does not the kindness and ingenuity of a friend, but the office and pertness of a schoolmaster. . . .

8. When you admonish your friend, let it be without bitterness; when you chide him, let it be without reproach; when you praise him, let it be with worthy purposes, and for just causes, and in friendly measures; too much of that is flattery, too little is envy: if you do it justly, you teach him true measures; but when others praise him, rejoice, though they praise not thee, and remember that if thou esteemest his praise to be thy disparagement, thou art envious, but neither just nor kind.

9. When all things else are equal, prefer an old friend before a new. If thou meanest to spend thy friend, and make gain of him till he be weary, thou wilt esteem him as a beast of burden, the worse for his age: but if thou esteemest him by noble measures, he will be better to thee by thy being used to him, by trial and experience, by reciprocation of endearments, and an habitual worthiness. An old friend is like old wine, which when a man hath drunk, he doth not desire new, because he saith "the

old is better." But every old friend was new once; and if he be worthy, keep the new one till he become old. . . .

SIMONE WEIL

From FRIENDSHIP

"Friendship is an equality made of harmony," said the Pythagoreans. There is harmony because there is a supernatural union between two opposites, that is to say, necessity and liberty, the two opposites God combined when he created the world and men. There is equality because each wishes to preserve the faculty of free consent both in himself and in the other.

When anyone wishes to put himself under a human being or consents to be subordinated to him, there is no trace of friendship. Racine's Pylades is not the friend of Orestes. There is no friendship where there is inequality. . . .

A friendship is tarnished as soon as necessity triumphs, if only for a moment, over the desire to preserve the faculty of free consent on both sides. In all human things, necessity is the principle of impurity. All friendship is impure if even a trace of the wish to please or the contrary desire to dominate is found in it. In a perfect friendship these two desires are completely absent. The two friends have fully consented to be two and not one, they respect the distance which the fact of being two distinct creatures places between them. Man has the right to desire direct union with God alone.

Friendship is a miracle by which a person consents to view from a certain distance, and without coming any nearer, the very being who is necessary to him as food. . . .

Translated by Emma Craufurd

C. S. LEWIS

From FRIENDSHIP

. . . Those who cannot conceive Friendship as a substantive love but only as a disguise or elaboration of Eros betray the fact that they have never had a Friend. The rest of us know that though we can have erotic love and friendship for the same person yet in some ways nothing is less like a Friendship than a love-affair. Lovers are always talking to one another about their love; Friends hardly ever about their Friendship. Lovers are normally face to face, absorbed in each other; Friends, side by side, absorbed in some common interest. Above all, Eros (while it lasts) is necessarily between two only. But two, far from being the necessary number for Friendship, is not even the best. And the reason for this is important.

Lamb says somewhere that if, of three friends (A, B, and C), A should die, then B loses not only A but "A's part in C," while C loses not only A but "A's part in B." In each of my friends there is something that only some other friend can fully bring out. By myself I am not large enough to call the whole man into activity; I want other lights than my own to show all his facets. Now that Charles is dead, I shall never again see Ronald's reaction to a specifically Caroline joke. Far from having more of Ronald, having him "to myself" now that Charles is away, I have less of Ronald. Hence true Friendship is the least jealous of loves. Two friends delight to be joined by a third, and three by a fourth, if only the newcomer is qualified to become a real friend. They can then say, as the blessed souls say in Dante, "Here comes one who will augment our loves." For in this love "to divide is not to take away." Of course the scarcity of kindred souls—not to mention practical considerations about the size of rooms and the audibility of voices—set limits to the enlargement of the circle; but within those limits we possess each friend not less but more as the number of those with whom we share him increases. . . .

That is why those pathetic people who simply "want friends" can never make any. The very condition of having Friends is that we should want something else besides Friends. . . .

Hence (if you will not misunderstand me) the exquisite arbitrariness and irresponsibility of this love. I have no duty to be anyone's Friend and no man in the world has a duty to be mine. No claims, no shadow of necessity. Friendship is unnecessary, like philosophy, like art, like the universe itself (for God did not need to create). It has no survival value; rather it is one of those things which give value to survival. . . .

Part XVI

Fables, Legends, and Folktales

I had three chairs in my house; one for solitude, two for friendship, three for society.

—Henry David Thoreau

AESOP

Birds of a Feather

A man who was intending to buy an ass took one on trial and placed it along with his own asses at the manger. It turned its back on all of them save one, the laziest and greediest of the lot; it stood close beside this one and just did nothing. So the man put a halter on it and took it back to its owner, who asked if he thought that was giving it a fair trial. "I don't want any further trial," he answered. "I am quite sure it is like the one that it singled out as a companion."

¶A man's character is judged by that of the friends whose society he takes pleasure in.

A Friend in Need Is a Friend Indeed

Two friends were travelling together when a bear suddenly appeared. One of them climbed up a tree in time and remained there hidden. The other, seeing that he would be caught in another moment, lay down on the ground and pretended to be dead. When the bear put its muzzle to him and smelt him all over, he held his breath—for it is said that a bear will not touch a corpse. After it had gone away, the other man came down from his tree and asked his friend what the bear had whispered in his ear. "It told me," he replied, "not to travel in future with friends who do not stand by one in peril."

¶Genuine friends are proved by adversity.

Translated by S. A. Handford

JEAN DE LA FONTAINE

FABLE 8.11: THE TWO FRIENDS

Two bosom friends once lived in Hyderab,
Sharing in common everything they had.
(I've heard that friendships are at least
As strong as ours are in the East.)

One night when both were busy sleeping,
Profiting from the absence of the sun,
One of them woke in alarm and, leaping
Out of his bed, ran to the house of the other
And roused his servants—for by now the Lord
      Of Slumber had set foot
Within the palace gates. The sleeping one,
Startled, reached for his purse and sword
And left his room to meet his brother.
      "It's a rare thing for you," he said,
"To be abroad when all the world's in bed:
You've always struck me as a man who'd put
To better use the sacred hours of night.
Have you lost a fortune gambling? Well, if so,
Here's money. Have you got into a fight?
      I've brought my sword—let's go!
      Are you tired of lying in the dark
      Night after night on your own?
      I've just come from beside
A pretty concubine. She's yours on loan—
Shall I call her over?" "No," his friend replied.
      "You haven't hit the mark.
But thank you for your kind zeal all the same.
      The truth is that I dreamed
      A dream in which you seemed
      Unhappy, so I came
      Rushing across, fearing the worst.

It was my accursed
Nightmare that was to blame."

Which of these two was the fonder?
There's a good question to ponder.
What do you think, reader, I wonder?
   A true friend is a pearl. He reads
   Your deepest needs
   And so spares you the shame
Of giving your heart's hidden desires a name.
   When somebody is very dear,
A dream, anything, nothing stirs your fear.

Translated by James Michie

SIR THOMAS ELYOT

From THE GOUERNOUR

. . . Horestes and Pilades, beinge wonderfull like in all features, were taken to gider and presented unto a tyrant who deedly hated Horestes, but whan he behelde them bothe, and wolde haue slayne Horestes onely, he coulde nat decerne the one from the other. And also Pilades, to deliuer his frende, affirmed that he was Orestes; on the other parte Orestes, to saue Pilades, denied and said that he was Orestes (as the trouthe was). Thus a longe tyme they to gither contendinge, the one to die for the other, at the laste so relented the fierse and cruell harte of the tyrant, that wondringe at their meruailous frendship he suffred them frely to departe, without doinge to them any damage.

Pitheas and Damon, two Pythagoriens, that is to say, studentes of Pythagoras lerninge, beinge ioyned to gither in a parfeite frendship, for that one of them was accused to haue conspired agayne Dionyse, king of Sicile, they were bothe taken and brought to the kinge, who immediately gaue sentence, that he that was accused shulde be put to dethe. But he desired the kinge that, er he died, he mought retourne home to set his householde in ordre and to distribute his goodes; whereat the kinge laughinge demaunded of him skornefully what pledge he wolde leaue hym to come agayne. At the whiche wordes his companyon stepte furthe and saide, that he wolde remayne there as a pledge for his frende, that in case he came nat againe at the daye to hym appointed, that he wyllingly wolde lose his hede; whiche condicion the tyraunt receyued. The yonge man that shuld haue died, was suffred to departe home to his house, where he set all thinge in ordre and disposed his goodes wisely. The day appointed for his retourne was commen, the tyme moche passed; wherfore the kynge called for him that was pledge, who came furthe merely without semblaunte of drede, offringe to abide the sentence of the tyraunt, and without grudginge to die for the sauinge the life of his frende. But as the officer of iustyce had closed his eien with a kerchiefe, and had drawen his swerde to haue striken of his hedde, his felowe came runninge and cryenge that the daye of his appointment was nat yet past; wherfore he desired the minister of iustice to lose his felowe, and to prepare to do execution on hym that had giuen the occasion. Whereat the tyraunt being all abasshed, commaunded bothe to be brought in his presence, and whan he had ynough wondred at their noble hartes and their constance in very frendship, he offring to them great rewardes desired them to receyue hym into their company; and so, doinge them moche honour, dyd set them at liberte. . . .

ELIE WIESEL

From SOMEWHERE A MASTER

Rebbe Uri, the celebrated Seraphin of Strelisk, needed money to marry off an old maid, orphan to boot. Where could he go? To people who had money. The problem was, he didn't know any; he knew only people who needed money—for themselves or for others. One of them was his friend Reb Moshe-Leib of Sassov, who also was running around the country collecting funds for beggars. He went to see him. At first, the two remained quiet for several hours, reflecting. Then Reb Moshe-Leib turned to his friend and said, "Uri, my friend, I wish I could help you with money but I have none. Still, there is something I can do for you: I shall dance for you." And he danced for his friend all night. Next morning, after prayers, he told his friend: "I must go. Wait for me." He left and returned two days later, with a considerable sum of money. "Let me tell you what happened," he said. "Years ago, I came into a strange city and was lucky enough to find a young boy who consented to be my guide. In return I promised him that I would come and dance at his wedding. Passing through Zlotchov after I left you, I heard music and singing. There was a wedding going on. Though I was not invited, I went closer—and recognized the bridegroom. I remembered my promise and kept it: I danced for the young couple and did my best to give them joy. When they heard my story—your story, Uri—they felt sorry for the poor old maid and they and their guests opened their hearts and their pockets. Here is the money, Uri, go and tell the girl that now it is her turn to rejoice."

Concluded Reb Moshe-Leib, "When somebody asks something impossible of me, I know what I must do: I must dance."

From the encounter of the two Rebbes we thus learn that there is always *something* one can do for one's friends. What is Hasidism if not the belief that man must have faith in God *and* in people? You suffer? Pray to God but speak to your friend.

Translated by Marion Wiesel

YORUBAN FOLKTALE

(In this West African myth, Esu is the traditional trickster figure.)

Everyone knows the story of the two friends who were thwarted in their friendship by Esu. They took vows of eternal friendship to one another, but neither took Esu into consideration. Esu took note of their actions and decided to do something about them.

When the time was ripe, Esu decided to put their friendship to his own little test. He made a cloth cap. The right side was black, the left side was white.

The two friends were out in the fields, tilling their land. One was hoeing on the right side, the other was clearing the bushes to the left. Esu came by on a horse, riding between the two men. The one on the right saw the black side of his hat. The friend on the left noticed the sheer whiteness of Esu's cap.

The two friends took a break for lunch under the cool shade of the trees. Said one friend, "Did you see the man with a white cap who greeted us as we were working? He was very pleasant, wasn't he?"

"Yes, he was charming, but it was a man in a black cap that I recall, not a white one."

"It was a white cap. The man was riding a magnificently caparisoned horse."

"Then it must be the same man. I tell you, his cap was dark—black."

"You must be fatigued or blinded by the hot rays of the sun to take a white cap for a black one."

"I tell you it was a black cap and I am not mistaken. I remember him distinctly."

The two friends fell to fighting. The neighbors came running but the fight was so intense that the neighbors could not stop it. In the midst of this uproar, Esu returned, looking very calm and pretending not to know what was going on.

"What is the cause of all the hullabaloo?" he demanded sternly.

"Two close friends are fighting," was the answer. "They seem intent on killing each other and neither would stop or tell us the reason for the fight. Please do something before they destroy each other."

Esu promptly stopped the fight. "Why do you two lifelong friends make a public spectacle of yourselves in this manner?"

"A man rode through the farm, greeting us as he went by," said the first friend. "He was wearing a black cap, but my friend tells me it was a white cap and that I must have been tired or blind or both."

The second friend insisted that the man had been wearing a white cap. One of them must be mistaken, but it was not he.

"Both of you are right," said Esu.

"How can that be?"

"I am the man who paid the visit over which you now quarrel, and here is the cap that caused the dissension." Esu put his hand in his pocket and brought out the two-colored cap saying, "As you can see, one side is white and the other is black. You each saw one side and, therefore, are right about what you saw. Are you not the two friends who made vows of friendship? When you vowed to be friends always, to be faithful and true to each other, did you reckon with Esu? Do you know that he who does not put Esu first in all his doings has himself to blame if things misfire?"

And so it is said,

Esu, do not undo me,
Do not falsify the words of my mouth,
Do not misguide the movements of my feet.
You who translates yesterday's words
Into novel utterances,
Do not undo me,
I bear you sacrifices.

Translated by Ayodele Ogundipe

PABLO NERUDA

From CHILDHOOD AND POETRY

One time, investigating in the backyard of our house in Temuco the tiny objects and minuscule beings of my world, I came upon a hole in one of the boards of the fence. I looked through the hole and saw a landscape like that behind our house, uncared for, and wild. I moved back a few steps, because I sensed vaguely that something was about to happen. All of a sudden a hand appeared—a tiny hand of a boy about my own age. By the time I came close again, the hand was gone, and in its place there was a marvellous white sheep.

The sheep's wool was faded. Its wheels had escaped. All of this only made it more authentic. I had never seen such a wonderful sheep. I looked back through the hole but the boy had disappeared. I went into the house and brought out a treasure of my own: a pine cone, opened, full of odor and resin, which I adored. I set it down in the same spot and went off with the sheep.

I never saw either the hand or the boy again. And I have never again seen a sheep like that either. The toy I lost finally in a fire. But even now, in 1954, almost fifty years old, whenever I pass a toyshop, I look furtively into the window, but it's no use. They don't make sheep like that any more.

I have been a lucky man. To feel the intimacy of brothers is a marvellous thing in life. To feel the love of people whom we love is a fire that feeds our life. But to feel the affection that comes from those whom we do not know, from those unknown to us, who are watching over our sleep and solitude, over our dangers and our weaknesses—that is something still greater and more beautiful because it widens out the boundaries of our being, and unites all living things.

That exchange brought home to me for the first time a precious idea: that all of humanity is somehow together. That experience came to me again much later; this time it stood out strikingly against a background of trouble and persecution.

It won't surprise you then that I attempted to give something resiny, earthlike, and fragrant in exchange for human brotherhood. Just as I once left the pine cone by the fence, I have since left my words on the door of so many people who were unknown to me, people in prison, or hunted, or alone.

That is the great lesson I learned in my childhood, in the backyard of a lonely house. Maybe it was nothing but a game two boys played who didn't know each other and wanted to pass to the other some good things of life. Yet maybe this small and mysterious exchange of gifts remained inside me also, deep and indestructible, giving my poetry light.
. . .

Translated by Robert Bly

DAVID THOMSON

From THE PEOPLE OF THE SEA

". . . 'twas a hot summer's day when my mother was a little girl. 'Twas she told me this herself for she was there. And this family McKinley was living next door to my mother's house in the village of Altmore. On that day there was no one at home in the McKinley's house, only the woman of the house and a little boy of hers, about three or four years old. The man o' the house was away line fishing that day, for mackerel, with some others of a crew, and the weather being good there was no man at home in the village. So there was no way for her, only to go herself to drive her cattle off o' the neighbour's crops. They were stopped by the wall beyond, you understand, and when she came to them they were eating the green corn, grazing a piece and running on another piece, the way they are when they're uneasy in themselves."

"Yes, yes," said Patrick Sean. "They are devils when they hear the fly."

"Well they had plenty of damage done and a terrible bawling and shouting out of them when she made to go to them. But to bring the little gossoon with her was a thing she could not do. She could not carry him and drive the cattle, and I suppose if she let him follow her she'd be afraid he might be hurted by those beasts. So she put him in a garden of potatoes that was behind the house, himself and the little dog with him, and she told him to play there for himself with the dog and not move from that place until she'd be back. Well, she gathered the beasts and put them into a piece of grassland that was fenced with a wall away from the crops. She didn't trouble to put them back on the mountain, because she was thinking of the little gossoon. But quick and all as she was, she had to close a gap in the wall, and when she came into the garden of potatoes, the little boy was gone."

"She was distressed, I'm sure," said the man with the slow voice.

"She made then a desperate search. She went to every house to see would she get word of him. But no one had seen him. No trace of him, nor the dog, no word of them. She remembered then how the child's father used to bring him with him sometimes to the strand, to the boat, and it put the heart across her to think of it, so she ran down to the sea, and there sure enough her heart was nearly broken, for, in a soft patch of sand beside the water's edge, there she saw the footprints of her child."

"He was drowned," said the man with the slow voice.

"She made sure to herself he was drowned. And every woman of the village of Altmore was searching the shore for that little gossoon. And she herself left them there. She was distracted. She went along by the cliff tops then, above, and she running, and she crying and wailing for the child. But very soon she heard another crying like herself, and 'twas a woman, and she stood still to listen, but she couldn't tell from where it came, and she ran to and hither, and she stood still again, and she listening for this cry. So she went to where she thought she heard the voice. On then she ran to a place where the cliff dipped down in a kind of a cleft, and there she thought the voice was stronger. And there what did she see when she climbed down but a great seal standing up in the sea a little way off from the shore and crying out and wailing like a woman. So she climbed down further, down this cleft o' the cliff, and there by a piece of rock that stood between her and the water, she did hear the crying of a child. And the crying of the seal was in her ears too. So down further she travelled among the rocks, and there she did find her boy, himself and the dog that was with him."

"I am sure she was thankful," said the man with the slow voice.

"She was of course. Herself and the McKinley man when he came home from the fishing that night—they knew well the child was lost only for that seal. He would never, being only a little gossoon, be able to climb back up the cliff, d'ye see, and his cries were lost in that lonely place. So she brought him home and she was glad. And by this the McKinley man was home too."

"He would be thankful," said the man with the slow voice.

"He was indeed. He heard every kind of story when he came from the shore about how the child was drowned in the sea. But he was thankful when he saw the gossoon. So whenever the father came back from the fishing after that day, he would bring a lock of fish to that cleft o' the cliff and put it on a rock for the seal. And the seal would swim in close when he saw the McKinley man come near. The seal would eat the fish and swim away. She was well known, that seal."

I said, "How was she known?"

"She was known by everyone in that place. She was oftentimes about. And the McKinley man put fish for her on to this rock for years. Until, at the end, she came no more. She would have died, or maybe she was killed. There is no way to know. But it was many years that the McKinley man was feeding her."

The man with the slow voice said, "They are noted for their longevity, the seals," and I asked what age they would live to.

"There is no way to know."

PART XVII

AFFINITIES: GROUP 4

A man that hath friends must shew himself friendly:
And there is a friend that sticketh closer than a brother.

—*Proverbs 18:24*

ROBERT LOWELL

School

1 FOR PETER TAYLOR

That doleful Kenyon snapshot: you ham-squat on your bed,
jaw hung sidewise, and your eyes too glossy;
chest syrup, wicked greens of diesel oil;
you the same sickly green, except you are
transparent. I can almost touch and smell
those pajamas we were too brush-off to change,
and wore as winter underwear through our trousers.
When the snapshot was developed, I saw you couldn't
live a week, and thought you might have died,
squatting upright, a last dynasty mummy.
You live on: earth's obliquities of health,
though Adams knew the Southerner must go under—
love teases. We're one still, we are weaker, wilder—
stuck in one room again, we want to fight.

Our Afterlife II

Leaving a taxi at Victoria,
I saw my own face
in sharper focus and smaller
watching me from a puddle
or something I held—*your* face
on the cover of your *Collected Stories*
seamed with dread and smiling—
old short-haired poet
of the first Depression,
now back in currency.

My thinking is talking to you—
last night I fainted at dinner
and came nearer to your sickness,
nearer to the angels in nausea.
The room turned upside-down,
I was my interrupted sentence,
a misdirection tumbled back alive
on a low, cooling black table.

The doctors come more thickly,
they use exact language
even when they disagree on the mal-diagnosis
in the surgeon's feather-touch.

Were we ever weaned
from our reactionary young masters
by the *schadenfreude* of new homes?

America once lay uncropped and golden,
it left no tarnish on our windshield . . .
In a generation born under Prohibition,
the Red Revolution, the Crash,
cholesterol and bootleg—
we were artisans
retained as if we were workers
by the charities of free enterprise.

Our loyalty to one another sticks like love . . .

This year for the first time,
even cows seem transitory—
1974
of the Common Market,
the dwarf Norman appletree
espaliered to a wall.
The old boys drop like wasps
from windowsill and pane.
In a church,
the Psalmist's glass mosaic Shepherd
and bright green pastures
seem to wait
with the modish faithlessness

and erotic daydream
of art nouveau for our funeral.

PETER TAYLOR

From ROBERT TRAIL SPENCE LOWELL

I believe Lowell was about as good a correspondent as you will find in our generation—especially during the last years. He sometimes wrote me two or three times a week. I suppose he was often lonely in England. He said, "England is a better country to live in than America—more comfortable and pleasant generally. But I am still more comfortable with Americans than with Englishmen." When he and I parted company after college he said, "You write me long letters often, and I'll come long distances to see you." It turned out quite the reverse, for the most part. He wrote often, and I travelled great distances to hear him talk. We did a lot of visiting back and forth. Our visits were just like being at Kenyon again, in a way. A big part of the time was spent reading—reading aloud. It is something he did with all of his close friends, I suppose. The first thing he ever read aloud to me was *The Education of Henry Adams.* He liked especially to read to me the passage about Rooney Lee. But mostly we read poetry—or *he* did. It was established early that he would do the reading. At Kenyon, we decided to make our own anthology of English poetry, beginning with the Metaphysical poets. He made all the selections, really. Over the years any close friend of his heard him read a lot of poetry, including his own. Whenever there was a reunion with an old friend, he would read all of his new work as well as poems by the old poets, the dead poets, that he had rediscovered and been in communion with, so to speak, since the last meeting. And he would always talk with great intensity about what he was writing then. *What is art but an intense life?*

I was last with him in London two years ago next month. At his and Caroline's place in Redcliffe Square he read aloud, and we talked away the better part of the five days. On the final afternoon he asked me if I remembered William Cory's "Heraclitus." I said I did, but only vaguely.

He said, "Look at it and tell me the best line in it." That was his way. I read aloud the first phrases my eye fell on: "How often you and I/Had tired the sun with talking." "That's it," he said with delight. When I got back to my hotel I found that I had memorized the two stanzas that make up the poem:

> They told me, Heraclitus, they told me you were dead,
> They brought me bitter news to hear and bitter tears to shed.
> I wept as I remembered how often you and I
> Had tired the sun with talking and sent him down the sky.
>
> And now that thou art lying, my dear old Carian Guest,
> A handful of grey ashes, long, long ago at rest,
> Still are thy pleasant voices, thy nightingales, awake;
> For Death, he taketh all away, but them he cannot take.

SEAMUS HEANEY

From GULLIVER IN LILLIPUT:
REMEMBERING ROBERT LOWELL

(This speech was delivered in 1987 at Harvard to commemorate the tenth anniversary of Lowell's death.)

The Penguin Book of Contemporary American Verse came into my hands in the late nineteen-fifties. I was an undergraduate at the time, a student in the Honours English course at Queen's University, Belfast, and I remember slugging around with bewildered, slightly anxious pleasure in the opaque linguistic element of "The Quaker Graveyard in Nantucket." Ten years later I found Hugh Staples's book, *Robert Lowell, the First Twenty Years,* where I read his illuminating account of the poem with great profit and an unthinking assent to its half-stated message that Robert Lowell was already a classic. So when I was introduced to Cal in London in 1972, in the corner of a party in honour of his marriage to Lady Caroline Blackwood, I felt both gagged and agog. The party was at Sonja Orwell's. Cyril Connolly was there. And Stephen

Spender. And Lord knows who else. I was hampered by a lingering shyness and an Irishman's unease in the presence of upper middle-class clamour, a noise which Evelyn Waugh once likened to the baying of hounds.

I was also, I must admit, wary of Robert Lowell's knee-melting flattery. When he invited me to visit Milgate, I remembered not only Staples's accounts but Norman Mailer's: the portrait Mailer painted in *Armies of the Night* of an effortlessly winning yet too cajoling patrician had put me on my guard.

But of course my guard dropped. Cal's courtesy and power were such that he would confer upon his interlocutor the delightful illusion of equality, by the mere inclination of his bespectacled head or a passage of his deftly languid hand. Over the next five years, I grew to know and love these gestures and to feel also his benevolences and bemused interest. After that evening he was a presence, he was *there,* and his very assent to one's identity as a poet—rather than any comment he might make upon the poems—was of real importance. Lowell was one of those who verify poetic vocation by simply being themselves and discharging the ray of their presence. He did happen to write one of the most delicious comments I could ever have desired on some of my "Glanmore Sonnets," saying that "they seem to have come through a grief." His real importance to me, however, had little to do with that kind of workshop praise. I suppose I was like many other friends who knew him far longer than I did, in that I experienced a sense of privilege in being close to so much intellectual stamina, personal force and attractive rascality. You never felt quite safe with him but neither did you ever feel sold short.

Oddly enough, the moment when I felt most bewildered in his presence was a moment when he was bereft of his capacity to unnerve. I went with him in January 1976 to two acupuncturists in Harley Street. He was at that time confined in a small private hospital where I had called to see him earlier in the afternoon and had been given a restorative nip from his Imperial After Shave bottle, which he had assured me contained Benedictine. Then, almost it would seem in order to atone, he carried me away in a taxi, with his ever present male nurse. And the next thing we had penetrated to the inner sanctum of two friendly and, it appeared to me, slightly quackish acupuncturists, stealthy, stooped and vaguely insinuating elders from the city of Leeds.

They called him Professor. They spoke calmingly to him and he became calm. He answered their questions about what they called his tension with an unexpected childlike candor. He allowed them to palp along the line of his neck and over his temples and down the back of his skull. He took off his shirt. He bowed a little and accepted the needles, one by one, in a delicate gleaming line, from the point of his shoulder to the back of his ear. I had a great feeling of intimacy and honour and heartbreak as I watched it all from behind, yet I could not stop myself from turning that accidental moment into an image, there and then, as it was happening. Gulliver in Lilliput, disabled, pinned down, yet essentially magnificent. The bull weakened by the pics of the picador. St. Sebastian. At any rate, it remains with me as an emblem of his afflicted life, his great native strength and his sorrowful, invigilated helplessness. Richard not himself, then Richard himself again.

But there was a happier moment which preceded that. This was in our cottage in Co. Wicklow, 1975. A very small gate-lodge, peopled by my wife, myself, our two small sons and our then two year old daughter. We were necessarily thrown together in a way in which Cal, who was then the inhabitant of a stately English country house, was not at all used to. I remember with great pleasure *his* pleasure when he said scampishly, "You see a lot of your children." He did continue to visit, on and off, our house, and the children. I suppose Marie and myself seemed very domestic, when he and Caroline came occasionally out of their big country house—at Castletown—into this suburban house where youngsters were running about. I now believe that it gave them a chance to masquerade as a domestic couple for a while themselves, and that that masquerade in part provoked the strange tenderness and merriment that pervaded those meetings. At any rate, there was both great joyfulness, tenderness, and a kind of blank knowledge also. So to commemorate his laconic joys in marriage, his great self-knowledge, and his great tenderness, I'll read the poem from *Day by Day* called "Marriage."

ROBERT LOWELL

Ford Madox Ford

1873–1939

The lobbed ball plops, then dribbles to the cup. . . .
(a birdie Fordie!) But it nearly killed
the ministers. Lloyd George was holding up
the flag. He gabbled, "Hop-toad, hop-toad, hop-toad!

Hueffer has used a niblick on the green;
it's filthy art, Sir, filthy art!"
You answered, "What is art to me and thee?
Will a blacksmith teach a midwife how to bear?"
That cut the puffing statesman down to size,
Ford. You said, "Otherwise,
I would have been general of a division." Ah Ford!
Was it war, the sport of kings, that your *Good Soldier,*
the best French novel in the language, taught
those Georgian Whig magnificoes at Oxford,
at Oxford decimated on the Somme?
Ford, five times black-balled for promotion,
then mustard-gassed voiceless some seven miles
behind the lines at Nancy or Belleau Wood:
you emerged in your "worn uniform,
gilt dragons on the revers of the tunic,"
a Jonah—O divorced, divorced
from the whale-fat of post-war London! Boomed,
cut, plucked and booted! In Provence, New York . . .
marrying, blowing . . . nearly dying
at Boulder, when the altitude
pressed the world on your heart,
and your audience, almost football-size,
shrank to a dozen, while you stood
mumbling, with fish-blue-eyes,
and mouth pushed out
fish-fashion, as if you gagged for air. . . .
Sandman! Your face, a childish *O.* The sun
is pernod-yellow and it gilds the heirs
of all the ages there on Washington
and Stuyvesant, your Lilliputian squares,
where writing turned your pockets inside out.
But master, mammoth mumbler, tell me why
the bales of your left-over novels buy
less than a bandage for your gouty foot.
Wheel-horse, O unforgetting elephant,
I hear you huffing at your old Brevoort,
Timon and Falstaff, while you heap the board
for publishers. Fiction! I'm selling short
your lies that made the great your equals. Ford,
you were a kind man and you died in want.

From RANDALL JARRELL, 1914–1965

When I first met Randall, he was twenty-three or -four, and unsettlingly brilliant, precocious, knowing, naïve, and vexing. He seemed to make no distinction between what he would say in our hearing and what he would say behind our backs. If anything, absence made him more discreet. Woe to the acquaintance who liked the wrong writer, the wrong poem by the right writer, or the wrong lines in the right poem! And how those who loved him enjoyed admiring, complaining, and gossiping about the last outrageous thing he had done or, more often, said. It brought us together—whispering about Randall. In 1937, we both roomed at the house of John Crowe Ransom in Gambier, Ohio. Ransom and Jarrell had each separately spent the preceding summer studying Shakespeare's *Sonnets,* and had emerged with unorthodox and widely differing theories. Roughly, Ransom thought that Shakespeare was continually going off the rails into illogical incoherence. Jarrell believed that no one, not even William Empson, had done justice to the rich, significant ambiguity of Shakespeare's intelligence and images. I can see and hear Ransom and Jarrell now, seated on one sofa, as though on one love seat, the sacred texts open on their laps, one fifty, the other just out of college, and each expounding to the other's deaf ears his own inspired and irreconcilable interpretation.

Gordon Chalmers, the president of Kenyon College and a disciple of the somber anti-romantic humanists, once went skiing with Randall, and was shocked to hear him exclaiming, "I feel just like an angel." Randall *did* somehow give off an angelic impression, despite his love for tennis, singular mufflers knitted by a girlfriend, and disturbing improvements of his own on the latest dance steps. His mind, unearthly in its quickness, was a little boyish, disembodied, and brittle. His body was a little ghostly in its immunity to soil, entanglements, and rebellion. As one sat with him in oblivious absorption at the campus bar, sucking a fifteen-cent chocolate milk shake and talking eternal things, one felt, beside him, too corrupt and companionable. He had the harsh luminosity of Shelley— like Shelley, every inch a poet, and like Shelley, imperiled perhaps by an arid, abstracting precosity. Not really! Somewhere inside him, a breezy, untouchable spirit had even then made its youthful and sightless promise to accept—to accept and never to accept the bulk, confusion, and defeat of mortal flesh . . . all that blithe and blood-torn dolor!

Randall Jarrell had his own peculiar and important excellence as a poet, and outdistanced all others in the things he could do well. His gifts, both by nature and by a lifetime of hard dedication and growth, were wit, pathos, and brilliance of intelligence. These qualities, dazzling in themselves, were often so well employed that he became, I think, the most heartbreaking English poet of his generation.

Most good poets are also good critics on occasion, but Jarrell was much more than this. He was a critic of genius, a poet-critic of genius at a time when, as he wrote, most criticism was "astonishingly grace-less, joyless, humorless, long-winded, niggling, blinkered, methodical, self-important, cliché-ridden, prestige-obsessed, and almost autono-mous." . . .

Randall was the only man I have ever met who could make other writers feel that their work was more important to him than his own. I don't mean that he was in the habit of saying to people he admired, "This is much better than anything I could do." Such confessions, though charming, cost little effort. What he did was to make others feel that their realizing themselves was as close to him as his own self-realiza-tion, and that he cared as much about making the nature and goodness of someone else's work understood as he cared about making his own understood. I have never known anyone who so connected what his friends wrote with their lives, or their lives with what they wrote. This could be trying: whenever we turned out something Randall felt was unworthy or a falling off, there was a coolness in all one's relations with him. You felt that even your choice in neckties wounded him. Yet he always veered and returned, for he knew as well as anyone that the spark from heaven is beyond man's call and control. Good will he demanded, but in the end was lenient to honest sterility and failure. . . .

It all comes back to me now—the just under thirty years of our friend-ship, mostly meetings in transit, mostly in Greensboro, North Carolina, the South he loved and stayed with, though no agrarian, but a radical liberal. Poor modern-minded exile from the forests of Grimm, I see him unbearded, slightly South American–looking, then later bearded, with a beard we at first wished to reach out our hands to and pluck off, but which later became him, like Walter Bagehot's, or some Symbolist's in France's *fin de siècle* Third Republic. Then unbearded again. I see the bright, petty, pretty sacred objects he accumulated for his joy and solace: Vermeer's red-hatted girl, the Piero and Donatello reproductions, the photographs of his bruised, merciful heroes: Chekhov, Rilke, Marcel Proust. I see the white sporting Mercedes-Benz, the ever better cut and more deliberately jaunty clothes, the television with its long afternoons of professional football, those matches he thought miraculously more graceful than college football . . . Randall had an uncanny clairvoyance for helping friends in subtle precarious moments—almost always as only he could help, with something written: critical sentences in a letter, or an unanticipated published book review. Twice or thrice, I think, he must have thrown me a lifeline. In his own life, he had much public acclaim and more private. The public, at least, fell cruelly short of what he deserved. Now that he is gone, I see clearly that the spark from heaven really struck and irradiated the lines and being of my dear old friend—his noble, difficult, and beautiful soul.

SEAMUS HEANEY

THE SOUNDS OF RAIN

i.m. Richard Ellmann

I

An all-night drubbing overflow on boards
On the verandah. I dwelt without thinking
In the long moil of it, and then came to
To dripping eaves and light, saying into myself
Proven, weightless sayings of the dead.
Things like *He'll be missed* and *You'll have to thole.*

II

It could have been the drenched weedy gardens
Of Peredelkino: a reverie
Of looking out from late winter gloom
Lit by tangerines and the clear of vodka,
Where Pasternak, lenient yet austere,
Answered for himself without insistence.

"I had the feeling of an immense debt,"
He said (it is recorded). "So many years
Just writing lyric poetry and translating.
I felt there was some duty . . . Time was passing.
And with all its faults, it has more value
Than those early . . . It is richer, more humane."

Or it could have been the thaw and puddles
Of Athens Street where William Alfred stood
On the wet doorstep, remembering the friend
Who died at sixty. "After 'Summer Tides'
There would have been a deepening, you know,
Something ampler . . . Ah well. Good night again."

III

The eaves a water-fringe and steady lash
Of summer downpour: *You are steeped in luck,*
I hear them say, *Steeped, steeped, steeped in luck.*
And hear the flood too, gathering from under,
Biding and boding like a masterwork
Or a named name that overbrims itself.

PART XVIII

LETTERS: GROUP 5

*I don't think I'd ever imagined a place and people
in which and with whom one felt so perfectly happy
that one felt suspended the whole time, and at the
same time wanting to smile,* and *smiling, continuously,
like a dog.*

　　　—Elizabeth Bowen to Virginia Woolf, *after a visit*

WILLIAM BUTLER YEATS

To Olivia Shakespear

82 Merrion Square
April 25, 1928

My dear Olivia,
For once I am dictating a letter. We got back a week ago, and there has been so much to do that I am tired. Two Dublin doctors have sat upon me; the Cannes man said "Lungs and nervous breakdown can be neglected, nothing matters but blood pressure" and gave me a white pill. The Monte Carlo man said "Blood pressure and lungs can be neglected, nothing matters but nervous breakdown," and gave me a brown pill. The Dublin men say "Blood pressure and nervous breakdown can be neglected, nothing matters but lungs," and have given me a black pill, and as a sort of postscript I am to have a vaccine injection once a week for the next three months. However I shall cut out one week in order to spend ten days in London in June. We came direct from Cherbourg to Queenstown so I have seen nobody.

The Tower is a great success, two thousand copies in the first month, much the largest sale I have ever had. I do nothing at present but potter over a new edition of *A Vision* which should be ready some time next year. When I get back to Rapallo I hope to write verse again but no more bitter passion I think. Re-reading *The Tower* I was astonished at its bitterness, and long to live out of Ireland that I may find some new vintage. Yet that bitterness gave the book its power and it is the best book I have written. Perhaps if I was in better health I should be content to be bitter.

Is Dorothy with you? Tell her that steak and onions are a disappointment. It was our first meal. She is forgiven. But I still sigh for badger's flesh. She will understand.

Will you be in London in June? I want to see you, and George is bringing Michael through London on his way to Ireland for the holidays. Omar is still at the happy age. We are struggling with Anne's desire to debauch her intellect with various forms of infantile literature presented by servants etc.

Yours always
W B Yeats

82 Merrion Square
May 22 [1928]

My dear Olivia:

Since I came back I have been writing all morning in bed and getting up for lunch and this has meant a continuous putting off of letters. I write all morning in a big MS book, and my note paper is all downstairs. After lunch I have said each day I will write a letter but at first I was tired and now that I am much better Lady Gregory has been here and so on. At the moment my head is all frozen hard because of a morning of mystic geometry, and I am trying to melt it.

Half hour later.

I have read a chapter in a detective story and that has melted my head.

We have sold this house to a Professor of Architecture who is attracted by its beauty, and we must be out by August 1, unless he will hire to us, as we have reason to hope, the upper part as a flat. I say goodbye sadly to this beautiful room, but I shall have the mountains of Rapallo in exchange. It will be a delight to get there for quiet winters—here all is storm. Perhaps I say that because we have refused Casey's new play—a sort of secret a good many people know because he has told, but you are the first I have told and theoretically I should not. He has written furious letters and has threatened to publish our opinion of the play. However in the end I think we have avoided a quarrel. He will get a London performance I am afraid and injure his fame. The play is all anti-war propaganda to the exclusion of plot and character . . . Of course if we had played his play, his fame is so great that we would have had full house for a time, but we hoped to turn him into a different path. Do not be surprized if you read in your morning newspaper extracts from a Casey preface quoting my opinion and denouncing it.

My blood-pressure was normal three weeks ago and though Casey and late hours have sent it up a bit I am really very well. Next month I shall be in London. George on her way to Switzerland to fetch Michael will drop me there and pick me up again.

Yours always
W B Yeats

Via Americhe 12–8
Rapallo
Nov 23 [1928]

My dear Olivia,
Here is often bright sun, sometimes so hot that I am driven in from my balcony, but to-day it is cold, not cold enough to make a fire necessary, but enough to make me light my paraffin lamp. The furniture arrived this morning and George is at the flat settling things in order. We move in next Tuesday and have tried to persuade the Pounds to join us in a vigorous house-warming but Dorothy seems to classify champagne with steak and onions and badger's flesh, and other forms of the tinsel of this world. I write each morning and am well, much better than I ever am at home and am already sunburnt. I am finishing a little book for Cuala to be called either *A Packet* or *A Packet for Ezra Pound*. It contains first a covering letter to Ezra saying that I offer him the contents, urging him not to be elected to the Senate of his country and telling him why. Then comes a long essay already finished, the introduction to the new edition of *A Vision* and telling all about its origin, and then I shall wind up with a description of Ezra feeding the cats ("some of them are so ungrateful" T. S. Eliot says), of Rapallo and Ezra's poetry—some of which I greatly admire, indeed his collected edition is a great excitement to me. He constantly comes round to talk of Guido who absorbs his attention.

We bought some furniture in Genoa, but when we explained to the maker of it that it must be without his favourite curves and complications he said he once made such plain furniture for an English family but it was "brutto." However he has been obedient and the results are excellent. The flat is our great excitement, it will be full of electric gadgets, but if you do not come to Rapallo who shall we have to describe them to? Indeed I see no reason in the world why you and Omar should not presently settle here or in the next little town which would give us all exercise walking the mile and a half between.

If one had not to take exercise life would be perfect, but 3.30 when I must go out for mine has just come—at 4.30 it will be the chill of evening.

Yours affectionately
W B Yeats

Riversdale
March 9 1933

Dear Olivia,

. . . I wish I could put the Swami's lectures into the Cuala series but I cannot. My sister's books are like an old family magazine. A few hundred people buy them all and expect a common theme. Only once did I put a book into the series that was not Irish—Ezra's Noh plays—and I had to write a long introduction to annex Japan to Ireland.

I have finished my essay on *Louis Lambert.* How one loves Balzac's audience—great ladies, diplomatists, everybody who goes to grand opera, and ourselves. Then think of Tolstoy's—all the bores, not a poor sinner amongst them. . . .

Joyce and D. H. Lawrence have however almost restored to us the Eastern simplicity. Neither perfectly, for D. H. Lawrence romanticises his material, with such words as "essential fire," "darkness" etc, and Joyce never escapes from his Catholic sense of sin. Rabelais seems to escape from it by his vast energy. . . .

Yours affectionately
W B Yeats

Riversdale
May 22 1933

. . . You are leaving London on I think June 15 or thereabouts. Please let me know your plans, as I rather forget them.

My two sensations at the moment are Hulme's *Speculations* and *Lady Chatterley's Lover.* The first in an essay called *Modern Art* relates such opposites as *The Apes of God* and *Lady Chatterley.* Get somebody to lend you the last if you have not read it. Frank Harris's *Memoirs* are vulgar and immoral—the sexual passages were like holes burnt with a match in a piece of old newspaper; their appeal to physical sensation was hateful; but *Lady Chatterley* is noble. Its description of the sexual act is more detailed than in Harris, the language is sometimes that of cabmen and yet the book is all fire. Those two lovers, the gamekeeper and his employer's wife, each separated from their class by their love, and by fate, are poignant in their loneliness, and the coarse language of the one, accepted by both, becomes a forlorn poetry uniting their solitudes, something ancient, humble and terrible.

Yours affectionately
W B Yeats

I write no more that I may catch the post.

Riversdale
May 25 [1933]

My dear Olivia,

I have changed my plans. I go to London on Friday June 2, so please keep some portion of Saturday and Sunday for me. On Monday I go to Oxford where I spend the night at the Eights' Club and then go to Cambridge for my degree and will be back in London on June 9.

Of course Lawrence is an emphasis directed against modern abstraction. I find the whole book interesting and not merely the sexual parts. They are something that he sets up as against the abstraction of an age that he thinks dead from the waist downward. Of course happiness is not where he seems to place it. We are happy when for everything inside us there is an equivalent something outside us. I think it was Goethe said this. One should add the converse. It is terrible to desire and not possess, and terrible to possess and not desire. Because of this we long for an age which has the unity which Plato somewhere defined as sorrowing and rejoicing over the same things. How else escape the Bank Holiday crowd?

I have bought a suit of rough blue serge.

Yours
W B Yeats

Read *Twenty Years a-Growing* or some of it. I once told you that you would be happy if you had twelve children and lived on limpets. There are limpets on the Great Blasket.

Riversdale
July 13 [1933]

My dear Olivia,

Heaven knows where you are but I suppose this will find you. The garden is full of roses and there are lilies in the lily pond and the croquet goes on from day to day and I can still beat my family. All is well, what more is to be said? I am revising a one-volume edition of my poems and doing odds and ends. I am to write my memory of Coole and Lady Gregory for Macmillan and have made peace with—— ——, who has suddenly and inexplicably turned amiable. . . .

Yours affectionately
W B Yeats

Tell me always where you are and what you are doing.

Riversdale
July 23 [1933]

My dear Olivia:

I have a lot of dull letters to write, and to make myself sit down on this hot day I have bribed myself by saying that I would begin by writing to you. Yet do I write to you as to my own past. . . .

Yours affectionately
W B Yeats

Riversdale
August 17 1933

My dear Olivia,

. . . I have corrected the proofs of my new book *The Winding Stair* (not the little book published in America but all work I have written since *The Tower*). "Crazy Jane" poems (the origin of some of these you know) and the little group of love poems that follow are, I think, exciting and strange. Sexual abstinence fed their fire—I was ill and yet full of desire. They sometimes came out of the greatest mental excitement I am capable of. Now for a year I have written some twenty or thirty lines in all—result of recovered health, this crowded Dublin life which always incites me to prose, and the turn given to my mind by a lecture tour. When my essay on the Swami is finished I think of interpolating a little dance play in between the essay and my book about Lady Gregory. It does not matter whether I do or not, one's life is a whole and my account of Coole will add to the solidity of what I have already written.

Yours affectionately
W B Yeats

Riversdale
Sept 20 [1933]

My dear Olivia,

My new book goes to you this post I hope—it depends on George, brown paper and string. . . .

You will know the poems in my book, and have written me of them before when they came out at Cuala or another press, yet write again. Say what you think of Crazy Jane (I approve of her) and of the poems on pages 76, 77, 78. . . .

Yours affectionately
W B Yeats

Riversdale
Oct 24 1933

My Dear Olivia,

   . . . Study the little angels on the new Irish postage stamps. The artist brought the design, much larger of course than the stamp, to the proper officials. The officials said the expression of the angels' eyes must be changed. He said they would be all right when reduced in size. Officials would not believe and he went home in a rage. He kept the design for two weeks and sent it back unaltered. The officials thought it was changed and sent it to the printer. When the artist got the proof, being still in a rage, [he] said that it was all wrong and must be altered, though there was nothing wrong, and altered it was. He considers that the cost of this alteration was necessary punishment. I don't think much of his stamp but he is a competent person, a designer of stained-glass in the best studio here.

A number of the reviews of my book have quoted that poem ending

<blockquote>
Young
We loved each other and were ignorant.
</blockquote>

I wonder if you remember those autumn evenings when I was on my way to Rapallo.

Yours affectionately
W B Yeats

LADY GREGORY

From JOURNALS

Jan. 28, 1930. A good day altogether. In my letter to G.B.S. I copied Yeats' rendering of Swift's epitaph, for G.B.S. has said when I spoke of them, that a translation might be very fine. He wrote them here on a half sheet of paper:

> Jonathan Swift is at the goal,
> Savage indignation there
>   Cannot lacerate his soul,
> Imitate him if you dare,
> World estranged man for he
>   Saved human liberty.

And then another:

> Jonathan Swift's in port,
> Savage indignation there
>   Cannot lacerate his heart:
> Imitate him if you dare.
> World-besotted wanderer, he
>   Served human liberty.

(I liked the first best, Yeats the second.)

EVELYN WAUGH

To Henry Yorke*

[Salisbury, 1926]

I have just finished reading *Blindness*. At the risk of appearing officious, I am impelled to write to you and tell you how very much I like it. It is extraordinary to me that anyone of our generation could have written so fine a book—and at Oxford of all places. I am seldom there now but, if I am, may I look you up?

---

*Henry Yorke (1905–75). Novelist under the pseudonym Henry Green. *Blindness*, his first book, had been started while he was at school.

M Tokatliyan Oteli,
Pera, Rue Istiklal,
Istanbul
[4 May 1929]

Dear Henry,

Well I must say that I *do* think it most extraordinary to be called "Diggy,"* (but I once knew a young man called Geoffrey Biddulph who had very eccentric habits as he had spent most of his life in James Joyce's Dublin; he had a sister called Hermione who lived in sin with a genealogist who kept pet squirrels. However all this is neither here nor there.) Evelyn† and I are thrilled about your engagement. You must be married *at once* very obtrusively—a fashionable wedding is worth a four column review in the *Times Literary Supplement* to a novelist. It was a great sorrow to me that circumstances deprived us of a real wedding. I have a great many ideas about them. May I come and stage manage yours. No Florentine maids or picture hats, I can tell you.

We are also enormously looking forward to reading your novel & it is maddening that I shall have to wait so long to see it. I think it is hopeless trying to send it out. There is a bottle of hair wash from Dellaz which has been following me round the Mediterranean since the end of February & meanwhile I am rapidly becoming bald.

I cant remember when I wrote last but I think it was a long time ago. From Egypt we went to Malta, some horribly picturesque streets—cobbles & steps & even *"native costume"* but the fortifications were clean and sensible looking and some remarkable baroque churches. Then we got onto the *Stella Polaris* again & have thrown ourselves into the social life of a "pleasure cruise." I am a member of the Sports Committee which is very serious indeed and Evelyn had to organise a fancy dress dance. I have a great rival for leadership of the bright young people in a stout Belgian. Today he appeared on deck in a Royal Yacht Squadron cap so I know when I am beaten.

All the sailors on the ship took to seamanship late in life. The Captain was a bank manager until a few years ago, the Purser the editor of a humorous Norwegian weekly, and the First engineer taught dancing. It seems very easy to be a captain because whenever there is any navigation to be done they hire a special pilot.

At Constantinople, we went to luncheon at the Embassy ten minutes after they had all sat down. When I recovered consciousness I found myself completely surrounded by Sitwells while H.E. the Ambassador with gallantry & tact of the corps diplomatique was making extensive &

---

*Adelaide Biddulph, whom Yorke was about to marry.
†Waugh's wife, Evelyn Gardner.

accurate quotations from *Decline & Fall* to a woman next to him, having been told by a secretary that one of his guests had written it, &
thinking it was her.

We had fun at Athens with Mark & Alastair [Graham]. Their new
hobby is to talk Greek with a cockney accent so it is all very much like
home from home.

Mark very sweet & skittish feeling relieved of the burden of keeping
up appearances & having terrific affairs in an atmosphere of garlic &
Charlie Chaplin moustaches.

When you are married will your father make you head of all his
factories and will you still be poor. Do come and live in Islington. Will
Diggy like me and Evelyn?

Sachy Sitwell met a German on the boat who said "Ah you English
know how to do your guesswork. The red face tells me you like champagne, eh?"

Love from us both,
Evelyn.

145 North End Road, N.W.II.
[June 1929]

Dear Henry,

I have just got back and read *Living*. Someone told me, Harold I
think, that it has not been getting very good notices. Has it been done in
Life and Letters yet, do you know, because I want very much to say in
print how enormously I admire it.

I really think that besides being a delightful book, it is an *important*
one. I admire so much the way you have written it—like those aluminum
ribbons one stamps out in railway stations on penny in the slot machines.
The absence of all that awful thing they call "word pictures," the way in
which no appearances are described. The telegraphic narrative which
might have been all wrong if you had used a present tense and is so
perfectly right in the past. Indeed I don't see how else you could have
made a framework for the dialogue which is magnificent. You seem to
have invented an entirely new language, doing for Birmingham born
people what Singe [*sic*] did with Irish—making an artistic form out of a
dialect so that every word is startling. In fact I would have liked *all* the
purpler patches eliminated—but that I know from experience is the
thing one cannot bear to be told. It reminded me just a little of Opal
Whitely's *Diary.*

I liked the rich people parts less than the poor and envied you the way
in which you just stopped writing about them any more—though I
thought the Tom Tyler incidents brilliant—"but it is quite true to say

that there was nothing dirty in all this" and "Dropping suddenly to be intimate" page 147. (I'm not sure that isn't the best sentence in the book.) and "goodness she did like it" p. 155. Another sentence I loved was "He spoke like he was sorry Lil was as she was."

But I mustn't start copying out all the book because I expect that after writing it and reading it how many times in proof you know most of it well.

The thing I *envied* most was the way you managed the plot which is oddly enough almost exactly the way Firbank managed his.

I thought the incident of the courtesan and old Mr Dupret had more in it than you made.

I liked the way Bert wanted to go to the lavatory in the train—in fact the various ways they talked to each other about lavatories all through.

Evelyn is well again and is going to Canonbury Square to live in my flat with Nancy Mitford while I write a book in a pub.

I hear Robert [Byron] has beaten us all by going to India in an aeroplane which is the sort of success which I call tangible.

A bald Norwegian with one eye fell in love with Evelyn so we spent all the last ten days eating caviar and drinking too much champagne.

We found bills of over £200 waiting for us and each overdrawn at our banks so I must write a lot quickly. I would rather fly to India. *The Birth Control Review* of New York have asked me for an article!

Do go and see Evelyn & Nancy—they would love it. When will you be married, where?

Love
Evelyn

Abingdon Arms,
Beckley,
Oxford.
[20 July 1929]

Dear Henry,

I was relieved to get your letter because once when I wrote a book a young man called Carew whom I had always liked wrote to tell me how good he thought my book was and I was so disgusted by his letter that I never could speak to him again without acute embarrassment and I thought perhaps my letter had had that effect on you well I am glad it hasn't.

I have written 25,000 words of a novel in ten days. It is rather like P. G. Wodehouse all about bright young people. I hope it will be finished by the end of the month & then I shall just have time to write another book before your party.

By the way would you like a seventeenth (or eighteenth I'm not sure) century water colour of the Prodigal Son which I bought in Malta for a wedding present or are you against "antiques" & would rather have a labour saving device for the kitchen?

Nancy Mitford came & drove us to Savernake on Sunday & I formed a clear impression that she & Robert are secretly married or is that my novelists imagination?

In the evenings I sit with the famous in the kitchen drinking beer. I like so much the way they don't mind not talking. Rich people always get shy when there's a silence or else they start thinking but in this public house they will all sit mute for five or ten minutes and then just go on talking at exactly the place they left off. Were they like that at Birmingham. By the way _did_ you say what the papers said you said about being jolly good pals with the boys at the works & all that? (I didn't know about Ld. Rosebery and was rather impressed.)

Do go and see Evelyn & Nancy. I've just sent them some caviar so you could eat that.

Are you going to Bryan & Diana's party. I might go up for it if I thought there would be anyone who wouldn't be too much like the characters in my new book.

I know what you mean about purple patches. My new book is black with them—but then I live by my pen as they say and you don't.

Yours
Evelyn

My distinguished sentiments to your young lady. I hope she's still firm about Talkies

The Royal George,
Appledore,
N. Devon.
[September 1929]

Dear Henry,

I put off going abroad and came here to make a last effort at finishing my novel. It has been infinitely difficult and is certainly the last time I shall try to make a book about sophisticated people. It all seems to shrivel up & rot internally and I am relying on a sort of cumulative futility for any effect it may have. All the characters are gossip writers. As soon as I have enough pages covered to call it a book I shall join Bryan & Diana [Guinness] in Paris.

Do you & Dig share my admiration for Diana? She seems to me the one encouraging figure in this generation—particularly now she is pregnant—a great germinating vat of potentiality like the vats I saw at their brewery.

I suppose it would be absurd to suggest you coming here for a week end? It is a very long journey and not very comfortable when you get here but it is lonely and there is very interesting bathing if either of you like that full of unexpected cross currents. I can't remember how much I told you in my letter about the details of my divorce—but I expect you know all about it now.

I had a harrowing time with my relatives & Evelyns. The only parents to take a sensible line were the basement boy [Heygate]'s who stopped his allowance, cut him out of their wills and said they never wanted to see him again.

There is some odd hereditary *tic* in all those Gardner girls—I think it is an intellectual failing more than anything else. My horror and detestation of the basement boy are unqualified. There is practically no part of one that is not injured when a thing like this happens but naturally vanity is one of the things one is most generally conscious of—or so I find.

Can you suggest anything for me to do after Christmas for six months or so—preferably remunerative but that is not important—but essentially remote & unliterary? I might go and dig in Lord Redesdale's bogus gold mine if he would let me. Or there is a man called Spearman who says I can hunt whales. Do think of something?

Evelyn

P.S. If you hear any amusing opinions about my divorce do tell me. Particularly from the older generation. The Gardner line is that I am very "unforgiving."

P.P.S. It is extraordinary how homosexual people however kind & intelligent simply dont understand at all what one feels in this kind of case.

17A Canonbury Square.
[December ? 1929]

Dear Henry,

You must not think from this address that I have gone to stay with the Heygates. I am living at Thame at Mr Fothergill's & expect to be here off and on until Christmas. Why do not you & Dig come for a week end (as my guests of course.) It would be such fun. Bryan & Diana have just left. It is really quite comfortable.

I am so delighted to hear of your creating a scene at a night club with the Heygates. I have decided that I have gone on for too long in that fog of sentimentality & I am going to stop hiding away from everyone. I was getting into a sort of Charlie Chaplinish Pagliacci attitude to myself as the man with a tragedy in his life and a tender smile for children. So all that must stop and one conclusion I am coming to is that I do not like Evelyn & that really Heygate is about her cup of tea.

That novel about Vile Bodies is being printed off and I will send a copy as soon as I get them dreading your verdict very much because now when anyone says they liked *Decline & Fall* I think oh how bored they will be by *Vile Bodies*.

I see Hamish & Maurice & I saw Harold [Acton] yesterday.

I am afraid this is all about myself. What I really set out to do was to ask after Digs tonsils. I do hope everything was completely successful. Did you go to the Brighton Pageant. Alex Waugh was Nelson which I think is very funny.

I envy you the Metropole.

> Love to you both,
> Evelyn

> *Chez M le Curé,*
> *Cabris,*
> *Près de Grasse,*
> *Alpes Maritimes.*
> *[Summer 1931]*

Dear Henry,

Canadel on whenever you like. Do engage a room for me & let me know the address of the hotel so that I can make arrangements.

I shall probably be there awaiting you. I got claustrophobia in the Nina-Maugham milieu and so came here into the hills where I am living in great discomfort with a crazy priest. He talks very fluently about wars all the time—sometimes the last one and sometimes the next. I never quite know which he means. Lloyd George is responsible for both apparently.

Patrick fell into bad company at the sea-side.

I am finishing that very dull travel book & shall soon begin on a novel which is genuinely exciting for me.

I know what you must feel about your office. I have a corresponding longing for some kind of routine in my life.

How well do you speak French? I can't say anything at all.

> Love to you both,
> E

[Villefranche, Summer 1931]

Dear Henry,

I have dragged Patrick away from Mont Parnasse and we are at present staying at the Welcome at Villefranche.

I look forward so much to your coming to St Tropez. When you write for rooms do book one for me—a large one if possible. I hope those fine Misses Ruthven (?) are coming too. The district is full of chums, Connolly, Aldous H, Willy Maugham, Nina, Eddie S-West, Alex Waugh, etc. I meant to do work but it is all very gay and we bathe a lot and get sleepy.

Do write and tell us some gossip.

We are going to live on an island at the end of the week but this address will be

Welcome Hotel
Villefranche sur Mer
Alpes maritimes.

An awful afternoon man called Keith Winter has arrived. Also Godfrey Wynne also Tennyson Jesse—too literary by half.

Will it make Dig shy if I appear in fisherman's clothes.

I have more scandal and baddish blood about Robert [Byron] in Paris.

I have found out more very shady things about Maurice's continental relaxation.

Do write,

Love,
Evelyn

Grand Pump Room Hotel,
Bath.
[May 1933]

Dear Henry

Just back after a journey of the greatest misery. So I came to Bath which was absolutely right and live in a suite of rooms overlooking a colonnade with servants as it might be a club and a decanter of Crofts 1907 always on my sideboard and am getting rid of some of the horrors of life in the forest. Soon I hope to feel up to London—on the 15th in fact when I shall arrive at the Savile & mean to stay intermittently until the end of July at least. I am longing to see you & Dig again. So much to discuss. Guinness—well it will keep. I've seen literally no one except my parents for a brief passage—five months mail to go through mostly

Christmas cards and press cuttings all requiring legal action. Heavy
Catholic trouble. Income Tax, dentist and so on. Now Bath is most
satisfactory.

Woodruff married.

Don't tell Hazel [Lavery] I am back.

Think of the horror of finding an article you wrote describing the
Rupununi cattle district rechristened MY ESCAPE FROM MAYFAIR. I have
written to Esmond Harmsworth about it and hope to get an apology.

Do both write to me & tell me scandal

Yours
Evelyn

[Written on Central Hotel,
Glasgow, paper with the
address crossed out.]
[13 November 1940]

Dear Henry,

I am writing to Forthampton—tho I suppose it is now an asylum of
some kind—because I tried to telephone you in London & to trace you
in other ways, but without result.

The Hogarth Press sent me a copy of your book "for review" but as I
don't review now I take it to be a present from you & thank you very
much indeed.

I read it in increasing delight. It got better and better, I thought,
towards the end. I never tire of hearing you talk about women & I wish
there had been very much more indeed about them & the extraordinary
things they say. Thank you by the way for "charlies" an entirely new
word to me.

I wish there had been twice as much about Oxford, four times as
much about hunt balls, twice as much about the factory.

Only one thing disconcerted me—more in this book than any of the
novels. The proletarian grammar—the "likes" for "ases," the "bikes" for
bicycles, "hims" for "hes" etc. and then the sudden resumption of gentleman's language whenever you write of sport. And I thought the school
"down the river" a pity—as tho' you hadn't got over snobbery. Both
these things upset me—school "by the river" and the correct hunting
terms. But it was a book no one else could have written and it makes me
feel I know [you?] far less well than I did before which, in a way, I take to
be its purpose.

I hope the shadow of death that hangs over it has lightened. You must
be finding plenty to do with your hands. After returning with head
unbloody but bowed from Dakar, marine life became too humiliating

and I have transferred to something more unusual under Bob Laycock whom you may remember in the first post–Duggan Maimie period. It is corps of Buck's toughs doomed no doubt to ignominy like the marines, but at the moment promising. Anyway a change.

Laura is having another baby at Xmas poor girl—regretted by all. I saw her for a week at Pixton.

My fondest love to Dig.

(There is a chap called Biddulph in my commando. Any relation?)

Evelyn

Piers Court.
[November 1946]

My dear Henry,

I have finished reading *Back* with intense interest. No one but you could have written it or any part of it (except the French pastiche of which hereafter). The ingenious symbolism—roses roses all the way—excited envy & I delighted in the gradual breaking of dawn from madness to normality which could not have been better done & which, I hope, symbolizes for you a cosmic process which is entirely invisible to me. And the "married & lived happy ever after" was conclusive for your couple this time as it was not for that beastly butler.

I should have liked it clearer whether in fact there was a marked physical likeness between Rose & Nance. She hints once that she is constantly plagued by being mistaken for the half sister but no one except Charlie seems to see it & then only when he is deranged.

The office scenes and the episode of the secretary seemed perfect. In fact the story is a triumphant success.

From all this I must except the Grand Siècle interpolation. A story within a story is a tricky device & I don't think this comes off. It is as if you wanted to show you can jolly well write with old world elegance if you care to—and you cant. Sentences like ". . . as well born as he, ill as he is as well" are excruciating to me. Apart from the jingle of it the syntax "well—ill—well" each time in different sense, "as—as—as—as" all different again. People did not write like that in civilized ages. It is like the time you told me poor Andrew Scott was a "cunt."

I get encouraging reports of the house I am thinking of buying in Ireland so I think soon I shall shake off the dust of your industrial state for ever.

You will think me a prig of course for what I have said above. Well I suppose I am.

Love to Dig
Evelyn

Piers Court.
12 November [1946]

Dear Henry,

I confess I hadn't realized the "pastiche" was authentic. I have re-read it & find my credulity strained. As a matter of literary morals should you not have put a note to this effect? To introduce someone elses work into your own fiction seems to me reprehensible.

The story is deep as a well and wide as a church door without it. If, as you kindly say, you value my opinion, do consider cutting it right out. Apart from its teeming inadequacies, it is, surely, false to the main story to make James read anything of that kind.

Laura and I greatly look forward to your visit. The only thing that might interfere with it, is our going to inspect the house in Ireland which I am thinking of buying. But if we go it will be for only a day or two. After 18th Dec all will be a slum here, with the return of my children from school, so come before then please.

Evelyn

VIRGINIA WOOLF

To Gerald Brenan

Monk's House, Rodmell,
Near Lewes, Sussex
Christmas Day 1922

Dear Gerald,

Very stupidly I came away without your letter, though I have been putting off writing till Christmas, hoping to have time and some calmness. It interested me, very much, and now I can't take it up and answer it as I had meant. But no doubt this is as well. What one wants from a letter is not an answer. So I shall ramble on, until the cook goes off to tea with Mrs Dedman, when I must scramble the eggs.

First however, we certainly hope to come to you about the end of March, or beginning of April. This depends on things that can't be settled now; so may we leave it, and write definitely later? Apart from talking to you, as we want to do, at leisure, fully, at night, at dawn, about people, books, life, and so on and so on, my eyes are entirely grey with England—nothing but England for 10 years; and you can't imagine how much of a physical desire it becomes to feed them on colour and crags—something violent and broken and dry—not perpetually sloping and sloppy like the country here. (This is a very wet Christmas day).

I have been thinking a great deal about what you say of writing novels. One must renounce, you say. I can do better than write novels, you say. I don't altogether understand. I don't see how to write a book without people in it. Perhaps you mean that one ought not to attempt a "view of life"?—one ought to limit oneself to one's own sensations—at a quartet for instance; one ought to be lyrical, descriptive: but not set people in motion, and attempt to enter them, and give them impact and volume? Ah, but I'm doomed! As a matter of fact, I think that we all are. It is not possible now, and never will be, to say I renounce. Nor would it be a good thing for literature were it possible. This generation must break its neck in order that the next may have smooth going. For I agree with you that nothing is going to be achieved by us. Fragments—paragraphs—a page perhaps: but no more. Joyce to me seems strewn with disaster. I can't even see, as you see, his triumphs. A gallant approach, that is all that is obvious to me: then the usual smash and splinters (I have only read him, partly, once). The human soul, it seems to me, orientates itself afresh every now and then. It is doing so now. No one can see it whole, therefore. The best of us catch a glimpse of a nose, a shoulder, something turning away, always in movement. Still, it seems better to me to catch this glimpse, than to sit down with Hugh Walpole, Wells, etc. etc. and make large oil paintings of fabulous fleshy monsters complete from top to toe. Of course, being under 30, this does not apply to you. To you, something more complete may be vouchsafed. If so, it will be partly because I, and some others, have made our attempts first. I have wandered from the point. Never mind. I am only scribbling, more to amuse myself than you, who may never read, or understand: for I am doubtful whether people, the best disposed towards each other, are capable of more than an intermittent signal as they forge past—a sentimental metaphor, leading obviously to ships, and night and storm and reefs and rocks, and the obscured, uncompassionate moon. I wish I had your letter for I could then go ahead; without so many jerks.

You said you were very wretched, didn't you? You described your liver rotting, and how you read all night, about the early fathers; and then walked, and saw the dawn. But were wretched, and tore up all you wrote, and felt you could never, never write—and compared this state of yours with mine, which you imagine to be secure, rooted, benevolent, industrious—you did not say dull—but somehow unattainable, and I daresay, unreal. But you must reflect that I am 40: further, every 10 years, at 20, again at 30, such agony of different sorts possessed me that not content with rambling and reading I did most emphatically attempt to end it all; and should have been often thankful, if by stepping on one flagstone rather than another I could have been annihilated where I stood. I say this partly in vanity that you may not think me insipid; partly as a token (one of those flying signals out of the night and so on) that so we live, all of us who feel and reflect, with recurring cataclysms of horror: starting up in the night in agony: Every ten years brings, I suppose, one of those private orientations which match the vast one which is, to my mind, general now in the race. I mean, life has to be sloughed: has to be faced: to be rejected; then accepted on new terms with rapture. And so on, and so on; till you are 40, when the only problem is how to grasp it tighter and tighter to you, so quick it seems to slip, and so infinitely desirable is it.

As for writing, at 30 I was still writing, reading; tearing up industriously. I had not published a word (save reviews). I despaired. Perhaps at that age one is really most a writer. Then one cannot write, not for lack of skill, but because the object is too near, too vast. I think perhaps it must recede before one can take a pen to it. At any rate, at 20, 30, 40, and I've no doubt 50, 60, and 70, that to me is the task; not particularly noble or heroic, as I see it in my own case, for all my inclinations are to write; but the object of adoration to me, when there comes along someone capable of achieving—if only the page or paragraph; for there are no teachers, saints, prophets, good people, but the artists—as you said—But the last sentence is hopelessly unintelligible. Indeed, I am getting to the end of my letter writing capacity. I have many more things to say; but they cower under their coverlets, and nothing remains but to stare at the fire, and finger some book till the ideas freshen within me, or they once more become impartible.

I think, too, there is a great deal of excitement and fun and pure pleasure and brilliance in one's fellow creatures. I'm not sure that you shouldn't desert your mountain, take your chance, and adventure with your human faculties—friendships, conversations, relations, the mere daily intercourse. Why do young men hold books up before their eyes so long? French literature falls like a blue tint over the landscape.

But I am not saying what I mean, and had better stop. Only you must write to me again—anything that occurs to you—And what about something for the Hogarth Press?

Leonard adds his wishes to mine for the future.

Yours
Virginia Woolf

P.S.
I add a postscript, which is intended to explain why I say that one must not renounce. I think I mean that beauty, which you say I sometimes achieve, is only got by the failure to get it; by grinding all the flints together; by facing what must be humiliation—the things one can't do—To aim at beauty deliberately, without this apparently insensate struggle, would result, I think, in little daisies and forget-me-nots—simpering sweetnesses—true love knots—But I agree that one must (we, in our generation must) renounce finally the achievement of the greater beauty: the beauty which comes from completeness, in such books as War and Peace, and Stendhal I suppose, and some of Jane Austen; and Sterne; and I rather suspect in Proust, of whom I have only read one volume. Only now that I have written this, I doubt its truth. Are we not always hoping? and though we fail every time, surely we do not fail so completely as we should have failed if we were not in the beginning, prepared to attack the whole. One must renounce, when the book is finished; but not before it is begun. Excuse me for boring on: you may have said nothing of the kind. I was wondering to myself why it is that though I try sometimes to limit myself to the thing I do well, I am always drawn on and on, by human beings, I think, out of the little circle of safety, on and on, to the whirlpools; when I go under.

To Dora Carrington

52 Tavistock Sqre. [W.C.1]
Sunday *[31 January 1932]*

Carrington dearest, I hope you dont mind my writing to you some-times—it is such a comfort because there is nobody to talk to about Lytton who knew him as you did—and of course dont answer. One hates so the feeling that things begin again here in London without him. I find I cant write without suddenly thinking Oh but Lytton wont read this, and it takes all the point out of it. I always put away things in my mind to say to Lytton. And what it must be for you—I wish some time I could see you and tell you about the time, after Thoby's [Stephen] death, before you knew him, when I used to see him. But I could never give him what you did. I used to laugh at him for having grown so mellow and good tempered (you know how I loved laughing at him) and he said, "Oh but you know, it is rather wonderful—Ham Spray and all that—and its all Carrington's doing." This is no help to you now, but it is for us. Before he knew you, he was so depressed and restless—and all that changed when you had Tidmarsh.

Tell Julia that she's still got to come and see us, and bring her book. Please do the pictures for it. I know Lytton would have liked that.

Yes of course I'll write about him some day, but it must be for you, only.

And some time I want to come to Ham Spray again (if this is not being like [Sibyl] Colefax). How lovely it was that night—I shall never forget it. Pippa dined here the other night—she seemed well; but very broken, I thought.

Well, Carrington, I must stop and please forgive me for droning on—but you are the person who understands best about Lytton.

                                                              Virginia
Leonard sends his love.

52 T. [avistock]S. [quare, W. C. I]
2nd March [1932]

I loved those little pictures, darling Carrington. How it seizes upon one, the longing for Lytton, when one sees them. But then how happy he looks—that is one comfort—and then again I thank you. We would always have come to Ham Spray: it was only the feeling we had that that belonged to another side of Lytton's life: I dont mean that you didn't want us, but that it was simpler for him to come here. But heavens— how I wish we had brushed aside all that, and come and stayed: or made him come here oftener. Of course one gets involved in things, and there is always the press, and Leonards different things—how worthless it seems now compared with one hour of being with Lytton. Yes, I think it does get harder—I cant describe to you the sense I have of wanting to tell Lytton something. I never read a book even with the same pleasure now. He was part of all I did—I have dream after dream about him and the oddest sense of seeing him coming in the street.

Oh but Carrington we have to live and be ourselves—and I feel it is more for you to live than for any one; because he loved you so, and loved your oddities and the way you have of being yourself. I cant explain it; but it seems to me that as long as you are there, something we loved in Lytton, something of the best part of his life still goes on. But goodness knows, blind as I am, I know all day long, whatever I'm doing, what you're suffering. And no one can help you.

I've read Julia's story. I think it astonishingly good. We shall publish it I hope: but will you try to keep her at it—and will you do pictures? I'm sure thats what would make it a success—Couldn't there be woodcuts in the text? It seems to me full of scenes that want illustrations. Its extraordinarily complete and sharp and individual—I had no notion it would be so good. But I feel she may tear it up at any moment—She's so queer: so secret, and suppressed.

Goodbye, darling Carrington

your old attached friend
Virginia

From DIARY

Saturday 12 March [1932]. So we went to Ham Spray—a lovely bright day, & got there at 1.30. "I thought you weren't coming" said C. She came to the door, in her little jacket & socks with a twisted necklace. Her eyes were very pale. "I sent a telegram; but I do everything wrong. I thought you didn't get it." She was pale, small, suffering silently. very calm. She had hot soup for us. I looked at the trees. We sat in the cold dining room. I didnt light the fire, she said. She had cooked us a nice hot lunch, succulent, with her own hands. We talked of Mary & Lytton. She had discovered whom Mary loves, owing to an indiscretion. But Lytton made her swear not to tell. So she didn't. We talked with effort; did she want us? Did she resent our coming to spy on her? She was bitter, laughing at Barbara [Bagenal]. "She asked how she could help. I told her to cut sandwiches. But she took an hour, talking to Tommy." Then we sat on the verandah. We asked her to make us woodcuts for notepaper. And to do designs for Julia's book. We tried to gossip—about Mrs Keppel: about Saxon; she laughed once or twice: & her eyes seemed to get bluer. Then it got cold & we went & sat in Lytton's study —all beautifully neat, his notepaper laid out—a great fire; all his books exactly fitting the shelves, with the letters over them. We sat on the floor round the fire. Then L. suggested a walk. She took us to her grove. She said the trees had a flower wh. smelt very sweet in summer. She said she had some notes to write & would we go by ourselves. We only walked to the bottom of the long low down. Then L. went to do the car, & I wandered in the garden & then back into the sitting room. I was taking out a book when C. came in & asked if we would have tea before we went. She had made it. She & I went upstairs, arm in arm; & I said Let me see the view from the window. We stood looking out—She said Dont you think one ought to keep a room exactly as it was? We went to Dorothy Wordsworth's house. Her room has been kept exactly as she left it. There are even the same prints & little things on the table. I want to keep Lytton's rooms as he had them. But the Stracheys say this is morbid. Am I romantic about it d'you think? Oh no, I'm romantic too, I said. And we went back to L.'s sitting room. She burst into tears, & I took her in my arms. She sobbed, & said she had always been a failure. "There is nothing left for me to do. I did everything for Lytton. But I've failed in everything else. People say he was very selfish to me. But he gave me everything. I was devoted to my father. I hated my mother. Lytton was like a father to me. He taught me everything I know. He read poetry & French to me." I did not want to lie to her—I could not pretend that there was not truth in what she said. I said life seemed to me sometimes hopeless, useless, when I woke in the night & thought of Lytton's death. I held her hands. Her wrists seemed very small. She seemed helpless, deserted, like some small animal left. She was very gentle; sometimes laughing; kissing me; saying Lytton had loved his old friends best. She said he had been silly with young men. But that was only on the top. She had been angry that they had not understood how great he was. I said I had always known that. And she said I made too much of his young friends. She said Roger was "as Lytton said, very dim in the intellect." He could never have a real intimacy—it wasn't sharing everything—only Roger was very high spirited & liked going to Rome, & rather liked Lytton reading aloud to him—but they couldn't talk. And this last year Lytton made up his mind to be middle aged. He was a realist. He faced the fact that Roger could not be his love. And we were going to Malaga & then he was going to write about Shakespeare. And he was going to write his memoirs, which would take him ten years. It was ironical, his dying, wasnt it. He thought he was getting better. He said things like Lear when he was ill. I wanted to take you to see him the day you came, but I was afraid to—James & Pippa said one must not run any risk, & it might have upset him. "No, of course not" I said. "Roger will take the books of course—he will have to." And what else did we say? There was not much time. We had tea & broken biscuits. She stood by the fireplace. Then we said we must go. She was very quiet & showed no desire for us to stay.

Then, as we were leaving the room to go she suddenly picked up a little French box with a picture of the Arc de Triomphe upon it & said "I gave this to Lytton. Take it. James says I mustnt give away Lytton's things. But this is all right. I gave it him." So I took it. There is a coin in it. How frightened she seemed of doing wrong—like a child who has been scolded.

She came down into the front of the house. She kissed me several times. I said "Then you will come & see us next week—or not—just as you like?" "Yes, I will come, or not" she said. And kissed me again, & said Goodbye. Then she went in; & turned & I waved & she waved back & she went into the house. Next morning at 8.30 the gardener heard a

noise in her bedroom. He went in & found she had shot herself through the thigh. She died in 3 hours. . . .
Thursday 17 March. So Carrington killed herself; & again what L. calls "these mausoleum talks" begin again. We were the last to talk to her, & thus might have been summoned to the inquest; but they brought it in an accident. She maintained this, even to Ralph. Her foot slipped as she was shooting a rabbit.
And we discuss suicide; & I feel, as always, ghosts [dwindling] changing. Lytton's affected by this act. I sometimes dislike him for it. He absorbed her, made her kill herself. Then the romantic completeness which affects Mary. "a beautiful gesture—her life & her death." Nonsense says Leonard: it was historic: the real thing is that we shall never see Lytton again. This is unreal. So we discuss suicide. and the ghosts as I say, change so oddly in my mind; like people who live, & are changed by what one hears of them. . . .

ELIZABETH BOWEN

To William Plomer

Bowen's Court
9th September [1952]

My dear William
Thank you for your sympathy. You have always been one of the most understanding as well as the dearest of our friends, seeing us in and out of so many scenes and places and times and houses, and I do particularly value your thoughts now. Also, there could not have been a happier time to have had your book—I mean a time at which *Museum Pieces* could be more welcome. The inscription, to both of us, gave me nothing but pleasure; my only wish is that Alan *could* have read the book. To me, it came at a time when I couldn't otherwise read anything, and yet was longing for the pleasure that reading can be—the mental equivalent of nervous hunger coupled with indigestion. To have something of yours— and one of the best I think that you've ever done—and at the same time to be in Tony's company was ideal. Apart from all the praise and reclame

Museum Pieces is having and will have, remember also that if it had been written, for a special friend at a special moment it could not have brought more happiness—and, in a way I can't explain, consolation.

At any time, William, and speaking objectively (awful word), *Museum Pieces* is a great piece of work. The balanced, apparently casual, up-springing build of the narration is so good. And, you have accomplished what I had always taken to be impossible—the bringing of "real" people into the dimension of art.

Funny, elegant, tragic, and with the [two?] of them floated in and added to by the element of your sensibility, your perception—oh William, it *is* a beautiful book!

Also, judging it on another (I mean the personally-knowing plane) as a bringing to life of beloved Tony and of his mother, it's quite uncanny. I see all of those changes of his face, the dilation of his eyes, and hear his laughter and the tones of his voice.

So you can imagine that to be both in your company and in his has peopled, has somehow saved, these last otherwise terrifyingly empty days for me.

All my love
Elizabeth.

Bowen's Court
6 May [1958]

Dearest William,

I only got back from America a week ago; one of the best things about home-coming was to find your *At Home.* It, I have been reading over these last days, with deliberate slowness, to make it last. Thank you for it twice over: I deeply appreciate having your name, and indeed my name in your hand, inside. This book is really magnificent; the best account of your and my times, and of having such times as one's own times, that I know. And I don't know how to tell you how I admire, and envy, the brilliance *and* depth, suppleness and yet no less precision, of the writing.

Best of all, the book is you, as we know and love you. (I don't know why I use the first person plural instead of the first person singular.) Again and again reading it I felt as though you were in the room: at the same time, I remained rightly in awe of that non-personal greatness one recognizes in a friend. On the whole, I haven't cared very much for most of my contemporaries' autobiographies (such as, though don't tell them) Stephen's and John Lehmann's. Most people do better to keep their traps shut; but you are an exception.

I was grateful, apart from many other things, for the return to life, for me, of Virginia and Tony: they are the only two of the dead whom I *truly* miss. (Alan never seems dead, in the sense that he never seems gone: I suppose that if one has lived the greater part of one's life with a person he continues to accompany one through every moment.)

Only you seem able to bring back Virginia's laughter—I get so *bored* and irked by that tragic fiction which has been manufactured about her, since 1941. As for Tony, I have so often tried (and so invariably felt, tried in vain) to give any idea of him to people who did not know him or barely knew him.

I *can't* believe—though I'd believe it if you say so—that I went to tea at Virginia's, and met you there, on the afternoon of George V's funeral. My cousin Noreen, who was staying with us, and Billy Buchan and I had got up at 4 A.M. to watch the procession in Edgware Road; and I remember nothing else about the afternoon except being anaesthetized by tiredness, plus in vain looking for food for that night's dinner (to which I do remember you and Tom Eliot came) with all shops shut: a condition I'd forgotten to foresee. I remember finally coaxing a large veal-and-ham pie, at black market price, out of [a] little restaurant in the understructure of Baker Street Station where I sometimes ate.

If I were a marker of books (out of sympathy; approbation) I should be drawing constant pencil-marks down your margins. You crystallise things I didn't know I had felt or thought. Also you say intransigent things with which I occasionally disagree; but I couldn't go into those unless I had both you and the book here at the same time, which I fear is unlikely.

What an agreeable life we all had, seeing each other *without* being "a group." Perhaps ours was, is, the only non-groupy generation: the younger ones now sound as though they'd started doing that again—or haven't they, really?

I wonder how you feel in the 1950s? Personally I am enjoying this epoch—it is really the first one, it seems to me, in which I've enjoyed being "grown up" as much as I expected to do when I was a child. The only sad thing is that, owing to the necessity to work so hard, I have altogether ceased to be able to write letters—as I used to do, if you remember, copiously in the 1930s. Not that that's probably a great loss to anyone else; but it *is* a loss to me, because writing to anybody is one great way of making oneself feel one is in their presence. It's unnecessary for me to say, I wish I saw you; say that I greatly miss you. I somehow fatalistically know you'll never come here; yet against all hope I continue to imagine you someday again will. While there's life there's hope— which is the major distinction between one's relations with the living and one's relations with the dead. Here I *am* (I continue to state) with

Eddy Sackville-West, who'd also love to see you, living nearby for the summer part of the year. Towards the end of October I'll be going back to New York for another two months.

My reasons for not more often coming to London are of the most banal kind: it's all so expensive. In New York I earn money as well as spend it. And the snag about going to London, but not living there is that it's harder to see those who don't live there either. How well we all do by living elsewhere, all the same.

Dear William, my best love and, again, thanks.
Elizabeth.

To Virginia Woolf

2 Clarence Terrace
Regent's Park
N.W.I.
July 1st [1940]

Dearest Virginia,

Ever since I got back here I have been thinking about Rodmell—this sounds nonsense, but you must know how some part of one's thoughts or one's imagination can go on contemplating a place amost continuously. And when I say Rodmell I mean Monks House and you and Leonard and everything indisassociable from it. It doesn't seem to me that I've ever been so perfectly happy—This seems to me to be all "I . . . I . . . I . . . ," but how impossible, quite wrongly, it is to write about any feeling without identifying oneself, with it. I don't think I'd ever imagined a place and people in which and with whom one felt so perfectly happy that one felt suspended the whole time, and at the same time wanting to smile, *and* smiling, continuously, like a dog.

I still feel very homesick.

At the end of which I can only say, thank you both very much. I loved everything that we did.

I do hope the Co-operative sent the sugar and that Mabel got on well with the currants and raspberries. You will be coming up to London today, I think, so I'm writing to Mecklenburg Square. I wondered if you had any more sirens: there haven't been any here since.

I read your lecture, which I'm sending back in this envelope, coming up in the train, with great excitement. The leaning tower metaphor seemed to me perfect. I'd never thought *into* those young men's position before, and your leaning tower, with the sense at once of unnatural angle and panic, made it (their position) suddenly comprehensible. The element of *fuss* about their work is explained, though not, I think, excused—and you don't excuse it. I didn't think you over-severe—did you think you were?—only deadly accurate. The quotations were damning.

I liked very much the early part—the part about family, books descending from books. I feel sure art ought to breed. The leaning tower people may be imitated (now) but they can breed nothing: they seem to me like mules or something.

I saw Cyril Connolly on Saturday he asked if you liked *Horizon*. I said (I hope truly) you liked his wish that things should be done well. He and Stephen and the young man Watson who finances *Horizon* are all living in a villa in Devonshire, coming up to London just now and then. They don't seem to like it very much.

The cactus travelled very well and had none of its white bloom knocked off. The garlic did well too: I left it with my suitcase and the cactus in the very refined porter's lodge of the English Speaking Union while I was having tea there with my aunt. I think the garlic must have been commented on, as the porter looked at me rather severely when I came to take it away again. I sat in this park on Saturday afternoon and read the Gorky book, notes, about Tolstoi with very great joy, in fact read it twice.

I think I told you I had asked the Ministry of Information if I could do any work, which I felt was wanted in Ireland. On Saturday morning I had a letter from them saying yes, they did want me to go. Now it has come to the point I have rather a feeling of dismay and of not wanting to leave this country. I am to see Harold Nicolson on Thursday and go to Ireland on Friday night next. I don't expect it will be for very long. I shall be at Bowen's Court first, but I expect they will also want me to move about the place. I don't know much till I've seen Harold Nicolson. I hope I shall be some good: I do feel it's important. As far as my own feeling goes I feel low at going away, so can only hope to be some good when I'm there. It will all mean endless talk, but sorting out talk into shape might be interesting. I suppose I shall also finish my book. But Ireland can be dementing, if one's Irish and may well be so now. If there's to be an invasion of Ireland, I hope it may be while I'm there— which I don't mean frivolously—but if anything happens to England while I'm in Ireland I shall wish I'd never left, even for this short time. I suppose the Ministry will give me a come-and-go travel permit.

If I find the letter I began to you at Bowen's Court I'll send it but it will be *very* old.

This letter is already very wandering. If I began to write about affection for you, Virginia, I should degenerate into sheer gush.

I'll write from Ireland, and may I tell you when I come back? Meanwhile my love to you both, and all the thoughts of the most continuous kind, that one can only stodgily call good wishes. Good wishes to you both, at all times and thank you for those lovely two days.

Love from Elizabeth

2 Clarence Terrace
Tuesday 18 Feb [1941]

My dear Virginia,

At this moment Lady Jones is having lunch with you (it's 1.45) and I do feel the strongest desire to ring you up—only I expect that, rather than harrying Lady Jones, which is as I should wish, it would be a bother for you. I expect she is really much nicer than one thinks: she has that smoothest Kensington surface but there is a slight rattle in her inside. I hope you'll have a nice afternoon with the Women's Institute, or as we used to call it when I was in the Headington one, the *W.I.* I expect the W.I. will have a nice time anyway. As a matter of fact I do very much miss W.I. dos: since I came to live in London I feel I don't live in England at all.

I was miserable coming away on Saturday. It was absolutely *lovely* at Monks House, all the time. I do hope happiness didn't make me too bouncing: I felt so awfully happy. I still can't see much but your upstairs room with the cyclamens on the window-sill—not actually on the window-sill but on a table, but at window-height—and those two arum lilies, and your embroidery. I mean, even apart from you and Leonard. All I have got to look at are scratches from the beautiful apache cat. The moss is now in the middle of my dinner table, in a sort of white Wedgewood basket dish.

I still haven't written to poor [Sagan?]. Did you?

It was worth while not cutting the theatre with that cousin, because he is obviously very homesick. He is nice, but the chief thing is that his father (long before he *was* his father) was very good to my mother when my father was ill. That is more than thirty years ago, but one has to work out that sort of understanding kindness from one generation to another, like the inverse of a vendetta. This boy, Jack, used to work in Guinness's brewery in Dublin, and has now been drafted to the brewery outside London. He has never been in England before except at school, and it is interesting to hear what he thinks of everything.

Today, this morning, I went and talked to Lord Cranbourne at the Dominions Office about Ireland. I say talked, because he listened with very sympathetic and charming Cecil politeness. I knew he had seen the reports I'd been sending in, and there were things I wanted to say that I couldn't write. So I had asked David to put me in touch with him.

Getting into the Dominions Office was such a business: I had had no exact idea where it was, so took a taxi, which didn't know either and aroused far more suspicion than if I had come on my feet. We were challenged by bayonets, and I said each time in a more quavering but more aggressive voice that I had an appointment. Then inside there were forms to fill in, then the long passages that though very hot still manage to smell of stone. There were outer courts of rooms of gentlemen-secretaries and files, then his room, which was nice and long, with boarded-up windows, a stretch of Turkey carpet, a roaring fire. Unfortunately it was just as I had imagined (the scene, I mean) there were almost no surprises. The last time I was in London I went to the War Office, also on an Irish errand, and there, because it was eleven o'clock, they were all drinking glasses of milk, which *was* something that I had not imagined.

Stephen Spender rang up this morning, just when I got in. He is laid up in Mr Worsley's flat, near Sloane Square, with what appeared to be a boil on the knee but what he now thinks must be water on the knee really. So I said I would go to tea with him on Thursday.

Otherwise I have done almost nothing since I came back but try to finish my Bowen's Court book. I have got to the part where my mother and I go and live in Folkestone, which is nothing to do with Bowen's Court except the fact of nobody being *there*, so I am trying to compress Folkestone into a paragraph.

I extremely stupidly left behind at Monks House some things that were on a lower shelf of my dressingtable and that, packing up quickly and absentmindedly, I didn't see. The only point of saying they're there is to say, don't bother about them; they are rather squalid, a green-backed hand mirror (*not* embossed, like Susie's hairbrush) and two rather greasy jars of cold cream. May I make them an excuse to come back to you before I go back to Ireland? I have another hand-glass, and have got to get some more cold cream anyhow, as those two jars were nearly finished.

I told Alan all about your omelette, and he said he would like to have a competition with you. I rather tactlessly said that I thought your omelette would win.

Thank you very, very much, Virginia and all my love.
Elizabeth

PART XIX

FAREWELLS

Anaktoria so far away, remember me.

—*Sappho*

LI PO

On Seeing Off Meng Hao-Jan

My friend bade farewell at the Yellow Crane House,
And went down eastward to Willow Valley
Amid the flowers and mists of March.
The lonely sail in the distance
Vanished at last beyond the blue sky.
And I could see only the river
Flowing along the border of heaven.

The Yellow Crane House stood till a recent date not far from the city of Wu-chang, Hupeh, on a hill overlooking the Yangtze-kiang.

Once upon a time a dead man of Shuh, traveling on the back of a yellow crane, stopped here to rest. Hence the name of the house.

There is another interesting story just as authentic, according to which: there stood here a tavern kept by a man whose name was Chin, to whom one day a tall rugged professor in rags came and asked very complacently, "I haven't money, will you give me wine?" The tavern keeper was game; he readily offered to the stranger the biggest tumbler and allowed him to help himself to all the wine he wanted day after day for half a year. At last the professor said to Chin, "I owe you some wine money. I'll pay you now." So saying, he took lemon peels and with it smeared on the wall a picture of a yellow crane, which at the clapping of his hands came to life and danced to the tune of his song. The spectacle soon brought a fortune to the tavern-keeper; he became a millionaire. Then, the professor left, flying away on his bird, whither no one knew. The grateful tavern-keeper built the tower-house in commemoration thereof, and called it the Yellow Crane House.

Willow Valley (Yang-chow), in Kiangsu.

Translated and annotated by Shigeyoshi Obata.

Taking Leave of a Friend

Blue mountains to the north of the walls,
White river winding about them;
Here we must make separation
And go out through a thousand miles of dead grass.
Mind like a floating wide cloud,
Sunset like the parting of old acquaintances
Who bow over their clasped hands at a distance.
Our horses neigh to each other
        as we are departing.

Translated by Ezra Pound

Exiles' Letter

To So-Kin of Rakuyo, ancient friend, Chancellor of Gen.
Now I remember that you built me a special tavern
By the south side of the bridge at Ten-Shin.
With yellow gold and white jewels, we paid for songs and laughter
And we were drunk for month on month, forgetting the kings and
        princes.
Intelligent men came drifting in from the sea and from the west
        border,
And with them, and with you especially
There was nothing at cross purpose,
And they made nothing of sea-crossing or of mountain-crossing,
If only they could be of that fellowship,
And we all spoke out our hearts and minds, and without regret.
And then I was sent off to South Wei, smothered in laurel groves,
And you to the north of Raku-hoku,
Till we had nothing but thoughts and memories in common.
And then, when separation had come to its worst,
We met, and travelled into Sen-Go,
Through all the thirty-six folds of the turning and twisting waters,
Into a valley of the thousand bright flowers,
That was the first valley;
And into ten thousand valleys full of voices and pine-winds.
And with silver harness and reins of gold,
Out came the East of Kan foreman and his company.
And there came also the "True man" of Shi-yo to meet me,

Playing on a jewelled mouth-organ.
In the storied houses of San-Ko they gave us more Sennin music,
Many instruments, like the sound of young phoenix broods.
The foreman of Kan Chu, drunk, danced because his long sleeves
    wouldn't keep still
With that music playing,
And I, wrapped in brocade, went to sleep with my head on his lap,
And my spirit so high it was all over the heavens,
And before the end of the day we were scattered like stars, or rain.
I had to be off to So, far away over the waters,
You back to your river-bridge.
And your father, who was brave as a leopard,
Was governor in Hei-Shu, and put down the barbarian rabble.
And one May he had you send for me, despite the long distance.
And what with broken wheels and so on, I won't say it wasn't hard
    going,
Over roads twisted like sheep's guts.
And I was still going, late in the year, in the cutting wind from the
    North,
And thinking how little you cared for the cost, and you caring enough
    to pay it.
And what a reception:
Red jade cups, food well set on a blue jewelled table,
And I was drunk, and had no thought of returning.
And you would walk out with me to the western corner of the castle,
To the dynastic temple, with water about it clear as blue jade,
With boats floating, and the sound of mouth-organs and drums,
With ripples like dragon-scales, going glass green on the water,
Pleasure lasting, with courtezans, going and coming without hindrance,
With the willow flakes falling like snow,
And the vermilioned girls getting drunk about sunset,
And the water, a hundred feet deep, reflecting green eyebrows
—Eyebrows painted green are a fine sight in young moonlight,
Gracefully painted—
And the girls singing back at each other,
Dancing in transparent brocade,
And the wind lifting the song, and interrupting it,
Tossing it up under the clouds.
    And all this comes to an end.
    And is not again to be met with.
I went up to the court for examination,
Tried Layu's luck, offered the Choyo song,

And got no promotion, and went back to the East Mountains
    White-headed.
And once again, later, we met at the South bridgehead.
And then the crowd broke up, you went north to San palace,
And if you ask how I regret that parting:
It is like the flowers falling at Spring's end
    Confused, whirled in a tangle.
What is the use of talking, and there is no end of talking,
There is no end of things in the heart.
I call in the boy,
Have him sit on his knees here
    To seal this,
And send it a thousand miles, thinking.

                            Translated by Ezra Pourd

TU FU

To Wei Pa, a Retired Scholar

The lives of many men are
Shorter than the years since we have
Seen each other. Aldebaran
And Antares move as we have.
And now, what night is this? We sit
Here together in the candle
Light. How much longer will our prime
Last? Our temples are already
Grey. I visit my old friends.
Half of them have become ghosts.
Fear and sorrow choke me and burn
My bowels. I never dreamed I would
Come this way, after twenty years,
A wayfarer to your parlor.
When we parted years ago,
You were unmarried. Now you have
A row of boys and girls, who smile

And ask me about my travels.
How have I reached this time and place?
Before I can come to the end
Of an endless tale, the children
Have brought out the wine. We go
Out in the night and cut young
Onions in the rainy darkness.
We eat them with hot, steaming,
Yellow millet. You say, "It is
Sad, meeting each other again."
We drink ten toasts rapidly from
The rhinoceros horn cups.
Ten cups, and still we are not drunk.
We still love each other as
We did when we were schoolboys.
Tomorrow morning mountain peaks
Will come between us, and with them
The endless, oblivious
Business of the world.

Translated by Kenneth Rexroth

MEI YAO CH'EN

AN EXCUSE FOR NOT RETURNING THE VISIT OF A FRIEND

Do not be offended because
I am slow to go out. You know
Me too well for that. On my lap
I hold my little girl. At my
Knees stands my handsome little son.
One has just begun to talk.
The other chatters without
Stopping. They hang on my clothes
And follow my every step.
I can't get any farther

Than the door. I am afraid
I will never make it to your house.

Translated by Kenneth Rexroth

WANG WEI

To Ch'i-wu Ch'ien Bound Home After Failing in an Examination

In a happy reign there should be no hermits;
The wise and able should consult together. . . .
So you, a man of the eastern mountains,
Gave up your life of picking herbs
And came all the way to the Gate of Gold—
But you found your devotion unavailing.
. . . To spend the Day of No Fire on one of the southern rivers,
You have mended your spring clothes here in these northern cities.
I pour you the farewell wine as you set out from the capital—
Soon I shall be left behind here by my bosom-friend.
In your sail-boat of sweet cinnamon-wood
You will float again toward your own thatch door,
Led along by distant trees
To a sunset shining on a far-away town.
. . . What though your purpose happened to fail,
Doubt not that some of us can hear high music.

Translated by Witter Bynner

HORACE

From To the Ship in Which Virgil Sailed to Athens

(Odes, I, 3)

So may the auspicious Queen of Love,
And the twin Stars (the seed of Jove),
And he who rules the raging wind,
To thee, O sacred ship, be kind,
And gentle breezes fill thy sails,
Supplying soft Etesian gales,
As thou, to whom the Muse commends
The best of poets and of friends,
Dost thy committed pledge restore,
And land him safely on the shore;
And save the better part of me
From perishing with him at sea.

Translated by John Dryden

GEORGE GORDON, LORD BYRON

To Thomas Moore

My boat is on the shore,
   And my bark is on the sea;
But, before I go, Tom Moore,
   Here's a double health to thee!

Here's a sigh to those who love me,
    And a smile to those who hate;
And, whatever sky's above me,
    Here's a heart for every fate.

Though the ocean roar around me,
    Yet it still shall bear me on;
Though a desert should surround me,
    It hath springs which may be won.

Were't the last drop in the well,
    As I gasp'd upon the brink,
Ere my fainting spirit fell,
    'Tis to thee that I would drink.

In that water, as this wine,
    The libation I would pour
Should be—peace to thine and mine,
    And a health to thee, Tom Moore.

ROBERT PENN WARREN

To a Friend Parting

Endure friend-parting yet, old soldier,
Scarred the heart, and wry: the wild plum,
Rock-rent axe-bit, has known with the year bloom,
And tides, the neap and spring, bear faithfully.
Much you have done in honor, though wrathfully.
That, we supposed, was your doom.

O you who by the grove and shore walked
With us, your heart unbraced yet unbetrayed,
Recall: the said, the unsaid, though chaff the said
And backward blown. We saw above the lake

The hawk tower, his wings the light take.
What can be foresaid?

Follow the defiles down. Forget not,
When journey-bated the nag, rusty the steel,
The horny clasp of hands your hands now seal;
And prayers of friends, ere this, kept powder dry.
Rough country of no birds, the tracks sly:
Thus faith has lived, we feel.

MAHAMMED ABDILLE HASSAN

To a Friend Going on a Journey

Now you depart, and though your way may lead
Through airless forests thick with *hhagar* trees,
Places steeped in heat, stifling and dry,
Where breath comes hard, and no fresh breeze can reach—
Yet may God place a shield of coolest air
Between your body and the assailant sun.

And in a random scorching flame of wind
That parches the painful throat, and sears the flesh,
May God, in His compassion, let you find
The great-boughed tree that will protect and shade.

On every side of you, I now would place
Prayers from the Holy Koran, to bless your path,
That ills may not descend, nor evils harm,
And you may travel in the peace of faith.

To all the blessings I bestow on you,
Friend, yourself now say a last Amen.

Translated by M. Laurence

SAPPHO

ANAKTORIA

Handsome horses O shiver and admire,
Long ships and symmetries of archers,
But black earth's fine sight for me
Is her I love.

Heart's hunger all can understand.
Did not she up and leave the best of men,
Helen that beautifullest of womankind?
[   ]*

And forgot her kin and forgot her children
To follow however far into whatever luck
The wild hitherward of her headlong heart
[   ]*

[   ]*
[   ]*
Anaktoria so far away, remember me,
Who had rather

Hear the melody of your walking
And see the torch flare of your smile
Than the long battle line of Lydia's charioteers,
Round shields and helmets.

                    Translated by Guy Davenport

*Illegible words in the manuscript.

FORD MADOX FORD

From Return to Yesterday

(Ford writes of Henry James at Lamb House when W. H. Hudson, Joseph Conrad, and Stephen Crane were all his neighbors.)

. . . Crane would sit writing, hour after hour and day after day, racked with the anxiety that he would not be able to keep going with his pen alone all that fantastic crew. His writing was tiny; he used great sheets of paper. To see him begin at the top of the sheet with his tiny words was agonising; to see him finish a page filled you with concern. It meant the beginning of one more page, and so till his death. Death came slowly but Brede was a sure death-trap to the tuberculous.

Then James' agonies began. He suffered infinitely for that dying boy. I would walk with him for hours over the marsh trying to divert his thoughts. But he would talk on and on. He was for ever considering devices for Crane's comfort. Once he telegraphed to Wanamaker's for a whole collection of New England delicacies from pumpkin pie to apple butter and sausage meat and clams and soft shell crabs and minced meat and . . . everything thinkable, so that the poor lad should know once more and finally those fierce joys. Then new perplexities devastated him. Perhaps the taste of those far off eats might cause Steevie to be homesick and so hasten his end. James wavered backwards and forwards between the alternatives beneath the grey walls of Rye Town. He was not himself for many days after Crane's death.

So the first of those four men to die was the youngest. Taken altogether, they were, those four, all gods for me. They formed, when I was a boy, my sure hope in the eternity of good letters. They do still. Long ago the greatest pride of my life used to be that Crane once wrote of me to a friend . . .:

"You must not mind Hueffer; that is his way. He patronises me; he patronises Mr. Conrad; he patronises Mr. James. When he goes to Heaven he will patronise God Almighty. But God Almighty will get used to it, for Hueffer is all right!"

And the words are my greatest pride after so many years.

They are now all dead, a fact which seems to me incredible still. For me they were the greatest influence on the literature that has followed after them—that has yet been vouchsafed to that literature. Young writers from Seattle to the Golden Gate and from Maine to Jacksonville, Florida, write as they do because those four men once wrote—and so with old writers in old houses in Greenwich Village. That fourfold tradition will not soon part. To that tradition I will one day return. For the moment I have been trying to make them live again in your eyes. . . . "It is, above all, to make you see."

ROBERT BURNS

Auld Lang Syne

Should auld acquaintance be forgot
And never brought to mind?
Should auld acquaintance be forgot,
And auld lang syne!

Chorus

For auld lang syne, my jo,
For auld lang syne,
We'll tak a cup o' kindness yet
For auld lang syne.

And surely ye'll be your pint stowp!
And surely I'll be mine!
And we'll take a cup o' kindness yet,
For auld lang syne.
For auld, &c.

We twa hae run about the braes,
And pou'd the gowans fine;
But we've wander'd mony a weary fitt,

Sin auld lang syne.
  For auld, &c.

We twa hae paidl'd in the burn,
 Frae morning sun till dine;
But seas between us braid hae roar'd,
 Sin auld lang syne.
  For auld, &c.

And there's a hand, my trusty fiere!
 And gie's a hand o' thine!
And we'll take a right gude-willie-waught,
 For auld lang syne.
  For auld, &c.

ENVOI

The Irish Dancer

I am of Ireland
And of the holy land
    Of Ireland.
Good sir, pray I thee,
Of sainte charity
Come and dance with me
    In Ireland.

THE AUTHORS

Aesop (c. 6th cent. B.C.), Greek fabulist.

Agnon, S. Y. (1888–1970), Israeli novelist and short story writer.

Akhmatova, Anna (1888–1966), Russian poet.

Arendt, Hannah (1906–1975), German-American political theorist.

Aristotle (384–322 B.C.), Greek philosopher.

Auden, W. H. (1907–1973), Anglo-American poet, critic, and essayist.

Bacon, Francis (1561–1626), English philosopher, essayist, and statesman.

Benjamin, Walter (1892–1940), German critic, philosopher, and essayist.

Berg, A. Scott (1949–), American biographer.

Bishop, Elizabeth (1911–1979), American poet.

Blake, William (1757–1827), English poet and artist.

Bonhoeffer, Dietrich (1906–1945), German theologian.

Borges, Jorge Luis (1899–1986), Argentine poet, critic, and short story writer.

Boswell, James (1740–1795), Scottish biographer.

Bowen, Elizabeth (1899–1973), Anglo-Irish novelist, short story writer, and memoirist.

Brecht, Bertolt (1898–1956), German playwright and poet.

Browning, Robert (1812–1889), English poet.

Burney, Fanny (1752–1840), English novelist.

Burns, Robert (1759–1796), Scottish poet.

Byron, George Gordon Lord (1788–1824), English poet.

Camus, Albert (1913–1960), French novelist and essayist.

Carducci, Giosuè (1835–1907), Italian poet and scholar.

Carroll, Lewis (1832–1898), English writer and mathematician.

Carver, Raymond (1938–1988), American poet and short story writer.

Chekhov, Anton (1860–1904), Russian playwright and short story writer.

Cicero (106–43 B.C.), Roman orator, politician, and philosopher.

Coleridge, Samuel Taylor (1772–1834), English poet, critic, philosopher, and theologian.

Colette (1873–1954), French novelist.

Cowper, William (1731–1800), English poet.

Dante Alighieri (1265–1321), Italian poet.

Davenport, Guy (1927–), American short story writer, critic, poet, translator, essayist, and artist.

Davidson, Angus (1898–1980), English biographer, translator, editor, and memoirist.

de la Mare, Walter (1873–1956), English poet and novelist.

Dickinson, Emily (1830–1886), American poet.

Donne, John (1572–1631), English poet and divine.

Douglass, Frederick (1817–1895), American autobiographer, abolitionist, and politician.

Eliot, T. S. (1888–1965), American-English poet, playwright, critic, and essayist.

Eliot, Vivien (1888–1947), English book reviewer, editor, and first wife of T. S. Eliot.

Elyot, Sir Thomas (1490–1546), English essayist, translator, and lexicographer.

Emerson, Ralph Waldo (1803–1882), American poet and essayist.

Epicurus (341–270 B.C.), Greek philosopher.

Faulkner, William (1897–1962), American novelist and short story writer.

Finch, Anne, Countess of Winchilsea (1661–1720), English poet.

Fitzgerald, Edward (1809–1883), English poet, translator, and aphorist.

Fitzgerald, F. Scott (1896–1940), American novelist and short story writer.

Flanner, Janet (1892–1978), American essayist, journalist, memoirist, and translator.

Flaubert, Gustave (1821–1880), French novelist.

Ford, Ford Madox (1873–1939), English novelist, critic, essayist, and memoirist.

Forster, E. M. (1879–1970), English novelist and essayist.

Frost, Robert (1874–1963), American poet.

García Lorca, Federico (1898–1936), Spanish poet and playwright.

Gordimer, Nadine (1923–), South African novelist and short story writer.

Gregory, Lady Augusta (1859–1932), Irish playwright.

Hardy, Thomas (1840–1928), English novelist and poet.

Harper, Michael S. (1938–), American poet.

Hassan, Mahammed Abdille (1864–1920), Somali poet.

Hawthorne, Nathaniel (1804–1864), American novelist and short story writer.

Hazlitt, William (1778–1830), English essayist and critic.

Heaney, Seamus (1939–), Irish poet.

Hellman, Lillian (1905–1984), American playwright and memoirist.

Hillard, George S. (1808–1879), American lawyer, politician, critic, biographer, and editor.

Homer (c. 8th cent. B.C.), Greek poet.

Horace (65–8 B.C.), Latin poet.

Housman, A. E. (1859–1936), English poet and scholar.

Hughes, Langston (1902–1967), American poet, playwright, novelist, and autobiographer.

Hurston, Zora Neale (1891–1960), American novelist, short story writer, folklorist, travel writer, and autobiographer.

James, Henry (1843–1916), American novelist, short story writer, critic, and essayist.

James, William (1842–1910), American philosopher.

Jewett, Sarah Orne (1849–1909), American novelist and short story writer.

Johnson, Samuel (1709–1784), English essayist, poet, critic, and lexicographer.

Jonson, Ben (1572–1637), English poet and playwright.

Joyce, James (1882–1941), Irish novelist and short story writer.

Kahler, Erich (1885–1970), Czechoslovakian-American sociologist, philosopher, and literary historian.

Keats, John (1795–1821), English poet.

Kennan, George F. (1904–), American diplomat and historian.

Kleinzahler, August (1949–), American poet.

La Fontaine, Jean de (1621–1695), French poet and fabulist.

Lamb, Charles (1775–1834), English essayist, poet, and critic.

Lear, Edward (1812–1888), English humorist, poet, and artist.

Le Guin, Ursula K. (1929–), American novelist, poet, and short story writer.

Lewis, C. S. (1898–1963), English scholar, critic, essayist, and fantasy writer.

Li Po (c. 700–762), Chinese poet.

Lowell, Robert (1917–1977), American poet.

Mann, Thomas (1875–1955), German novelist, short story writer, and essayist.

Martial (c. 40–104), Roman poet.

Marx, Groucho (1891–1977), American comedian.

Maxwell, William (1908–), American novelist and short story writer.

Mei Yao Ch'en (1002–1060), Chinese poet.

Melville, Herman (1819–1891), American novelist and short story writer.

Mencken, H. L. (1880–1956), American editor, critic, philologist, essayist, and autobiographer.

Michelangelo Buonarroti (1475–1564), Italian sculptor, painter, architect, and poet.

Mistral, Frédéric (1830–1914), French Provençal poet and memoirist.

Montaigne, Michel de (1533–1592), French essayist.

Mozart, Wolfgang Amadeus (1756–1791), Austrian composer.

Nash, Ogden (1902–1971), American poet, humorist, and playwright.

Neruda, Pablo (1904–1973), Chilean poet, diplomat, and politician.

O'Connor, Frank (1903–1966), Irish short story writer, poet, critic, and historian.

Owen, Wilfred (1893–1918), English poet.

Parkman, Francis (1823–1893), American historian and horticulturalist.

Pasternak, Boris (1890–1960), Russian poet and novelist.

Philips, Katherine (1631–1664), English poet.

Po Chü-I (772–846), Chinese poet and politician.

Pope, Alexander (1688–1744), English poet.

Price, Reynolds (1933–), American novelist, poet, playwright, and short story writer.

Pritchett, V. S. (1900–), English novelist, short story writer, essayist, critic, and autobiographer.

Rich, Adrienne (1929–), American poet and essayist.

Rilke, Rainer Maria (1875–1926), German poet.

Robinson, Edwin Arlington (1869–1935), American poet.

Roethke, Theodore (1908–1963), American poet.

Rousseau, Jean-Jacques (1712–1778), Swiss-French philosopher, novelist, political theorist, and autobiographer.

Sappho (c. 6th cent. B.C.), Greek poet.

Schwartz, Delmore (1913–1966), American poet, editor, and short story writer.

Sexton, Anne (1928–1974), American poet.

Shakespeare, William (1564–1616), English playwright and poet.

Shelley, Mary Wollstonecraft (1797–1851), English novelist.

Spenser, Edmund (1552–1599), English poet.

Swift, Jonathan (1667–1745), Irish satirist, poet, essayist, and divine.

Taylor, Jeremy (1613–1667), English bishop, theologian, and devotional writer.

Taylor, Peter (1917–), American short story writer and novelist.

Thomson, David (1914–1988), English folklorist, novelist, essayist, and autobiographer.

Thoreau, Henry David (1817–1862), American essayist and naturalist.

Thurber, James (1894–1961), American humorist, essayist, and artist.

Tolstoy, Leo (1828–1910), Russian novelist, short story writer, and philosopher.

Tu Fu (712–770), Chinese poet.

Turgenev, Ivan (1818–1883), Russian novelist, playwright, and short story writer.

Ungaretti, Giuseppe (1888–1970), Italian poet and translator.

Walcott, Derek (1930–), St. Lucian poet and playwright.

Wang Chien (768–833), Chinese poet.

Wang Wei (699–759), Chinese poet and painter.

Warren, Robert Penn (1905–1989), American novelist, poet, critic, essayist, and short story writer.

Waugh, Evelyn (1903–1966), English novelist, biographer, autobiographer, and travel writer.

Weil, Simone (1909–1943), French philosopher and essayist.

Whitman, Walt (1819–1892), American poet.

Wiesel, Elie (1928–), Romanian-American novelist, essayist, and memoirist.

Wilbur, Richard (1921–), American poet and translator.

Wilde, Oscar (1854–1900), Irish playwright, novelist, critic, and essayist.

Woolf, Virginia (1882–1941), English novelist, critic, short story writer, and essayist.

Wordsworth, Dorothy (1771–1855), English diarist and poet.

Yeats, William Butler (1865–1939), Irish poet and playwright.

PERMISSIONS

Kennan, George F.: Reprinted from *Sketches from a Life* by George F. Kennan by permission of Pantheon Books, a division of Random House, Inc. Copyright © 1989 by George F. Kennan.

Kleinzahler, August: "Friends Through at New Year's" from *Earthquake Weather.* Copyright © 1989 by Moyer Bell Ltd.

La Fontaine, Jean de: "The Two Friends" from *Selected Fables* by Jean de La Fontaine, translated by James Michie (Allen Lane, 1979), translation copyright © James Michie, 1979.

Le Guin, Ursula K.: "Vita Amicae" from *Hard Words,* Harper & Row, 1981. Copyright © 1979 by Ursula K. Le Guin; first appeared in *The Kenyon Review,* reprinted by permission of the author and the author's agent, Virginia Kidd.

Lewis, C. S.: Excerpt from "Friendship" in *The Four Loves,* copyright © 1960 by C. S. Lewis and renewed 1988 by Arthur Owen Barfield, reprinted by permission of Harcourt Brace Jovanovich, Inc.

Li Po: "Taking Leave of a Friend" and "Exiles' Letter" from *Personae,* translated by Ezra Pound. Copyright 1926 by Ezra Pound. Reprinted by permission of New Directions Publishing Corporation. "On Seeing Off Meng Hao-Jan" from *The Works of Li Po,* translated by Shigeyoshi Obata. Copyright 1922 by E. P. Dutton, renewed 1950 by E. P. Dutton. Reprinted by permission of the publisher, Dutton, an imprint of New American Library, a division of Penguin Books USA Inc.

Lowell, Robert: Excerpt from "Randall Jarrell" from *Collected Prose* by Robert Lowell. Copyright © by Farrar, Straus and Giroux, Inc. Reprinted by permission of Farrar, Straus and Giroux, Inc. "Our Afterlife II" from *Day By Day* by Robert Lowell. Copyright © 1975, 1977 by Robert Lowell. Reprinted by permission of Farrar, Straus and Giroux, Inc. "Ford Madox Ford" from *Life Studies* by Robert Lowell. Copyright © 1956, 1959 by Robert Lowell. Renewal copyright © 1987 by Harriet Lowell. Reprinted by permission of Farrar, Straus and Giroux, Inc. Excerpt from "School" and "Letter with Poems for a Letter with Poems" from *Notebook* by Robert Lowell. Copyright © 1967, 1968, 1969, 1970 by Robert Lowell. Reprinted by permission of Farrar, Straus and Giroux, Inc.

Mann, Thomas, and Kahler, Erich: From *An Exceptional Friendship: The Correspondence of Thomas Mann and Erich Kahler.* Copyright © 1975 by Alice L. Kahler. Reprinted by permission of Alice L. Kahler.

Martial: Excerpts from Lucius Valerius Martialis, *Epigrams of Martial Englished by Divers Hands.* Copyright © 1987 The Regents of the University of California. Reprinted by permission of the University of California and the University of California Press.

Marx, Groucho, and Eliot, T. S.: Excerpt from *The Groucho Letters* by Groucho Marx. Copyright © 1967 by Groucho Marx. Reprinted by permission of Simon & Schuster, Inc.

Maxwell, William: "The Fisherman who had no one to go out in his boat with him" from *The Old Man at the Railroad Crossing and Other Tales* by William Maxwell. Copyright © 1957, 1958, 1965, 1966 by William Maxwell.

Mei Yao Ch'en: "An Excuse for Not Returning the Visit of a Friend" from *One Hundred Poems from the Chinese,* translated by Kenneth Rexroth. Copyright © 1971 by Kenneth Rexroth. All rights reserved.

Mencken, H. L.: Excerpt from *Letters of H. L. Mencken,* selected and annotated by Guy J. Forgue. Published by Alfred A. Knopf, Inc., 1961. Reprinted by permission of Alfred A. Knopf, Inc.

Michelangelo Buonarroti: "Veggio co'be' vostr' occhi un dolce lume" reprinted from *Michelangelo: Life, Letters and Poetry,* translated by George Bull and Peter Porter. Copyright © 1987 by George Bull. Reprinted by permission of Oxford University Press.

Mistral, Frédéric: Excerpt from *The Memoirs of Frédéric Mistral* by Frédéric Mistral. Copyright © 1986 by George Wickes. Reprinted by permission of New Directions Publishing Corporation.

Thomson, David: From *The People of the Sea* by David Thomson. Reprinted by permission of Paladin/Granada, HarperCollins Publishers.

Thurber, James: "My Friend McNulty" from *Credos and Curios,* published by Harper & Row. Copyright © 1962 by Helen Thurber. Copyright © 1990 by Rosemary A. Thurber. Reprinted by permission of Rosemary A. Thurber.

Tu Fu: "To Wei Pa, a Retired Scholar" from *One Hundred Poems from the Chinese,* translated by Kenneth Rexroth. Copyright © 1971 by Kenneth Rexroth. All rights reserved. Reprinted by permission of New Directions Publishing Corporation.

Ungaretti, Giuseppe: "In Memoriam" translated by Henry Taylor. Copyright © 1975 by Henry Taylor. Reprinted from *An Afternoon of Pocket Billiards* by permission of the author.

Walcott, Derek: "Forest of Europe" from *The Star-Apple Kingdom* by Derek Walcott. Copyright © 1977, 1978, 1979 by Derek Walcott. Reprinted by permission of Farrar, Straus and Giroux, Inc.

Wang Chien: "Hearing That His Friend was Coming Back from the War" from *Translations from the Chinese,* translated by Arthur Waley. Copyright 1919 and renewed 1947 by Arthur Waley. Reprinted by permission of Alfred A. Knopf, Inc.

Wang Wei: "To Chi Wu Ch'ien Bound Home After Failing in an Examination" by Wang Wei from *The Chinese Translations* by Witter Bynner. Copyright © 1978 by The Witter Bynner Foundation. Reprinted by permission of Farrar, Straus and Giroux, Inc. "To the Bachelor of Arts" from *Translations from the Chinese,* translated by Arthur Waley. Copyright 1919 and renewed 1947 by Arthur Waley. Reprinted by permission of Alfred A. Knopf, Inc.

Warren, Robert Penn: "To a Friend Parting" from *Selected Poems 1923–1975,* by Robert Penn Warren. Copyright © 1976 by Robert Penn Warren. Reprinted by permission of Random House, Inc.

Waugh, Evelyn: From *The Letters of Evelyn Waugh* edited by Mark Amory. Copyright © 1980 The Estate of Laura Waugh. Copyright © 1980 in the introduction and compilation of Mark Amory. Reprinted by permission of Ticknor and Fields, a Houghton Mifflin Company.

Weil, Simone: "Friendship" reprinted by permission of The Putnam Publishing Group from *Waiting for God* by Simone Weil (translated by Emma Craufurd). Copyright © 1951 by G. P. Putnam's Sons, renewed © 1979 by G. P. Putnam's Sons.

Wiesel, Elie: Excerpt from *Somewhere a Master* by Elie Wiesel, translated by Marion Wiesel. Copyright © 1982 by Elirion Associates, Inc. Reprinted by permission of Summit Books, a division of Simon & Schuster, Inc. Excerpt from *Night* by Elie Wiesel. Translation copyright © 1960 by MacGibbon & Kee. Renewal copyright © 1988 by The Collings Publishing Group. Reprinted by permission of Hill and Wang, a division of Farrar, Straus and Giroux, Inc.

Wilbur, Richard: "What is the Opposite of Two" from *Opposites,* copyright © 1973 by Richard Wilbur, reprinted by permission of Harcourt Brace Jovanovich, Inc.

Wilde, Oscar: Excerpt from *De Profundis* by Oscar Wilde, published by Vintage Press, 1964. Reprinted by permission of Philosophical Library.

Woolf, Virginia: "Letter to Gerald Brenan, Christmas Day 1922" from *The Letters of Virginia Woolf, Volume Two: 1912–1922* by Nigel Nicholson, copyright © 1976 by Quentin Bell and Angelica Garnett, reprinted by permission of Harcourt Brace Jovanovich, Inc. "31 January 1932" and "2 March 1932" from *The Letters of Virginia Woolf, Volume Five: 1932–1935* by Nigel Nicholson, copyright © 1979 by Quentin Bell and Angelica Garnett, reprinted by permission of Harcourt Brace Jovanovich, Inc. "12 March 1932" from *The Diary of Virginia Woolf, Volume Four: 1932–1935* by Anne Olivier Bell, copyright © 1982 by Quentin Bell and Angelica Garnett, reprinted by permission of Harcourt Brace Jovanovich, Inc.

INDEX